The British Invasion
of the River Plate
1806–7

The British Invasion of the River Plate 1806–7

How the Redcoats Were Humbled and a Nation Was Born

BEN HUGHES

Pen & Sword
MILITARY

First published in Great Britain in 2013 by
PEN & SWORD MILITARY
An imprint of
Pen & Sword Books Ltd
47 Church Street
Barnsley
South Yorkshire
S70 2AS

ISBN 978-1-78159-066-6

Typeset by Concept, Huddersfield, West Yorkshire, HD4 5JL.
Printed and bound in England by CPI Group (UK) Ltd, Croydon CR0 4YY.

Pen & Sword Books Ltd incorporates the imprints of Pen & Sword Aviation,
Pen & Sword Family History, Pen & Sword Maritime, Pen & Sword Military,
Pen & Sword Discovery, Wharncliffe Local History, Wharncliffe True Crime,
Wharncliffe Transport, Pen & Sword Select, Pen & Sword Military Classics,
Leo Cooper, The Praetorian Press, Remember When, Seaforth Publishing and
Frontline Publishing.

For a complete list of Pen & Sword titles please contact
PEN & SWORD BOOKS LIMITED
47 Church Street, Barnsley, South Yorkshire, S70 2AS, England
E-mail: enquiries@pen-and-sword.co.uk
Website: www.pen-and-sword.co.uk

Contents

List of Plates vii

List of Maps ix

Acknowledgements x

Prologue xi

Introduction xiv

Author's Note xvi

Glossary xvii

Part 1: Sir Home Popham, 'A Damned Cunning Fellow!' 1

  1. 'The Secret is Unravelled' 3

  2. The Capture of Cape Town 12

  3. Into the Unknown 22

  4. The Viceroyalty of the River Plate 31

  5. The Occupation of Buenos Ayres 43

  6. The Resistance 59

  7. *La Reconquista* 67

Part 2: Reinforcement 81

  8. 'For he's a jolly good fellow!' 83

  9. Revolution! 88

10. Maldonado 96

11. The Siege of Monte Video 109

12. Captive! 128

13. The Occupation of Monte Video 134

Part 3: La Defensa 145

14. General Whitelocke 147

15. The Advance on Buenos Ayres 157

16. The Western Suburbs 174

17. The Battle of Buenos Ayres 183

18. Surrender 206

Epilogue: Echoes 217

Appendix I: British Troops Numbers and Casualty Statistics 226
Appendix II: Money 227
Appendix III: Weights and Measurements 229

Notes 230
Bibliography 272
Index 278

List of Plates

Sir Home Popham – 'a modern Pizarro'. Engraving, 1807.

Sir David Baird – 'a rough diamond ... with one or two rather repulsive traits'. Portrait by Sir John Watson-Gordon, *c.*1860.

William Pitt the Younger. The man behind Britain's Blue Water policy. Portrait by Thomas Gainsborough, 1792.

James's Town at St Helena. Built along a single street nestled between two cliffs, the town had a population of 1,200 and a 'pleasing' appearance. Engraving from a drawing by Edward S. Blake, 1830.

The Port of Buenos Ayres. As the South Atlantic's premier trade hub, Buenos Ayres was considered a rich prize. Painting, 1823.

Fort Santa Teresa. One of the Viceroyalty of the River Plate's most outlying defences, Fort Santa Teresa in modern-day Uruguay was the scene of the first contact between Popham's men and the Spanish forces. Photograph by Alexandra Sweeney.

The Plaza Mayor at Buenos Ayres. A bustling, open space of compacted earth, used for military parades, public executions, religious festivals and markets. Emeric Essex Vidal, watercolour, 1820. (*Anne S.K. Brown Military Collection, Brown University Library*)

The Cabildo at Buenos Ayres. Built in the first half of the eighteenth century, the Cabildo, or town hall, played a vital role in the British invasions. Photograph, 2005.

The militia of the River Plate. A tawdry mixture of 'long-haired Indians, and whiskered Spaniards' with little regularity in dress. Emeric Essex Vidal, watercolour, 1820. (*Anne S.K. Brown Military Collection, Brown University Library*)

Taking the city of Buenos Ayres by the British forces. Although roundly celebrated in the British press, Beresford's capture of Buenos Ayres was a relatively straightforward affair. Only one of his men was killed. *c.*1806. (*Anne S.K. Brown Military Collection, Brown University Library*)

The British troops entering the Citadel. *c.*1806. (*Anne S.K. Brown Military Collection, Brown University Library*)

The dunes at Maldonado. Now Uruguay's premier beach resort, in October 1806 the beach at Punta del Este saw a 'determined advance by the grenadiers of the 38th'. Photograph by the author, 2012.

Blandengues barracks at Maldonado. Irregular light cavalry originally raised to fight the Indian tribes of the frontier, the Blandengues were amongst the best troops the Spaniards had. Photograph by the author, 2012.

Sir Samuel Auchmuty was the most competent of all the senior British officers sent to the River Plate. 'We all thought [him] … most excellent', recalled Private William Lawrence of the 40th Foot. Engraving.

Colonia del Sacramento. Situated directly opposite Buenos Ayres, the port of Colonia has long been of the utmost strategic importance in the history of the River Plate. Photograph by the author, 2012.

Robert Craufurd. Forced into a humiliating surrender, 'Black Bob' was haunted by his experiences at the River Plate until his death at Ciudad Rodrigo in 1812.

The British advance on Buenos Ayres, June 1807. After trudging over the sodden flats of the west bank of the River Plate for four days, the redcoats' spirits were lifted by the sight of the spires of Buenos Ayres cresting the horizon. Drawing, José María Cardano y Bauzá. 1807.

Simptoms of Courage – La Defensa. Whitelocke's plan of attack was fatally flawed. In the confusion of 5 July 1807, 311 British soldiers lost their lives. Cartoon by George Cruikshank, 1808. (*Anne S.K. Brown Military Collection, Brown University Library*)

La Merced Church in Buenos Ayres was held by members of the 5th Foot throughout the morning and early afternoon of 5 July, 1807. Photograph by the author, 2012.

Whitelocke and the Ghost of Byng. When news of the British defeat reached London there was outrage. Some, including Brigadier-General Craufurd, called for Whitelocke to be shot, invoking the precedent established in 1757 when Admiral John Byng was executed for his failure at the Battle of Minorca. Cartoon, 1808. (*Anne S.K. Brown Military Collection, Brown University Library*)

The tower of Santo Domingo Church. Occupied by Craufurd's Light Brigade throughout the morning and early afternoon of 5 July 1807, Santo Domingo was fired on by the Spanish artillery in the fort of Buenos Ayres. The roundshot can still be seen today. Photograph by the author, 2012.

List of Maps

1. British Atlantic Voyages (1805–1807) 000
2. The Capture of Cape Colony (1806) 000
3. The River Plate (1806–1807) 000
4. Beresford's Invasion and the Reconquista (June and August 1806) . . . 000
5. Buenos Ayres and Environs 000
6. Central Buenos Ayres 000
7. Viceroyalty of the River Plate 000
8. The Reconquista 000
9. Maldonado and San Carlos 000
10. The Advance on Monte Video 000
11. The Siege and Assault of Monte Video 000
12. Naval Operations, North Colonia 000
13. Colonia del Sacramento and Environs 000
14. Whitelocke's Advance on Buenos Ayres 000
15. La Defensa 000
16. The Battle for El Retiro 000
17. Lumley's Attack 000
18. Craufurd's Attack, the Left Wing 000

Acknowledgements

This work is the result of two years of primary research. Whilst a considerable amount of previously unused material was unearthed in the British Library, the National Army Museum, the Colindale Newspaper Library and the National Archives in Kew, a limited budget permitted no more than a two-week perusal of the archives in Buenos Aires and Montevideo. Because of this, I drew heavily on some excellent secondary sources to flesh out the Spanish side of the conflict. First amongst them was Carlos Roberts' *Las Invasiones Ingleses*, still regarded as the standard history on the subject despite being published over eighty years ago. More recent, specialised histories such as Lyman Johnson's *Workshop of Revolution: Plebian Buenos Aires and the Atlantic World* and Susan Socrow's *The Merchants of Buenos Ayres* were also helpful. English-language histories are thin on the ground. Ernestina Costa's *English Invasions of the River Plate* is a slim and unambitious volume written from an Argentine point of view as a counter to British ignorance. The only other English-language history is Ian Fletcher's *The Waters of Oblivion*. While providing a much-needed British perspective, it adds little in terms of original research.

I am indebted to Rupert Harding of Pen & Sword Books for taking on this project and John Fletcher of Grenadier Productions and Les Waring for reading and commenting on early drafts. The insight they provided has been invaluable and resulted in several alterations to the text. I would also like to thank my wife, daughter and mother-in-law for excusing me from domestic duties for countless mornings, and especially my most tireless collaborators and proof-readers, my parents Jane and Dave Hughes. It is to them that this book is dedicated.

Santo Domingo Church, Buenos Ayres, the Viceroyalty of the River Plate

Midday, 5 July 1807

For Brigadier-General Robert Craufurd, it was the last throw of the die. The Spaniards had his men surrounded. If he failed to unite with the 45th in La Residencia, a fortress-like monastery five blocks to the south, he would have little choice but to surrender. In the last three hours, the church had become a death trap. Cannon and musket fire had shredded the gates, shattered the windows and pockmarked the walls. Filled with gun smoke, the interior resembled an abattoir. Dozens had been killed, a hundred wounded were seeking shelter amongst the overturned pews and several Dominican monks, one of whom had been shot in the chest while trying to prevent the redcoats looting, had been herded together before the altar. The surviving redcoats were returning fire. Outside, elusive targets dressed in improvised uniforms or civilian garb crouched on the rooftops, whilst others sheltered behind barricades erected along the streets. The green-jacketed riflemen occupying the adjacent rooftops and the church tower, from which the British colours still flew, had killed and wounded several. Amongst them was an aide de camp who had had the audacity to demand the British surrender and had been shot through both thighs by Private Thomas Plunkett as a result. Craufurd's men were amongst the best soldiers in the world, but the urban environment was a great leveller. The enemy outnumbered them two to one and was determined to defend their town to the last.

Leading the column tasked with linking up with the 45th was one of Craufurd's most exceptional officers. Citing a preference for 'a dashing service' over endless drill and a dreary colonial social life, Major William Trotter had given up a staff role at Cape Town to volunteer for the campaign. In October, after sailing across the southern Atlantic, he had led the grenadier company of the 38th across the sand dunes at Maldonado. In February he had been one of the first into the breach at Monte Video and in June he had been wounded fending off a night attack at Colonia del Sacramento. Alongside him were a handful of light infantry, 100 grenadiers of the 45th led by Captain John Payne and the regiment's thirty-three-year-old lieutenant-colonel, William Guard.

At one in the afternoon, Trotter formed his men into a compact column, burst out of the church gates and charged down the street. At first the enemy held their fire. When the distance closed, a volley thundered out. The front two ranks of Trotter's command were killed or wounded to a man. Lieutenant-Colonel

Guard's sword was shattered by three musket balls and Captain Payne was shot through the lungs. Trotter was bloodied and had his coat torn to shreds, but pushed on. The Spaniards fell back, but the fire from the windows and rooftops increased. Pausing to look through his telescope at a street corner, Trotter was shot through the head and chest. The survivors hesitated. A few turned back to the church leaving blood trails on the cobblestones as they dragged their wounded behind them. Soon all were in full retreat.

Three blocks to the south, lying squat beside the muddy waters of the River Plate, was the fort of Buenos Ayres. Inside, General Santiago de Liniers was struggling to comprehend what his men were about to achieve. Just three days before, when the Spanish vanguard had been routed on the outskirts of town by Craufurd's Light Brigade, the fifty-two-year-old had thought all was lost. Whilst Liniers had spent the night hiding in an outbuilding, the *alcalde de primer voto* (chief councillor), Martín de Álzaga, had taken charge. Mobilising the people with the aid of Bishop Benito Lué y Riega's impassioned rhetoric, Álzaga had turned the town centre into a fortress. Trenches had been dug across the main streets, paving stones ripped up and piled into barricades, cannon positioned to cover the major intersections, sharpshooters posted, grenades and incendiary devices made from pitch-filled clay jars handed out to the women and children and arms stockpiled on the town's flat-topped roofs.

Two hours after Trotter's death, Brigadier-General Craufurd surrendered. The other British columns taking part in the attack had fared little better: both wings of the 88th had been cut to ribbons; the 5th and 36th had been hemmed in to north of the *Plaza Mayor* (main square); and in the centre Colonel Peter Kington had been mortally wounded and his dismounted cavalrymen forced to fall back. Aside from Major Jasper Nicolls in the Residencia, only Brigadier-General Samuel Auchmuty had had any success. Having routed the enemy in El Retiro and bayonetted dozens in the surrounding houses, his troops had captured the town's bullring. Two miles to the west, in an imposing ranch in the suburbs, Lieutenant-General John Whitelocke, the commander-in-chief, remained ignorant of his troops' predicament. When the extent of the catastrophe dawned on him the following day he surrendered his entire command.

The River Plate campaign was a humbling experience for the British army. In open combat the troops had been consistently successful, but a combination of arrogance, muddied aims and two decisive defeats in the cramped streets of Buenos Ayres had undone them. Of 20,000 soldiers and sailors involved, over 500 had been killed, 1,500 wounded and 3,000 taken prisoner by a 'rag-tag' collection of Spaniards, creoles, Indians and blacks, whom the British officers thought beneath contempt. Many never recovered from the experience. General Whitelocke was court-martialled; the musket ball that pierced Captain Payne's lungs killed him the following year as he climbed a hill at the Battle of Roliça; and Robert Craufurd was haunted by his failure in South America until his death at the siege of Ciudad Rodrigo in 1812.

Other veterans went on to cover themselves in glory. Lieutenant-Colonel Guard and Major Nicolls were promoted to lieutenant-general for their exploits in the Peninsular War and rifleman Plunkett recorded the British army's most celebrated feat of marksmanship when he killed General Auguste Colbert at Cacabelos at a range of 650 yards. The inhabitants of Buenos Ayres realised even greater achievements. Emboldened by their success against one of the world's most powerful nations, they demanded the right to self-determination. Although a decade of internecine warfare followed in which Álzaga, Bishop Riega and Liniers all lost their lives, in 1816 the inhabitants would wrest their independence from Spain.

Introduction

In 1805, with the Napoleonic Wars entering their third year, the British found themselves in an unenviable position. The French dominated Western Europe and by the end of the year victory against the Russians and Austrians at Austerlitz would leave the rest of the continent exposed. Knowing the British economy was dependent on overseas trade Napoleon had implemented the Continental System, closing all European ports outside Sweden and Portugal to her merchant fleet. Over the next two years exports fell by 12 per cent, corn prices rose by a third, unemployment skyrocketed and wages slumped.[1]

The British Army was also in decline. In 1793 the Revolutionary Wars had started promisingly enough with an expeditionary force driving inland from the north Holland coast with Austrian, Dutch and Hanoverian support. The French withdrawal allowed the allies to capture the stronghold of Valenciennes, but the victory proved short-lived. The following winter, a counter-offensive pushed the allies back to the sea and by 1796 Prime Minister William Pitt had turned his attention further afield. That summer the largest expeditionary force to leave the British Isles sailed to the West Indies under Sir Ralph Abercrombie. St Lucia, Grenada and St Vincent were taken and the following year saw some success against the Spanish: Trinidad fell, but by the end of 1797 Abercrombie's army had been devastated by yellow fever and malaria and the sixty-three-year-old returned home. 1798 was a year of reconstruction. New recruits were drafted, equipped and trained and the following year an Anglo-Russian landing was made on the coast of Holland. Support expected from Dutch insurgents failed to materialise and with the French rushing reinforcements into the region, the allies were only saved by a last-minute armistice. In 1800 worse was to come. A series of poorly planned expeditions were launched against French and Spanish possessions at Belle Isle, Ferrol, Cádiz and on the Italian Riviera. All ended in defeat or withdrawal. In 1801, after their Austrian allies had been humbled at Marengo and agreed terms with the French, the British sued for peace. The country's economy was in decline, invasion seemed imminent and poor harvests had caused severe food shortages. The only positive note was the capture of Egypt, but even that was blighted by news that the victory had cost the life of Britain's most gifted commander, Sir Ralph Abercrombie, mortally wounded at the Battle of Alexandria on 21 March 1801. The Peace of Amiens proved short-lived. For Napoleon, it had never been more than a breathing space. The British were equally bullish. Having been forced to concede their recent gains, they were eager to rejoin the fight.

In 1803, with the recommencement of hostilities, Pitt changed strategy. Unable to compete with the French in mainland Europe and loathe to re-engage in the disease-ridden Caribbean, the Prime Minister played to his strengths. Although the British Army was in decline, the Royal Navy was at the height of its powers. By launching a series of combined operations against his enemies' overseas possessions, Pitt hoped to disrupt their colonial trade, while simultaneously opening up new markets for the British merchant fleet. The strategy, known as 'Blue Water' policy, appealed to the economic interests of the City and had been successfully employed nearly half a century before during the Seven Years' War. In 1805 the first mission was authorised. It is with this expedition that our story begins.[2]

Author's Note

Italics have been used for the titles of publications and the Spanish and military terms included in the glossary. I have omitted the terms 'foot' or 'regiment of foot' when referring to British regiments – therefore the Highland Light Infantry are simply the '71st'. Cavalry regiments are given their full titles. I have used the old British spellings of 'Buenos Ayres' and 'Monte Video' and refer to the 'Viceroyalty of the River Plate' as these terms were consistently employed by the invaders. In all other cases modern Spanish spellings are used. I refer, holistically, to the English, Irish and Scottish soldiers and sailors who took part in the campaigns as British. Similarly, the inhabitants of the Viceroyalty of the River Plate are termed Spanish. *Porteño* denominates residents of Buenos Ayres; 'creoles' are those born in the viceroyalty; and *peninsulares* are immigrants from mainland Spain. A summary of British troop numbers and casualties, a note on currency and exchange rates and a conversion chart of weights, distances and measurements are included in the appendices.

Glossary

Audiencia – senior court in the viceroyalty.

aquardiente – a popular South American spirit.

arroyo – stream.

bastion – defensive feature jutting out from the walls of a fortification allowing the defenders to enfilade enemy attacks.

Cabildo – both town council and council hall.

cabildo abierto – extraordinary general meeting.

Cortes – government set up in Cádiz on Ferdinand VII's abdication.

coup de main – the act of taking a town or city by assault.

creole – person born in the colonies.

Cuerpo de Invalidos – reserve infantry consisting of soldiers unfit for regular duty.

chevaux de frise – defensive barrier constructed of a tree trunk or plank of wood studded with sword blades or knives.

estancia – ranch or rural estate.

falucho – small, coastal sailing ship with one or two masts and triangular sails.

fascine – bundles of brushwood positioned in front of breaching batteries in siege warfare to protect gunners from enemy fire.

gabion – wicker baskets packed with soil positioned in front of breaching batteries in siege warfare to protect gunners from enemy fire.

goleta – small sailing ship, similar in size and appearance to a bergantin, typically with two masts.

intendencia – a local administrative region. The Viceroyalty of the River Plate was divided into eight *intendencias* and four *gobernaciones*.

Jesuit Bark – bark of the Cinchona tree valued for the curative effects of the quinine it contains.

ladron/a – thief.

matadero – slaughter yard.

mestizo/a – person of mixed European and Indian parentage.

misiones – Jesuit missions in the Guarani Indian community of modern-day Paraguay.

mulatto/a – person of African and European parentage.

pampas – flat, open grasslands of eastern Argentina, Uruguay and southern Brazil.

pampero – gale force wind originating in the *pampas* (grasslands).

pasquin – anonymous lampoon or political slogan.

peninsulares – people of Spanish birth.

peón(es) – rural worker(s).

permiso – licence granted by the Spanish crown permitting trade with South America.

peso – unit of currency in Spain's South American colonies.

porteño/a(s) – resident(s) of Buenos Ayres.

quintal – Spanish unit of weight equivalent to 46 kilogrammes.

glacis – area of flattened, cleared ground, sloping gently upwards to the walls of a fortification providing defenders with a clean field of fire.

quinta – suburban house with gardens enclosed by walls or hedges.

ravelin – defensive outwork built to channel attacks into interlocking fields of fire.

real – unit of currency in Spain's South American colonies.

Reconquista – Spanish and creole victory over the British in Buenos Ayres on 12 August 1806.

rhea – large, flightless bird native to the *pampas* of southern South America.

siège en forme – formalised siege warfare.

Te Deum – a Catholic hymn of praise, traditionally sung at celebrations.

vaqueria – wild cattle round-up and slaughter in colonial Buenos Ayres.

yerbamate – a tea-like herbal infusion grown in the *misiones* in Paraguay.

zorilla – skunk.

zumaca – small twin or triple-masted coastal schooner.

PART 1

SIR HOME POPHAM

'A Damned Cunning Fellow!'

Chapter 1

'The Secret is Unravelled'

The Atlantic Ocean
August 1805 – January 1806

The fleet gathered off Cork was the largest the Reverend Henry Martin had ever seen.[1] Since June ships had been arriving daily and by August there were over seventy-five crammed into the bay. Seven belonged to the Royal Navy. Three were towering two-deck ships-of-the-line. The flagship, HMS *Diadem*, and HMS *Belliqueux* boasted sixty-four guns, whilst HMS *Diomede* mounted fifty. Each was crewed by over 350 sailors and marines. Martin also counted two frigates – HMS *Leda* of thirty-eight guns and HMS *Narcissus* of thirty-two – HMS *Espoir*, an eighteen-gun brig-sloop, and a twelve-gun brig, HMS *Encounter*.[2] Twelve of the vessels were hospital or store ships and thirty-seven were army transports.[3] On board were over 6,000 soldiers, sixty women and forty children.[4] The vast majority were infantry divided into two brigades.[5] The first consisted of the 24th, 38th, and 83rd Regiments commanded by Brigadier-General William Carr Beresford. The second, the Highland Brigade, was made up of the 71st, 72nd and 93rd, led by Brigadier-General Ferguson. On board the *King George* transport were three companies of Royal Artillery under General Yorke and two squadrons of the 20th Light Dragoons provided the army with a cavalry detachment.[6]

Also with the fleet were fourteen armed merchantmen of the East India Company.[7] Besides the reverend Henry Martin, whose financial difficulties had led him to accept a missionary role in Adeen, the Indiamen carried the 59th and several detached companies, including one from the 21st which had been ordered to garrison the company's posts at Bombay and Calcutta.[8] One of the Indiamen was destined to travel even further afield. Much to the amusement of Captain Fletcher Wilkie, a quick-witted veteran of the 38th, the *Pitt* was carrying 120 female convicts bound for Botany Bay, who entertained the troops 'with choice specimens of their conversational powers, whenever ... [they] came within hail.'[9]

On board HMS *Diadem* was the commander of the fleet. Born in 1762 in Tetuan, Morocco, Sir Home Popham was the fifteenth son of the resident British consul. His mother had died one hour after his birth. In 1778, after turning down a place at Cambridge University, Popham had been assigned to HMS *Hyaena*, a twenty-four-gun frigate, as a first-class volunteer. Having learned the basics of his craft, he had sailed to the West Indies and received his baptism of fire in January 1780 when HMS *Hyaena*, in company with twenty-two sail-of-the-line and

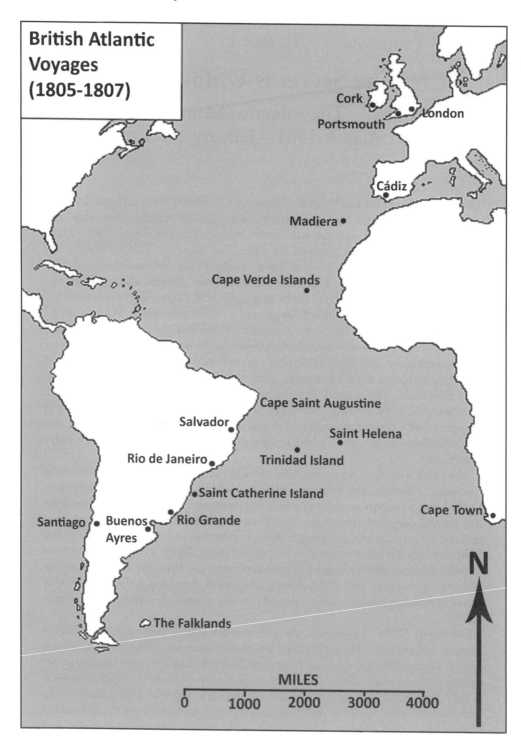

British Atlantic
Voyages
(1805-1807)

Cork

London

Portsmouth

Cádiz

Madiera •

Cape Verde Islands
•

Cape Saint Augustine

Salvador
•

Saint Helena
•

Rio de Janeiro •

Trinidad Island
•

•Saint Catherine Island

Cape Town •

Santiago •   Buenos •   Rio Grande
Ayres

The Falklands

N

MILES

0   1000   2000   3000   4000

frigates under Admiral Sir George Rodney, defeated eleven Spanish warships. The victory, which took place when Popham was just seventeen, would be his first and last experience of battle.[10] Over the intervening years, Popham had developed a new signal system for the navy and masterminded several combined operations (missions involving the navy and the army working in concert). Added to the fact that his principal patron was no less than William Pitt, the most powerful politician in Westminster, this expertise led directly to Popham's current command.

The soldiers packed into the transports were led by Major-General Sir David Baird. Born into an Edinburgh merchant family, the forty-eight-year-old was 'a rough diamond' with 'one or two rather repulsive traits' and thoroughly unpopular with his men for his insistence on precision drills, 'pipe-claying' and 'heel-balling'. Nevertheless, he was an effective soldier and had acquired a modicum of fame for the two occasions on which he had achieved the remarkable during his thirty-two-year career. In 1780, whilst serving in Mysore as a captain with the 73rd Highlanders, he had been severely wounded and captured by Hyder Ali. Conditions in the dalwai's dungeons were notorious and Baird was one of just a handful to survive four years' imprisonment.[11] In 1801, as a major-general, he had led an army from Kosseir on the Red Sea to Kena on the Nile and on to Cairo as part of the British mission to expel the French from Egypt. 'The March across the Desert' caught the imagination of the public and was roundly celebrated by the press.

The destination of Popham and Baird's expedition was secret. Official orders stated it was bound 'for the Mediterranean', but the presence of the East Indiamen made this most unlikely.[12] As Lieutenant Robert Fernyhough, one of four brothers in the armed services, pointed out 'the secret is not [yet] unravelled, nor will it be, till we get out from the land.'[13] Elsewhere speculation was rife. On board HMS *Diadem* Captain Alexander Gillespie of the Royal Marines conjectured they were destined for a diplomatic mission to Constantinople; the Reverend Henry Martin had heard rumours that they were to invade Brazil; John Graham, Paymaster's Clerk of the 71st, surmised that they were bound for Jamaica; Surgeon Richard Thompson of HMS *Narcissus* had heard talk of an attack against Tenerife; and Captain Wilkie believed Caracas a distinct possibility. When Gillespie saw a number of horses stamped with the mark of Sir David Baird all doubt ceased.[14] With both Baird and Popham on board there was only one destination which fitted the bill – Cape Town. Both commanders knew the Dutch colony well and as the primary stopover en route to India it also made a suitable target for Pitt's Blue Water policy.

In mid-August Popham and Baird oversaw a field exercise to practise the landing in Africa. The target was Haulbowline Island, a naval arsenal and dockyard 300 metres off shore. 'The boats were all drawn up in divisions,' Captain Wilkie recalled, 'and we proceeded to the attack ... with the greatest regularity, landed and embarked again without loss.'[15] Whilst Wilkie, a veteran of landings on the coast of Flanders during the Revolutionary War, was distinctly unimpressed, two young officers of the 71st were wildly excited by the theatre of it all. Ensign Thomas Lucas had absconded from the regiment's 2nd Battalion in Glasgow to ensure he did not miss out on the action and Ensign John Graham was equally thrilled.[16] 'My Dear Father,' he wrote on the eve of the expedition's departure, 'I am happy to inform you that our Regiment is ... to hold themselves in readiness for foreign service. My mother cannot be startled ... knowing, as she does well, that I am a soldier ... I trust, when I am called upon to act against the enemies of my country, I may be no disgrace to the cloth. I am at present, thank God, in good health and excellent spirits. We are ordered to hold ourselves in readiness at twenty-two minutes' warning. Send me your blessing! Farewell!'[17]

On 28 August Popham gave the order to set sail. The Blue Peter was hoisted and signal guns fired to warn the officers to repair on board ship. Tars raced up the rigging, sails were set and anchors hauled up by men sweating at the capstan. That afternoon the fleet proceeded out of the harbour with HMS *Diadem* at its head. 'The wind proving westerly, and the ships making a great deal of lee way, we came to anchor again under the windward shore', Reverend Martin noted in his journal. The swell grew and the reverend 'passed the rest of the day in dejection: being scarcely able to keep from vomiting'.[18] On 1 September a favourable wind sprung up out of the northeast and over the next three and a half weeks the fleet sailed south through the Bay of Biscay, skirted the Iberian Peninsula and trailed round the coast of northwest Africa.[19]

Once he had found his sea legs the Reverend Martin spent the voyage meditating, reading passages from his bible and learning 'Hindostanee' from grammar books and conversing with Lascar sailors. On HMS *Diadem* Lieutenant Robert Fernyhough of the Royal Marines was also studying, but with considerably more warlike intent. Having been appointed adjutant to the Sea Battalion, a force of sailors and marines that Popham was training to support the army, he buried himself in General Dundas's *Rules and Regulations* and played out battle scenarios with wooden miniatures in his cabin.[20] For Captain Gillespie, a seasoned sailor, the voyage proved 'tedious', with only two incidents of note. On 6 September a storm scattered the convoy and late one afternoon 'a large squadron' was spied from the mastheads, 'supposed to have been enemies'.[21] Trafalgar was still a month away and admirals Villeneuve, Allemand and Willaumez were known to be at large in the Atlantic. As Popham moved to engage the ships, his sailors cleared for action, ran out the guns and began to fire into the leading stranger until she hoisted Portuguese colours. Norbert Landsheit, a German sergeant serving with the 20th Light Dragoons, noted that some of the men were disappointed. 'There was much lamentation over bulk-heads knocked away, and sea-stock displaced', he explained, '[but] no bones were broken; and we steered our course again, only half pleased with the result.'[22]

On Sunday 28 September the fleet reached Madeira. Portuguese neutrality and the island's location on the principal sea-routes to Asia and the Americas guaranteed it visitors on a regular basis. Ships from all over the world stopped to refill their water casks and stock up on fresh fruit, vegetables and the famous local wine. When Popham arrived an English merchant fleet bound for the West Indies under convoy of HMS *Dart*, an eighteen-gun sloop, and HMS *Raisonnable*, a sixty-four-gun ship-of-the-line due to join Popham's command, had already occupied the choicest moorings.[23] After anchoring at midday in twenty-four fathoms, the men were presented with a breath-taking view. Funchal was built on the slopes of a gentle hill rising from the beach. '[Its whitewashed] houses [were] interspersed with trees, promiscuously towering above one another,' and 'luxuriant vineyards [grew] upon the sloping sides of the adjacent mountains in the shape of an amphitheatre, finely diversified by streams and villas'.[24] Rising above town was a large castle and gun batteries built on a finger of black rock.[25]

At 2.00 pm the officers went ashore. After splashing through the surf, they walked into town 'by a winding road over a steep hill planted ... with vines'. Prickly pears, vegetables and banana, peach, orange and lemon trees were also in evidence. Despite the natural abundance, Captain Gillespie was unimpressed. Whilst he thought Funchal beautiful from a distance, up close 'the fairy picture vanishes, as little but ruinous houses, and dirty streets, in a constant bustle from sledges, and men bearing down to the beach the wines of the island for shipment, are to be observed.'[26] Reverend Martin also had mixed feelings. Although delighted to be on *terra firma* after a month at sea, he was appalled that people were doing business on the Sabbath and scandalised on visiting the local Catholic church. 'The splendour of the' place 'was beyond any thing I had conceived' he recalled '[and I] was shocked beyond measure at the absurd ceremonies'. Martin's consternation grew as the day progressed. 'At dinner, [I] met a party of about twenty. [There were] several colonels and ladies [present]; everything was in the same grandeur as in London; I was disgusted at the thoughtlessness of the company on this day. We had great profusion of fruit, apples, pears, grapes, raisins, walnuts, almonds, and bananas, a fruit I did not like.'[27] Lieutenant Robert Fernyhough was considerably more upbeat. Visiting a convent on the cliffs above the town, he 'passed two hours very agreeably, accompanied by a brother officer, chatting with the nuns at the grating.'[28] Captain Wilkie also enjoyed the island. The water stored on his transport had grown rank and he and his fellow officers were 'under the influence of extreme thirst' by the time they landed. 'We drank Madeira and water by the bucket,' he recalled 'and devoured grapes by the bushel.'[29]

On 30 September Popham held a meeting with 'all the [Royal Navy] captains and [army] colonels' on HMS *Diadem*, at which the expedition's destination was revealed and orders delivered. The next day HMS *Protector*, a twelve-gun brig, joined the fleet and on 2 October, after the ships had watered and taken on fresh stores, the signal to re-embark was given. A last-minute rush ensued. 'The streets [were] crowded with Englishmen,' Surgeon Thompson recalled. '[They] emptied the different wine cellars completely and purchased up all the seastock they could procure.'[30] The fleet set sail at sunrise 'with a favourable breeze'. With HMS *Raisonnable* and *Protector* and the convoy bound for the West Indies in company, it cut a 'fine aspect' with a total of 120 sail.[31]

On 4 October the West Indies fleet parted company and Popham 'hoisted his broad pendant' indicating that he had assumed the rank of commodore.[32] HMS *Diadem* duly 'hove too, most of the squadron cheered [and] several of the men of war saluted the flag' with thirteen-gun cannonades.[33] Afterwards Popham ordered Captain Ross Donnelley of HMS *Narcissus* to 'cruise for intelligence' off the Cape of Good Hope and the frigate soon disappeared to the south, leaving the rest of the fleet in her wake.[34] For the next six days the weather was 'fine and pleasant' and the voyage routine. The sailors of Popham's Sea Battalion exercised with small arms, drilled and fired at 'marks' suspended from the yards. Others busied themselves repairing their ships' sails, hulls and rigging, 'blacking the masts', 'knotting yarns and small rope' and inspecting and maintaining the stores. The soldiers slept, gambled and fought amongst themselves and their officers passed their days at ease, reading, writing or fishing for tuna, shark or dolphin.[35]

On 10 October the fleet crossed the Tropic of Cancer and three days later the first casualty was recorded. At 2.00 am, James Turner fell overboard from HMS *Protector*, having lost his balance when 'reaching at a flying fish [caught] in the for-chains'. With the brig clipping along at five knots, within seconds he was lost from sight.[36] On 15 October the Atlantic echoed to the sound of broadsides as Captain Josias Rowley of HMS *Raisonnable* exercised his gun crews.[37] Two days later the fleet reached the trade winds which would carry them southwest across the Atlantic towards Brazil.[38] On 21 October, as Nelson became legend off Cape Trafalgar, word spread that the fleet was to call in at São Salvador da Bahia. Several of the Indiamen were running short of fresh water and there would not be another opportunity to stock up before the Cape.[39] Four days later HMS *Protector* and the *Britannia* East Indiaman had a minor collision, the latter carrying away the former's bowsprit with her mizzen chains. By 2.00 pm the damage had been repaired and the fleet sailed on.[40] The next morning Popham split his command. The fastest sailing transports, the Indiamen and HMS *Leda* were ordered to make all sail for Salvador, where the rest of the fleet would join them.

On 30 October Reverend Martin's Indiaman passed the equator and the sailors aboard practised the ceremony of 'The Crossing of the Line'. Those who had never been to the southern hemisphere before were obliged to pay a tribute of cash or alcohol to the veterans or face the ritual of shaving. On HMS *Protector* this involved being placed on a plank above a large tub of water, having one's face smeared with 'a mixture of tar, paint, grease, and filth', being roughly shorn with a blunt iron hoop, dunked into the tub and soaked with 'twenty buckets of water'. The whole was presided over by sailors dressed as Neptune and his Nereides and, surprisingly, endured with good humour by all concerned.[41]

That night a 'heavy gale' blew the advance party into The Racers, a treacherous shoal off Cape San Augustin.[42] At 4.00 am the *King George* transport ran aground.[43] The impact was immense. The ship was driven across the rocks until her 'bowsprit and jib-boom' projected over the sand on the far side. 'Along these [spars], the officers, artillerymen, and ships' company, made their way,' and jumped to safety. Others launched the ship's boats. Packed with women and children they rowed round the rocks and found a safe landing point on the beach beyond. Amongst the last to abandon ship was General Yorke of the Royal Artillery, who insisted on leaving via the bowsprit and jib-boom. 'Either from misjudging the distance, or trepidation, he dropped too soon' and fell into the sea.[44] Breaking the surface, Yorke was picked up by a wave and 'thrown with such violence against the side of the ship that he sunk, and was seen no more.' A private died attempting to save him and a sailor was also killed. Refusing to quit the ship, which was carrying £300,000 in captured Spanish *pesos* bound for China, he went below to gather some of the treasure, 'saying, he had lived poor, and he would be d—d if he would not die rich.' Having 'filled his shirt bosom' with coins, he 'came upon deck, shouting huzza! till the ship was nearly under water.' Several comrades tried to save him, but he threatened them with a cutlass until they departed. By the time she sank, the *King George* had drifted several miles out to sea into deep water. As she bubbled beneath the waves, the stubborn sailor 'took off his hat [and] gave three cheers'.[45]

The *Britannia* East Indiaman, 'a powerful, fine ship, built of teak', was also in trouble.[46] Seeing his course was taking him dangerously near the shoals, the duty officer on the forecastle called out a warning, but too late. 'In a few minutes [the ship] struck with tremendous force upon a perpendicular rock [and] every man . . . was thrown down . . . After . . . some time [she] . . . got off . . . and floated into deep water about two miles from the rocks'.[47] By now dawn had broken and the *Britannia* began firing her guns as a signal of distress.[48] Several Indiamen went to her aid. They rescued all aboard before she sank while the boats of HMS *Leda* picked up the survivors of the *King George* who were stranded on the shoals. By morning all had been saved, including a baby who had been born the night before.[49] Despite the loss of two ships, one of which had been carrying over 400 recruits for the East India Company, only three men had died.[50]

When Popham and the rest of the fleet passed the shoals in daylight on 3 November they avoided the danger with ease. HMS *Leda* and the advanced party were waiting for them. Several of the survivors of the *Britannia* and *King George* were transferred to the ships-of-the-line and the fleet sailed on.[51] As they neared the coast of Brazil the temperature soared and by 4 October, when land was sighted, HMS *Diomede*'s thermometer registered eighty-one degrees.[52] Two days later a squall dispersed the ships and it wasn't until 12 October that they re-formed and sailed into Salvador Bay. To European eyes the sheer scale was overwhelming. 'This vast bay . . . seemed only bounded by the far horizon,' Captain Wilkie recalled. 'On the right hand, [were] a line of gently-swelling hills, covered from their summit to the . . . water's edge with all the rich and luxuriant verdure of the tropics; on the left, the bay [was] partially shut in by the beautiful island of Taparica, [which was] feathered in like manner to the seashore . . . [and] crowned with . . . lofty groups of cocoa nuts, and other palms . . . Here all appears life, and hope, and everlasting spring'.[53]

After the fleet had anchored, a flotilla of small boats approached HMS *Diadem* from the shore. 'A person without stockings ascended, and came on board', Lieutenant Fernyhough recalled. 'The sailors, without ceremony, put him on one side to make way for the expected [official, but] . . . our stockingless visitor sat down very deliberately, and . . . [to our surprise] was announced as the Governor of St. Salvador.' Despite this inauspicious start, Popham and Baird were invited ashore. Landing at 'an excellent dockyard' hidden amongst the trees, they were received by an 'honour' guard whose cartridge boxes were filled with their morning porridge ration.[54]

The lower town of San Salvador consisted of a single street running 'along the margins of the water', lined with warehouses, wine vaults, a customs house and a row of shops selling rum, beef and an incredible variety of fruit. '[The lower town was] full of filth and the fumes of the coarsest tobacco' Captain Gillespie remarked, and Lieutenant Keith was appalled to find that the storekeepers had trebled their prices.[55] 'A gradual and pleasant ascent' led to the upper town. Above the chaos of the docks, the area boasted several fine churches, convents and monasteries, a theatre, which the British officers would frequent, and the leading merchants' houses. In the centre was a small square. On one side stood 'the common jail'. The governor's residence was opposite.[56]

Once the formalities had been concluded, the British officers were free to explore the town provided they returned to the ships each night.[57] Captain Wilkie was struck by the inhabitants' racial diversity. The people were of all colours, 'varying from the sickly yellow of the Mestizo, like a faded cabbage-leaf, through every shade of yellow, copper, burnt umber, and jet black'. To the inhabitants the British were equally fascinating. 'Whenever any of us used to bathe in the bay,' Wilkie recorded, 'we were surrounded by all ages and sexes, lost in astonishment at the whiteness of our hides.' Particularly entrancing was the daughter of the paymaster of one of the Indiamen. A young woman with a 'fine figure ... regular features ... [and] a complexion of the most beautiful clearness and transparency', she was followed by crowds of onlookers wherever she went.[58]

Several officers were permitted to venture inland.[59] Lieutenant Fernyhough went tiger-hunting in the hills and Captain Gillespie enjoyed a day trip up a river that emptied into the bay in search of livestock.[60] Meanwhile the soldiers and sailors were growing restless, and on board HMS *Diadem* an altercation ensued. After drinking heavily, Rene Renard and Henry Foster 'assembled on the Poop [deck] to fight each other with loaded Musquets'. They were only prevented from doing any damage by the swift intervention of the provost and his guard. Two days later they were led onto the deck by the master at arms, stripped to the waist, tied to a grating by the wrists and knees and flogged with a cat-o-nine-tails in front of the entire crew. Renard was given thirty-six lashes. Foster got forty-eight.[61]

Meanwhile, the business of preparing the fleet continued: the water butts were filled; fresh provisions, cattle and 'sixty or seventy' horses procured for the cavalry and infantry officers were loaded; the sails were mended and the hammocks scrubbed. A new bowsprit was made for HMS *Protector*; HMS *Leda* received a foremast made 'of one stick of very heavy [local] wood'; and HMS *Encounter's* rigging was repaired.[62] Those who had succumbed to scurvy or fever were carried ashore to the upper town, where they slept in the open air. Fed on fresh fruit and attended by the medical staff they recovered quickly.[63]

The longer the British stayed in Salvador the more strained relations with the locals became. Linguistic, cultural and religious differences all proved a cause of friction and the blundering Doctor Emerson committed a considerable *faux pas*.

When allowed to play the organ in one of the churches of the upper town 'he instantly struck off God save the king, Britons strike home, Britannia rules the waves, and some other grand national airs with admirable effect'. Captain Gillespie thought the show was marvellous. The locals were less impressed.[64] Later, 'two wild thoughtless officers' of the 20th Light Dragoons committed a much more serious indiscretion. When visiting another of the town's churches, one was asked to kiss a priest's crucifix to receive his blessing, but 'had the great impudence' to apply it to the mouth of his pet poodle instead. The officers were forced to flee for their lives.[65]

On 24 November this antipathy came to a head. After landing 'to pass the day, dine, and go to the theatre', the captain and lieutenant of the *Globe* Indiaman, a civilian and an officer of the 74th sent their boat back to their ship, 'meaning to take the chance of [hiring] a shore one [that] night.' When the time came 'they found a boat manned by black fellows, and ... a mulatto skipper, with whom they agreed to be taken on board for a certain sum.' Halfway to the anchorage the crew demanded the fare. The officers promised to pay once they reached their ship, 'some angry parleying took place, and ... another boat full of black fellows pulled up alongside'. Several of the newcomers 'leaped into their boat armed with knives, and began stabbing directly, right and left.' The civilian and the captain and lieutenant of the *Globe* were mortally wounded, but the officer of the 74th, 'although wounded, and encumbered with a tight regimental coat, [dove] ... out of sight ... and ... swam, till picked up by another boat'.[66] The next morning the body of the chief officer was found, and 'exhibited on the beach ... and many a wish was breathed to attack the whole villainous population ... The General and Commodore ... stirred themselves ... and several persons were ... confined; but ... the difficulty of fixing on an individual in the dark, amongst a set of black savages, was too great to give any hopes of success'.[67]

Following this incident all were keen to leave and when the Blue Peter was hoisted on HMS *Diadem* on 29 November the officers returned to their ships with pleasure.[68] The bullocks HMS *Raisonnable* had taken aboard were found to be unhealthy just one day after leaving shore. The ship's log recorded that they 'had been overdrove'. As each perished its body was thrown overboard, leaving a trail of corpses in the fleet's wake.[69] The rest of the passage passed without incident. As Captain Wilkie put it, 'a voyage across the Southern Atlantic, even in summer, is cold and dreary'. Apart from the occasional whale sighting, there was little to distinguish one day from another.[70] Popham used the time to continue training his Sea Battalion. The men were drilled twice a day, exercised with pikes and muskets and outfitted in 'white jackets [with] blue cape and cuffs, white trousers and gaiters'. On 3 January, the entire fleet awoke to an ominous prospect.[71] Rearing up ahead through the mist were the mountains of South Africa. Training was over. The time for action had come.

Chapter 2

The Capture of Cape Town
Southern Africa
January – March 1806

On 4 January the ships sailed into Table Bay. Battling strong winds, they proceeded in line and passed 'close under the Cape'. English colours were hoisted and broadsides fired as a sign of intent. From the deck of HMS *Diadem*, Lieutenant Fernyhough noted that the demonstration achieved the desired effect. 'The town appeared in great confusion' he recalled, '[and] we saw a party of cavalry, riding in various directions.'[1] With the Dutch panicking, Popham sailed into deep water and dropped anchor at 5.00 pm 'between the Blaauwberg [Mountain] and Robin Island' with Cape Town to the southeast.[2] The infantry were issued 'thirty-six rounds of ball cartridge' and ordered to ready themselves for landing the next morning. 'It was a melancholy sight', the Reverend Henry Martin recalled. 'The privates [of the 59th] were keeping up their spirits by affecting to joke about the approach of danger', whilst 'the[ir] ladies [were] sitting in the cold night upon the grating of the after-hatchway overwhelmed with grief.'[3]

That evening Baird and Popham searched for a suitable landing site. Undeterred by the Dutch batteries, they sailed up the coast on HMS *Leda* until 'a small bay, sixteen miles to the northward of Cape Town', was found.[4] At first light the men of the Highland Brigade readied themselves to lead the attack. Whilst the Dutch gathered on the heights above them, their boats formed up around HMS *Espoir*, but as Baird was about to give the signal 'it came on to blow fresh' causing a 'great swell'.[5] The sea was whipped up into a 'high surf' which rolled in and pounded the beach, leaving Baird no choice but to delay.[6] One hour before midday, with no sign of improvement, the boats were recalled and the soldiers returned to their ships. Exhausted, they collapsed below decks and were soon asleep.[7]

Popham and Baird had no time for such luxuries. With water supplies running low and the prospect of a French fleet appearing to their rear, they had to get ashore without delay. That afternoon they boarded HMS *Espoir* and sailed 'from Lospard's Bay', a 'small inlet' about twenty miles to the north, 'to within gunshot of the batteries of Cape Town' looking for a sheltered cove, but without success. Becoming desperate, Baird detached Brigadier-General Beresford with the 38th Foot, 20th Light Dragoons 'and a proportion of the artillery' under convoy of HMS *Diomede* and HMS *Espoir* to Saldanha Bay, a sheltered cove sixty miles to the north 'where the disembarkation could be accomplished with

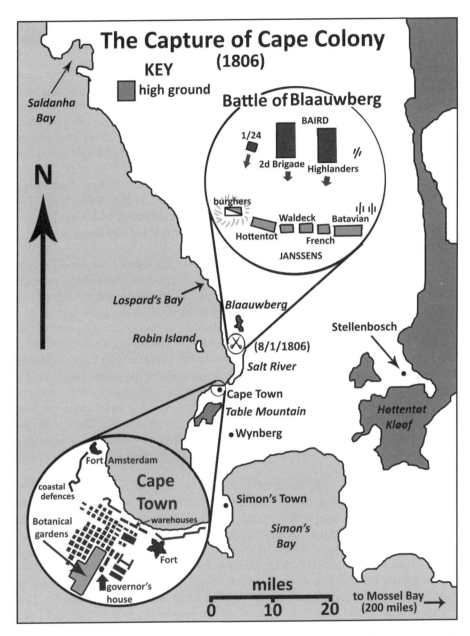

The Capture of Cape Colony (1806)

KEY

high ground

Battle of Blaauwberg

BAIRD

1/24

2d Brigade Highlanders

burghers

Waldeck Batavian

Hottentot French

JANSSENS

Saldanha Bay

N

Lospard's Bay

Blaauwberg

Robin Island

(8/1/1806)

Salt River

Stellenbosch

Cape Town

Table Mountain

• Wynberg

Hottentot Kloof

Fort Amsterdam

coastal defences

Cape Town

Botanical gardens

warehouses

Fort

governor's house

Simon's Town

Simon's Bay

miles

0   10   20

to Mossel Bay (200 miles)

facility'. If there was no improvement in the weather, the rest of the army would follow the next day.[8] At dawn, Baird got his first good news since arriving off South Africa. Overnight the surf had lessened and a landing appeared practicable. Lospord's Bay was chosen for the attempt.[9] Guarding it was a patrol under Colonel Le Sueur, who had positioned his native Hottentot riflemen along a series of sand dunes dominating the beach. Whilst the 71st and 72nd Regiments boarded their boats, HMS *Encounter* and the boats of HMS *Diadem* and *Belliqueux* were sent inshore to bombard the enemy. As they opened fire, HMS *Protector* joined in the cannonade.

With the round shot and shells falling ever closer, Le Sueur withdrew to a second line of hills and at 11.30 am the Highlanders were sent in. Their pipers playing, they rowed through 'a dense tangle of seaweed', leapt into the surf and splashed ashore.[10] On the far side of the line, a boat from the *Charlotte* transport carrying thirty-six of the 93rd overturned in the breakers.[11] 'Every soul in her went to the bottom and was drown'd'.[12] The rest of the brigade formed up on the beach. Led by Lieutenant-Colonel Denis Pack, a powerful man with a fierce temper, the light company of the 71st were the first to move inland.[13] Although bruised by a spent rifle ball, Pack urged his men up the sand dunes to dislodge the enemy.[14] The regiment's two pipers drew their broadswords and joined in the charge. A brief skirmish ensued. Two defenders were killed and three wounded. The survivors fled inland.[15]

With the bay secure, the rest of the infantry and the marine battalion landed. The operation was immense. Horses, guns, provisions and ammunition were all rowed ashore. The men who had already landed relaxed amongst the dunes and started the three days' rations Popham had ordered them to cook before disembarking. Haunted by a presentiment of death, Captain Andrew Foster of the 24th used the time to say goodbye to his friends. On the voyage from England he had become well-acquainted with the officers of the 71st and with Captain Henry Le Blanc of the grenadier company in particular. 'We went round together' Le Blanc recalled, 'and he bid good-bye to all the officers ... though I did not remark on it at the time.' With the farewells over, Foster turned his attention to his best friend. 'Now', he said, 'my hardest task is to take leave of you.' Le Blanc, a thirty-year-old of excellent connections, dismissed his friend's solemn manner: 'We shall beat the Mynheers to-morrow', he replied, 'and then we will have a jolly day in Cape Town.'[16]

On 7 January the 59th, the East India troops and Popham's Sea Battalion landed. At the same time Baird ordered the marines to re-embark. Word had reached him that Lieutenant-General Jan Willem Janssens, the governor of Cape Town, had encamped his army by a farmhouse six miles to the south. Baird could not believe his luck. Rather than settling in for a protracted siege behind Cape Town's formidable defences, Janssens had 'imprudently' committed himself to battle. Baird ordered the marines to sail to the south under convoy of HMS *Diadem*, HMS *Leda* and one of the gun-brigs and cut off his retreat. The plan was sound, but involved the marines landing at the beach that had been judged too dangerous on 5 January. For Lieutenant Fernyhough, it was a terrifying ordeal. 'The nearest point we could get to the shore was forty or fifty yards [out], so that we were obliged to wade ... up to the middle, before we could reach it', he recalled. 'In getting out of the boat, a sea came, and dashed me over the head, and I thought I should have ... to swim for it, but another wave set me on my legs again; I then took to my heels, and ran till I got [in] safely. To my great annoyance, I found an excellent pistol spoiled ... and all my ammunition rendered useless.'[17] By this time, Janssens' army had marched to the north to confront Baird, leaving only a small rear-guard to defend the position. 'Just as we were leaving the boats', Fernyhough recalled, 'the gun-brig opened a fire of grape shot among them, killed two, and the rest retreated.' A second enemy detachment attempting to manhandle a gun on to a hill was also repulsed 'by a well-directed fire' from the gun-brig and the marines were able to move inland. 'As soon as we had formed and our piece of artillery was properly manned ... we advanced up the hill, expecting to find the enemy there, but to our disappointment they had vanished.'[18]

At 4.00 am on 8 January Baird's army advanced down the road to Cape Town via the heights of the Blaauwberg, or Blue Mountain. Progress was slow. Ahead of the main body, the light troops fought a running battle through the scrub with the skirmishers of the enemy. Behind came the two infantry brigades. At the rear the Sea Battalion and East India recruits dragged 'two howitzers, and six light field-pieces' through the 'soft, burning sand'.[19] The land was covered with thorn bushes, which tore at the soldiers' clothes, and in the arid conditions the men were 'dreadfully in want of water'. Several died on the march. 'One man of the name of Taylor dropped close by me,' Ensign William Gavin of the 71st recalled, '[and] turned quite black in a moment.'[20]

At 6.00 am the army crested the heights. The enemy was drawn up on the far side of a wide plain beneath them. Having spent thirty-four years in the army, Lieutenant-General Janssens was well aware that his force of 2,000 was both outnumbered and outmatched, but 'the honour of the fatherland demanded a fight.' Janssens' left flank was anchored on a low hill slightly in advance of the main line held by a company of mounted riflemen, or burghers, and a battery of mounted artillery. Next was a Hottentot infantry regiment commanded by Colonel Le Sueur, the officer who had contested the British landing on 6 January, then two battalions of Waldeck infantry, mercenary units recruited from the Germanic and Hungarian principalities, and 200 French marines and sailors from the frigate *Atalante* and the *Napoleon* privateer, both of which had been trapped at anchor in Cape Town by Popham's sudden arrival. Beyond were the 22nd and 9th Regiments of Batavian infantry and on the right flank, 'advanced considerably in front of [the] ... line', were fifteen 'light guns' manned by slaves from Mozambique and Javanese gunners.[21]

At 7.20 am Baird called his men to arms. The Highland Brigade took the left whilst the second brigade, led by the commander-in-chief's brother in Beresford's absence, formed up on the right in regimental columns 200 yards behind. When the advance began the Highlanders progressed swiftly across the plain, following the cart track to Cape Town, but the second brigade was hampered by the terrain and fell further behind. Ordered to dislodge the mounted riflemen and artillery from the hill on Janssens' left, Henry Le Blanc's fatalistic friend Captain Foster of the 24th became the first casualty of the day. After dismounting and taking careful aim over the back of his horse, a burgher shot him through the neck.[22]

At 8.00 am the Javanese gunners opened fire. The round shot bounded across the plain, bowling over thorn bushes and plunging through the British lines.[23] On the far side of the field the Royal Artillery returned fire. The first shots fell amongst the Waldeck mercenaries in the centre of Janssens' line. Several were killed or wounded and the survivors edged backwards. Janssens implored the regiment to remain firm, but after a few more shot ploughed through their ranks they routed. By now the leading elements of the Highland Brigade had begun to fire volleys of musketry at the 22nd Batavian Regiment. Although at too great a range to be truly effective, the gunfire weakened their resolve and when the 71st charged the Batavians ran. With his centre crumbling, Janssens ordered the rest of his army to retreat before the defeat turned into a disaster. The Javanese abandoned two cannon to the 71st, but the rest withdrew in good order covered by the fire of the mounted artillery which was the last Dutch unit to leave the field.[24] The Highlanders were in no condition to contest their retreat.[25] Having slaked their thirst at a nearby stream, they collapsed on the field.

At sunset Reverend Martin walked to the battlefield to care for the wounded. The first he saw were three Highlanders making their way to the rear. All had been shot through the hand. Some six miles on Martin came across another Highlander. Shot through the thigh, the Scot had dragged himself to the edge of the battlefield and was resting under a thorn bush. Later Martin reached the hill where the grenadier company of the 24th had fought. The staff surgeons were taking care of three men who had been mortally wounded. 'One who was shot through the lungs was spitting blood and yet very sensible', Martin recalled. '[I] spread a great coat over him ... [and] talked ... a little of the blessed gospel ... [he] feebly turned his head in some suprize, but took no further notice'. Climbing higher Martin reached the body of Captain Foster. 'His face and bosom were covered with thick blood,' the reverend recalled, 'and his limbs rigid and contracted as if he had died in great agony.'[26]

The army camped on the field. 'Just as the moon began to appear above the mountains', the enemy's mounted riflemen began harassing the pickets, and in the small hours the temperatures plummeted. Lieutenant Fernyhough 'felt the cold very severely' having 'nothing to lie upon but the bare sands'.[27] The next morning, the British counted their losses. They had suffered 212 casualties to Janssens' 353. In the fight for the hill, the 24th had had four killed, including Captain Foster, and sixteen wounded. Most of the rest of the losses were suffered by the Highlanders on the left. The 71st, which bore the brunt of the enemy cannon fire, had five killed and sixty-seven wounded and Colonel Grant of the 72nd had been shot and 'thrown from his horse'.[28]

On 8 January Janssens marched to Hottentot Kloof, a table land 'by nature impregnable', while Lieutenant-Colonel van Prophalow, left in command of the capital, asked for a ceasefire of forty-eight hours. Baird encamped just outside the Dutch lines at Salt River and granted him six, threatening to assault the city immediately afterwards.[29] Prophalow was in no mood to call his bluff and on 10 January signed the capitulation.[30] The 59th took possession of the town's defences and at 3.00 pm the next day the British flag was hoisted on the castle. A royal salute was fired by the artillery and answered by Popham's ships at anchor in the harbour. Over the next few days several outposts were established. On 12 January Stellenbosch was occupied and on 15 January the 83rd Regiment took control of Mossel Bay and the 71st occupied Wynberg, a village seven miles to the south of Cape Town. With Janssens and the bulk of the Dutch army still at large, Brigadier-General Beresford was ordered into the mountains with the 59th and 72nd to pursue him. Janssens entered into negotiations and conceded on 18 January, giving the British undisputed possession of the entire colony. The victors were delighted. For such a major capture casualties had been light and the prize money was considerable. 'I expect [my] share [to be] between 200 and 300 pounds', Lieutenant Fernyhough estimated. Another officer recorded that field officers stood to make £1,400 each.[31]

Cape Town was the largest European settlement in sub-Saharan Africa. Built in an arid valley, it was surrounded on three sides by peaks, the highest of which, Table Mountain, rose over a thousand metres above town. To the north lay Table Bay. Beyond were the Blaauwberg Mountain and the plain where the battle had been fought. The waterfront was dominated by the cavernous warehouses of the Dutch East India Company and defended by numerous blockhouses, batteries, redoubts and a pair of forts. The town itself, which Lieutenant Keith of HMS *Protector* thought 'neat, clean, and well-built', was laid out in a regular grid pattern.[32] The streets were paved with coarse gravel cemented with red clay and lined with rows of pine trees. A small stream, bounded by a low stone wall, ran through the centre. Aside from the flat-roofed private houses, which Surgeon Thompson of HMS *Narcissus* believed the 'handsomest [he] ... ever saw in any part of the world', there were several buildings of particular note, including two churches, one Lutheran and the other Calvinist, a theatre, a vast hospital and the governor's residence. The latter was surrounded by extensive botanical gardens and contained a small zoo housing a couple of lions, a wild ass, an ostrich, and two or three flamingos.[33]

The majority of Cape Town's 6,500 free inhabitants were from Holland. Many were employees of the Dutch East India Company. There were also several English, a legacy of the colony's brief history as a British possession during the French Revolutionary Wars. Having suffered under restrictive Dutch trade laws, they were delighted when Popham and Baird declared Cape Town an open port shortly after Janssens' capitulation. Outnumbering the Europeans were over 9,000 slaves. The majority were 'Malays', natives of the Dutch East India Company's possessions in the Far East, forcibly impressed into service after being captured as prisoners of war.[34] There were also 800 freed men, and numerous Khoikhoi, local tribesmen, who wandered freely in and out of town. Known as Hottentots to the Europeans, the Khoikhoi were polygamous agriculturalists who had lived in the region for 1,500 years. Lieutenant Keith observed that they were 'as tall as most Europeans', but 'more slender', with skin of a 'yellowish brown ... and ... the finest set of teeth imaginable'.[35]

Whilst Janssens was permitted to return to Holland with his men out of respect for his prolonged resistance, the soldiers who had been garrisoning Cape Town were imprisoned in Amsterdam Fort and the casements under the shore batteries. Baird offered them an unappealing choice: remain confined for the duration of the war or enlist in the British regiments.[36] 'Of the two evils, they choose the least' and on 25 January seventy-seven 'volunteers' from the Waldeck Chasseurs, the German mercenary unit that had performed so poorly during the battle, joined the 71st. Recruited under duress and promised a bounty of twenty Spanish *pesos* which failed to materialise, they began to desert from the start. On 27 January Private Simon Blost fled and on 5 February Private John Domas absconded. After the provost guard was strengthened several offenders were caught. The first were flogged, but when the problem continued six were sentenced to death. 'The whole ... were shot the same day', Wilkie recalled, 'three at Cape Town and three at Simon's Bay.'[37]

As well as being a firm believer in corporal punishment, Baird was also obsessed with drill. According to Captain Wilkie, he 'retained two Serjeants of the 59th' especially to train the men in his most inexplicable parade ground peccadillo – 'the mystery of standing on one leg'. Men and officers alike were forced to practice daily from 5.00 to 7.00 am 'until ... complete in this noble art, so useful to a man in after life', Wilkie noted dryly. 'Guard mounting' followed, 'then our regimental parade ... [and] at two we dined, in order to be ready at four to repeat the goose-step; this until six; then our regimental parade in the evening; after which it was dark.'[38] This schedule was more than some officers could stomach. Colonel Sir Robert Wilson, the popular commander of the 20th Light Dragoons, preferred to exercise his men by organizing sporting tournaments on the plains outside Cape Town. When Baird got wind of the practice a bitter argument followed, and on 18 February, to the 'great grief' of his men, Wilson resigned his commission in protest and returned home on HMS *Adamant* the same day.[39]

The rest of Baird's officers endured and some even found ways of amusing themselves. Hunting expeditions were organized, the Cape wines, including a fine vintage named 'Constantia', were sampled and dances to which the local ladies were invited were held. Surgeon Thompson thought the young Dutch women very beautiful, 'thin and genteel', whilst lamenting that they 'turn[ed] very clumsy and corpulent as soon as they become mothers.'[40] Captain Gillespie agreed, attributing the phenomena to a diet of 'fish [soup] swimming in the fat of sheep's tails ... [and] beef steaks with onions'.[41] Other officers spent their free time riding in the countryside, a party was held when news arrived of the victory at Trafalgar and one Sunday Captain Wilkie and several of his fellow officers climbed Table Mountain.[42] Setting out before dawn, they strolled through a landscape of vineyards and gardens until reaching a solitary watermill, where a diagonal fissure in the vertical rock face provided the only means of ascent. As they climbed, the officers saw several baboons and Wilkie 'had one or two shots with a rifle', but with no success. The three-and-a-half-hour ascent was 'sharp' and required several 'sundry halts', but on reaching the summit the exertion proved worthwhile. 'It was a beautiful morning', Wilkie recalled. '[Far below] Cape Town ... looked like a child's city built with cards, [and] the ships in the bay [were] diminished to "cock-boats". The troops were on parade previous to

Church ... and when they broke into column to march past, [they] ... looked like a line of ants ... in motion.'[43]

On the morning of 4 March a French frigate was spotted offshore. A scout detached by Admiral Willaumez, who was planning to waylay the British China Fleet on its homeward voyage, the forty-gun *Volontaire* had been ordered to sail to the Cape prior to the arrival of the ships-of-the-line.[44] HMS *Raisonnable* and HMS *Narcissus* were the first to spot her. At 7.30 am they observed 'the stranger hoist French colours' and gave chase, keeping to seaward to prevent her escape. Seeing the Dutch flag flying above Cape Town (a common ruse to lure un-suspecting ships into a hostile harbour), Captain Britel sailed into Table Bay at 11.00 am 'and stood towards' HMS *Diadem*. Popham waited until the frigate was within hailing distance, raised the British flag and fired a single shot across her bows. Seeing the situation was hopeless, Britel struck his colours. Popham had lived up to his reputation once again – he had a gift for accruing considerable prize money with minimal risk, the capture of the *Volontaire* being a perfect example.[45]

Lieutenant Fernyhough was sent to take possession. 'As soon as I got on board, I saw a number of English officers and soldiers [confined beneath the hatches],' he recalled. 'One of the officers came and shook me by the hand, and burst into tears, he was so overjoyed [and] the poor soldiers were [so desperate to escape] ... that they appeared ready to jump overboard.' Their reaction was unsurprising. Returning to England after four years of garrison duty at Gibraltar and active service in Abercrombie's Egyptian campaign, the men, who were of the 2nd and 54th Foot, had been captured off Brest and held in appalling conditions. In the past three months a dozen had died 'from want of air' and some were so weak that they expired shortly after liberation.[46] As part of the surrender, Lieutenant Fernyhough was presented with three swords. 'One ... I returned to [the French commander after he had signed his parole]; another I gave to the Hon. Lieut Percy', (a son of Lord Beverly whom Popham had instructed to command the boarding party) and 'the third was an Arabian scimitar, which I kept myself ... It was handsomely mounted [with jewels]' and 'the hilt [was] in the form of a cross'.[47]

Popham and Baird spent the rest of March preparing to receive Willaumez's fleet. Additional batteries were thrown up, outworks built and furnaces kept burning to provide the gunners with red-hot shot. The ships were anchored in positions where their broadsides could aid the shore gunners or patrolled the coast, their firepower increased by the addition of detachments of redcoats from the 71st.[48] The tension was heightened in mid-March by a number of false alarms, including one deliberately started by 'a goose of a Dutchman' who was flogged after confessing 'it was all his own invention.'[49] By April, with still no sign of Willaumez, the fear of an attack began to wane and Popham turned his attention to a half-formed plan with which he had been preoccupied for some time – the capture of Buenos Ayres.

The concept of a British descent on the River Plate was not without precedent. The idea had first been mooted in 1711 and in the Seven Years' War two separ-ate expeditions had been planned. An official British venture had been redirected at the last minute, while a joint Anglo-Portuguese plan financed by private merchants had reached its destination, only to turn back in 1762 after the loss of the flagship. Twenty years of peace with Spain had put any further plans on hold, but ever since the recommencement of hostilities in the last decade of the eighteenth century William Pitt had been toying with the idea.[50] His reasons were economic. It was widely believed that South America had enormous potential as a market for British goods, but as the Spanish insisted on restrictive trade laws, their removal was a prerequisite. With this in mind in 1790 Pitt had given an audience to Francisco de Miranda, a Venezuelan revolutionary who had dedicated his life to South American independence. Miranda's proposal for an invasion briefly appealed to Pitt, then involved in a diplomatic spat with Spain over navigation rights in the Nootka Sound, but was dropped when the crisis was resolved. Nevertheless, the idea was not entirely abandoned. In 1797 Henry Dundas, Pitt's Secretary for War, considered using the garrison of Cape Town combined with the police force of New South Wales for a similar project and the following year Miranda was invited back to Westminster as the renewal of hostilities once more rendered his plan palatable.[51] With the threat of French invasion Pitt's priority, Miranda was turned down once more. Undaunted, the Venezuelan remained in London and in 1803 found a firm ally in Sir Home Popham.[52]

Drawn by Miranda's adventurism and the promise of rich rewards, Popham was converted to the cause and in November 1803 prepared a report for the Admiralty entitled 'Appreciation of the attack on Rio de la Plata'. Tying in with Pitt's Blue Water policy, several other plans for attacking South America were considered by the Admiralty and War Office over the next two and a half years. Most were ill-informed flights of fancy, erroneously assuming the Spanish colonies were teetering on the brink of revolution, whilst ignoring the geographical and logistical barriers to success. Lieutenant George Briarly of the Royal Navy thought 'the whole Province [of Venezuela] might be taken without the loss of twenty men'; an anonymous 'expert' claimed 'that the inhabitants of [the River Plate] only wait an attack to fly to the assistance of the invader'; another believed that Monte Video could be pounded into submission by a single seventy-four-gun ship-of-the-line and two frigates; and Lord Selkirk envisioned 10,000 men conquering the entire continent from the Caribbean to Patagonia within two years.[53]

Although Popham's plan was rejected by the Admiralty along with all the others, when he learnt of his appointment to capture the Cape his South American ambitions had been rekindled. In the summer of 1805, shortly before departing for Portsmouth, he had had a meeting with 'Mr. Wilson, an eminent merchant of the city of London', who informed him that Monte Video was 'defenceless' and that Buenos Ayres would cede to British rule if free trade was allowed. Popham had then sent a letter to Robert Patten, the governor of St Helena, priming him to provide troops for a future attack, and a few months later in Salvador he interviewed 'an Englishman who had been eleven months a ship-carpenter at Monte Video'. Although he had no official sanction, Popham was convinced that Pitt would support him and in March 1806, with a powerful fleet at his disposal, he was finally ready to act.[54]

The only obstacle remaining was Sir David Baird. Although he had command of the fleet, Popham required infantry, which meant persuading the Scot to part with one of his regiments. Unlike Popham, a man of the mould of Francis Drake who possessed an adventurous spirit and self-belief that bordered on arrogance, Baird was conservative and unsuited to the wild gamble that Popham had in mind. On 24 March, after a series of interviews with Sir Home, Baird wrote to his friend, Lieutenant-Colonel Gordon of the 72nd, expressing his doubts. 'Popham is pushing me hard to make a dash at Buenos Ayres' he confided. 'From the information he has obtained he believes we would carry it with the greatest ease if I would spare him ... five or six hundred men. Although I am aware of the great advantages that would be derived ... I cannot consent [to the plan] ... without first hearing from England'.[55] Baird's misgivings were well-founded. After capturing the Cape, Popham had been ordered to forward the bulk of the troops to India and send the surplus transports back to England. The only mention of South America had been in a letter from John Barrow, the Second Secretary of the Admiralty, suggesting a single frigate be sent to cruise off the east coast of the continent to procure intelligence.[56] Aside from this flimsy pretext and the assumption of support from Pitt, Popham's plan was entirely his own initiative. Such schemes had been relatively commonplace in the sixteenth and seventeenth centuries, but the contemporary Royal Navy had less room for mavericks. Only absolute success could protect Popham. If he captured Buenos Ayres, the press would laud him a hero. Defeat would most likely end his career.

By early April Popham had convinced Baird to change his mind. That he succeeded was partly due to his remarkable powers of persuasion, a skill honed in the courtroom defending himself from long-running accusations of involvement in contraband, in the House of Commons as a Member of Parliament for Yarmouth and during a diplomatic mission to secure the support of the Russian Tsar. Another influence was the recent arrival of Captain T. Wayne, an American slaver who had sailed into Cape Town on 28 March from Buenos Ayres. As well as confirming the viceroyalty was rich and ripe for the plucking, Wayne volunteered his services and those of his ship and crew. Also key in Baird's decision was the prospect of prize money. Although the mines of Potosí did not produce the quantities of silver they had churned out in their heyday and the legendary city of El Dorado had never been found, South America retained a reputation for wealth and, according to a report that later surfaced in *The Times*, 'Sir David absolutely refused to let [Popham] ... have a single man' until he had signed 'a special agreement' stipulating that the Scot would receive two-eighths of all property captured compared to Popham's one.[57]

Chapter 3

Into the Unknown

Cape Town, the Southern Atlantic and the River Plate
March – June 1806

By early April Cape Town was in a state of great agitation: rumours of a secret mission to South America abounded, the sailors of Popham's Sea Battalion were in training and down at the docks the 300-strong crew of HMS *Leda* was preparing to put to sea.[1] On 1 April the frigate 'rec'd [a] New Main Top [Mast] from the Dock Yard'. Supplied in two halves, the timber was fitted together and raised on board ship.[2] Two days later Captain Robert Honeyman received orders from Popham detailing his mission. 'You will ... proceed [across the South Atlantic] for the purpose of cruising off and within the headlands of Cape St Mary and Cape St Antonio. Intelligence ... respecting Maldonado, Monte Video, and Buenos Ayres is wanting ... You will therefore take every means by close examination of prisoners that may fall into your hands to ascertain the strength of each place, the number of troops, its defences by sea and land, and the disposition of its inhabitants.'[3] At dawn on 4 April 'live Oxen & Sheep [&] Vegetables' were loaded and at 10.00 am Honeyman weighed anchor. With a 'fine Pleasant wind' filling her sails, HMS *Leda* soon left Table Bay behind her.[4]

The frigate's departure heightened the rumours onshore. Some thought an attack on Macao, Manilla or Isle of France (Mauritius) a possibility, but the majority believed the target was South America.[5] 'At length', Captain Wilkie recalled, 'the guessers settled it down ... to a marauding expedition along the coast of Peru'.[6] On the morning of 11 April Popham was rowed ashore to meet Sir David Baird and cement the details of the expeditionary force. Popham pushed for a regiment whose commanding officer was his close friend, but Baird 'insisted' he take the 71st instead.[7] Three Royal Engineers led by Captain George Kennett, and twenty artillerymen with four 6-pounders under Captain James Ogilvie were also assigned, along with five dismounted light dragoons of the 20th under Sergeant John Henry. The whole was commanded by Brigadier-General William Carr Beresford, a competent, if unimaginative, thirty-eight-year-old professional who had fought at Toulon, Egypt and South Africa and had won respect for his expertise at logistics. Corpulent, balding, prone to sweating profusely and blind in one eye, Beresford was later described as both 'the ablest man in the army' and 'a low-looking ruffian with damned bad manners.'[8] As further insurance that his wishes would be met, Baird appointed his nephew, Ensign

Alexander Gordon, an Eton-educated twenty-year-old who had served with the fashionable 3rd Guards, as one of Beresford's aides-de-camp. The other was Captain Robert Arbuthnot, a twenty-three-year-old from County Mayo who had fought his countrymen in the Irish Rebellion eight years before.[9] Totalling just over 950 men, Beresford's was a small force, barely meriting the title of an expedition. Popham had pressed for more, but it was all Baird had been willing to spare.

On 12 April the embarkation began. As well as the soldiers, sixty women and children boarded the fleet, which consisted of three ships-of-the-line, HMS *Diadem*, *Raisonnable* and *Diomede*, the frigate, HMS *Narcissus*, the *Encounter* gun-brig and five transports – the *Walker*, *Willington*, *Melantho*, *Triton* and *Ocean*.[10] The operation lasted two days. As well as the men's equipment, baggage and ammunition, several months' water and provisions were loaded and 'seven casks of Dollars' hoisted on board HMS *Diadem* to pay the 71st.[11] On HMS *Raisonnable*, seamen Thomas Gooch and John Norton were given twenty-four lashes for drunkenness and neglect of duty, on HMS *Diomede* the sailors made hammocks for the troops, while Lieutenant Fernyhough wrote a letter home from HMS *Diadem*. 'We sail this evening for South America', he began, '[and] calculate upon making considerable prize money ... you may be assured that we will do our best.'[12] The next morning the ships gathered in the bay awaiting a favourable breeze. That evening, William Love, a twenty-year-old ordinary seaman from Galway, and Thomas Cook, a forty-three-year-old from Sussex, stole one of HMS *Encounter*'s boats, rowed ashore and deserted.[13]

On HMS *Diadem* Popham spent the evening writing to William Marsden, Secretary of the Admiralty. After outlining his intentions and the intelligence he had received, he made a plea for understanding: 'I hope the view I have given their Lordships of my conduct, and the motives by which I was induced [to undertake this] project ... promising so much honour and prospects of advantage to the Empire, will be considered ... preferable to ... allowing the squadron ... to moulder away ... in a state of cold defensive inactivity.'[14] Popham's plea was disingenuous. Having been instructed to defend Cape Town from French attack, he had wilfully disobeyed orders and taken it upon himself to launch an invasion 4,500 miles away. A second letter was addressed to Robert Patten, the governor of St Helena. A small, mountainous island in the south Atlantic, St Helena had been occupied by the British East India Company since 1658. It served as a way station for ships returning to England from the Far East and would make a convenient stopover for Popham's fleet en route to the River Plate. Having received a positive reply to the letter he had sent from London several months before, Popham felt the time was right to ask Patten for a more concrete contribution. 'My object in addressing your Excellency', he wrote, 'is, to request you will spare a company of Artillery ... to aid this enterprise; and ... [send] them ... to meet me at Monte Video'. Popham was convinced his request would not fall on deaf ears. St Helena would benefit from trade with the fertile River Plate, and if the area was in British hands, Patten need not fear a Spanish attack. [15]

The next morning, with 'a fine … breeze' from the southeast, the fleet sailed out of Table Bay.[16] The first part of the voyage was routine. On 16 April HMS *Narcissus* 'spoke an American ship bound to St Helena' and Richard Coan, an ordinary seaman on board HMS *Encounter*, who had been sick for some time, died and his body 'was committed … to the deep'.[17] On 20 April a squall blew up. By nightfall it had grown into a storm. As it began to scatter the ships Popham made the signal for all to steer northwest by north and ride it out. On board HMS *Narcissus* Captain Donnelley close reefed the top sails and took down the top gallant yards to lessen the strain, but the master of the *Ocean* transport reacted too late.[18] A sudden gust filled the sails. The pressure split the mizzen mast and wrenched it over the side.[19]

The next morning the *Ocean* transport was missing. 'During the whole of the day the Commodore used every effort by laying too & sending vessels to windward … [but] we could not get sight of her', Brigadier-General Beresford recalled. The loss was catastrophic. Some 200 men of the 71st – over a quarter of Beresford's ablest fighting force – were on board. 'This struck Sir Home in exactly the same light it did me' Beresford recalled, 'and after some consideration he determined to proceed to [St Helena] … where we had every reliance that a reinforcement would be given'.[20] After sending HMS *Narcissus* ahead to warn Governor Patten of the squadron's imminent arrival and HMS *Encounter* to the River Plate to intercept the *Ocean* should she arrive there before them, Popham set sail for St Helena.[21]

Several dozen miles to the west, the *Ocean* was adrift. 'When Daylight appeared', Ensign Gavin recalled, 'no ship of the fleet was to be seen'. With no sign of help, the master took charge and soon 'all hands [were] employed in getting up a jury mast'. On the morning of 29 April a sail was spotted astern. The stranger gained rapidly and that evening fired a warning shot across the transport's bows. As a boat was sent to board her, the soldiers were hidden below decks and the transport disguised as a merchantman. 'We were in the greatest suspense,' Gavin recalled, 'but to our joy [the stranger] … turned out to be an East India pacquet, bound for England'. Later that night, having reached the required latitude, the master opened his sealed instructions and learnt they were destined for the River Plate.[22] The men were in low spirits. Provisions were scarce and the soldiers feared that they would 'be too late to share in the conquest'. Captain Henry Le Blanc was able to reassure them. 'You need be under no apprehension' he informed his 'brother officers', ' "[as] you will be [in] time enough, for I shall lose my leg there." I said this,' Le Blanc recalled, 'fully assured in my own mind that it would be so; but if you ask me from whence that assurance arose, I am unable to answer.'[23]

At 4.00 pm on 30 April Popham's fleet arrived off St Helena.[24] Nine miles in circumference, the barren rock made an imposing spectacle. Rising perpendicularly out of 'the bosom of the deep', the cliffs were crowned with heavy batteries and two forts guarded the approaches.[25] The ships dropped anchor in twenty-six fathoms while the fort fired a seventeen-gun salute answered by HMS *Diadem*.[26] That evening Beresford and Popham were rowed to James Town for an audience with Governor Patten. Built along a single street nestled between two cliffs, the town had a population of 1,200 and a 'pleasing' appearance. The houses were 'well-built' in the English style, interspersed with coconut palms and boasted 'a nice looking church in the midst of them.'[27] As Popham and Beresford arrived, the fort fired a second salute and Patten greeted them on the beach. 'An old man … intelligent and good natured', the governor led the commanders to his residence where a regiment of East India troops received them. The meeting went as well as Popham and Beresford could have hoped. 'I am happy to inform you that we have not been disappointed', the latter wrote to Sir David Baird the next morning. '[Patten] has given … [us] a detachment [of 150 infantry, 100 artillerymen and] two 5.5-inch howitzers.'[28] The expedition was also reinforced by three merchantmen at anchor in the bay, amongst them the *Justina*, an English ship of twenty-six guns belonging to Messrs Princeps and Saunders of London. Persuaded that their cargo of 'sundries for speculation' would fetch a high price in a 'liberated' Buenos Ayres, William Dunn, the ship's supercargo, and Robert Morris, her captain, abandoned their original venture – a trip to Botany Bay via Cape Town – and joined Popham's squadron instead.[29]

Reading the latest papers to arrive from London, Lieutenant Robert Fernyhough learnt of the death of his brother, John, a royal navy lieutenant who had drowned whilst attempting to save the crew of the *Rayo*, a Spanish prize wrecked off St Lucar the day after the Battle of Trafalgar.[30] Popham was appraised of some equally disastrous news.[31] 'I heard of … the death of Mr Pitt, which I consider the greatest national calamity that ever [struck] our country' he recalled. 'To my personal feelings it has been such a shock that I shall not easily recover.' Normally confident to the point of arrogance, the news caused Popham a crisis of self-doubt. Pitt had been his principal patron and had protected Sir Home from his political enemies. His death would leave a power vacuum in Westminster and allow the Tories, who distrusted Popham's wilder instincts and had previously attempted to orchestrate his downfall, to rise. 'I am now toiling under such speculative promise of approbation, either from different policy or different sentiment that I proceed with little pleasure', Popham confessed in a letter to Viscount Melville, First Lord of the Admiralty, 'but as Sir David is equally committed with myself in this enterprise I trust I shall neither be wanting in zeal or firmness to accomplish it'.[32]

Meanwhile, the ships replenished their water supplies, the officers explored the island and the commissaries purchased cloth to make uniforms for the 100 sailors of the Sea Battalion, a ploy designed to convince the South Americans they were regular troops.[33] In the morning of 2 May the Blue Peter was hoisted. The St Helena troops, under vice-governor Lieutenant-Colonel William Lane, were accommodated on board the newly recruited merchantmen.[34] Ill-disciplined and poorly paid, many were foreign born and there were even a few Spaniards in the ranks.[35] The rest of Beresford's troops returned to the ships that had brought them from the Cape, with the exception of Private Patrick O'Brien of Captain Paley's company of the 71st. Deemed too sick to continue, O'Brien was left in

James Town to convalesce.[36] That evening, to a seventeen-gun salute from the fort, the squadron weighed anchor and sailed out of the bay.[37]

The rest of the voyage passed smoothly with 'fine pleasant weather'.[38] The men of the Sea Battalion were exercised with pikes and small arms daily. As they drilled and practised volley fire with blank cartridges, their comrades made their uniforms – blue jackets with red capes and cuffs, belts, white trousers and gaiters and black feathered caps.[39] On 17 May Jonathon Patterson, a thirty-three-year-old able-seaman from Lewick, fell overboard from HMS *Narcissus* and drowned; three days later the uninhabited island of Trinidad was sighted and on 22 May HMS *Encounter* spoke to a passing American merchantman and the lookouts on HMS *Diomede* spotted a strange sail running for the horizon.[40] Popham sent the cutter to give chase.[41] Too slow to escape, the stranger struck her colours. She proved to be the *Emmanuel* merchantman, several weeks out from Accra with a cargo of African slaves for the River Plate. Popham put several soldiers on board and took her in tow.[42] On 27 May Popham transferred aboard HMS *Narcissus*. Anxious for intelligence on his destination and having heard nothing from Captain Honeyman of HMS *Leda*, Sir Home used the frigate to scout ahead. With him went Lieutenant Groves of HMS *Diadem* and Mr Wayne, the American who had volunteered his services as a guide at Cape Town. 'Not liking … to leave the troops', Beresford ordered his secretary, Captain Kennett of the Royal Engineers, to go along as the army's sole representative.[43]

As Popham approached the River Plate, the weather deteriorated. On 5 June there was an electrical storm and the next day HMS *Narcissus* entered a fogbank, reducing visibility to a few dozen yards.[44] Inching his way forward into the muddy, shallow water, Popham knew he must be close to his destination, a fact confirmed by numerous flights of sea-birds breaking out of the fog, but it wasn't until noon on 7 June that he had his first sight of land.[45] The island of Lobos, a barren rock five miles from the east bank of the River Plate, loomed ahead. 'We were astonished at the number of seal[ion]s playing around the ship,' Surgeon Richard Thompson recalled. 'The island [was] … covered with them, [and they were] making a most hideous noise imaginable … [It] put me in mind of being near Smithfield market, [in] London.' That afternoon HMS *Narcissus* crept forward into the unknown. In the shallow waters, the sounding lead was in constant use and the anchor was carried cock-billed, hanging from the cathead, ready to drop at a moment's notice.[46] At sunset Popham ordered Captain Donnelley to come to a halt and the frigate dropped anchor in eight fathoms.[47]

As the Royal Navy officers were beginning to realise, navigating the River Plate was a hazardous undertaking. The waters were riddled with hidden shoals. English Bank began twenty miles southeast of Monte Video and the Chico and Ortiz banks were 100 miles upriver. To make matters worse, the water level could change from day to day with little warning. As well as the unpredictable tide, bitingly cold *pampero* winds, which gathered strength on the vast plains to the west of Buenos Ayres, could force the water out to sea, causing it to fall by as much as eighteen inches in half an hour.[48] Further complicating matters was the difficulty of finding a solid anchorage on the muddy bottom and the problems

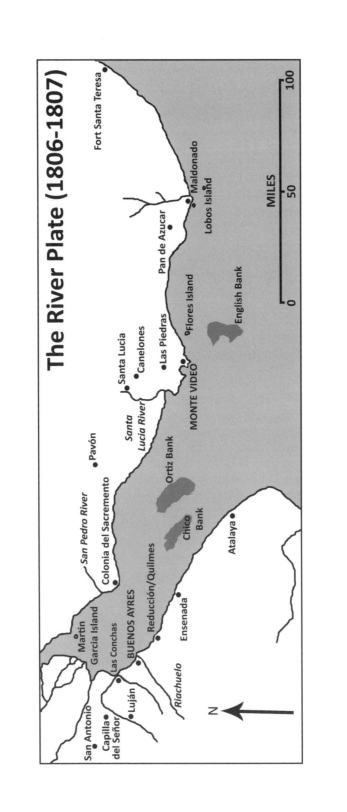

The River Plate (1806-1807)

Fort Santa Teresa

Maldonado
Lobos Island
Pan de Azucar

Flores Island

English Bank

Santa Lucia
Canelones
Las Piedras

Santa
Lucia River

MONTE VIDEO

Pavón

Ortiz Bank

San Pedro River

Colonia del Sacremento

Chico
Bank

Reducción/Quilmes

Martín
Garcia Island

BUENOS AYRES

Las Conchas

Ensenada

Atalaya

San Antonio
Capilla
del Señor

Luján

Riachuelo

N

MILES

0   50   100

navigators had in ascertaining their precise position. Even when the fog lifted, the land provided precious few points of reference. Whilst a few low hills rose to the east, to the west was as featureless a landscape as could be imagined: mile after mile of swaying grassland rolled on as far as the eye could see, with barely a tree to break the monotony.[49]

On the morning of 8 June, the fog having dispersed, Popham reconnoitred Monte Video. '[We] saw several vessels in the harbour', Surgeon Thompson recalled 'but at too great a distance to make them out distinctly. The town seems large.' 9 June dawned bright and clear. After hoisting American colours, Popham continued his scout, hoping to catch a local ship unawares. At 3.00 pm he succeeded. Spotting a schooner wending her way upriver near English Bank, Popham ordered Donnelley to sail toward her. By the time her captain realised the danger, it was already too late and when Popham hoisted British colours, the schooner struck without a shot being fired. Although Portuguese and bound for Rio de Janeiro, the *Bankege* was carrying Spanish goods and was therefore a legitimate target. After her seventy-five crew had been imprisoned below decks on HMS *Narcissus*, midshipman White and eight men were sent on board. Some 114 cured cowhides and 39,000 Spanish *pesos* were found.[50] As well as several paying passengers, the governor of Valdivia in Chile and the ship's pilot, a Scot named William Russell, were on board.[51] Having lived in the viceroyalty for twenty-four years and knowing the river's shoals and hidden banks intimately, Russell was a particularly valuable addition to Popham's growing list of informants. Besides confirming Buenos Ayres's poor state of defence, he informed Sir Home that the viceroy had reinforced Monte Video on learning of the British squadron's visit to Salvador and that a caravan from the silver mines of Upper Peru had recently arrived in Buenos Ayres. Popham's legendary good fortune had held. If he was quick, he would seize a fortune.[52]

The next morning, Popham sailed to the mouth of the river to rendezvous with the fleet. On 10 June the *Ocean* transport was sighted. Those on board were delighted when the *Narcissus* hove to alongside. For the last eight days they had been reduced to a diet of wheat boiled in salt water, a mutiny had only narrowly been avoided and when they learnt they had not missed out on the action and the prize money their joy was complete.[53] Popham, who had given them up for lost, was equally glad and only Captain Henry Le Blanc, obsessed with his impending doom, failed to raise a smile.[54] The next day the fog descended once more. On 11 June HMS *Narcissus* chased a strange sail which turned out to be HMS *Encounter*, on 12 June able-seaman Edward Cherril, a twenty-seven-year old from London, fell overboard and drowned and it was not until 13 June, guided through the murk by the sound of HMS *Raisonnable*'s signal guns, that Popham finally rejoined the fleet.[55]

That afternoon a council of war was held on HMS *Diadem*. Brigadier-General Beresford, Lieutenant-Colonel Denis Pack of the 71st, the Honourable John Deane (the expedition's brigade-major), captains James Ogilvie of the Royal Artillery and George Kennet of the Royal Engineers, and Captain Robert Arbuthnot and Ensign Alexander Gordon, Beresford's aides-de-camp, represented the army, whilst Popham was joined by captains Ross Donnelley (HMS *Narcissus*), William King (HMS *Diadem*), Josias Rowley (HMS *Raisonnable*), Joshua Edmonds (HMS *Diomede*) and Lieutenant James Talbot (HMS *Encounter*). Though Beresford and his officers pushed for an attack on Monte Video, the Royal Navy closed ranks and Popham insisted on moving against Buenos Ayres. Beresford's concerns were strictly military. He argued that the walled town of Monte Video would be easier to hold and, as it boasted a relatively deep water anchorage, it would enable the troops to maintain contact with the fleet. Popham's preoccupations were political and economic. Buenos Ayres, having neither significant defences nor a regular garrison, would make a softer target, and as the capital of the viceroyalty its capture was likely to lead to a domino effect rendering an attack against Monte Video unnecessary. Popham's arguments won out. 'What finally determined me to accede', Beresford explained, 'was that the Fleet was in want of everything, the Troops had no Bread ... [the] Provisions ... in the Transports [had been] ... consumed ... and ... we had reason to believe ... that supplies would be more certainly attained'. What Beresford failed to mention, and what was perhaps his true motivation, was that Buenos Ayres was holding a fortune in Peruvian silver and gold.[56]

That evening the infantry, artillery, marines and Sea Battalion were transferred to the ships with the shallowest draughts (the five transports, the *Justina* and HMS *Encounter* and *Narcissus*) and on 15 June the naval captains and field officers of the army signed a document ensuring 'a mutual Participation of all seizures & captures'. The following evening the fleet split once more. HMS *Diadem*, *Raisonnable* and *Diomede* sailed north to blockade Monte Video, whilst Popham took the smaller ships northwest to Buenos Ayres. Although only ninety miles by Beresford's reckoning, the voyage took nine days.[57] As well as 'the shoalness of the water, adverse winds and currents, continual fogs, and the great inaccuracy of the charts', Popham and his captains had to contend with 'the inequality of the sailing in some of the transports'. The unarmed vessels lagged behind and frequent halts had to be made.

On the first day HMS *Narcissus* ran aground. 'We got eight of the guns forward ... hove up the rudder, [and sent] out all the boats,' Surgeon Thompson recalled. It was a nervous time for those on board. If the tide pushed the frigate further onto the shoals she would break up under the pressure. The boats were kept out all night to tow her free, but it wasn't until the following morning that they succeeded.[58] Subsequently, HMS *Encounter* and the *Justina*, both of which drew considerably less water, led the way.[59] Guided by William Russell, the Scottish pilot taken from the Portuguese brig, Lieutenant Talbot proceeded upriver, constantly sounding and signalling his readings with cannon fire.[60] Nevertheless, on 22 June HMS *Narcissus* grounded on Chico Bank. Several cannon were run forward to raise the stern and the stream anchor was thrown overboard in an attempt to haul her off, but to no avail. That night an electrical storm descended. With howling wind, rain and lightning, the men, women and children on board panicked. All seemed lost until Lieutenant Talbot ran HMS *Encounter* alongside and transferred sixteen 18-pounders, some shot and fifty-seven people on board.

With the frigate lightened, she hauled off at 6.30 am. 'We have had a miraculous escape', Thompson noted, '[as] the ship must have gone to pieces had she not got off.'[61]

The rest of the voyage was uneventful and at 7.00 am on 24 June a lookout on the masthead of HMS *Encounter* 'saw Buenos Ayres bearing WSW'. After making a feint against the port of Ensenada de Barragán, a muddy cove forty miles down-river where they were fired upon by an artillery detachment, the fleet anchored off Quilmes, a shallow bay eight miles southeast of the suburbs, which Russell deemed 'an excellent place' for a landing.[62] Popham hoisted signals for the war-ships to clear for action, and the troops were ordered to cook three days' pro-visions for the campaign that lay ahead. That morning Beresford announced his assumption of 'the rank of major-general under the authority of Sir David Baird'. This meant that he was now senior to all the Royal Navy captains and second only to the commodore himself. Sir Home wrote a letter to the Admiralty venting his disapproval: 'I make no reference [to the matter] from pique or any personal motive', he claimed disingenuously, failing to mention the true source of his displeasure – the promotion would afford Beresford a greater share of the prize money than even Popham was entitled to claim.[63]

That evening orders were circulated that the landing would begin at dawn.[64] Although the men were nervous, they were convinced victory lay within their grasp. Only Captain Henry Le Blanc remained fatalistic. Earlier that day John Pooler, the surgeon of the 71st, had told him that his instruments had 'contracted a little rust' during the crossing. '[He] asked [me] . . . who could best put them in order', Le Blanc recalled. Thinking he would be next under the knife, the captain assigned the task to one of his best men then sought out the assistant-surgeon, Jason Evans, to learn how to apply the tourniquet to his leg. Le Blanc had little sleep that night. After practising with the apparatus into the small hours, he lay awake in his cot, dreading what the morning would bring.[65]

Chapter 4

The Viceroyalty of the River Plate

Buenos Ayres
June 1806

Rafael de Sobremonte y Núñez del Castillo, the viceroy of the River Plate, had first been alerted to the possibility of a British attack back in November.[1] Stung by Popham's tars' disrespect, the governor of Salvador had 'sent an extraordinary express ... to the viceroy ... giving a most detailed account of the squadron' and warning Sobremonte that it might be headed his way.[2] Believing Monte Video the most likely target, the viceroy sent the garrison of Buenos Ayres across the river and 2,000 militia were raised and encamped outside town.[3] In late February, after four months had drifted by, news arrived of Baird's capture of Cape Town. Although the regulars remained in Monte Video, the threat of British attack was put out of mind until the morning of 20 May, when HMS *Leda* dropped anchor opposite Fort Santa Teresa after a voyage of six weeks.[4] Captain Honeyman's mission had been dogged by mishap from the start. The ship's gunner, George Thompson, had turned into a full-blown alcoholic; an anchor had been lost off Cape Santa Maria in a storm and whilst sounding the bay off Fort Santa Teresa, the master and four sailors were taken by a Spanish detachment. Lieutenant Parker, sent to negotiate their release, only succeeded in getting himself and two other sailors captured and, after further attempts at arbitration had failed, Honeyman sailed for the island of Santa Caterina to resupply.[5]

When a report of the incident arrived at Buenos Ayres, Sobremonte was unconcerned. HMS *Leda* was but a single frigate. Her presence did not necessarily herald a full-scale attack, and it was hardly the first time that armed British ships had been sighted in the river. The eighteenth century had seen numerous visitations: British smugglers were commonplace and just eight months previously an English privateer had terrorized Spanish merchantmen for several weeks before being captured by the *Joaquina* off Callao.[6] The viceroy, a sixty-year-old nobleman, soldier and colonial administrator who had been Madrid's third choice for the position, had more pressing concerns. In 1802 a drought had caused food prices to soar and by 1806 wages were at an all-time low. Emboldened by the revolutions in the United States and France, the working class was becoming ever more vociferous, mysterious *pasquines* (lampoons) anonymously posted in the main square advocated republicanism and liberty, and a recent influx of African slaves fuelled rumours of a Haitian-inspired revolt.[7] Besides, the viceroy also had personal business to take care of. Augmenting his salary of 40,000 *pesos* by fair

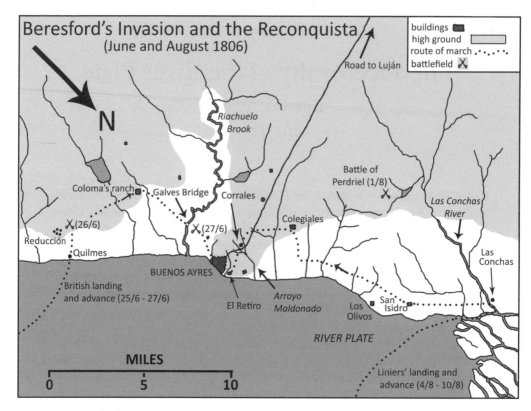

Beresford's Invasion and the Reconquista
(June and August 1806)

buildings
high ground
route of march
battlefield

Road to Luján

N

Riachuelo
Brook

Battle of
Perdriel (1/8)

Las Conchas
River

Coloma's ranch   Galves Bridge   Corrales

Colegiales

X(26/6)

X(27/6)

Reducción

Quilmes

Las
Conchas

BUENOS AYRES

British landing
and advance (25/6 - 27/6)

Arroyo
El Retiro   Maldonado   Los   San
Olivos   Isidro

RIVER PLATE

MILES

0   5   10

Liniers' landing and
advance (4/8 - 10/8)

means or foul, and marrying off his eleven children, were far more important than marshalling the defences against some nebulous threat.[8]

In June the rumours intensified. Reports of a British fleet off southern Brazil by the Governor of Rio Grande were given added credence by the accounts of several fishermen who had seen strange sails through the fog.[9] On 15 June, a naval ensign, José de la Peña, spotted a fleet of warships from his schooner, *Nuestra Señora del Carmen*, whilst patrolling the river, and a week later several ships were sighted from Maldonado watchtower. Even so, the viceroy continued to procrastinate. Rather than mobilising his gunboats and armed schooners, he merely ordered two cavalry piquets to the riverside hamlets of Las Conchas and Quilmes, while sending a small detachment of soldiers under Santiago de Liniers, a French-born captain in the Spanish navy, to occupy Ensenada. Despite the evidence to the contrary and the fears of several of the viceroyalty's senior figures, including Pascual Ruiz Huidobro, the governor of Monte Video, Sobremonte insisted the 'enemy fleet' was nothing more than smugglers involved in the contraband that had blighted his dominion for so long.[10]

On 24 June Sobremonte's nonchalance appeared vindicated. That morning Liniers had fired on a flotilla of ships which had attempted to land at Ensenada. The Frenchman's report was dismissive. 'These ships are [no more than] despicable pirates, without order or discipline,' he wrote. 'Warships of any nation, [would] have [had] more resolution in attack.' Adding a request for 100 men to make sure he could repulse any further attempts at landing, Liniers dispatched his letter to the capital. Sombremonte was attending a performance of 'El sí de las Niñas', the latest offering from the celebrated Madrid playwright Leandro Fernández de Moratín at the Nuevo Coliseo – a dilapidated theatre on the corner of Calles San Martín and Merced whose straw roof had been burnt by an errant firework during a religious festival several months before.[11] Reassured that there was no cause for alarm, he settled back to enjoy the play, but at 9.00 pm Martín Jacobo Thompson, Captain of the Port of Buenos Ayres, informed the viceroy that numerous British warships were at anchor off Quilmes point. 'I saw considerable movement in the viceroy's box', remembered Lieutenant Rodrigo Muñoz – also present that night – '[then] the news that the enemy were closing on our coast swept through the theatre'. As the stalls were thrown into chaos, Sobremonte stole out. Only after he had prepared his family to leave for the interior did he begin organizing the defence.[12]

On the viceroy's arrival at the fort, a squat building in the centre of town whose eastern ramparts were lapped by the River Plate, the signal fires were lit to alert the boats in the harbour.[13] Messengers were sent to gather the senior militia officers and two patrols were despatched to Quilmes. The first, four soldiers and an artilleryman led by Sergeant Gerónimo Tabares of the *Cuerpo de Invalidos*, was ordered to man the signal gun at Quilmes and fire a single cannon shot should the enemy appear. The second, twelve men under Ensign Manuel Sanchez, was to search the marshes nearby.[14] When the militia officers arrived a council of war was held. Amongst those present were Colonel Nicolás de la Quintana, the commander of the Blandengues, a body of irregular light cavalry raised to protect the frontier from Indian attack; Pedro de Arze, sub-inspector of military forces at Buenos Ayres; Juan Ignacio de Elía, the Basque commander of the city's Cavalry Volunteers; and Colonel Eustaquio Gianninni, the town's chief military engineer, who was best known for his restoration of a Galician lighthouse eighteen years before. After outlining the threat, Sobremonte issued his orders. Quintana was to gather his Blandengues at Galves Bridge, the highest crossing point of the Riachuelo Brook two and a half miles to the southeast, and advance to the village of Reducción, a cluster of 'detached houses of inferior description' clustered round a church on the heights overlooking Quilmes Bay.[15] The officers of the Cavalry Volunteers were to summon their men to their barracks at the end of Calle Catedral, issue arms and ammunition, and be ready to join Quintana the following morning. The Infantry Volunteers would remain in reserve. After assuring Sobremonte their task was impossible – the troops were spread throughout the town and its environs and such urgency was unprecedented – the officers rushed from the meeting to gather their men.[16]

As was becoming clear, the troops at Buenos Ayres were hopelessly unprepared. The bulk of the regulars had been transferred to Monte Video and, aside from a handful of infantry and artillerymen garrisoning the fort, the only professional units at Sobremonte's disposal were a company of horse artillery and Quintana's Blandengues. This 'standing army' was supported by four part-time militia units: the Cavalry Volunteers under Colonel Elía; the Infantry Volunteers, led by Miguel Ignacio de Azcuénaga; the *Cuerpo de Invalidos*, an under-strength regiment of incapacitated regulars; and the Urbanos, a body of merchants 'organised' into six companies under Colonel Jaime Alsina y Verejes. Although the militia was theoretically capable of mustering some 4,000 men, only half that number would be deployed. The rest were too old, unwilling to fight or lived far from town and would take several days to mobilise. Even those who were available were poorly trained and lacked ammunition, arms and experience. Most of their officers were old men, unaccustomed to the advances of modern warfare. Elía and Quintana were in their sixties, Gianninni was fifty-five, Ignacio and Azcuénaga were fifty-two, and even the youngest, Colonel Alsina of the Urbanos, was over forty.[17] Although several had fought Indians on the frontier, such actions had been little more than skirmishes and the last had occurred over twenty years before. The younger generation was no better equipped. Captain Manuel Belgrano, a thirty-six-year-old creole in Azcuénaga's unit who would go on to achieve great things in the Wars of Independence, readily admitted his incompetence: 'I [had] accepted [the commission] more to have another uniform to wear, than out of any interest in the military profession', he confessed. '[When] the English invaded I was not only ignorant of how to form a company in line of battle or column, but also of how to order the men to shoulder arms, and had to … rely on one of my subalterns or corporals to give the command.'[18] Mariquita Sánchez de Thompson, the wife of the captain of the port of Buenos Ayres and a chronicler of the town's social history, was equally damning: 'it didn't even cross anyone's mind that there would be a war here', she observed. 'The old men had forgotten what war was and the young … didn't even preoccupy themselves with such things.'[19]

Although the majority of *porteños* would later put the poor state of the militia down to the viceroy's incompetence, in some part it was the result of active design. Whilst the threat of a working-class revolution was as yet a dim one, by arming and improving the militia Sobremonte would have been providing those he feared the most with the means to overthrow him. He was thus content to allow the organisation to atrophy, while its equipment and munitions were squandered and fell into disrepair.[20] King Carlos IV's ministers were also culpable. Since 1792 viceroys had been requesting reinforcements and as recently as June 1805 Sobremonte had warned that Buenos Ayres was in no state to resist a determined attack. His pleas were ignored. At war with England and subject to Napoleon's frequent demands, Spain was in no position to reinforce her colonies. Besides, King Carlos' ministers shared Sobremonte's concerns. The more militarised the colony, the harder it would be to control.[21]

At dawn on 25 June, any doubts about the scale of the British threat evaporated. From the flat roofs of the two-storey buildings in town, the fleet could be seen eight miles away at anchor in Quilmes Bay and at 7.00 am the general alarm was raised.[22] The cannon fire echoing down the cobbled streets threw the town into chaos. Civilians and soldiers rushed back and forth and men and boys of all ages ran to the fort to beg for weapons to defend themselves.[23] At the barracks of the Cavalry Volunteers in Calle Catedral the situation was equally confused.[24] Roused from his bed at midnight, Captain Manuel Martínez, a native of Santander in Spain who had got married less than two months before, was appalled. The men of several different companies were mixed together and their captains were unsure who had been issued with weapons and who had not. Several had carbines, others had pistols, some were armed with swords and others had nothing at all. Even those who had firearms had only been issued with four cartridges and many had already lost their flints. Outside, some volunteers were mounted, their horses whinnying in alarm. Others had turned up with just their saddles slung over their shoulders. At lunchtime some officers returned home. If they were going to die, at least they would do so with a full stomach.[25] Eight miles to the southeast at the village of Reducción, Sergeant Gerónimo Tabares was also in a panic. Ever since firing his signal gun at first light, he and the five men under his command had been watching the British fleet and praying for reinforcement. At 4.00 pm, with Quintana's Blandengues still several miles away, Tabares' worst fears were realised: the offshore breeze let up and the landing began.[26]

HMS *Encounter* was the first to weigh anchor. Despite only drawing twelve feet, the gun-brig could get no closer than a mile to shore.[27] Deliberately running aground on the muddy bottom, Lieutenant Talbot ordered his men to load the two long 12-pound chasers.[28] With the gun-brig covering them, the rest of the fleet lowered their boats, a flotilla of twenty-one small craft, and Beresford's 1,641 men disembarked.[29] On board HMS *Narcissus*, at anchor in four fathoms a mile further out, Surgeon Thompson watched as Popham's Sea Battalion boarded the frigate's boats. 'The poor fellows [were] ... in the highest spirits imaginable', he recalled. 'One of them got wounded in the side by a pike by accident, yet his zeal was such, as soon as he got his wound dressed he slipped off into one of the boats unknown to me.'[30] A quarter of a mile from the beach, the boats grounded and the men waded ashore, marshalled by Captain William King of HMS *Diadem*, who spent the entire afternoon up to his waist in the water. Beresford and his suite were amongst the first to reach land. After setting up a perimeter, the major-general had two local fishermen pressed into service as guides.[31]

At 5.00 pm Colonel Quintana and his Blandengues arrived on the heights above the bay. One hour later Sub-Inspector Pedro de Arze joined them with 200 Cavalry Volunteers and at dusk a third body of cavalry appeared accompanied by one howitzer and two light cannon of the first division of the Horse Artillery, giving Arze a total of 600 men.[32] Compared to their elegantly accoutred and uniformed officers, the rank-and-file were a tawdry mixture of 'long-haired Indians, and whiskered Spaniards' with little regularity in dress.[33] Some wore short jackets of coarse cloth. Others had blue, white or red ponchos and many wore narrow-brimmed hats fastened under the chin with cords of tanned cowhide.[34] Their horses were dirty and badly looked after and their weapons old and rusted.[35] As each body arrived the men deployed across the rising ground and lit fires to warm themselves. After observing the invaders, Arze sent out a picket and dashed off a note to Sobremonte stating that he believed the enemy looked more like marines than regular troops and that so far only 1,000 had disembarked. At dusk, the temperature dropped and a heavy rain fell.[36]

Two miles below Arze's position, beyond a wide bog bordered by a barely perceptible rise, the British were forming up on the beach.[37] In the darkness, the pipers and drummers of the 71st played to call the men into position, the officers of the light company sounded their whistles and the ships' boats made a third and final journey, bringing the cannon and howitzer to shore.[38] Each was hauled through the shallows by four men and set up on the beach.[39] By 8.00 pm the disembarkation was complete.[40] 'After a close view of our position', Captain Gillespie recalled, 'it was ascertained that we were insulated ... owing to a flow of tide into a ravine which surrounded it. But an ebb, and an immediate advance placed us beyond it, near to the margin of a green morass.'[41] Militarily, the position was strong. It had the advantage of a low bank of rising ground to its front which screened the troops from the observations of the enemy.[42] Beresford threw out a picket under Lieutenant George Landel of the Royal Marines and gave the order for the men to encamp.[43] One mile out, Lieutenant Talbot's job was done. At midnight he hove HMS *Encounter* off the muddy bottom, stood out from shore and anchored alongside HMS *Narcissus* in three and a half fathoms.[44]

With an unknown number of the enemy on the high ground ahead, and the muddy waters of the River Plate behind, the British had a nervous night. 'It was just dark when an alarm was heard from unsteady fellows [to our front]', Gillespie recalled. Seeing some wild horses grazing the marsh, a number of Popham's Sea Battalion had attempted to catch them, but only succeeded in making them stampede the British line. Hearing the hooves thundering towards them, the picket 'discharged their muskets' and fell back on the main body. Panic was only averted by Lieutenant Landel. Ordering his men to stay firm, he 'maintained his ground until the main body formed'.[45] Elsewhere, Captain Henry Le Blanc was having another sleepless night. Fixated on his premonition of death, he huddled up under his great coat and listened to the 'incessant rain.'[46]

At 7.00 am on the morning of 26 June, as the British were breaking camp, Sub-Inspector Arze despatched a message to Colonel Elía of the Cavalry Volunteers, six miles off at Galves Bridge, requesting him to join him. Mounted on a 'richly caparisoned' steed and dressed 'in [a] superb ... poncho', Arze was feeling confident: by all accounts, the enemy was little more than a bunch of ill-disciplined brigands.[47] After gathering his scouts, he rode down the hill to the edge of the swamp that separated the two armies and composed a report to Sobremonte. 'I have just personally observed the enemy', he began. [They are] in a column of 800 to 1000 men ... [but] it's impossible to say whether there are more [hidden] between the rise and the beach as my scouts suspect ... I am once more of the mind that their project is not a great design. Nevertheless, it would be most convenient if Elía could join me with the second division of the Horse Artillery.'[48] One hour later, having formed his men up in line along the heights with his right flank secured by the village of Reducción and his artillery in the centre, Arze changed his mind.[49] 'It's now nine thirty', he wrote to Sobremonte, 'and I have just returned from a [second] reconnaissance ... I am now inclined to believe that they exceed 2,000 men, the most part troops of the line amongst whom I have seen a proportion of grenadiers ... they have artillery, I have clearly seen two pieces with their ammunition carriages, and suspect they have more'.[50]

At 10.30 am, as Arze's confidence was evaporating with the morning mist, the British 'drum[s] beat to arms.'[51] Abandoning his baggage in the overnight camp, Captain Le Blanc was feeling decidedly nervous. 'I saw our surgeon,' he recalled, 'ran to him and said, – "Look out for me, I shall be the first that falls"'. With that, Le Blanc took up position near Lieutenant-Colonel Denis Pack and ushered his men to fall in.[52] 'Our troops formed in two columns' Captain Gillespie recalled, 'and after a forward movement of 800 yards they deployed into line.'[53] Beresford ordered the 71st to take the right and the marine battalion to deploy to the left. Two of Captain Ogilvie's 6-pounders, manhandled by sailors, were positioned on each flank, and a pair of howitzers was placed in the centre. Some 120 yards behind the first line were the St Helena troops with two more field pieces. Their orders were to follow the main advance and deploy to either flank should it be threatened by cavalry.[54]

'We had not proceeded far', Captain Gillespie recalled, 'when we got entangled in the morass'. The small rise had hidden the impediment and its presence came as a surprise.[55] The guns on the right and in the centre embedded up to their axles and had to be hauled out by the sailors in reverse. Whilst Popham's tars were sweating at their harnesses, Arze ordered his cannon to open fire 'with an oblique direction to the [British] right'. The moment Henry Le Blanc had been dreading had arrived. 'I had been speaking to [Lieutenant] Colonel P[ack], as we were advancing, when the first shot was fired,' he recalled. 'The second took away the musket of the man on my right ..., passing between his head and mine'. The crew of the Spanish 6-pounder 'six or seven hundred yards' to the captain's front then reloaded and fired for a third time. 'I saw [the ball] ... coming all the way from the gun', Le Blanc recalled. 'My covering sergeant called out "Stoop." [but] I said – "Stand up, it is coming low."' The ball smashed into the captain's calf, ripping away the greater part of the muscle, then tore off 'the fleshy part of the thigh of' Sergeant William Anderson standing behind.[56] Appalled, several of the new recruits ran for the rear, but Beresford drew his sword and forced them back into line.[57]

At midday Colonel Elía's Volunteer Cavalry, supported by a company of grenadiers under Captain Juan Florencio Terrada and the second division of the Horse Artillery, arrived on the far right of the field. Cheering 'Long live the King!' they advanced to link up with Arze's men.[58] Determined to break the main body of the enemy before they were reinforced, Beresford abandoned Ogilvie's guns and ordered his infantry to advance at the double. Whilst the marines switched round to the far right to block the new arrivals, the 71st waded through the marsh and clambered up the rise.[59] When the British were still a hundred yards away Arze's cavalry fired a ragged volley with their pistols and carbines. Moments later, the two cannon on the far left of the British line, which had avoided the swamp and advanced with the infantry, opened fire. The round shot drilled through Arze and Quintana's men before bounding on into Elía's rein-forcements.[60] Cresting the heights, the 71st fired three volleys of close-range musketry, fixed bayonets and charged. Arze and Quintana's men had had enough. Turning his horse's head to the northwest, the sub-inspector gave the order to retreat. His men hastily complied, leaving two of their cannon behind them. Carried along by the human tide, Arze berated his men, asking 'what will the women of Buenos Ayres think of you?'[61] His words had little effect. As his cavalry passed through Elía's men, they threw them into confusion, and two cannon shots, fired by the British from the Spaniards' abandoned guns, completed the rout.[62] Watching the battle through his telescope from the deck of HMS *Narcissus*, Popham 'had the satisfaction of seeing ... [the] Spanish cavalry flying in every direction'.[63]

Few casualties had been caused on either side. A handful of Spaniards had been killed by the Highlanders' musket volleys and Captain Ogilvie's cannon fire. Several more had been wounded and carried from the field. On the British side, Captain Le Blanc and Sergeant Anderson were the only casualties. Once the captain's mangled leg had been amputated above the knee, HMS *Encounter* sent a boat to pick him up and Le Blanc took up residence on board HMS *Narcissus*.[64] The rest of the troops returned to camp to collect their belongings. While Captain Donnelley and several sailors hauled the guns out of the swamp, Beresford allowed the men a two-hour rest, then ordered a headcount. Lieutenant-Colonel Lane, the commander of the St Helena Regiment, realised that Mr Halliday, his assistant-surgeon, was missing. He had last been seen as the troops advanced that morning. In his official return, Beresford marked Halliday as 'missing'. It was later discovered that he had been 'barbarously murdered' by a group of enemy horsemen who had ridden round the British advance.[65]

Seven miles to the northwest, colonels Azcuénaga and Gianninni were setting up camp on the north bank of the Riachuelo next to Galves Bridge. Charged with holding the position by Viceroy Sobremonte, Azcuénaga and Gianninni had 400 men under their command. As well as a few hundred of Azcuénaga's battalion, there were thirty-six regular grenadiers and three 2-pounder cannon under Lieutenant-Colonel Juan de Olondriz, fourteen Blandengues under Lieutenant Ignacio Warnes, and eighty convicts released on the condition they fight. The Urbanos, citing the fact that they were only required to serve inside the bound-aries of the town, had refused to march.[66] Since arriving at 3.30 pm, Azcuénaga and Gianninni had been busy preparing their position. A waist-high barricade of cut thorn bushes had been formed and a shallow trench dug for the infantry. Beyond, Olondriz's cannon were positioned. Without picks and shovels little more could be achieved. The boats moored on the southern bank had also been brought across the river and the bridge partially destroyed, leaving just a single span to allow communication.[67]

At 4.00 pm the first of Arze's cavalry arrived from Reducción. Galloping up to the bridge, they paused to tell their comrades exaggerated tales of the strength of the British forces, then raced on into town.[68] William Pius White, a thirty-six-year-old smuggler and slave trader from Boston who had spent the last nine years resident in the viceroyalty, saw one of them gallop by his house in the suburbs.[69] Urging him to stop, White listened as he blurted out his news: the enemy numbered 6,000, were all elite grenadiers and 'as big as Patagonians'. With that the cavalryman sped on 'with all possible expedition ... till he got to Cordova, 400 miles in the interior.'[70] White, on the other hand, went out to receive the invaders. An old business acquaintance of Sir Home Popham's, it seems likely the American had known about the invasion for some time. The two men's paths had first crossed in India in 1800 while Popham was working as a merchant captain and their dealings had resulted in the Englishman owing the American a considerable sum of money. While planning the invasion of the River Plate, it could not have escaped Popham's notice that a renewal of their aquaintence would prove mutually beneficial. White was an influential figure. He had strong links with both the fledgling independence movement and the merchant class and would act as a go-between in exchange for a lucrative postion under the new British regime.[71]

At 5.00 pm Sub-Inspector Arze reached Galves Bridge.[72] With him were the men he had managed to rally from the battle at Reducción. After crossing to the far bank, Arze hailed Colonel Azcuénaga. 'The enemy troops number between three and four thousand', he declared, 'they are well-disciplined veterans and are close on my heels, do what you can to delay them and then fall back before you're overrun.' After leaving Azcuénaga and Gianninni two 4-pounders and the single mortar he had saved from the battlefield, Arze ordered the final span of Galves Bridge burnt and continued into town.[73]

Some seven miles to the southeast the British were also on the move. With the light company of the 71st forming the vanguard and the artillery hauled by Donnelley's seamen bringing up the rear, they made good progress. The landscape they traversed under a glowering sky was undulating grassland, featureless aside from the occasional tree, ridgeline or small rise. Vast herds of wild cattle and horses parted before them and startled quail, partridge and teal broke into flight.[74] Exhausted following the fight at Reducción, Ensign William Gavin's thoughts had turned to where he would make his bed for the night. 'On the march through a country without stone or stick, I picked up a bleached horse skull, in order to make a pillow ... but after carrying it for about two miles ... was obliged to cast it away, and continue the march.' An hour later, Gavin had a stroke of good luck. Spotting an isolated hut, he made his way towards it to find a horse tethered to the door. To the young ensign's delight 'the bedding of the owner [was hidden] under the saddle'.[75]

On reaching an *estancia* (ranch) belonging to a merchant named Santa Coloma shortly before sunset, the British 'observed a large fire' two miles ahead.[76] Beresford immediately realized its significance. As the last natural barrier between his army and Buenos Ayres, he had suspected the Spaniards would make a stand at the Riachuelo Brook, but had been hoping that they would leave Galves Bridge intact. Instead, the major-general 'had the mortification of seeing it in flames long before ... [he] could reach it.' Halting his march, Beresford ordered the majority of his men to make camp for the night, whilst he, Lieutenant-Colonel

Pack, Captain Kennet of the Royal Engineers and three companies of the 71st continued with a pair of Ogilvie's howitzers. The major-general's impatience was fostered by two pressing concerns. His troops were low on ammunition and his water supplies were nearly exhausted. If he could capture the bridge before it was completely destroyed, he might be able to take possession of Buenos Ayres that night.[77] Left behind with the main body, Captain Gillespie enjoyed a brief respite in the weather. 'The evening was beautiful', he recalled. 'We beheld ... the lofty spires of Buenos Ayres a league off; the grand aim of our hopes, and the period of our labours.'[78]

At 8.00 pm, after crossing the Riachuelo Valley – a 'low marshy flat', the advance party arrived at a hamlet on the south bank of the river.[79] Beresford and Kennet crept forward to reconnoitre the position and found the bridge 'entirely consumed' by flames. Disappointed, Beresford decided to wait till morning before making an attack.[80] Ensign Gavin was relieved. 'Lieut. [Edmund] Le Estrange and myself got under the wall of a brick store and huddled together,' he recalled. '[We] were composing ourselves to rest, when some of our men went down to the River ... to bring water.' Seeing the British by the light of the flames, the Spanish sentries on the far bank opened fire and Azcuénaga's men soon began blazing away with what little ammunition they had. The British returned fire and Olondriz's light cannon started firing blindly into the night. With the enemy alerted, Beresford ordered his men to withdraw. Gavin found the march intolerable. '[It was] very dark' he recalled, '[and we stumbled around blindly] scarcely knowing in what direction we were proceeding.'[81] The fire-fight had cost the British a handful of wounded and one of Terrada's grenadiers had been shot in the head.[82]

That evening Colonel Gianninni sent word of his 'success' in repulsing the enemy to Sobremonte. At 9.30 pm the messenger returned with orders for all but four of the cannon to be taken back to town. The others were to be withdrawn several hundred yards to the north of the bridge into the centre of the hamlet of Barrancas along with the bulk of the infantry, leaving just two companies to guard the river crossing. The order was obeyed, even though the officers thought it a mistake – the Riachuelo provided the best means of halting the enemy and by positioning the cannon in the hamlet, they were neither defending the river nor the outskirts of town. As a result of the officers' misgivings a council of war was convened. Second-Lieutenant Leornardo de San Pedro y Pazos suggested holding the buildings on the south bank to prevent the British occupying them and rigging a few boats with explosives in mid-river. Gianninni refused to alter his orders. 'He ... shrugged his shoulders', Lieutenant Pedro Joubert of the Volunteer Infantry recalled, '[and said] that that was what he had been told to do'.[83]

Captain Kennet was ordered to make a second reconnaissance before dawn. '[He] found that ... the enemy were drawn up behind hedges, houses, and in the shipping on the opposite bank,' Beresford recalled, '[and that] the river [was no more than] ... thirty yards wide.'[84] The light company of the 71st, commanded by Lieutenant L'Estrange, and the grenadiers, now led by Lieutenant William

Mitchell in Captain Le Blanc's absence, were ordered to engage the enemy whilst the Sea Battalion hauled the army's eleven cannon towards the only cover available, a house and *pulperia* (bar and general store) close to the burning bridge.[85] Under a brooding sky and constant drizzle, L'Estrange and Mitchell's men stole down to the river, took up position amongst a stand of willows whose lower branches dipped into the water, and opened fire.[86] The enemy responded and soon both sides were blazing away. Watching the confrontation from a low rise, Beresford ordered Ensign Gavin to remind the men to be frugal with their fire. 'This was not [a] very pleasing duty', Gavin recalled. 'I had to proceed through a plain of upwards of 300 yards, exposed to the musquetry and ... cannon [fire] of the Spaniards, who peppered away at me with the same eagerness as if they had the whole British force before them. I ran in desperation ... but the bullets whistled so thick about my ears that I thought diverging a little towards the right might be safer. When I got into a dyke ... a [cannon] ... shot came by me (*en ricochet*). I resumed my old situation on the plain, and arrived under the bank of the river a great deal more frightened than hurt.'[87]

By now the British cannon had been dragged into position. Captain Ogilvie directed the sailors to place the guns inside the house and *pulperia*, their muzzles poking out of the doors and windows, while the two howitzers were positioned behind.[88] Realising the importance of the position, Gianninni ordered his men to form column and advance towards the river bank, then open out into line with the cannon on their left flank after 200 paces and force the enemy to retire. Ogilvie soon found his range and his 6-pounders caused carnage as they ploughed through the Spanish ranks. The howitzers were also a success. Loaded with Lieutenant-Colonel Shrapnel's new invention, 'spherical case' shot, they sent a number of shells fizzing high over the river to explode in mid-air above the Spanish line. Colonels Gianninni and Azcuénaga, safe behind some thorn bushes several hundred yards to the rear, ordered their cannon to reply, but the shot of their 2- and 4-pounders could barely reach the British position.[89] After a few more rounds of cannon fire, the Spanish left broke, split up into small groups and dispersed from the field.[90]

Sensing victory was within his grasp, Beresford moved the rest of his men to the river bank and ordered several sailors under Captain King to swim across and bring back some boats which the Spaniards had tethered to the willows on the far side. 'Three or four of the small craft' were lashed together and planks placed over them to form a pontoon bridge.[91] As the first British troops crossed the Spanish right fled. Using the cover of the buildings, thorn hedges and ditches, they ran back to town. Three of Gianninni's cannon were overturned and abandoned in the rush. Colonel Azcuénaga attempted to rally some of his men in a side street, but when a cannonball crashed through some nearby houses, he abandoned the attempt, leaving just a handful of holdouts led by a brave young creole cadet named Juan Vasquez to contest the field. Wishing to salvage some pride, Vasquez and his men fired a few volleys then hauled three of the abandoned cannon from the field as the British skirmishers closed on their position.[92]

By 11.00 am the bulk of Beresford's men were formed up on the north bank. Having defeated the enemy twice in two days at the cost of just a handful of wounded and one dead – James Rogers, a thirty-two-year-old sailor from Devonshire with Popham's Sea Battalion – Beresford was feeling magnanimous. 'Seeing no symptoms of further opposition, and learning that the [enemy] troops in general had deserted the city, motives of humanity induced me to send, by the Hon. Ensign Gordon, a summons ... to [surrender]'.[93] Beresford's terms were outlined in the letter. He would only accept an unconditional capitulation, but promised to respect the inhabitants' lives, religion and private property.[94] Acting as Gordon's interpreter was William Pius White, whom Beresford had gladly employed. By the time they reached Buenos Ayres, Sobremonte had already fled. After riding six miles out of town to the village of Monte Castro, the viceroy packed his family and personal belongings into his state coach and set off with a detachment of dragoons for Córdoba.[95] His last actions were to leave orders for Brigadier José Ignacio de la Quintana, the seventy-year-old military governor of Buenos Ayres, to take charge of the surrender and forward the viceroyalty's riches to Córdoba.

Brigadier Quintana stalled. 'He returned to me an officer', Beresford recalled, 'to ask some hours to draw up conditions, but I could not consent to delay my march.'[96] With the British column on the verge of advancing, White and Gordon were sent back to town, whereupon Brigadier Quintana accepted the original conditions, only asking for time to draw them up in writing. Beresford consented and halted his troops on the outskirts of town.[97] In the fort, a farce was unfolding. The Spanish officials were unsure what an official surrender document actually looked like. Eventually an old copy of *El Mercurio*, a Spanish newspaper, was found and the terms printed therein, pertaining to the British surrender of Pensacola in Florida twenty-five years before, were used as a template.[98] Clutching the document, a deputation filed out of the fort to meet the British. As well as Brigadier Quintana, various other military, administrative and clerical officials were present, including Benito Lué y Riega, the Bishop of Buenos Ayres. To Beresford's soldiers, starving and filthy after three days marching across the sodden *pampas*, the contrite officials, dressed in full regalia, were a welcome sight.[99] Beresford had done it. Buenos Ayres was his.

Chapter 5

The Occupation of Buenos Ayres

Buenos Ayres
June 1806

Beresford's 'gallant little army marched triumphantly into' town at 3.00 pm on 27 June. Despite their exhaustion and the near constant rain, for the British it was a joyous affair. The regimental and King's colours and the pipers and drummers of the 71st led the way. As they marched down Calle San Francisco, slipping on the wet cobblestones, Beresford ordered the column to adopt double spacing 'to give a more imposing shew' and the citizens flocked to their balconies to watch them pass. Amongst the elegantly veiled *porteñas* who 'smiled a welcome' was Mariquita Sánchez de Thompson, the wife of the captain of the Port of Buenos Ayres.[1] A romantic girl of just twenty years of age, whose family owned a sizeable property on Calle Correo, Mariquita was enchanted. 'The Scots of the 71st Regiment, [were] the most handsome troops I had ever seen', she recalled. '[They had] boots tied up with latticed ribbons, [with] a part of the bare leg showing, a short kilt, a beret with black feathers and a Scottish ribbon worn as a belt with a tartan shawl'.[2]

Not all the locals were so enamoured. On learning of the surrender several wept with rage and a mob gathered at the fort. Whipped up by agitators blaming the defeat on the viceroy's 'cowardice', they spoke openly of disobeying the order to surrender. By late afternoon, with their numbers swelled by several of the Infantry Volunteers who had fought at Galves Bridge, they began chanting – 'War! War! – We don't want to surrender: we want to die fighting!', but when an officer appeared on one of the balconies to warn them that the death penalty would be imposed on any who disobeyed the order of the viceroy, their resolve crumbled. Moments later a thunderstorm broke overhead, lashing the streets with rain, and the protestors dispersed.[3]

By 4.00 pm Beresford had established his headquarters in the fort and began debating whether to pursue the viceroy's convoy into the interior.[4] At one stage he went as far as to procure 400 horses, but later changed his mind. Learning of the viceroy's unpopularity and having witnessed his incompetence first-hand, Beresford reasoned that his continuing presence as the de facto head of resistance would 'in a great degree counteract the efforts of any [more able] officers that might have the will and ability [to oppose us] ... It was with such expectations', he later explained in a letter to Sir David Baird, 'that I made no attempts to stop [him]'.[5] Meanwhile, the key buildings were occupied, the men of the 71st and St Helena Corps were quartered in the Rancheria Barracks, patrols were

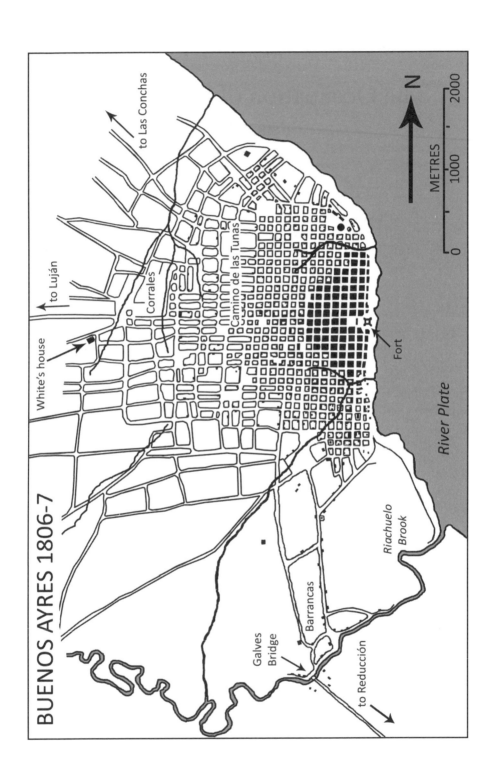

BUENOS AYRES 1806-7

N

METRES

0 1000 2000

to Las Conchas

to Luján

White's house

Corrales

Camino de las Tunas

Fort

River Plate

Riachuelo Brook

Barrancas

Galves Bridge

to Reducción

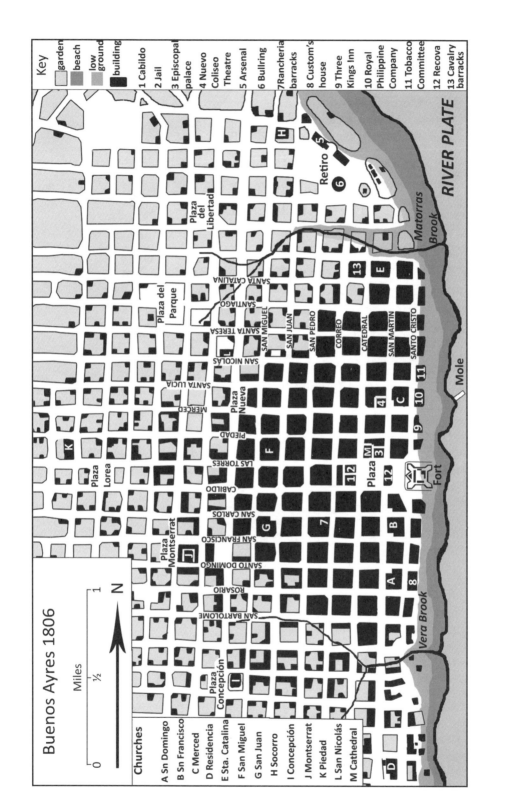

Buenos Ayres 1806

Miles

0   ½   1

N

Key

garden	
beach	
low ground	
building	

1 Cabildo
2 Jail
3 Episcopal palace
4 Nuevo Coliseo Theatre
5 Arsenal
6 Bullring
7 Rancheria barracks
8 Custom's house
9 Three Kings Inn
10 Royal Philippine Company
11 Tobacco Committee
12 Recova
13 Cavalry barracks

Churches

A Sn Domingo
B Sn Francisco
C Merced
D Residencia
E Sta. Catalina
F San Miguel
G San Juan
H Socorro
I Concepción
J Montserrat
K Piedad
L San Nicolás
M Cathedral

RIVER PLATE

Matorras Brook

Retiro

Plaza del Libertad

SANTA CATALINA

Plaza del Parque

SANTIAGO

SAN MIGUEL

SANTA TERESA

SAN JUAN

SAN PEDRO

SAN NICOLAS

SANTA LUCIA

MERCED

Plaza Nueva

CORREO

CATEDRAL

SAN MARTIN

SANTO CRISTO

PIEDAD

Plaza Lorea

LAS TORRES

CABILDO

SAN CARLOS

Plaza Montserrat

SAN FRANCISCO

SANTO DOMINGO

ROSARIO

SAN BARTOLOME

Plaza Concepción

Plaza

Fort

Mole

Vera Brook

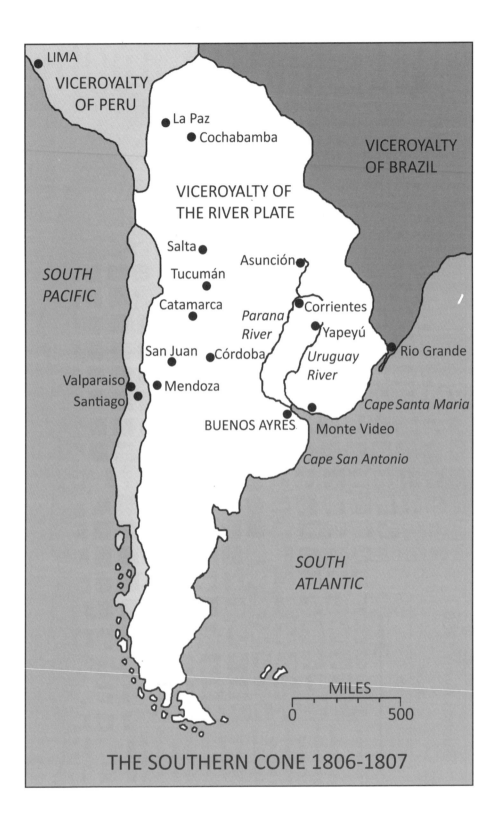

LIMA

VICEROYALTY
OF PERU

La Paz
Cochabamba

VICEROYALTY
OF BRAZIL

VICEROYALTY OF
THE RIVER PLATE

SOUTH
PACIFIC

Salta
Tucumán

Asunción

Catamarca

*Parana
River*

Corrientes

Yapeyú

San Juan   Córdoba

*Uruguay
River*

Rio Grande

Valparaiso
Santiago

Mendoza

BUENOS AYRES

Cape Santa Maria

Monte Video

Cape San Antonio

SOUTH
ATLANTIC

MILES

0   500

THE SOUTHERN CONE 1806-1807

organised, and sentries posted in the suburbs, the Plaza Mayor and at the major intersections. Elsewhere the 755 Spanish officers, sergeants and rank and file who had surrendered were processed by Captain Gillespie. After their weapons had been sent off to be secured in the holds of the British ships, the men were allowed to return to their homes on condition that they reported in 'four days in the week'. The officers, having signed their paroles and promised not to take up arms until officially exchanged, were also dismissed.[6]

His duty done, Captain Gillespie sat down to 'a repast of eggs and bacon' in the Three Kings tavern on Calle Santo Cristo, to find himself sharing a table with several Spanish officers. Noticing the hostess appeared somewhat reluctant to serve his companions, Gillespie asked what the matter was. 'She instantly turned to her countrymen' and began berating them 'in a loud and most impressive tone. "I wish that you gentlemen had informed us sooner of your cowardly intentions to surrender", she announced, "for I will stake my life that had we known it, the women [of Buenos Ayres] would have turned out unanimously and driven back the English with stones."'[7] Later Gillespie was 'accosted by several of ... [his] countrymen' who turned out to be former crew members and 'passengers' of the *Lady Jane Shore*, a convict transport which had gone missing nine years before. While en route to Botany Bay in August 1797 several of the crew, in large part composed of French deserters, had mutinied. After killing the captain and setting his officers adrift in a longboat off the coast of Brazil, they had landed at Monte Video. Some had been imprisoned by the Spanish authorities, others had become citizens and by the time of Beresford's arrival 'some of the female convicts were well-married and the males [were] working at their different trades'.[8] Surprisingly, Beresford took no action against them. The British soldiers got on well with the former convicts and two, Patrick Carey and a man named Smith, joined the 71st.[9]

At 7.00 am British colours were hoisted on the fort and a salute fired by the cannon. Watching from the deck of HMS *Narcissus* four miles off shore, Popham was delighted. Due to the shallowness of the water and adverse weather, he had been unable to contact Beresford since the landing three days before. Popham had witnessed the victory at Reducción and seen 'some firing near the banks of the River Chuello' on the morning of 27 June, but the sight of the king's colours flying from the fort was the first confirmation he had had of Beresford's success.[10] HMS *Narcissus* and HMS *Encounter* fired their broadsides in salute whilst Popham clambered aboard one of the frigates' boats and was rowed ashore for his first glimpse of the British Empire's latest acquisition.[11]

* * *

Although a prosperous commercial hub by the time of the British invasion, Buenos Ayres' early history was far from glamorous. Founded in 1536 by an expedition led by Pedro de Mendoza, for the first 200 years it had been little more than a provincial garrison town. Located on the wild southern frontier of the Viceroyalty of Peru and governed from far-away Lima, Buenos Ayres lived in the shadow of Spain's Pacific colonies and was frequently besieged by the Querandíes, a local tribe of hunter-gatherers. In 1541 the original settlement finally suc-cumbed and was burnt to the ground and abandoned. Thirty-nine years later a second expedition, led by Juan de Garay, refounded the town and, with the Querandíes brought low by war and disease, over the next two decades the settle-ment grew. By 1602 its population had reached 500, most of whom were soldiers, but as just two ships per year were permitted to trade directly with Spain, the colony relied on contraband with neighbouring Brazil. All imports, legal or otherwise, were paid for with the only commodities – cured cow hides and tallow obtained from the vast herds of wild cattle which grazed on the grasslands outside town. As the meat itself could not be preserved long enough to reach European markets, the *vaquerías* (round-ups) were horrendously wasteful. The cattle were corralled and slaughtered. Their hides were stripped and cured, their fat rendered into tallow and their tongues removed as the choicest cut. The rest was left to rot or to feed the packs of wild dogs that roamed the plain.[12]

In 1680 the Portuguese founded the village of Colonia del Sacramento on the far side of the River Plate. After issuing an ultimatum, the governor of Buenos Ayres, José de Garro, attacked with 480 soldiers and 3,000 Guarani Indian auxili-aries from the Jesuit *misiones* in Paraguay. Heavily outnumbered, the Portuguese were defeated and, although the town was returned by treaty the following year, news of the victory was well-received in Madrid. Belatedly realising the damage caused by restricting foreign trade, King Carlos II granted several merchants special *permisos* (royal licences allowing trade between Europe and Spanish South America) and the colony's growth gathered pace. By the middle of the eighteenth century, Buenos Ayres had a population of 10,000 Europeans and creoles aug-mented by a similar number of *mestizos*, Indians and African slaves. Another 6,000 lived in the surrounding countryside. As a result of continuing conflicts in Europe, the Spanish monarchs issued *permisos* with ever-increasing frequency. Struggling to keep pace with the demand for hides, the *vaquerias* were replaced by large rural estates or *estancias*. A further fillip came in 1767 with the expulsion of the Jesuits from the *misiones* in Paraguay, giving Buenos Ayres direct access to the Guarani Indians and control of the lucrative *yerbamate* trade. The town's prosperity was crowned nine years later when it was named capital of the newly formed Viceroyalty of the River Plate, thus freeing it from subservience to Lima.

The first viceroy, Pedro de Cevallos, arrived in the river in 1777 with six ships-of-the-line, six frigates and an army of 10,000 men. After recapturing Colonia del Sacramento, which had become a hub for smuggling operations, Cevallos took up residence in Buenos Ayres and implemented a new directive from Madrid. The Law of Free Commerce permitted the town's merchants to trade directly with Cádiz through the use of *flotas*, fleets convoyed by Spanish warships which made the Atlantic crossing once or twice a year. Cevallos also introduced laws which stimulated agriculture and regulated workers' hours and pay. As a further con-sequence of the town's new status, the riches of Upper Peru (modern day Bolivia) began to pass through Buenos Ayres and in 1788 individual merchants began to trade directly with Spain, although import taxes of up to 34.5 per cent ensured contraband continued to flourish.[13]

Under Cevallos' successors, Juan José de Vértiz y Salcedo and Nicolás de Campo, the population of Buenos Ayres reached 40,000, the central streets were paved, clay street lamps were installed on the main thoroughfares, educational institutions developed and the Nuevo Coliseo theatre opened. In 1791 the outbreak of war in Europe saw dozens of French privateers take to the high seas. Unable to protect his merchant fleets, Carlos IV permitted limited foreign trade. This led to the rise of a new breed of merchants. Engaging foreign partners, they inundated the continent with cheap British goods and amassed huge wealth. As a result the traditional merchant class went into a slow yet steady decline, leading to a divide which would dominate local politics for decades.[14] During the governorship of Viceroy Pedro Melo (1795–97) merchant fleets from the Philippines began stopping in the river. In 1796 imports and exports of 3 million and 5 million *pesos* respectively were recorded and by the turn of the nineteenth century Buenos Ayres had become an important hub for international trade. In exchange for the cured hides of the *pampas*, *yerbamate* of the *misiones*, and precious metals and minerals from Upper Peru, African slaves and luxury European trade goods were imported. In a town with virtually no manufacturing or industry, by 1806 this trade, and the regional traffic which grew from it, was able to support a population of 70,000 souls.[15]

At the pinnacle of *porteño* society were the administrative, clerical and military elite.[16] The first consisted of three separate bodies. The *Audiencia* (high court) advised the viceroy on policy and acted as a high court of appeal, while the *Consulado* was a ministry of transport, agriculture and trade. Both had juristriction over the entire viceroyalty, whereas the authority of the third body, the *Cabildo*, only covered the *intendencia* of Buenos Ayres. Composed largely of high-ranking members of the mercantile class, the latter's duties were obstensibly municipal, but its political influence was growing.[17] Both the administrators and the clerical elite were almost exclusively Spanish-born: Sobremonte was from Seville; Huidobro, the governor of Monte Video, was from Galicia; and Bishop Benito Lué y Riega, the spiritual head of Buenos Ayres' 1,100 priests, monks, nuns and clerics, hailed from Lastres, a small village in Asturias.[18] The senior officers of the armed forces were a mixture of creoles and *Penisulares*. Although his father was from Vizcaya in the Basque Country, Brigadier Quintana hailed from Buenos Ayres, as did Colonel Azcuénaga of the Infantry Volunteers, whilst Colonel Elía was from Navarre and Colonel Giannini had been born in Badajoz.

Beneath the ruling elite was the merchant class, itself divided into several tiers. The highest dealt exclusively in intercontinental traffic and was split between those who had emerged in the 1790s with the rise of foreign trade, and the original merchant families who had prospered under the old Spanish monopoly. The former included several Catalans and Gallegos. The latter was dominated by Basques. Amongst the most influential monopolists at the time of the British invasion were Don Antonio Gaspar de Santa Coloma, a sixty-four-year-old from Alava whose ships took silver to Cádiz and returned with European trade goods, and Martín de Álzaga, the *alcalde de primer voto* (town mayor) and another of the town's leading Basques, who had enjoyed a rapid rise since his arrival in the River

Plate as an eleven-year-old apprentice unable to speak a word of Castilian. Amongst the most prominent internationalists were Tomás Antonio Romero and Pedro Duval. Slave traders and associates of William Pius White, Romero and Duval smuggled tobacco into the viceroyalty from Brazil and imported the mercury used in the amalgamation of the silver mined in Potosí.[19]

Beneath these two factions were the merchants who dealt in regional trade – coarse woollen textiles from Cochabamba, Córdoba and Corrientes, carts, cigars and ponchos from Tucumán, dried fruit and olives from Mendoza, embroidered handkerchiefs from Salta and wines and *aquardiente* from San Juan, Mendoza and Catamarca.[20] Next was a 'middle class' of lawyers, large-scale retailers, cattle ranchers and farmers. These top three tiers totalled 8,000, or a ninth of the town's population.[21] Most were white and a few were foreign born. As well as a significant minority of Portugese, there were some French, Genovese, Napolitans, Dutch, Germans, Irish, North Americans and a handful of English.[22] The rest of the population, as Captain Gillespie noted, were a 'compound breed': a mixture of Indians, whites and blacks 'through various stages of connexion, and … hue'.[23] The most successful worked as peddlers, clerks, tavern owners, 'shoe-makers, taylors, barbers … keepers of dram shops, carpenters … little retail-traders' and soldiers.[24] Beneath them were *peónes*, or day workers, employed in the town's farms, small businesses, tanneries and *mataderos* (slaughter yards). Many were *mulattos*, but there were also some Indians and a handful of free blacks who had received manumission in their owners' will.[25]

At the bottom of the pile were the slaves. The trade in human cargo was big business in Buenos Ayres, with an individual worth an average of 300 *pesos*.[26] Some were sent to Paraguay or Chile to toil on plantations and cattle ranches. Others went to the silver mines of Upper Peru, but from the 1790s until the end of the colonial period, the majority remained in Buenos Ayres where they worked as coach men, seamstresses, pages, cleaners, cooks, shop assistants, warehouse workers, labourers or artisans.[27] This surge in the slave population had had a destabilising effect. Whilst many of those who had previously entered the city had had prior residence in Spain, the recent influx was imported directly from West Africa. Their language, dress and culture were alien and considered threatening and, although the Cabildo had attempted to ban their traditional gatherings, the free *porteños* were haunted by the thought of a Haitian-inspired revolt.[28]

Despite its political status, Buenos Ayres remained architecturally provincial.[29] Spread out for two miles along the west bank of the River Plate, about 200 miles from its mouth, the town formed a triangle composed of 100 blocks, each 100 metres across.[30] Its base, facing the waterfront, was bordered to the north and south by the Matorras and Vera brooks.[31] In the centre, situated two blocks from the river, was the Plaza Mayor. A bustling, open space of compacted earth, it was used for military parades, public executions, religious festivals and markets. On the northwest corner was the cathedral, 'a large edifice, with a lofty dome and parapet' and 'elegant' exterior which housed several religious treasures including 'a fine historical painting of the Acts of the Apostles'.[32] The main door opened on to a flight of stone steps, which were often crowded with market traders.

Beyond was Calle Catedral, a handsome cobbled thoroughfare running the length of the town. On the west side of the plaza was the prison and the town hall. The former was squalid and overcrowded with prisoners who begged passers-by for scraps of food.[33] The latter was built of stone and surmounted by a large square tower. Inside was a chamber where the Cabildo met named the Sala Capitular.[34] To the northeast was the Episcopal Palace. To the south was 'a range of mean, low shops, with a broad pavement in front,' which sold 'every kind of small European Hardware' and the recently finished Recova, a two-storey arcade, was situated to the east. During the day its elegant arches housed the principal stores in town. At night they provided shelter for the homeless.[35]

To the east of the Recova was a smaller square named the Plazoleta del Fuerte, on the far side of which stood the fort. A squat stone and brick building overlooked by the surrounding two-storey houses, its eastern ramparts were lapped by the waters of the River Plate. A dry ditch crossed by a drawbridge ran round the other three sides, each corner was flanked by a small bastion and forty bronze cannon were mounted on the walls. Inside was a small courtyard ringed by several mud and brick buildings, including the governor's residence, the royal treasury, a guardroom, an armoury and a small chapel. Although a fine building when it was finished at the start of the eighteenth century, the fort had fallen into a state of disrepair. 'The cannon were honey-combed, [and] their carriages rotten, the walls [were] low and in part demolished towards the square, and the ditches [were] choked up with rubbish' Gillespie recalled.[36] Some 200 metres to the north was the mole, a pier built of rough stone projecting 200 yards into the River Plate, capped by a battery of three guns. Clustered around its base were the customs house and a watchtower designed to prevent smugglers sneaking ashore.[37] Nearby were the post-office and several warehouses. Some belonged to private merchants. Others were property of the Spanish crown's Tobacco Administration Committee or the Royal Philippine Company. Both operated state-enforced monopolies, denying all but the smugglers access to their particular trade.[38]

Buenos Ayres boasted several religious buildings of note. There were two convents, of the Capuchin and Catalina denominations, four monasteries and twelve churches.[39] The most important were the Santo Domingo, a stone building with a single crenelated tower and adjacent Dominican monastery which stood four blocks to the west of the Plaza Mayor, and La Merced, a Jesuit construction situated on a small square two blocks to the north. On the southern outskirts of town next to the river was La Residencia, a fortress-like monastery with barred windows and thick walls which covered an entire block. As well as housing a Bethlemite monastery, the building contained a chapel and a large hospital with 150 beds whose barred windows overlooked a courtyard to the southwest.[40] Approximately 1,000 yards to the north of the Plaza Mayor was El Retiro, a park spotted with several large buildings where the elite drove their mule-drawn carriages on the Sabbath.[41] Situated on rising ground it was used for military parades as well as civilian promenades and afforded a fine view across town. In the centre was the bullring, a large wood and brick amphitheatre where up to 8,000 watched the shows held every Sunday in the summer months.[42] Also present was the artillery barracks, a small fort and the arsenal, the latter 'an open spot, upon which lay blank shells, and pyramids of shot'.[43] To the north were several *quintas*, large houses surrounded by orchards, which backed onto a cliff beyond which the ground fell away to a beach and the river.[44]

The houses in central Buenos Ayres, built eight to a square, were constructed of whitewashed brick or stone.[45] Most had a single storey. Others, such as that owned by the slave trader Pedro Duval, boasted two.[46] While the majority housed the town's elite, others had been converted into hives of tiny studios and apartments rented out to poor families and single working men.[47] Each resembled a miniature fortress and was built facing inwards towards a courtyard perfumed with orange and lemon trees.[48] The windows were small, barred and blocked with heavy wooden shutters. Thick, double doors were set in masonry frames, topped with crenelated arches boasting family crests, and the contiguous roofs were flat and protected by four-foot high parapets.[49] The further one strayed from the town centre, the more ramshackle the houses became.[50] The streets followed the same trend. Whilst those of the centre were clean, well-lit with clay storm lamps and paved with wide cobblestones, on the outskirts, especially to the north, they were dark, dirty, dangerous places.[51] Formed of hard packed earth and clogged with festering waste, putrefying livestock and the corpses of abandoned slaves, muggings and knife fights were common and in winter deep trenches were gouged by torrential rain.[52]

A mile from the centre were the suburbs where several of the richer residents lived, including the Bostonian William Pius White. Here each 'block' contained one or two houses ringed by a high thorn hedge of aloe and prickly pear enclosing orchards of orange, lemon, peach, fig and olive trees.[53] There were also three *mataderos*, where cattle were butchered and flayed and hides dried and tanned for export. The stench, even in winter, was appalling. 'A few privileged hogs ... fed entirely on the bullock's heads and livers' grazed the yards, and carrion birds, drawn in from the surrounding *pampas*, flocked to devour the remains.[54] Beyond were flimsy shanty towns of adobe shacks with straw roofs which housed the city's poor.[55] Then the *pampas* began. Threaded with narrow tracks leading to the towns of the interior, aside from a scattering of *estancias* built on low rises and ringed with slave and *peon* huts, the grasslands were uninhabited and ran on flat and featureless for miles.[56]

Aside from an annual carnival, when the slaves, women and working classes overturned the sexual, social and racial boundaries which governed colonial society, everyday life in Buenos Ayres was uneventful. As Mariquita Sánchez noted, 'praying and eating ... were the only distractions'. Religious festivals were celebrated with great enthusiasm and the rivalry between the town's seven parishes, each of which was determined to outdo the others in the elaborateness of their costumes and processions, was intense.[57] The only book widely available was the Bible. Others, particularly those of foreign origin, were censored or had been banned by the Inquisition and although there were several schools, education was limited. 'All that was taught was to read and write and the four basic rules of arithmetic,' Sánchez recalled.[58] In 1772, the Colegio de Huérfanas, opened two years before to educate orphans, had begun admitting the daughters of 'decent and distinguished people'. For two *pesos* one *real* a month they learnt 'letters, sewing, Christian doctrine and other tasks befitting their sex.'[59] The only secondary school was the Colegio de San Carlos, where theology, metaphysics and logic were taught for an annual fee of 100 *pesos*. Those amongst the elite who wished to further their education were sent to the universities of Córdoba, Lima, Upper Peru or Madrid.[60]

Entertainment was limited. The Three Kings was the town's only restaurant. 'There were so few passers through that there was no need for more', Sánchez observed. A certain Monsieur Ramón provided a catering service and also took on house slaves as apprentices in his kitchen, returning them to their owners as fully fledged chefs after a year. On Calle San Francisco was a French confectioner's famed for its coffee, cakes and pastries. Three other large cafés, where residents could snack on barley sugars, drink, gossip and play billiards were scattered round the Plaza Mayor, the town had several *canchas de bolos* where a form of lawn bowls was played and the Basque community enjoyed *pelota*, 'a species of Tennis', in which a ball was hit between two opposing teams using a glove 'faced with very thick leather'. As much as fifty *pesos* could change hands on each set.[61] For the poor, there was cock fighting and a staggering 700 *pulperias*, general stores-cum-grog shops, which sold liquor by the dram and were 'often ... crowded by the scum of society'.[62]

*   *   *

On 28 June Popham and Beresford began establishing British control. Their first job was to secure funds to maintain the army and fleet. Over 430,000 *pesos* were seized at the wharves, customs house, post office, Tobacco Administration Committee and Royal Philippine Company.[63] The money was transferred to the Royal Treasury in the fort where 208,519 *pesos* had been captured and a thorough search of town unearthed a further 4,825 hidden in the house of a local priest.[64] Some 1,309 kilograms of tobacco, a million cigars and a number of live vicuñas, alpacas and guanacos, originally intended as gifts to Napoleon's Empress Josefina, were also liberated. Within two weeks a local buyer was found for the tobacco and cigars and the 11,000 *pesos* raised were added to the British haul.[65] Even so, Popham was obliged to add £3,773 from his own pocket to ensure the coffers did not run dry.[66]

The commanders' next task was to secure provisions.[67] Only ten days' supply of bread was left on board the ships and salt rations were running low. As the farmers who kept Buenos Ayres supplied with fruit and vegetables had fled several days before, Beresford sent messengers into the countryside via the local magistrates to assure them that he was willing to pay for fresh produce.[68] The farmers returned and, in July alone, the British spent £3,619 on provisions.[69] Popham was also involved in the search for supplies. 'I ... found ... [200 casks of meat] in possession of [a merchant named] Mr Jackson, who had salted in two years ago' he recalled. 'I agreed to take such a proportion ... as was good and fit for the men to eat.'[70] The men found their own ways of dealing with hunger. Adopting a local

Indian custom, several took to roasting the armadillos that lived on the plains outside town.[71]

Beresford's next concern was security. A garrison of 400, including the Royal Marines, Popham's Sea Battalion and Ogilvie's artillery, was stationed inside the fort and four permanent guard posts were established: thirty men were sent to El Retiro; eighteen were assigned to the mole; eighteen took up quarters in the prison beside the Cabildo; and twenty occupied a post at El Picquete.[72] Popham took possession of five armed Spanish schooners and four gunboats and on 2 July, after the terms of surrender had been finalised and signed by the Cabildo, Beresford wrote to Baird asking for reinforcements from the Cape.[73] The dispatches were sent by the *Melantho* transport as soon as the wind was favourable.[74] Beresford then attempted to convince the residents that his army was more formidable than it actually was. As well as his ploy of using double spacing on the march into town, detachments were embarked on board the boats, then landed dressed in different uniforms.[75]

The first two nights of the occupation were tense.[76] The British thought a popular uprising imminent and Beresford went as far as to term the situation 'somewhat critical ... The surrounding countryside I can have no hopes of ... conciliating', he confessed in his dispatches to Baird. 'The whole of it is at present in ... insurrection.'[77] Beresford need not have worried. The opposition was disorganised, the viceroy had taken most of his soldiers to Córdoba and the majority of those that remained had already surrendered. Without leadership the rest were in no mood to fight. Following the capitulation several 'were seen skulking ... in the outskirts of the town, peeping out from the hedges, with their muskets in their hands,' but 'returned quietly to their habitations' within two or three days.[78]

By 1 July Popham's thoughts had turned to profit. Establishing himself in the fort, he wrote to the mayors of the principal manufacturing towns in England. 'I ... consider it a duty to the commercial interests of Great Britain ... to state ... that the conquest of [Buenos Ayres] opens an extensive channel for ... [her] manufactures', he began. 'Hitherto ... trade ... has been cramped beyond belief ... but from this moment it ... will be thrown open. I need not point out ... how beneficial the commerce of this hitherto neglected country will be ... this city ... alone contains 70,000 inhabitants, wanting all sorts of goods of European manufacture. The productions of this country are indigo, tobacco, Vincenta wool, cotton, tiger skins, seal skins, copperas, figs, dried tongues, beef and hams, saffron, cochineal, cocoa, hemp, hair, wheat, gums, drugs, gold, silver, and precious stones, exclusive of hides and tallow, which I consider the great staple, 1,400,000 of the former being annually exported.'[79] In a private letter to his London-based agent, Popham asked for a large quantity of silk stockings, stressing that the order should not be made public. Having learnt of an item in high demand, the commodore was determined to get the jump on his competitors. Down by the riverside, the merchantmen that had joined the expedition at St Helena were doing a roaring trade. Having sold all their merchandise at a profit of 250 per cent, two of the ships, loaded with as many cured hides as they could carry, set sail for

England, while the *Justina*, useful to Popham due to her heavy armament and shallow draught, was persusaded to stay.[80]

On 3 July Lieutenant Groves of HMS *Diadem*, one of the commanders of Popham's Sea Battalion, was sent to take possession of Ensenada, a small port frequented by smugglers forty miles downriver. Beresford and Popham wanted to ensure that the army would have a post to fall back on should they be forced to leave in a hurry.[81] The same day, having learnt that Sobremonte had been abandoned by his escort and had had to leave his treasure caravan at Luján, a small village on the road to Córdoba twenty-five miles to the west, Beresford ordered Captain Robert Arbuthnot, one of his aides-de-camp, to set out in pursuit. With him went Sergeant John Henry and five troopers of the 20th Light Dragoons and twenty mounted privates of the 71st led by lieutenants Charles Graham and Thomas Murray. The whole was guided by William Pius White, the Bostonian who had already made himself an indispensable part of the British regime. Their progress was slow. On the outskirts of Buenos Ayres the road deteriorated into a simple track which the rains had churned into a morass. Thirty-five miles northwest, after crossing the River Conchas, Arbuthnot sighted the spire of the church of Luján, and spurred his men on. Parties of irregular horsemen shadowed their advance, but did not attack and on arriving in the village, 200 single-storey mud houses clustered round an elegant church, Arbuthnot commandeered the town hall.[82] Over the next few days, when not enjoying boisterous games of football in the main square or feeding their fire with benches from the village school, Arbuthnot's men unearthed 631,684 *pesos*, seventy-one pigs of silver, weighing between 56 and 100 lbs, and seventy-two pigs of copper.[83] Some of the money had been bundled up in animal skins, over 100,000 was found tied up in linen bags or packed into boxes and 'a great portion of' the rest 'had been thrown into wells'.[84] The treasure was loaded onto nineteen wagons and escorted to Buenos Ayres by the infantry, whilst Arbuthnot and his dragoons rode ahead to give Popham and Beresford the good news.[85]

Back at Buenos Ayres the major-general was busy issuing proclamations. Printed by Juan José Perez for a fee of 118 *pesos* on the only press in town, the notices were designed to dispel the *porteños'* worst fears – that the heretics would attempt to convert them or liberate their slaves or rob them of their wealth and means of continuing their livelihoods.[86] '[The citizens of Buenos Ayres are] to enjoy the full and free exercise of their Religion', the first proclamation promised. 'All private property ... shall receive the most ample protection ... a free trade will be opened ... [and] all good citizens will enjoy ... the advantages of a commercial intercourse with Great Britain where no oppression exists'. The documents stated that merchant vessels would not be seized as a means of encouraging trade and promised that import and export taxes would be reduced. The new rates were not fixed until 4 August. Duty on imported British goods was cut from 34.5 per cent to 12 per cent. All other imports were taxed at 17 per cent. Export duties were also in Britain's favour. Hides dispatched to her ports were taxed at 6 per cent plus one *real* per unit, compared to a rate of 6 per cent and two *reales* on those sent elsewhere.[87]

The proclamations were well received. At midday on 7 July all the members of the administrative elite reported to the fort to swear allegiance to the British crown and from 10 July private citizens were also invited to record their loyalty.[88] 'Almost every evening, after dark, one or more ... [came to the fort] to attest their names in a book' Captain Gillespie recalled. 'The number finally amounted to fifty-eight ... most of [whom] ... concurred ... that many others were disposed to follow their example, but were kept back from diffidence as to the future ... [rather than] political scruples, or a want of attachment towards us.'[89] Self-interest motivated the majority. Many came from a rising class of ambitious young merchants who stood to profit from free trade, were involved in slavery as well as smuggling and had extensive foreign contacts. Now that their business had become legal, a fortune was to be made.[90] The priests of Buenos Ayres also appeared to befriend the British. They swore allegiance alongside the administrators on 7 July, Popham noted their 'practical assistance' and Bishop Lué y Riega in particular gave 'a shew of the most obsequious respect, and ... friendship to General Beresford'. By the end of the first week of July, 'everything [in Buenos Ayres had] assumed the face of happiness. Hospitality reigned, the laws had their course, and the worshippers of the sanctuary attended as usual, without any one to make them afraid'.[91]

With security seemingly assured, the British made themselves comfortable. A house was rented for 70 *pesos* a month for the commissary general's department and 579 *pesos* were spent hiring carts and slaves from the Cabildo for the 'conveyance of public stores'. Richard Dalton, the purser of HMS *Diadem*, was appointed as the Royal Navy's liaison officer, Captain John Thompson was assigned the role of port captain, Lieutenant Peter Adamson of the 71st was made mayor of Buenos Ayres, and Beresford was appointed a secretary from the Cabildo to facilitate cooperation between the British and Spanish authorities.[92] Furniture was purchased for the troops in the Rancheria Barracks and the women and children who had sailed from England with the 71st were transferred ashore.[93] Captain Henry Le Blanc, who was already able to hobble around on crutches, was deemed fit enough to leave his quarters on HMS *Narcissus*, and billets were acquired for the commissioned officers in town.[94] As Beresford's secretary, Captain Kennet of the Royal Engineers took up residence in the fort. Once installed, he had his writing desk, which had been brought all the way from England via the Cape on HMS *Narcissus*, hoisted out of the frigate's hold and rowed ashore.[95] Captains Gillespie, Herbert and Forbes rented rooms in the Three Kings, Lieutenant Fernyhough was accommodated by 'a most hospitable merchant' and Lieutenant-Colonel Robert Campbell of the 71st, Pack's second-in-command, was put up by Tomas Antonio Romero, one of Buenos Ayres' most prominent slave traders, for 12 *pesos* a month.[96]

The upper-class *porteños* proved great hosts. '[The] families ... paid [us] ... the kindest attentions,' Captain Gillespie recalled, '[and] afforded many examples of a natural goodness of heart ... as to convince us that benevolence was a national virtue.' On sunny afternoons, the band of the 71st held impromptu concerts by the waterfront and in the evenings, *tertulias*, or formal dances, were held by prominent families such as the Barredas, Duvals, Romeros, Terradas and Galveses.[97] Dressed in long cloaks and elegant black lace *mantillas*, 'all the neigh-bouring females' attended. Several brought a particular breed of lap dog – hair-less aside from the head and tail – and all were accompanied by elderly female chaperones.[98] Whilst some British officers attempted small talk in faltering Spanish, others invited the young *porteñas* to dance.[99] 'Waltzes were the vogue,' Gillespie observed, 'accompanied by the guitar or piano.'[100] At one of these gatherings Captain George Kennet fell in love. His dancing partner, Mariana Sánchez Barreda, was equally smitten.[101] When not attending dances, Captain Gillespie spent his time poring over 'three duodecimo volumes' on the history of the Incas lent to him by a friendly Spanish officer. Other officers founded Buenos Ayres' first Freemason Lodge or attended the theatre and regular Sunday parades were held in the Plaza Mayor at which Colonel Pack led the men in prayer.[102]

On 13 July, a bright, clear day that 'was excessively cold', the nineteen treasure wagons from Luján came clattering into town.[103] Along with the money and hides seized from the *Bankege*, the gunboats and schooners captured in the port and the goods found in the warehouses and wharves, the total prize money amounted to over 1,250,000 *pesos*. As commander-in-chief, Baird, despite never having left the Cape, received a staggering £23,990 5s 8d. Beresford's haul amounted to £11,995 2s 10d, whilst Popham, bound by the secret deal he had arranged in Cape Town, received just £5,997 7s 5d. Although a handsome amount, which dwarfed the £18 6s the common soldiers were given, Sir Home was far from satisfied; his thoughts turned to the capture of Monte Video and he spent the second week of July rattling off letters to the Admiralty demanding reinforcements and supplies. Having experienced the dangers of navigating large ships of war round the River Plate, 'four frigates, three or four sloops, and ten of the largest gun-brigs,' were requested. Winter clothing and ships' supplies were also needed. 'I trust ... the navy board ... [will] send out a great proportion of warm clothing,' Popham wrote, 'particularly the Guernsey frocks which in tem-perate weather can be worn alone and in cold, such as we have here now, can be worn under their jackets ... We also want nails for the 64-gun ships, some cables, ... and two bower anchors for the *Diomede*.'[104]

Sir Home's next task was to organise his fleet. As Buenos Ayres was an open town, Beresford's men would be exposed should the troops at Monte Video cross the river. Accordingly, HMS *Encounter*, the *Walker* transport, and the captured Spanish sloops of war were ordered to patrol the bays and creeks upriver from Colonia del Sacramento, from where any invasion was likely to be launched. The ships-of-the-line, meanwhile, remained on blockade duty in the deep water off Monte Video. On 20 June HMS *Diadem* had given chase to a strange sail which later 'proved to be the Spanish ship *La Denia* from Barcelona bound for Monte Video'. As *La Denia* fled, she hoisted American then Spanish colours, but struck after a few warning shots had passed close under her bows. At the end of June two more Spanish brigs, the *San Francisco de Paula* and *Buen Viage*, were detained. Seventeen pipes of port, four rolls of cloth and 850 stacks of firewood were confiscated. The captains were provided with IOUs before being sent on their way. On 1 July a Russian ship with a cargo of African slaves was taken and in the days that followed several Prussian and Portuguese merchantmen were apprehended.[105]

On 19 July, an unusually warm and sunny day, HMS *Narcissus* set sail from Buenos Ayres for England.[106] After two days spent at anchor off Monte Video with the rest of the fleet (bolstered by the recent return of HMS *Leda* from Santa Caterina) Captain Donnelley proceeded downriver. Crammed into the frigate's hold were over a million *pesos* worth of coin, trade goods and precious metals, the rest of the booty having been retained in the Royal Treasury in the fort. Also on board were glowing despatches to the War Office and Admiralty, the latter carried by Brigade-Major John Deane, and several private letters. One, written by Beresford to Viscount Castlereagh, former Secretary of State for War and the Colonies, espoused particular confidence. 'This town & neighbourhood ... remain[s] ... tranquil', he boasted, '[and] each day [has] increased the satisfaction of the people ... every inhabitant not a Spaniard most earnestly desires to remain under the protection of His Britanick Majesty'.[107] By the middle of July all seemed calm. Beresford was convinced that the Spaniards posed no threat and was even considering raising a local militia.[108]

Not all was as it seemed. While two vocal factions of the city's population, namely those who stood to profit from a relaxation of Madrid's strict trade laws and a small group who saw British rule as a stage on the road to emancipation were pleased, two other factions were vehemently opposed to the invaders. The first, a small but growing band of creole radicals tired of the corrupt, self-seeking and incompetent rule of Spain, desired absolute independence from the Old World. The second, and by far the most numerous, remained loyal to Carlos IV. Composed chiefly of Spaniards and enjoying the covert support of elements of the clergy as well as the monopolists amongst the merchant class, the loyalists abhorred foreign, Protestant rule.[109] Both groups, although diametrically opposed in their politics, were united by the presence of a mutual enemy, and as early as the end of June two separate plots had been hatched to retake Buenos Ayres.

Chapter 6

The Resistance

Buenos Ayres
29 June – 1 August 1806

Amongst the first to voice their opposition to British rule were two patriotic young Catalans, Felipe de Sentenach and Jerado Estebe y Llach. A seventeen-year-old engineer from Barcelona, Sentenach had arrived in South America in 1804. After spells in Monte Video and Paraguay, he had travelled to Buenos Ayres on the eve of the British invasion. The twenty-five-year-old Llach, on the other hand, had been resident in the capital for several years.[1] After being introduced by a mutual acquaintance, on 29 June they confessed their desire to be rid of the invaders. Their first step was to draft a report for Pascual Ruiz Huidobro, the governor of Monte Video, detailing the strength of their opponents. By quizzing the British officers and counting the daily rations ordered for the troops, the Catalans saw through Popham's and Beresford's ploys to mask their numerical weakness. By 3 July the report was ready. Included was a diary covering the events of June, notes on the number, armament and location of the fleet and the whereabouts of Beresford's garrison, guard posts and patrols. The letter concluded with a scheme for the town's reconquest and a request for military aid. With 1,000 men, twelve 24-pounders, twelve gunboats and four bomb ketches, Sentenach and Llach assured Huidobro that Buenos Ayres would be theirs.[2]

A few days later, Captain Santiago de Liniers, the Frenchman who had bombarded Popham's fleet from Ensenada on 25 June, also decided to take action. A fifty-two-year-old career soldier from Nirot, Liniers had entered military school in Malta at the age of twelve, graduating three years later with the Cross of Chevalier to serve as a cavalry sub-lieutenant in the Piedmont. In 1774 he volunteered to fight for Spain in the campaigns being waged against the Moors in Algiers. Afterwards, Liniers travelled to Cádiz and transferred to the Spanish navy and in 1776, with the rank of ensign, sailed for the River Plate under Viceroy Cevallos to fight the Portuguese. Liniers later saw action in the American War of Independence and distinguished himself at the Siege of Port Mahon in Minorca, resulting in a promotion to lieutenant. A diplomatic role in the war against the Barbary pirates followed. When Madrid was forced to negotiate with the Bey of Algiers, Liniers secured a favourable treaty and persuaded the tyrant to release his Christian slaves. A promotion to captain and senior naval commander at Buenos Ayres followed. In the muddy backwaters of the River Plate, the thirty-five-year-old held a variety of posts including interim governor of the *misiones* in Paraguay, and after the death of his first wife, Juana de Menviel, he married Martína

Sarratea, daughter of one of the wealthiest merchants in town, cementing his social standing. The couple had several children, but Liniers strayed into the arms of Ana Perichon, a young French woman of Mauritian pedigree. This, combined with a preference for a relaxation of trade restrictions, connections with a growing French faction and suspected links with a secretive and as yet insignificant independence movement, rendered Liniers undesirable in the eyes of the establishment. His responsibilities were curtailed and aside from chasing the occasional pirate, his chief preoccupations became spending time with his family at his ranch and going on hunting expeditions with his dogs.[3] The best part of the next decade was idled away until the arrival of Popham's squadron kickstarted the Frenchman's career.

Liniers' plan began with subterfuge. Having spent a few days holed up in the *estancia* of a friend outside town, at the end of June he sent a letter to Beresford asking for permission to deliver his parole. Beresford accepted and on 29 June Liniers arrived in Buenos Ayres. The Frenchman assured the major-general 'that he was disgusted with the Spanish Service for wrongs received, & that he had long wished to throw off the Military Habit & set up as a merchant to support a Family'. Although a written parole was not required – 'through interests of delicacy' – Liniers swore not to take up arms again and was granted the freedom of town.[4] On 1 July Martín de Sarratea, Liniers' father-in-law, threw a dinner party at his house near Santo Domingo Church. Both Liniers and Beresford were invited and the two appear to have got on well. The Frenchman divided the next few days between furthering his friendship with the British and clandestine meetings with members of the Cabildo before stealing out of Buenos Ayres on the night of 10 July. Riding to the port of Las Conchas, Liniers sailed across the river to Colonia del Sacramento and travelled overland to Monte Video to garner support.[5]

The clergy of Buenos Ayres, although ostensibly collaborating, were also keen to be rid of the invaders. Secretly outraged that the British refused to kneel in his presence, Bishop Riega encouraged his priests to denounce them from the pulpit.[6] Friar Gregorio Torres of the Santo Domingo Church made a solemn vow to dedicate the British colours to the Virgin Mary should she bless the *porteños* with victory and at least two priests crossed to Monte Video to drum up support.[7] Another who made the journey was Juan Martín de Pueyrredón, a nineteen-year-old creole patriot. The eldest son of a French-Basque merchant, Pueyrredón was educated in Europe and spent his formative years in revolutionary France, returning to Buenos Ayres in 1805 fully versed in the ideals of the Enlightenment. Pueyrredón believed a temporary British occupation the best way to achieve his long-term aim of an independent South America and had initially collaborated with the invaders along with his associate William Pius White, but on realizing the British merely intended to replace one colonial power with another, he decided that his destiny lay with the resistance.[8] On 9 July, after being secretly commissioned by the Cabildo, he too crossed to the east bank.[9]

By the second week of July Sentenach's and Llach's plan was gathering pace. Five more Catalans had joined them, including Juan de Dios Dozo, a young scribe and bookkeeper from Cádiz, who persuaded his employer, Martín de Álzaga, a monopolist and one of the richest merchants in town, to join the cause. A ruthless and xenophobic man, whose naked ambition had driven him to secure the Cabildo's key role of *alcalde de primer voto* over a decade before, Álzaga wielded great influence, and, with his network of informants, would prove the Catalans most important recruit yet.[10] On 8 July Álzaga hosted a meeting in his town house. Several key points were agreed: at least 500 men would be recruited; an *estancia* outside town would be rented and fortified to serve as a training base and arms, ammunition and supply store; several houses in the town centre would be procured as arms caches; and two mines would be dug and filled with explosives – one under the Rancheria Barracks and the other beneath the fort. When the army from Monte Video arrived, the fuses would be lit and the attack would begin.

On 9 July the Catalans elected Sentenach as their commander. Llach was chosen as his second and Tomás Valencia, a young bookseller who took his surname from the city of his birth, was appointed sergeant-major.[11] The next day recruitment of the lower ranks began. With several conspirators in town, the Catalans conducted the process in secrecy. Each of the four captains recruited a lieutenant who in turn enlisted four subalterns. The lieutenants and subalterns then recruited five sergeants who went on to enlist the privates, each group being unaware of the identity of the others. By 15 July 1,900 men had been enlisted and the captains put their founding principles into writing. Their loyalty to Carlos IV was reiterated, the Virgin Mary of Conception was chosen as their patron saint and Álzaga agreed to pay each man four *reales* a day. The document also noted that the captains felt it was their right to elect their own governors in the event of victory, a clause reflecting Álzaga's future plans. Over the next two weeks 2,000 unpaid volunteers were enlisted to act as a reserve and on 16 July the Chacra de Perdriel, an isolated farmhouse twelve miles northwest of Buenos Ayres, was rented as a base for the army. The site was chosen for its proximity to the port of Los Olivos (thought to be the most likely point of arrival for reinforcements from Monte Video) as well as its natural strength. With a lake to the north, a brook to the west and mud walls to the south and east, the defenders believed they could hold out against anything the British could send against them.[12]

At Monte Video preparations were also under way. On 1 July, having heard rumours of the fall of Buenos Ayres, a public meeting was held at the convent of San Francisco. The people agreed to aid the capital, the resolution was backed by the officers of the army and navy and by the evening of 2 July a bellicose crowd had gathered at the governor's palace, where Pasquil Ruiz Huidobro was leading a council of war. A fifty-six-year-old Galician, Huidobro had been governor of Monte Video since 1803. Having ascended the ranks of the Spanish navy, he had sailed to the River Plate in 1776 with Pedro Cevallos' expedition. Good-looking and never less than exquisitely dressed, Huidobro suffered from poor health and was more of a statesman than a soldier. He loved military parades, but consistently avoided the battlefield and was one of the few leaders on the Spanish side who would die of natural causes.[13] Insisting he was too ill to lead the expeditionary force, Huidobro ordered his officials to mobilise the troops.[14] The next morning one of Popham's ships-of-the-line sailed into the bay. Tacking out of gunshot, she dropped anchor off Carretas Point. The sight only added to the townsfolk's enthusiasm for war. Over the next few days Huidobro was inundated with offers of help: Juan Franco Garcia, a militia colonel, volunteered his salary; the rancher Juan José Seco offered to maintain a unit of 200 cavalry and contributed 1,600 horses; a merchant named Francisco Antonio de Castro loaned three ships armed with cannon and mortar and crewed by sailors and slaves; Francisco Antonio Maciel, a wealthy creole farmer, meat-curer and philanthropist, offered the use of a barn to quarter the troops; and Felipe Contrusi donated 4,000 *quintales* of rice and his gold and silver jewellery.[15]

On 4 July three units of militia were formed. Volunteers who hailed from France, Navarre and Vizcana served under Augustín Abreu Orta, a forty-year-old retired naval lieutenant from Andalucía employed by the Spanish Philippine Company. The second unit, made up of Galician and Asturian volunteers, was commanded by Roque Riobo, an infantry captain of the Spanish regulars, whilst the third, known as the Miñones, consisted of Catalan and creole volunteers. Uniformed in blue and yellow and armed with pistols, carbines and sabres, the Miñones were formed around a backbone of sixty retired regulars and led by lieutenants Rafael Bofarull and José Grau. Hundreds of peasants also came into town to sign up as mounted irregulars. Each was expected to bring their own horse and was paid twelve *pesos* a month.[16]

On 10 and 11 July a naval squadron was organised. It consisted of six gunboats, crewed by fifty sailors each, eight transports and six armed sailing ships. Four were *zumacas*, small twin or triple-masted coastal schooners, one was a single masted *balandra* and the last, the flagship, was a large armed sloop equipped with oars as well as sails enabling her to manoeuvre in a dead calm. The squadron was placed under the command of Juan Gutiérrez de la Concha, a forty-six-year-old Cantabrian trained in astronomy and cartography at the Naval Academy in Cádiz, who had recently arrived at Monte Video after mapping the Patagonian coast.[17] Hipólito Mordeille, a colourful forty-eight-year-old privateer from Bormes-les-Mimosas in France, was de la Concha's more than capable second. Known as Mancho as the result of losing his left arm during a boarding operation in the Mediterranean a decade before, Mordeille had recently returned from a privateering sweep off the African coast during which he had captured four British slavers.[18]

On 14 July Martín de Pueyrredón arrived at Monte Video. The next day Governor Huidobro sent a letter to Sentenach and Llach approving their plan and promising them reinforcements, and on 17 July Pueyrredón was sent to Luján to take command of some troops due to convene there from several towns in the interior. Later the same day Santiago de Liniers arrived.[19] After consulting with the Cabildo, Huidobro appointed the Frenchman commander-in-chief of the expeditionary force.[20] With Popham's squadron still in sight, Abreu and Riobo's volunteers were ordered to remain in town and on 21 July, when Liniers reviewed the troops he would command, they amounted to no more than

600 men. As well as a unit of regulars, there was a detachment of Blandengues, a squadron of dragoons, a corps of militia, the 150-strong Miñones, a number of priests and surgeons and an artillery train led by Captain Francisco Agustini made up of two howitzers and three cannon and manned by 110 Indian volunteers.[21] As the expeditionary force was preparing to march, a letter arrived from Sobremonte. Having reached Córdoba on 12 July, the viceroy had named it his temporary capital and had been raising troops to return to Buenos Ayres.[22] The citizens of Monte Video were unimpressed. 'This letter is as bold as it is inappropriate' one resident noted in his diary '[and] caused such a commotion and occasioned such disgust that I don't feel up to making further comment.' The next morning Liniers' first detachment marched out of the San Pedro gate to the east. On 23 July the rest of the army departed and de la Concha's fleet set sail for Colonia. Cheering townsfolk crowned the walls to watch them leave.[23]

Across the river the Catalans' plan was progressing. Troops had been installed in the ranch at Perdriel, the stockpiling of arms and ammunition was gathering pace and on 17 July Álzaga rented a town house next door to the Rancheria Barracks from which the mine would be dug. Two sappers, Bartolome Tast and Pedro Arnau, took up residence, tools were carried inside hidden in wooden barrels and a lookout posted in a billiard hall across the street. The next morning Sentenach snuck into the British barracks in disguise. Pacing out the building, he noted the locations of the officers' bedrooms and the dormitories of the troops.[24] By the second half of July rumours of the coming insurrection were rife. Word of the missions to Monte Video and the Catalans' efforts to raise troops in the city reached Beresford, who also learnt of the Cabildo's complicity and the existence of an armed camp on the outskirts of town.[25] Most of the intelligence was unspecific, but when his informants told him of the whereabouts of an enemy magazine at Fleuris, nine miles from town, Beresford ordered Captain James Ogilvie of the Royal Artillery to destroy it. On arrival the artillerymen gathered as much ammunition as they could carry, but whilst they were filling their tumbrils the powder caught light. Two men were killed in the ensuing explosion and several badly wounded. The rest returned to town.[26]

Another cause for concern for Beresford was an increase in the rate of desertion. Seduced by offers of land, marriage and employment, several Catholics in the ranks had absconded.[27] As early as 3 July three Spaniards from the St Helena Regiment had been given 500 lashes each for attempted desertion and by the middle of the month the malaise had spread to the 71st.[28] Private Thomas Deal ran on 17 July. A Spanish resident named San Genes was sentenced to death for aiding him, but the punishment was later dropped at the request of Bishop Riega. Jacob Echart of Captain Paley's company, one of the Germans forcibly recruited in Cape Town, absconded soon after.[29] On 19 July Beresford published a proclamation reiterating his threat to execute any locals involved. The document had immediate results. Rather than run the risk of being discovered, one resident murdered the soldier he had been harbouring and on 20 July several citizens were arrested and a military court martial convened to try them.[30] Amongst the judges was Samuel Pococke, a captain in the 71st who spent his nights pining for his 'dearest Eliza', whom he had married in Reading two and a half years before, and making pessimistic entries in his journal. 'This looks like a cloud hanging over our heads', he noted in reference to the upcoming trial, 'which one day or other will burst'.[31]

A further concern was the disappearance of the prisoners of war taken in June. Many of the Spanish officers, despite signing their paroles, had absconded and most of the rank and file had followed suit. Having heard that they were not receiving sufficient rations, on 24 July Beresford directed Captain Gillespie to pay them a month's allowance. Gillespie ordered the prisoners to report to him to receive it, but 'of more than 500 only 12 appeared at the appointed time.' Most of the rest had joined the resistance.[32] That evening the *Santo Cristo del Grao*, an unsuspecting Spanish merchantman from Cádiz, dropped anchor off Buenos Ayres and was seized by a detachment of eighteen men under Captain John Thompson of the Royal Navy. 'The master was thunderstruck on seeing the English come on board', Captain Pococke recalled '[and] said he had only been a few months released from an English prison.' From newspapers seized on board, the British learnt of Vice Admiral Duckworth's victory at the Battle of Santo Domingo on 6 February. That evening, the officers toasted his success and Beresford ordered a salute fired by the cannon in the fort to celebrate.[33]

On 25 July word spread that 'the Spaniards' intended to rise up and attack at midnight, their plan to seize Beresford whilst he attended a performance at the Nuevo Coliseo, then assault the fort. The major-general ordered the pickets and patrols strengthened and the fort's cannon made ready to fire, then went to the theatre as planned accompanied by a number of his officers. 'We were all on our guard', Lieutenant Fernyhough recalled, 'but nothing occurred, although a number of suspicious persons were about, and a great crowd at the door on our return to the castle.'[34] Alone in his lodgings Captain Pococke went to bed fully dressed, his sword at his side and both pistols loaded. The next day there was still no sign of an attack. Pococke realised it was a temporary reprieve. 'I am inclined to think that their reports will come true in the end', he noted, '[and] perhaps when we least expect it.'[35]

By now the Catalans' preparations were coming to a close. On 22 July they had received Huidobro's reply. Although the cannon they had requested were needed at Monte Video, the news of Liniers' imminent arrival encouraged them to redouble their efforts and the next day a house was hired on Calle San Juan to be used as an armoury. Muskets, pistols, swords and gunpowder were smuggled past the British sentries in covered wagons, empty barrels and pipes. Inside, five men worked round the clock making cartridges from scraps of twisted paper, pinches of gunpowder and lead shot. On 24 July Tast, Arnau and eight other sappers began digging the first mine. Outside sentries carrying sawn-off muskets under their cloaks patrolled whilst Sentenach snuck back into the barracks to ensure the sappers had not been heard. Two days later Juan de Dios Dozo rented a house on the Plazoleta from which the second mine would be opened and a carpenter was hired to prepare the struts needed for the shafts. Once more Sentenach risked his life to ensure success. Entering the fort in disguise, he measured the distance between the curtain wall and the interior barracks and magazine.[36]

Twenty-five miles to the northwest Juan Martín de Pueyrredón had reached Luján where 1,000 riders were awaiting him. Antonio de Olavarría, a sixty-year-old Basque who had taken part in the defeat at Quilmes four weeks before, had brought 200 Blandengues and two 2-inch mortars from the forts on the Indian frontier. Approximately 100 others had been recruited from the surrounding farms, paid by Pueyrredón and a local landowner and uniformed in sky blue sashes donated by a local priest. On 28 July the riders departed for Perdriel.[37] The first mine was completed that morning. After just four days the sappers had dug ninety feet under the road and excavated two side tunnels, each terminating in a small chamber. One was fifteen feet under the principal dormitory of the 71st. The other was positioned under the key structural wall of the barracks. Both were packed with thirty-six barrels of gunpowder, primed and ready to explode.[38]

By the end of July fewer and fewer citizens were taking to the streets and the British were feeling decidedly vulnerable.[39] In the Rancheria Barracks the men were particularly concerned. One night a drummer of the 71st was kept awake 'by a noise ... [seemingly] proceeding from labourers beneath him.' He informed a sergeant and 'an expedient was adopted by laying several muskets, barrels uppermost ... upon the floor, upon which some pins were placed, so as to be deranged by the smallest concussion.' The next morning 'they were found upon the ground' and a thorough search of the surrounding buildings was carried out. The Spaniards disguised the mine head and nothing was found. Beresford remained calm. 'All this gave me but little uneasiness', he recalled, 'as I did not think those from Monte Video could ever effect a passage across [the river], & the disaffected [of Buenos Ayres] were acting as I wished in leaving the Town, [the only place] where ... they could be dangerous to us.'[40]

On 28 July, Beresford learned that Liniers' expeditionary force had arrived at Colonia and ordered HMS *Encounter* to perform a reconnaissance. The following morning a show of force was made in town.[41] 'The whole garrison marched out ... in different directions, in order to show the Spaniards that we were ... ready to meet them in the field', Captain Pococke recalled. 'The inhabitants were greatly alarmed, and fled in all directions'. That night, Pococke confided his fears to his journal. 'There is no doubt something is in agitation', he wrote. 'I think the wisest thing that we could do would be to be off, while we [still can] ..., with the treasure and the property'.[42]

At midday on 30 July HMS *Encounter* dropped anchor ten miles off Colonia. Lieutenant Talbot sighted 'a considerable number of vessels' at anchor in the bay. Liniers, who had arrived the day before, ordered de la Concha to attack.[43] At 1.30 pm Talbot 'counted 10 gunboats, 2 schooners & 6 launches' all 'full of men' sailing towards him and 'got the two long 12-pounders ... astern' to engage them. At 2.45 pm, as the enemy 'began to come up ... very fast', Talbot's gunner opened fire. One of the Spanish ships, a schooner donated by the Montevidean merchant Francisco Antonio de Castro, was armed with a 32-pounder and by 4.45 pm Talbot was in some difficulty.[44] Unable to manoeuvre due to a contrary wind and having had several shots go whistling past the rigging and one crash through the poop deck, he broke off the engagement.[45] On his arrival off Buenos Ayres Talbot sent a boat inshore.[46] The messenger landed to find soldiers dashing back and forth and arms and ammunition being issued. That afternoon Beresford had learnt that Pueyrredón was due to join the volunteers from Buenos Ayres at Perdriel and was mobilising his men to confront them.[47]

Chapter 7

La Reconquista

Buenos Ayres
1 August – 12 August 1806

Leaving Lieutenant-Colonel Campbell in command in the fort, Beresford led a column of 500 of the 71st and fifty of the St Helena Regiment out of town at 1.30 am on 1 August. The troops were accompanied by Colonel Denis Pack and a local guide. As they marched through the Plaza Mayor, Captain Ogilvie joined them with thirty artillerymen, six cannon and six howitzers. The men filed down the cobbled streets 'in the greatest silence', passed through the suburbs and out of town. Sentries placed at every junction arrested passers-by to prevent word reaching the enemy. 'The stars were bright overhead' and later a perfect dawn revealed 'a beautiful plain'. Captain Pococke thought the pampas the 'most delightful' landscape he had ever seen.[1] Beresford was preoccupied with more serious matters. Twice misled by his guide, it wasn't until 8.00 am that his advanced guard caught sight of the enemy.

Only 100 of the 950 volunteers the Catalans had gathered at Perdriel remained. Keen to spend some time with their families before the Reconquista, the rest had returned to Buenos Ayres. Most of those that remained had never experienced combat before. One exception was their leader, Corporal Juan Pedro Cerpa. Another was Jacob Echart, the former Waldeck Chasseur who had deserted from the 71st and was now in command of one of Cerpa's six cannon. Also present were 100 men under Pedro Anzoategui. Having spent the previous night hauling four 18-pounders out to the farm from Buenos Ayres, they were exhausted. Encamped on a low hill one mile to the west were the 1,050 cavalrymen who had arrived from Luján with Juan Martín de Pueyrredón the night before. The vast majority would play no role in the coming battle. As Anzoategui's men positioned their guns beside Cerpa's on the low ground before the farmhouse, a lookout rode into camp warning the British were near. Cerpa drew his men up behind a line of earthen walls and shallow ditches to the rear of the artillery and, as the British deployed for battle, Pueyrredón, mounted on a fine Chilean thorough-bred, led his escort of fifty men to the farm and formed up on the right. Olavarría and the rest of the cavalry remained in reserve.[2]

At 8.30 am Beresford ordered the 71st to advance. Lieutenant John Graham and Ensign Gavin stepped six paces to the front. The men formed line around them and marched forward supported by the guns, while Beresford, his staff and escort remained on a low rise. When within 1,000 yards of the enemy, Captain Ogilvie unlimbered his 6-pounders and opened fire. It was the moment Olavarría had been waiting for. Turning his horse to the north, he led his 1,000 riders from the field, later claiming that he had orders to wait for Liniers' arrival before committing to a fight. Down by the farm the Spanish cannon returned fire, but their round shot flew wide. When within musket range, Pack ordered the 71st to fire by companies from left to right and after 'seven or eight' volleys, the Highlanders charged. Corporal Cerpa and a handful of men briefly held out, but the bulk of the Spaniards mounted their horses and fled to the north. Cerpa and the rest followed suit, leaving a handful of dead and wounded and Jacob Echart behind. Serving his cannon singlehandedly, the German was overrun and knocked to the ground. The redcoats wanted to kill him immediately, but their officers insisted on placing Echart under guard.

Meanwhile, having ridden unseen round Beresford's left flank, Pueyrredón and ten of his escort charged the British supply train. Most of the drivers managed to flee with their wagons, but one cart loaded with grain for the mules was cut off. Severely wounding the driver with their sabres, the Spaniards hauled their prize from the field. While Ogilvie fired a few round shot after them, killing one man and cutting a horse in two, Pueyrredón charged Beresford and the gaggle of British staff officers watching from the rise. Recognizing the young creole from his involvement with the Cabildo, Beresford reached for his sword, but it stuck fast rusted into its scabbard. Captain Arbuthnot and Colonel Pack held the riders at bay until Lieutenant Mitchell and a section of redcoats arrived and blasted them from their saddles. His Chilean thoroughbred shot beneath him, Pueyrredón was on the verge of being captured when Captain Lorenzo López rode to his aid. Leaping up behind his fellow officer, the young patriot was carried from the field.[3]

The British rested for two hours before returning to Buenos Ayres. At sunset they marched through the Plaza Mayor with Echart, seven other prisoners and the ten captured cannon at their head. 'The town was greatly crowded to see us' Pococke recalled. Having heard rumours of a British defeat, the *porteños* hid their disappointment well. Beresford was greeted by Bishop Riega and several senior members of the Cabildo still keen on maintaining their charade of support.[4] Having marched forty-two miles in a single day, the redcoats were exhausted and Captain Pococke's 'feet were a good deal blistered'. Nevertheless, the victory provided a much-needed tonic and at a celebratory dinner that evening, Beresford opined it 'would ... insure ... tranquillity till reinforcements from England or the Cape should [arrive]'.[5]

The defeat was a major setback for the Catalans. Juan Trigo, the commander at Perdriel, had left all his correspondence at the farmhouse and the conspirators were worried that their plans would be betrayed. As soon as word reached town, Sentenach called an emergency meeting. All agreed that they had gone too far to turn back and swore they would never surrender. Sentenach commanded them to disperse into the countryside and await his call whilst advancing the pace of his preparations. On 2 August several more houses on the eastern side of the Plazoleta were rented to provide cover for the sappers, the neighbours were bribed to ensure their silence and work on the mine under the fort began.[6] That afternoon, as a British court martial made short work of Jacob Echart's trial, Popham was rowed ashore from HMS *Leda*. Having learnt of Lieutenant Talbot's brush with de la Concha at Colonia, he spent the day adapting the *Triton* and *Walker* transports to attack the enemy fleet. Armed sailors and marines, heavy cannon and six and a quarter barrels of gunpowder were transferred on board and they set sail while Popham and Captain King assembled a second flotilla at Buenos Ayres.[7] At 4.30 pm the next day the *Walker* reached Colonia and exchanged fire with a battery that Liniers had set up in the main square. Little damage was done and when 'a dreadful hurricane blew up' out of the southeast, the transport was forced to break off the encounter.[8] That night, as Popham's gun-brigs and armed transports were trapped in-shore, Liniers' expeditionary force boarded de la Concha's ships and was swept across the river.[9] Joined by a unit of local militia under Captain Pedro García and Martín Pueyrredón and a few other survivors from Perdriel, their numbers were swollen to 1,400 men. The crossing was chaotic. Amidst the swirling rain and howling winds, de la Concha's ships stole across the water, each captain having no idea of the whereabouts of the other members of the fleet. Liniers' vessel had a particularly fortunate escape. Approaching the west bank, a break in the clouds revealed HMS *Leda* half a cannon shot away. Putting on more sail, the Spaniards were swept on before the British could react. At dawn the fleet landed at Las Conchas, a hamlet of huts built on marshy ground fifteen miles to the northwest of Buenos Ayres.[10] Within two hours the disembarkation was complete. Several horses and mules fell into the water and were drowned, but not a single man was lost. Hauling the ships up Las Conchas River, Liniers camped half a mile inland. Without tents and low on provisions, his men spent the night lashed by driving rain awaiting a British attack.[11]

By 5 August Liniers had consolidated his position. One hundred and fifty local volunteers and a number of de la Concha's sailors and Mordeille's privateers swelled his army to over 2,000, pickets were thrown out, an advanced guard organised, horses and mules requisitioned to replace those lost during the landing, regular patrols set up, and several huts occupied. The next day the Catalans made contact, requesting that Liniers delay his attack to allow the sappers to complete the mine under the fort. A letter also arrived from Sobremonte. Approaching with an army of 2,500 raised in Córdoba, the viceroy also requested that Liniers postpone the fight. The Frenchman refused. With little shelter, few supplies and the storm continuing unabated, he was keen to strike as soon as possible.[12]

At Buenos Ayres the weather was causing havoc. Whilst Popham rode out the gale with the yards and topmasts of HMS *Leda* struck, the flotilla of small ships and armed boats he and Captain King had gathered was devastated. On 6 August two gunboats were driven on shore and smashed to splinters and two others foundered at their anchors. HMS *Diadem*'s launch and barge were swamped, the *Triton* transport had her rudder ripped off and the yawl and launch belonging to HMS *Leda* were sunk.[13] Onshore, news of Liniers' arrival had spread and the townsfolk were in a belligerent mood. 'Every one resumed a degree of con-temptuous insolence,' Captain Gillepsie recalled, and on the night of 4 August a mob attacked the Three Kings.[14] The British occupants abandoned their belong-ings and sought shelter elsewhere. The following night, having received intel-ligence of an attack planned against the fort, Colonel Pack mounted a strong guard in the Plaza Mayor under Captain Pococke. 'It was very cold and dis-agreeable, and I got ... intolerably wet', Pococke complained. The attack failed to materialise, but at about 10.00 am four Spaniards accosted a British sentry and stole his firelock. 'There was no great courage in doing so', Pococke observed '[as] he was only a boy of sixteen'.[15]

On 7 August Beresford hosted another dinner in the fort. The atmosphere was tense and the conversation soon turned to reinforcement. The General and Captain King 'feel confident that the "Melantho" is at the Cape by [now]', Pococke wrote in his diary. 'If so, it cannot be long till we have a reinforcement. God knows what may happen in the interim'. Later a priest arrived to beg for a reprieve for Jacob Echart. Bishop Riega had been to the German's cell to administer the sacrament and the messenger explained that he could not be executed until at least a day afterwards. The request was granted. Pococke and his fellow officers slept fully clothed that night with their weapons loaded beside them.[16]

On 8 August the rain ceased and Beresford and Pack rode out of town to check on the state of the roads. They were keen to meet Liniers in the open field where their troops' superior organisation would give them the upper hand, but the tracks leading to Las Conchas were a quagmire. Only now did Beresford begin to countenance defeat. If Liniers attacked, he might be forced to abandon Buenos Ayres and retire on board Popham's fleet. Ensenada provided the most obvious means of escape. Although the port was a few days' march from town, the water was deep enough to allow the boats within a few hundred yards of shore. 'That ... I might not be unprepared' Beresford recalled, 'I sent Capt. Kennet of the Royal Engineers to examine the Bridge over the Riachuelo ... and to note what it would require to make it passable, at the same time ... [preparing] my plan of defence in case of being attacked'.[17] Beresford's strategy had two stages. On the enemy's advance the fort's signal cannon would be fired. The 71st and St Helena Regi-ments would take up position in the Plaza Mayor and seven cannon, each cover-ing one of the main streets, would be positioned to support them. If the square became untenable, all would fall back to the fort.[18]

The next morning dawned bright and clear. At 11.00 am Jacob Echart was led into the Plaza Mayor where the garrison was drawn up to witness his execution. After Lieutenant-Colonel Campbell had read out the sentence, Echart was blind-folded and shot. '[He] met his [end] ... with firmness', Captain Gillespie observed. 'His anxious last request was that his parents might for ever remain strangers to [his fate].'[19] At midday a sentry from the St Helena regiment was attacked in one of the outlying squares. Two mounted Spaniards knocked him down and a third stole his firelock. Lieutenant Sampson went to his aid, but was stabbed in the shoulder. His attacker was bayonetted several times and seized.

'Even while the surgeon was dressing his wounds, [he] seemed to set everyone at defiance', Lieutenant Fernyhough recalled. 'We suspected that he was an emissary from the Spaniards; but he said that he would sooner suffer death than [reveal] ... from whence he came'.[20]

That afternoon, Captain King sailed for Las Conchas on HMS *Encounter* to engage the enemy fleet. The gun-brig was supported by HMS *Belem* and HMS *Dolores*, two schooners captured from the enemy six weeks before. Each was armed with a pair of 18-pounders and crewed by sailors from HMS *Diadem*.[21] Lieutenant Herrick, in command of HMS *Dolores*, was the first to encounter the enemy – a band of Liniers' men encamped by the river bank. Herrick fired a few round shot, but by the time HMS *Belem* and *Encounter* had come up the enemy had retired inland.[22] That night de la Concha's fleet were spotted off San Isidro. The Spaniard's four schooners and six gunboats were anchored in shallow water, making it impossible for the British to engage them. Dropping anchor, King ordered his men to clear for action in case the enemy should set sail during the night.[23]

Whilst the majority of the Royal Navy officers were doing their utmost to engage the enemy, there was a distinct feeling that Popham, safe on board HMS *Leda* in mid-river, was happy to leave the army and marines to their fate. Captain Pococke thought the commodore had only ever been interested in the prize money and Captain Gillespie was also disappointed. 'I can only regret that his mental resources were no way equal to meet the difficulty, and that his professional exertions in this hour of danger, fell far short'.[24] On the morning of 9 August Liniers advanced, arriving at the slaughteryard of Corrales de Miserere, three miles west of Buenos Ayres, at 1.00 pm on Sunday 10 August, where a number of local recruits and a few of those defeated at Perdriel joined them. While Chaplain Dámaso Antonio Larrañaga of the Monte Video Infantry Volunteers performed mass, Liniers composed a letter to Beresford demanding his surrender.[25] 'The fortune of arms is variable', he wrote. 'A little more than a month ago Your Excellency entered this capital without opposition and with a small number of troops ... but today, with the highest enthusiasm to throw off your hated dominion, we will soon show you that ... courage ... is not unknown to the people of Buenos Ayres. I am at the head of an army of well-organized troops who are much superior to those under your command ... the navy ... will not let you escape ... [and] thousands of the townsfolk ... await no more than my signal to throw themselves against [you]'.[26] After dispatching his letter, Liniers advanced once more. The road from Corrales was atrocious, but with the aid of hundreds of local boys who dragged the cannon through the mud, Liniers made his way across the Arroyo Maldonado and arrived near El Retiro at dawn.[27]

The British had just concluded divine service when a lookout reported the enemy's arrival. Beresford called his men to arms and retired to the fort for a meeting with the Bishop and Cabildo. At 2.00 pm Liniers' aide-de-camp, the thirty-five-year-old Lieutenant Hilarión José de la Quintana, arrived with the Frenchman's dispatch.[28] 'He had a great drum beating before him', Lieutenant Fernyhough recalled, 'an unusual mode of procession [which] made some of us smile.' Beresford treated Quintana with contempt and kept him waiting. Unwilling to delay, the creole returned to Liniers only to reappear one hour later when Beresford agreed to receive him. After reading Liniers' missive, the major-general composed a reply. 'I have no doubt that your army is numerically stronger than mine, but any comparison of their relative discipline is futile: neither did I enter this city unopposed, to execute it I had twice to defeat the enemy – its fate arms will decide.'[29] Beresford ordered the signal cannon fired and put his plan into action. Colonel Pack marched the 71st and St Helena Regiments to the fort two companies at a time, where they deposited their packs and proceeded to their positions in the Plaza Mayor. At 4.30 pm, with the process half complete, musketry was heard from El Retiro where twenty-one men under Sergeant Peter Kennedy of the 71st had been posted. Beresford ordered Captain Ogilvie to take 'two guns' and a small detachment of artillery to their aid.[30]

On learning of Beresford's rebuttal, 100 Miñones and two 6-inch howitzers which Captain Francisco Agustini had loaded with broken nails and scrap metal attacked El Retiro. The skirmish with Kennedy's men was brief. The redcoats fired a volley killing a sergeant and private and wounding a first and second lieutenant before their position was overrun. Although fatally wounded, Sergeant Kennedy and one of his men escaped. Six others were taken prisoner. The rest were cut to pieces. Privates James Archibald, Hugh Bryn, William Mckinon and Jason Robins were killed on the spot. The others were herded one by one into a ring of fifty of the enemy, 'so that each might have a stab at them', and dispatched by a hundred cuts. Their ears and genitals were cut off and 'worn as cockades' and their remains thrown on the river bank for the dogs.[31] By the time Ogilvie arrived it was all over. Setting up his two cannon, the captain briefly exchanged fire with Agustini's howitzers, but when the Miñones began to outflank his position, Beresford ordered him to retire.[32] Riding back to the Plaza Mayor, Ogilvie was accosted by two men. The first 'attempted to startle his horse, by stepping before him and shaking his cloak … whilst … [the other] ran out of a house behind, and stabbed at Ogilvie with a sword'. Badly wounded above the buttocks, the captain galloped back to the fort.[33]

By 5.00 pm the men of the 71st and St Helena regiments were in position. Eight of the ten Highland companies were formed up under the arches of the Recova and outside the Cabildo on the east and west sides of the Plaza Mayor. The East India Company troops were posted on their flanks and the Royal Marines and sailors of Popham's Sea Battalion garrisoned the fort. Seven cannon were deployed, their muzzles pointing down the streets providing access to the Plaza Mayor. The Royal Artillery detachment, led by Lieutenant Alexander Macdonald in Captain Ogilvie's absence, set up two guns in the Plazoleta covering Calles Santo Cristo and San Martín, while Captain Benjamin Hudson of the St Helena Artillery commanded the guns in the Plaza Mayor covering the centre and the left.[34] The grenadier and light companies of the 71st were divided into pickets of thirty to forty men. Several were ordered to occupy the rooftops of the most prominent buildings in the centre, whilst the others held a loose ring of advanced guard posts.[35] Throughout the afternoon, they were in action. The enemy advanced under cover by knocking through the walls of the buildings and kept up a constant fire from the rooftops, wounding several redcoats who were carried back to the fort. As the sun fell the temperature plummeted. In the Plaza Mayor the men huddled together, listening to the skirmishing a few blocks away.[36]

That evening the Spanish and creole cavalry cut off British communications with the interior, while Liniers and his infantry set up camp in El Retiro.[37] The Frenchman's headquarters was in the bullring. The perimeter was protected by five 24-pounders and outlying pickets were set up two blocks away.[38] Although the British had destroyed all the ammunition in the artillery park, Liniers salvaged two 18-pounder carriages which were mounted with cannon requisitioned from de la Concha's gunboats. Throughout the day reinforcements arrived and Sentenach and Llach promised to return on 11 August with 700 men. The troops spent the night under arms. They had little shelter and although the rain had ceased an icy wind was blowing hard from the northwest.[39]

In the fort Beresford and Pack discussed the possibility of an attack. Whilst the St Helena Regiment would remain in the Plaza Mayor, the 71st would advance to El Retiro in three columns. The first was to march along the riverbank and engage the enemy with musketry, whilst the second and third made bayonet charges from the flank and rear. At 3.00 am, with the firing in the centre having ceased, the officers of the 71st were called into a huddle and the plan discussed. Pack 'was fully bent on the business', but Pococke and several others had their doubts. A night attack was a risky affair. Although if successful they would almost certainly rout the enemy, they would soon regroup and without cavalry the victory would not be total. Failure would be catastrophic and if the townsfolk attacked the troops remaining in the fort and the Plaza Mayor in the 71st's absence, the Highlanders would have nowhere to fall back to. The thought of scattered bands being hunted by the mob was nightmarish. The plan was rejected.

An hour after dawn, the enemy reoccupied the houses surrounding the British outposts, took to the rooftops and opened fire. 'Our advance picquets and sentries … were not tardy in returning it', Pococke recalled and the pattern of skirmishing that had characterised the previous day continued.[40] Fighting alongside the Spaniards and creoles were several women and children including Manuela Hurtado de Pedraza who had joined her husband, a corporal of dragoons, on the front line. When he was killed on the afternoon of 11 August, Manuela dispatched the redcoat who had slain him with a bayonet, took up her husband's musket and continued the fight.[41]

That morning the Spanish flag was hoisted on the bullring. The sight was greeted with vivas and Liniers held a parade and counted his troops. As well as the 640 regulars and 134 Catalan volunteers from Monte Video, he had 100 militia from Colonia, 323 sailors from de la Concha's fleet and 200 Blandengues. When Sentenach and Llach joined at 8.00 am with 700 local volunteers it brought the total to over 2,500 men.[42] At 10.00 am Liniers ordered Captain Agustini to take an 18-pounder and engage the British shipping. Advancing along the beach, they opened fire on a captured gunboat, forcing the crew to row out into the river, and at 11.00 am turned their attention to the *Justina*, the British merchantman that had joined Popham's squadron at St Helena. Commander Robert Morris ordered his crew to run out the merchantman's twenty-six cannon and an artillery duel began. Two Spaniards were wounded, several balls were fired through the *Justina*'s hull and at midday 'a shot struck her mizzen-mast, and ... down dropped the English ensign' into the river. 'This occasioned a general huzzah from the enemy', but the *Justina* was soon reinforced by Captain King's flotilla which had sailed back to town. Anchoring near the head of the mole, HMS *Dolores* and *Belem* opened fire and at 1.15 pm the Spaniards were forced to retire.[43]

That afternoon Popham came ashore from HMS *Leda*. Beresford knew the time had come to abandon town and the two commanders discussed the details of the evacuation. Once the sick, wounded and civilians had been embarked a signal gun would be fired from the fort, Popham would sail to Ensenada and the troops would march overland to meet him.[44] As soon as the commodore had returned to HMS *Leda*, Captain John Thompson began the operation. The women, children, sick and wounded lined up on the mole to be rowed out to the ships, but with the weather worsening after a few dozen had embarked the plan was put on hold until morning.[45] Meanwhile, the skirmishing continued. Under cover of darkness, the enemy occupied the churches near the Plaza Mayor.[46] Several redcoats were wounded by marksmen posted in the bell towers and carried to the fort. That night William Pius White tried to instigate an eleventh-hour negotiation. Hoping that Liniers would agree to a bloodless British withdrawal, the Bostonian wrote a letter to Martín de Pueyrredón requesting a meeting between the lines early the following morning. He spent the rest of the night anxiously awaiting a reply.[47]

At 3.00 am Beresford ordered Lieutenant Macdonald to advance two blocks and 'throw a couple of [howitzer] shells into ... [Liniers'] lines'.[48] The situation in the Spanish camp was already chaotic. False alarms had been raised; the men called to arms then dismissed; huge bonfires burned out of control; packs of wild dogs roamed about barking and scavenging food; the different units became mixed up and the volunteers left to join in the skirmishing if and when they pleased. Liniers had little control. His plan to wait until midday before launching a general attack appeared unmanageable and when Macdonald's shells came fizzing through the night and exploded amidst the trees, the confusion was complete.[49] Meanwhile, Pueyrredón had received White's letter and replied proposing a meeting at 9.00 am in Catalina Square.[50]

An hour before first light on 12 August, the 71st were paraded in the Plaza Mayor. Two watches were organised and at 7.00 am the pickets rotated. Amongst the replacements was Lieutenant William Mitchell. In command of Captain Henry Le Blanc's grenadier company, the young lieutenant was thrilled at the prospect. 'On leaving the fort, he shook hands with us all', Lieutenant Fernyhough recalled, 'and dashed out of the gates. Pausing only to call back "we will show them some sport", he led his men into the Plaza Mayor.'[51] As the sun rose over the river, the Miñones moved out despite Liniers' orders that they wait and

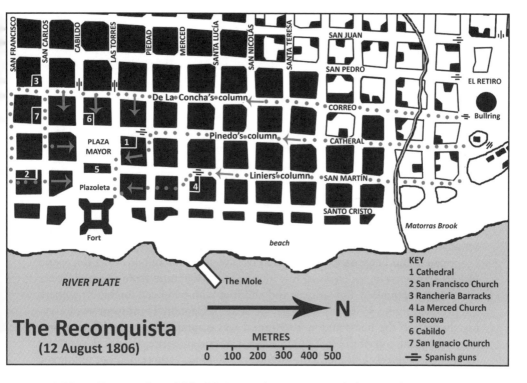

The Reconquista
(12 August 1806)

KEY
1 Cathedral
2 San Francisco Church
3 Rancheria Barracks
4 La Merced Church
5 Recova
6 Cabildo
7 San Ignacio Church
≡ Spanish guns

at 8.00 am Sentenach and Llach's 700 volunteers joined them. Advancing down Calle Correo with an 18-pounder under the cover of a lingering fog, they turned at the corner of Calle Merced and came under fire from a thirty-five-strong British picket posted in the small square in front of the church. Sentenach ordered forty of his men to occupy the roof of a nearby house. Taking position behind the parapets, they forced the redcoats to withdraw to the archway at the rear of the church, allowing the Catalans to deploy their 18-pounder. After two discharges of grape, the British fell back once more and the 18-pounder was placed in front of the church, from where it was able to fire down Calle San Martín directly into the Plaza Mayor. Leaving forty men to serve the gun, Sentenach led the rest towards the cathedral.[52] The picket led by Lieutenant William Mitchell was also under attack. The lieutenant was shot and killed and Ensign Thomas Lucas, the young officer who had absconded from the 2nd Battalion of the 71st to join the expedition to the Cape, was wounded by a ball through his knee. Refusing to leave Mitchell's bloodied body, the grenadiers surged forward and carried it back to the Plaza Mayor.[53] Meanwhile, William Pius White was picking his way through the streets to Catalina Square to meet Martín de Pueyrredón, but with the skirmishing intensifying, he was forced to turn back.[54]

At 9.00 am, seeing he could no longer prevent a full-scale confrontation, Liniers threw his troops into the fray. They advanced in three columns. The first, led by the Frenchman, proceeded up Calle San Martín. The second, under Colonel Augustin Pinedo, took Calle Catedral, while the third, commanded by de la Concha, advanced up Calle Correo, its mission to sweep round the far side of the Plaza Mayor and attack the British from the rear.[55] Most of the remaining outposts were soon forced to fall back and the firing became general. Squinting out of his one good eye, Beresford noted large parties of the enemy manoeuvring down the streets whenever the breeze plucked away the gunsmoke. 'Considerable bodies [were] advancing against our right flank,' he recalled, 'others [were] passing our front to get to our left, whilst the Front was also attacked.' To counter, Beresford ordered Lieutenant Macdonald to 'throw shot, shell and grape wherever a party [of the enemy] was seen'.[56]

Down by the waterfront the left flank of Liniers' column came within range of the *Justina*. Having worked his way into the shallows until the merchantman was 'nearly on her beam ends', Captain Morris opened fire. The thirteen-gun broadside flailed the Spaniards with grapeshot. They returned fire with their 18-pounder and lieutenants Grove and Herrick, in command of HMS *Belem* and *Dolores* respectively, sailed in to join the fight.[57] Watching from the mole were the sick and wounded and women and children who had been unable to embark the previous night. With the wind having abated, Captain Thompson was hurrying them onto the boats and at 10.30 am it was Captain Henry Le Blanc's turn. 'As I was going out of the fort on crutches, Captain [George] K[ennet], overtook me' he recalled. '"L[e Blanc]," the engineer called out, "you remember telling me you would lose your leg – now, observe, I have not half an hour to live; take my writing desk with you … [and] if ever you reach England … see my father … [and] tell him [of my fate]"'. Before Le Blanc could reply, Kennet ran towards the Plaza Mayor.[58]

By 11.00 am all the British pickets had been forced to retire. The rooftops surrounding the Plaza Mayor were crowded with the enemy, the Rancheria Barracks had fallen to the Miñones and the towers of the San Francisco and San Ignacio churches had been occupied.[59] With a hail of fire raining down upon them, more and more of the British troops fell. Amongst the casualties was Captain Kennet. Whilst standing beside Beresford he was struck in the back and 'soon after expired'.[60] From the fort one block to the east, Captain Gillespie observed the enemy through his telescope. 'I could perceive the inferior clergy [were] particularly active in directing their troops beneath them' he recalled. When a cannon was set up in one of the church towers, Beresford gave his gunners permission to open fire.[61] A ball struck the target and the priests ducked inside.[62]

Two blocks to the north, from a temporary headquarters inside La Merced Church, Liniers organized his artillery. A mortar was placed alongside the Catalans' 18-pounder outside the church, two 4-pounders were positioned to command Calle Cabildo, an 18-pounder and mortar were set up along Calle San Martín and a 4-pounder was sited to fire canister and grape shot down Calle Catedral. With his guns in position, Liniers ordered his cavalry to charge into the Plaza Mayor and seize Beresford's artillery as a prelude to a final infantry assault.

As they galloped down Calle San Martín, the British guns opened fire with grape-shot and the redcoats positioned under the Recova poured a volley of musketry into their flank as they burst into the open. With a final close-range cannonade from Macdonald's guns, the cavalry fled, leaving the cobbles slick with blood.[63] Amongst the wounded was José María Miranda, a marine ensign who had got caught up in the charge. His horse killed, his hand bleeding and his sword shattered by grape, the young officer managed to drag himself clear.[64]

Several more unsuccessful frontal assaults were launched before Liniers restricted himself to a combat of attrition. Whilst his regulars remained in reserve, the volunteers, townsfolk and irregulars occupied the buildings surrounding the British position. Encouraged by their priests, who spent the morning offering the men absolution, they threw themselves into the fight. De la Concha's marines scaled the rooftops as if they were the rigging of a warship and several of the Infantry Volunteers of Monte Video used over 600 cartridges and had to be issued more.[65] The redcoats returned fire as best they could. Others hurled grenades at the enemy and several had personal duels. One was fought between a grenadier of the 71st and 'a Spaniard, with a long red feather [in his hat]'. After firing from the window of one of the houses bordering the Plaza Mayor, the latter ducked inside to reload. 'One of this man's shots fell very near the grenadier', Lieutenant Fernyhough recalled. The Highlander picked up the ball, 'put it in his own musket, in addition to the charge, and when the Spaniard appeared again from his hiding-place, [he] fired, and shot him dead.'[66]

By midday Beresford realised it was only a matter of time before his position became untenable. While the enemy fire was increasingly deadly, his men were having difficulty finding a target. Those serving the guns were especially vulnerable. During the course of the morning Lieutenant Macdonald lost three rank and file, and Captain Hudson of the St Helena Artillery had nine killed and fourteen wounded. Reinforced by redcoats, the survivors stuck to their task and each of the seven gun crews fired over ninety rounds that morning. Lieutenant Macdonald led by example. Although severely burnt in the face when one of his ammunition carts exploded, he returned to the fight as soon as the wound had been dressed and only abandoned his post when he was shot through the thigh later that morning and could no longer stand.[67]

At 12.30 pm the focus of the battle swung to the northwest corner of the Plaza Mayor where Sentenach's men were engaging the British troops positioned round the cathedral. The Catalan had sent fifty men to a nearby rooftop whilst the rest manhandled a 36-pounder to the corner of Calle Piedad. Loading canister, they swept the British lines.[68] Some 200 redcoats countered by swarming round the side of the cathedral and taking the Catalans in the rear. Informed of the movement by his lookouts, Sentenach ordered forty men, supported by a body of Miñones led by Lieutenant Victorio Garciade Zuñiga and a number of marines and sailors from de la Concha's fleet to occupy a rooftop flanking their advance. Firing from behind the parapets, they forced the redcoats to fall back then surged forward once more.[69] Advancing down Calle Catedral, they set up two cannon within a few yards of the Plaza Mayor. Beresford, by now sweating so profusely

that his red jacket looked black, ordered Lieutenant Thomas Murray of the 71st
to counterattack. With bayonets fixed, the redcoats took the guns, but without
nails to spike them or drag ropes to haul them clear, their attack proved futile.
Sentenach responded by occupying yet more houses on both sides of the street
and when Lieutenant Cristobal Salvañach and Corporal Pedro Rosendo of the
Miñones charged, Murray's men fell back to the Recova.[70] Martín de Pueyrredón
rode into the Plaza Mayor behind them, snatched a banner from a piper and
galloped back to his lines.[71]

By 1.00 pm Beresford realised the game was up. His guns were down to their
last few rounds of ammunition; three of his officers and forty-six of his men were
dead and over 100 were wounded. The hospital in the fort was packed and the
gateway and drawbridge were crowded with casualties. Unable to fall back to
Ensenada without abandoning the wounded, the major-general decided to parley,
but he first needed to disengage from the enemy. As his pipers and drummers
played the retreat, the guns were hauled across the Plazoleta into the fort. The
British ensign was lowered and a flag of truce raised in its place. With the last
of his men inside, Beresford ordered the drawbridge raised. Two guns double-
loaded with round shot and grape were positioned in the courtyard, while the
sailors and marines manning the cannon on the battlements were ordered to
retire 'to prevent any breach of the Flag of Truce'.[72]

The majority of the enemy had no such qualms. As Captain Hilarión de la
Quintana, Liniers' aide-de-camp, crossed the Plazoleta to find out what Beresford wanted, the militia and local volunteers 'set ... up a most hideous yell' and
swarmed across the cobblestones behind him. Cries of 'behead the infidels' and
'knife them' were heard, and several guns 'planted within fifty paces of the gateway'. Others surged up against the walls, 'brandishing their knives, [and] threatening [the British] with destruction'. Beresford was outraged. According to the
code of honour that governed European warfare, with the raising of the flag of
truce the battle had been put on hold. Both sides were required to retain their
positions until terms of surrender were agreed or hostilities recommenced. The
majority of those he faced knew nothing of such niceties. Believing that the
British had already surrendered, they demanded they raise the Spanish flag.
When the idea was dismissed eight of Mordeille's privateers climbed the walls
and began brawling with the redcoats until Gillespie threatened to open fire if
they did not retire. 'Curiosity [then] induced me to look over the parapet,' the
marine captain recalled and 'above fifty musquets were discharged at my head
from various quarters of the square'. Although Gillespie escaped unscathed,
Captain Alexander Mackenzie of the marines was shot through the shoulder. 'It
was a severe wound. When [the] ... ball struck him ... the blood spirted out[,] ...
he ... immediately dropped' and was carried below.[73]

Although appalled by his countrymen's behaviour, Captain Quintana begged
Beresford to diffuse the situation by raising the Spanish flag. 'Specifying that it
should not be considered as affecting the British Rights, or placing us in a different situation', the major-general reluctantly agreed. 'Some daring, ill-looking
fellow [then] climbed up and planted the Spanish colours over the gate'. The

British troops were mortified. 'Some of them, with tears in their eyes, requested ... to be permitted to die with arms in their hands'. Others had to be physically restrained in order to prevent them shooting the Spaniard by the gate. 'God only knows what would have been the consequence' Captain Pococke opined.[74] At 3.00 pm, Beresford and Quintana left the fort. Escorted by a company of Spanish regulars who struggled to keep the mob at bay, they made their way to Liniers in the Plazoleta. The Frenchman embraced his opponent. Congratulating Beresford for his spirited defence, he apologised for his own side's lack of knowledge of the rules of war. The two men then agreed that the British should be treated as if they had surrendered with full honours. The officers would be allowed to retain their swords while the men would be imprisoned for their own safety. As soon as Popham could send transports, they would be exchanged for the prisoners Beresford had taken at the end of June and embarked for England.[75]

At 4.00 pm, having agreed to meet Liniers in the town hall later to finalise the arrangements, Beresford returned to the fort and addressed his men. He began by 'admiring the great gallantry of every individual and concluded by saying that for the sake of saving the lives of so many noble and brave fellows ... he was induced to act as he had done.' The gates were opened, the drawbridge lowered and the men, accompanied by the women and children whom Captain Thompson had been unable to evacuate, filed into the Plazoleta. 'We hung down our heads sorrowfully', Lieutenant Fernyhough recalled, 'and instead of carrying our swords erect, we dropped them by our sides.' The humiliation was complete when the 71st were ordered to surrender their colours. The men were then marched into the prison by the town hall between two lines of Spanish regulars. 'It appeared as if Liniers had selected this guard of honour ... from the dregs of his troops, to mortify us', Captain Gillispie observed. 'Amongst the crowd one of the ex-convicts from the *Lady Jane Shore* Indiaman called out: "Look, look my brave fellows, at the set of ragged cowards to whom you have given in".'

At the prison gates the officers were separated from the men. The latter were searched and ordered to give up their weapons. Several dashed their muskets against the ground before being bundled inside while the officers signed their paroles. Most returned to the fort where they were crowded into a small room by sentries who attempted to steal the few possessions they retained. Nearby, the British troops who had been mortally wounded breathed their last. The surgeons did the best they could to ease their suffering, while Father Dámaso of the Monte Video Infantry Volunteers gave the last rites to the Irish and German Catholics.[76] The British officers were allowed to return to their lodgings in town. En route Colonel Pack and Ensign Gavin were accosted by 'a frantic mob' dragging the colours of the 71st through the gutter. The crowd began 'crying out for the head of an Englishman' and they were only saved by the intervention of 'a worthy Spanish gentleman' who happened to be passing nearby.[77]

A mile to the east, the British gunboats and schooners were having difficulties of their own. Having seen the Spanish colours hoisted on the fort, they were attempting to work their way out to mid-river when there was a sudden drop in the water level. Whilst HMS *Dolores* and the majority of the ships' boats were able to escape, the *Justina*, HMS *Belem* and a boat from HMS *Raisonnable* ran aground. When the enemy moved several cannon down to the beach and opened fire, Lieutenant Groves of HMS *Belem* ordered his men to abandon ship. Boarding their boats, they rowed out to the fleet. Those on HMS *Raisonnable*'s settee and the *Justina* were less fortunate. Riding their mounts into the water, a patrol of creole cavalry led by a young cadet from Salta named Martín Miguel de Guemes boarded and forced their surrender.[78] Watching through his telescope from the deck of HMS *Leda*, Popham was deeply concerned. Beresford's capture was a disaster and with Pitt dead, Sir Home knew his enemies in Westminster would take full advantage of his humiliation. The debacle could end his career.

PART 2

REINFORCEMENT

Chapter 8

'For he's a jolly good fellow!'
London
12 September – 5 October 1806

News of Beresford's capture of Buenos Ayres reached England on 12 September. The initial reports, via merchantmen who had spoken with HMS *Narcissus* on the high seas, were treated with caution, but when the frigate arrived at Portsmouth the following morning the celebrations began. Beresford's and Popham's dispatches were delivered to Downing Street by Major John Deane and published in a *Gazette Extraordinary*. Word spread throughout the capital and that night cannon were fired in Hyde Park and at the Tower to mark the good news. On 14 September the committee of the Patriotic Fund met at Lloyd's Coffee House and resolved 'that Vases of £200 value each, with appropriate inscriptions, be presented to Major-General Beresford and Commodore Sir Home Popham, for their gallant and disinterested conduct in this successful and important enterprise. Inferior honorary awards were also voted to the wounded junior officers ... and provision is to be made for the wounded, and for the families of those who so gloriously fell.'[1] The dispatches were published in the press on 15 September and glowing editorials were written. *The Courier* termed the capture 'a brilliant achievement' and even *The Times* celebrated Popham's success.[2]

On 17 September the treasure was unloaded from HMS *Narcissus*. The thirty-two-ton haul included '334 boxes of dollars, 71 pigs of silver, weighing from 56 to 100lbs ... 72 pigs of copper ... and 114 hydes'. The booty was packed into eight wagons, each emblazoned with the legend 'TREASURE', which set off for London with an escort of thirty-six marines and former members of Popham's Sea Battalion dressed in the uniforms which they had worn when they had broken the Spanish line at Reducción two and a half months before. After a brief stop in Esher, Surrey, the convoy reached the capital three days later where its escort was swelled by 'Loyal Britons and the Lambeth Volunteers'. Proceeding through Parliament Street, they passed along Pall Mall to St James's Square and afterwards to the Bank, flanked by cheering crowds. Seated on the wagons' roofs, the sailors waved captured Spanish flags and the whole was preceded by a prize brass cannon.[3]

On 15 September the Chamber of the Board of Trade met to discuss the commercial opportunities presented by Popham's success. Several members of the cabinet were present. 'It was at first suggested that Neutrals should be admitted to participate', *The Times* reported, 'but the disadvantages that would accrue were so clearly pointed out, that the idea was abandoned. Had the trade been thrown open in this way, it would have given ... the [North] Americans a decided advantage over this or any other country. The Meeting, therefore, was of opinion, that the trade ought to be carried on in British bottoms exclusively.' Furthermore, the board decided that a tax of 20 per cent would be placed upon all German linens exported to Buenos Ayres to benefit Scottish and Irish manufacturers, a measure *The Times* considered 'equal to a prohibition'. The results of their deliberations were then forwarded to Buenos Ayres, 'for the guidance of those ... entrusted with the Government of that Colony.'[4]

Popham's letter to the mayors of Britain's manufacturing towns was also in circulation. Whilst Sir Home's agent contacted Mr B. Frere, a supplier of silk stockings, to complete the commodore's private order, several merchants prepared to make the voyage to South America.[5] 'The ... letter ... set every brokendown clerk and supercargo on the *qui vive*,' one contemporary recalled. Soon 'all the stores in Manchester and Liverpool' were emptied of their stock, and the merchant fleets were loaded with 'as much long cloths, printed calicoes, and sheetings, as would have reached [from Buenos Ayres all the way] across the *pampas* to S[an]t[i]ago [de Chile].'[6] Lancashire, Glasgow and Carlisle were also caught up in the frenzy, the like of which had not been seen since the days of the South Sea Bubble, and a 'meeting of the inhabitants of the towns and neighbourhood of Salford and Manchester' voted to publically thank Popham for opening up South America to British trade. A copy of their resolution was dispatched to Sir Home, another was sent to Lord Auckland and others were printed in *The Morning Chronicle*, *The Morning Herald*, *The Star*, *The Sun*, *The Courier* and *The Statesman*.[7]

Amongst the goods shipped were snuffboxes and medals engraved with political mottos. 'The arts, Industry and Light will flourish' read one. 'Religion and its holy ministers will be protected' promised another. Others boasted the slogan 'free people, minds and commerce' and the most blatant insisted 'It's not conquest, but union'. With the vast majority of the population of the River Plate illiterate, images were also employed. Crude portraits of Popham and Beresford were emblazoned on handkerchiefs alongside those of George Washington and Francisco Miranda. Hand fans were printed with depictions of Justice and Liberty and Britannia breaking America's chains, at her feet a humbled Spanish lion and ships carrying goods from a myriad of nations.[8]

One of the merchants involved was William Eastwick, 'a skilful and fearless sailor' of thirty-four who had spent the last fourteen years working for the British East India Company.[9] Defrauded of his fortune by an unscrupulous agent and with a newborn son to provide for, Eastwick leapt at the chance when invited by Mr Holloway, a friend who also happened to be Popham's brother-in-law. '[He] had received a private letter' Eastwick explained, 'pointing out that there was much to be done by those who were first in the field ... on the strength of this, Mr Holloway's agent, Mr Davison, of St James' Square, ... offered ... him a credit of £100,000 to establish a house of business at Buenos Ayres and Monte Video ... the ship *Anna* [was] ... purchased, and command of her, together with such a share in the venture as I could take up, was offered to me ... I ... sent a letter by return post to say I would be in London the next day [and] ... bade my loved ones farewell.'[10] Eastwick's first task was to choose what cargo to take. 'The country I was going to was new to me', he admitted, 'and I had not any personal knowledge of what description of goods was best suited ... However, where there are British troops and fighting, there is always drinking, and where there is victory there is toasting, and so ... I laid in eighty pipes of Spanish wine and forty casks of Brandy.' With the rest of the *Anna*'s hold filled with 'a vast number of trunks containing printed cottons', Eastwick set sail from Gravesend in early November. His ship was just one of over a hundred merchant vessels that would sail to the South Atlantic that winter.[11]

While the City was overjoyed at Popham's success, the government's reaction was mixed. Having known nothing of Pitt's interest in South America, The Ministry of All the Talents, a shaky coalition government that had replaced his second ministry, had to devise its strategy as it went and was handicapped by that fact that it was working with information several months out of date. On 28 July, having learned of Popham's departure from the Cape, but still unaware of his capture of Buenos Ayres, the Admiralty had decided to replace him with Rear-Admiral Charles Stirling. Whilst Baird was also to be recalled, Beresford was to escape censure and reinforcements, under Brigadier-General Sir Samuel Auchmuty, were to accompany Stirling's fleet.[12] News of Popham's subsequent success presented the government with a conundrum. Public and mercantile support was widespread and Popham also enjoyed the backing of several politicians, one of whom, Sir John Sinclair, MP for Caithness in Scotland, went as far as to term him 'a modern Pizarro'.[13] Others were determined to see Popham and Baird punished. 'I was one of those who advised their recall,' wrote Viscount Grey, First Lord of the Admiralty, 'upon the ground that they [acted] ... without orders ... They did not leave a single ship of the line at the Cape, and they diverted ... a frigate bound for India with pay for the troops. Such conduct ... I consider reprehensible and a subdiversion of all discipline and good government.'[14]

Lord Thomas Grenville, President of the Board of Control and future First Lord of the Admiralty, advocated a more measured approach. 'I should myself be ... forgiving enough to extend an amnesty to Popham,' he wrote to Lord Buckingham on 13 September. 'Though very blameable in the project, [he] has certainly had great merit in the execution, but I know not whether my colleagues will be as mercifully disposed as I'.[15] Grenville's colleagues proved more accommodating than he anticipated. The War Office and Admiralty agreed that although it was too late to prevent Sir Home's recall, they would not ruin him upon his return. At a time when Napoleon bestrode Europe, Popham's success provided a much-needed fillip to national pride, whilst also providing those keen on a negotiated peace with a bargaining chip. Equally importantly, the capture of Buenos Ayres would provide an outlet for the manufactured goods that had been idling in warehouses across the country since Napoleon's implementation of the Continental System.

Brigadier-General Auchmuty, the leader of the reinforcements destined for the River Plate, was a rare example of the War Office selecting a commander purely based on his competence for the job.[16] An American loyalist from New York, Auchmuty had had his baptism of fire with the 45th Foot in the American War of Independence. Afterwards, he had transferred into the 52nd Regiment and sailed to India. Over the next fifteen years he fought throughout the subcontinent, was involved in the campaigns against Hyder Ali and the Tipu Sultan and returned to England a lieutenant-colonel. In 1801 he was appointed adjutant-general to Sir David Baird in the Egyptian campaign, sailed to Suez on board HMS *Romney*, commanded by Sir Home Popham, and went on to take an active role in the celebrated march across the desert and capture of Alexandria.[17] By 1806, Auchmuty had three decades of experience and was a brave, talented, popular and diplomatic soldier with an innate dislike of dandyism. 'We all thought Sir Samuel ... most excellent', recalled a young private bound for the River Plate. 'He always delighted most in a good rough-looking soldier with a long beard and greasy haversack, who he thought ... the sort of man most fit to meet the enemy.'[18]

Auchmuty's orders left room for interpretation. He was to travel to Plymouth where his command was assembling and sail to the River Plate via Cape Town under convoy of the fleet commanded by Rear-Admiral Stirling. Once there he was to put himself under the command of Major-General Beresford. If Beresford had been defeated or was 'indisposed', Auchmuty was to recover any lost ground 'if possible', then await further reinforcement, the War Office assuring him that 3,000 men would follow 'at the interval of about three weeks'.[19] Under Auchmuty's command were two regiments of foot – the 40th, an 'excellent corps' of 'seasoned troops', many of whom had fought under Abercrombie in Egypt, and the 87th, a regiment recently raised in Ireland 'chiefly, if not altogether, composed of very young men'.[20] The former was led by Colonel Gore Browne, an Irishman originally educated for the church, whilst the latter was under the command of Colonel Sir Edward Gerald Butler, a thirty-six-year-old who had received his peerage in 1794 after rescuing the Austrian Emperor at the Battle of Viller-en-Cauchies during the French Revolutionary Wars.[21] The infantry were supported by the 17th Light Dragoons, 'a very fine regiment' of 628 troopers led by Colonel Evan Lloyd; the 'Death or Glory Boys', as they were known, were to operate as infantry.[22] Auchmuty was also given an artillery company commanded by Captain Alexander Dickson and three companies of the 2/95 led by Major Thomas Gardener, amongst whose officers was a nineteen-year-old lieutenant named Harry Smith.[23] Two final elements of Auchmuty's command, the 9th Light Dragoons and a detachment of reinforcements for the 71st, would not travel with the main expedition. The former would be long delayed in England due to a lack of transports and would not reach the River Plate until a month after the main body had arrived.[24] The latter, a seventy-strong detachment under Captain William Brookman, 'which consisted chiefly of striplings belonging to Glasgow', would be picked up at the Cape, bringing the total number of reinforcements to 3,000 men.[25]

On 3 October the 40th Regiment spent a final night in Portsmouth before embarking for the fleet rendezvous at Falmouth. Private William Lawrence, a builder's apprentice who had run away from home to escape a tyrannical master, was glad to leave. Many of his comrades were distraught. 'Only about six women to a company of a hundred men being allowed to go with us, many who were married had to leave wives and children behind. When the order was given to embark, the scene was quite heartrending: I could not see a dry eye in Portsmouth, and if the tears could have been collected, they might have stocked a hospital in eye-water for some months.'[26] On 8 October the twenty-five transports gathered at Falmouth were joined by Stirling's fleet. The rear-admiral's flagship was HMS *Ardent*, a sixty-four-gun ship-of-the-line under Captain Ross Donnelley, who had been promoted from HMS *Narcissus* on his return with Popham's dispatches. Also present were two thirty-two-gun frigates, HMS *Unicorn* and HMS *Daphne*, two sloops-of-war, the eighteen-gun HMS *Pheasant* and the sixteen-gun HMS *Charwell*, a store ship bound for Cape Town and a merchantman whose ultimate destination was the East Indies.[27] On 9 October the fleet weighed anchor and set sail with a 'fair breeze'. Billy Pitt, a young officer on board HMS *Charwell* who had already made several transatlantic voyages, watched from the taffrail as 'Old England' sank beneath the waves behind him.[28]

Chapter 9

Revolution!

Buenos Ayres
13 August – 10 October 1806

With the British defeated there was a power vacuum in Buenos Ayres. Armed mobs roamed the streets and a revolutionary note was in the air. The British prisoners were in a perilous situation. On 13 August Ensign Gavin came close to falling prey to an armed gang sweeping through town. 'During the frenzy . . . [my Spanish hosts] concealed me under a bed' he recalled.[1] That afternoon Captain Pococke went to see his men. Half of the rank-and-file remained imprisoned in the jail beside the Cabildo. The rest had been moved to a building in El Retiro. It was a depressing experience. En route Pococke noticed that Popham's fleet had disappeared downriver and in the prison conditions were squalid.[2] The cells were overcrowded and the inmates 'huddled in filth'.[3] The women and children were packed in alongside their men, food supplies, aside from a small portion of bread provided by the British officers, were non-existent and 'most of the noble fellows [were] in tears at their unfortunate situation'. The captain was not the only one to visit. Earlier a Spanish officer had offered the British troops pay and board and a plot of land in the interior on retirement in return for joining Liniers' army. Several of the St Helena Regiment and fifty-five of the 71st found the proposal too good to refuse.[4]

Next door Beresford and Liniers were discussing the terms of the surrender. They agreed that the British would be exchanged for the Spanish prisoners taken on 27 June, and that the former would be returned to the fleet on condition they sail directly to England or the Cape. Copies of the capitulation were made 'in rough English & French' while final drafts were composed in English and Spanish and a letter dispatched to Popham requesting he bring the transports to Buenos Ayres and embark the men.[5] Elsewhere, the wounded were attended to. The Spaniards struggled to cope. Official reports stated that fifty of their men had been killed on 12 August and 136 wounded.[6] Dozens more died under their surgeons' knives, the medics claiming that Beresford's men had poisoned their musket balls to cover their own incompetence.[7]

The ninety-nine British rank-and-file who had been wounded were well looked after. A hospital was set up by the town's friars and the British surgeons worked alongside.[8] The wounded officers were treated in private houses. Captain Alexander Mackenzie was looked after by the Escurras family, whose ladies spent five months tending to his wounds. 'Their attentions and hospitality were unrelaxed, and unbounded'.[9] Ensign Thomas Lucas was less fortunate. His knee shattered by a musket ball, the young officer feared infection and urged the surgeons 'to amputate ... if they had the smallest doubt respecting his life.' John Pooler and his assistant Jason Evans consistently refused.[10] Elsewhere the dead awaited burial. Whilst the forty-six British rank-and-file who had been killed were thrown into trenches dug in the dry ditch round the fort, at El Retiro and by the water-front, the three dead officers lay in state. Lieutenant Mitchell's corpse, in a house near the Plaza Mayor, was stripped of everything of value. Pococke noted that the Spanish guard even took the sheet draped over his body.[11]

The day of 14 August dawned bright and cold as reports of Sobremonte's imminent arrival at the head of the army he had raised in Córdoba circulated round town. Whilst the viceroy had been following protocol by moving his headquarters and treasury, his behaviour had incensed the *porteños*.[12] Their ire stoked by agitators, several began openly accusing him of cowardice and a *cabildo abierto* (extraordinary general meeting) was called in the Sala Capitular to discuss the official reaction to his return. Under pressure from a crowd of 4,000 in the Plaza Mayor, several of whom forced their way into the meeting hall, the assembly decreed that Sobremonte was forbidden to enter town.[13] Liniers was chosen as the interim military and political commander of Buenos Ayres in his stead. With the defeat of the British to his credit, the Frenchman had the backing of the mob, and as an advocate of free trade he also enjoyed the support of a powerful faction of the merchant class. Meanwhile, Martín Álzaga and the monopolists entrenched themselves within the Cabildo and bided their time. The situation remained volatile and, with the British fleet still in the river, now was not the moment for open revolt. Besides, Álzaga believed Liniers ignorant of the complexities of the situation – a puppet who could easily be swayed.[14]

A few blocks to the north, Captain Kennet and Lieutenant Mitchell were buried. The British officers, Liniers and several leading Spaniards and creoles formed the cortège. Amongst the civilians was Mariana Sánchez Barreda, the young girl who had fallen for Kennet several weeks before.[15] As the 'heretic' officers were not allowed to be interred in hallowed ground, a single grave was dug for both in El Retiro. Captain Pococke read a prayer, a company of Liners' grenadiers fired a salute and the party returned to town. 'As we were going back to the fort [Liniers] was met by the ... Cabildo' Pococke recalled, 'and greeted as Governor and Commander of the troops of Buenos Ayres'. The townsfolk were delighted. The still of the morning was broken by dozens of celebratory cannon shots, a *Te Deum* was held in the cathedral and the mob chanted 'viva' as Liniers paraded through the Plaza Mayor.[16]

That afternoon Juan Martín de Pueyrredón was dispatched with a unit of dragoons to intercept Sobremonte on the road from Córdoba. On the pretext that the viceroy risked being lynched by the mob, Pueyrredón was ordered to prevent his return. Meanwhile, at Buenos Ayres the victory parade was in full swing, but the British officers were in no mood for celebration. Ensconced in the fort, Beresford blamed Popham's avarice for his misfortune, while Pococke spec-ulated about the consequences of the day with admirable accuracy. 'I am firmly of the opinion that the 12 August 1806 will be the origin of the independence of this country', he noted in his journal. 'The seeds are sown, and before many years pass ... their production will be arrived at maturity. The Court of Spain will forever ... lament both the conquest of Buenos Ayres ... and the recapture ... by Liniers.'[17]

Thirty miles to the southeast Popham's fleet was at anchor off Ensenada de Barragán. Having embarked the detachment of the Sea Battalion stationed there and thrown their two field pieces into the river, on 14 August Popham sailed to Monte Video and transferred his flag to HMS *Diadem* along with the sick and wounded who had been evacuated from Buenos Ayres. He then attempted to secure Beresford's release.[18] Popham began by issuing Governor Huidobro with a thinly veiled threat. After reminding the Spaniard of his country's recent humiliation at Trafalgar and the number of his compatriots currently languishing in British jails, he proposed a prisoner exchange. 'A reflection [on] how much such ... conduct tends to alleviate the miseries of war will ... induce your Excellency to order all the prisoners now in your hands to be immediately restored', he wrote. Insulted by the commodore's tone, but unsure as to the strength of his position, Huidobro penned an evasive response, later followed, on his learning of the extent of the British defeat, by a determined rebuttal. Popham prevaricated until 16 August when Liniers' messenger arrived. Seeing a chance to restore his reputation, the commodore ordered two transports to sail for Buenos Ayres and pick up the troops.[19]

The situation in the capital remained tense. The leading citizens continued to manoeuvre for power, the mob held sway on the streets and the British officers were targeted. Lieutenant Fernyhough was so concerned that his scimitar would be stolen that he entrusted it to a Spaniard whom he had befriended during the occupation and on 15 August Captain Gillespie had had his quarters ransacked.[20] All his possessions were stolen, including the history of the Incan emperors lent to him by a Spanish officer three weeks before. 'Even the paper from the walls was taken' he recalled.[21] Two days later captains Pococke and Mackenzie received a visit from an officer and several men of the Miñones who demanded to search their trunks. The captains refused and the matter was referred to Liniers. 'The Governor seemed excessively hurt' at his men's 'intrusion', Pococke recalled 'and denied that that any such examination should take place'.[22] Robberies were not the British officers' only concern. 'Whenever I went into the streets', Captain Gillespie recalled, 'I was commonly followed by several attendants with drawn knives, who appeared ... to watch for a favourable opportunity of using them, but guarding one side by the wall, and the other with a sword under my arm, the villains were kept in awe.'[23]

The first of Popham's transports arrived on the evening of 17 August. 'Beholding [it] ... riding at anchor off ... town', Captain Pococke noted that 'there [was] ... some probability of being off'.[24] In the Town Hall other plans were afoot. Seeing the prisoners as their only insurance against further British attack, the Cabildo pressured Liniers into going back on his word. Chief amongst the protaganists was Martín de Álzaga, who no doubt enjoyed the Frenchman's discomfort. At first Liniers attempted to steer a middle course. On 18 August he tried to persuade Beresford to allow him to add the proviso 'en quanto puedo' (as far as I am able) to the terms of the surrender document.[25] The major-general flatly refused. Two days later, with still no definite timetable for their departure, Beresford 'thought it right to remonstrate against any further delay'. Liniers assured him 'that the delay was occasioned by forms only and that he need not have any anxiety on the subject.'[26] Nevertheless, the British officers remained concerned. 'Many began to despair of our going away', Pococke noted, 'and think we shall be sent into the country.'[27] Three days later a rumour flew round town that the British soldiers had escaped from prison. The general alarm was sounded and the garrison paraded in the Plaza Mayor. Although the rumours were un-founded, the mob was incensed and prowled through the streets looking for British officers on whom to vent their rage. Benjamin and Charles Hodson, captains in the St Helena Regiment, were their first victims. Seized as they were returning to their quarters from an evening at the Three Kings, the brothers were tied up and paraded through town. 'Several fellows held knives to their breasts', Pococke recalled, their watches were stolen 'and a rascal walking behind the younger made several blows at him with a sword'. Fortunately, the blade was blunt and when the Hodsons were rescued by a young Spanish officer, the mob turned its attention elsewhere. Gathering outside Gillespie's quarters, they dragged his servant boy into the street and murdered him 'in a most brutal manner'.[28]

On 26 August Ensign Thomas Lucas died of his wounds. His condition had been deteriorating for days. 'If the doctors had taken his leg off in the first instance he would most likely be ... living ... now', Pococke opined.[29] That afternoon Beresford had another meeting with Liniers. 'As soon as we were seated [he] ... communicated to me that the British troops were to be detained' the major-general recalled '[and] so fully launched out in condemnation of the breach of faith ... and declaring his own inability to resist ... that I had nothing to add'. Driven to desperation by his desire to keep his word, Liniers sent his aide-de-camp to Beresford's quarters that evening. '[He] inform[ed] me of his [master's] resolution to embark our people', the major-general recalled, 'but as the people of the town were against it and in a state of insurrection ... [he] requested ... that I ... order the transport[s] to a certain place out of sight ... and [said] that he would ... send our men off in the night time.' Beresford stayed awake till dawn, but no more was heard of the plan. Liniers had been betrayed and the Cabildo had threatened to have him arrested should he insist on liber-ating the British prisoners. From that day on the Frenchman denied any knowl-edge of the agreement he had made.[30] On 27 August the Cabildo announced their decision to transfer the British rank-and-file to the interior while the fate of the officers remained in the balance. '[We] were either to remain in Buenos Ayres or be sent to London', Pococke was informed.[31] The next day, 100 miles to the northwest, Juan Martín de Pueyrredón met Sobremonte at the village of Fontezuelas. Having warned the viceroy that he risked the wrath of the mob should he return to Buenos Ayres, Pueyrredón rode back to the capital with his detachment of hussars, whilst an enraged yet impotent Sobremonte set off for Monte Video.[32]

In late August Liniers and the Cabildo began raising a new army. They knew the British would be back and were determined to be prepared. Their first job was to secure funds. The citizens were asked to donate and over the next five months 118,878 *pesos* were raised.[33] The majority came from the administrative, clerical and merchant classes. Gaspar de Santa Coloma and Bishop Riega pledged 3,000 *pesos* each, Álzaga gave 2,000 and even the humblest citizens contributed. Several donated a single *peso* and Doña Mercedes Robles gave just six *reales*.[34] Loans were also solicited. Francisco Antonio Letamendi, a friend of Liniers who owned a 1,000-yard plot of land along the banks of the Riachuelo, lent 10,000 *pesos*, Esteban Romero, a fifty-two-year-old shop owner who had fought alongside Sentenach during the Reconquista, made a similar pledge, as did Manuel de Arana. All three negotiated an interest rate of 5 per cent.[35]

With the war chest filling, recruitment began. On 6 September a proclamation called for volunteers to procure arms and present themselves for duty and 'a military enthusiasm broke forth in every rank of society … All the youths of the most respectable families hastened to enrol their names' Captain Gillespie recalled, 'and … recruiting parties daily paraded through the streets, beating up for volunteers'. By the end of October twenty-two units had been formed. Ten were battalions of infantry. Uniformed in blue jackets and white trousers, each was classified by the origin of its volunteers. Five were raised from among natives of mainland Spain – the Cuerpo de Gallegos and the Tercios de Andaluces, Catalanes, Montañeses and Asturianos and Vizcainos each contained between 200 and 600 men.[36] These recruits were mainly middle class. The Montañeses included waiters, tailors, shepherds, hat-makers, silversmiths, builders, barbers, writers, cobblers, carpenters, shopkeepers, blacksmiths and tradesmen.[37]

Two specialised infantry companies were also raised: the Granaderos (grenadiers), led by Juan Florencio Terrada, one of the few veterans whose reputation had survived the debacle at Galves Bridge, and the Cazadores Correantinos, a company of light troops. The remaining three infantry units had a distinctly plebian character. The 1,359-strong Regimiento de Patricios was composed of creoles born in Buenos Ayres and led by Corenelio de Saavedra, a prominent local merchant and part of the internationalist faction. Conceived as an elite unit from the start, the Patricios were proud of several idiosyncrasies. The privates enjoyed the right to wear their hair in ponytails, elected their own officers and played an active role in regimental politics, creating a proto-revolutionary bond between the commissioned and non-commissioned ranks previously unheard of.[38] The Arribeños were a unit of volunteers from the interior of the viceroyalty led by Pio de Gama; and the 352-strong Regimiento de Indios, Morenos y Pardos was an Indian and mixed race unit raised from amongst the lower class residents in town.[39] Many were attracted by wage of twelve *pesos* a month, a considerable attraction given Buenos Ayres' volatile economic climate.[40] Those who could not bring their own arms were supplied with captured British muskets and gunpowder brought from the arsenal at Monte Video and, as a special allowance for their poverty, the Cabildo issued the Indios, Pardos and Morenos and Arribeños 3,500 *pesos* to purchase uniforms.[41]

Four units of artillery and eight of cavalry were formed. The former included the 395-strong Patriotas de la Unión and the Indios, Morenos y Pardos, a unit of 426 men led by Captain Francisco Agustini, the commander of Liniers' artillery during the Reconquista. The Unión was recruited from Sentenach and Llach's Catalan volunteers and were the only militia to be regularly paid, a privilege recognising the part they had played in the Reconquista. The cavalry included three squadrons of hussars under Juan Martín de Pueyrredón and Martín Rodríguez. With the officers raised from amongst the young separatists' friends, the hussars also had a somewhat radical character. In defiance of Spanish norms, the sergeants and corporals were given titles taken from the armies of republican Rome and the troopers wore a ribbon of sky blue, a colour later associated with an independent Argentina. Several deserters from Beresford's army also joined the hussars, amongst them an Irish trumpeter named Michael McCarthy, whose knowledge of British army calls would confuse his former comrades in the months to come. The remaining cavalry units were the Cazadores, whose troopers were Andalucian in orign, the Migueletes, who were issued with red coats taken from the 71st, the Caribineros de Carlos IV, the Escuadron de Labradores y Quinteros, and Liniers' personal escort of seven men.[42] The new army was fundamentally different in character to anything raised in Spanish South America before. The regular military had lost face during the debacle of June 1806 and while professionals such as Colonel César Balbiani, an experienced Spanish officer recruited as he passed through town on his way to Peru, remained important, a new breed of civilian officers, many of whom hailed from the ranks of the town's commercial elite, came to the fore.[43]

With each new regiment raised, the *porteños* pride grew. '[They] possess every confidence in their ability and courage', Captain Pococke noted, '[and claim they] will defy any force that England can send against them.'[44] By October over 8,500 men were under arms. Drills were carried out every morning, the Cabildo organised victory parades and the captured British colours were consecrated in the cathedral and dedicated to the Virgin Mary, completing the pledge made by Friar Gregorio Torres two months before.[45] The local children were also caught up in the excitement and at least three died as a result of firearms accidents whilst 'playing at soldiers', Captain Pococke recalled.[46] Another side-effect was a growing rivalry between the *porteño* troops and those from Monte Video and in early September, after several scuffles, the majority of the latter were sent home to avoid further confrontations.[47] One of the few to remain was Juan Gutiérrez de la Concha. The forty-six-year-old Spanish naval captain who had led the right-hand column at the Reconquista was charged with commanding the *porteño* fleet of four armed *zumacas*, a dozen small ships, and six gunboats.[48] Unable to compete with Popham's frigates and ships-of-the-line, de la Concha would limit his operations to the maze of islands and shallow channels to the northwest of Colonia. Another issue for the Cantabrian was a lack of firepower. Aside from the two schooners donated by Francisco Antonio de Castro, which mounted one 18- and one

32-pounder, most of his ships carried cannon ranging from 3.5- to 6-pounders and were outgunned by even the smallest British schooners.[49] To compensate, de la Concha packed his ships with militia and marines and ordered his commanders to board the enemy at every opportunity.

One hundred and twenty miles to the east Popham remained locked in dispute with Governor Huidobro. A staggering total of forty-four letters had been exchanged concerning the British prisoners and the commodore's mood was darkening. Several of his ships needed refitting and a lack of fresh food had resulted in scurvy claiming several victims on board HMS *Diomede*.[50] The thirty merchantmen Popham had detained during the blockade also needed supplies and, although he had sent HMS *Raisonnable* to Rio de Janeiro on 26 July for anchors, cordage, canvas, wine, port and provisions, there had been no word from her captain, Josias Rowley, since he had parted company.[51] On 28 August Popham learnt the identity of his new masters in Westminster from an American ship 'just arrived in the river'. The Ministry of All the Talents, the coalition that had come to power following Pitt's demise, included representatives from across the political spectrum. William Windham had been appointed Secretary of State for War and the Colonies and the new First Lord of the Admiralty was Lord Howick, a reform-minded Whig with whom Popham immediately began an unctuous correspondence.[52]

Back at Buenos Ayres, the fate of the British rank-and-file was sealed. On 1 September the Cabildo's version of the capitulation was printed and distributed around town. 'It was announced ... that our surrender was at discretion', Colonel Pack recalled, 'and that it was the determination of ... [Liniers] that the British troops should be sent to the interior, and the officers on their parole to Europe'.[53] Two days later the first detachment left town. Before marching under escort, their packs were looted and their uniforms taken to clothe Liniers' recruits.[54] Dressed in rags and civilian garb, the Highlanders made a sorry sight. 'They hoped their country would not forget them', Lieutenant Fernyhough recalled, and 'hung about us ... much distressed, and parted ... in despair.'[55] On 10 September the second detachment departed, leaving just sixty-three British rank and file in town. Most were skilled craftsmen who had been permitted to set up shop.[56] Others had taken domestic positions or converted to Catholicism and married local girls, amongst them a St Helena cadet who was given a captain's commission in a unit of Spanish regulars.[57] The band master of the 71st was also allowed to remain. 'Such was the female passion for music ... [that he] was invited to become [a] teacher', Captain Gillespie explained. 'Many pupils pressed upon him, and being an excellent composer, his little productions were keenly brought up ... [and] he amassed [a considerable sum of] money'.[58]

Meanwhile, Popham had tightened his blockade of Monte Video. Several more merchantmen were detained and on 9 September *El Carmen*, a *zumaca* several weeks out from the Falkland Islands, was sighted making a dash for the Santa Lucia River. HMS *Leda* weighed anchor and gave chase. Laying on all sail, Captain Honeyman cut the brig off and forced her to run into the shallows near

El Cerro de Monte Video to escape. The crew hoisted Spanish colours, abandoned the brig and rowed ashore, where they hid amongst the sand dunes and were joined by a passing patrol of the Monte Video Cavalry Volunteers led by Juan Benito Aguiar. Honeyman dropped anchor as close as he dared and sent his large cutter, pinnace and launch under lieutenants Parker and Stewart to cut the brig out or burn her. As soon as the lieutenants had boarded the *zumaca*, Aguiar's men opened fire. Others braved HMS *Leda*'s broadside to ride into the water and get a better shot and a few dozen swam out towards the British launch with knives between their teeth. Lieutenant Stewart was shot through the left arm and three seamen including Abdula, a twenty-three-year-old from Bengal, were wounded before the British abandoned the attempt. They made off in the cutter, but were forced to leave the launch behind. The Spaniards were delighted with the prize. On board was an eighteen-pound carronade, twenty-six muskets, twenty-five pairs of pistols and an officer's sword. When the Cabildo at Monte Video learnt of their success, Aguiar's men were rewarded with 150 *pesos* and a barrel of *aquardiente*.[59]

On 15 September HMS *Raisonnable* rejoined Popham's fleet from Rio de Janeiro. '[She] was so heavily laden [with provisions] ... that her lower deck ports were caulked down'. The next morning a strange sail was sighted approaching from the south. The new arrival was HMS *Medusa*, a thirty-eight-gun frigate and the forerunner of a convoy one month out from Cape Town. Baird's long anticipated reinforcements had arrived. When the news reached Buenos Ayres the remaining British rank-and-file were locked up as a precaution and the Cabildo made preparations to send their officers into the interior. Beresford was furious; the others resigned to their fate. On the morning of 11 October, they gathered in the Plaza Mayor. Whilst the Cabildo paid their respects to Beresford, the officers said farewell to the citizens who had befriended them. Wishes of goodwill were exchanged and Ensign Gavin was presented with 'as much ... biscuit as a huge black could carry' by a contractor who had supplied the British with bread. After a final meal at the Three Kings, a carriage was provided for Beresford and and at 3.00 pm they got under way. 'We took leave of Buenos Ayres with heavy hearts' Lieutenant Fernyhough recalled, 'not expecting to see it again for some time'.[60] The young marine's words were portentous. Most of the British officers would spend the next twelve months in the interior. Some would never see their homeland again.

Chapter 10

Maldonado
May 1806 – 5 January 1807

Baird had dispatched the reinforcements from Cape Town in three waves. The first sailed from Simon's Bay on 17 August. Under convoy of HMS *Medusa*, a thirty-eight-gun frigate, and HMS *Protector*, the twelve-gun brig involved in the victory at the Cape, were the *Diadem*, *Adamant* and *Columbine* transports and HMS *Howe*, a twenty-four-gun store ship. On board the flotilla were half of the 38th – a crack unit, 811 strong, many of whom had been recruited in Ireland; two troops of the 20th Light Dragoons; and 103 of the 54th Foot – the remnants of those who had been rescued from the hold of the *Volontaire*.[1] The voyage was a difficult one. On the first day a storm split the fleet, forcing each ship to continue independently. On 4 September HMS *Protector* reached St Helena where she was joined by the *Diadem*, *Columbine* and *Adamant*. The following day they continued in convoy to Monte Video, arriving on 6 October to find HMS *Medusa* and *Howe* awaiting them.[2]

On 21 August the second wave, consisting of the *Rolla* and *Melantho* transports set sail from Cape Town. On board was another detachment of the 38th and two 10-inch mortars. Eight days later, 'in the midst of wet weather', the final wave, escorted by Captain William Fothergill of the sixty-four-gun HMS *Lancaster*, departed from Simon's Bay.[3] Under his protection were the *Fanny*, *Royal Charlotte*, *Pretty Lass*, *Alexander*, *Hero*, *Caledonia* and *Polly* transports. The rest of the 38th, under Lieutenant-Colonel Spencer Vassal, were on board, as was the 685-strong 47th, which had been due to embark for India until Beresford's dispatches had induced Baird to change its destination, and 140 of the newly arrived 20th Light Dragoons.[4] In overall command of the reinforcements was Lieutenant-Colonel Joseph Backhouse of the 47th. A cautious officer, whom Popham would accuse of having a propensity for 'torpitude', Backhouse had fought in the West Indies during the American War of Independence and had taken part in the inglorious plundering of the Dutch island of St Eustatius.[5] Backhouse's subordinates were considerably more bellicose. Born in Boston to a loyalist militia officer, Lieutenant-Colonel Vassal had joined the army as a twelve-year-old ensign and had served at Gibraltar, Egypt, Flanders, the West Indies, France, Spain, Ireland and the Cape. At the latter he had left his pregnant wife and three children to lead his men to the River Plate. A competent officer and strict disciplinarian, Vassal was cool under fire and commanded great respect.[6] The expedition's deputy-adjutant-general, Major William Trotter of the 83rd, was of a similar stamp. Brave and decisive where Backhouse was irresolute and weak, Trotter was admired by his comrades and had served in France, India, Egypt and the Cape. Bored by garrison duty and Baird's draconian regime, he had begged Backhouse to take him to the Plate.[7]

Captain Fletcher Wilkie of the 38th was also delighted to leave Africa. He thought HMS *Lancaster* 'a fine roomy vessel, well-calculated for carrying troops', the weather was delightful and the passage across the Atlantic 'very pleasant' indeed.[8] Below decks was a different story. Conditions were cramped and unsanitary and two men of the 38th, privates William Leeche and John Jeffreys, died during the voyage.[9] Their bodies were tossed into the ocean along with several bullocks loaded at the Cape, which succumbed to disease. Captain Fothergill was a notorious flogger. On one day alone he dished out a total of 228 lashes and on 15 September a sailor named Neil Curry 'was entangled in ye coil, dragg'd overb'd and drown'd'. Shortly afterwards the island of Trinidad and the Martinvas Rocks were sighted and on 10 October HMS *Lancaster* arrived in the River Plate.[10] 'The Spring was just begun', Captain Wilkie recalled, 'and the river covered in fog, so ... we groped our way [forward] very carefully with the lead always going ... After two days ... the fog suddenly cleared [and] ... we found ourselves close to the fleet anchored ... [off] Monte Video.'[11]

The British fleet was now the most impressive that had been seen in the river since Viceroy Cevallos' expedition. Four ships-of-the-line, two frigates, two gun-brigs, one navy victualler, twelve transports and over forty merchantmen, both neutral and enemy vessels detained for attempting to run the blockade, were at anchor in the roads.[12] Only the *Rolla*, which Popham had sent to Rio Grande to purchase flour, biscuit and live cattle, was missing.[13] On learning of Beresford's defeat, Backhouse was mortified and Sergeant Norbert Landsheit of the 20th Light Dragoons 'grievously chagrined', while Wilkie claimed to be saddened 'but not much surprise[d]'.[14] On the evening of 12 October, a council of war took place. A safe anchorage was needed: supplies were running low; scurvy was rife; and the ships would soon be exposed to the summer storms should they remain in mid-river. 'After several projects were canvassed', Popham, Vassal and Backhouse decided to make an attempt against Monte Video.[15] Built on the shore of a shallow bay, the town boasted two strong forts and was ringed by a ditch and high stone walls studded with bastions and mounted with heavy cannon. Any assault would require artillery, and as Backhouse's troops were bereft of cannon, a joint operation was required. Two ships-of-the-line, the frigates, gun-brigs and five armed transports would manoeuvre as close as possible to the town's south gate. As each passed she would fire broadsides to silence the batteries and blast a breach in the walls. An infantry assault would follow.[16]

The next morning, whilst Backhouse searched for a landing site on HMS *Leda*, the ships were prepared. The 10-inch mortars were mounted on the *Fanny* and *Columbine* transports; the *Triton*, *Hero* and *Royal Charlotte* were loaded with ten to twelve 24-pound carronades and four long 18-pounders, and HMS *Lancaster* and *Diomede* were lightened to a draft of seventeen and a half feet.[17] The process took several days. The weather worsened and the fleet had to take shelter in the lee of the island of Flores. Sick of eating preserved rations and hard tack, Captain

Fothergill sent a foraging party to the island of Lobos to hunt sealions. Several were shot, butchered and prepared for the officers' table, along with hundreds of sea-fowl eggs. By 27 October the winds had abated and the bomb ships were ready. Captain Wilkie was astonished at HMS *Lancaster*'s transformation. 'She had only ballast left to keep her from upsetting,' he recalled. 'Her upper guns [had been] taken away [aside from one long 9-pounder, and] the topmasts and all her spars [had been] removed'.[18]

The next morning the *Rolla* arrived from Rio Grande with cattle which were distributed around the fleet and at 9.00 am the ships moved inshore.[19] Leading the line was the *Triton* transport under Captain Joshua Edmonds. Having lost command of HMS *Diomede* to Hugh Downman, a senior captain who had arrived with Backhouse's reinforcements, Edmonds had 'very handsomely' volunteered for the role. Next came the *Hero* and *Royal Charlotte*, the two bomb ships, the gun-brigs and the frigates. HMS *Lancaster* and *Diomede* brought up the rear. His sounding lead in constant operation, Captain Edmonds brought the *Triton* in as close as he dared with Spanish 24-pound round shot splashing into the river around him. At two and three quarter fathoms, still two miles distant from the southern walls, he signalled his findings to the rest of the fleet, shortened sail and hauled into the wind. The ships tacked one by one, ran parallel to the shore and opened fire. The British sailors would fire over 3,000 roundshot. Several fell amongst the batteries, but few carried over the walls.[20] The Spanish enjoyed more success. While Governor Huidobro rode through the streets to volleys of 'vivas!', scores of civilians volunteered in the batteries. The round shot were placed in braziers until they glowed red-hot and fourteen Spanish gunboats, moored under the walls, added their fire. Three defenders were wounded, amongst them a young child and a woman whose leg was badly mauled.[21] Several of the British ships were also hit. One sailor was wounded and a shot sunk HMS *Encounter*'s cutter. At 11.00 am it was HMS *Lancaster*'s turn. Unlike the *Diomede*, which had had all her upper guns removed, Captain Fothergill had insisted on leaving a single long 9-pounder on his quarter deck. 'From this gun being higher, and the ... deck allowing more elevation, he was able to throw the shot right into ... town ... [He] hit the church twice, and was ... delighted afterwards to learn that he had killed a priest', Captain Wilkie recalled.[22]

At 11.30 am Popham called off the attack. The Spanish gunboats proved too slow to cut off the *Fanny* bombship and at midday the British fleet reassembled four miles off shore.[23] That afternoon Popham proposed an attack on Maldonado, a coastal village of 1,000 inhabitants with a deep-water bay eighty miles to the southeast.[24] Backhouse, who could never be accused of alacrity, was reluctant, but when the commodore 'begged' he 'at last acceded' and at midnight the troops were transferred onto the frigates.[25] They proceeded in company with HMS *Diadem*, *Protector* and *Encounter* to Maldonado whilst the rest of the fleet sailed to the island of Flores to mislead anyone watching onshore.[26] At 5.00 pm on 29 October Popham and Backhouse arrived off Maldonado. After skirting the island of Gorriti, a rocky outpost mounting four batteries of heavy guns, the ships anchored in five fathoms a quarter of a mile from the beach.[27] The assault force –

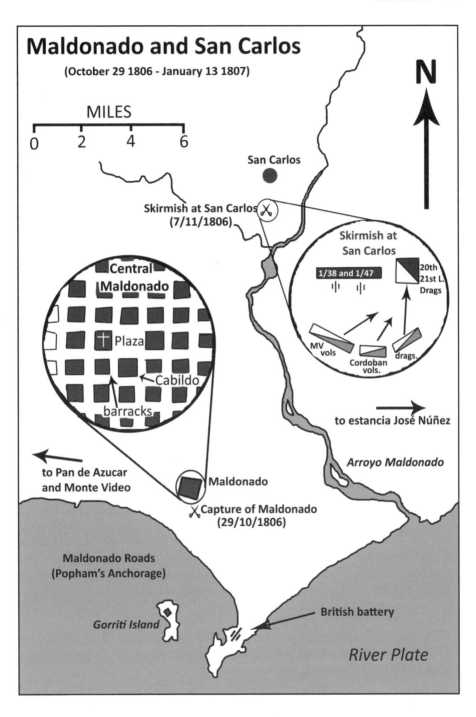

Maldonado and San Carlos

(October 29 1806 - January 13 1807)

MILES

0   2   4   6

N

San Carlos

Skirmish at San Carlos
(7/11/1806)

Skirmish at
San Carlos

1/38 and 1/47

20th
21st L.
Drags

MV vols
Cordoban vols.
drags.

Central
Maldonado

Plaza

Cabildo

barracks

to estancia José Núñez

Arroyo Maldonado

to Pan de Azucar
and Monte Video

Maldonado

Capture of Maldonado
(29/10/1806)

Maldonado Roads
(Popham's Anchorage)

Gorriti Island

British battery

River Plate

the grenadiers and light company of the 38th, two sections of dragoons and a few companies of marines and armed sailors – clambered into the ships' boats and were rowed ashore. A handful of Spanish musketeers in the dunes were dispersed by a shower of grapeshot and Colonel Vassal formed his infantry into an echelon line unopposed. The 38th under Major Trotter took the lead on the right, the dismounted dragoons were deployed as light infantry on the left and the cavalry, sailors and marines formed the reserve.[28] Delighted to be on dry land after two months at sea, the men were 'in the highest spirits, and in full confidence of success'.[29] Vassal had been informed that the Spanish garrison had deserted the village and expected little resistance.[30] Ordering his men to hold their fire, he led them over the sand dunes towards the village, three miles distant from the shore.[31]

Contrary to what Vassal had heard, the Spanish had not abandoned their posts. On sighting the British ships in the bay, the mayor, Ventura Gutierrez, sounded the general alarm and the soldiers and militia, joined by several villagers, formed two units. An artillery train of four guns, including a 6-inch brass howitzer and a long brass 6-pounder, were mobilised under second Lieutenant Francisco Martínez, whilst the infantry and cavalry were led by a captain of the Blandengues named Miguel Borrás. The artillery took up position by the customs officers' watchtower on the outskirts of the village, whilst Borrás' men, numbering 230, hid themselves on the rooftops of two of the principal buildings on the main square.[32] As the British descended from the sand dunes and ran across the plain, Martínez ordered his artillerymen to open fire.[33] The first round shot flew high and wide, but when the British got 'within about forty yards' Martínez discharged 'a howitzer loaded with grape'. Private Joseph Harrison of the grenadiers was shot through the head and died instantly.[34] The survivors 'rushed forward, and drove the enemy from their guns'. Seventy were bayonetted in the charge.[35] In over a decade of active service it was the first time Captain Wilkie had seen a bayonet used to kill a man. 'One of our soldiers had his ... bent like a hoop in forcing it into a fellow's chest', he recalled.[36] Re-forming his men, Vassal drove on down the main street, which was flanked by a row of 'low and mean' houses. As they approached the main square, dominated by a gigantic half-finished cathedral, Borrás' regulars and militia opened fire from the rooftops.[37] Three of the 38th were hit.[38] Their comrades smashed their way into the houses and bayonetted all they found. Within a few minutes the town was won and at 9.00 pm the British flag was hoisted on the custom officers' watchtower. Out in the bay Popham fired a salute while Lieutenant-Colonel Backhouse and the 47th rowed ashore to consolidate control.[39]

Fifty Spaniards and creoles had been killed in the fighting, amongst them two officers of the Maldonado militia.[40] Many of the survivors fled to San Carlos, a village of 500 inhabitants ten miles to the north. The rest surrendered and a few were executed on the spot.[41] Seeing one of the Spanish officers about to be bayonetted, Vassal intervened. As he pushed the redcoats back, the Spaniard pulled a pistol and fired at point blank range. Somehow the ball missed, but the powder flash 'scorch[ed] the Colonel's pantaloons.'[42] Taking the officer prisoner,

Vassal ordered the ends of the streets barricaded with barrels, overturned carts and furniture in case of counterattack. Several of his troops obeyed. The rest ran amok. Following several weeks cramped on board ship and the exhilaration of the fight, Vassal allowed them 'three hours license. Never surely did men make better use of the opportunities afforded them', Sergeant Landsheit recalled. Several ransacked the houses for liquor. Others assaulted any male Spaniards they found before locking them in the Blandengues barracks on the Plaza Mayor.[43] The rest 'stole clothes, money, jewellery and kitchenware and smashed all the furniture and anything else that didn't serve their needs'. Religious effigies were targeted and the women roughly searched for hidden coins. Some had their clothes torn from their backs and others were sexually abused.[44] The officers tried to regain control by pouring the 'liberated' liquor into the gutters and defending some of the richer houses, but most of the town remained exposed. After helping himself to the contents of 'a deserted mansion', Sergeant Landsheit emerged with 'a dozen silver-handled knives and forks' and a bundle of fine silk, lace and linen shirts, chemises and stockings, to find the village quiet. His comrades had drunk themselves into a stupor. Snoring loudly, the conquerors of Maldonado were fast asleep in the streets.[45]

The next morning, Backhouse ordered Vassal to assault the shore batteries to the south whilst he established control in the village.[46] Vassal achieved his aims with ease. The battery faced the sea and when the British infantry appeared to his rear the Spanish commander surrendered, leaving the island of Gorriti the last outpost in enemy hands. Popham promptly demanded its capitulation. 'Any opposition on your part', he informed the commander, 'must be fruitless, and if you do not allow the officer who is charged with this letter to hoist His Majesty's colours ... you will have to answer for the ... consequences'. Captain Augustin de Loris conceded. Twenty 24-pounders were captured and the garrison – four officers and 104 men – were transferred aboard the British ships as prisoners of war. In the village, Backhouse was having more difficulty. After assigning the few men fit for duty to the outposts, he had the provosts shake awake the rest. Eventually the men responded to the threat of corporal punishment and 'betook themselves to the work of fortifying and rendering the post tenable.'[47] With his immediate security concerns dealt with, Backhouse had 'the walls of the houses ... posted with proclamations inviting the inhabitants to return home ... assuring them ... that the English were not ... conquerors but ... friends'.[48] Despite the chaos of the previous night, the proclamations were a sign of intent. Backhouse had the men's belongings searched and returned the looted goods he found; sentries were posted to protect the main buildings; an open letter forbidding any local to sell wine or *aquardiente* to the troops was published; and the Cabildo were invited to return to work.[49] The prisoners of war were also reviewed and only eighty, whom the British were convinced were soldiers, were kept in custody.[50] Meanwhile, an officer was despatched to San Carlos to demand its surrender, horses were commandeered for the cavalry, and a headquarters was established in a house on the Plaza Mayor.[51]

The commander at San Carlos, a Portuguese officer in Spanish service named Cardoso, conceded to Backhouse's demands and on 31 October 200 men with two field-pieces marched inland to accept his surrender. After commandeering a few horses and cattle and ceremoniously receiving the commandant's baton, the troops returned to Maldonado, allowing Cardoso to remain in de facto command.[52] That afternoon HMS *Diadem* and *Raisonnable* anchored 'within a cable's length of the shore' bringing 'the whole of the peninsula ... under cover of ... [their] guns.' The ships would spend several months in Maldonado roads and the sailors made themselves at home. 'We found ... [our stay] remarkably pleasant', Lieutenant Samuel Walters recalled. After the thunderstorms and freezing temperatures of winter, November brought sunshine and warmth and 'fishing, shooting, hunting, and riding was the order of the day'.[53] Even Popham relaxed and 'soon put in practice his powers of telegraph', Captain Wilkie recalled. Watching from the customs tower the soldiers deciphered his messages. "A ship to windward', in the code, was altered into 'bread'; 'one to leeward', into 'butter'; in place of 'boats to go on shore', it was 'have horses on the beach'; 'reef topsails' [became] 'send us some fresh beef'; 'weigh anchor' – 'have you any poultry?' and 'an enemy in sight' – 'I am coming to dine with you'.[54]

With an insufficient force for further conquest and no threat from the Spanish by land or sea, the British soldiers were also at ease. Aside from visiting their colleagues in the navy and the occasional journey into the interior to round up cattle and horses, there was little to occupy them and their domestic arrangements were soon made. 'The soldiers were gathered together in one or two large buildings', Wilkie recalled, '[whilst] the officers occupied the best houses, which we designated hotels, and named after some peculiarity of the senior officer, or some of the inmates. Sketches were drawn on the white-washed walls, and a MS. newspaper was published once a week, detailing the news of the village.'[55] On 4 November the *Willington* transport sailed for England. On board was Henry Le Blanc, the captain of the 71st who had lost his leg at Reducción four months before, Popham's and Backhouse's dispatches and several private letters.[56] 'At present every thing is conjecture,' one, penned by an officer on HMS *Howe*, related. 'I believe the general opinion is, that we shall remain here, until we have a reinforcement from England ... [but] our prospect of making a fortune [in prize money] is, I am afraid, all over'.[57] A letter from Captain Richard Howard of the *Alexander* transport was equally pessimistic. 'We have at present possession of Maldonado', he wrote, 'but I do not think we shall keep it long.'[58]

Two days later Lieutenant Augustin Abreu Orta arrived at San Carlos determined to make Howard's prediction come true. Born in the town of Tarifa, Andalucia in 1766, the forty-year-old Abreu was a former naval officer. Following a distinguished career, he had left active service and emigrated to Monte Video where he married in 1804. With the arrival of the British, Abreu had volunteered for the militia and had been due to travel to Buenos Ayres with Liniers, but Governor Huidobro had ordered him to remain to protect the city from assault. With Beresford's defeat, the threat of attack was over and on 2 November Abreu was ordered to take 350 cavalry, a mixture of regular dragoons and volunteers from Córdoba and Monte Video, and harass the British at Maldonado.[59] Despite being commanded not to engage in open battle, at the very first opportunity this was exactly what Abreu did.[60]

At 10.00 pm on 6 November a column of 100 British infantry with two light swivel guns and fifty light dragoons set out on a routine mission to corral live-stock in the interior.[61] So blasé had the British become that they considered such sallies good sport and had christened the practice 'bullock-hunting'. This par-ticular party had the village of San Carlos as its destination and was led by Lieutenant-Colonel Henry Fox Brownrigg, Backhouse's quarter-master-general. The son of an Irish peer, Brownrigg had joined the army in 1801 and was known for his 'military prowess, connexions, rank, situation, youth, healthy constitution and noble mind'.[62] Under his command were Backhouse's adjutant-major, Captain Blake Ebrington, a man who 'seldom failed to be present whenever anything like fun or fighting was likely to take place', and Sergeant Landsheit of the 20th Light Dragoons.[63]

The day of 7 November dawned with a thick, persistent fog. As the troops advanced over a series of low granite hills brightly coloured birds broke into flight and occasionally flocks of the ostrich-like rhea were seen through the gloom.[64] At 10.00 am, with the fog lifting, the British arrived outside San Carlos. 'The bishop and his clergy ... came out to salute us', Landsheit recalled and assured Brownrigg that a number of cattle had already been rounded up and would shortly be delivered. 'We planted our videttes and sentries ... on small eminences at a little distance from the road, after which we dismounted, and ... began to eat and drink and be merry – but no cattle came.' As the British were beginning to get suspicious, they were attacked. 'First one vidette, then another, held up his helmet in his hand, fired his carbine and came galloping to the rear ... for at the distance of perhaps a quarter of a mile, about [three] ... hundred horse made their appearance, pushing towards us at full speed, and in excellent order.'[65] With his infantry in line on the right supported by the swivel guns, Brownrigg formed his cavalry in column on the left. Captain Ebrington and three other officers walked their horses six paces to the front and prepared to receive the charge.[66]

Abreu's men had been trailing the British all day. Leaving their baggage at a nearby *estancia*, they had ridden through the morning, only for their initial enthusiasm to dissipate when, on cresting a rise, they had spotted the British troops exercising in Maldonado and began to worry that they would crushed between two enemy forces. Abreu insisted, however, and on sighting Brownrigg's men all the Andalucian's cavalry had begun the charge. As they closed, the bulk of the Cordoban and Monte Videan volunteers, facing the British infantry, shied away and after receiving a couple of musket volleys and watching a few grenades hurled at hopelessly long range exploding to their front, they took cover behind a line of thorn hedges, leaving Abreu and eighty dragoons to engage the British cavalry alone.[67] The British hussars fired their carbines, then drew their swords and charged. 'Through and through we rode,' Landsheit recalled, 'hacking and cutting and receiving in our turn some hard blows'. Lieutenant Abreu was one of the first to fall. Shot in the side, he was spilled from his saddle and set upon by Private Thomas Marshall of the 20th Light Dragoons. A former corporal demoted for a drunken incident at the Cape, Marshall severed Abreu's left wrist with the first blow of his sword.[68] His second split the Andalucían's helmet, scalp and skull, exposing his brains.[69] A number of Abreu's men were also wounded and his second-in-command, Captain José Martínez, was shot through the right arm. Privates William Barrit and John Combly and Sergeant Charles Fulcher of the 20th and 21st Light Dragoons were also killed. One endured a particularly unpleasant fate. His horse bolting across the field, he was chased by thirty of the creole cavalry volunteers who had been watching from the thorn hedges. After a brief pursuit, the Briton's horse stumbled. The creoles pulled him to the ground and stabbed him to death with their knives.[70]

Eleven minutes after the mêlée had begun the British cavalry disengaged. 'This was done to get us clear from the range of the infantry and [swivel] guns', Landsheit explained, 'both of which were ... eager to take part in the fray.' Disorganised and leaderless, the dragoons were thrown into confusion by the first British volley and 'in three seconds ... were rolling one upon another, or scattered like sheep over the plain'. Several riders were killed, including Antonio Bessot, a Catalan whose chest and body were perforated with musketry, before the redcoats finished him off with their bayonets. A few others managed to reach the British line, where their sabres were put to good effect. Privates James Kearney and George Bell of the 38th were killed and Private John Horton fatally wounded, before the re-formed British dragoons chased the remaining Spaniards and creoles from the field.[71] Enraged at the villagers' duplicity, Brownrigg ordered his men to burn San Carlos to the ground. 'We ... set it on fire in several quarters,' Landsheit recalled, 'and ... helped ourselves to such valuables as could be easily removed'. One resident, who shot at the looters with a musket, was set upon and mortally wounded before the British withdrew.[72] 'We brought back such of our [casualties] ... as could bear the jolting of cars', Landsheit recalled, '[and] left the rest, with all the Spaniards, under the care of an English surgeon'. As the British rode back to Maldonado, the villagers doused the flames and buried the dead. The redcoats and blue-jacketed dragoons were tossed into a nearby marsh, while the Spaniards and creoles were interred in the graveyard. Taken to a nearby *estancia*, Abreu lingered on for a few hours before expiring.[73]

On learning of the skirmish, Backhouse and Popham drew up a plan of evacuation. If the Spanish attacked Maldonado in force, the troops would retreat to a low peninsula to the south where they could be evacuated by the fleet. On 10 November HMS *Lancaster* and three armed transports dropped anchor in the roads, adding their firepower to that of HMS *Raisonnable* and *Diadem* and the same day two 18-pounders were hoisted ashore and a battery constructed on the sand dunes facing town.[74] In the village, the barricades were reinforced. Trenches were dug, dry stone and brick walls erected and *chevaux de frise* positioned at the major intersections.[75]

With Abreu dead and Martínez wounded, the Spaniards restricted themselves to driving the wild cattle and horses beyond Backhouse's reach. The tactic proved successful and the 'bullock-hunting' expeditions had to go further and further inland. Some casualties were caused, but never with the intensity of the fight at San Carlos. On 17 November Private Thomas Leake of the 38th was killed and Private Patrick Hennessey of the 47th died on 10 December.[76] In Maldonado, food supplies began to run low. Sergeant Landsheit complained of a lack of rum and Captain Wilkie and his fellow officers were forced into culinary experiments.[77] Armadillos were sampled, as were 'two varieties of partridge'. Fish, one of which 'was as large as a cod', were caught in the Arroyo Maldonado, and a rather dangerous trial was conducted with some local greens, thought to be wild spinach.[78] 'The plant turned out to be 'a species of night-shade', Captain Wilkie recalled. It made 'all the mess foolish for twenty-four hours ... [and gave us] the most curious delusions.'[79]

At the end of October Popham chartered the *Kitty*, a British privateer which had hoped to trade at Buenos Ayres, to sail to Rio de Janeiro for supplies. Mr Blennerhasset, the purser of HMS *Raisonnable*, was placed on board with £15,000 of certified bills.[80] Popham also authorised the fleet's pursers to buy provisions from the neutral merchantmen gathered in Maldonado Roads. On 1 December there were twelve Americans, three Danish and one Portuguese. Twelve had been detained for being in breach of the British blockade, two had been denied entrance to Monte Video and two had arrived from Rio de Janeiro with the express purpose of selling goods to the British army and fleet. With their cargoes expiring, even those captains who had been detained were willing to do business.[81] In November the *Superb* of Boston sold eighteen casks of wine to HMS *Lancaster* and a cargo of West Indian rum and flour was purchased from a merchantman from Philadelphia. Ovens were built on the island of Gorriti and fresh bread sent ashore.[82]

On 26 November 140 Spanish and creole prisoners were transferred from the ships to the island of Lobos. Although Popham claimed it was for their benefit – they were 'unused to sea provisions ... and still more to confinement' – conditions were extreme. Aside from a few tents there was no shelter and provisions were scarce.[83] Driven to desperation thirty-seven of the prisoners escaped in makeshift boats fashioned from sealskin. When they reached Monte Video, the story of their deprivations spread, further damaging the British cause.[84] Another problem at Maldonado was a high rate of desertion. On 16 November two privates of the 38th absconded and another followed two weeks later.[85] The first pair arrived at Monte Video within three days. Each was given twenty-five *pesos* and assigned work in the defensive batteries. They told their hosts that many of their comrades wanted to join them. The Spaniards pressed the men to write letters encouraging further desertions, which were smuggled into Maldonado, and a fund was set up to pay 100 *pesos* to each new arrival.[86]

On 3 December several strange sails were sighted off Maldonado. The convoy consisted of a number of victuallers and two East Indiamen – the *Earl Spencer* and *Sir Steven Lushington* – under convoy of HMS *Sampson*, a sixty-four-gun ship-of-the-line.[87] The Indiamen, whose captains had been hoping to trade at Buenos

Ayres, brought some welcome diversion to the men under Backhouse's command.[88] 'There were ... several English ladies of a speculative nature [on board]', Captain Wilkie explained. These were part of the phenomenom known as 'The Fishing Fleet' – single women who travelled to India, where many eligible young bachelors were to be found, in the hope of marrying above their station. The ladies 'favoured' Wilkie and his fellow officers 'with a visit' but were distinctly unimpressed by the 'half-starved bachelors' they found. '[Maldonado] held small chances of "settling," Wilkie explained, 'and still less of the Captain getting rid of his "investment." So round went the capstan ... and off all the shes did go, leaving us again to our own resources'.[89]

HMS *Sampson* was carrying a less welcome passenger. Charles Stirling, the forty-six-year-old rear-admiral who had orders to replace Popham as naval commander-in-chief, was a seasoned professional who had fought at the Glorious First of June and the Battle of Algeciras and served as second-in-command at the Battle of Cape Finisterre.[90] For Stirling, Popham's adventure had been ill-conceived from the start and he was convinced that the British were unwelcome in South America. Whilst success would hold little reward and would be difficult to achieve, failure would result in sanction. 'With this impression', noted a contemporary, 'he [had] made every objection, consistent with his sense of duty, to the acceptance of the command: indeed, had it not been his opinion that it is the duty of an officer to go wherever his country calls, he would not have accepted it.'[91]

Stirling's first challenge was to wrest control. Realising that he might well have reached the end of his career, Popham was desperate to score one last success before leaving. To this end he volunteered his services in the event of an attack being made on Monte Video when Auchmuty arrived. Popham envisioned a role as Stirling's 'honorary aide-de-camp, or [employed] in any situation where he could impart ... the result of seven months' local experience'. Stirling declined. His orders were to send Popham home at the first opportunity. As far as the Admiralty was concerned, the commodore no longer had any role to play in the River Plate. Neither side was willing to compromise and the dispute grew increasingly acrimonious as the days dragged by. 'The moment one argument failed another would be started, or something else suggested', Stirling recalled.[92] A further issue was that when Popham did eventually leave, he was determined to do so in a warship sailing directly for England, thus avoiding an awkward landing at Cape Town en route. Such extravagances Stirling was unwilling to grant.[93]

On 11 December HMS *Pheasant* arrived. On board was Major John Deane, the officer who had carried Beresford's victory dispatches to London and now brought word that Auchmuty's reinforcements were three weeks away. With the prospect of more mouths to feed and supplies running ever lower, the troops made more and more frequent forays, ever further into the interior, to gather cattle. Although casualties remained low, the enemy was gathering strength. A new commander, Colonel Santiago Allende of the Córdoba Cavalry Volunteers, had replaced Abreu. Based in the village of Pan de Azucar, at first he had toyed with the idea of a full-scale attack on Maldonado, but had since changed his mind and deployed four pickets, each containing 100 men, around the village instead. Allende's tactics proved effective and the British grew afraid of venturing beyond the limits of Maldonado.[94] This resulted in further desertion and in December at least thirteen men absconded.[95] One of the officers of the 47th summed up the situation in a letter home. 'There are now 5,000 Spanish troops encamped about eighteen miles from this place ... [They] are expected to attack ... every day ... are all mounted on most excellent horses ... [and] have a most curious method of fighting, with a long rope and a noose at the end, which they throw with the greatest nicety to the distance of thirty yards ... as soon as they have caught their object, they gallop off, and drag him to death in five minutes; several of our men have been taken in this way.'[96] Another of the creoles' tactics – riding up to within extreme musket range, firing a single shot across the back of their horses and galloping away – was considered equally unsporting by the British.[97]

A 'bullock-hunting' expedition on Christmas Eve proved particularly disastrous. Some 600 men, amongst them Sergeant Landsheit, set out before dawn, their target an *estancia* by the riverbank belonging to José Núñez.[98] 'We reached [it] ... about three o'clock in the morning,' Landsheit recalled 'and saw ... between two and three hundred cattle, with some valuable horses, gathered within a pen. To drive off the keepers ... and turn the animals' heads towards Maldonado was the work of a minute ... but we had not proceeded far, when the day being fully broke, we saw the wide plain ... covered with scattered bands of horsemen, who began sounding their cow-horns ... and riding in a direction parallel to that which we ... were pursuing ... we pricked our ears up, and moved like men preparing for battle, till suddenly ... the natives, putting each a finger in his mouth, sent forth a loud and peculiar cry ... Up went the tail of each ... bullock ... and away they galloped immediately ... till the whole herd had dispersed ... suddenly there opened up upon us, right and left, in front and in rear, a terrible fire of musketry. The Spaniards ... had laid ... an ambuscade'.[99]

Lieutenant Francis Rundell of the 54th, 'a very fine young man' who had been rescued from the hold of the *Volontaire* nine months earlier, was hit in the chest. Mortally wounded, he was picked up by his comrades and carried back with the retreat.[100] 'Nothing now remained but to leave the cattle to themselves and fight our way back to Maldonado', Landsheit recalled. 'We were driven ... to the water's edge and ... surrounded. Some tall rocks that lay within [the] low-water mark afforded some cover to the infantry, while the cavalry had nothing for it but to skirmish at every disadvantage ... We maintained the fight as best we could, charging from time to time ... and then retreating ... so as to be in some degree protected by ... the infantry, when the officer who commanded ... sent off three dragoons, one after another ... along the edge of the water towards headquarters. Happily ... none of them was cut off ... and Colonel Backhouse lost not a moment in getting his people under arms ... the Spaniards ... retreated on the first appearance of his scouts'.[101]

On 26 December Popham finally deigned to return home. The move may have been prompted by the receipt of some private letters from London delivered by William Eastwick, the English merchant who had left Portsmouth in November

1806 on the *Anna*. The Ministry of All the Talents was said to be already on the verge of collapse and was likely to be replaced by one composed of Popham's political allies.[102] The latest newspapers from London also contained reassuring news. 'They say you, Beresford, and myself have the freedom of the city', Popham wrote to Baird. 'It is also hinted that all [will] be well with me if I don't ride too high.' The commodore's self-confidence had returned. 'If any energy had existed in our government ... and they had sent us out some reinforcement, we should have had all of South America by now' he opined. 'I will draw a good contrast between the promptness of our decision and ... the inertness of theirs; as General Tarleton says they have behaved on this occasion like a set of drones.'[103] On the eve of his departure on the *Rolla*, an American brig detained by HMS *Medusa*, Popham asked Stirling if Captain William King and the coxswain and signalman from HMS *Diadem* could join him. 'I would with great pleasure direct [these] ... men to be sent to the *Rolla* for your personal convenience', Stirling replied drolly, 'if I was assured that you would actually proceed'. Popham sailed the next day.[104] On 6 January Auchmuty's 'long awaited reinforcement' arrived.[105] Leading the flotilla were HMS *Ardent* of sixty-four guns, the frigate HMS *Unicorn*, the gun-brig HMS *Staunch* and the *Charwell* sloop of war. Twenty-five transports carrying 3,000 men were in convoy.[106] Backhouse's troops were delighted. Wilkie spoke of the sight affording him and his fellows the 'greatest pleasure', whilst Sergeant Landsheit recalled his 'indescribable joy'.[107] Having suffered the ignominy of two months' virtual imprisonment in a 'deserted village', the British were about to go on the offensive once more.[108]

Chapter 11

The Siege of Monte Video
5 January – 3 February 1807

Brigadier-General Samuel Auchmuty disembarked at Maldonado at 5.00 pm on 5 January. The men took to the American instantly. 'He ... expressed his high admiration of our conduct', Sergeant Landsheit recalled, 'inquired into our wants – and assured us that it would be his business to make us comfortable.' Auchmuty was true to his word. 'That ... night a supply of rum, which we had not seen for a long while back, reached us' and over the next three days '18 cwt of rice', ten barrels of flour, three puncheons of spirits, and 'five kegs of dollars' were distributed.[1] On 6 January the new arrivals disembarked. Landsheit and his comrades were glad of the reinforcement, but for Private Thomas Todd, one of the 'young boys' in Captain Brookman's company of the 71st, it was a rude awakening. '[The troops] were in the greatest want of every necessary ... and quite disheartened', he recalled.[2] That evening Auchmuty and Stirling agreed to abandon Maldonado: the anchorage was not as sound as the navy had thought; the town was exposed to attack; and it 'was of no consequence' strategically.[3] Besides, Auchmuty had a bigger prize in mind – Monte Video. The next day the men were divided into divisions. The best troops – Major Thomas Gardener's riflemen, Vassal's 38th and an elite Light Battalion (consisting of the combined light companies led by Lieutenant-Colonel Brownrigg and Major Trotter and supported by four guns) were designated the First Division under the overall command of Brigadier-General the Honourable William Lumley. A veteran of the 1798 Irish Rebellion, the Egyptian campaign of 1801 and Baird's capture of the Cape, Lumley was the archetypal dashing cavalryman and Auchmuty's second-in-command. The Second Division, commanded by Colonel Gore Browne, consisted of the 40th, 47th and 87th Regiments and Captain Brookman's company of the 71st supported by one howitzer. The rest of the infantry, the cavalry and the remainder of the artillery formed the reserve under Lieutenant-Colonel Backhouse.[4]

On 6 January the outposts pushed inland to confuse the enemy. Meanwhile, Stirling's sailors prepared 3,000 sandbags from old sail canvas stored on HMS *Howe* and on 12 January haversacks and drag belts were made for the seamen who were to be landed to haul the guns.[5] The next morning, a storm 'of incessant and heavy rain; thundering and lightning' having abated, the embarkation began.[6] It was a textbook operation. 'We were instructed to evacuate ... without beat of drum and ... every man and horse returned on board of ship ere the Spaniards were ... aware of our intentions', Sergeant Landsheit recalled.[7] By 9.30 am the embarkation was complete.[8] Backhouse's troops were glad to put Maldonado behind them. 'A ship on foreign service seems like an epitome of home', Captain Wilkie explained, 'and we tumbled on board the "lobster smacks" with considerable delight.'[9] That afternoon two officers and twenty-five men from HMS *Lancaster* were landed on Gorriti Island to man the batteries.[10] Along with HMS *Lancaster*, they were to remain off Maldonado with the neutral merchantmen, while the rest of the fleet – three ships-of-the-line, four frigates, three sloops, four gun-brigs, forty transports and twenty-seven English merchantmen – sailed due west for an assembly off Flores Island.[11] By 14 January the assembly was complete. The ships' captains signed an agreement promising all prizes would be divided equally, the army was supplied with three days' provisions, and HMS *Leda* was dispatched to Monte Video with a summons for the viceroy to surrender.[12]

Barracked on his arrival the previous October, Sobremonte had long since departed Monte Video for the village of Las Piedras, leaving Governor Huidobro in charge in town. A dandy 'whose body exuded more scents than a perfumery', Huidobro commanded little respect amongst the military and authority effectively divulged on several officers and the Cabildo. These disparate parties had some 3,500 men under their command. Several units, such as the Miñones and the Monte Video Infantry Volunteers, had taken part in the Reconquista. Another of merit was the Húsares del Gobierno, a militia regiment built around Hipólito Mordeille's privateers. Others, such as the Galician and Asturian volunteers and the 250 prisoners who had been released on condition they fight, were of dubious worth. Fifteen miles to the north, Sobremonte had another 2,500 men. These mounted regulars and militia included the Cordoban volunteers under Colonel Santiago Allende and brought the total number of defenders to 6,000 men. The Spaniards' numerical strength gave them the courage to rebuff Auchmuty's summons, but their indiscipline and splintered chain of command would give the British the upper hand.[13]

On the morning of 15 January Stirling's fleet sailed to Carretas Point six miles east of Monte Video.[14] The rear-admiral and his senior officers spent the day reconnoitring the coast and found 'two small bays … protected by a chain of rocks from easterly winds' which 'seemed exactly the place we wanted'.[15] That afternoon orders were distributed for the landing. At first light HMS *Raisonnable*, with the British merchant ships in convoy, was to sail west and blockade Monte Video. The rest of the fleet would cover the disembarkation. HMS *Diadem* and *Ardent* would form an outer cordon, dropping anchor in five fathoms, five miles out. The frigates would form an inner ring, while HMS *Charwell*, *Encounter*, *Daphne* and *Pheasant* would cover the landings in the eastern and western bays respectively. All would use springs to bring their broadsides to bear, whilst the launches of HMS *Raisonnable* and *Diomede*, armed with carronades, were to 'touch the beach if necessary.' The troops would disembark by divisions. The first was to land at dawn, the last would reach shore late the following afternoon.[16]

At first light the operation began.[17] At 7.00 am HMS *Charwell* and *Encounter* dropped anchor within musket-shot of the eastern beach, while HMS *Daphne* and *Pheasant* covered the western bay, and at 10.00 am the troops of the first division clambered into their transports' flat-bottomed boats.[18] As they gathered round the sloops, gun-brigs and launches, 800 lancers and six cannon commanded by Colonel Allende made an appearance on the heights.[19] Some of the cavalry began to descend, but when the ships opened fire the majority retired, leaving just 'a few fool-hardy' riders to brave the British guns. 'One hero, in a fine … flowing poncho, galloped down to the extreme point where the ships were moored', Captain Wilkie recalled. 'Not satisfied … he returned along the beach, giving a few bravado flourishes of his hands, in token of defiance. After getting … a certain distance, he began to suspect that the fire of the ships was not the pleasantest accompaniment to a canter … gave spurs to his horse, and our soldiers gave him a cheer. He had not … gone many yards when … a cannon shot … nipped off his head'.[20]

At 10.30 am the crews of the landing boats pulled for shore.[21] Ploughing through the surf, the tars hauled them up the beach, the first division formed up on the sands, the wind freshened and a heavy rain began. With Auchmuty commanding and Major Gardener's riflemen fanning out ahead, the first line of sand dunes were swiftly secured. 'We could see [our] … troops in motion', Stirling recalled, 'and the Spaniards retreating before [them]'.[22] By the time the second division had landed, the riflemen had secured the next ridgeline and it wasn't until 2.00 pm that Sobremonte's troops began to provide any real resistance, opening a long-range cannonade from the hills.[23] Two men and Lieutenant Edward Chawner of the rifles were wounded and John Pridenoze, a drummer with the 95th, was killed.[24] 'The evening was beautiful', Stirling recalled. 'All night long the boats … were in motion. Guns, stores, ammunition, and all the materiel of an army were landed'.[25] Horses were brought ashore for the artillery and the wounded were rowed back to the hospital ships.[26]

At sunset Sobremonte's troops remained frozen on the heights, their commander bereft of ideas. In Monte Video Governor Huidobro was equally anxious. That afternoon he had sent a naval lieutenant, José de Cordova, to ask Sobremonte if he should advance with the entire garrison and push the enemy into the sea. The viceroy dismissed the idea, requesting only the support of Mordeille's Húsares del Gobierno. Hudiobro sent them 'without losing an instant' only for a second letter to arrive from Sobremonte 'asking for the Militia Battalion to be dispatched … The troops [marched and] passed the night in the field [but] the next morning the Viceroy ordered them to return to town without having employed them in anyway'.[27]

On 17 January the cavalry's horses, 310 gallons of spirits, three days' provisions and a detachment of 300 seamen under Captain John Palmer of HMS *Pheasant* were landed.[28] HMS *Encounter* and an armed transport covered the army's left flank, driving off 'strong bodies of the enemy' with showers of round shot and grape and the men of the 1st Division continued skirmishing with Allende's troopers on the heights.[29] 'There was a good deal of firing today', Stirling recorded. 'We lost another man, and had two wounded. A great many of the enemy fell.'[30] The next day passed without loss for the British. While

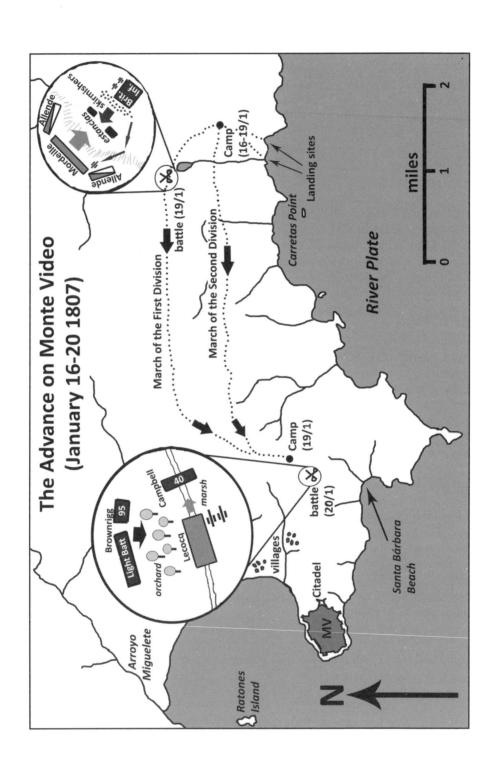

The Advance on Monte Video (January 16-20 1807)

Arroyo Miguelete

Ratones Island

Brownrigg
95
Light Batt
orchard
Lecocq
Campbell
40
marsh

villages

MV
Citadel

Santa Bárbara Beach

battle (20/1)

Camp (19/1)

March of the First Division

March of the Second Division

battle (19/1)

Mordelle
Allende
Allende
estancias
Skirmishers
Brit. Inf.

Camp (16-19/1)

Carretas Point

Landing sites

River Plate

N

miles
0   1   2

Sobremonte procrastinated and Huidobro sent a messenger to Buenos Ayres requesting reinforcement, Stirling conducted divine service on board HMS *Diadem*, seventy-four light dragoons and provisions were landed and that evening Auchmuty sent word that he intended to move out the next morning.[31] In response Stirling ordered his sloops, gun-brigs and the armed launches of HMS *Diadem*, *Ardent* and *Howe* to shadow the advance.[32]

The British moved out in two columns at daybreak. On the right was Lumley's 1st Division. The 2nd Division, under Colonel Browne, advanced closer to shore, while Backhouse's reserve followed behind. At first the going was slow. Captain Palmer's sailors sweated into their drag belts as they hauled the guns over the sand dunes, but once the army reached the plain inland, the pace increased. At 6.00 am Lumley's column was confronted by Sobremonte. Reinforced by Mordeille, the viceroy had over 2,500 men.[33] 'They were drawn up on some heights, and formed, with their wings thrown forward, three sides of a square', Sergeant Landsheit recalled. '[Auchmuty] examined the[m] ... carefully for a minute, and then ordered the advance'. Thus began a race to occupy two *estancias* commanding the field. Although Mordeille's infantry ran to keep up with Allende's cavalry on their flanks, the British, with the 95th and light dragoons fanned out in skirmish order and the infantry in column behind, outpaced them. On reaching the buildings, they deployed their cannon and opened fire. Sobremonte's gunners promptly answered. The British dragoons had 'several men and horses ... killed' and a round shot 'took [Auchmuty's] horse in the hip, and knocked [its] ... leg to shivers'. Shaken but unhurt, the brigadier-general remounted and ordered the dragoons to charge the enemy guns. 'On we rushed at a gallop', Landsheit recalled and '[after] sabring the cannoneers, [captured one brass gun]'. Colonel Allende's cavalry subsequently fled, leaving Mordeille's infantry exposed to the full weight of British fire and, when the Light Battalion charged, they too dispersed bringing the battle to a close. British casualties were twenty-five killed and wounded. Spanish deaths were not recorded, but Major John Tucker, Auchmuty's assistant-quarter-master-general, thought 'their loss ... considerable'.[34]

Following the battle, the British columns advanced over a verdant plain leading to a granite peninsula at the end of which was Monte Video. Broken by numerous gullies cut by winter rains, the rock sloped down into the river and sheltered a circular bay to the northwest.[35] Although it was subject to *pamperos* and relatively shallow, the bay was the best anchorage in the river, a fact that had resulted in Monte Video's rapid growth since its foundation as a counter-balance to regional Portuguese ambitions in 1726. On Auchmuty's arrival, the town boosted a population of 10,000. Many were involved in trade. Legal business was restricted to sending dried meat and hides to Cuba in exchange for sugar and a single ship was permitted to ply the route to La Coruña every two months. Contraband was bigger business and slavery a principal source of revenue. Others were employed in the whaling and seal-skinning industries or by the Spanish navy. As well as guarding the River Plate, the latter sent regular patrols to Patagonia and the

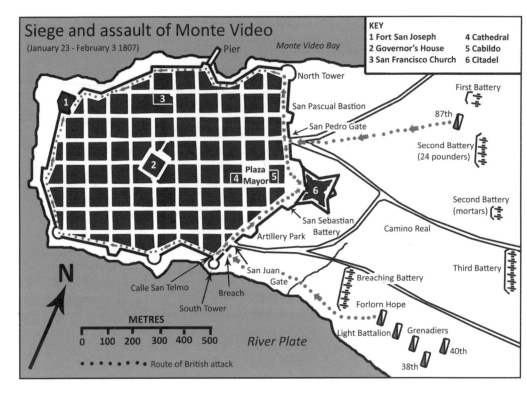

Falkland Islands. Monte Video was also home to several hundred French, Maltese, Sardinian, Genovese and Corsican privateers. Along with its population of 1,000 slaves, the majority recent arrivals from West Africa, this afforded the town a cosmopolitan character.[36]

At midday the British arrived in the eastern suburbs. The houses had been pulled down on their approach, leaving a maze of gardens ringed by fences constructed of the 'horns and skulls of cattle' and hedges of prickly pear. Only one building remained intact. At 600 yards from the walls, the cover afforded by the Casa de Seco would prove invaluable.[37] While the advanced guard under Major Francis Miller of the 87th advanced to within cannon range of the walls, the bulk of Auchmuty's army halted on some heights two miles from town. That afternoon they were joined by Captain Donnelley of the Royal Navy and 790 marines and sailors landed at Santa Bárbara Beach.[38] With the ships-of-the-line anchored in the bay to the northwest and the army strung out across the peninsula, Monte Video's communications were hampered, though not entirely cut off. Under the protection of the cannon on the walls and a battery of ten guns on Ratones Island, a number of boats, including six donated by the local merchant Francisco Anotonio de Castro, ferried supplies between the town's stone pier and the Arroyo Miguelette, a creek which emptied its muddy waters into the north of the bay where a communications trench gave further protection. In this way the defenders could be kept provisioned indefinitely.[39]

By evening the British troops had thrown up a forest of tents, bullock-hide bivouacs and lean-tos.[40] The men were delighted with their new home. In the ruined suburbs were orchards of peach, lemon, nectarine, fig and orange trees, to the west 'the country ... abounded with ducks, geese, turkeys, fowls ... sheep and bullocks' and from the heights they had a grandstand view of town. The most pertinent feature was the curtain wall. Built of stone, it was four feet thick and fifteen feet high. Its eastern face was pierced by two gates, San Pedro to the north and San Juan to the south, and strengthened by the San Sebastian and San Pascual *bastions*, each mounted with 24-pound brass cannon and heavy mortar. To the south, where the wall met the sea and turned westward, stood a high round tower and in the centre was a square fort named the Citadel. A regular work, it boasted bastions, a ditch, a small *ravelin* riveted with brick, and a *glacis* sloping down towards the east. Between the South Tower and the Citadel was the Artillery Park, a bulwark mounted with seven cannon. The British could see little of the interior of town aside from the tiled dome and twin square towers of the cathedral, the tallest building in Monte Video.[41]

Inside, the citizens were in uproar. Furious at the viceroy's retreat, they demanded action. Although loathe to throw the remains of his forces against an enemy superior in number, discipline, armament and training, Huidobro was overruled. 'In these heated circumstances', he recalled, 'I decided to hold a council of the leading military officers to which the Cabildo were also invited'. Dressed in powdered wig and perfectly pressed pantaloons, the governor did his best to dissuade them from attacking, but the outcome was a foregone con-clusion. 'All agreed on a sally,' Huidobro reported. A messenger was sent to the viceroy at Las Piedras asking for support and that afternoon the officers were ordered to parade their men in the main square. Some 1,642 deployed, many of them unblooded militia who knew nothing of manoeuvre or volley fire. Others were African slaves. 'With this number it was impossible to attack', Huidobro opined, 'but just then 600 cavalry arrived from the viceroy ... and it was agreed that the sally would take place at dawn'. That evening two companies of marines and sailors joined the force, bringing the total to 2,372. With the viceroy absent, command went to General Bernardo Lecocq. A Spaniard from La Coruña, Lecocq was the chief military engineer and just twenty-one days shy of his seventy-second birthday. Due to his age and lack of battlefield experience, efforts were made to prevent him, 'but he was senior and obstinate' and insisted on command. Lecocq's second was the garrison's sergeant-major, Francisco Javier de Viana, a forty-two year-old *porteño* and former governor of the Falkland Islands.[42]

At 6.00 am on 20 January, having spent the entire night drinking, the Spanish marched unsteadily out of town in two columns.[43] The first, led by Lecocq and supported by four cannon under Captain Pablo Colombo, advanced east down the Camino Real. Its mission was to hold the enemy, whilst the second column, which consisted of cavalry, would sweep round the British army's left flank, cutting it off from the fleet. At 6.30 am the first column's advanced guard – two companies of Miñones and the recently-arrived marines – encountered the

British outposts in the suburbs. Major Miller, in command of several detached companies amounting to 400 men, managed to repulse them. Learning of this reverse, Lecocq's men began yelling 'Attack! Attack!' Rushing forward with little order, they forced Miller to retreat.[44] Two wounded grenadiers of the 40th were left behind. The Spanish 'hacked and mangled [them] with knives' before continuing their advance.[45] Colonel Gore Browne, in charge in the suburbs, ordered Major Donald Campbell of the 40th to take three companies and block them.[46] Campbell formed his men across the road in a marshy hollow carpeted with twenty foot high bulrushes. When Lecocq's column came up, wildly firing grape shot from their cannon, the 40th charged. '[The Spanish, bolstered by Dutch courage,] gallantly received [them] ... and great numbers fell on both sides.'[47]

Watching the battle develop on the rise one mile to the east, Auchmuty ordered Lieutenant-Colonel Brownrigg to advance with the Light Battalion and the three rifle companies to the north of the Camino Real and attack Lecocq's flank.[48] By the time Brownrigg was in position, hidden by a peach grove, the fighting had become desperate. Cannon, musketry, hand grenades, swords and bayonets were all deployed.[49] More intent on his snuff box than what was going on around him, Lecocq had had his hat shot from his head, dozens of his men had been killed, Captain Colombo's guns had become separated from their ammunition cart, all his mules had been killed and the Spanish and creoles were starting to inch backwards under the 40th's fire.[50] Sensing the moment was right, the Light Battalion and rifles gave three cheers and charged with fixed bayonets through the peach grove.[51] Lecocq's militia failed to notice until it was too late. The septuagenarian ordered a disciplined retreat, but as Brownrigg's troops crashed into his flank the militia scattered through the ruins and made for the safety of the walls. Captain Colombo somehow got all but one of his cannon back to town and the Infantry Volunteers retained their colours after a desperate fight. The standard bearer, Vicente Figueroa, was shot through the hand and the officers had to join in the mêlée with swords and pistols before they broke free.[52] Hundreds of their comrades were killed by the Light Battalion and the riflemen and the survivors 'pressed ... so closely that the Spaniards on the ramparts could not ... fire ... for fear of hurting their own men'.[53] 'This was the first blood I had ever shed in battle', Thomas Todd, a sixteen-year-old private from Edinburgh, recalled. 'During the action, the thought of death never once crossed my mind ... a still sensation ... a firm determined torpor, bordering on insensibility ... stole over my whole frame'.[54]

The second Spanish column retired without drawing their swords.[55] Rear-Admiral Stirling ordered HMS *Encounter* to 'annoy the[ir] retreat'.[56] Sailing close in to shore, Lieutenant Talbot anchored opposite a prominent sand dune. As well as protecting the brig from the cannon on the walls, it concealed it from the cavalry, allowing Talbot to wait until the riders came alongside before firing a broadside into their flank. 'The carnage was dreadful', Sergeant Landsheit recalled and by the time Talbot's gunners were finished 'the road was ... heaped with slain'.[57] Riding through the gaps in the British line, the survivors returned to

Sobremonte's camp at Las Piedras.[58] That afternoon Stirling sent other boats inshore to pick up prisoners or transfer the wounded to the fleet.[59] Amongst the former were several African slaves and Sergeant Isidoro Revoredo of the Monte Video Cavalry Volunteers. After having the ball which had entered his right thigh removed from his left hip, Revordeo was locked below decks with dozens of his comrades.[60]

By 8.30 am it was over.[61] Seventy-two British soldiers had been killed or wounded. The three companies of the 40th who had held Lecocq's men amongst the bulrushes had borne the brunt. Sergeant H. Bowles would be awarded a gallantry medal for his bravery.[62] Twelve of his men and Lieutenant Timothy Fitzpatrick had been killed and twice that number wounded.[63] The Light Battalion had also suffered. Two of the 95th had been killed, Captain William Crookshank wounded and Major Trotter had had his horse killed under him and been shot through the hand.[64] British casualties were as nothing compared to those of their foes. As well as losing one cannon in the rout, Lecocq estimated that as many as seven hundred of his men had been killed, wounded, dispersed or captured. British estimates of Spanish losses ranged up to 1,500 men.[65]

With the sun still rising, the rifles and Light Battalion returned to their camp. 'We passed, in our way … over the field of the dead', Private Todd recalled. With the carrion birds flocking, the corpses were thrown into a giant pit. 'It was too much for my feelings [and] I was obliged to turn aside my head from the horrid sight … Men, who, in the morning … trode forth in strength … now lay shockingly mangled … a prey to animals … [and] I had been an assistant in this work of death!'[66] Given sentry duty near the spot, another young private, nineteen-year-old William Lawrence of the 40th, was also affected. 'It was the most uncomfortable two hours … I had ever spent', he recalled. 'I kept my eyes more on the place where the dead were than on the road I was placed to watch, not having altogether forgotten the absurd ghost stories of my own country. I … began to think … that I had done a good many things I should have liked not to, and to regret for the first time leaving my apprenticeship, my father, mother, and friends, to follow a life so dangerous as I now found this to be'.[67]

The next morning Brigade-Major Captain Philip Roche was sent to treat with Huidobro. The guns fell silent as he approached the walls under a flag of truce. After being blindfolded and escorted through 'the clamorous … mob', several of whom fired their muskets as he passed, Roche proposed a daylong ceasefire to bury the dead and return the wounded to town 'on parole of honour'. Huidobro agreed, but declined terms of surrender, insisting that he and his men would 'defend their town and fortress with the last of their blood.'[68] Despite his bombast, the governor was worried. Safe in Las Piedras, Sobremonte seemed content to leave Monte Video to its fate, the recent action had proved that a major sally was not an option and it now seemed the siege would roll on to its inevitable conclusion. Huidobro's only hope was that a relief force would arrive before it was too late. With this in mind, he wrote a second letter to the Cabildo in Buenos Ayres 'asking for troops or militia [to be sent] with all possible haste'.[69]

Later that day, the governor's first dispatch arrived in Buenos Ayres to a decidedly mixed reception. Since learning of Backhouse's landing at Maldonado, the *porteños* had been divided as to whether to aid the east bank, an antipathy due to the growing rivalry between the two towns. As the chief naval base in the region, Monte Video was home to a disproportionate number of *peninsulares*; it had been founded 150 years after the capital, so had had less time to develop creole politics; and its relatively deep-water port ensured it enjoyed a disparate share of ocean-going trade.[70] All this raised hackles across the river. Since Sobremonte's exile to the east bank, many *porteños* also disingenuously associated their pretentious younger neighbour with support for the viceroy. Besides, while the British remained in the river, Buenos Ayres needed all the men it had. In November 1806, when Huidobro's envoys had first attempted to recruit in the Plaza Mayor, a unit of ponytailed Patricios had torn their banners to shreds and forced them to flee.[71] Later an argument about whether gunboats should be sent had flared up, but on 20 January the Cabildo decided to act. Within three days 108 militia of the Regiment of Buenos Ayres, 325 Blandengues and seventy-eight dragoons were mobilised.[72] Command was given to Brigadier-General Pedro de Arze, the Spaniard who had presided over the defeat at Reducción six months before.[73] Leading the Blandengues was Colonel Nicolás Quintana, another survivor of June 1806. Amongst his riders were the brothers Antonio, Marcos, Diego and José González de Balcarce – three of whom would play prominent roles in Buenos Ayres' turbulent future.[74]

Meanwhile, Rear-Admiral Stirling had sent HMS *Charwell* and *Protector* to patrol upriver around Colonia. As well as intercepting enemy vessels, lieutenants Edwin Chamberlayne and Thomas Blainey were to head off any British merchantmen that came their way. Whilst some had still not heard of Beresford's defeat, others were well aware that Buenos Ayres was in enemy hands. Fully insured, they could claim the cost of their cargo and ships from the underwriters in the event of capture – an outcome some considered preferable to an unprofitable trip.[75] Back at Monte Video preparations for the siege continued. On the afternoon of 21 January 360 gallons of spirits, three days' provisions and two 24-pounders with 300 rounds of ammunition were landed at Santa Bárbara Beach; 1,031 sandbags were made and a transport was converted into a hospital ship.[76] That night a sally took place. Undaunted by the previous day's bloodshed, Sergeant Pablo Martínez and twenty men stole through British lines. Before the redcoats realised what was happening, they had herded 200 pigs corralled in the suburbs back inside.[77]

On 22 January the *siège en forme* began. Auchmuty's first task was to deal with twelve enemy gunboats moored in the bay to the northwest.[78] 'I was aware that their [fire] ... would annoy us' he explained, '[so] a two gun battery was constructed to keep them in check'.[79] After being dragged up the beach, the 24-pounders were wheeled inland, where Captain John Squire of the Royal Engineers constructed an earthwork to house them. It was backbreaking work. 'The thin, superficial soil was baked hard by the sun' Captain Wilkie recalled, entrenching tools were scarce and the fire from the bastions and the Citadel a constant menace.[80] At 6.00 pm, after Able-Seaman Ralph Blair, a twenty-six-year-old from Durham, had been killed by round shot, HMS *Staunch* and *Encounter* were ordered 'to ... throw [some] shot into ... town' as a diversion.[81] Misunderstanding the signals, lieutenants Benjamin Street and James Talbot anchored in eighteen feet of water under the heaviest batteries on the west side of town and began a prolonged artillery duel. As well as a regular fort, named San Joseph, the seaward approaches had seven independent batteries built into the curtain wall mounting forty-six guns. In the thirty-five minutes it took the lieutenants to notice Stirling's signal to break off, the gun-brigs were badly mauled. HMS *Encounter* 'had five men wounded and rec'd several shot [through the] ... Hull, sails & rigging'. On HMS *Staunch* 'three men [were] slightly wounded ... Thomas Start lost his right leg [and later died as a result]' and the main mast was shot through. Lieutenant Street was forced to leave a cable and anchor behind in his haste to sail out of range.[82]

On 23 January a thunderstorm descended. With a 'strong gale' blowing in from the Atlantic the river rose five feet, forcing the ships to stand out from shore.[83] The *Charlotte* transport lost an 18-pounder and the siege was brought to a temporary halt. On shore, Auchmuty used the time to resupply. Whilst well stocked with food, the expedition was running low on gunpowder and spirits. Stirling tried to make up for the deficit by appealing to the merchantmen with the fleet, who were only too happy to charge exorbitant prices. One of the beneficiaries was William Eastwick, the captain of the *Anna*, who had had the foresight to purchase forty casks of brandy back in London.[84] On the morning of 24 January the outposts skirmished with a unit of Sobremonte's cavalry while the British battery kept up 'a partial fire' answered from the walls. The Navy spent the afternoon landing supplies and four 24-pounders and two mortars for a second battery and Captain Robert Honeyman and the master of HMS *Leda* sounded the river near the South Tower. Auchmuty had decided to breach the walls of the Citadel and realised that the guns in the tower would be able to flank the assault. If they could be knocked out from the sea, it would save the army significant casualties. Honeyman eventually found a point within cannon range where the frigate could anchor in three fathoms and a buoy was laid to mark the spot.[85]

The second battery was constructed half a mile east-northeast of the Citadel.[86] Around 300 men of the 40th cut down an orchard of peach trees to build *gabions* and *fascines*. Others dug an entrenchment, amongst them Private Thomas Todd of the 71st.[87] A former drama student who had quit after suffering stage fright, Todd found the work exhausting. 'We were forced to labour night and day', he complained. 'My hands, when I left home, [had been] ... white and soft, now they were ... as hard as horn.'[88] When the battery was finished on 25 January Auchmuty and Stirling agreed on a joint bombardment to begin at 4.00 pm. HMS *Leda*, *Medusa* and *Daphne* and three armed transports were used. Sailing in under single-reefed top sails, the former grounded on the muddy bottom in two and three-quarter fathoms one mile to the west of Fort San Joseph.[89] Although the frigates were too far out to be effective, the shallower draught transports managed to throw several shells into town. Exploding in the narrow streets, they damaged some houses and killed a number of civilians.[90] In the San Sebastian Battery, Captain Pablo Colombo was having more success. Taking deliberate aim with a pair of 24-pounders, at 6.00 pm he shot away HMS *Leda*'s main top gallant mast.[91] Half an hour later Stirling hoisted the signal to break off the attack.[92]

On the far side of town the royal artillery, led by Captain Alexander Dickson, were also disappointed. 'When the fireworks were all ready, the frontpiece was thrown down, and away rattled the 24-pounders against the parapet', Captain Wilkie recalled. 'It was soon found, however, that both from the distance, and the wall being of tougher materials than was supposed, it would be ... a doubtful affair making a practicable breach'.[93] The mortars were better placed. Their shells exploded amongst the houses and 'did execution' and Governor Huidobro ordered the eastern portion of town evacuated as a result.[94] That evening Sergeant Isidoro Revoredo of the Monte Video Cavalry Volunteers escaped from the British hospital ship in the bay. Dragging himself from his hammock, he staggered to the deck and threw himself over the side. Despite his wound he managed to swim to shore and within three weeks had rejoined his comrades and was back in the fight.[95] Six more naval 24-pounders were landed on the morning of 26 January.[96] Informed that the southeast bastion of the Citadel 'was in so weak a state that it might be easily breached', Auchmuty ordered the third battery dug within 1,000 yards. That afternoon one of the Spanish boats ferrying supplies into town from the creek to the northeast strayed into deep water.[97] Judging her an easy prize, Captain Josias Rowley of HMS *Raisonnable* 'sent two cutters in shore ... to bring [her] out'. The Spanish responded by deploying seven large launches and two gunboats and a fire-fight broke out. Supported by the battery on Ratones Island, the Spanish got the upper hand, but when another British cutter and the frigate HMS *Daphne* joined the fight, the launches and gunboats withdrew to the shallows.[98]

On 27 January the ships landed 620 gallons of spirits and 300 rounds of ammunition for the guns. At Auchmuty's request, the African slaves captured on 20 January were also disembarked – presumably to help finish the third battery.[99] The gunners opened fire the next morning. So close to the walls, the position came under heavy fire. Sergeant William Luxton of the 40th risked his life by seizing a live shell and hurling it over the parapet; Timothy Connor, a landsman from HMS *Daphne*, was wounded; and two privates of the 17th Light Dragoons and Captain Charles Beaumont of the 87th were killed.[100] The duel was not entirely one-sided. 'The parapet [on the Citadel] was soon in ruins,' Auchmuty noted, 'but the rampart received ... little injury, and I was soon convinced that ... the only prospect of success ... was to erect a battery as near as possible to a wall by the South [San Juan] Gate ... and endeavour to breach it.'[101]

Although a *siège en forme* was normally a slow, deliberate process, at Monte Video Auchmuty did not have the luxury of time. Stocks of spirits were low; dysentery had hospitalised dozens and killed two; a steady trickle of men, mostly Irish Catholics, was deserting to the enemy; and the gunpowder supply would be exhausted within a week.[102] With the Portuguese in Brazil reluctant to sell the

British war materiel, the nearest point of resupply was Cape Town, two months' round trip away. The only alternative was to purchase the supplies belonging to the merchantmen attached to the fleet. As with the spirits, Stirling found them 'disposed to take advantage of the times'. Issuing bonds, the rear-admiral took all they had to offer, instructing the merchants to get the money from the government on their return to Britain.[103] Equally pressing was the possibility of enemy reinforcement. Auchmuty was aware that Arze's troops were en route and several other individuals and small groups had already made their way inside.

Some 120 miles to the west a second relief column of six guns and 3,000 militia led by Santiago de Liniers was preparing to leave Buenos Ayres.[104] Amongst the troops were 229 volunteers from the Patriotas de la Unión, the artillery regiment that had fought at the Reconquista led by Felipe de Sentenach. After a chaotic departure from Buenos Ayres in a flotilla of twenty-three launches and small boats, they crossed to the east bank on 30 January.[105] At 5.00 pm Liniers sent a dispatch to Huidobro urging him to hold out. 'I am at this moment ... come to Anchor, between the Rivulets of St. Juan and St. Francisco', he began. 'Endeavour to hold out, till my arrival, which will be within four days. I am at this instant going to commence my march, with an army full of impatience to measure Arms with the Enemy ... Hold out ... and the vile enemy, who now annoys you shall soon receive the punishment which he so richly deserves.'[106]

In Monte Video the situation was desperate. The third British battery was able to hurl round shot and shells into the heart of town. On 28 January three civilians had been killed and nine wounded and the Cabildo and several houses on the Plaza Mayor were badly damaged. The cathedral, serving as a temporary hospital and packed with wounded, was hit by several round shot and its façade badly scarred.[107] The gunners were also having a torrid time. Since the siege had begun they had been under arms without relief. On 28 January alone over 1,000 24-pound round shot were fired. None had slept and adrenaline and a steady supply of beef and hard biscuit was barely enough to keep them going. In the South Tower a cannon had blown up due to metal fatigue killing two artillerymen. Two more guns had burst in the San Sebastian Battery and on 28 January Captain Colombo was killed by a British round shot which came whipping over the walls. Three more men were slain in the Citadel, one by a round shot and two by a shell and that night an attack was made by a British column on the commmunciations trench by the Arroyo de Miguelette. Although the redcoats were repulsed by a squad led by Corporal Juan Francisco Armada of the Monte Video Cavalry Volunteers, if the supply route was cut, the situation would deteriorate.[108] At a council of war Sergeant-Major Viana and Mordeille went as far as to suggest surrender, but Huidobro insisted they fight on.[109] Arze was about to arrive and Liniers was not far behind. If they could hold out for a few more days, the British would be forced to fight on two fronts.

Six long 24-pounders were landed for the breaching battery on the morning of 31 January. The entrenchment was begun that evening 600 yards from the walls. The Caso de Seco provided some cover, but it was gruelling work.[110] As well as facing enemy cannon fire, the men had to dig through bare rock.[111] That afternoon, Stirling sent HMS *Staunch* and three armed transports to engage the South Tower. Watching them close over the muzzle of their 24-pounder were Sergeant Manuel Sans and his crew of veterans, militia and slaves. The transports expended a good deal of powder, but their fire had little effect and they broke off the encounter.[112] HMS *Staunch* was next. Sailing as close as possible, she opened fire at 11.00 am with grape and round shot from her twin chasers. Five minutes later Sans sent a 24-pound shot crashing through her bow. Ordinary Seaman Richard Walker was killed and 'considerable damage [done] on board'. Undaunted, Lieutenant Street wore the gun-brig round and returned for two more passes. Sans found his range once more. After the gunner had crippled the gun-brig's mainmast, Street broke off the action and committed Walker's body to the deep.[113] Elsewhere, the crew of HMS *Diadem* was landing supplies for Dickson's batteries. Amongst the materiel were 400 shot, 340 cartridges, 300 quill tubes, forty-five pounds of matches, two port-fires and eighty barrels of powder. Dickson's gunners continued firing late into the evening. On the walls, Lieutenant Miguel Espina and two artillerymen were wounded and a fire broke out in the suburbs which burnt all night and illuminated the entire area.[114]

By daylight on 1 February the breaching battery was ready. In command was Captain Lewis Carmichael of the Royal Artillery, a zealous young man who vowed not to shave until the siege was won. 'When the ruddy stubble of his chin was well-begrimed with ... nitre, sulphur, and charcoal, with a slight varnish of cannon smoke, his face might have been a good study for a dealer in ... burnt amber' Captain Wilkie recalled.[115] Carmichael and his men worked tirelessly. 'Every shot now took away large pieces of the wall ... and [there was] such a repetition of shot and shells that the Spanish Artillerymen could scarce make their appearance! ... [In] the east part of the town, the houses were all in a most wretched condition, and the church was much cut up.'[116] By 2 February an eleven-metre wide breach had been made ten metres from San Juan Gate.[117] Although sufficient for the town to be taken by storm, few of the guns that flanked it had been knocked out.[118] In the San Sebastian Battery one cannon had had its carriage 'shattered to pieces' and in the Artillery Park, El Insatiable, 'a very fine [brass 24-]pounder ... emblazoned with the arms of Spain', had been struck on its muzzle preventing it from firing.[119] Four other guns in San Sebastian and two 24-pounders in the South Tower 100 metres to the south remained unscathed.[120]

That afternoon Stirling was rowed ashore. After he and Auchmuty had agreed that the breach was practicable, an officer was sent into town with a final summons for surrender. Huidobro was in no mood to receive him. The night before Arze's men had arrived along with 465 troops from the missions in Paraguay and the town of Yapeyú on the Uruguay River, bringing the garrison back to its pre-sally strength of 3,000.[121] The mob, increasingly the real power in Monte Video, would not contenance surrender.[122] Besides, Huidobro thought the breach too narrow and his interpreter, Captain Pablo Colon, had been killed by a cannonball on 1 February.[123] The British officer was ignored for half an hour then returned to British lines. Once he was under cover, the siege guns opened fire once more.

Up on the heights, Auchmuty briefed his leading officers on the assault. 'I cannot ensure your success', he told them, 'but now or never is the moment; our ammunition will not hold out another day … We must make one bold effort, or abandon South America.'[124]

Auchmuty's plan was simple. The guns would fire until 3.00 am when the main assault column, gathered round Carmichael's battery, would advance into the breach with fixed bayonets. A second column would move against San Pedro Gate. Although equipped with scaling ladders, their attack was a feint. Once inside the walls the main column would split into two.[125] The first half would turn right. Sweeping round the interior, they would neutralise the batteries in the Artillery Park and the San Sebastian Battery, take the Citadel and open San Pedro Gate to the second column. The second half would turn left, take the South Tower, the batteries on the curtain wall and Fort San Joseph. All would then meet in the central square.

The main column was to be headed by a forlorn hope – thirty-three volunteers led by Lieutenant Mathias Everard. The second son of an Irish peer, Everard had been rescued from the hold of the *Volontaire* at the Cape eleven months before. His unit was made up of desperate men who had staked their lives on the prospect of promotion. As well as a sergeant of the 38th, there were thirty-one privates, the majority from the detachment of the 54th that had been rescued with Everard.[126] Next in the order of attack was the Light Battalion led by Lieutenant-Colonel Brownrigg, then two companies of rifles, a newly-formed grenadier battalion, led by majors Campbell and Tucker, and the 38th under Lieutenant-Colonel Vassal. In support was the 40th under Major John Dalrymple. The 87th, under Major Francis Miller, and the remaining rifle company, were to attack San Pedro Gate. Overall command was given to Colonel Gore Browne, who would direct the assault from a forward position and assume the role of commandant once the town was won.[127]

Inside the walls Huidobro was writing a letter to Liniers urging him to make all possible haste while his senior officers made their final preparations. Bullock-hides filled with earth were stacked up in the breach; grenades were distributed; two cannon manned by forty men from the Buenos Ayres Regiment under 2nd Lieutenant Juan Jasca were positioned in Calle San Telmo to fire on the attackers the moment they came through the wall; other guns were sited behind barricades at the major intersections; leaflets were distributed threatening death to any who surrendered; and Francisco Viana and Hipólito Mordeille were given key commands.[128] The former was assigned to the Citadel, the latter to the San Sebastian Battery and Artillery Park.[129] Mordeille's 300-strong Húsares del Gobierno were amongst the best troops Huidobro had. As well as Spaniards and creoles, the unit contained several French privateers, some American merchantmen and at least twenty British deserters. Having fled their units at Maldonado, the latter knew death was their only alternative to victory.[130]

That night the British took up their positions. Wrapped in their greatcoats, some talked nervously amongst themselves. Others tried to snatch a few hours' sleep, despite the guns booming about them. At 2.30 am Lieutenant-Colonel

Vassal addressed his men. 'I am a damned bad hand at a speech', he began. 'Spare the women and children; for the rest, you know what to do'. Moments later the cannon fell silent and the attack began. Led by Everard's forlorn hope, the Light Battalion, grenadiers and the 38th picked their way forward, glancing nervously up at the walls. 'There was not the slightest appearance of stir or movement in or about the town' one recalled. The night was pitch-black. 'The moon was in the last quarter, gradually sinking in the west, and obscured for the most part by clouds', but 'the stars were out in thousands'.[131] Suddenly a flare was sent up by the defenders. The brass guns in the San Sebastian Battery, Artillery Park and South Tower scoured the approaches to the breach with grapeshot, whilst the infantry defending the walls opened fire with their muskets.[132] 'The whole scene … was lighted up as if by a magician', Wilkie recalled.[133] Only one of Everard's men was hit by the opening volley. The second discharge felled twenty-five.[134] Disguised by the bullock-hides, the breach was barely discernible in the darkness and Everard led the head of the column off course. For fifteen minutes they groped their way along the wall under a terrible crossfire until Captain Charles Rennie of the light company of the 40th located the breach. Urging his troops to follow him, the twenty-four year-old from Montrose clambered up the rubble, but was killed as he reached the top.[135] Lieutenant Harry Smith of the rifles was wounded by his side. The rest of the Light Battalion and grenadiers drove on. Under the fire of six heavy cannon, loaded with canister each packed with 400 musket balls, the carnage was appalling.[136] Over the next hour 386 soldiers were killed or wounded on the spot.[137] Amongst the latter was Lieutenant-Colonel Brownrigg. Several others were wounded by their comrades' bayonets in the crush.[138]

Placing scaling ladders against the heaped bullock-hides, the survivors climbed upwards under attack from hand grenades and musketry from the troops in the street below. Scores more were killed. The rest pushed the dead aside and climbed on. Broaching the top of the hides three abreast, they leapt fifteen foot down into Calle San Telmo.[139] Sergeant José Gonzalez of the Buenos Ayres Regiment briefly resisted, but was cut down and the rest of the Spaniards and creoles fled. The Light Battalion and the grenadiers chased them with their bayonets. Both 2nd Lieutenant Jasca and an officer of Basque descent named Faustinio Gaxeia were mortally wounded. The latter managed to drag himself back to the door of his house before he expired. Others were slaughtered on the spot. 'There were men who had been shot twice that [tried to] surrender', one of Jasca's comrades recalled, '[but they] were bayonetted twenty times'.[140] Back at the breach Major Trotter was having 'a personal conflict in one of the embrasures'. Lifting his adversary off his feet, Trotter 'threw him down' onto the rubble below, formed his men up and charged towards the San Sebastian Battery. Nearby some of the grenadiers under Major Campbell were also involved in a bitter fight. Major Charles Turner was bayonetted in the arm before the Spaniards were overpowered and the grenadiers swept towards the South Tower and Fort San Joseph.[141]

Outside the walls, the 38th were having problems of their own. With the cries of the wounded and the noise of the guns, grenades and musketry, they 'mistook the breach partly effected for the real one, and were for some minutes thrown out of their course.'[142] Vassal was inspirational. 'When he observed any of the men stoop' Sergeant Benjamin Matthews recalled, 'he cried out … "Brave 38th … don't flinch; every bullet has its billet. Push on, follow me!"'[143] By the time they found the breach, several Spanish gunners were back in position. '[They] were very liberal in their distribution of grape and canister', Wilkie recalled. 'The distance was so short … that these missiles had not space to scatter, and many a poor fellow … was carried off by … a dose of leaden pills enough to have doctored a whole section.'[144] The survivors forced their way upward and dropped into the unpaved street below. One detachment, under Major David Ross, advanced towards the cathedral on the main square. Vassal took the rest to aid the Light Battalion in the fight for the first bastion.[145]

The 40th had also lost their bearings.[146] By the time they located the breach, the regiment had passed through the crossfire twice and twenty-six men had been killed, amongst them Major Dalrymple and Lieutenant Thomas Alston.[147] The wounded included a captain, four lieutenants and an ensign. The survivors climbed the scaling ladders and jumped into the street below.[148] To the south, Major Campbell's grenadiers had captured the South Tower. After bayonetting Sergeant Sans and his gun crew of three veterans, three militia and two African slaves, they raced on to Fort San Joseph.[149] The defenders promptly surrendered and by 4.45 am the Union Jack was flying from the battlements.[150] On the other side of town progress was not so swift. Although the artillery park had been taken, the struggle for the San Sebastian Battery went on. Mordeille's Húsares del Gobierno refused quarter and held the Light Battalion at bay until the arrival of the 38th swung the tide. '[Vassal] was advancing when a grape shot broke his leg' Sergeant Matthews recalled. 'As soon as he fell he cried out, "Push on … my good soldiers, charge them, never mind me; it's only the loss of a leg in the service."'[151] As Vassal attempted to staunch the bleeding with his handkerchief, his men stormed the battery. The guns were overrun, several of the defenders ran to the Citadel and resistance collapsed. The British were in no mood for mercy. 'The carnage … was dreadful,' one officer observed, 'every Spaniard being bayonetted on the spot.' Mordeille was amongst the casualties. Shot through the breast, he fell and was bayonetted twenty times.[152]

To the north Major Miller's men had outdone themselves. Although their attack had only been intended as a feint, they had forced their way inside. Whilst the 87th drew the defenders' attention by charging San Pedro gate, a detachment of Captain Elder's rifle company climbed the walls with scaling ladders.[153] Casualties amongst the 87th were heavy. In Captain John Evans' company, leading the charge, nineteen privates and Lieutenant Hugh Irvine were killed by the gunners' first fire. Dozens more, including captains Evans and Rawston McCrea, lieutenants William Boucher and Francis Cockburne, Ensign Richard Lawrenson and Assistant-Surgeon Hugh Wilder were badly wounded.[154] Their sacrifice allowed Captain Elder's rifles to ascend the ramparts. The defenders not killed by their Baker rifles or sword bayonets quickly surrendered. Amongst the prisoners were several slaves who had been chained to the guns, one of whom was destined to become the personal servant of Lieutenant Dudley St Leger Hill, Elder's second-in-command.[155] Once the walls were cleared, the rifles opened the gates and the 87th stormed inside.[156]

By 5.00 am, aside from a few holdouts in the Citadel under Sergeant-Major Viana, organised resistance had collapsed. With no prearranged rally points, disparate bands of Spanish and creole survivors dashed through the streets, firing on one another as frequently as they did on their enemies. Many made their way to the pier and fled across the bay on small boats. Others locked themselves in their houses, hoping the redcoats would vent their fury elsewhere, while a few managed to fight their way inside the Citadel.[157] The British, largely leaderless following the bloodshed at the breach, prowled the streets and for a brief period the situation was out of control. Any defenders found in the open were killed, several *pulperias* were broken into and some looting occurred. One of the buildings attacked was the town hall on the main square. As the redcoats battered down the gates, the Cabildo cowered upstairs. 'We were rescued by the exertions of a gallant and amiable officer' one recalled. Their saviour, Captain Henry Powell, kept the Cabildo safe until Colonel Gore Browne arrived to assume command. After receiving 'the sword and insignia of justice' from the councillors, Browne placed a guard at the gates and called a general parade in the main square.[158]

'The drums beat to assembly' Private Lawrence recalled 'and orders were given for the massacre to be stayed, but that all the prisoners were to be taken that we could lay our hands on.'[159] Spreading through town, the redcoats rounded up hundreds of the enemy, Governor Huidobro amongst them. Escorted to Auchmuty's encampment, he surrendered at 5.30 am. 'He requested terms for the garrison, and the "honours of war"', Major Tucker recalled. 'The General would [not] grant [them] ... and a surrender at discretion ensued.'[160] At 6.00 am the attackers turned their attention to the holdouts in the Citadel. Learning that Viana refused to surrender, Captain Elder of the 95th ascended one of the towers of the cathedral with a section of his best marksmen and a sailor from the fleet. Whilst the latter hoisted the Union Jack on the steeple, the former opened fire.[161] The men on the battlements had nowhere to hide. At 6.30 am, after several had been killed and the rest driven inside, Viana raised a flag of truce and by 8.00 am the fighting was over.[162]

The Royal Navy spent the morning securing control of the bay. 'Lieutenant William Milne, with the armed launches, took possession of the island of Ratones ... which surrendered without any resistance'. Seventy prisoners were taken along with ten iron guns. Twelve armed ships, forty-four merchant vessels ranging from 100 to 1,000 tons, fifteen gun-boats and six armed launches were captured and one of the boats donated by Francisco Antonio de Castro was handed over to the British by his own slaves. Several other boats escaped and a 'very fine frigate mounting twenty-eight guns' was set on fire by her crew.[163] The flames reached the magazine just as a party of British soldiers and sailors was rowing out to douse them. 'As we got in line with her, and under her stern, she blew up', Captain Wilkie recalled. Three of the captured gunboats were set alight by burning debris. The rest were secured.[164]

The storming of Monte Video was the bloodiest event of the campaign so far. Some 118 British troops were killed and 279 wounded. Casualties were particularly heavy amongst the commissioned ranks. One major, three captains and two lieutenants were killed, whilst the wounded included two lieutenant-colonels, three captains, eight lieutenants and four ensigns.[165] The 40th and 87th bore the brunt. Twenty-seven of the former were killed as they marched before the guns and twenty-four of the latter died as they stormed San Pedro Gate.[166] Spanish losses were higher still: 500 were killed, 800 wounded and 2,000 taken prisoner. Amongst the slain were Mordeille, who survived a few hours before succumbing to his wounds, the philanthropist Francisco Antonio Maciel, and José González de Balcarce, one of the four brothers who had arrived from Buenos Ayres. The wounded included Thomás Ruis, a private of the Miñones and hero of the Reconquista who was wounded seven times and left for dead. The three surviving González de Balcarce siblings were made prisoners of war, as were Governor Huidobro, brigadiers Lecocq and Arze, Sergeant-Major Viana, Colonel Nicolás Quintana and all the other men and officers who had survived.[167]

Chapter 12

Captive!

Buenos Ayres and Environs
11 October 1806 – 22 February 1807

At 3.00 pm on 11 October 1806 the British officers captured at the Reconquista rode northwest out of Buenos Ayres. Including their servants and military escort the column numbered 150 men. It was a fine spring day. The temperature was in the mid-twenties and not a cloud spoiled the sky. Leaving the centre, they passed through extensive gardens bordered by hedges of quince and prickly pear. After a few miles the suburbs gave way to open grassland populated by vast herds of cattle and at dusk they halted at the ruins of an abandoned Jesuit college six miles northwest of town. As the provisions and baggage had gone ahead with Beresford and his carriage, the officers had no supper. 'A few hides were our beds', Captain Gillespie recalled, 'and our saddles with their sheep skin trappings ... our pillows.'[1] The journey continued at dawn. Traversing the waist-high clover undulating in the breeze, Captain Pococke was put in mind of 'the swell of the sea after the raging of a storm'. At 10.00 am the column breakfasted on bacon and eggs at a roadside *pulperia*, that afternoon they passed a caravan of sixty wagons carrying Mendocinian wine and, after fording the River Conchas, arrived at Luján at twilight. The officers thought the village a 'miserable' place. Its 200 mud houses were poorly built and the inhabitants had little to do aside from 'basking in the sun ... [and] picking the vermin from [one another's] ... heads'.[2]

On 14 October the officers were divided into two parties. Beresford, Lieutenant-Colonel Pack, Captain Arbuthnot, Captain Ogilvie of the Royal Artillery, and six others were put up in the town hall with their servants. At 5.00 am, after several had purchased new mounts, the rest rode north out of town. The commander of the guard wishing to disorientate them, they followed 'a road but rarely frequented' and were soon lost amongst the swaying grasses and trailed by packs of curious wild dogs. These companions 'yielded great amusement' Captain Gillespie recalled. 'When any game started [up from the side of the track], there was a general pursuit ... [and] though our pack were at first ignorant ... the taste of blood soon made them eager for the chase.' Hares, armadillo and burrowing owls were caught, but a *zorilla* proved a harder quarry. Temporarily blinded by its putrid spray, Lieutenant Wade of the Royal Navy 'plunge[d] ... headlong [into a nearby river] to relieve himself'.[3] At 2.00 pm the officers reached Capilla del Señor. 'Pleasantly situated' on 'a small ascent' besides a river 'abound-ing ... in fish', the village lay twenty miles north of Luján. For fourteen of the prisoners, the most senior of whom was Major Tolley, the village would be their home for the next few months. The remaining thirty-three continued their odyssey west northwest across the *pampas* at noon. 'The country afforded no novelty whatever', Captain Pococke, the 71st's perennial pessimist, recalled. 'We had no sooner dismounted than it came on to rain excessively hard, and continued about an hour.'[4] Later, Lieutenant Ballingall of the St Helena Regiment enticed two wild dog pups from their den by imitating their mother's calls. He kept them thereafter as pets and they 'proved in the end very faithful [companions]' Captain Gillespie recalled. That evening the officers slept on a marshy plain close to a small hut, whose inhabitants sold them sheep which they butchered and cooked for dinner.[5]

On 16 October the remaining officers reached San Antonio de Areco, their final destination. Lieutenant Fernyhough thought it 'a much better and neater village than either of the former two ... [they] had passed'. Centred round a brick church, the village stood on rising ground, was surrounded by acres of peach, fig, walnut and pear trees, 'which afforded very pleasant walks', and had 'a fine river ... well-stocked' with catfish.[6] Even Pococke had to admit that the countryside was 'pretty enough' and the officers soon settled into their new homes.[7] Pococke shared a house with Colonel Campbell and five others; Gillespie and a fellow officer rented a small hut for three *pesos* a month which had formerly served as a flour granary; and Lieutenant Fernyhough stayed at a cattle ranch owned by Felipe Ortorala fifteen miles from town.

Although guarded by a small detachment of dragoons, the officers were given considerable freedom. 'Our amusements consisted, chiefly, in fishing, shooting, and hunting', Lieutenant Fernyhough recalled, '[and, at one stage,] we destroyed upwards of 500 [wild dogs] ... in four days'. Rhea proved more of a challenge. 'We sometimes chased them for hours', he recorded, 'but seldom ... could come up with them, although mounted on swift horses, as they always run before the wind spreading their wings, which act as sails on a ship'.[8] Pococke preferred fishing in the river: 'the Spaniards are greatly astonished at our success', he recalled, '[as] they catch very few themselves, which must be attributed to the rudeness of their tackle'. On 25 November the officers founded the Areco Cricket Club, the first in South America, and 'two weekly papers were established.' These 'amused us for a while', Captain Gillespie recalled, 'but soon degenerated into channels of satire and were abandoned.' On Saturday nights the officers met 'under a friendly tree that stood in the fields. Each ... brought his stool, his bottle, and his jug, and ... a fire was kindled, around which, everyone in his turn, was obliged to sing a song, or tell a story.'[9]

The officers were also permitted to visit each other and by questioning travellers and writing letters they kept up with national and international news. On 1 November Lieutenant Peter Adamson of the 71st received a letter from Doctor Forbes in Luján informing him of Backhouse's arrival at Maldonado; ten days later Captain Duncan MacKenzie, the paymaster of the 71st, was informed that his wife had arrived at Cape Town; on 24 November Pococke learnt of the skirmish at San Carlos from a letter from Captain Ogilvie; one month later news spread round San Antonio that Henry Le Blanc, the officer of the 71st who had

had his leg amputated after the battle of Reducción, had been promoted to major; and on New Year's Eve the officers learnt that Prussia and France were at war.[10]

Another source of information was the merchant-cum-spy William Pius White. Due to his impeccable connections, the Bostonian continued to enjoy freedom of movement, despite his continuing collaboration with the British. After arriving at San Antonio on 30 November with news of the military build-up in Buenos Ayres, he visited the prisoners in the area before travelling to Luján for a meeting with Beresford. Afterwards White returned to Buenos Ayres and compiled a report on the strength of Liniers' troops which was delivered to Backhouse at Maldonado.[11] Whilst seemingly ignorant of the threat posed by White, the Cabildo kept Beresford under constant scrutiny. 'During the time I was at Luxan, I knew myself to be surrounded by spies', he recalled. 'I was ... [suspected] not only of having communication with Bues. Ayres, but with our Fleet & Army and that from the latter I used to get frequent expresses at night.'[12]

One Saturday afternoon at the end of November an ugly incident took place at Capilla del Señor. Whilst standing at the door of his billet, Alexander Kirie, a British officer's servant and private of the 71st, 'was suddenly lassoed' by a stranger. Putting spurs to his horse, the creole dragged Kirie to the end of the village where his 'throat was ... cut from ear to ear' and his body stripped of everything of value.[13] One week later on a fine spring day, Captain Ogilvie was out riding with Lieutenant-Colonel Pack on the outskirts of Luján. Two miles from the village a rider approached claiming to have letters from Buenos Ayres for Beresford which he had left with an accomplice nearby. After accompanying the stranger for a mile, the officers grew suspicious and said they would go no further. The creole drew a pistol and fired at Ogilvie, upon which Pack charged. 'I directly rode at the fellow', he recalled. 'He ... dropped [the pistol] ... and ... struck at me [with his sword], but so awkwardly, as only to cut my jacket ... [he then] ... sheered off'. The bullet had hit Ogilvie under the shoulder and buried itself in his lungs. He died fourteen days later and was buried behind the church at Luján.[14]

At first the British presumed robbery had been the motive, but later a conspiracy involving the Cabildo was suspected.[15] Shortly afterwards an officer and thirty dragoons were sent to Luján 'under the pretence of looking ... [for] the assassin'. Beresford believed their real mission was to spy on the British prisoners and intercept their communications. '[Their officer was] zealous, active & cunning', the brigadier-general recalled, '& had always night sentries placed at some distance from the village ... but in spite of all his efforts and precautions he returned after some weeks as wise as he came.'[16] A few days later word arrived of Auchmuty's imminent arrival at Maldonado and by mid-January the news was confirmed. Combined with the arrival of a month's pay from Buenos Ayres, it prompted a wave of optimism amongst the British officers.[17]

On 5 February a deputation from the Audiencia arrived at Luján. Amongst the members were Guido Bass, 'and ... Señor Garcia, an Attorney ... [and] Lt Colonel' in Liniers' army. After placing Beresford and his fellow officers 'under a close sentry', the Spaniards searched their quarters seizing all the documents they found. '[This was done] on the pretext of discovering some traces [of clandestine correspondence with revolutionary factions in Buenos Ayres],' Captain Gillespie recalled, 'but in reality [their motive was] to seize upon the original of the treaty [made on 13 August]'.[18] The document was an embarrassment to the Cabildo. Amongst the terms was one stating that the prisoners were supposed to have been released into British custody – an agreement that had been blatantly ignored. Due to the quick thinking of Captain Robert Arbuthnot, who secreted the document in an orchard, the Spaniards returned to Buenos Ayres empty-handed.[19] Two days later new orders arrived. With Monte Video's capitulation, the prisoners were to be moved 400 miles inland to Córdoba. It was the excuse Beresford had been waiting for. As the Spaniards had broken the terms of his parole, he considered himself free to escape with his honour intact.[20]

In Buenos Ayres the news of the fall of Monte Video was met with outrage. A scapegoat was needed and once more Sobremonte fitted the bill. *Pasquines* appeared in the Plaza Mayor proclaiming 'Death to the Viceroy!', 'Down with the *Audiencia*!', and 'Let's Raise the Republican Flag!'[21] Álzaga cited the viceroy's refusal to aid the sally on 20 January as the main cause of Huidobro's defeat, while others believed his failure to supply Liniers' relief column with horses had prevented them arriving in time.[22] A *cabildo abierto* was called, the upshot of which was nothing short of revolutionary.[23] On 10 February, under pressure from a 4,000-strong mob in the Plaza Major chanting its support for Liniers, those gathered in the Sala Capitular decided that Sobremonte should be arrested and the Frenchman named viceroy in his place. The Audienca was appalled. They withdrew from the chamber, but nevertheless accepted the duty of informing Sobremonte of his fate.[24] With an infantry and cavalry escort, two of its members crossed to the east bank and arrested him on 16 February in the village of Pavón. He was then held under arrest in a convalescence house on the outskirts of Buenos Ayres.[25] The move was indicative of just how far the *porteños* had travelled down the road to independence. Sobremonte was the representative of the crown, chosen by the king of Spain himself. To defy the monarch's will so blatantly was unprecedented.[26] In an attempt to protect themselves from reprisals, the Cabildo sent a dispatch to Asunción in Paraguay. As well as informing the authorities of the decision regarding Sobremonte, the letter ordered Bernardo Velasco, the resident intendant, to make all haste to the capital to aid in its defence. By enlisting a high-ranking official, the Cabildo hoped to avoid incurring the wrath of Spain. A second motivation was to to install a counter to balance Liniers' growing power. Although the Cabildo themselves had originally elevated the Frenchman to facilitate the removal of Sobremonte, the man Álzaga had once presumed a puppet had begun to display a will and ambition of his own.[27]

Whilst the news of the fall of Monte Video reinforced the will of the majority of *porteños* to rid themselves of the invaders, a minority saw the defeat as a signal to compromise, amongst them two of Beresford's new contacts, Manuel Aniceto Padilla and Saturnino Rodríguez Peña. A twenty-six-year-old law student from Cochabamba in Upper Peru, Padilla had moved to Buenos Ayres as a young man and become involved in contraband trade with British smugglers. In 1806 he had been arrested and was under threat of execution on Beresford's arrival, but had since attained the rank of captain in the Arribeños militia. Padilla considered himself a realist. Spain was a fading power whilst Britain was in the ascendancy. If the viceroyalty was to be conquered it made good sense to be with the winning side. Padilla's co-conspirator, the forty-two-year-old *porteño* Saturnino Rodríguez Peña, had different beliefs. A merchant, lawyer and captain in the Patriotas de la Unión, Peña had developed a deep admiration for the British while working as a saltmeat agent in their colonies in the West Indies. Both a patriot and an Anglophile, Peña's politics coincided somewhat with those of Francisco Miranda, the Venezuelan revolutionary. Both saw British help as a stage on the road to independence.

Padilla and Peña were not alone. Manuel Belgrano, a militia officer who would go on to become one of Argentina's principal liberators, the journalist and politician Juan José Castelli, Francisco González – the watchman of the Buenos Ayres Cabildo, and Mariano Moreno, a lawyer representing foreign ranchers' interests, all participated in the plot to enlist British aid. A shadowy 'principal person' co-ordinated their efforts. Although his identity is unknown, Liniers seems a strong possibility. The plan that was to unfold was too intricate and reliant upon the complicity of too many of his officers for the Frenchman not to have been involved. Liniers also had motive. His honour troubled by his duplicitous role in the surrender agreement and the British prisoners' subsequent mistreatment, the Frenchman remained keen to secure Beresford's release. One option he had considered had been an exchange for José Fernando de Abascal, the newly-appointed viceroy of Peru. Learning he had been taken prisoner by the Royal Navy whilst crossing the Atlantic, Liniers had suggested an exchange. Several letters followed, but the plan had been shelved on Abascal's escape.[28]

In early 1807 Peña contacted Beresford at Luján. He proposed releasing all British prisoners and securing favourable trading rights for the country's merchants in exchange for Britain's official recognition of the viceroyalty's independence from Spain. Beresford agreed to discuss the plan with Auchmuty and on 7 February Padilla organized a meeting with Álzaga to table his proposal. The creole had badly misjudged the situation. Álzaga remained loyal to Spain and Padilla only escaped immediate imprisonment as the Basque hoped he would lead him to his accomplices. Without the Cabildo's support, Padilla and Peña hastily adopted a second, less ambitious plan. Essentially one of self-preservation, it would not only protect them from their enemies in Buenos Ayres, but also ingratiate them with the invaders. They decided to help Beresford escape.[29]

On 10 February Manuel Luciano Martínez de Fontes, a captain of the Blandengues, arrived at Luján to escort the British officers into the interior. 'Without having any opportunity of providing ourselves with either comforts, or … necessaries … we left [that afternoon]', Beresford recalled.[30] Proceeding across the *pampas*, the convoy of eight officers, four women and two children passed La Encrucijada where the road to Córdoba began, then stopped at a ranch owned by Bethlemite Monks on the outskirts of Arrecifes. On 16 February Padilla and Peña arrived claiming they had a verbal order from Liniers to escort

Beresford to Buenos Ayres. Whether by coincidence or design, Captain Martínez was related to Peña by marriage. Inclined to trust his in-law, Martínez handed the brigadier-general into his custody. 'After assuring me of their ... devotion ... and of the abhorence of the whole town for the conduct held towards me & my troops ... [they] proposed ... to take me to the British army at Monte Video', Beresford recalled. Believing the chance to deliver the intelligence he had gathered in Luján was worth the risk involved, the major-general agreed on condition that Pack be allowed to accompany him.[31]

The next morning the party rode southeast. 'After ... a variety of perils, and ... the most excessive fatigue, [they] arrived in Buenos Ayres' and secreted themselves in the house of Francisco González.[32] On the evening of 21 February, with Beresford and Pack disguised as Spaniards, they made their way to the mole, talking their way past several patrols, but there was no sign of the boat that was supposed to be awaiting them. Growing desperate, they decided to wade through the water towards a strange sail offshore. After half an hour they reached the vessel, the Portuguese sloop *Flor del Cabo*, paid the sailors 1,000 *pesos* for a rowing boat and set off downriver towards Ensenada.[33] By morning they were exhausted. 'The weather was tempestuous, the wind adverse, and they had remained so long in wet clothes that they were chilled and weary'. The entire party was 'beginning to despair ... when ... to their great joy they descried the sloop of war [HMS] *Charwell*' patrolling the area. After taking the fugitives on board, Lieutenant Chamberlayne wore the sloop round to the east and made all sail for Monte Video.[34]

Chapter 13

The Occupation of Monte Video
3 February – 10 May 1807

Before the gun smoke had even dissipated from the streets, Monte Video returned 'to a state of comparative tranquillity. Some of the troops were marched out of town until arrangements could be made for their accommodation, and everything soon became quiet and regular.'[1] Considering the difficulty of maintaining discipline in the aftermath of a *coup de main* this was a remarkable feat. 'The only instances of disorder', Wilkie recalled, 'were occasioned by some of the sailors of the transports, who got ashore, and began to plunder. One fellow was brought to the main guard with his Guernsey frock swelled out in front by the accumulation of nearly one hundred watches ... His delivery from this inconvenient load furnished a good deal of laughter.'[2] Colonel Gore Browne, appointed commandant of the garrison, decided to make an example. After the 2,000 Spanish and creole prisoners had been confined in the ships, a punishment parade was held in the main square. Several men were flogged 'with the utmost severity'. Two others, who had been condemned to death, were given a last-minute reprieve due to the intervention of the Cabildo. Seeing fit to grant the Spaniards' 'earnest entreaties' for clemency, Browne had the culprits imprisoned instead.[3]

That afternoon, as the British dead were buried in 'a rude grave' by the South Tower, Auchmuty made a proclamation.[4] He encouraged the residents to return to work and assured them their property and religious freedom would be respected, if 'they behave[d] themselves as becometh good subjects' and took an oath of allegiance to George III.[5] Meanwhile, accommodation was arranged for the troops. Whilst the cavalry remained encamped to the east under Brigadier-General Lumley, 'the bulk' of the army was put up in town.[6] 'I was billeted upon a young widow', Private Todd recalled, '[who] did all in her power to make me comfortable ... [even though] her husband had been slain'.[7] Captain Wilkie also stayed with a widow whose two 'fair daughters' made his accommodation 'the most envied in town.'[8] On board the fleet the prisoners were processed. After signing their paroles the officers were given the freedom of town. One exception was Brigadier-General Arze. Having broken the parole he had signed in June 1806, he was confined to the fleet. Many of the local soldiers were also allowed to return to their families, but those from elsewhere in the viceroyalty were locked in the holds of ten transports and guarded by armed marines.[9] The men of Mordeille's old unit, the Húsares del Gobierno, heard rumours that they would be 'put to the knife' for having killed so many during the assault. Although there was no substance to the rumour, over the next few weeks it inspired several to escape. Leaping from the ships, they swam ashore and made their way into the interior to join the guerrillas harassing the British outposts.

Twenty British deserters and three American merchant sailors captured fighting for the Spanish during the siege were court-martialled and sentenced to death. Also facing execution were the crew members of the *Lady Jane Shore* who had made Monte Video their home.[10] Unlike Beresford, who had shown their former comrades leniency in Buenos Ayres, Auchmuty used the full weight of the law. The executions took place on 4 February. 'We all had to march up ... and take example from [them]', Private Lawrence recalled. Amongst the condemned was 'a large-sized Irishman' who had a miraculous escape. 'When they turned the ladder round to swing him off [the gallows], the rope broke, and he fell to the ground'. He 'begged hard for mercy and the rope had made such a terrible mark on his neck that I suppose the general thought he had been hanged enough: so he was sent to hospital, and when he recovered, transported' to Australia.[11]

In the temporary hospital in the cathedral the 279 British troops who had been wounded were treated. Musket balls and canister were removed, heavy bleeding cauterised with boiling pitch and mangled limbs amputated.[12] Many of the casualties, especially those who had been hit in the leg, contracted lock-jaw (tetanus).[13] While there were some successful operations, such as that performed on Captain John Whetham of the 40th who had his right leg amputated above the knee, dozens died of their wounds.[14] On 7 February Lieutenant-Colonel Vassal passed away.[15] 'Great hopes were at first entertained that his ... life might be saved by the amputation of the leg, but the heat of the climate brought on the symptoms of mortification with ... rapidity'. Vassal's body was carried through Lieutenant-Colonel Brownrigg's room en route to burial. 'There goes one of the best and bravest of men!' Brownrigg exclaimed, 'I shall soon follow him'. The lieutenant-colonel was right. He died of his wounds later that day.[16] During the Napoleonic Wars illness was a far bigger killer than combat and the campaigns in the River Plate were no exception. By 21 April a third of the grenadier company of the 87th were too ill to attend roll call. Most were put up in the general hospital in town, the rest on board the hospital ships off shore.[17] Several officers also fell ill. Lieutenant Harry Smith of the 95th 'was afflicted with a most severe fever and dysentery'. Having lost much of his body weight, he was confined to bed for several weeks. The family upon whom he had been billeted cared for him as if he were one of their own. '[I] owe my life to the[ir] kind attentions', Smith later admitted. 'My gratitude ... can never be expressed'.[18]

On 7 February Auchmuty wrote to Westminster detailing a catalogue of logistical issues. Supplies were the most pressing. With Liniers' troops to the northwest and Sobremonte's cavalry occupying Las Piedras, Auchmuty had to prepare to be besieged. Gunpowder, flour, spirits and salt meat were all needed. On 10 February HMS *Leda* set sail for England with the request for resupply, while HMS *Rolla* was sent to Rio Grande and HMS *Medusa* to Rio de Janeiro. Both sailed with army commissaries on board to purchase what they could from the Portuguese.[19] Auchmuty's second priority was administration. On the eve of the town's capture the majority of the Spanish officials had fled with their papers, leaving the British to start the process from scratch. Several army and naval officers were appointed to replace them. All received additional salaries as well as their normal pay. Lieutenant John Tylden, Auchmuty's nineteen-year-old nephew, was made the town's treasurer; John Tyrell was appointed Collector of Customs, a post that paid a salary of £1,500; John Culverhouse was named Captain of the Port; and Mr Wilkinson, formerly the purser of HMS *Lancaster*, was appointed Acting Naval Storekeeper.[20] As no legal authority was left in town, a regular garrison court martial was established to try both military and civil cases. Its agenda was eclectic. 'One day', Captain Wilkie recalled, 'it was to try a Spanish spy for attempting to seduce our soldiers; another, to settle a squabble between two merchants' clerks; or try a sailor for having a *lark*; or some other persons for robbing the King's stores.'[21]

Desertion was another problem. Particularly susceptible were the young recruits of the 87th or Prince of Wales' Irish. As well as sharing the locals' religion they could sympathise with their resentment of English occupation.[22] Twelve would desert during their first two months in Monte Video compared to just three of the 47th and 38th and two of the 20th Light Dragoons, whilst the 40th and the three companies of the 95th registered no deserters at all.[23] The Monte Videans encouraged the men to abscond. '[One] case of desertion was that of an officer's servant', Private Lawrence recalled, 'who went away with the greater part of his master's clothes, taking with him likewise a Spanish lady; he was lucky to get off safe and nothing was heard of him afterwards.'[24]

On 4 February the customs house was reopened under British control. The first merchant ship was inspected on 9 February and by the end of May 1807 sixty-six vessels had been registered.[25] On 7 February new rates of tax were introduced. Initially 12.5 per cent was charged on imports and the port was open to ships of all nations, prompting a complaint from a British consortium. Feeling hard done by due to the loss of their main market at Buenos Ayres, they wanted neutrals forbidden from trading as well as a suspension of taxes on British bottoms. Auchmuty compromised. Unwilling to deny himself his main source of revenue, he kept the British tax rates the same, whilst raising those imposed on neutrals to 18.75 per cent and introducing a levy of 10 per cent on all foreign exports.[26] These concessions were not enough to tempt 'the great merchants'. Riding at anchor in the roads, they 'would [not] condescend to "break bulk" until ... [they reached] Buenos Ayres'. Those 'who liked to "turn the ready penny,"' on the other hand, promptly opened shops in town.[27] Amongst them was William Eastwick. 'I rented a large house', the merchant recalled, '[where] Mr Holloway, myself, and two clerks took up residence and met with immediate and considerable sales'.[28] Another who set up shop was Mr Arthur Crauford. From his premises at number 53 Calle San Pedro, he catered to the wealthier Spanish and creole inhabitants and the British officers in town. Crauford's inventory included Irish linens, 'of every description, White calicoes, Cambric and Muslin, Woolens and Haberdashery, New Wearing Apparel ... Earthernware ... Saddles and Bridels, Boots and Shoes, Tin ware ... Metal Pots ... Irish

Butter ... [French and Spanish] Brandy ... Old Jamaica Rum, Port, Claret, [and] Tenerife and Madeira Wines in Wood and Bottles.'[29]

The speed and quantity of trade was dizzying. By April 1807 over £1 million of goods had been sold, 500,000 *pesos* paid in taxes and over 2,000 merchants and merchant sailors had arrived. Combined with the 4,000 British soldiers resident, Monte Video took on the appearance of an English town on market day. Travelling via the tried and tested riverine smuggling routes, the goods were resold as far afield as Peru and Brazil, enriching the Monte Videan middle men beyond measure. Many in Buenos Ayres were also involved. Taking advantage of the low prices, Liniers bought up several shipments of British cloth and buttons to uniform his men. Other *porteños*, particularly those who had prospered from Spanish trade restrictions, were appalled and the Cabildo issued a decree threatening to hang anyone involved. Patriotism played only a small role in their decision. Local producers were being undercut and the thought of Monte Video surpassing Buenos Ayres as the principal trade hub in southern South America was galling.[30]

Auchmuty's next task was to secure the release of the prisoners taken with Beresford. In early February he wrote to Sobremonte at Las Piedras 'demanding that ... [they] should be delivered up ... and declaring that all the prisoners that we have taken, should ... be sent to England, if the demand was not complied with'. Sobremonte replied that the decision would have to be made by Carlos IV. Auchmuty was not prepared to wait. 'This answer I communicated to the late Governor and the Cabildo [of Monte Video],' he recalled, 'assuring them ... I should certainly send away the prisoners [I had taken, if Beresford's men were not released], I was now requested to write to the Cabildo at Buenos Ayres, and was informed that they alone could comply with my demand, as the ... Province was under their orders.'[31]

On 14 February a British convoy arrived. Four transports, carrying the 9th Light Dragoons, and three British merchantmen were escorted by a thirty-six-gun frigate, HMS *Nereide*.[32] The troops, the long-delayed final detachment of Auchmuty's reinforcements, had sailed from Portsmouth on 12 November with a separate expedition under Brigadier-General Robert Craufurd, whose ultimate destination, as was then understood, was the Pacific coast of Chile. Ignorant of Beresford's defeat and the difficulties of campaigning in the region, the War Office had dreamed up another outlandish plan for South American conquest. Craufurd's expedition was to sail to Cape Town and on to the Pacific, either by way of Buenos Ayres or Australia depending on the season, the winds and the inclination of Rear-Admiral Sir George Murray, the commander of the flotilla convoying Craufurd's troops. The expedition was to land on the central Chilean coast and capture the port of Valparaiso and the capital, Santiago, then establish a chain of armed posts across the Andes and the Argentine *pampas* to Buenos Ayres, over 500 miles away. When HMS *Nereide* had left Craufurd at the Cape Verde Islands on 6 January, the plan had still been operational, but news of the Reconquista had since reached London and the Minstry of All the Talents had ordered the Admiralty to dispatch HMS *Fly*, one of the Royal Navy's fastest

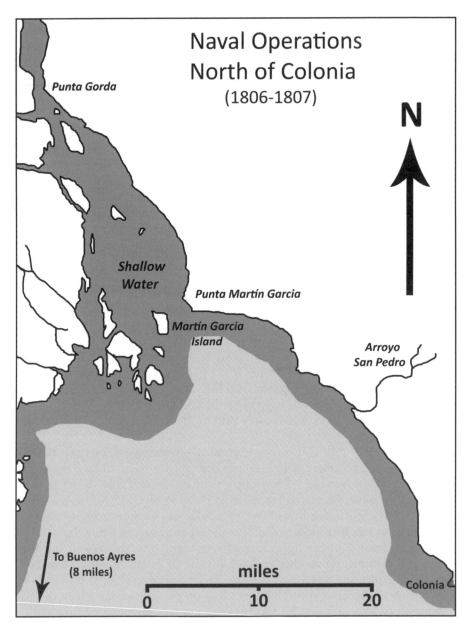

Naval Operations
North of Colonia
(1806-1807)

Punta Gorda

N

Shallow
Water

Punta Martín Garcia

Martín Garcia
Island

Arroyo
San Pedro

To Buenos Ayres
(8 miles)

miles

0   10   20

Colonia

sloops, to Cape Town to divert Craufurd to the River Plate. As the troops in the
region would soon amount to 10,000, a senior officer would also be required to
lead them.[33] William Windham's first choice had been the victor of the Battle of
Maida, Lieutenant-General Sir John Stuart; Lord Grenville had proposed Sir
George Prevost, a former governor of St Lucia and Dominica in the West Indies
and there had even been runmours that Arthur Wellesley, a young officer who

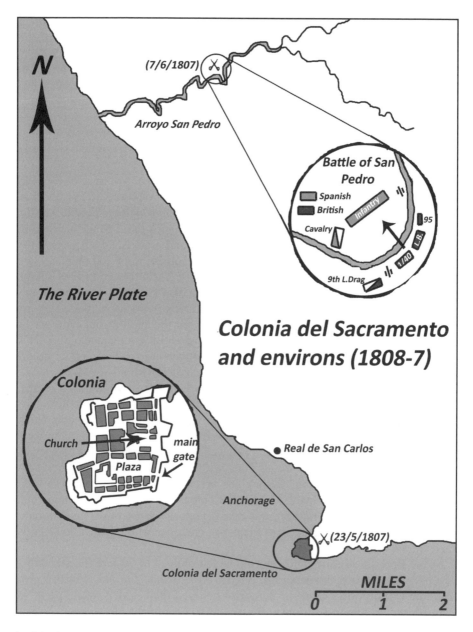

had had spectacular success in India, might be selected, but the position was eventually given to a relatively untried yet eminently well-connected lieutenant-general named John Whitelocke instead.[34]

Auchmuty and Stirling's next task was to consolidate their position.[35] To this end the latter amassed a fleet of small ships suitable for patrolling the shallows to the northwest of Colonia. Overall command was given to the commander of

HMS *Staunch*, Lieutenant Benjamin Street.[36] As well as his own gun-brig, Street had HMS *Encounter*, *Pheasant*, *Charwell*, *Dolores* and *Protector* at his disposal and had recently acquired the use of HMS *Olympia*, a ten-gun schooner which Rear-Admiral Murray had sent to patrol the River Plate only for Stirling to press her into service as she was 'particularly adapted for th[e] river'. The rear-admiral had also commissioned HMS *Paz*, a twelve-gun schooner captured at Monte Video.[37] Despite out-gunning the enemy, Lieutenant Street was unable to prevent the Spaniards moving freely in the shallower reaches. 'Without the army occup[ying] ... posts on the river up to Pt. Garcia so as to enable gunboats to take shelter in the creeks', the situation would continue, he recalled.[38]

Auchmuty, meanwhile, concentrated on extending his control into the interior. An advanced guard was ordered to move against Sobremonte at Las Piedras. Characteristically, the viceroy avoided combat, withdrawing seventy miles to the village of Pavón where the detachment sent from Buenos Ayres would arrest him. On 20 February the British occupied Las Piedras and established outposts in the villages of Santa Lucia and Canelones, the latter consisting of 200 men and two field pieces under Colonel Backhouse.[39] This gave Auchmuty control of a large area of farmland and solved his supply problem at a stroke.[40] The American's next move was to contact the authorities at Buenos Ayres as suggested by ex-governor Huidobro. HMS *Encounter* was chosen for the mission, but came across HMS *Charwell* with Brigadier-General Beresford and Lieutenant-Colonel Pack on board in mid-river. Believing their escape might have a direct effect on his mission, Lieutenant Talbot returned to Monte Video with all speed.[41]

No doubt Auchmuty had mixed feelings on learning of Beresford's escape. Whilst the addition of two competent senior officers would undoubtedly aid his cause, Beresford's reappearance could also deny the American overall command. Beresford had other plans, however. He felt uncomfortable assuming command without the War Office's consent and believed he could best serve his country by sharing his knowledge of the River Plate with the policy makers in London.[42] Another possible motivation, despite his certainty that his parole had been rendered invalid by the Spaniards' actions before his escape (an opinion soon supported by a court of enquiry), was that Beresford's sense of personal honour prevented him from taking up arms against an enemy to whom he had so recently surrendered his sword.[43]

Before Beresford returned to England he felt obliged to explore the possibility of a negotiated peace. If successful, Buenos Ayres would become a British protectorate without force of arms. Beresford believed there was 'a strong party' of sympathisers in senior positions in town and was confident of success.[44] Nearly all the British officers who had arrived since his imprisonment disagreed. Lieutenant-Colonel Richard Bourke, the army's quarter-master-general, thought 'that the prejudices of religion were not to be overcome', Rear-Admiral Stirling, as has previously been explained, was also a sceptic, and Colonel Gore Browne believed that the British were without a single friend in the entire continent. 'The People here are not that soft, effeminate race they are in Old Spain', he explained. 'On the contrary they are ferocious ... if England is serious in keeping this fine country a force of 15,000 men [would be needed to] ... beat them in the field ... stifle insurrection & ... convince the People that G. Britain is determined to effect the conquest and maintain it – for at present they do not think [we] ... are serious.'[45]

On 6 March Major Donald Campbell boarded HMS *Charwell* to complete the mission that Beresford's appearance had interrupted one month before.[46] The sloop dropped anchor six miles from Buenos Ayres, Campbell was rowed ashore and transferred aboard a Spanish gunboat, blindfolded and dropped at the mole. 'After landing ... [I] proceeded in the midst of a mob to the citadel ... [where] I found a great crowd of officers and people of all descriptions ... pressing in so much, that the doors were ... shut, and sentries placed, to prevent more from entering.' Campbell then gave Liniers the dispatch that Auchmuty and Stirling had prepared.[47] After deploring the treatment of the British prisoners of war, it threatened to send the soldiers captured at Monte Video to England should those taken with Beresford not be exchanged. The letter closed by imploring Liniers to surrender.[48] The Frenchman replied that 'the sword must decide [the matter]', and assured Campbell that there would be no prisoner exchange. The major then returned to the gunboat, despite the wishes of a voluminous part of the crowd who demanded his arrest. 'The dispute ran so high that General Liniers ... sent one of his aid de camps ... to clear away the mob, that I might get on board', Campbell recalled. 'From what I could see there seemed to be a great deal of party work amongst them ... Genl Liniers was in a disagreeable situation, and had little authority ... in short there seemed to be no subordination'.[49]

Upriver Lieutenant Street had noticed an increase in enemy naval activity. Gutiérrez de la Concha had four armed schooners, the *goleta Remedios*, the *falucho San Antonio*, two armed launches, and six gunboats operating between Buenos Ayres and the maze of islands and shallow straits to the northwest of Colonia.[50] In mid-February HMS *Staunch* and *Encounter* captured a schooner and several small boats and on 10 March, during a fierce storm, HMS *Staunch* was hit by a bolt of lightning. '[It] shivered the [fore top gallant] mast to pieces, set fire to the fore topsail and tore it in several places, split and shivered the fore topmast ... broke one of the hammock stanchions and drove in the starboard bulwark about four feet square ... [before going] out through the supper hole and melting the copper [sheeting covering the hull] at the water's edge.'[51] On 13 March HMS *Staunch* was in action again. Whilst escorting several prizes to Monte Video, she was attacked by two schooners, two gunboats and a *falucho* under Lieutenant Juan Ángel de Michelena.[52] Steering alongside the lead schooner, Lieutenant Street unleashed a 'broadside of Grape & Round', knocking her out of the fight. The rest of the enemy vessels returned fire. Second master John Walkie was wounded and, with '[her] running and rigging being shot away', HMS *Staunch* hauled off to make repairs.[53] At first light, HMS *Encounter* was spotted approaching from the north and by the afternoon Lieutenant Talbot had joined the fight. 'After being roughly handled [by the enemy]', he recalled, 'we obliged them to seek shelter in the harbour of Buenos Ayres with a number of killed and wounded'. The British brigs chased the enemy as close in as they dared, before breaking off the engagement at 7.30 pm. '[We] received several shot in our masts and sails', Talbot recalled, '[and the] cutter ... was cut away by a shot and could not be recovered.' HMS *Staunch* was even more badly mauled. As well as having 'seven of her ten 18-pound carronades dismounted', the 'main shroud, main topmast shroud and the sails were much damaged by grape'.[54]

The same morning Auchmuty launched his second major offensive of the campaign. Wanting to place a buffer between Monte Video and Buenos Ayres, the American had decided to capture Colonia del Sacramento. Before first light six companies of the 40th, the Light Infantry Battalion, commanded by Major Trotter following Lieutenant-Colonel Brownrigg's demise, the three companies of the 2nd Battalion of the Rifles and a detachment of the 9th Light Dragoons climbed aboard their transports. Weighing anchor at 5.20 am, they were escorted upriver by HMS *Pheasant, Charwell, Protector, Paz, Dolores* and *Olympia*.[55] In overall command was Lieutenant-Colonel Pack. Unlike Beresford, the Scot had no qualms about taking up arms again against the Spanish. The squadron anchored five miles off Colonia on 15 March. Whilst the troops were disembarking, the local commander hoisted a flag of truce from the fort and an officer was sent ashore to discuss terms.[56] The commander duly surrendered and the troops 'landed with ease'. Unwilling to accept the decision, some militia put up a token resistance, but 'retreated ... after firing a few shots'.[57]

Colonia del Sacramento had been founded by the Portuguese in 1680. Due to its strategic position, it had changed hands six times over the next hundred years until Viceroy Cevallos definitively won the village for the Spanish in 1777. Built on a rocky promontory, Colonia resembled Monte Video in miniature. It had a population of 2,800 and a 'good small harbour' which could accommodate 'a few ships'. Although many of the houses were in 'a state of ... neglect', groves of orange and peach trees 'gave it a pretty appearance' and a ruined church which had been used as a magazine stood as 'a shattered and curious monument of the united powers of lightning and gunpowder.' Colonia's once-strong walls were also in poor repair. A large breach rendered them ineffective, but Pack improved the defences. A 200-strong picket was posted in the house of an amiable soap-boiler and tallow chandler 'some distance from town'; batteries were dug on the hills; and a *chevaux de frise* was wedged in the gap where the gate had once stood.[58]

Back in Monte Video, on 22 March Beresford was rowed aboard HMS *Diomede*. The next day Captain Downman set sail for England.[59] Meanwhile, news had reached Buenos Ayres of the capture of Colonia. Desperate not to concede possession of such an important port so close to the capital, the Cabildo raised 600 men to retake it. Most were volunteers encouraged by the promise of a 4,000 *peso* reward for the capture of Lieutenant-Colonel Pack – 'the escaped prisoner, who ... [had] violated his sacred oath and word of honour.'[60] The troops included two companies of Miñones led by Captain José Grau and a body of Patriotas de la Unión equipped with four 6-pounders and two 6-inch howitzers. Overall command was given to Francisco Javier de Elio. A forty-year-

Sir Home Popham – 'a modern Pizarro'. Engraving, 1807.

Sir David Baird – 'a rough diamond ... with one or two rather repulsive traits'. Portrait by Sir John Watson-Gordon, c.1860.

William Pitt the Younger. The man behind Britain's Blue Water policy. Portrait by Thomas Gainsborough, 1792.

James's Town at St Helena. Built along a single street nestled between two cliffs, the town had a population of 1,200 and a 'pleasing' appearance. Engraving from a drawing by Edward S. Blake, 1830.

The Port of Buenos Ayres. As the South Atlantic's premier trade hub, Buenos Ayres was considered a rich prize. Painting, 1823.

Fort Santa Teresa. One of the Viceroyalty of the River Plate's most outlying defences, Fort Santa Teresa in modern-day Uruguay was the scene of the first contact between Popham's men and the Spanish forces. Photograph by Alexandra Sweeney.

The Plaza Mayor at Buenos Ayres. A bustling, open space of compacted earth, used for military parades, public executions, religious festivals and markets. Emeric Essex Vidal, watercolour, 1820.

The Cabildo at Buenos Ayres. Built in the first half of the eighteenth century, the Cabildo, or town hall, played a vital role in the British invasions. Photograph, 2005.

The militia of the River Plate. A tawdry mixture of 'long-haired Indians, and whiskered Spaniards' with little regularity in dress. Emeric Essex Vidal, watercolour, 1820.

Taking the city of Buenos Ayres by the British forces. Although roundly celebrated in the British press, Beresford's capture of Buenos Ayres was a relatively straightforward affair. Only one of his men was killed. *c.*1806.

The British troops entering the Citadel. 'The Scots of the 71st Regiment, [were] the most handsome troops I had ever seen' recalled Mariquita Sánchez de Thompson, one of dozens of *porteñas* watching Beresford's men enter town. '[They had] boots tied up with latticed ribbons, [with] a part of the bare leg showing, a short kilt, a beret with black feathers and a Scottish ribbon worn as a belt with a tartan shawl'. *c.*1806.

The dunes at Maldonado beach. Now Uruguay's premier beach resort, in October 1806 the beach at Punta del Este saw a determined advance by the grenadiers of the 38th. Photograph by the author, 2012.

Blandengues barracks at Maldonado. Irregular light cavalry originally raised to fight the Indian tribes of the frontier, the Blandengues were amongst the best troops the Spaniards had. Photograph by the author, 2012.

(*Left*) Sir Samuel Auchmuty was the most competent of all the senior British officers sent to the River Plate. 'We all thought [him] ... most excellent', recalled Private William Lawrence of the 40th Foot. Engraving.

(*Right*) Robert Craufurd. Forced into a humiliating surrender, 'Black Bob' was haunted by his experiences at the River Plate until his death at Ciudad Rodrigo in 1812.

Colonia del Sacramento. Situated directly opposite Buenos Ayres, the port of Colonia has long been of the utmost strategic importance in the history of the River Plate. Photograph by the author, 2012.

The British advance on Buenos Ayres, June 1807. After trudging over the sodden flats of the west bank of the River Plate for four days, the redcoats' spirits were lifted by the sight of the spires of Buenos Ayres cresting the horizon. Drawing, José María Cardano y Bauzá. 1807.

Simptoms of Courage – La Defensa. Whitelocke's plan of attack was fatally flawed. In the confusion of 5 July 1807, 311 British soldiers lost their lives. Cartoon by George Cruikshank, 1808.

(*Left*) La Merced Church in Buenos Ayres was held by members of the 5th Foot throughout the morning and early afternoon of 5 July, 1807. Photograph by the author, 2012.

(*Right*) The tower of Santo Domingo Church. Occupied by Craufurd's Light Brigade throughout the morning and early afternoon of 5 July 1807, Santo Domingo was fired on by the Spanish artillery in the fort of Buenos Ayres. The roundshot can still be seen today. Photograph by the author, 2012.

Whitelocke and the Ghost of Byng. When news of the British defeat reached London there was outrage. Some, including Brigadier-General Craufurd, called for Whitelocke to be shot, invoking the precedent established in 1757 when Admiral John Byng was executed for his failure at the Battle of Minorca. Cartoon, 1808.

old colonel from Pamplona and veteran of numerous European wars, Elio had recently arrived from Spain as military commander of the east bank.[61]

At dawn on 12 April Elio's troops embarked on six schooners, six gunboats and nine small boats, under the command of Juan Gutiérrez de la Concha. They set sail the following morning. Twenty miles to the northwest, off the island of Martín Garcia, Lieutenant Street's flotilla was ill-prepared to receive them. Two days earlier lieutenants Treacher, Blainey and Stewart of HMS *Dolores*, *Protector* and *Staunch*, had gone ashore to bag a few water fowl, only to be captured and taken inland. Deprived of these officers, the flotilla failed to react when de la Concha's ships were spotted and Elio's landing, at the mouth of Las Higueritas Brook fifty miles north-northwest of Colonia, was unopposed. The Spaniard's march progressed well and by the evening of 21 April his troops had closed to within striking distance of the walls.[62]

The speed of Elio's march caught Lieutenant-Colonel Pack unawares. At 1.00 am on 23 April his troops snuck past the British picket and advanced to the breach in the walls under cover of a sunken lane. Fortunately for the defenders, one man broke orders by taking a shot at a British sentry and Lieutenant John Scott managed to hold Elio at bay with a section of rifles whilst the rest of the garrison got under arms. In the bay Captain Palmer heard 'a great firing of musketry' and 'sent all hands armed on shore' and by 3.00 am Elio had been repulsed. Fleeing through the night in disorder, his men were pursued for three miles to the village of Real de San Carlos. Losses were light. The Spaniards suffered twenty-four casualties, half of which Elio believed had been caused by his own men in the confusion and just three of Pack's soldiers had been hit. Major Trotter 'received a severe wound through the body' and Captain Wilgress of the Royal Artillery had his arm shattered by a musket ball.[63]

On 26 April the 600 Spaniards and creoles captured at Monte Video were embarked on HMS *Lancaster* and *Howe* and nine army transports bound for England. Huidobro and his family were allotted an entire ship to themselves. The officers were also well accomodated, but the men suffered terribly. They were locked in the ships' holds and lacked winter clothes. HMS *Lancaster* leaked and fresh provisions were scarce. Although Stirling assigned Doctor William Miller to attend them, many would die of scurvy on the voyage across the Atlantic.[64] On 10 May, two weeks after the Spaniards had departed, HMS *Thisbe*, a thirty-four-gun frigate two months out from Portsmouth, arrived off Monte Video. On board was Lieutenant-General John Whitelocke, the newly-appointed commander-in-chief in the River Plate.

PART 3

LA DEFENSA

Chapter 14

General Whitelocke

The River Plate
10 May – 27 June 1807

Lieutenant-General John Whitelocke was hopelessly out of his depth. Unlike many of his subordinates, who had won their laurels on the field, Whitelocke was renowned only for his 'coarse manners' and 'antipathy to the smell of gunpowder' and had had but a single experience of combat over a decade before. The incident, which had taken place when Whitelocke had been a thirty-six-year-old lieutenant-colonel, was the talk of the army for months. Tasked with spear-heading the attack on Port-Au-Prince in Santo Domingo, he had attempted to bribe his opposite number, Governor Étienne Laveaux, into capitulating. A member of the *noblesse oblige*, Laveaux was appalled and demanded the imper-tinent Englishman grant him the satisfaction of a duel. Whitelocke refused and reluctantly marched to the attack. After an initial reverse, reinforcement and victory followed. Whitelocke's prize was to carry the dispatches to London, an honour frequently given to the most connected rather than the most meritorious officer. Whitelocke's case was no exception. Son of the fourth Lord of Aylesbury, a year before his inglorious debut he had married into the family of the Deputy Secretary of War and amongst his legion of patrons was no less than the Prince of Wales.[1] On returning to Britain Whitelocke was made a full colonel and given a staff role at Horse Guards. Over the next decade promotions to brigadier-general, major-general and lieutenant-general had followed, as had the lucrative colonelcy of the 89th and an appointment as governor-lieutenant of Portsmouth. By 1806 Whitelocke was also dabbling in army reform. As this was one of the pet projects of William Windham, the Secretary of State for War and the Colonies of the Ministry of All the Talents, he was thus fostering yet another valuable connection which led directly to his latest command.[2]

Whitelocke's orders for the River Plate were open to interpretation. After waiting for Craufurd's arrival, he was to recapture Buenos Ayres, but only if he felt he had sufficient men to hold it. 'You will consider as the object of your enterprise,' the document stipulated, 'not the annoyance or distress of the enemy, but the occupation of such particular stations or portions of the Territory as ... would not be easily recoverable'. A further warning not to alienate the locals followed. This was to be achieved, Whitelocke was advised, 'by abstaining from everything which can shock their religious opinion or Prejudices [and] by respecting their persons and Property'. His orders also revealed the War Office's belief that the South Americans were not only desperate to shake off the mandate of Madrid, but also open to the idea of British rule. 'Individuals [in positions of local authority] it may be necessary to change,' they stated, 'and in doing so a preference should as much as possible be given to the native inhabitants over Persons of Old Spain.'[3]

Once in Monte Video, Whitelocke tried to make up for his inexperience with a combination of bluster and micro-management. Whilst he would prove adept at the latter, the former was hopelessly ill-conceived. Riddled with insecurities and all too aware of his reputation as a parade-ground martinet, he adopted a personality based on an ill-conceived idea of how a general ought to behave. The result, resembling a caricature of a salty old sergeant-major, was a mixture of arrogance, rudeness and vulgarity which alienated his men and officers alike. Tied to this, and equally damaging, was Whitelocke's jealousy of the true soldiers under his command. This led him to refuse to allow them to act on their own initiative, and resulted in an inability to listen to the advice of the very men on whose counsel he should have relied.[4] Chief amongst them was Brigadier-General Auchmuty. Indeed, the only person to whom Whitelocke appeared to pay any heed was his second, Major-General John Leveson Gower, a thirty-two-year-old aristocrat who suffered from the same failings as his commander.[5] Having also arrived on board HMS *Thisbe*, Gower was equally ignorant of the situation on the ground. Furthermore, he lacked active experience and suffered from a personality that estranged his subordinates. Whilst such qualities may well have struck a cord with Whitelocke, they made the major-general an eminently unsuitable confidant and incompetent second-in-command.[6]

Whatever his faults, Whitelocke proved an energetic administrator. On 15 May, when a rumour swept round Monte Video that the inhabitants had stockpiled arms in their houses and intended to rise up and massacre the garrison, he divided the town into districts, allotted each to a regiment and began a thorough search at first light. Although Captain Wilkie thought it 'rather ungallant to turn out so many Señoras and Señoritas from their warm beds at that unseasonable hour', several weapons were found and confiscated, amongst them 'fowling-pieces inlaid with ... silver, pistols mounted in the most costly manner, [and] swords and daggers ... [with] gold ... handles'.[7] A quantity of property belonging to the Royal Philippine Company was also unearthed. It included 'Chinese work-boxes and fancy articles, fans, card-boxes, &c., which had been intended as presents to ... Napoleon's family'. All was sold at auction 'and swelled very considerably the amount of ... prize-money.'[8]

In the second half of May Whitelocke tried to form a cavalry brigade. The British infantry had consistently out-fought the Spaniards and creoles, but their victories had proved indecisive. Given an effective cavalry, Whitelocke could turn a reverse into a bloody rout. Although he had the troopers he required, they lacked mounts and on 15 May Brigadier-General William Lumley, Whitelocke's highest-ranking cavalry specialist, was ordered to ride between Monte Video and Colonia with an escort from the 17th Light Dragoons and round up whatever horses he could find. Lumley's journey proved far from fruitful. Enemy guerrillas had driven the best horses into the interior and foiled his efforts to gather the few that remained. Heavy rainfall made the frequent river crossings particularly hazardous and by the time he returned, Lumley had only gathered 100 horses, leading Whitelocke to command all the British residents, military and civilian alike, to surrender theirs to the army. Some 500 more were thus obtained, but the second of Whitelocke's problems proved insurmountable. '[South American horses are] extremely clever', Lumley explained, 'and as good as any I saw ... But the total want of dry food rendered them useless in a very few days'. Fed on grass, the horses were suitable for irregular light cavalry, but did not have the stamina required for the more heavily accoutred British dragoons. As a result, the grain stores in Monte Video were seized and four ships dispatched to Brazil to buy further supplies. The horses would not take to the diet, however, and Whitelocke was forced to give up on his dream of a mounted brigade.[9]

Whitelocke's next task was to choose a landing site near Buenos Ayres. The job fell to Lieutenant-Colonel Bourke, the army's quarter-master-general. Having interviewed Rear-Admiral Stirling and Major John Deane (the only British officer in Monte Video who had set foot on the far bank), Bourke was able to rule out Quilmes: since Beresford's landing Liniers had constructed a heavy battery over-looking the beach and the nearby marsh rendered the passage impractible.[10] Ensenada de Barragán, a bay twenty miles downriver, was a better possibility and on 19 May Bourke boarded HMS *Fly* to see the area for himself. 'We examined ... a considerable extent of the coast', he recalled, 'from at least sixty miles east-ward of the Ensenada, as far as six or seven miles westwards of Buenos Ayres: the result ... was that we believed that there was no other place where the troops could be landed, under cover of [even] the smallest ships of war'.[11] There appeared to be only two disadvantages. The first, the distance between Ensenada and the town, was countered by the space the site offered for a pitched battle should Liniers choose to fight in the field, as Whitelocke hoped he would, and the second, a thin band of marshland running parallel to the beach, was believed to be a lesser barrier than Beresford had dealt with the year before.[12]

Whitelocke next began investigating the overland route from Ensenada. As most travellers went by boat and no local wished to be branded a traitor, only 'three or four' informants could be found.[13] One was the ever-present Bostonian, William Pius White. Another was John Mawe, an English geologist who had arrived in the River Plate in 1805 to perform a geological survey, only to be arrested as a British spy and imprisoned.[14] According to these men there were three routes from Ensenada to Buenos Ayres. The first lay along the coast; the second skirted the river through boggy ground; the third crested a series of shallow heights between two and six miles inland. As Whitelocke intended to take cannon, the latter was deemed the most suitable. It also connected with a path leading to the high ground at El Retiro via a ford over the Riachuelo Brook. Although Whitelocke later held that he had always intended to be guided by circumstances, a plan was beginning to form in his mind. From El Retiro he could establish contact with the navy and dig in his heavy guns. The enemy would then have but two choices: surrender or be bombarded into submission.[15]

On 20 May Whitelocke began procuring transports to cross the river. As many of those which had carried the troops across the Atlantic were too large to operate in the shallows of the Plate, he commissioned several merchant ships. Some, such as the *Lord Chesterfield*, were offered freely. Others had to be commandeered. Whitelocke next turned his attention to defence. After dispatching the rest of the 40th to Colonia, a rampart, riveted with brick, was constructed inside the walls of Monte Video opposite Auchmuty's breach and a unit of 400 militia, grandly entitled the Royal British South American, was raised from amongst the British merchants in town.[16] On 23 May Whitelocke founded Monte Video's first newspaper. Edited by the adjutant-general, Lieutenant-Colonel Thomas Bradford, and translated by Manuel Aniceto Padilla, one of the men who had orchestrated Beresford's escape, *The Southern Star* presented classified adverts for merchants' wares, local news and official proclamations, as well as reproducing articles from *The Times*. All were printed in English and Spanish and selected to show the invaders in a glowing light. In an early edition Nelson's Trafalgar dispatches were reproduced. A later copy informed readers of developments in mainland Europe and reported that a forty-five year-old local slave had given birth to triplets, and on 27 June 'a most melancholy incident' was related. Whilst hunting sealions off the island of Flores, two merchant sailors from Liverpool, Mr Isaac Griffin and 'a fine boy, aged fifteen', had their boat overturned by the breakers and were never seen again. 'It is ... feared they were devoured by sea-wolves' *The Star* speculated, 'as these monsters kept up ... a frightful howling, and collected in immense numbers about the fatal spot.'[17]

As Whitelocke's planning entered its final stages, winter began. 'The nights were frosty, with now and then a little snow', Private Todd recalled. During the day there were 'great showers of hail as large as beans' and 'dreadful rains deluged all around. We had ... thunder and lightning [and] one night in particular, the whole earth seemed one continued blaze'.[18] Winter also brought an upturn in enemy activity. On 1 June Lieutenant Street's flotilla saw action in the narrows off Martín Chico Point. Spotting *La Mosca de Buenos Aires*, a lightly-armed schooner commanded by Juan Bautista Azopardo, a thirty-four-year-old Maltese privateer and former crew member of Mordeille's, whom Liniers had granted a letter of marque, the lieutenant sent HMS *Staunch*'s gig and HMS *Protector*'s cutter in pursuit. Crewed by two dozen 'well-armed' men and commanded by Midshipman Morrison and Master Miller, the boats caught up with the chase off Gorda Point to find de la Concha's entire fleet 'of seven sail' at anchor. Despite being heavily outgunned and outnumbered, the British boarded the nearest sloop with pistols, knives, axes and swords. The crew leapt into the water and swam to *La Mosca*, which opened fire as soon as their comrades were clear. None of the British sailors were hit. Sailing downriver, they rejoined HMS *Staunch* off Martín Garcia Island with their prize before the enemy had even mustered a pursuit.[19]

The next day Lieutenant Street ordered Lieutenant Douglas on HMS *Dolores* to accompany Morrison and Miller's boats on another sortie upriver. At 4.00 pm they sighted a *falucho* and two schooners sailing northwest. Douglas gave chase until nightfall when the Spanish grounded their ships two miles from Gorda

Point. As they made camp round a large fire on shore, the British dropped anchor in mid-river. Anticipating a nightime attack, Douglas sent out boats to sound the area, double-shotted HMS *Dolores*' bow guns with round shot and grape, issued small arms and cleared the decks for action. At 3.00 am the alarm was raised. In the moonlight the lookout spotted the *falucho* and one of the schooners sailing directly towards them. 'When I got on deck', Douglas recalled, '[I] saw them broad on the starboard bow. They ... cheered each other and gave us several guns loaded with grape.' Cutting the anchor cable and hauling up the jibs, Douglas wore round to bring his guns to bear and, at half pistol range, fired the bow chasers at the schooner followed by a double-shotted starboard broadside. Small arms fire was also exchanged and the Spaniard sheered off. '[The *falucho* then] ... came under our stern', Douglas recalled, 'and kept peppering us with grape, till the bowsprit was on our Taff rail.' Unable to bring his guns to bear, Douglas ordered his sailors to open fire with small arms. The creoles 'several times cried out 'boardo' and made some attempts' the lieutenant reported, 'but never mustered ... the courage to go through with it.' With the British sailors' musketry sweeping their deck, the Spaniards broke off the action and sailed to the south. HMS *Dolores* was too badly damaged to pursue. Although only two men had been 'slightly wounded', her sails and rigging were shredded and the main topsail and foretopsail braces had been shot away. Drifting dangerously close to the bank, Douglas dropped anchor and ordered his men to make repairs. Dawn revealed the Spanish sailing for Buenos Ayres. Douglas sent his boats to pursue them, 'but [they] could not come near'.[20]

Just before the action the Spaniards had dropped off a detachment of marines under Josef Corbrera and a unit of Patricios from Buenos Ayres who made their way overland to Colonel Elio's encampment to the north of Colonia. With the addition of several men who had escaped from Monte Video, the Spaniard's army was now 2,000 strong. On 6 June he advanced to within twelve miles of the British lines and set up camp by Arroyo San Pedro.[21] Since the disastrous night attack on Colonia in April, morale had deteriorated. Insubordination, desertion and in-fighting had become commonplace and Elio had even had to deal with a minor revolt. In a series of letters to the Cabildo, he complained that the only troops he could rely on were those who had deserted from the enemy. Mostly German and Irish Catholics, they were well-trained and their actions had irrevocably tied them to the cause.[22]

Thanks to Lieutenant Street's flotilla, Pack was well aware of Elio's movements.[23] After leaving a garrison under Major Pigot of the 9th Light Dragoons, he took 1,013 men to attack the Spaniard in the field.[24] 'We were called under arms at midnight', Private Lawrence recalled, '[and] a little after two in the morning we left the town with an Indian for our guide'. As they approached Arroyo San Pedro, Pack ordered the fifty-four riders of the 9th Light Dragoons to fan out ahead under Captain Frederick Carmichael. On falling in with Elio's picket, a skirmish took place. Trooper James Turner was mortally wounded and a few Spaniards and creoles taken prisoner. The rest fired some signal rockets and fled to the north.[25] At 7.00 am the British arrived at Arroyo San Pedro. Elio's troops were drawn up on an elevated piece of ground on the far side. The Spaniard had placed his infantry in the middle, 180 hussars and ten Blandengues under Pedro Núñez on his right and six light guns crewed by the Patriotas de la Unión on his left. The whole was protected by the river and bracketed by marshy ground. A single ford, covered by Elio's guns, provided the only line of advance. Pack attacked immediately. Whilst the three companies of the 2/95th under Major Gardener thinned the enemy ranks with their Baker rifles and Lieutenant Shepherd opened fire with two 6-pounders, the 40th and Major Trotter's Light Battalion crossed the river with fixed bayonets. 'Reduced to a front of less than two sections' they waded into the muddy water 'up to their middles, and under a heavy fire' from Elio's guns. Two privates of the 40th were killed whilst crossing. The rest formed line on the far bank and advanced towards the enemy 'without firing a shot.' Núñez's cavalry fled as the British climbed the rise, but the infantry stood firm and fired a volley. 'Every shot seemed to rise up over our heads', Private Lawrence recalled. Thirty yards out Pack ordered his men to charge. With the steel-tipped line hurtling towards them, the majority of Elio's infantry broke, leaving a single company of the pony-tailed Patricios commanded by Lieutenant José Quesada to briefly hold their ground. Quesada and ten others paid the price for their bravery. The rest fled after their comrades to the north.[26]

The battle had lasted twenty minutes. Some 120 of Elio's men had been killed and 'a great many' wounded. Although Elio escaped to Buenos Ayres with 400 men, a lieutenant-colonel, a major, two captains, two lieutenants and over 100 rank and file were captured as well as a standard, six cannon, 300 muskets and carbines, ammunition and stores. Elio blamed the cowardice and insubordination of the militia for the defeat. His men claimed the Spaniard was responsible. Many contemporaries felt that they might have had a point. Despite the proximity of his camp to Colonia, Elio was poorly prepared and had fled the field with such haste that he had left his sword behind.[27] Pack's performance, on the other hand, had been exemplary and British losses were light. The two privates who had been killed crossing the river were the only fatalities and just a handful were wounded, amongst them Major Trotter of the Light Battalion who always seemed to be in the thick of the action. Whilst the surgeons attended his wounds, the men looted their prisoners. '[Pack] ordered everything to be taken from [them] ... as that was how he had been served himself ... at Buenos Ayres', Lawrence recalled. 'We set to clearing them of all they possessed, their money, which amounted to about 2,000 dollars, their clothes and even their boots.' Added to the six captured cannon, later valued at £40 each, it was a fine haul. 'We gave ten dollars to each of the widows of the men killed,' Lawrence recalled, 'and ... divided [the rest amongst ourselves]'.[28]

Eighty miles to the east, the cavalry detachment at Santa Lucia had also come under pressure. Skirmishes had been occurring throughout April and May, several men had been killed and one officer, Lieutenant Thomas Jones of the 21st Light Dragoons, taken prisoner. In late May and early June these clashes intensified. On 24 May Trooper George Hoare of the 17th Light Dragoons was killed and two others taken prisoner; on 5 June another trooper was snatched; and ten days later three officers were captured in Santa Lucia.[29] 'They had been in the habit of visiting some ladies', an observer recalled, 'and a meeting was appointed with them on ... [the] evening [of 15 June] about three miles from their quarters. While engaged with the fair ones, the house was surrounded by [twenty] ... armed men ... six or seven of whom violently entered ... and demanded the Englishmen within ... The ... gentlemen [surrendered and were] carried off'.[30] At Canelones Colonel Backhouse's force had also been attacked. Since April enemy horsemen had been hovering around the village, in May several skirmishes had taken place and in the first week of June an ultimatum was delivered by a Spanish aide.[31] If the British failed to surrender on 12 June, they would be attacked by overwhelming odds. Backhouse, never one to take a risk, 'thought it prudent to retire'. Falling back, he met a relief force of 500 under Colonel Thomas Mahon of the 9th Light Dragoons on the outskirts of Monte Video. After taking Backhouse's two guns, Mahon advanced on Canelones to find that the enemy had withdrawn.[32] When he returned to Monte Video on 14 June, he found a forest of masts six miles off shore. Brigadier-General Craufurd's troops had arrived.[33]

At forty-two years old Robert Craufurd, or 'Black Bob' as he would come to be known, was a seasoned professional. Having fought under Lord Cornwallis in India in the early 1790s, he had gone on to serve General Gerard Lake as deputy quarter-master-general during the Irish uprising of 1798, before a series of staff and attaché roles and a brief period as Member of Parliament for East Retford in Nottinghamshire. He had been promoted to colonel in October 1805 and reached brigadier-general two years later. Nepotism had also been instrumental in his rise. Craufurd's sister-in-law, the dowager duchess of Newcastle, owned his former borough and his primary patron was William Windham, the current Secretary of State for War and the Colonies. Craufurd's appointment as leader of the expeditionary force tasked with the invasion of Chile had been a dream posting. Success would have enabled him to establish a formidable reputation and set him 'on the road to fame and fortune'. The arrival of HMS *Fly* at the Cape had changed everything.[34] As well as redirecting Craufurd to the River Plate, Windham had appointed Whitelocke over his young protégé's head. Craufurd had been 'mortified beyond description' when he heard the news. His first reaction had been to ask for a recall, but by the time he reached the River Plate he had decided to try to put his disappointment behind him.[35]

The fleet escorting Craufurd's troops was immense. There were two sixty-four-gun ships-of-the-line – HMS *Polyphemus*, which served as Rear-Admiral Murray's flagship, and HMS *Africa*. Both had fought at Trafalgar. The thirty-six-gun frigate HMS *Nereide* was also present; as were HMS *Fly* and HMS *Saracen*, two sixteen-gun sloops; HMS *Haughty*, a twelve-gun brig; and HMS *Flying Fish*, a four-gun schooner. Twenty-five transports and five victuallers and store ships completed the convoy.[36] On board were over 4,800 troops. The 5th, 36th, 45th and 88th Foot were present in their entirety. There were five companies of the 1/95th, 243 artillerymen and the 299-strong 6th Dragoon Guards or Carabiniers. Brigadier-General Craufurd and Rear-Admiral Murray were rowed ashore on

15 June. Their boat took an hour and a half to reach the pier on the far side of Monte Video. After a tour of town, during which Whitelocke pointed out the defensive strength of the flat-topped houses, the plan for the first stage of the advance on Buenos Ayres was revealed. The 8,000 troops to be used in the operation would be divided into four brigades led by brigadier-generals Craufurd, Auchmuty, Lumley and Mahon. The first would proceed upriver the next morning. After rendezvousing at Colonia, the army would cross the river and land at Ensenada de Barragán. Although one last regiment of foot (Whitelocke's own 89th) and some horse artillery were yet to arrive under General Wroth Palmer Acland, Whitelocke was concerned by the lateness of the season and determined to attack without delay.[37]

On 16 June Craufurd's troops were transferred into the shallow draught vessels that Stirling and Whitelocke had prepared. For men who had been on board for up to ten months, the new accommodations were far from satisfactory. '[We] were packed in something like herrings into a barrel', Lieutenant George Miller of the 1/95th recalled. 'The officers swung in the cabin in three tiers, like chests of drawers. I happened to swing in the middle, and the man who slept below me adopted the precaution of fixing a preventer brace round my cot during the night'.[38] Beef, spirits and bread for 10,000 men for forty-five days and twenty-eight cannon were loaded.[39] Three iron 24-pounders, three brass 12-pounders, two Spanish brass 12-inch mortars and two 6-pounders were to be left on board as a siege-train. Captain Augustus Frazer, the senior Royal Artillery officer, had persuaded Whitelocke that they might be used to bombard Buenos Ayres once the troops were within striking distance of town. The remainder, six 6-pounders, five Spanish 4-pounders, two 3-pounders from St Helena and five 5.5-inch howitzers would be landed with the army at Ensenada. Each was supplied with 200 rounds of ammunition. Over 2.5 million musket ball cartridges, 20,000 carbine cartridges and 40,000 rifle rounds were also embarked.[40]

Some 150 miles to the northwest, off Martín Chico point, HMS *Staunch* had picked up two of Beresford's officers. Major Henry Tolley and Lieutenant Peter Adamson, both of the 71st, had managed to escape from the Colegio de San Ignacio, an isolated retreat 100 miles south of Córdoba.[41] Evading armed pursuit, they had travelled over 200 miles to the Paraguay River and obtained a boat. '[By] hiding during the day and rowing all night, [and] levying contributions of provisions on any house where no male person was to defend it', they sailed downriver to the confluence with the Plate and crossed to the east bank, where they came across HMS *Staunch*'s cutter. The odyssey had seen them traverse 400 miles in twenty-two days.[42]

At midday on 17 June, having been delayed for one more day by contrary winds, Whitelocke's first division departed.[43] The twenty-four transports sailed under convoy of HMS *Saracen*, *Encounter* and *Paz*. Before they had proceeded more than seven miles, violent south-easterly winds forced them to drop anchor to avoid being blown into the Atlantic. The next morning a thick fog descended making 'it … impossible to see a ship's length off'.[44] Back at Monte Video Whitelocke had attempted to placate Craufurd by giving him command of the elite Light Brigade, a post which had previously been reserved for Brigadier-General Acland – still somewhere in the mid-Atlantic with the 89th. '[As] the light troops ... [were] mostly at Colonia, it became necessary to embark immediately' recalled Lieutenant-Colonel Lancelot Holland, an officer on Craufurd's staff, and at 3.00 pm the next day Craufurd and suite were rowed aboard the *Lord Chesterfield*.[45] The south-easterlies continued for two more days, stranding the transports in mid-river, and on 19 June Holland returned to Monte Video for supplies.[46] The next day the winds continued and a swell of flood water rushed down the river into the Atlantic.[47]

Onshore, Whitelocke was having doubts about his prospects of success. '[England] has assuredly derived no benefit from our first operations under ... Sir Home Popham', he explained in a letter to William Windham. 'The whole system appears to have been galling to the Inhabitants, and instead of an impression favourable to Great Britain, I am persuaded that it will be difficult ever to do away the idea that individual interest influenced the whole of those proceedings ... [As a result] we have scarcely one friend in the Country.'[48] On the morning of 21 June the wind swung to the north and the last division embarked on twenty-one transports under convoy of HMS *Thisbe*, *Rolla*, *Olympia* and *Medusa*.[49] Having left a garrison of 1,353 men in Monte Video under Colonel Gore Browne of the 40th, Whitelocke and his staff bid farewell to the Cabildo and were rowed out to HMS *Nereide*.[50] Captain Corbet saluted with seventeen guns and got under weigh at noon with HMS *Flying Fish* in company.[51] That day the fleet made good progress and by nightfall all three divisions dropped anchor forty miles upriver. The next morning 'was foggy and the wind foul'. The ships remained at anchor and the men were given mugs of cocoa to ward off the cold.[52] On board the *Lord Chesterfield* Lieutenant-Colonel Holland and Craufurd's brigade-major, Sir John Campbell, 'employed the morning ... making [sea]pyes and puddings' and at 4.00 pm the transports got under weigh. Sailing through the night, the fleet threaded its way between the Chico and Ortiz banks, the latter marked by a beacon on board HMS *Charwell*.[53] The next day the transports were becalmed yet again. On HMS *Nereide* Whitelocke 'had a long conversation' with his quarter-master-general, Lieutenant-Colonel Richard Bourke, about the practical and moral issues involved in bombarding Buenos Ayres. Still the lieutenant-general remained undecided. At day break 'a fair wind' blew from the south.[54] HMS *Flying Fish* and *Nereide* went direct to Ensenada de Barragán. The rest arrived off Colonia on 24 June.[55]

Hampered by thick fog, the embarkation of Pack's men was a laborious process. The 9th Light Dragoons, light artillery, stores and the sick and wounded boarded on 25 June. A number of iron 24-pounders, too cumbersome to load, were spiked and thrown into the sea and their carriages burned to prevent them falling into the hands of the enemy, while Lieutenant-Colonel Holland took advantage of the delay to go for a ride to the village of Real de San Carlos three miles to the northwest. Inland the sun had burned off the fog and 'the day was clear and lovely.' The next morning the three companies of the 2/95th, the Light Battalion and the 40th were embarked. At 10.00 am the fleet made sail and at

4.00 pm dropped anchor off Ensenada de Barragán. United for the first time, it made quite a spectacle. HMS *Nereide*, *Medusa*, *Thisbe*, *Saracen*, *Pheasant*, *Fly*, *Rolla*, *Encounter*, *Haughty*, *Flying Fish*, *Dolores*, *Paz* and *Olympia*, two armed transports, six gunboats and seventy-two unarmed transports were all anchored between four and six miles offshore.[56] That night a heavy rain fell, but the next morning dawned bright and clear. Scanning the shore through his telescope, Lieutenant-Colonel Holland was reminded of the Curragh of Kildare.[57] 'The coast … appeared flat', he recalled, 'with some wood and the country covered in cattle.' Throughout the day the wind remained in the east. There was thunder, lightning and heavy rain and it wasn't until the morning of Sunday 28 June that the troops were able to land.[58]

Chapter 15

The Advance on Buenos Ayres

Buenos Ayres and Environs
28 June – 4 July 1807

Compared to the debacle of 1806, the *porteños* were well-prepared. By June 1807 over 9,000 men were under arms.[1] A garrison of 2,000, consisting of the Cuerpo de Invalidos under Francisco Agustini, a company of Miñones and a battalion of Patricios, were assigned to guard town, while the rest were organised into four mobile divisions, each between 1,500 and 2,000 strong. The Red Division was led by General César Balbiani, a recently-recruited Spaniard who had previously held military commands in the Chilean regions of Chiloe and Osorno; the White Division was under General Bernardo de Velasco, a forty-two-year-old from Burgos and the intendant of Paraguay; the Blue Division was commanded by Colonel Javier Elio, the Spaniard whom Pack had defeated at Colonia; and the Reserve Division was led by the Spanish naval captain Juan Gutiérrez de la Concha. In support were over sixty cannon, howitzers and mortars gathered from as far afield as the upper Paraná River and ranging in calibre from 32- to 3-pounders. The lighter pieces were attached to the four divisions. The larger were divided into two independent batteries. One consisted of eight guns, the other of ten.[2]

The bullring in El Retiro had been transformed into a state-of-the-art arsenal. Over 600 90-pound barrels of gunpowder, thousands of shot and shells, millions of small arms cartridges, hundreds of home-made grenades, entrenching tools, fuses, dead-matches and port-fires had been stacked in orderly rows.[3] Some of the munitions had been captured from two English merchantmen which had sailed too close to Buenos Ayres. Others had been sent from as far afield as Lima and Santiago. A new battery, named Abascal in honour of Peru's newly-appointed viceroy, had been built on the cliff by the bullring to protect El Retiro from a waterborne attack. The three brass 18-pounders and two 13-inch mortars installed covered the roadstead. Thousands of horses had been corralled for the cavalry; in January a grand review and battlefield exercise had been held; the infantry regiments were regularly drilled in the plazas; and provisions of all sorts had been prepared, dried, salted, packed and stored. Over 1 million *pesos* had been donated locally and another 500,000 *pesos* had been sent from Peru. The women of Buenos Ayres had cut and stitched thousands of uniforms; others had set up military hospitals throughout town to aid the monks at La Residencia; sixteen Indian chiefs had offered the services of their people; children as young as twelve

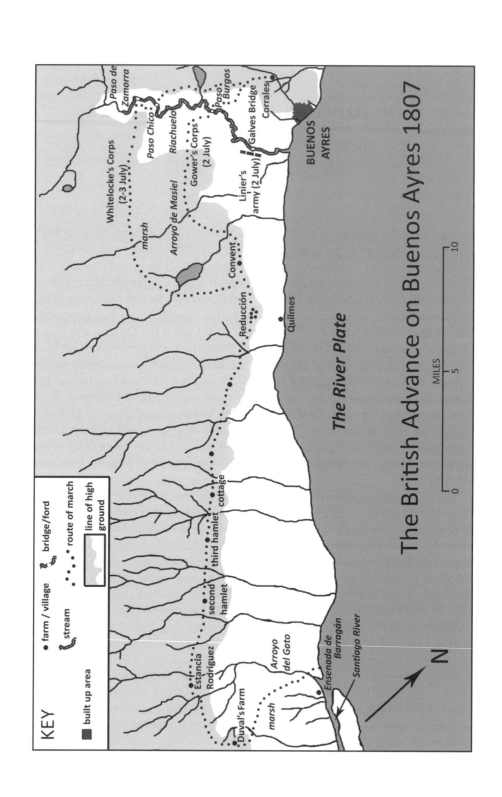

KEY

- ● farm / village
- ⌇ stream
- ⌇ bridge/ford
- ⋯ route of march
- ▨ line of high ground
- ▨ built up area

The British Advance on Buenos Ayres 1807

The River Plate

BUENOS AYRES

Corrales
Galves Bridge
Paso Burgos
Linier's army (2 July)
Riachuelo
Paso Chico
Paso de Zamorra
Whitelocke's Corps (2-3 July)
Gower's Corps (2 July)
Arroyo de Masiel
marsh
Convent
Reducción
Quilmes
cottage
third hamlet
second hamlet
Estancia Rodriguez
Duval's Farm
marsh
Arroyo del Gato
Ensenada de Barragán
Santiago River

N

MILES
0   5   10

had volunteered for the militia; and the worshippers at the San Telmo Church had raised enough money to found their own gun.[4]

In June the pace of mobilisation stepped up. Thousands of women and children were evacuated and artillery and cavalry detachments were sent to Quilmes and Los Olivos.[5] At the former two batteries were dug. The first overlooked the bay. The second commanded the marsh which Beresford had had to cross the year before. The north bank of the River Chuelo was also fortified and at Galves Bridge several heavy guns were dug in.[6] On 20 June reports arrived from Atalaya, a naval garrison eighty miles to the southeast, of a British fleet gathering in the river. On 24 June a final grand review and battlefield exercise was held. The next day the general alarm was sounded. The British fleet was on the move. The troops were deployed to previously assigned defensive positions and a party of 2,000 marines was dispatched to Colonia to harass Pack's evacuation. Back in Buenos Ayres Liniers inspected his men.[7] They cheered the Frenchman as he rode past and he praised them and assured them of victory. Confidence was high and the atmosphere celebratory.[8] 'Nothing was to be heard but concerts of music in all quarters' a local merchant recalled '[and] the people passed the night ... full of spirits, and calmly expecting an opportunity of coming to action'. As the British fleet gathered off Ensenada de Barragán on 26 June, Liniers' army was further augmented by a last-minute rush of volunteers.[9]

The British landing began at 6.30 am on 28 June. It was a cold, hazy morning with light winds. Commanding HMS *Dolores* and four gunboats armed with 18-pounders, Captain Thompson of HMS *Fly* put down a series of buoys marking the deep water channel leading into shore by the estuary of the Santiago River. At 8.30 am they anchored in ten feet of water half a mile out, their cannon bearing on a line of low hills four miles inland, while the transports joined them. At 9.15 am they arrived and Admiral Murray, on board HMS *Flying Fish*, raised the signal for the disembarkation. A flotilla of small boats were lowered into the muddy water, the men clambered aboard and were rowed ashore.[10] The landing was somewhat chaotic. 'They ... pushed off without any order or regularity', Lieutenant-Colonel Holland recalled. 'Not only men of the first brigade, but some of almost every regiment of the expedition set out together.' A quarter of a mile out, the boats ran aground on a sand bar and the men waded ashore.[11]

Brigadier-General Craufurd was amongst the first to reach land, a curving strip of sand one mile to the northwest of the village of Ensenada. As he strode up the beach, a company of the 1/95th fanned out ahead of him.[12] Once they had secured the area, Craufurd formed up the Light Brigade and by 10.00 am they were moving inland. After a mile and a half they encountered the Arroyo del Gato, a stream twenty yards across and five feet deep that was the first of many problems they would face that day. Craufurd got a message back to the ships and the rest of the army was landed to the southeast in the mouth of the Santiago River while the Light Brigade crossed via a pontoon bridge thrown up by Captain John Squire of the Royal Engineers.[13] By 11.00 am Craufurd had secured Ensenada, a small village consisting of several 'bad houses', a few huts, a church and an abandoned fort. In the bay four ships, one American, one Portuguese, one

Prussian and one English prize, were secured.[14] All the inhabitants had fled aside from two men who were pressed into service as guides. Also present was William Pius White and a group of mounted *peónes* whom he had recruited to round up wild cattle for the army on the march.[15] They sold Craufurd and Holland a pair of horses with saddles and bridles for 16 *pesos*. 'We were [later] told we [had] paid at least twice their value', Holland complained.[16]

At midday the Advanced Corps pushed five miles inland, their destination 'a small tract' of raised ground crowned by three farm buildings and a scattering of trees. As well as Craufurd's Light Brigade, consisting of the combined light companies, Captain Brookman's company of the 71st and four companies of riflemen led by Major Robert Travers, the Advanced Corps, which was commanded by Major-General Gower, included Auchmuty's brigade (the 38th and 87th with the detached grenadier company of the 47th) and two 3-pounders from the 1st Artillery Battery hauled by fifty artillerymen and thirty six sailors under Captain W.D. Nicolls.[17] The march began badly and conditions got progressively worse. Marshy ground gave way to a bog a mile and three quarters in breadth.[18] The colour of ink and consistency of pea soup, the mud came up to the men's knees and turned their red, blue and green uniforms consistently black.[19] Private Thomas Todd of the 71st had his shoes sucked from his feet, Major-General Gower's thoroughbred pitched him into the slime on two occasions and the twelve horses assigned to the artillery were buried up to their bellies and the cannon 'stuck fast' in the sludge. Only after a superhuman effort by the sailors were they dragged clear.[20]

At 3.00 pm the Advanced Corps reached the heights. To Frazer's relief, the footing was firm and the horses were reharnessed to the guns. With Major Travers' riflemen forming a loose screen ahead, they marched for a mile across a sea of waist-high clover inhabited by vast numbers of birds. On reaching the three buildings they had spotted from the river, Gower ordered the men to make camp. The Light Brigade held the right and the 87th and 38th were positioned on the left.[21] After pickets had been set up, the men built fires, dried their clothes and plundered poultry, lemons and oranges from the farm.[22] Inside the building on the far right, a 'rude' hut of three rooms, Craufurd and Holland met Pedro Duval, a slave trader, smuggler and associate of William Pius White's. As a proponent of free trade, Duval had welcomed Beresford and hoped to profit through an early association with his successors. '[He] did not seem very much concerned [at the army's presence],' Holland recalled, '[and] laughed and talked a great deal.' After Duval had informed them of Liniers' defensive preparations, the officers drank a bottle of wine and dined on the 'sea pie' they had prepared on the *Lord Chesterfield*.[23]

Five miles to the rear, Auchmuty's and Mahon's brigades had taken possession of Ensenada. The troops were quartered in the fort and the buildings surrounding it.[24] Although most had a supper of salted pork, Private Stephen Morley and his comrades in the 5th caught 'killed, roasted, and devoured' an 'immense pig' they found roaming the village.[25] At 6.00 pm one of Gower's aides arrived with news of the difficulties the Advanced Corps had encountered crossing the swamp. Lieutenant-Colonel Bourke ordered the engineers to 'mend the worst passes' with fascines and planks at first light.[26] Down by the beach, the disembarkation continued. Landing the cannon proved particularly difficult and although all the guns would eventually be unloaded, the 5.5-inch howitzers were left on board. Disembarking the horses was also problematic. 'Through the awkwardness of the persons employed, upwards of forty made their escape'. Two others were injured and had to be destroyed.[27]

News of the landing was met with bemusement in Buenos Ayres. Whitelocke had placed fifty miles of sodden ground between himself and his destination. With the skies threatening rain, the Spaniards knew the route would turn into a morass and the British would exhaust their supplies, energy and patience long before they came within striking distance. One merchant thought the decision 'a desperate measure', explicable only by Whitelocke's fear of the batteries covering the landing sites to the north and south of town.[28] The move had also gifted Liniers the initiative. After recalling the detachments from Quilmes and Los Olivos, the Frenchman deployed the bulk of his forces at Galves Bridge while ordering the First Hussars to ride to Ensenada. The unit's commander, Martín Rodríguez, split his men into three squadrons.[29] After driving all the horses and cattle in the area beyond Whitelocke's reach, his orders were to harass the British march.[30]

The morning of 29 June dawned cold and damp.[31] Shivering round their campfires, the Advanced Corps stamped their feet and turned their thoughts to breakfast. Lieutenant Miller 'went out with a few [rifle]men, and shot a bullock. [We] dragged him home with a horse in triumph', he recalled.[32] Meanwhile, Craufurd and Holland rode out to inspect the pickets. The officer in charge, Captain George Elder of the 2/95th, had organised them well.[33] 'Had I placed them myself, I could not have done it better' Craufurd was heard to declare.[34] Later, Craufurd and Holland 'went on ... reconnaissance about three miles in front' with an escort of riflemen commanded by Major Norman Mcleod. In the distance they spotted sixty of Rodríguez's hussars, dressed in sky blue and white and armed with pistols, sabres and short barrelled carbines.[35]

Five miles to the rear the Main Corps were in motion. Under Whitelocke's command were Lumley's brigade (the 88th, 36th and 5th with two 6-pounders) and Colonel Mahon's brigade (four dismounted squadrons of 9th Light Dragoons, the 45th, five companies of the 40th, five companies of riflemen and four dismounted squadrons of the 6th Dragoons or Carabiniers). The swamp beyond Ensenada proved even more difficult to cross than the day before. 'It was not possible to get through it with a greater front than one section', one officer recalled, 'or to march in more than a single column ... For two miles and a half we were constantly up to our knees in mud and water.' The Carabiniers found it particularly galling. Having had their carbines replaced with unwieldy long-barrelled Spanish muskets, the troopers had to endure the indignity of slogging it out on foot with the infantry. 'With their white breeches and jack-boots, [they] looked very picturesque when we got into the black swamp of Ensenada', one observer recalled.[36] Whitelocke's senior Royal Artillery officer, Captain Augustus Frazer, also found the march exhausting. 'It is hardly possible to conceive a swamp more difficult to overcome', he opined. With his cannon up to their axles and the horses proving a hindrance, Frazer requested assistance and 300 of the 38th were sent back to help.[37] 'We found the drivers spurring and flogging away at the poor horses', Captain Wilkie recalled. 'They were ... kicking and plunging ... [and] making ... [the] footing ... worse [still].' After the horses had been unhitched, the guns were eventually dragged free.[38]

Arriving at the camp on the heights, Whitelocke decided that Lumley and Auchmuty's brigades should swap corps. The former would accompany Gower's Advanced Corps on the onward march, whilst Auchmuty's men would remain with Whitelocke. The decision caused considerable head-scratching in the days to come. Auchmuty's men (the 38th and 87th Regiments) had been in the River Plate for six months. They were acclimatised and had adapted to the enemy's tactics. Lumley's (the 36th and 88th) had spent the same period on board transports with no opportunity to exercise. Furthermore, Auchmuty's had been resting since they had arrived at the heights the previous afternoon, while Lumley's had been struggling through the marsh all morning. While the 36th contained several veterans and was up to the challenge, the 88th would prove particularly unsuitable. The regiment had had an influx of recruits just before sailing and included 'a vast number of very young men'.[39]

At midday Craufurd returned from his morning reconnaissance. Seeing Major Mcleod galloping into camp alongside the brigadier-general, Whitelocke burst into a rage. The rifle major had left on his own initiative, a quality that the lieutenant-general despised. '[Whitelocke] was in a great passion', Holland observed, 'and ... attacked ... [Mcleod] with great fury.' Craufurd intervened on the major's behalf. Dark and intense and still fuming about losing overall command, the brigadier-general was not a man to be meddled with. Whitelocke backed down and at 1.00 pm the Light Brigade moved out.[40] A screen of skirmishers led the march and two companies of riflemen were positioned on each flank. Two 3-pounders followed 200 yards behind. Then came the main body of the Light Brigade with a small rear-guard and a few flankers on either side.[41] Riding beside Craufurd was Señor Duval. 'Much against his inclination', the merchant had been pressed into service as a guide. 'Being sickly and leaving his family in the midst of an army, [he] was very unhappy', Holland recalled. Compared to the trials of the swamp the march was easy-going. 'The country is almost all level', Private Todd recalled, 'and covered with long clover that reached to our waists.'[42]

After a long, gradual descent under leaden skies, the men splashed across a knee-deep stream. Captain Nicolls' guns were hauled across by the artillerymen and seamen, then rehitched to the horses on the far side. One mile further on, on the crest of a low rise, was Estancia Rodríguez, a collection of small farmhouses where the sixty horsemen Craufurd had spotted earlier awaited. Dismounting, the hussars sighted their carbines across the backs of their horses and fired a volley at 500 yards. Not a single shot found its mark and when two companies of riflemen advanced 'in double quick time ... [the creoles] got on their horses and went off at a full gallop ... There was not a soul left in the village', Holland recalled. 'All had abandoned it, leaving their corn, cattle, furniture, etc., behind'. After looting the buildings, the troops pushed on. Two miles to the northeast was another low rise topped with a second hamlet to which the horsemen had retreated. Deploying into line, the riflemen fired a few shots. One of the rider's sabres was shattered by a rifle bullet, in a flurry of feathers, a hen another had trussed to the side of his saddle was killed and when the rifles fixed their sword bayonets and charged the hussars fled once more.[43] The Light Brigade marched on to a third hamlet on a third rise where they halted for the night. After organising a string of pickets, Holland and Craufurd retired to a three-room hut. 'We contrived to make a tolerable supper about 9 o'clock,' the former recalled, 'after which we smoked cigars, and then wrapping ourselves in our cloaks lay upon some skins [and went to sleep]'.[44]

Two miles to the rear, Lumley's brigade had occupied the second hamlet which the Light Brigade had passed earlier in the afternoon. Having marched all the way from Ensenada, the men of the 36th and 88th were exhausted.[45] They had already eaten the three days' rations they had landed with, so Lumley ordered the *peónes* William Pius White had supplied to round up some cattle. Lassoed and dragged into camp, their throats were slit with 'a stream of gore and foam' and bloody sides of beef were doled out along with a half ration of spirits. Whilst the officers packed into the abandoned huts, the troops tore up the railings the locals had used as cattle enclosures and made fires to cook the meat. Afterwards, they slept in the open covered by blankets and greatcoats hoping the rain would hold off for another night.[46]

Back at Ensenada, Lieutenant-Colonel Bourke had had another frustrating day supervising the ongoing disembarkation of guns, horses and stores. Guarded by four companies of the 40th under Major Donald Campbell, Rear-Admiral Murray's sailors had rowed back and forth throughout the afternoon. Enough spirits, bread and salted pork to last the army three days were landed, as were all the guns remaining on board intended for the mobile batteries aside from the two 5.5-inch brass howitzers which Frazer now considered surplus to requirements. Also disembarked were the army's entire complement of horses and mules. Including those of a few troopers already inland, there were 320 of the former and thirty-six of the latter, which Whitelocke had purchased in Monte Video from a supercargo bound for the Cape. 'Before sunset everything [was] landed that could be conveyed'. After ordering Campbell's four companies to march inland at dawn with the guns and as many provisions as they could carry, Bourke made his way to Ensenada to find somewhere to sleep for the night.[47] That evening the creole hussars probed the British encampments. 'One of them advanced right up to the bonfires [of the Light Brigade]' and, 'having observed them, fired a carbine volley' and rapidly withdrew. Whipping through the dark, the bullets killed one sentry and wounded another. The British returned fire and Captain Nicolls discharged his two 3-pounders into the night.[48]

Before dawn on 30 June Commissary-General Bullock, in charge of the supplies landed at Ensenada, prepared to march inland. 'The greatest difficulty was experienced in getting any of the horses to bear the pack-saddles', he recalled. Used to living wild on the *pampas*, the horses bucked and kicked and threw off their burdens. Several escaped. The rest were eventually persuaded to carry the army's supply of 17,000 pounds of biscuit. The spirits landed the day before were loaded onto two small carts and hitched to the mules and the column, accompanied by Major Campbell's four companies, ten guns under Captain James Hawker of the Royal Artillery and 200 sailors under captains Josias Rowley and John Joyce of the Royal Navy, set out at daybreak. On reaching the swamp the march deteriorated into farce. The mules got stuck and the spirits were unloaded. Some casks were staved in. Others sunk into the mire. Just one was salvaged and carried back to the beach. The horses were also having difficulties. Plunging and kicking they threw off their burdens. Several more escaped and all but 250 pounds of biscuit was lost. Watching the charade from the heights above, Captain Frazer authorised Hawker to abandon his heavier guns. The four Spanish 6-pounders were duly spiked and their carriages smashed and allowed to sink into the mud. '[I] gave my consent', Bourke recalled, 'supposing Capt. Frazer to write by the Genl's order.'[49]

Meanwhile, the commander of the 5th, Lieutenant-Colonel Humphrey Davie, had had a stroke of good fortune which would go some way to compensating for the supplies lost in the swamp. Having set out before daylight from his camp on the heights on a foraging party, Davie had come across a herd of 'about 4,000' sheep.[50] Whilst the find resolved the issue of meat supply, the men still lacked biscuit and their all-important spirit ration and, to make matters worse, before all the sheep could be butchered, let alone cooked, Whitelocke ordered the troops to march.[51] Leaving Colonel Mahon with five companies of the 40th and a few dragoons at Duval's house to wait for Captain Hawker's arrival, the rest of the Main Corps set out across the heights, following in the tracks the Advanced Corps had made the day before.[52] During the march, Captain Wilkie observed Whitelocke's behaviour with amusement. 'Our chief would often dismount, march in among the sections, and talk to the soldiers about their kits, their tots, grub, and soft tommy', he recalled. '[This] occasioned some surprise at first; but I soon saw that the fellows "smelt a rat," – and I could observe some of them walking cheek-by-jowl with their general, with their tongues in their cheek an evident symptom of not liking gammon.'[53]

As the lead elements of the Main Corps reached the second hamlet, Lumley's troops advanced, leaving behind the half-butchered remains of the cattle their *peónes* had caught that morning. The 45th halted, while the 87th detached from the Main Corps to join Lumley's march, taking up position in the rear of the 36th and 88th. At the head of Lumley's column was Captain Frazer with the four 6-pounders of the 2nd Artillery Battery. Following the previous day's exertions, Lumley's troops were glad of the late start. Although they had not had a chance to cook their beef, the delay had allowed a small ration of liquor to reach them and the men were in high spirits. 'We advanced ... over one of the finest plains I ever beheld' Captain George Monkland of the 36th recalled. 'The prospect [was] only bounded by the horizon, except [for] an occasional eminence on view of the river on our right ... this day's march was good, but still we experienced the inconveniences of being wet, having to ford two *arroyos*. The Advance had some skirmishing with ... [some mounted] *ladrones* (Robbers) which infest the country in gangs'.[54]

The 'Robbers' were the Escuadron de Labradores y Quinteros, a body of 300 light cavalry armed with lances, knives, lassos, long-barrelled muskets and pistols led by Lieutenant-Colonel Antonio Luciano de Ballester, whom Liniers had ordered to relieve Rodríguez's Hussars. A former rancher in his early sixties who owned a *patisserie* a few blocks from the Plaza Mayor, Ballester had recruited his men from amongst the peasants of the *pampas*. They proved more effective at the guerrilla tactics Liniers required than the young gentlemen of the hussars and were particularly adept at lassoing British stragglers.[55] On the afternoon of 30 July Lieutenant Robert Crosse of the 36th had a narrow escape. 'Being a short distance in the rear a fellow ... rode him down and threw the snare at him, which fortunately only knocked off his hat' Captain Monkland recalled. The creole tried again, 'but just as the noose was falling over [Crosse's] head, he ... threw it off with his sword' and ran for the protection of the British column. 'The horseman snapped his pistol at him, [but] missed, and being nearly within shot of the rear-guard, after this failure, rode off.'[56] Two of Colonel Mahon's Reserve Brigade were less fortunate. Having waited all morning for Captain Hawker's guns to reach him, Mahon had decided to make camp at Duval's farm. Two privates and a corporal of the 40th took advantage of the delay to loot 'an Indian Hut' on the outskirts. Fully occupied, they failed to notice the approach of Ballester's men until it was too late. The corporal was lassoed round the neck, dragged off and butchered and one of the privates knocked down and killed with knives. The other escaped 'after receiving a sabre-wound which carried the skin and hair off the back of his head. This [incident] was a great glory to the natives', Private Lawrence recalled. 'They stuck the corporal's head on a pole and carried it in front of their little band when on the march'.[57]

Ten miles to the northwest, Craufurd's Light Brigade had had an uneventful day. After a routine morning reconnaissance, the brigadier-general had received a dispatch from Gower obliging him to await Lumley's brigade before marching and it wasn't until 2.30 pm that they moved out. 'We were ordered to advance four or five miles;' Holland recalled, '[but] after having advanced between two and three, we were stopped by two small streams running parallel to each other along our front'. Informed he would be unable to arrive at the next set of huts before nightfall, Craufurd called a halt. 'There was a small dirty, abandoned cottage on the left of our outposts', Holland recalled, 'in which we passed the night after making a hearty supper on the provisions we [had] brought with us in our canteens'.[58]

At dawn on 1 July, Holland was ordered to throw a bridge over the streams. At 9.00 am Gower and the lead elements of Lumley's brigade arrived and the whole Advanced Corps moved out as a single body.[59] After crossing the streams and mounting the crest of a rise beyond the far bank, the rifles in the vanguard encountered a detachment of enemy horsemen and several shots were exchanged.[60] These skirmishes continued throughout the day and at one point two men of the 95th were nearly killed. 'One had actually the noose about his neck', an officer recalled, 'when his companion shot the fellow, and saved his ... life. The other ... had only time to get upon his legs when he beheld his brave preserver "*lasooed*," ... he fired, and repaid the obligation by knocking the man off his horse'.[61] An artilleryman was also attacked. 'A Dragoon or two were despatched' to aid him, but the enemy stabbed him and rode off before they could get within carbine range.[62]

After two miles the column was brought to a halt by the arrival of Whitelocke and a gaggle of mounted staff officers.[63] '[He] came to us full of doubts and difficulties', Holland recalled, '[and] appeared not to know what to do'.[64] Whitelocke was in a quandary. Concerned that indiscriminate slaughter was contrary to his orders, he was unhappy with the plan to bombard the city, but had no fixed alternative.[65] '[The] General ... took me aside', Craufurd recalled, '[and explained] that he had thought of detaching a part of the army towards the higher part of the Chuelo, in order to turn the position in which he understood the enemy had entrenched himself on that river, whilst the rest of the army should advance against that position, and that General Gower agreed with him that it was an advisable operation.' Craufurd warned Whitelocke against dividing the army and the lieutenant-general 'ended the conversation with saying, "Well, I think you are right."'[66] Unsure of his own judgement and reluctant to follow his subordinates' advice, Whitelocke was in an uncomfortable position: his army was about to make contact with the main body of the enemy, yet he still had no definite plan.

After an hour Whitelocke and his escort rode back to the Main Corps, leaving Gower with orders to march on Reducción, seven miles to the northwest. 'We were delighted to get quit of him and advance', Holland recalled.[67] For Captain Monkland, to the rear with the 36th, the march was a delight. There was 'incredibly fine ... herbage' and the abundance of wildlife was remarkable. 'Notwithstanding the exertions that had been used to drive the cattle out of our reach, herds innumerable were to be seen and horses gregariously plunging over the plains. The space above [was] filled with birds of every species, game of all descriptions, from the pheasant to the snipe, and peacocks, turkeys, [and] geese'. As the afternoon wore on the mist lifted opening up a heartening view of Murray's fleet at anchor off Quilmes Bay and a mile before Reducción the men were further cheered when the spires of Buenos Ayres broke the horizon.[68] Of more concern was a plume of smoke spotted to the northwest, which Colonel Pack believed indicated that the Spanish had fired Galves Bridge.[69] His assumption was incorrect. The smoke was actually coming from the brig *Dos Hermanas* and the *zumaca Reconquista*, which the Cabildo had fired to prevent them falling into British hands.[70] Galves Bridge was still intact and remained central to Liniers' plans. Having ordered Colonel Elio's Blue Division to encamp on the north bank on 29 June, the Frenchman spent the afternoon and evening of 1 July moving the rest of his army up to join them.[71]

At 3.00 pm Gower's Corps reached the outskirts of Reducción. Built on a low hill surrounded by ploughed fields, the hamlet consisted of a number of 'detached houses of inferior quality' clustered round a simple church.[72] 'Here the enemy [cavalry] had formed themselves in some irregular figure', Captain Monkland recalled. 'More resembling columns than anything else; they were divided in two parties in number perhaps 200 ... An order was given to form column of Companies right in front, and in this manner [we] advanced over the ploughed field'. Using their long muskets, the enemy opened fire while the redcoats were still out of range. Gower ordered Captain Frazer to unlimber one of his 3-pounders and return fire. Once three round shot had been sent hurtling across the field, the Light Brigade opened into line and charged through the gun smoke. The enemy mounted and scattered to the north.[73] Craufurd's men pursued them for two miles before halting by a Dominican convent on the edge of a band of marshy ground where they made camp for the night.[74] 'We took our quarters in a chapel on the left flank' Holland recalled. '[It was] the best [quarters] we had met with: there was not only the Chapel room, but a large house, all a ground storey connected with it.' Two miles to the east, the 36th and 88th were still on the march. As they passed through Reducción, several collapsed with exhaustion. Assigning a guard to remain in the village and protect them, Gower pushed on and at sunset made camp midway between the last of the houses and Craufurd's position. 'The 88th [were] in the rear of the 36th [who] were thrown back in echelon', Monkland recalled. 'On the right flank were ... the Grenadiers ... Our left was covered by a dwelling and flanked by small pickets which communicated with those of General Craufurd's brigade'. Gower commandeered the house and a number of sheep were found in the grounds. Although there was no bread or spirits, combined with a supply of wheat Craufurd's men had uncovered, they proved sufficient to feed the entire corps.[75]

Meanwhile, Whitelocke's Main Corps had made camp in Reducción. The dismounted 9th Light Dragoons and Carabiniers had suffered terribly on the march. Unused to slogging it out on foot with the infantry, the troopers were exhausted. At dusk Lieutenant-Colonel Bourke arrived. After organising a supply of beef to be delivered to the men, he met Lieutenant William Blight, a Royal Navy officer from HMS *Nereide*, whom Rear-Admiral Murray had sent ashore at Quilmes to organise the landing of some supplies. '[He] was directed to have a quantity of spirits & biscuits sent ashore in the morning', Bourke recalled. Later a dispatch arrived from Gower explaining that he had made camp two miles away and that he believed the enemy had burnt Galves Bridge. Whitelocke decided 'to reconnoitre the Enemy's position on the Riachuelo' at dawn. The lieutenant-general was still unsure as to his plan of attack, but informed Bourke that he intended to halt for a day to allow Mahon's Reserve Brigade to join them. Within hours he would change his mind yet again. Amongst the reasons for his vacillation was the weather.[76] Overhead, the storm clouds were gathering. If they burst overnight and Galves Bridge had indeed been destroyed, the only means of reaching Buenos Ayres – a series of fords over the Riachuelo (the Paso de Zamora, the Paso Chico and the Paso Burgos) – would grow increasingly difficult to cross.[77]

That night the temperature plummeted and there was thunder, lightning and heavy rain. Knowing his army was unlikely to hold firm in open battle, Liniers marched across Galves Bridge, deploying 300 metres beyond the south bank. It was a desparate measure. With their backs to the Riachuelo, the militia would have to fight. If they were defeated, however, British victory would be total. The Red Division took the right flank, the White Division took the left and the Blue Division held the centre. The heavy guns, including a formidable masked battery of brass 24-pounders, were dragged into position by seventy oxen; gunboats were anchored in the river; several buildings were pulled down to clear the field of fire; and at sunset the infantry practiced volley fire with live ammunition. Despite the weather and a lack of tents and provisions, morale was high. '[The men] endured with the greatest constancy', one witness recalled, 'the Officers who went the rounds hearing on all sides nothing but expressions of confidence and alacrity during the night.' Liniers' second, General Velasco, was considerably less confident. Having little faith in his men's ability, he thought Liniers' decision to deploy with the Riacheulo at his back was suicide.[78]

That evening the Quinteros were replaced by a unit of hussars who made probing attacks throughout the night.[79] Particularly bothersome were the antics of Michael McCarthy, the Irish trumpeter who had joined the Spanish after deserting from the 71st. Riding upwind of the British positions, he played a series of alarm calls causing chaos in the camps.[80] 'We were twice under arms during the night', Monkland recalled: 'the first ... occasioned by the drums of the 88th ... in consequence of the firing kept up by the pickets'; the second due to 'a great sound of the galloping of horses', believed to signal an enemy attempt to retake Reducción.[81] One mile to the north, having polished off a bottle of 'liberated' wine, Lieutenant George Miller had fallen asleep in 'a great-leathern armchair' in the Domincian convent when one of the enemy's skirmishers passed by the sentries unnoticed. 'He then remounted,' Miller recalled, 'rode handsomely into the very centre of our picket, around the watch fire in the middle of the court-yard, and got clear off before the alarm could be given. He did it neatly,' the lieutenant conceded, 'and we gave him credit for his adroitness.'[82] Twelve miles to the south Mahon's Reserve Brigade also encountered the enemy. Whilst leading a foraging party, Lieutenant Jason Lloyd of the 17th Light Dragoons was lassoed by an Indian who burst out of the darkness. 'Fortunately', Private Lawrence recalled, 'he had the presence of mind to ride after him and ... managed to cut the lasso with his sword.'[83]

At 2.00 am, during a heavy shower, Whitelocke had another change of heart. Calling for his military secretary, Lieutenant-Colonel Francis Torrens, he dictated a dispatch ordering Gower 'to advance that morning ... [,] feel his way over the Chuelo at any place he might find it practicable above the bridge, [and] to take a position on the [northern] ... suburbs of Buenos Ayres'. The major-general was also instructed to 'communicate with the shipping, and ... send ... a summons to the Spanish General [to surrender]'. The dispatch concluded with a vague promise that the Main Corps would come to his support.[84] Both Torrens and Lieutenant-Colonel Bourke reminded Whitelocke of the folly of dividing his troops and urged him to stick to his previous plan – reconnoitring the enemy before advancing with the entire army on 2 July. '[We] earnestly endeavoured to dissuade him', Bourke recalled, 'but in vain'. Whitelocke had finally made up his mind.[85]

Bourke delivered the dispatch at first light. Gower was 'much dissatisfied' with Whitelocke's orders. Lumley's brigade was in no state to march – the 88th were 'nearly knocked up' and the 36th were in little better condition. Having thrown away their blankets on the previous day's march by Whitelocke's order, they had endured a miserable night. 'I wished ... [Gower] to communicate to the Genl. on the subject', Bourke recalled, 'in hopes that the measure might be abandoned altogether'. Gower refused. Although he disagreed with the plan, he had received a direct order and at 8.00 am broke camp. Reaching Craufurd an hour later, the Advanced Corps moved out in a single column. After a hurried conference between Gower, Craufurd and William Pius White, they marched northwest to within sight of Galves Bridge before wheeling left at 10.30 am and proceeding along a line of high ground running parallel to the Riachuelo.[86]

Liniers' morning had started well. Dawn had seen the Frenchman riding up and down his lines 'animating his soldiers with the watch-word "Saint Jago and victory"'. With his cavalry reporting the enemy en route, it appeared that Whitelocke would offer a pitched battle, but at 10.30 am the red-coated column veered off to the southwest instead of filing down to the river. By the time he realised that they intended to outflank him, Liniers had lost the initiative and decided to split his forces to counter the move. The Reserve Division was left to guard the bridge with the heavy artillery, the cavalry were sent up the south bank to find a suitable position to hold up the enemy advance, Balbiani's Red Division were ordered to shadow Gower by marching along the south bank behind them, while Liniers led Velasco's White Division and Elio's Blue Division back across the Riachuelo in an attempt to reach the western outskirts before the British arrived.[87]

Seven miles to the southeast, Whitelocke was writing to Rear-Admiral Murray. As well as appraising him of the change of plan, he requested that he have the heavy guns and the rest of the provisions ready to land to the north of Buenos Ayres where the army would re-establish contact with the fleet. A dispatch was also sent to Colonel Mahon desiring him to march to Reducción and take charge of the supplies that Murray had already landed. Leaving the dismounted Carabiniers and 9th Light Dragoons at Reducción with Major William Gwyn of the 45th and 300 others who were too exhausted or sick to continue, Whitelocke broke camp at 10.30 am.[88] Following a local guide, he took a looping line of march to the southwest, intending to trace the tracks of the Advanced Corps, but on cresting a rise at midday, as the skies cleared, it became apparent that the two columns had diverged. '[We] saw [Gower far in the distance] ... moving more to the [north]westward' Bourke recalled. '[The guide] explained this by saying that when we had crossed the Arroyo de Masiel ... that we should move more [north]westwards likewise.' After an hour spent wading through a marsh, it was clear that the guide was mistaken and once they had reached dry ground a second halt was called.[89] Whitelocke had a decision to make. The lieutenant-general was inclined to camp for the night, but Lieutenant-Colonel Bourke was vehemently opposed. For a moment Whitelocke 'seemed wavering', but then referred the matter to Brigadier-General Auchmuty. '[Whitelocke] observed that the guide had deceived him', the American recalled, 'that the ford of the Chuelo was still, by his account, many miles off; that there was no chance of reaching it before dark; that he had secured cattle for the troops; and that where he then was there was a sufficiency of fire-wood to cook the meat.' Auchmuty thought Whitelocke's decision sound. Gower was in no danger so long as he did not advance into town (a stipulation that Whitelocke had made in his orders), the men would benefit from a rest and a good meal, and the American could see no harm in making the attack one day later than planned.[90] After despatching an order to the Reserve Brigade telling Colonel Mahon to wait in Reducción until he received further instructions, Whitelocke gave the order to make camp.[91]

Five miles to the north, the Advanced Corps had made good progress. Three miles after wheeling to the left, Balbiani's Red Division had been spotted shadowing their march. The 36th formed column on the right flank to counter the threat and Gower ordered the men to press on. With Captain Frazer's two 3-pounders leading the line and Major Travers' riflemen skirmishing ahead against bands of enemy horsemen posted 'on every eminence, at every house and in ambush at every enclosure', they soon left Balbiani's men behind, prompting the Spaniard to give up the pursuit and march back to Galves Bridge. After traversing another three miles of marshy ground crisscrossed with shallow streams, the Advanced Corps descended into the Riachuelo Valley where 600 enemy horsemen had formed up on a stretch of dry land. The Spaniards' position was a strong one. A copse guarded their right flank and their left was anchored on a marsh bordering the river. Ordering the rifles to clear the wood, Gower formed the Light Brigade in line while Lumley's brigade (the 36th and 88th) formed column on their right. Once the copse had been secured, Captain Frazer rolled two 3-pounders and one 6-pounder to the front and opened fire. Watching from the treeline, Lieutenant George Miller noted that the sailors working the guns 'enjoyed the fun exceedingly. I observed one of them with seven canteens slung about him', he recalled. 'He looked like the planet Saturn, with his . . . satellites.' After three round shot had bounded across the plain, the horsemen dispersed. The route to the Riachuelo was open.[92]

Moving on, the Light Brigade reached a large marsh where their guides pointed out a track passing obliquely to the right leading to the Paso Burgos. 'After some consideration', Holland recalled, 'Gen. Gower determined that Gen. Craufurd should advance with his brigade, to . . . gain the Pass . . . if he succeeded, Gen. Lumley should follow'.[93] After two miles, the Light Brigade reached the brook. 'There was not a Spaniard near it', Lieutenant Miller observed with delight. Thirty yards across, and swollen by the recent rains, the Riachuelo proved the most formidable obstacle the men had faced since the swamp at Ensenada. Carrying their cartridge boxes and firearms above their heads, they waded across up to their waists in the icy torrent, struggling to keep their footing on the gravel bottom. Captain Frazer's guns had to be unlimbered and carried across. The ammunition boxes were taken by infantrymen who balanced them on their heads, whilst others hefted the cart over on their shoulders.[94] Soon the Light Brigade had formed on the far bank. 'The men cheered', Holland recalled, 'and could hardly be restrained from boisterous expressions of delight.'[95] As Lumley's brigade staggered into view, Major Robert Travers reported that a 'considerable body' of the enemy had been spotted several miles away by one of his riflemen. Formed in column, they appeared to be making for a height one mile distant, which overlooked the road to Buenos Ayres. Keen to reach the position before them, Craufurd received permission from Gower to push on. Advancing over a fine meadow, the Light Brigade left Frazer's guns and Lumley's men behind them.[96]

The enemy Travers' riflemen had spotted were part of Elio's Blue Division. Unable to match the speed of the Light Brigade's advance, the Spaniard had become bogged down on the north bank of the Riachuelo and decided to return to the centre of town. Liniers' advance with the White Division had been little better. Unused to the rigours of a forced march and having to drag several guns along tracks churned up by the recent rains, his militia struggled to cope. Hundreds dropped out and by the time Liniers reached the western suburbs, only 1,000 men and eleven cannon remained. Learning that the enemy had already taken the Paso Burgos, Liniers positioned his troops in Corrales de Miserere, an open slaughteryard on the road to Buenos Ayres three miles to the west of the Plaza Mayor. Bordered by several large *quintas* surrounded by fruit orchards and enclosed with tall, dense hedges of prickly pear, it made an ideal defensive position. Liniers divided his cannon into two batteries. The first, one 12-pounder, one 8-pounder and a 6.5-inch howitzer, was positioned on a slight rise covering the road from the ford. The remaining seven guns, cannon of between 8 lbs and 4 lbs in calibre, were lined up behind a prickly pear hedge on the far side of the slaughteryard. Two infantry battalions (the Vizcainos and Arribeños) and a squadron of hussars were in close support. Formed in line, they were divided into two wings on either side of the second battery.[97]

One mile to the southwest, as Craufurd's Light Brigade gained the height they had seen from the river, a messenger arrived from Gower with orders to halt. Craufurd disobeyed. 'The day was so far advanced, and the state of the operation so critical, I took the liberty . . . to proceed'. The enemy's skirmishers grew more numerous as the Light Brigade advanced and although they 'kept at a respectful distance', a rifleman named Fraser 'tumbled one of them' with a long shot from his Baker rifle. '[He] passed the body unnoticed,' Lieutenant Miller recalled, 'but one of those who came after undid his sash . . . [and] found fifty-two doubloons.'[98] As the Light Brigade entered the suburbs, the enemy fire ceased. Craufurd recalled his skirmishers and advanced in a tight column a section wide down a narrow road flanked by ditches and hedges of prickly pear. After winding to the left, they reached William Pius White's house, a large building marking the town's western boundary, when General Gower appeared and ordered them to halt whilst Lumley's brigade came up with the guns. Although they were just a quarter of a mile from Liniers' first battery, 'not a Spaniard was in view', dusk was rapidly approaching and 'many of the men leaned up against [the wall of White's] house, for a little ease'.[99] As Gower and Craufurd discussed their next move a shower of grape shot and musketry came scything through the hedges. 'The men shrunk' back and for a moment it seemed as if they might rout until Craufurd took control. 'Gower said something to me', the brigadier-general recalled, '[which] I understood ... as an order to attack ... and immediately obeyed.' Commanding the Light Battalion to form line on the lead company, Craufurd advanced against the enemy's centre, while Captain George Elder's rifle company swept round their flank. The light troops lost cohesion as they dashed through the hedges and gardens, but the cover prevented the enemy from seeing them until it was too late. The first battery was overrun in an instant. Charging out of cover and up a slight rise, the 'light bobs' and riflemen bayonetted any who opposed them. The rest of the gunners fled back to their main line in the square. As Craufurd's men emerged into the open with the setting sun behind them, the Spanish infantry and second battery opened fire. Two dozen men were cut down. The rest of the shot flew overhead and the British began firing rolling musket volleys in reply. At first the Spaniards resisted. The Vizcainos Regiment maintained a 'lively fire' and at one stage Juan Pio de Gana, the Basque commander of the Batallón de Arribeños, advanced from the right wing and attempted to outflank Craufurd's line. Dozens fell on both sides, but when de Gana was killed by the shockwave of a round shot passing within inches of his stomach and Elder's company began pouring repeated volleys into the Spaniards' flank, they routed.[100] Closely pursued by the Light Brigade, the left wing broke towards the centre, whilst the right fled to the northwest and scattered into the countryside beyond town.[101]

The pursuit was chaotic. The light troops and riflemen hunted the enemy with their bayonets and Liniers concealed himself in a farmhouse. Others hid in the cellars beneath Piedad Church, while a few continued to offer resistance. Captain George Elder of the 95th was shot in the groin by a group of holdouts hidden in a trench and at 7.30 pm Craufurd called off the pursuit. Having chased the enemy for half a mile, the Light Battalion had reached the crossroads of Camino de las Tunas with Calle Torres. A few hundred metres west of the fort, the area was dominated by two large houses and an extensive peach orchard lay to the south.[102] Some of the troops started looting and near Piedad Church several warehouses were broken into. With their owner, José Estarraquero, watching impotently from a nearby house, the soldiers stole Sevillian snuff, Brazilian tobacco, Paraguayan cigars, paper and playing cards.[103] While Craufurd and his officers attempted to regain control, Captain Squire of the Royal Engineers galloped up with orders from Gower. Craufurd was to fall back to Corrales immediately. Cursing his superior's caution, Craufurd sent Brigade-Major Campbell to inform Gower that nothing lay between his troops and the centre of town and that a decisive victory was within his grasp. As Lumley's brigade arrived and formed on Craufurd's right, a definitive order was returned. Reasoning that the enemy might cut off the British wounded, Gower refused to be swayed. Still Craufurd insisted and Gower was obliged to appear in person to ensure his orders were obeyed. Leaving three companies of the 95th under Major Thomas Gardener to hold the crossroads,

Craufurd reluctantly withdrew at 8.00 pm. His men picked their way back past the enemy dead, cursing Gower with every breath, and took up positions in the buildings round the slaughter-yard.[104]

The encounter had cost the British fourteen dead and forty-two wounded.[105] Major Robert Travers of the 95th had been shot through the shoulder and Captain Elder was carried immobile from the field.[106] Spanish losses were considerably higher – 100 had been killed and a similar number taken prisoner. Many of the wounded were hospitalised at La Residencia where a team of twenty surgeons worked through the night.[107] The survivors were scattered over several miles. Liniers' men had also lost two ammunition carriages for field pieces, one for small arms, numerous muskets and ten guns, all of which fell into British hands.[108] Two bakehouses filled with enough fresh provisions to last the entire army two days were also captured and a tilted waggon loaded with bread taken by Captain William Parker Carrol of the 88th was particularly well received.[109]

In and around the slaughter-yard, the Advanced Corps settled in for the night. The Light Brigade occupied the houses along the eastern edge of Corrales, Craufurd and his staff holed up in a nearby chapel, while Lumley's men remained exposed in the square. 'The position in the military point of view was advantageous,' Holland recalled, 'in every other [it was] detestable. The ground was covered with putrid offals, and the stench they sent forth was horrible.' Gower forbade the men from lighting fires. Unable to cook the bloody hunks of beef and mutton they had carried from Reducción, the troops passed another night with empty stomachs.[110] Sleep was rendered impossible by howling packs of dogs that prowled the lines and at 2.00 am an electrical storm began. 'The rain descended in torrents, accompanied by an exceedingly heavy fall of hail', Captain Monkland recalled. 'The repeated peals of thunder [were] ... the most tremendous I have ever heard [and] in a few moments all were drenched to the skin'. In this 'deplorable state [we] remained "biding the pelting of the pitiless storm," and anxiously looking out for ... dawn.'

Chapter 16

The Western Suburbs

Buenos Ayres
3–4 July 1807

When the downpour ceased in the small hours of 3 July, Lieutenant George Miller saw a 'corpulent person' come out of a building beyond his position with the rifle picket at the crossroads. '[The stranger] kept looking [back and] ... muttering to himself' the lieutenant recalled. 'I called out to him to surrender; upon which he took to his heels'. Miller's riflemen opened fire, 'but in the dark' the stranger got away.[1] As the lieutenant later learnt, the stranger was none other than Santiago de Liniers.[2] Having spent several hours hiding under a stretcher, the Frenchman had decided to escape past British lines. Heading northwest with General Velasco, he reached the village of Colegiales before dawn and took shelter in a farmhouse. By morning 500 of his men had joined him. Having sent a unit to Los Olivos to meet the marines returning from Colonia, Liniers composed a letter to the Cabildo detailing 'the disgraceful combat' at Corrales. With less than 2,000 troops between the enemy and the centre of Buenos Ayres, he presumed the capital was already lost.[3]

News of Liniers' defeat caused chaos in town. Spilling into the streets, the survivors of the left wing spread word that the British were hot on their heels and several senior officers panicked. Colonel Elio dismissed his men and scribbled a message to General Balbiani, urging him to abandon his position at Galves Bridge, while Francisco Agustini, commander of the artillery, galloped off to the suburbs to escort his wife to safety.[4] Several soldiers followed his lead. Throwing away their arms and uniforms they hid before the British arrived. The Cabildo, on the other hand, remained calm. A meeting of senior officers and councillors was held in the Sala Capitular and Martín de Álzaga began preparing the defence.[5] His plan was based on an idea which Liniers had previously rejected. Abandoning the suburbs, Álzaga would pool all the troops in the Plaza Mayor and draw the redcoats in after him. Once the enemy had committed to the narrow streets where their superior training and discipline would be nullified, the Spaniards would counterattack, destroying them or forcing them to surrender.[6]

The first step was to fortify the Plaza Mayor. At 5.30 am the general alarm was sounded and a message sent to Galves Bridge ordering the men of the Red and Reserve Divisions to spike the heavy cannon and fall back to town. On their arrival, the cobblestones were prised up to build barricades at the corners of the Plaza Mayor. Directed by Captain Azopardo, the Maltese privateer who had sailed with Mordeille, the men topped the fortifications with sandbags made from bullock-hides, leather sacks stuffed with *yerba mate*, and bales of wool. At 6.45 am Colonel Elio, having reformed his division, arrived. 24-pounders were dug in around the Plaza Mayor, a pair of 16-pounders positioned in each of the surrounding streets and the street lamps and barrels of pitch were lit to prevent a surprise attack. Cattle were driven into town and corralled in the fort's ditch and food, wine, *aquardiente*, arms and ammunition were stockpiled in the Plaza Mayor. Some 2,000 troops were assigned to defend El Retiro and others were ordered to hold La Residencia on the far left wing. The citizens also mobilised. Men and women armed themselves with knives, muskets, homemade grenades and clay pots filled with flammable pitch and took up positions on the rooftops. Hundreds of slaves were pressed into service, issued with fourteen-foot pikes topped with knives and organised into units. A second line of defence was established three to four blocks from the Plaza Mayor on Calles Santa Lucia, San Miguel and Santo Domingo. The 3rd Regiment of the Patricios manned strongpoints in the Rancheria Barracks, in houses near La Merced and San Francisco churches and along Calle San Miguel. The Andalucians held a house near San Miguel Church, the Arribeños were stationed around La Merced Church and several of Rodríguez's Hussars were spread out around the perimeter. Others, including the Miñones and a number of private citizens, made their way to the western suburbs to harass the British lines. Shortly before dawn Captain Francisco Agustini returned. Having escorted his wife to safety, he took command of the guns in the fort.[7]

The morning of 3 July dawned with fresh breezes, dark cloud and rain.[8] First light revealed the unburied victims of the previous evening's fight at Corrales lying amidst discarded offal that had been rotting for several days.[9] Later 'a naked Spaniard' was spotted running out of the chapel where Craufurd and his staff had spent the night. 'This caused an investigation', Holland recalled, 'and we found fifty of them ... armed in the building. They were frightened and laid down their arms.'[10] Meanwhile, Captain Frazer was ordered to cover the open space in front of the British lines and the roads leading to the Plaza Mayor with the captured cannon, while the guns brought from Ensenada were installed in the two large houses at the crossroads which had been occupied by Craufurd's advanced guard.[11] At dawn Captain Philip Keating Roche, Lumley's Brigade-Major, rode into town with 'a verbal summons' for Liniers' surrender. Accompanied by a flag of truce, a corporal of the 17th Light Dragoons and a trumpeter, Roche stopped at the crossroads where Major Gardener, whose riflemen had been fired on throughout the morning, lent him an officer and twelve privates for further protection. 'We proceeded with some difficulty', Roche recalled. '[There was] considerable firing' which increased in volume as the column picked its way forward. A quarter of a mile from the centre, after passing numerous armed bands holed up in fortified houses, they were stopped by a Spanish officer commanding an advanced guard. A message was sent back, and, after a 'considerable time', Colonel Elio arrived. He forbade Roche from visiting Liniers 'on any account', but promised that if he had 'any written communication ... he would convey it to him'.[12] Roche returned to Corrales, asked for a formal summons from Gower and made his way back through enemy lines.[13] This time a Spanish aide-de-camp received him. Whilst Roche waited for a reply, the Spaniard pressed him for details of the battle at Corrales. 'I took care not to diminish [it]' Roche recalled, '[and] told [him], with truth ... that they had lost a considerable number'.[14] After an hour and a half Elio's written reply arrived and Roche made his way back to Gower. The journey was the most perilous of all. 'All description of people, men and boys, were armed, and all drunk ... they paid very little respect to the flag of truce, and but for the rifle corps I am sure I could not have got back', Roche recalled.[15] Elio's reply held no surprises: 'Nothing relative to the laying down of our arms will be attended to ... [We have] a sufficient number of brave troops, commanded by brave chiefs, full of desire to die in defence of their country'.[16]

At 1.00 pm, 'under a heavy shower of rain', Liniers returned from Colegiales to cries of 'Long live the King!' and 'Long live our General!' Humbled after the battle of 2 July, he made only minor changes to Álzaga's plan. Trenches, twelve feet wide and nine feet deep and backed by barricades of bullock-hide sandbags, were dug across the main streets one block from the Plaza Mayor; a number of 12-pounders were sent to the Residencia; and the garrison at El Retiro was bolstered by the marines who had returned from Colonia, a company of Galician Grenadiers (part of the Tercio de Gallegos and led by Captain Jacobo Varela) and a company of Patricios, bringing the total number of defenders on the right wing to 2,500.[17] Juan Gutiérrez de la Concha was put in command. He placed half of his troops in the bullring, while the rest manned two mortars and twenty-seven cannon, ranging from 6-pounders to 36-pounders, positioned around the park.[18] That afternoon Bishop Benito Lué y Riega conducted an open sermon at El Retiro. Speaking to 'an immense congregation', he reminded the *porteños* that it was God's will that the British be defeated and urged those who had thrown away their arms to rejoin the fight.[19]

At 2.00 pm Whitelocke's Main Corps reached Corrales. Having broken camp at daybreak, they had spent all day marching through the rain and crossing the Riachuelo at Paso Chico.[20] After consulting Gower and Craufurd, Whitelocke established headquarters in William Pius White's house, one mile behind the front line.[21] A field hospital was set up in the same building and John Mawe, the English geologist turned military guide, was given command of the provost's guard and ordered to prevent the troops from looting the neighbourhood *pulperias*.[22] Under severe pressure ever since the landing, Whitelocke was beginning to crack. Chief amongst his delusions was the belief that his subordinates were plotting against him and that Gower was trying to usurp his command. A symptom of this paranoia was unprovoked attacks on his junior staff. Shortly after his arrival, he summoned Captain Squire of the Royal Engineers and Captain Frazer of the Royal Artillery to White's house to vent some steam. Even though he had permitted them to join Gower's advanced column during the march, he now felt it had been a betrayal. 'There was a long conversation, in which the General expressed himself with warmth on the subject', Squire recalled, 'and directed me not to hold as much communication in future with General Gower.'[23]

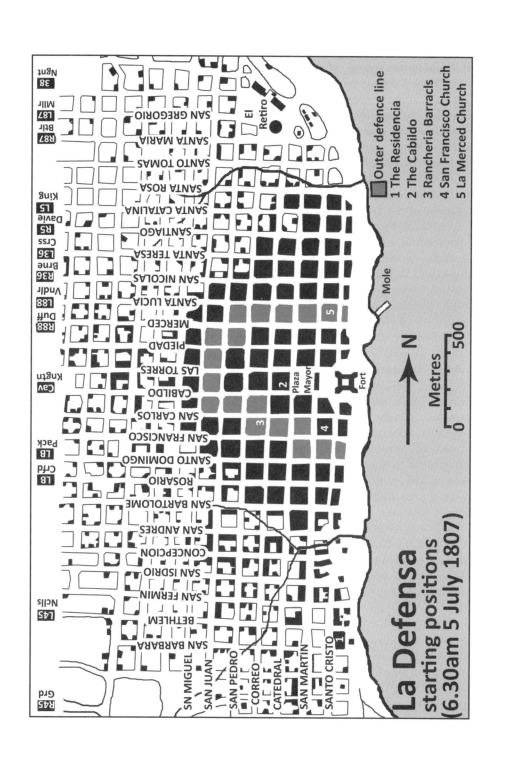

La Defensa
starting positions
(6.30am 5 July 1807)

Outer defence line

1 The Residencia
2 The Cabildo
3 Rancheria Barracls
4 San Francisco Church
5 La Merced Church

N

Metres
0   500

SAN GREGORIO
SANTA MARIA
SANTO TOMAS
SANTA ROSA
SANTA CATALINA
SANTIAGO
SANTA TERESA
SAN NICOLAS
SANTA LUCIA
MERCED
PIEDAD
LAS TORRES
CABILDO
SAN CARLOS
SAN FRANCISCO
SANTO DOMINGO
ROSARIO
SAN BARTOLOME
SAN ANDRES
CONCEPCION
SAN ISDRIO
SAN FERMIN
BETHLEM
SAN BARBARA
SN MIGUEL
SAN JUAN
SAN PEDRO
CORREO
CATEDRAL
SAN MARTIN
SANTO CRISTO

El
Retiro

Mole

Fort

Plaza
Mayor

38 Ngnt
187 Mlir
R87 Btlr

L5 King
R5 Davie
L36 Crss
R36 Brne
L88 Vndlr
R88 Duff

Cav Kngtn

LB pack
LB Crfd

L45 Nclls

R45 Grd

By the time of Whitelocke's arrival, the skirmishing at the outposts had been continuing for five hours. Lieutenant-Colonel Holland thought the enemy 'short, ill made, square figures, of a dark complexion', while reluctantly conceding they were 'remarkably good marksmen'.[24] Lieutenant George Miller, with Major Gardener at the crossroads, had to agree. 'I never saw the French shoot so well as they did', he opined many years later having fought his way from Roliça to Waterloo. 'Any one exposed for a single minute, at a range of two hundred yards, had no chance ... whatever.' Miller put the Spaniards' success down to their long-barrelled muskets. Twice the length of the British Brown Bess, they were cumbersome and slow to reload, but deadly accurate.[25] Private Patrick Desmond of the 2/95th and three men of the 88th were killed that day and the grenadier company of the 36th lost half a dozen.[26] Manning an advance post with one of Captain Frazer's guns, Captain Alexander Williamson charged an enemy cannon commanding a square to his front. The Spaniards were ready for him. As the grenadiers broke cover 'a dense shower of grapeshot ... tore the ... [grenadiers] to pieces'. Williamson and four others were killed and Lieutenant Wingfield 'severely' wounded.[27]

The Spaniards also suffered. The 95th killed several with their Baker rifles and on the left of Gower's line Captain Joshua Crosse and 'nine or ten men' of the 36th 'drove a body of horse, 150 strong, near a mile from the lines'. The redcoats 'killed two and wounded the officer who commanded them.'[28] At 3.00 pm Whitelocke ordered his centre to entice the enemy out of cover. Lumley's men concealed themselves in the peach orchard, while Craufurd's Light Brigade fell back to some heights beyond Corrales. 'The idea was, that ... the enemy ... would ... kindly come down to the place where we lay in waiting', one of Lumley's officers explained. All but a handful failed to comply. 'They were too ill-natured, or too knowing, to fall into so egregious a snare' and 'in the course of a quarter of an hour' the plan was abandoned. One of the few to fall into the trap 'was so indignant at [the thought of] being taken ... that he took a flying leap down a deep well'. At 4.00 pm the Light Brigade and pickets returned to their former positions. Auchmuty's men were ordered to hold the left of the line and Lumley's covered the right.[29]

At 5.00 pm Gower rode to the rear to propose a plan of attack he had been working on to Whitelocke.[30] The lieutenant-general was glad of the advice. With his troops committed to the western suburbs and having abandoned the scheme of bombarding the town from El Retiro, he was all out of ideas. Gower's plan was fiendishly complex. It involved attacking the town centre with the army divided into thirteen columns, each consisting of between 250 and 600 men. On the right, the 45th would advance in two columns on La Residencia, while the 38th, now led by Lieutenant-Colonel John Nugent following Colonel Vassal's demise, was assigned to take El Retiro on the far left. The rest of the columns, with the exception of the 6th Dragoon Guards, or Carabiniers, whose attack towards the heavily fortified Plaza Mayor was a feint, would advance up the streets assigned to them until reaching the river while Whitelocke, Gower and their staff remained at Corrales with a small reserve. Having reached the water's edge the troops were to break into any buildings suitable for defence with pickaxes and sledgehammers which would be supplied and await further commands. Gower stressed two particulars. Firstly, that the men advance with fixed bayonets and unloaded muskets – if they could stop and shoot at the enemy, the attack could become bogged down. Secondly, it was imperative that no column deviated from its given route and under no condition were they to directly engage the bulk of the enemy in and around the Plaza Mayor. Although Whitelocke accepted the plan, it was flawed on three counts. Firstly, it defied one of the principal maxims of war – never to divide one's forces in the face of the enemy. Secondly, it was incomplete. No plan for actually defeating the *porteños* was provided – the men were instructed to take up positions in enemy territory like islands in a hostile sea and wait for victory to materialise. Lastly, it surrendered the key advantage the redcoats enjoyed. While their discipline and training ensured them success in the open field, the urban battlefield was a great leveller.[31]

On various occasions before, during and after 'a bad scrambling dinner' at White's house that evening, Bourke, Torrens and Craufurd all had ample opportunity to express their doubts about Gower's plan. But whilst Bourke mentioned that it was 'a very novel kind of attack' which would 'be attended by the loss of a great many lives', and Torrens pointed out that with the 'weather having set in to rain' speed was of the essence, none raised any major opposition. Several believed the plan a poor one, but no one offered an alternative and no one seriously thought it would result in defeat. The officers' self-belief, bolstered by racist contempt for the enemy, made anything but victory inconceivable. The sole exception was Colonel Denis Pack.[32] Having been bested by the *porteños* before, he saw Gower's plan would lead to disaster. As a colonel and field officer, however, Pack's opinion carried little weight and when his chance to speak finally came 'something ... attracted the General's notice', Whitelocke 'rather abruptly broke off the conversation' and the moment was lost.[33]

Agreeing to a final briefing the next morning, the officers were dismissed and Craufurd, Pack and Holland returned to their quarters in the chapel at Corrales. 'The night was terrible', Holland recalled. '[There was] violent thunder, lightning and rain [and] I contrived to lose myself ... and wandered about in the dark, over bogs and ditches [for] two or three hours.'[34] At the front, beef, biscuit, mutton and liquor were distributed and despite the efforts of John Mawe, several *pulperias* were broken into and quantities of *aquardiente* and 'country wine' unearthed. A number of men became inebriated and, in a few cases, their officers lost control. 'Such a scene I never before witnessed', one captain recalled. 'Everything eatable and drinkable went to destruction', livestock was slaughtered, butchered and cooked, houses were looted, furniture was broken and burnt, and the men began 'halloing, laughing and [making considerable] noise!' Several civilians were caught up in the chaos. A number of women were raped. A few were murdered and a handful of children were also killed.[35]

On the morning of 4 July Whitelocke opened the briefing by announcing he would attack at midday. 'General Gower ... then proceeded to point out in the map his plan', Brigadier-General Lumley recalled. No significant changes had been made to the proposal of 3 July. The officers made copies whilst Gower fielded their questions. 'I ventured to ask what was to be done in case we met with greater opposition than we had reason to expect', Lumley recalled. 'I was told ... we were to possess ourselves of the houses, defend ourselves and await further instructions'.[36] Later, Whitelocke took Brigadier-General Craufurd to one side. '[He told me] that he felt so much reluctance in adopting a measure which must be attended with so great an effusion of blood ... that he had determined to send another summons to the Spanish General'. Craufurd felt the move a mistake: 'I told him ... that they would consider it as betraying a want of competence on our part', he recalled.[37] Whitelocke then asked Gower for his opinion, but when the major-general expressed similar doubts, Whitelocke exploded with rage. 'He said I was throwing cold water upon everything he did', Gower recalled, '[that] he considered me his declared enemy, and that he would supersede me from the situation I held'.[38] At 10.30 am William Pius White delivered a briefing. He informed the British officers that they were opposed by 6,000 men with numerous heavy cannon entrenched in the town centre. '[He also told us] that the enemy would surrender if we gained a position on each flank,' Lieutenant Colonel Torrens recalled.[39] What both White and Whitelocke remained ignorant of was that an outer defensive cordon had also been established. The British troops would not learn of the screen of heavily defended outposts running round Calles Santa Lucia, San Miguel and San Francisco until they blundered into them.[40]

At 11.00 am Whitelocke dismissed his staff and invited his brigadier-generals and Colonel Pack to express their opinions.[41] Auchmuty pushed for delaying the attack until the morning of 5 July. 'I apprehended that there would not be time [enough] to communicate ... [the plan] to ... [the men] ... and make the necessary arrangements for carrying it into action' the American recalled. 'I also observed ... that mid-day was an improper time to march through the streets of a populous city, ... [and] conceive[d] we should penetrate further, without serious loss, if we deferred the attack till day-break'.[42] Pack spoke up in Auchmuty's support. 'I remarked ... that from the turrets of Buenos Ayres the enemy would distinctly perceive every movement that we made'. After some discussion, the revision was agreed, although Gower only conceded with the utmost annoyance. Pack was desperate to point out the plan's more serious flaws, but understood from the second-in-command's demeanour that he would be wise to hold his tongue 'and the conference broke up with orders for the attack to take place ... the following morning.'[43] Whitelocke had the plan duplicated and copies delivered to each brigader-general. Those prepared for Craufurd and Pack by Lieutenant-Colonel Holland omitted one key paragraph. The officers of the Light Brigade would go into combat unaware of Gower's stipulation that under no circumstances were they to veer off their given path and attack the Plaza Mayor.[44]

Despite Craufurd's and Gower's counsel, Whitelocke was determined to give Liniers one final chance to surrender. After the officers had returned to their posts, he ordered Captain Samford Whittingham, one of his numerous aides, to take a final summons into town. Although fired on from several windows and rooftops, Whittingham made it to the Spanish advanced guard where an artillery officer despatched the summons to Liniers.[45] The Frenchman was busy inspecting the positions round the Plaza Mayor. At each gun emplacement he offered a few words of encouragement before moving on. On receiving Whitelocke's letter, he went to the town hall and called for a translator, but deemed it unworthy of a reply. Continuing his tour, he warned his men the attack would be coming soon.[46]

At noon Lumley's troops were ordered to replace the Light Brigade at the outposts.[47] The skirmishing had been intensifying throughout the morning, the Spaniards were growing in confidence and Sergeant Richard Blincowe of the 1/95th and Private Richard Richards of the light company of the 40th had been killed.[48] Without the 95th's Baker rifles to keep the enemy at bay, Lumley's brigade was badly mauled. 'On the march we were much annoyed by the prickly pear hedges', one officer recalled, 'and the enemy ... opened on all sides from bushes, houses, and every place that afforded the least cover, a continued and very handsome fire.'[49] Trained to exchange volleys on the open field, the 36th had no answer to the *porteños*' tactics. Several, including Lieutenant William Cotton, were wounded, others were killed and the survivors forced to abandon their positions on the left of Lumley's line.[50] As they fell back, Captain Joshua Crosse was wounded by a rifle shot whilst providing covering fire.[51] Occupying the houses left vacant, the Spanish and creoles were able to enfilade the flank and rear of the 88th. Captain Andrew Blake's company was particularly exposed. Privates Carrol, Faircloth and Flanagan were killed and several others wounded before Blake pulled back. The Spaniards remained in the position until one of Captain Frazer's 6-pounders was rolled forward to oppose them. After a few round shot had punched through the abode walls, they withdrew.[52]

To the left, Auchmuty's Brigade had also come under heavy fire. The 87th suffered the worst of it and privates John Donovan and John Grant were killed before Auchmuty received orders to fall back.[53] Whitelocke had decided to make another attempt to draw the enemy into an ambush. After withdrawing some distance, the men lined up behind a thick hedgerow through which several large holes had been cut to enable them to charge should the enemy make an appearance. 'At one time from the shouts that were heard, we eagerly expected their ... arrival', an officer recalled, '[but] they ... soon changed their intention and ... retired ... to their old system of warfare.' The ploy foiled once more, the troops reoccupied their old positions and the skirmishing continued as before.[54] Forty-seven British soldiers, including a captain and five subalterns, had been killed or wounded in the fighting so far and three others were listed as missing.[55]

At 5.00 pm the senior officers and staff, guided by William Pius White, rode out to inspect their starting positions for the attack. '[We] found much variance between the plan & the ground', Bourke recalled. '[I] reported [this to Gower and warned] ... that it was probable the Columns would not all be placed exactly as he wished ... and also stated ... that all communications ... would very soon be cut off by the enemy closing on their rear ... [but he] made light of these objections'.[56] After nightfall Gower visited the 45th, while the brigadier-generals on the left of the line briefed their field officers.[57] A few even added some extra details to the written orders. Having learnt of the presence of the San Miguel Church, one block to the south of the right wing of the 88th's line of advance, Brigadier-General Lumley advised Lieutenant-Colonel Duff to take possession, despite this being contrary to Gower's order that no column was to deviate from its given path.[58] The brigadier-generals then applied to headquarters for the pickaxes and sledge hammers mentioned in the plan. 'By this time it was dark,' Auchmuty recalled. 'Frequently ... it was reported to me that attempts had been made to obtain the tools without success.' Realising he could not rely on his superiors, Auchmuty had his men search the houses and several suitable implements were found.[59] Major Henry King of the 5th was also having difficulty. Eventually, a few of the regimental pioneers' tools were requisitioned and 'a crow-bar and a mattock or two' were found.[60] At headquarters Whitelocke was writing a circular letter imploring his brigadier-generals 'to impress on ... those under their command the necessity of desisting from violence towards unarmed men, women and children'.[61] He also dispatched a note to Colonel Mahon in Reducción instructing him to march with the Reserve Brigade to Galves Bridge.[62]

At midnight the Carabiniers and 9th Light Dragoons arrived from Reducción and were sent to relieve Lumley's brigade at the outposts.[63] The men of the 36th and 88th were delighted to retire and made short work of a meal of meat, wine, 'and a little biscuit'.[64] At 2.00 am they bedded down under their greatcoats, but would get little sleep that night. 'On a sudden the joyful intelligence arrived that we were to storm the town before daylight', one officer recalled. Most celebrated the news, congratulating each other that their sufferings were nearly over and that they would soon be masters of a foreign town. Others took the opportunity to wish their comrades luck, while the officers of the 87th argued over who would be left behind to command the baggage guard. With the quarter-master employed on the general staff, the task fell to Lieutenant Michael Barry. A 'high-spirited young man', Barry begged Lieutenant-Colonel Butler to allow him to fight. Butler conceded and the regiment's longest-serving sergeant, William Grady, was assigned the task in his stead.[65]

Chapter 17

The Battle of Buenos Ayres

Buenos Ayres
5 July 1807

At 5.00 am the men were shaken awake. Leaving their greatcoats, knapsacks and colours in the cantonments, they formed up shivering in the streets outside. It was pitch black and eerily silent.[1] The sun would not rise for two hours and cloud blanketed the moon.[2] Having left a section to guard their possessions, each of the fourteen columns was led to the starting line thirteen blocks to the west of the river. The men slipped and stumbled through the darkness. The unpaved streets were slick with mud and had been cut up by rain. By 6.00 am all but one of the columns were in position. As Colonel Peter Kington's dismounted dragoons got lost in the dark, the brigade commanders toured the lines. Offering whispered words of encouragement, Auchmuty, Craufurd and Lumley urged their men to make good use of their bayonets. As Auchmuty joined the right wing of the 87th on Calle Santa Maria, he heard several men cursing Whitelocke's name. The redcoats hated going into battle with unloaded muskets. Fourteen blocks to the south in Calle Santo Domingo, Colonel Pack's men were also worried. With the sky beginning to lighten across the river, they were anxious to move out before being fully exposed.[3]

On Calle Merced Lieutenant-Colonel Duff, in command of the right wing of the 88th, was particularly nervous. The second son of the Earl of Fife, Duff had seen action in the West Indies and Eygpt, but had never fought in the confines of a city before. Three of his ten companies had been ordered to remain at head-quarters as guards, and following the trials of the march from Ensenada, the remainder were seriously under strength. Looking at the 200 figures huddled round him in the gloom, he realised he was in desperate need of reinforcement. At 6.30 am his prayers seemed to be answered when two companies under Major William Iremonger appeared. Gower had sent them forward from White's house, but had ordered them to remove the flints from their muskets. Duff couldn't believe it. Glancing at his watch, he commanded Iremonger to round up as many spares as he could find. One block to the north Major Richard Vandeleur was in command of the regiment's left wing. As he was waiting for the signal cannon to fire, it suddenly occurred to him that his orders seemed terribly vague and when Brigadier-General Lumley passed by he asked him if he could be any more specific. '[Lumley] replied that he knew no more than I did,' the major recalled.[4] Meanwhile, as Kington's dismounted dragoons continued to blunder about in the dark searching for their starting position, one and half miles to the west Whitelocke was having doubts of his own. Lieutenant-Colonel Bourke heard him muttering that he was unhappy with the plan and had been forced to adopt it. 'Not seeing how this could be the case,' Bourke recalled, 'I made little or no reply'.[5]

At 6.35 am Captain Frazer fired the three signal cannon. The powder in the firing tubes fizzed through to the main charge and the cannon belched flame across the slaughter yard.[6] Moments later two round shot came down on the outskirts of the Plaza Mayor throwing clods of mud over Azopardo's gun emplacements. The third crashed through the western window of the Cabildo and into the packed chamber of the Sala Capitular.[7] On Calle Merced Lieutenant-Colonel Duff gave the order to move out. Several of Major Iremonger's men were still without flints. Cursing Gower, they put their trust in their bayonets. One block to the north, Major Vandeleur's wing advanced in a column seven men wide. The major was struck by how quiet the town was.[8] 'The utmost silence reigned' and even the dogs were quiet, he recalled.[9] On Calle Santo Domingo, Lieutenant-Colonel Pack had the same sensation. '[The peace was] only interrupted by a few random shots fired from a distance' he recalled. At the head of Pack's 600 a section of volunteers under Captain Brookman of the 71st 'heard ... voices in several of the houses'. Torn between investigating and pushing on, Pack decided momentum was of the essence.[10] The hidden enemy detachments allowed him to pass.

Commanding the left wing of the 5th in Calle Santa Catalina Major Henry King had an early sighting of the enemy. Some Spaniards were struggling to manouvere four cannon a few blocks ahead. As King drew closer, the Spaniards spiked the guns, shot the horses harnessed to them and fled down a side street. Without even pausing to claim the cannon, King rushed on.[11] Four blocks to the south on Calle Santa Lucia, Major Vandeleur of the left wing of the 88th saw two Spanish vedettes. 'As I approached, they retired down the street, occasionally looking up, as if speaking to people in the windows and tops of the houses', he recalled. As Vandeleur reached their position, the hidden Spaniards and creoles opened fire. The major ordered his men to quicken their pace. They cheered and ran on. As well as the musketry, grenades, stones, bricks and clay pots filled with flaming pitch were hurled from the rooftops. Several of the 88th were shot in the head, shoulders and neck. Others received shrapnel wounds in their calves and thighs and a few were badly burnt.[12] One block to the south, Duff's column was also taking casualties. With the leading men fifty yards from San Miguel Church, militia hidden on the flat roof tops to their left opened fire.[13]

Elsewhere, the advance was unopposed. In Calle Rosario Brigadier-General Craufurd saw nothing 'but small straggling parties of the enemy' who fell back before him; the 45th, advancing in two columns under Lieutenant-Colonel William Guard and Major Jasper Nicolls, met but trifling resistance as they moved on the Residencia; to the north both wings of the 5th and 36th had similar experiences; and the 38th received nothing more than a little musket fire from the roof of the Quinta Zuloaga, a large house on the northwest corner of El Retiro. Indeed, Captain Wilkie thought the greatest difficulty the 'muddy clay' of the

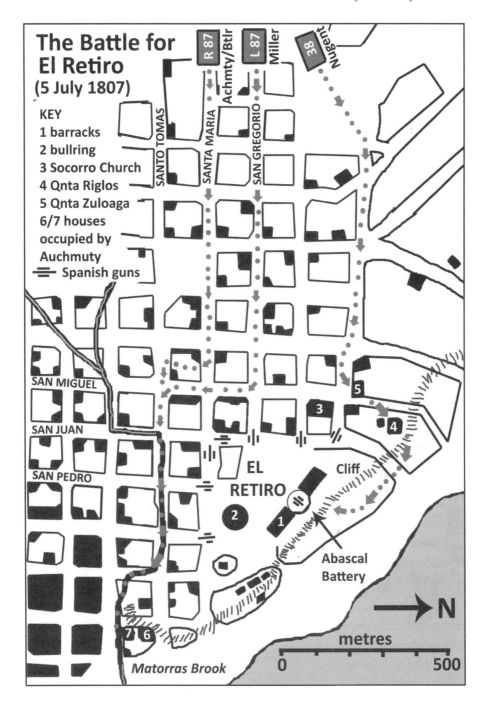

The Battle for El Retiro
(5 July 1807)

KEY
1 barracks
2 bullring
3 Socorro Church
4 Qnta Riglos
5 Qnta Zuloaga
6/7 houses occupied by Auchmuty
Spanish guns

R 87
Achmty/Btlr
L 87
Miller
38
Nugent

SANTO TOMAS
SANTA MARIA
SAN GREGORIO

SAN MIGUEL
SAN JUAN
SAN PEDRO

5
3
4

EL RETIRO
2
1

Cliff

Abascal Battery

N

metres
0   500

Matorras Brook

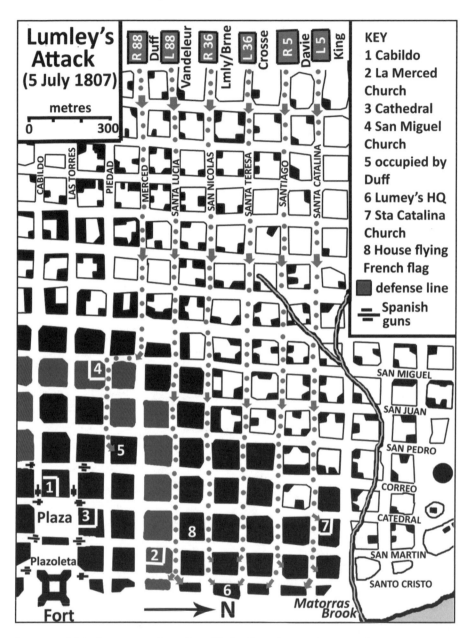

lane up which they were advancing. '[It had] such tenacity as to draw a great part of the men's shoes off their feet', he recalled.[14]

A few hundred metres to the south both wings of the 87th had also begun their advance unopposed, but after a third of a mile the peace was shattered by two 24-pounders in El Retiro. 'The day had not sufficiently dawned to see any objects at a distance, [when] we were suddenly assaulted by a discharge of grape'

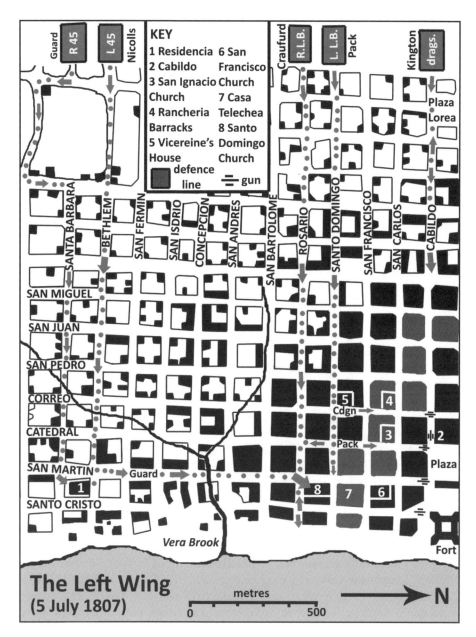

KEY
1 Residencia
2 Cabildo
3 San Ignacio Church
4 Rancheria Barracks
5 Vicereine's House
6 San Francisco Church
7 Casa Telechea
8 Santo Domingo Church
⬛ defence line ⚊ gun

Guard R 45 L 45 Nicolls

Craufurd R.L.B. L.L.B. Pack

Kington drags.

Plaza Lorea

SANTA BARBARA
BETHLEM
SAN FERMIN
SAN ISIDRIO
CONCEPCION
SAN ANDRES
SAN BARTOLOME
ROSARIO
SANTO DOMINGO
SAN FRANCISCO
SAN CARLOS
CABILDO

SAN MIGUEL
SAN JUAN
SAN PEDRO
CORREO
CATEDRAL
SAN MARTIN — Guard
SANTO CRISTO

5 Cdgn
4
3
2
Pack
Plaza
8 7 6

Vera Brook

Fort

The Left Wing
(5 July 1807)

metres
0   500
N

Auchmuty recalled. The tightly-packed columns were devastated. Single grape shot hit men in the front rank before tearing on through those behind. Limbs were ripped off, whole files decaptitated, skulls smashed and chunks of flesh punched from torsos. Dozens died, their bodies 'thickly strewed' about the muddy lane for 'some hundred yards'. The King's colour was shredded with grapeshot and the entire front section of the grenadier company, leading the right wing, was cut down by the first discharge. Lieutenant Michael Barry, the officer who had begged to take part the night before, was the first to die. Captain David Considine was also killed and Captain Alexander Rose was struck by three shot, one of which tore out his left eye.[15]

Some 300 metres to the north, the 38th also came under heavy fire. As they neared the northwest corner of El Retiro, the troops on the roof of the Quinta Zuloaga fired a concentrated volley against them. One officer and several men were killed. As the breeze whipped away the gun smoke to reveal the Spaniards reloading, Captain George Elrington of the detached grenadier company of the 47th rushed the main door. Yelling for his men to follow, he smashed it down and raced up the stairs. Several grenadiers were felled by a final volley. The rest burst onto the flat-topped roof. The seventy Spaniards they found were bayonetted to a man.[16]

On Calle Santa Maria the right wing of the 87th was being cut to shreds. As well as the grape shot scything through their ranks, they had come under long-range musket fire from the Spanish Marines positioned in the upper tiers of the bullring. The rear of the British column began returning fire. Several hit their own men and 'at length [the column] began to hover and fall back'. While Lieutenant-Colonel Butler attempted to rally them, Auchmuty hit upon a solution. Cutting a hole in the hedgerow to his right, the American ducked into the garden beyond. 'Follow me my brave lads', he called out. 'The day is ours'. The redcoats took his lead. Running through the garden they broke through the hedgerow on the far side and emerged into Calle Santo Tomas.[17]

Ten blocks to the south, the central column, composed of the dismounted Carabiniers, the 9th Light Dragoons and a pair of 6-pounders, had only just set off. Delayed by Colonel Peter Kington having missed his way in the gloom, they advanced down Calle Cabildo at 7.00 am. Positioning one of his guns at the head of the column, Kington left the other behind with a squad of thirty men. Despite his orders not to fully commit, the lieutenant-colonel was determined not to miss out on the action.[18] A few blocks to Kington's north the 5th and 36th were nearing their destinations. With the river within musket shot they remained virtually unscathed. Only Captain Joshua Crosse of the 36th, the officer who had distinguished himself on 3 July, had been slightly wounded. On the far right the 45th had already achieved its principal aim. Forced to take a detour on the advance, Lieutenant-Colonel Guard had arrived at the Residencia shortly before 7.00 am to find the left wing, under majors Nicolls and Tolley, had arrived three minutes before. Their men had dispersed an enemy party with a single gun positioned in front of the building and were breaking down the main gates. Once inside the redcoats killed or captured all those inside. Two companies were assigned to hold the Residencia, four took up positions in nearby houses and one was detached to sweep the area for sharpshooters. The entire operation had taken a little over half an hour and been achieved with the loss of just seven men. With Major Nicolls more than capable of controlling the situation alone, Guard set off with his grenadiers for the centre of town. Jogging one block up Calle

Santa Barbara they turned right on Calle Catedral hoping to join up with Craufurd's men.[19]

On the other side of the Plaza Major the 88th was having more difficulty. At the corner of Calles San Miguel and Piedad, Lieutenant-Colonel Duff tried to force his way inside San Miguel Church. With the gate wide open, the redcoats poured into the courtyard, but the church doors were barred from the inside. As the sergeants pounded on them with their sledgehammers, the Andalucians and Patricios positioned in the buildings around them opened fire from murderously close range. In the confines of the courtyard, the redcoats had nowhere to hide. Dozens were hit in the head, neck or shoulders. The heavy wooden doors resisted all the sergeants' efforts and the fleeting figures tormenting them offered little at which to return fire. Corpses soon lay heaped around the porch and the courtyard grew slick with blood. After thirty of his men had been hit, Duff 'deemed it prudent' to move on. Racing out of the gates into a hail of small arms fire, he turned east down Calle Piedad.[20]

Some 200 metres to the northeast in Calle Santa Lucia, Major Vandeleur and the left wing were also taking heavy casualties. When they crossed Calle Correo, a 16-pounder set up on the corner of Calle Torres discharged grapeshot into their right flank. As the dwindling band rushed on, Vandeleur noticed one of Major Iremonger's men struggling to fit a flint to his musket. A hidden marksman shot him dead. Crossing Calle Catedral the column was struck by a second discharge of grape, killing several men and one officer, and the survivors were confronted by an ominous sight. The enemy had erected a breastwork of bullock-hide sandbags blocking the path to the river 100 yards ahead.[21]

Meanwhile, Colonel Pack's column had halted at the corner of Calle Santo Domingo and Calle San Martín. As the troops at the rear caught up, the colonel discussed his next move with his second, Lieutenant-Colonel Henry Cadogan. 'Hearing firing to my left, and seeing nothing of the enemy in my front, or any post to occupy ... we agreed [to advance on the centre of town]'. Due to Lieutenant-Colonel Holland's error, Pack was about to throw his men at the heart of the defences despite Gower's intention that they stay clear of the Plaza Mayor. Telling Cadogan to take the rear half of the column and the 3-pounder north along Calle Correo, Pack took the rest on a parallel course up Calle Catedral. A wave of fire erupted as they advanced. With the lead section of Cadogan's troops, Private Todd of the 71st saw Captain Brookman fall. '"Mind your duty, my lads onwards, onwards, Britain for ever!" were [his] ... last words'. Cadogan urged the rest of the Glaswegians on. 'Down the Gallogate, my boys! Charge them!' As the British neared Calle San Carlos a regiment of Patricios stationed in the Rancheria Barracks fired a volley into their left flank, other militia and private citizens opened up from the surrounding rooftops and a 16-pounder discharged grapeshot into their front. 'On a sudden the whole of the leading company ... and every man and horse at the gun, were either killed or disabled", Cadogan recalled. Abandoning the 3-pounder, he ordered the survivors to fall back. They retreated to the corner of Calle Santo Domingo chased by the cheering Patricios, broke into two buildings and took refuge inside.[22] On Calle Catedral Pack was also facing stiff resistance. One and a half blocks from the Plaza Mayor, an enemy volley killed or wounded the entire lead section. Pack had his coat torn by five musket balls and was lightly wounded twice. Faced with overwhelming odds, the Scot ordered his men to take cover on Calle Santo Domingo while he ran to Cadogan's position to urge the lieutenant-colonel to retreat. Loathe to give up ground so dearly won, Cadogan refused. Pack left him to his fate, took seventy men and ran towards Calle Rosario to find Craufurd.[23]

Craufurd's advance, by contrast, had been straightforward. Having received no more than a smattering of musket fire on the approach, his men had been momentarily troubled crossing Calles Correo, Catedral and San Martín – swept with grapeshot by the 16- and 24-pounders in and around the Plaza Mayor – but negotiated them by splitting into small groups and dashing across the openings. At 7.30 am, as Cadogan's and Pack's men were being decimated just three blocks away, Craufurd was standing on the beach of the River Plate. Listening to the fire to his left, the brigadier-general decided it was time he entered the fray. Dispatching Brigade-Major Campbell to the Residencia with orders for Colonel Guard to support him with the 45th, Craufurd led his men back into town. 'I had not got far when I met Lieutenant-Colonel Pack', he recalled. The Scot was in a state of great agitation. For the second time in a year he had seen his men slaughtered by the *porteños* and urged Craufurd to fall back to the Residencia before he suffered the same fate. Craufurd refused. To retreat without having been fully engaged was unthinkable. Spotting the Santo Domingo Church one block away, he told Pack he was determined to take it.[24]

So far the British attack had had mixed results. On the far right, Major Nicolls and Colonel Guard of the 45th had occupied the Residencia. In the centre Craufurd's column and both wings of the 5th and 36th had reached the bank of the River Plate, but elsewhere the day was undecided. Pack and Cadogan's men had been decimated and forced to fall back from the Plaza Mayor; a few blocks to the north the 88th had suffered horrendously, but were still advancing, while on the far left of the line the battle for El Retiro was about to begin.

After breaking through the prickly pear hedge into Calle Santo Tomas, the right wing of the 87th had continued its advance. The fire from the guns in El Retiro and the Spanish marines in the bullring remained heavy. Dozens more were hit. Several, including a number of wounded officers, dispersed into the streets to the south seeking shelter. The rest pushed on to the corner of Calle San Juan where the Matorras Brook afforded some cover. Wading into the filthy water, Auchmuty led them to the River Plate where they broke into two large houses. The doors were breached and the troops took shelter inside. While the enemy in El Retiro fired on the buildings from the heights, the remains of the left wing of the 87th joined them. Having suffered equally from the cannon fire on their advance down Calle San Gregorio, Major Miller had also diverted to his right. He had since been wounded and disappeared with the colour party, but the remains of his column joined Auchmuty's men.[25]

Meanwhile the 38th continued its attack to the north of El Retiro. Having cleared the Quinta Zuloaga, Lieutenant-Colonel John Nugent charged the guns beyond. With no cover the attack was a bloody failure. Dozens were killed before Captain Wilkie pointed out an alternative – a path leading from the back of the *quinta* round the enemy's open right flank. Nugent gave his assent and Wilkie set off at a run with his grenadiers and a company of the line. After breaking through the hedgerow of prickly pear, the redcoats dashed through the orange grove where they were 'galled by an incessant fire of musketry' from the roof of the Quinta Riglos and a nearby outhouse. With the rest of the regiment covering them from the lane, the grenadiers broke down the door of the *quinta* with blows from their musket butts and cleared the rooftop, while a private 'who was always in scrapes, and of ... rather bad character', battered in the door of the outhouse alone. Partially forcing it open, he squeezed through the gap and rushed up the stairs, arriving 'alone, on the roof' to find 'fifteen' of the enemy 'fit for action'. The private bayonetted the first pair instantly. 'Several ... others threw themselves down, pretending death', while four gathered in a corner to counter-attack. As the private's comrades arrived and began searching those who had feigned death for hidden coins, the private rushed the quartet in the corner. 'He ... bayonetted one,' Wilkie recalled, and two others surrendered. The fourth took 'a leap off the house', but was bayonetted as he jumped. He died before he hit the ground.[26]

Six blocks to the south, Major King, leading the left wing of the 5th, had occupied the four corner buildings of the final block of Calle Santa Catalina. Ordering the regimental colour to be hoisted from the highest rooftop, he ran fifty yards to the south to get a clearer view, but began drawing fire from the Spaniards on the rooftops around La Merced Church. Slightly wounded, King ran back to his men to find they had taken several prisoners, amongst them John Smith, 'a soldier of the 71st' whom King 'concluded ... to be a deserter'. The major then detached two companies under captains George Clark and John Drury to communicate with Lieutenant-Colonel Davie in the street beyond. As they left, a number of casualties from the 87th arrived huddled around a single colour. Bloodied and bruised, with their uniforms hanging in tatters and the flag scorched and torn by grapeshot, they were a demoralising sight. Major Miller and Captain Rose, the latter's left eye socket a gaping hole, were amongst them. '[They] came ... calling for a surgeon', King recalled, 'stating that the 87th were dreadfully slaughtered ... and that Captain Considine and Lieutenant Barry of the grenadiers were killed.'[27]

At the intersections of Calles Santo Cristo, San Nicolás and Santa Teresa the 36th had also occupied a number of houses. Several of the enemy had been killed and dozens captured. Others flooded the nearby rooftops and opened fire. Leaving the majority of their men in the street below, Lieutenant-Colonel Robert Burne and Brigadier-General Lumley, in charge of the right wing, and Captain Joshua Crosse, commanding the left, sent detachments to the rooftops to return fire. '[They] scarcely ever [had] ... a better object to aim at than a hat, a bonnet rouge, [or] a glance through a loop hole, or window', Captain Monkland recalled.

Meanwhile, Lumley established his headquarters in a large two-storey house on the southwest corner of Santo Cristo and San Nicolás and ordered the King's colours raised. Sergeant Jackson of the grenadiers volunteered. Hoisting the flag on the most exposed corner, he ducked back inside. Aside from a single musket-ball which had torn through his jacket, waistcoat, braces and flannel shirt and grazed his chest, Jackson escaped unscathed. At the fort, four blocks distant, Captain Agustini's gunners loaded the three cannon they could bring to bear with round shot and grape and opened fire. The crews of two 24-pounders at the end of Calle Santo Cristo in the Plaza Mayor followed suit. Targeting a protruding corner, they attempted to knock Lumley's headquarters to the ground, but the round shot passed straight through the wattle and daub walls. One tore the legs off a British soldier. Another crashed through a room full of prisoners 'frightening the poor devils out of their lives.'[28]

At 8.15 am Lieutenant-Colonel Guard and the grenadiers of the 45th joined Craufurd in Calle Rosario. Bolstered by the reinforcement, the brigadier-general advanced on Santo Domingo Church, but on turning down Calle San Martín was forced back by a wave of fire. The enemy held a sandbag barricade at the end of the block. Others fired down from the nearby houses. Seeing a straightforward advance would cost him dearly, Craufurd ordered Lieutenant Robert Nickle of the 88th to break into some nearby houses with thirty men and return fire from the rooftops. The pickaxes Nickle had been issued proved inadequate. Half the party were hit and the lieutenant wounded before they forced their way inside. Having dragged the casualties under the cover of a nearby wall, the survivors raced up the stairs, dispatched the occupiers and opened fire on the barricade below. Meanwhile, covered by the Baker rifles of the 95th, the column's 3-pounder was manoeuvred to the corner of Calle San Martín. It 'was excellently served' and soon cleared the enemy from the barricade. The gunners then opened fire on the church's wooden gates. The first round shot broke them open in a shower of splinters and at 8.30 am Craufurd's men raced inside.[29]

On the far side of the Plaza Mayor the 88th's situation was deteriorating. Having abandoned his attempt to break into San Miguel Church, Colonel Duff advanced down Calle Piedad under an increasingly heavy fire only for resistance to intensify as he neared the Plaza Major. Citizens as well as slaves joined in the killing. Hunting rifles, grenades and homemade incendiaries were used and great cauldrons of boiling water were poured down upon them. 'Four grenadier officers being wounded; the major, the adjutant, and assistant-surgeon, being killed, and having lost ... from eighty to one hundred rank and file', Duff ordered his men to break open three houses on the right of Calle Piedad between Calles San Pedro and Correo. Desperate to get under cover, the sergeants set about the task with gusto. Sergeant-Major William Bone was wounded three times whilst breaking down one door, but continued attacking it with his pickaxe until he had forced his way inside.[30]

Three blocks to the northeast the left wing of the 88th was also in trouble. Confronted with the twelve-foot-high breastwork thrown up across Calle Santo Cristo, Major Vandeleur's men hauled themselves over the parapet and dropped into a six-foot ditch on the far side. Flanked by the 24-pounder in the Plaza Mayor and the militia manning the corner houses, the ditch was a death trap. Dozens were killed. The survivors boosted each other up under a 'dreadfully hot fire' and scrambled out. Others climbed upon the 'heaped bodies' of their fallen comrades, while Captain James Chisholme and his section sheltered in one corner to cover the rear. The rest ran down a short flight of steps to the river where Vandeleur ordered them to break into a single-storey house. Using their musket butts to splinter the heavy wooden doors, the survivors rushed inside.[31]

Two miles to the west, Whitelocke remained unaware of the carnage his troops were embroiled in. Pacing up and down Corrales, he spoke not a word to anyone and was particularly distant with his second-in-command. Having fallen out on 4 July, Gower and Whitelocke would barely exchange a word all day. At 9.00 am Whitelocke broke his silence to order Captain Whittingham and Lieutenant-Colonel Torrens to take forty-six light dragoons to the rear where several enemy horsemen had been seen 'hovering about'. Glad to have something to occupy themselves, Whittingham and Torrens left Whitelocke and Gower to their feud.[32] Meanwhile, captains Clark and Drury of the left wing of the 5th had reached Lieutenant-Colonel Davie's position and been sent to occupy Santa Catalina Church two blocks to the rear. The nuns cowered in the cellar while the redcoats looted the church and raised the King's colours on the tower. The sight prompted a cheer from both wings of the 5th. Major King's position, two blocks to the east, was becoming increasingly tenuous. Enemy guns at El Retiro and sharpshooters in the surrounding houses had been pouring on 'a galling fire' ever since he had raised his flag. Having had one man killed and two wounded on the rooftop in as many minutes, the major ordered the rest to kneel down. On the ground floor Assistant-Surgeon Hugh Bone had set up a temporary field hospital and was up to his elbows in gore. King's only hope was that the guns above him would be silenced. Several enemy bands had already run past his position fleeing from the fight for El Retiro. They were demoralised and easily captured by the parties King sent out to intercept them. It seemed as if the 38th were gaining the upper hand.[33]

Having taken the Quinta Riglos, Wilkie's two companies of the 38th sallied out of the back door. Cutting through the remains of the orange grove, they broke through the hedgerow on the far side and used the low ground beneath the cliff to work their way round the enemy's flank. On reaching the northeast corner of El Retiro, Wilkie ordered his men to attack the Abascal Battery. Rushing up the cliff, they charged the position with fixed bayonets. The sixty gunners barely had time to spike their cannon before fleeing towards a barracks beside the bullring. With the British hot on their heels they were unable to close the doors and the redcoats stormed inside. Only five of the gunners, taking refuge in the dungeon, survived. The rest were put to the bayonet. Wilkie's men then swarmed into El Retiro from the rear and charged the cannon that had been harassing the 87th and 5th throughout the morning. Spiking all but one of their guns, the crews fled. Several joined the Spanish Marines and Galician Grenadiers in the bullring. The rest surrendered or were hunted down, while Lieutenant-Colonel Nugent brought the other companies of the 38th into the action. Occupying the barracks and surrounding buildings, he raised his flag on the rooftop at 9.00 am and besieged the bullring from all sides.[34]

Two blocks to the southeast, the enemy had been attempting to drive Auchmuty and the 87th out of the houses they had occupied by the riverbank. The redcoats had held firm. Dozens of *porteños* had been killed and three guns and 100 men captured, and when the 38th silenced the guns in El Retiro, Auchmuty went on the offensive. Climbing the cliff behind the houses they had occupied, the 87th helped Nugent's men mop up the few pockets of resistance remaining, before turning their attention to the bullring. In the midst of the fighting, Billy Pitt, a young officer of the Royal Navy, arrived from HMS *Charwell*. Sent ashore by Captain Thompson to find out how the battle was progressing, Pitt made his way to El Retiro where he joined a company of the 38th taking cover behind a low wall. Having never witnessed a land battle before, Pitt was appalled: 'the heat was excessive; the roaring of cannons, the rattling of musketry, -shouts, -groans, -advancing, -retreating, -men falling, -and horrid shrieks [were] on every side. I never shall forget it ... The ground [was] strewed with Englishmen, Spaniards, and horses, tumbling one upon the other, and the blood of the whole [was] mingling into one stream.' Nearby, Lieutenant William Hutchinson of the 87th deployed the 12-pounder which the Spanish gunners had been unable to spike under the cover of the corner of a house from where it could bear on the bullring. With the aid of several privates of the 38th who had been instructed in gunnery whilst garrisoned in Ireland, Hutchinson loaded the gun with round shot and opened fire.[35]

Inside the bullring, the situation was desperate. De la Concha's men had been able to hold their own against the 38th, but when the 87th joined the fight and Hutchinson opened fire with the 12-pounder it became clear that the battle was lost. The round shot punched through the wood and brick walls and caused carnage inside. The Spaniards were running low on ammunition and there was no hope of relief. Some 250 men and ten officers had been killed or wounded and de la Concha had been hit twice. One bullet had broken his sword. The other had taken the top of his hat. Jacobo Varela, the captain of the Galician Grenadier company, was unwilling to give up the fight. Yelling 'For Santiago and Spain!' and 'Death before Slavery!' he sallied out of a side gate. Caught by surprise, the redcoats gave way. Several of Varela's men, including Lieutenant Cándido de Lasala, were cut down as they ran; the rest punched through the British cordon. Racing across the park to the southwest, they fought their way along Calle San Pedro and regained Spanish lines.[36]

Moments later de la Concha raised the white flag. Four hundred men, many of them wounded, were taken prisoner and Charles Dixon, a drummer who had deserted from the East India Company, was recognised by one of his former comrades. An epaulet was found in his pocket proving his guilt. Lieutenant-Colonel Nugent had the honour of accepting de la Concha's sword and at 9.45 am Auchmuty occupied the bullring with the 87th, the regimental colours were raised from the flag pole and the 38th were assigned positions around the perimeter. On his way back to the barracks Captain Wilkie met 'Corporal Mackay, a regular built Highlander' of his company carrying 'a sword well-stained in one hand and a pair of boots in the other. I asked him what he had been about' Wilkie recalled. Mackay replied that he had been 'putting all the wounded *out of pain*; and having seen that I had lost my shoes in the muddy lane ... had unbooted a dead Spanish officer ... however doubtfully acquired ... the boots fitted very well.'[37]

In Calle Cabildo Colonel Kington's column had come under heavy fire. Two 24-pounders hurling round shot from the fort were beginning to find their range and as Kington's men neared Liniers' outer defence line, the enemy infantry concealed on top of the buildings opened up and the dismounted British cavalrymen began falling fast. John and William Gun, two of three brothers in Captain John Baldwind's company, were killed and Colonel Kington was shot through the thigh. As he dragged himself into a side street, Captain Percy Burrell took command. When Burrell was mortally wounded moments later, Major George Pigot of the 9th Light Dragoons ordered the survivors to retreat. The enemy sharpshooters could not be seen let alone engaged, the round shot was ever more destructive and the houses impossible to break into with the tools the men had been issued. Sticking close to the sides of the houses to avoid the worst of the fire, the troopers fell back. Colonel Kington was left behind.[38]

Four blocks to the southeast Lieutenant-Colonel Cadogan's men were also in trouble. Having fallen back after the ambush at the Rancheria Barracks, they had broken into two buildings at the junction of Calles Santo Domingo and Correo. The main body, consisting of the lieutenant-colonel, twenty men of the 47th under Captain Robert Kelby, a section of the 36th, a handful of the 40th and 71st and a company of riflemen under Major Robert Travers, had installed themselves in the vicereine's house. The rest held out in 'a small dwelling on the opposite side of the street.' Making their way up to the rooftops, the Light Bobs and greenjackets returned fire. Initially the Baker rifles kept the enemy at bay, but by 10.00 am several of Saavedra's Patricios and a few hussars under Martín Rodríguez had worked their way into a commanding position in the twin towers of the San Ignacio Church. With British casualties mounting, discipline deteriorated and several men began looting. One sergeant mananged to fill his wooden canteen with stolen coins, only to be shot through the head 'as he came out ... The canteen burst' as it hit the cobblestones, Private Todd recalled, 'and a great many doubloons ran in all directions'. Eighteen men dashed into the open to gather the money, but all were picked off by the sharpshooters above. With his position untenable, Cadogan ordered an officer and ten men to contact Craufurd. If the brigadier-general could send reinforcements, they might just get out alive.[39]

Back at Corrales, Whitelocke's apprehension was growing. Although the sound of the fighting carried above the rooftops, he still had no idea of what was going on and at 10.00 am instructed his aide, Captain Foster, to investigate. Picking his way through the suburbs subjected to scattered fire, Foster and his escort of six men came across several Carabiniers and light dragoons retreating down Calle Cabildo. On meeting Captain Henry Davenport, Foster suggested they fall back to Plaza Lorea and the troops installed themselves in a house commanding the square as a party of the enemy with a single gun appeared to the east. Ascending to the rooftop, Foster trained his telescope on the centre of town. 'I observed the British colours flying about a mile distant on the left ... [and] the King's colours of some regiment ... on a large building at my right ... a mile distant, with an intermediate position which I took to be a church, from which I could plainly distinguish the rifle corps with two or three light infantry'. The positions Foster had observed were the bullring, the Residencia and Santo Domingo Church respectively. Having completed his mission, he returned to Corrales to give Whitelocke his report.[40]

Ten blocks to the east, Craufurd's troops were looting Santo Domingo Church. Gold and silver crosses and ceremonial plate were stolen. One friar had his arm shattered by a musket ball. Another was shot through the chest. Craufurd herded the rest to one side, detailed guards to protect them and soon regained control. Meanwhile, the colours of the 71st, captured a year earlier at the Reconquista, were found on display above the altar to the Virgin Mary. Lieutenant-Colonel Pack was delighted. He ordered a private to fly them from the church's single tower, while Craufurd marshalled the defence. After setting up a field hospital for the wounded, the 3-pounder was positioned in the street before the main gates. Riflemen were posted in the tower and across the rooftop and a crack shot named Private Thomas Plunkett was hoisted onto a low building enabling him to fire directly down Calle San Martín into the Plaza Mayor. The flag and rifle fire attracted the enemy's attention. Several occupied the surrounding rooftops and began firing into the church.[41]

By 10.30 am Colonel Cadogan's situation was desperate. The men he had sent to Craufurd had all been killed and the officer badly wounded. Holed up in the vicereine's house, the remains of his command were low on ammunition; fourteen privates and a sergeant had been killed and five officers and eighty-two rank-and-file wounded. Most had been shot on the rooftop. The gutters streamed with blood which poured into the street below. At 10.50 am a Spanish officer approached with a flag of truce. Although Cadogan was suspicious, after conferring with Major Travers and Captain Kelby, he allowed the Spaniard inside. As soon as the British stopped firing, the enemy occupied the most dominating positions which the riflemen's fire had previously denied them. When the firing started again, Cadogan realised the game was up and at 11.00 am waved the white flag.[42]

Half a mile to the northeast, the survivors of the left wing of the 88th were crammed into a courtyard ten yards square. One side opened to the river bank a dozen yards away. The others were backed by four tiny rooms whose sloping roofs terminated in a parapet. Beyond, the enemy had gathered in large numbers. Firing down into the courtyard, they killed or wounded any who had the temerity to step out into the open and Major Vandeleur's repeated attempts to take the rooftop were beaten back. Amongst those killed was Ensign 'Honest' John McGregor. Shot through the back when attempting to get a glimpse of the enemy, he bled to death in the courtyard. Several others managed to rush out into the street. Breaking into a two-storey house opposite, they got onto the roof and returned fire. For a few minutes, their musketry proved effective, but the height of the building exposed them to the 24-pounders on the northern rampart of the fort. Captain Agustini directed their fire himself. The redcoats engaged the gunners, killing a corporal and three men, but after a few rounds of grape had swept their position, they were forced to retire. Half a dozen made a dash across the rooftops to the north hoping to reach the 36th. The rest took cover inside and Agustini ordered his men to shoot out the main doors.[43]

At 11.00 am Agustini's adjutant major, Martín Cedaver, brought a light gun forward from the Plaza Mayor. Manoeuvring it to one side of the barricade on Calle Santa Lucia, he opened fire on Vandeleur's position. The round shot smashed through the walls adding to the carnage inside. Hidden in the ditch a few feet away, Captain Chisholme's men heard the report. Using the bodies of their dead comrades as a firestep, they fired a close-range volley into Cedavar's gunners, killing three and forcing the rest to fall back. Rallying the survivors, Cedaver returned to fire a second shot. Chisholme's men fired again, but their musketry was answered by dozens of enemy infantry on the rooftops and they were forced to return to cover. With Cedaver's gun free to fire on Vandeleur's position, at 11.15 am the major called a council of war. His officers concurred that they had to surrender. 'The situation … was … alarming', one explained. '[It was] certain death to quit … cover; to retreat was impracticable, and all hopes of support [had] vanished … half the division lay … dead or wounded, and one shell, or a few grenades, would have determined the fate of the remainder.' Waving a white handkerchief towards the enemy, Vandeleur ordered his men to cease fire.[44]

Some 500 metres to the southeast, the right wing of the 88th was also close to surrender. Having occupied three houses on Calle Piedad between Calles San Pedro and Correo, Lieutenant-Colonel Duff had been conducting an uneven firefight across the rooftops for the last three hours. With the firing to their left and right slackening, Duff feared the other British columns had withdrawn and began to countenance surrender. His position was commanded on all sides. Sharpshooters in the towers of the cathedral and the San Miguel Church could fire directly down onto his men and the number of casualties was rising. The rooftops were slick with blood and covered in dead. Even in the interior, the red-coats were exposed to enemy fire. Having run across town from the site of their victory over Lieutenant-Colonel Cadogan's column, Martín Rodríguez's Hussars were shooting through the windows and doors. Even the regimental surgeon was under fire and any man appearing in the apertures was soon hit. Duff was out of options. At 11.50 am the enemy was admitted to discuss terms.[45]

With three of the central columns defeated, the Spaniards and creoles re-deployed. After receiving more ammunition and wolfing down a bowl of broth or some bread and cheese at the field kitchens in the centre, they engaged the remaining British positions. The redeployment was spontaneous. Holed up in the fort and the Sala Capitular, Liniers and Álzaga had become passive observers. Although informed of developments by their staff, they had no way of exerting control. The militia units, mixed up with armed civilians and slaves, had become unresponsive to central command.[46] To the north the 36th bore the brunt of the pressure and Brigadier-General Lumley and Lieutenant-Colonel Burne also had to deal with growing indiscipline. Holed up by the riverside between Calles San Nicolás and Santa Teresa, they were surrounded by *pulperias*. Several men were already intoxicated and Burne ordered his officers to smash the remaining bottles of wine and stave in the casks of spirits before the situation got out of control. Meanwhile, the fighting continued. As the enemy fired from the surrounding rooftops and windows, the redcoats stormed the houses and slowly expanded their control along the waterfront. Any enemy horsemen who strayed into the area were killed in the streets. Most of the men inside the buildings were also put to the bayonet, although boys were taken prisoner.[47]

At 11.30 am the men of the left wing of the 88th who had escaped Calle Santa Lucia arrived at Lumley's headquarters. Having fought their way across the rooftops, they breathlessly delivered their report. The 88th had lost half their men and the remainder had surrendered. Lumley began to fear the worst. 'The enemy were … visibly superior … in numbers' he explained, 'they were protected from our fire, and we exposed to theirs; they were also in possession of a numerous artillery, and we had not a single gun.' At midday Colonel Elio approached under a flag of truce. After confirming the capitulation of the 88th and claiming that his troops held 1,000 prisoners, he demanded Lumley's surrender. The Englishman 'angrily desired him to be gone'. Up on the rooftop, a lookout had spotted 300 enemy approaching along the beach with two cannon.[48] 'It was now evident that the … truce was merely to divert our attention,' Captain Monkland recalled. A veteran of dozens of battles and sieges on the subcontinent, Lieutenant-Colonel Burne ordered thirty men to charge the guns. Approaching behind an aloe hedge bordering the river front, Captain William Swaine of the grenadiers led them at a run. The Spaniards spotted the redcoats' shako feathers over the hedge, unlimbered their 12- and 9-pounders and opened fire. The volley was devastating. Captain Swaine was shot through the thigh. Lieutenant John White was wounded in two places and several men were killed. Lumley ordered the rest to fall back. Captain Monkland was furious. 'This appeared the moment to pounce upon our prey before they could reload', he explained. Instead, the survivors had to dash through a storm of grapeshot fired down Calle Santo Cristo by the 24-pounders in the Plaza Mayor.[49]

Three blocks to the northwest, the right wing of the 5th had been joined by Brigadier-General Auchmuty. The American had left Colonel Nugent in charge at El Retiro to see how they were faring. Joining Lieutenant-Colonel Davie in the tower of Santa Catalina Church, he surveyed the scene beneath him. While the left wing of the 5th was under pressure, the right had only seen scattered action. Auchmuty ordered Davie to hold on for as long as possible and only fall back to El Retiro as a last resort. Moments later a dispatch arrived from Lumley recounting the surrender of the 88th. Auchmuty sent him the same orders he had given Davie and returned to El Retiro under scattered fire. Two blocks to the southeast Major King decided to take the fight to the enemy. Spottting a French flag flying from a building on Calle San Martín between Santa Lucia and San

Nicolás, he left Assistant-Surgeon Bone and twelve men with the wounded and led the rest of the left wing of the 5th outside. One block from their target, they came under heavy fire, broke into a nearby house and reformed in a covered courtyard, before sallying outside. Four men were killed in as many yards. The survivors fell back to the courtyard and King sent Captain Philips to Lieutenant-Colonel Davie for reinforcements.[50]

By midday Brigadier-General Craufurd's troops were also feeling the pressure. Since Cadogan's, Duff's and Vandeleur's surrender, the enemy had redirected a number of troops against them. Sharpshooters were situated behind every window and covered the surrounding rooftops and barricades had been thrown up across the streets leading to the Plaza Mayor. All the exits of the church had been enfiladed, forcing the men to take shelter inside, where they fell prey to shots fired through the windows. The tally of dead and wounded was rising rapidly. By the gates all but one of the crew of the 3-pounder had been hit and all the horses killed. The sole survivor, a sergeant-major, continued to load the gun with grape regardless and cut down any Spaniard who dared to show himself beyond the barricades. Above the crack of the Baker rifles and the duller reports of musketry, a regimental bugle was heard. The musician, a deserter from the 71st, repeatedly sounded the ceasefire. Several of his former comrades were taken in. Quitting their posts, they fell back to the church, allowing the enemy to close on their position. Rifleman Plunkett remained unmoved. He had already dispatched a dozen of the enemy and when Elio's aide-de-camp, Captain José de Pazos, approached under a flag of truce he decided to 'have a slap at the fellow with the white handkerchief'. Lining up his foresight, Plunkett pulled the trigger. The ball drilled through both of Captain Pazos' thighs.[51]

Despite the deterioration of his position, Craufurd remained convinced he had been right to take the church. 'I had no reason to suppose that any … disaster had befallen any part of our army,' he explained, 'and when … a [second] Spanish officer … approached the convent, I flattered myself that … General Liniers had judged it expedient to capitulate'. The Spanish emissary had something entirely different in mind. 'He came into the court-yard,' Craufurd recalled, '[and] informed me that the 88th … and some other corps … were taken prisoners; that all our attacks had failed, and that he was charged … to summon me to surrender.' Craufurd dismissed the demand, but the incident left him profoundly concerned. '[I began to] think the situation not an advisable one to remain in … [and] determined … to extricate myself from it'. Craufurd determined to wait until the enemy moved against him in force, then sally out and fall back to the Residencia.[52] At 1.00 pm the opportunity arose. 'A considerable column' of the enemy was spotted advancing down Calle San Martín intent on capturing the 3-pounder. Craufurd called in the outposts and ordered the colours lowered from the tower in preparation. As the troops gathered by the gates, Major Trotter offered to drive the enemy back, allowing the rest to withdraw to the south. As well as a section of his own light infantry, Colonel Guard and Captain John Payne of the grenadiers of the 45th volunteered to go with him. Lieutenant

George Miller of the 95th observed the eighty-five men leave. '[Trotter] looked desponding for the first time in his life', he recalled.[53]

Meanwhile, on Calle San Martín, Major King was preparing to make another attempt to capture the house flying the French flag. Rushing from the covered courtyard, his men reached the door, but were unable to force their way inside. With the enemy firing down from the rooftop, several privates were killed, Drummer Downie was mortally wounded, Captain Henry Ridge badly cut across his leg and King 'struck on the head with a spent ball' and shot in the left arm. Seeing the enemy bringing up two cannon, the survivors fell back. A section was ordered to keep the artillerymen's heads down, while King retreated to the north. Sergeant Maiden and the wounded withdrew to the house where Assistant-Surgeon Bone had established his field hospital and Drummer Downie and the dead were left behind in the courtyard. Turning right onto Calle San Nicolás, King found a house occupied by the 36th and took shelter inside.[54]

By 1.30 pm the situation of the 36th was becoming untenable. Although Captain Joshua Crosse and some of the left wing had joined the bulk of the regiment in the houses by the riverside, the enemy column moving down the beach had resumed its advance and a second detachment, also headed by a pair of field pieces, was advancing from the west. In danger of being caught in a pincer movement, Lieutenant-Colonel Burne insisted on leading a counterattack, but a number of men under Captain Crosse pre-empted the move by charging the guns on the beach. The enemy's first fire killed several. The survivors pushed home their attack. Abandoning their 12-pounder by the mole, the Spaniards fled to the fort dragging the 9-pounder behind them. While Crosse pursued them, Burne joined in the attack with fifty grenadiers. Reaching the abandoned 12-pounder, he spiked it with a bayonet just as Captain Agustini's gunners opened fire from the fort. Three rounds of grape shot forced Burne to retire. Running back the way they had come, he and his grenadiers took cover behind a house and low hedge by the river side.[55] Meanwhile, Crosse had caught up with the enemy outside the fort's gates. Drawing his sword, he charged the men dragging the 9-pounder, took the commander prisoner and was on the verge of charging into the fort, when he stole a glance over his shoulder to see how many had kept up with his advance. Only Sergeant William Vinicombe stood behind him. Retreating twenty paces, the two men threw themselves down behind a large rock just as the gunners in the fort opened fire with grapeshot. Back at his headquarters, Lumley ordered a detachment to drag the captured guns clear. With Agustini alert to the danger, they were driven back after reaching the drag rope of the 12-pounder. One private was left behind and threw himself beneath the barrel of the gun. It was repeatedly struck with grapeshot and a cannonball spun the tumbril round through 360 degrees. Somehow both the horses harnessed to the gun and the private underneath it survived.[56]

On the other side of the Plaza Mayor, Major Trotter's men burst out of the gates of Santo Domingo. The Spaniards received them with a volley. Colonel Guard had his sword shattered, Captain Payne was shot in the chest, and all those in the first two ranks were killed or wounded. With his coat torn to shreds,

Trotter charged on. The Spaniards fell back and he reached the corner of Calle Rosario with a handful of men, but whilst looking through his telescope, was shot through the head and chest by marksmen crouched on a rooftop. The survivors fled back to the church where Lieutenant Miller received them. 'They went out eighty-four, and returned . . . twenty-three' he recalled. '[It was the most] wanton sacrifice of human life [I have ever seen]'. As the news of Trotter's death spread, a wave of despondency fell over the defenders. Even Craufurd was moved. 'His eyes now seemed to be opened to the situation we were in,' Pack recalled, 'and [he began] to doubt that things were . . . so favourable as we had hoped'. Regaining his composure, Craufurd ordered the riflemen back to the outposts. If Buenos Ayres was to be his last stand, he was determined to make the *porteños* pay dearly.[57]

Meanwhile, on Calle San Nicolás, the second Spanish column, a mixed party of infantry and cavalry led by Manuel de Arze (the brigadier-general's son), was advancing on Lumley's position with two guns. The task of dispersing them was assigned to Major King and the left wing of the 5th. Forming his men into a compact column one section wide, King charged up the street, but 'on nearing the enemy, we observed them waving their hands, making signals not to fire;' he recalled, 'and an officer with a white handkerchief came forward, as we supposed, to surrender'. King halted and the officer, Manuel de Arze, moved towards him. 'His men followed him close,' the major remembered, '[and] I made signs to them to lay down their arms'. When the Spaniards refused, King 'seized two or three [of their guns], and threw them to the ground . . . one man presented at me . . . I parried the muzzle of his piece with my sword, and one of my men rushed forward and made a thrust with his bayonet at the Spanish officer, he . . . jumped aside, and the bayonet . . . tore open his clothes.' With the situation deteriorating, King disarmed Arze and sent him under guard to the headquarters of the 36th just as the Spanish and creole troops surged forward to seize the British colours. '[King] hesitated no longer [and] gave the order to charge'. In the melee Arze and twelve of his men were killed. The rest then fled, the riders bowing their heads close to their horses to avoid the British volley that followed them down the street.[58]

At 2.00 pm Lumley decided to fall back to El Retiro. 'We had been engaged . . . above six hours; our numbers were much reduced . . . all our ammunition was expended, and I well knew that, ere long, I must be completely surrounded and over-powered', he later explained. The outposts were ordered in before the withdrawal was made. Lieutenant-Colonel Davie (with the right wing of the 5th at Santa Catalina Church) was told to regroup with Major King; the remains of the left wing of the 36th fell back to headquarters; and the troops near the fort with Lieutenant-Colonel Burne and Captain Crosse were ordered to retreat when they saw the rest moving down the beach. Dashing forward from cover to cover, the remains of the left wing of the 36th avoided the grape fired at them from the 24-pounders in the Plaza Mayor, but progress was slow. Several men were carrying the corpse of Captain Henry Johnson, who had left a pregnant wife and six children in Monte Video, while others struggled with Lieutenant Robert Whittle who had been mortally wounded. At the rear was Captain Henry Vernon's company. Tasked with escorting the prisoners, the captain lost contact with the rest of the wing and decided to take a short cut. As he turned a corner two Spanish cannon were discharged at short range. The grape killed all but one of the lead section and Vernon was struck full in the chest. Although his ornamental breast-plate took the brunt of the blast, the captain was hurled across the street. Heavily brusied and badly cut on his left leg, Vernon limped back down Calle Catedral. 'Not thinking it worth their while to fire on a single man, [the enemy] suffered [him] ... to [withdraw] ... in safety'.[59]

At 2.30 pm Lumley led the remains of the 5th and 36th to El Retiro. A few were cut down by grape and round shot fired from the fort as they withdrew up the beach. Several others were left behind. Some deliberately missed the call, intending to desert as soon as their comrades had withdrawn. Others were forgotten in the confusion. A few made their way to El Retiro, while others were captured by the enemy. One detachment of the 5th had been left in Santa Catalina Church where a number of civilians and slaves besieged them. Watched by their comrades in El Retiro, the redcoats kept them at bay by firing from the church tower, but having expended their ammunition, they left the wounded, fixed bayonets and made a break for the park. Several broke through. The rest were taken prisoner and led to the fort.[60]

In the western suburbs Whitelocke was still unaware of the situation in town. Captain Foster had informed him of the fate of Colonel Kington's column, but he remained ignorant of the surrender of Cadogan's, Duff's and Vandeleur's and the rest of the army was out of contact. One hour previously, he had ordered Brigade-Major Charles Conway to the Residencia to see what had become of the 45th, but the staff officer had returned after a few minutes. The enemy were everywhere and it was impossible to force a way through. At 2.30 pm Whitelocke tried again. This time he hoped to establish contact with Auchmuty's left wing. Captain Whittingham, having returned from his reconnaissance with Lieutenant-Colonel Torrens, volunteered for the task. 'I immediately said I should be most happy to have an opportunity of rendering myself useful,' Whittingham recalled, 'and ... marched off [towards El Retiro] with a sergeant and ten dragoons, and thirty infantry.'[61]

By 3.00 pm all the *porteño* combatants in the centre of town had gathered around Santo Domingo Church. As well as firing their muskets through the broken windows and shattered gates, they deployed several cannon. One block to the north a field piece had been manhandled into the yard of the Casa Tellechea from where it could spray the front gates with grapeshot, a 6-inch howitzer, positioned at the corner of Calles Catedral and Santo Domingo, provided a flanking fire and several guns in the fort were firing round shot at the church's tower and roof. Inside, Craufurd's troops were in dire straits. 'We had a hundred wounded', Lieutenant-Colonel Holland recalled, and with the round shot crashing through the roof, 'expected soon to have the place about our ears, the troops were alarmed and jaded' and their small arms ammunition was running low. With no firing to be heard in the other parts of town, Craufurd concluded that his only option was to surrender. 'About half past three o'clock I assembled … Colonel Pack, Colonel Guard, and Major Mcleod', he recalled, '[and] told them, that in my opinion to retreat was utterly impossible; that it was completely in the power of the enemy to annihilate the remainder of the brigade … that all the rest of the army had been obliged to retreat, and … I did not think that the sacrifice of the remainder of the men, could … prove in any way advantageous. I added, that … I should do nothing with the view of ending the action, unless I had the[ir] entire concurrence'.[62] Pack and Guard agreed at once, but Mcleod, having known the shame of defeat in Holland in 1799, was reluctant. Noticing his hesitancy, Craufurd offered the major the command if he thought he could lead the column to safety. Appalled at the responsibility, Mcleod backed down and at 3.15 pm a flag of truce was waved towards the enemy. An officer came forward and Craufurd stepped out to receive him. '[He] said our troops were either taken, killed or retreated' Holland recalled. 'After some conference we sent him back with some proposals [and] he returned [with] … General … [Elio] … a dirty ill-dressed man … surrounded by a riotous armed rabble'. Elio would only accept an unconditional surrender. Believing he had little choice, Craufurd agreed.[63]

One mile to the northwest, Captain Whittingham was making his way to El Retiro. Having divided the infantry into two flanking columns, he posted the mounted dragoons in front and to the rear. 'Our whole route was one continual skirmish,' Whittingham recalled, 'and the enemy was constantly on the watch to surprize us.' An hour out from Corrales, the captain ordered his flankers to take the next men they met prisoner. 'They presently brought me three', he recalled. 'I gave them to understand that, if they wished to avoid the gallows, they must take care to conduct me safely to the Plaza de los Toros'. Unsurprisingly, the *porteños* agreed.[64]

By 3.30 pm Craufurd had agreed terms. Leaving 100 wounded in the church, his troops laid down their arms and marched out of the gates. 'It was a bitter task', Holland recalled. 'Everyone felt it … the men were all in tears.' Several smashed their muskets against the floor in frustration and Lieutenant Miller of the 95th was particularly galled. 'I could never see the necessity of [surrender]' he recalled. 'Night was not far off; we might have held on until dark, and then forced our way out'. At the head of the column, Holland was also feeling ashamed. 'Nothing could be more mortifying than our passage … amidst the rabble. They were very dark skinned people, short and ill made, [and] covered with rags.' Once in the town centre, the prisoners were herded into a walled courtyard and stripped of their possessions by their guards. 'The officers lost everything', one witness recalled. 'Even their watches, hats and boots' were taken. All were then received by Liniers in the Plaza Mayor. He and Craufurd exchanged pleasantries in French and the prisoners were divided by rank. The men were confined in make-shift prisons scattered round the centre. The officers were led to Liniers' quarters in the fort where they were relieved to find Cadogan's officers and the survivors of the 88th.[65]

At 4.00 pm Captain Whittingham arrived at El Retiro. 'I found Sir Samuel Auchmuty in complete possession', he recalled. 'He had taken thirty-three pieces of cannon, an immense quantity of ammunition, and 607 prisoners.' Having placed the 5th with the 87th in the bullring, Auchmuty had moved the 38th to the Quinta Riglos in the orange grove and the 36th to 'a sort of horse barracks' nearby. By the time Whittingham arrived, a field hospital had been established in Socorro Church, the prisoners were under guard in some nearby outbuildings, contact had been made with Captain Thompson's flotilla and the boats of HMS *Protector* had landed 1,200 musket cartridges. Auchmuty ordered Whittingham to ask Whitelocke for some gunners to man the captured cannon and suggested the commander-in-chief transfer his headquarters to El Retiro. Whittingham then galloped back to Corrales to deliver his report.[66] On Whittingham's arrival at 4.45 pm, Whitelocke dispatched eighteen artillerymen to El Retiro, but declined to follow them himself until he knew the fate of the columns on the right. Despite learning of the surrender of the 88th, he and his staff remained optimistic. 'The impression of complete success was not . . . on the mind of any one person present,' Lieutenant-Colonel Torrens explained, 'but great hopes were entertained of a favourable position having been taken up on the left flank of the enemy'. Not wanting to be caught on the open ground with nightfall imminent, Whitelocke and his staff retired to White's house for the night.[67]

Meanwhile, in the Sala Capitular a heated discussion was under way. Since learning of Craufurd's capitulation, Liniers had drawn up a draft surrender proposal for Whitelocke. The terms were more than reasonable. In exchange for the evacuation of all British troops from Buenos Ayres, the prisoners the Spaniards and creoles had taken (including those captured with Beresford the year before) would be released on condition that they sail immediately for England and not fight again until formally exchanged. Álzaga wanted more. He insisted the British withdraw entirely from the River Plate. Liniers feared the demands would back Whitelocke into a corner, but Álzaga was adamant. A letter was promptly drawn up. The Frenchman signed at 5.00 pm, but with chaos reigning in the streets, it would not be dispatched until morning.[68]

One mile to the south, the 45th were wondering what had become of their comrades. Having seen the colours of the 71st lowered over the Santo Domingo Church from the tower of the Residencia, Major Nicolls was beginning to fear the worst. On the other side of town in El Retiro skirmishing continued and at one stage the general alarm was raised. Forming two lines centered on the guns they had captured, the troops awaited an assault. Two miles to the southwest, Whitelocke and his staff had made themselves comfortable at White's house. Having despatched a letter to Rear-Admiral Murray requesting his presence at the bullring in the morning, the lieutenant-general sat down to dinner with his staff. Afterwards several junior officers were sent to the rooftop to keep watch, while Whitelocke retired to his quarters and the rest 'laid themselves down on various parts of the floor to sleep'.[69]

In the town centre, the British prisoners had a less comfortable evening. After being herded into jail, the rank and file had been searched a second time and those taken in Santo Domingo Church ordered to give up 'a gold crucifix of great value that was ... missing. We stood in a large circle of Indians and Spaniards ... [with] levelled muskets', Private Todd recalled, until, miraculously, the article reappeared. Others got away with their loot. 'One soldier, who had a good many doubloons, put them into his Camp-kettle, with flesh and water above them ... placed [it] all upon a fire and kept them [quite] safe'. In the fort the British officers signed their paroles and were 'crammed into two rooms' overlooking the river. With the mob baying for blood in the Plaza and a crowd on the beach drawing their swords across their necks theatrically, they were assigned a considerable guard. The outer chamber was designated a dining room. 'Some biscuit and a lump of flesh smoked and quite beastly' were served up and two tubs of water left on the floor. 'Some went to drink, some went to p[ee], and some went to drink again' Lieutenant Miller recalled. In the inner chamber others tried to snatch some sleep. While Craufurd was given a matress by Colonel Balbiani, the rest made do with the floor. 'We lay down, not quite sure whether our throats would be cut during the night' Miller recalled. Colonel Peter Kington had also been taken prisoner. Having dragged himself into a side street after being wounded on Calle Cabildo, the colonel had been on the verge of falling prey to a group of enraged creole militia, when an old Spaniard had saved him. '[He] dragged [Kington] ... into his house, and having bound up his wound, laid him on his own bed, and watched [over] him ... [throughout the] night with the tenderness of a parent'.[70]

The day of 5 July 1807 proved the costliest of the entire campaign. Of the 6,000 British troops who had taken part in the fighting, 311, including fifteen officers, had died. Fifty-seven officers and 622 men had been wounded and three officers and 205 men were missing. The casualties were not evenly distributed. The 88th, 87th and 95th lost 198, 186 and 132 men respectively, whereas the 45th had only nine men killed or wounded. The Spaniards lost 200 dead and 400 wounded. Both sides had also had a considerable number captured by the enemy. Auchmuty held 700 prisoners at El Retiro, while Liniers had 1,611 in the town centre. Whitelocke had not yet lost the battle, but the *porteños* had definitely won the first round.[71]

Chapter 18

Surrender
Buenos Ayres and Monte Video
5 July – 7 September 1807

After a restless night, Whitelocke sent Captain Whittingham to contact Colonel Mahon at Galves Bridge and the 45th at the Residencia. With an escort of ten dragoons and fifty infantrymen, he set out at 6.30 am. Looping through the suburbs as the sun peeked out from beneath the clouds over the River Plate, he fell in with Mahon's pickets an hour later and was conducted to the colonel's temporary headquarters by the Riachuelo. Whittingham ordered Mahon to move up to Corrales and, after leaving his infantry and a Spanish prisoner to show the colonel 'a circuitous way to Mr. White's house, without approaching too close to town', set out for the Residencia with his cavalry escort and 100 grenadiers of the 40th under Captain John Gillies.[1]

At El Retiro the troops had been under arms since 5.30 am. 'Everything remaining quiet ... after dawn had broke, [we] ... were dismissed with orders to fall in at a moment's warning', Captain Monkland recalled. Down by the beach, Captain Thompson's flotilla landed a 24-pounder which was hauled up the cliff by thirty men from HMS *Nereide* at first light. Biscuit and spirits were brought ashore while regimental butchers slaughtered a few cattle left in the bullring. Morale was high. 'It was to the no small joy of all that preparations were [being made] ... for a bombardment', Monkland recalled, 'and the gunboats [were] observed to anchor closer in shore'. This last was by Captain Thompson's order. Having assigned Lieutenant Heron of HMS *Saracen* and Lieutenant Fraser of HMS *Medusa* to command the four gunboats, Thompson signalled that they should anchor off the mole and engage the fort.[2]

At 8.00 am a Spanish messenger was admitted to the bullring carrying the letter Liniers and Álzaga had drafted the previous afternoon. Besides reiterating the surrender of the 88th, it announced the capture of Craufurd's and Pack's columns (the first time the British had had the news confirmed) and included Álzaga's terms. Liniers closed the letter with a threat: 'If these proposals are not agreed to, I cannot answer for the safety of the prisoners, as my Troops are so infinitely exasperated against them'. Despite the news, British spirits remained buoyant and the men believed they were only waiting to be united with Mahon's Reserve Brigade for a second offensive to be launched. Meanwhile, Auchmuty replied to Liniers saying that he would forward his message to Whitelocke and, while the negotiations continued, would order his own troops 'to abstain from firing on the town'. Sergeant Hamilton of the 17th Light Dragoons was then dispatched to Corrales with Liniers' message.[3]

Hamilton arrived at 10.00 am. Whitelocke had Liniers' letter translated, then called a council of war to consider his reply. The commander-in-chief was inclined to accept, if only to escape the pressures of command, and the threat against the prisoners proved particularly effective. Whitelocke's staff strongly advised him to decline. While Gower suggested agreeing to the ceasefire to buy time, Lieutenant-Colonel Bourke counselled dismissing the offer entirely, gathering the army at El Retiro and evaluating the plausibility of a bombardment or second attack. Whitelocke followed Gower's advice and at midday ordered Captain Brown to propose a twenty-four-hour ceasefire 'in the cause of humanity ... As to surrendering', the letter continued, 'having taken so many prisoners ... it is quite out of the question'. On Brown's return at midday, Whitelocke and his staff set off for El Retiro with an escort of dragoons and two 6-pounders commanded by Captain Frazer of the Royal Artillery.[4]

With their terms rebuffed, Liniers and Álzaga ordered Gerardo Esteve y Llach, one of the heroes of the Reconquista and the commander of the Patriotas de la Unión, to take the Residencia. Supported by 100 infantrymen under Lieutenant Miguel Mugía, Llach set out with two brass howitzers and a 9-pounder at midday. Leaving the Plaza Mayor, he advanced down Calle San Martín, but on reaching the Bethlemite Hospital at the corner of Calle San Bartolome, Mugía's troops deserted in droves. Llach pushed on and opened fire on the British position on crossing the Vera Brook. On the roof of the Residencia, majors Nicolls and Tolley and Captain Whittingham were discussing the events of the last thirty hours when Llach's first round 'shot tore overhead'. Nicolls and Tolley immediately organised a counterattack. Taking cover 300 metres from the enemy with eighty men, they fixed bayonets, formed column and charged down Calle San Martín. Private Peter McConnel was killed and five others wounded by a volley of grape and musketry before the Spaniards and creoles scattered. Several were bayonetted or shot in the pursuit and Llach's two howitzers were taken.[5]

At 12.30 am, using kedge anchors to hold their four gunboats in position off the mole, lieutenants Fraser and Heron opened fire on the fort with their 24-pounders. Agustini's men replied, but the British guns were better served and soon managed to send a round shot flying over the battlements and crashing through the adobe wall of Liniers' quarters. The Frenchman wrote to Whitelocke demanding the bombardment cease and Captain William Parker Carrol of the 88th and a Spanish aide volunteered to deliver it. Meanwhile, Agustini's gunners had found their range. After a round shot hit the bow of one of their gunboats, Heron and Fraser upped anchor and moved a few yards before sending two more rounds crashing into the buildings in the fort's interior.[6]

At 1.00 pm Whitelocke arrived at El Retiro. While Lieutenant-Colonel Bourke and captains Frazer and Squire examined the ground and captured ordnance, Gower selected sites for batteries to bombard the centre of town. After 'some considerable time' he decided six heavy guns could be housed in the bullring and a mortar battery positioned in cover of the buildings outside. Meanwhile, Captain

Frazer of the Royal Artillery had found thirty-six guns ranging in size from 8- to 36-pounders and 600 barrels of gunpowder. In his opinion El Retiro was a perfect site for bombarding the town, setting it on fire and reducing the fort. He thought the entire operation could be achieved in no more than 'a few hours'. Captain Squire of the Royal Engineers agreed, but Bourke, although no artillery expert, 'conceived any attempt to batter the town ... w[oul]d be ... useless'. As the houses were made of adobe, round shot passed straight through them and they could neither be burnt nor knocked down.[7]

Meanwhile, Captain Carrol and Liniers' aide were making their way across the Plaza Mayor. Outside the cathedral Carrol noticed that several children who been killed in the fighting had been placed in open caskets 'for the purpose of inflaming the populace against the British prisoners.' The effect was undeniable. Spotting the red-coated officer in their midst, the 'infuriated mob' dragged him off his horse to lynch him. Miraculously, Carrol managed to talk his way out. Comparing his would be executioners to the 'noble Castilians, from whom they were descended', he shamed them into releasing him. In a moment, 'the popular tide turned in his favour; they gave him back his epaulettes, hat and ... sword ... replaced him on horseback, and cheered him [on his way], "throwing up their greasy caps" in salute as he passed.'[8]

On the roof of the bullring, Whitelocke's meeting was underway. Gower began by stating 'that there were but two means' of continuing the offensive. 'The one by assault had been tried with only partial success; the second by bombardment ... would ... produce very little effect upon a town of so immense a size ... I moreover stated' he recalled 'that the number of troops remaining, even were the Spanish General disposed to give up ... were by no means adequate ... to control such a mass of armed inhabitants'. Next Sir Samuel Auchmuty 'reflected on the situation in which the army was placed ... Upwards of half the troops originally engaged, were now either killed, wounded, or prisoners ... the remainder were fatigued, without confidence, and exposed to the most inclement season'. Auchmuty also mentioned 'the difficulty of procuring ordinance stores, and provisions from the fleet ... [,] the loss [the army] ... must inevitably sustain if hostilities recommenced ... the difficulty of burning or destroying the town [and] ... the difficulty of making a retreat ... When I weighed all these circumstances', the American recalled, 'I had no hesitation in saying, that if better terms could not be obtained, and a period of six months given for the evacuation of Monte Video, with a facility to the merchants to dispose of their goods, it was my opinion they should be acceded to.' Captains Frazer and Squire spoke next. Both insisted Buenos Ayres could be bombarded, but despite their expertise as a royal artillery officer and royal engineer respectively, their appeals fell on deaf ears.[9]

Whitelocke had made up his mind. He had not wanted to fight in the first place and now that he had the backing of his two most senior officers he felt he could sail home to England with his pride intact. The only obstacle remaining was Rear-Admiral Murray. Unable to land due to contrary winds, Murray remained on HMS *Nereide* several miles off shore. Once the meeting had broken up, Whitelocke wrote to him again, assuring him that 'Spanish America never can be

English' and urging him to 'come ... [ashore] without loss of time'.[10] At 2.00 pm Captain Carrol arrived. Liniers' letter warned that unless the gunboats ceased fire, 'he could not ... be answerable for the lives of his prisoners'. Again the threat worked immediately. Whitelocke signalled Captain Thompson and lieutenants Heron and Fraser were obliged to silence their guns and stand out to deep water. A flag of truce was rasied on the bullring and at 3.00 pm Gower was sent into town to negotiate the surrender.[11]

Gower reached the fort as the captured British field officers were sitting down to a meal with their hosts. 'The dinner was ... carried off very well', Lieutenant-Colonel Holland recalled. Sitting nearby, Craufurd was desperate to have a word with Gower before the negotiations began. 'I thought it my duty to ... tell him, that ... I was quite convinced, that if the army attacked the town again in the same way they had done on the 5th, they would be completely defeated'. Afterwards, Craufurd accompanied Colonel Elio to the Residencia to give majors Tolley and Nicolls official confirmation of the ceasefire, while Gower and Liniers negotiated in private. The major-general insisted that the British be allowed to remain in Monte Video for at least four months and that a neutral zone be established around town; that no attempt should be made at disrupting British supplies; that the troops in Buenos Ayres be allowed ten days to evacuate with all their cannon and supplies from a point of Whitelocke's choosing; and that commerce in the River Plate would be open and free while the British remained. It was also agreed that each side should give the other three hostages to ensure all terms were adhered to. Liniers could not believe how little his opponents were demanding and was only too happy to agree. Gower returned to El Retiro at 7.00 pm with the preliminary terms 'written in Spanish upon [a piece of] ass's skin.'[12]

The reaction in El Retiro was one of anger and disbelief. '[A] conflict of passions ... pervaded every heart', Captain Monkland recalled. 'You mourn for your Country, [and] feel indignant at those who have ... tarnished her Honour.' Major King thought the agreement 'disgraceful' and 'ignominious', Private Morley called it 'deplorable' and Captain Wilkie noted that 'nothing could exceed the disgust of the men'. When the news spread to Captain Thompson's inshore fleet, the reaction was similar. 'To describe the surprise and vexation of everybody ... [was] impossible', Billy Pitt of HMS *Charwell* recalled. 'A little army, composed of the finest troops in the world, to be worsted by a rabble, appeared to every one incredible.'[13] At El Retiro, skirmishing continued throughout the night. 'The enemy ... annoy[ed] us from the bushes and gardens in front and wounded several men and officers walking about.' Later, a picquet of the 87th was attacked by a large party of the enemy. The redcoats drove them off, capturing two officers and seventy men for the loss of just two of their own.[14]

On the morning of 7 July Whitelocke showed Bourke the preliminary terms of surrender. '[I] thought it right ... to give my ideas on the subject', Bourke recalled, '[and] wrote a short sketch of our affairs ... concluding that ... in our circumstances such a treaty might be desirable.' At 7.00 am notice of the truce was sent to Mahon's Reserve Brigade at Corrales, while at the Residencia Major

Nicolls applied to Liniers for provisions as he was running low. 'I received a reply that provisions should be sent; however, none ... [but] a very small portion which was given to the sick and wounded [arrived]'. Having expended most of their ball cartridge, Nicolls' men spent the rest of the day manufacturing new ones from the canister shot they had captured on 6 July.[15] Elsewhere, the British spent the morning burying the dead. Assigned to clear the bodies from the road the 87th had used to approach El Retiro on 5 July, Captain Monkland was particularly affected. 'The impression the horrid spectacle made on me will not easily be erased', he admitted. 'The lane for some hundred yards was ... thickly strewed with dead ... lying in contemplation – fine young fellows, who, but a little [time] ... before [had been] in health and vigour, were now stretched lifeless in the dust, some in their countenances depicting writhing agony, others smiling in death'. In the centre, the *porteños* were also burying the dead. Hundreds were slung into mass graves along the beach between the fort and El Retiro. Others were buried at a cattle ranch near White's house, while many more were left to litter the streets.[16]

Admiral Murray arrived at El Retiro at 11.30 am to find Whitelocke on the roof of the bullring. 'He showed me the terms', Murray recalled, 'and said ... he thought as did the other generals that ... [they] ... should be agreed to'. Murray sought the advice of his second, Captain Henry Bayntun, the commander of HMS *Africa*. 'He told me he thought I could not possibly do otherwise than sign ... for the general must be the best judge of what the army could do, [and] that if I did not ... I must ... take ... responsibility ... for any consequences'. Once Murray had signed, Captain Whittingham, who had arrived that morning from Corrales, was sent to the fort to bring Liniers to El Retiro to conclude the formalities. The terms were swiftly settled and Liniers returned to prepare the official document.[17]

In the centre, the situation remained volatile. Three thousand had gathered in the Plaza Mayor, shouting, drinking and firing their weapons in the air. Ordered to communicate with Liniers, Captain Foster, one of Whitelocke's aides, was caught in the crush. 'The ... rabble ... refused to ... allow me to pass', he recalled '[and] insulted the escort and myself, by spitting at us and firing over our heads'. After half an hour several mounted Spanish dragoons left the fort, pushed through the crowd and conducted Foster inside. Baying for the blood of Colonel Pack, the mob surged in after them, forced their way up to Liniers' quarters where the Scotsman and his fellow officers had just finished dining and were only prevented from snatching him by three priests who stood round his chair. 'A vast bustle and confusion' ensued. Eventually Liniers restored order and the mob dispersed. The Frenchman then urged Pack to disguise himself 'like a Spaniard', slip out of the fort and ride for British lines before they returned. At 7.00 pm Liniers dispatched the official surrender document to El Retiro. Heading the procession was a bugle player who had deserted from the 71st and a number of gaudily dressed Spanish staff officers who caused sufficient distraction for Pack and Foster to escape to British lines. That night the people of Buenos Ayres celebrated. 'An illumination took place ... and great rejoicings were heard'. The *porteños* could barely believe what they had achieved and in a letter to a friend in Europe, General Bernardo Velasco went as far as to call their victory '[an] astonishing ... event, which cannot be ascribed but to a decided favour of Heaven.'[18]

By dawn the mob had dispersed and Liniers ordered the prisoner exchange to begin. While Craufurd and Holland remained behind, the rest of the officers were escorted to El Retiro along the riverfront. 'We passed heaps of our own dead', Lieutenant Miller recalled. Stripped of all their clothing save their black leather stocks, the corpses were beginning to rot and 'many ... appeared abused'.[19] Craufurd and Holland spent the morning visiting the wounded. Housed in several churches, monasteries and convents, '[they] were in a sad neglected state'. The monks and friars had little medical knowledge and were overwhelmed by the quantity of casualties. Over the next few weeks dozens of rank-and-file would die, many contracting lockjaw as their comrades had done following the siege of Monte Video. The officers fared better. Some were treated in the fort and others were taken in by wealthy families. Colonel Kington was looked after by Mrs O'Gorman, Liniers' lover, who had flown the French flag on 5 July. 'In [her] ... hospitable mansion' the colonel received daily visits from Liniers and the Spaniard who had rescued him. Other British officers had already succumbed to their wounds. Captain William Brookman of the 71st, who had been shot leading Pack's column on 5 July, had struggled on for two days in the fort before expiring.[20]

By mid-morning most of the British prisoners had reached El Retiro. Each group was escorted by an enemy 'rabble', dressed in rags and flushed with pride. At midday the 45th arrived from the Residencia. With their colours flying and the captured howitzers at their head, the sight boosted flagging morale. Later the hostages to be left in Buenos Ayres were chosen. Captain Carrol of the 88th, Captain Nicholas Hamilton of the 5th and Captain Leicester Stanhope of the Carabiniers all volunteered. Colonel Balbiani was amongst their counterparts. 'He was delighted at the prospect of going to England', Captain Monkland recalled, 'his highest ambition [being] ... to behold the Opera.' That afternoon Lieutenant-Colonel Bourke and General Bernardo Velasco settled the demarcation line between the two armies, while several *porteñas* went to El Retiro to flirt with the British officers and the transports and ships of war sent boats to the beach beneath the Abascal Battery in preparation for the evacuation the next day.[21]

At sunset Colonel Mahon's Reserve Brigade arrived from Corrales. En route the waggons carrying the sick and wounded had been cut off by a party of Spaniards. Although they had eventually been allowed to pass, the *peónes* guiding them had been detained. 'Whitelocke promised to [demand their release]', John Mawe recalled, 'but ... omitted to do so, and was very generally accused for this unfeeling neglect'. Considered traitors by the *porteños*, the *peónes* were dealt with severely. 'Some were executed,' Mawe recalled, 'and others condemned to hard labour. Thus not only were they disappointed of ... [the] reward [they had been promised for aiding the British], but [they were also] abandoned in their hour of need'.[22]

The evacuation began on 9 July. Loading the guns, men, horses and supplies was a massive undertaking which would continue for three days. While the walking wounded embarked at the mole, the rest of the troops waded eighty yards into the river off El Retiro where the boats were able to collect them. They were then rowed five miles out to the transports. Admiral Murray's sailors worked round the clock watched by a crowd of *porteños*, many of whom sported weapons and uniforms taken from the British dead. 'These were bitter pills to swallow', recalled William Pitt of HMS *Charwell*, 'but we were ... obliged to gulp them [down] ... while the flag of truce was flying'.[23] In El Retiro, discipline collapsed and desertion soared. On 9 July eleven men of the 45th disappeared, the next day twelve 9th Light Dragoons went missing and even the rifles lost a man. Corporal Noah Beavers was the only greenjacket to abscond from either battalion over the course of the entire campaign. Informed of the problem by Whitelocke, Liniers ordered the deserters rounded up and returned to El Retiro. 'Above fifty' were discovered and embarked in chains to stand trial at Monte Video. Many more were never found. Two sailors from HMS *Nereide* also deserted. Their captain, Robert Corbet, was a notorious flogger and would lose many more men before leaving the River Plate. John Mawe's job of policing the *pulperias* became increasingly difficult as the evacuation progressed. Many men were drunk by the time they boarded the transports and Corporal Hutchins of the 5th was so intoxicated that he fell into the river and drowned.[24]

On 9 July HMS *Rolla* sailed for Monte Video and HMS *Saracen* departed for England the next day. Auchmuty, Craufurd, Bourke and Holland were all on board.[25] On the afternoon of 11 July Whitelocke and Lumley and their staff dined in the fort. 'The dinner was excellent', Captain Whittingham recalled. '"God save the King" was played ... the healths of the Kings of England and Spain drunk ... [and] nothing exceeded the modesty and propriety of General Liniers'. The same could not be said of General Whitelocke. 'He observed the Spanish officers ... were ... very ill clothed', one contemporary recalled, '[and] expressed ... surprise ... at ... being invited to dine with ... blackguards.' By midday on 12 July the evacuation was complete. As well as the hostages and their servants, 400 of the most seriously wounded and a number of medical officers were left behind – their orders to catch up as soon as they could be moved. Captain Whittingham was the last to depart. At 2.00 pm he took a small boat from the mole and boarded the *Aurora* packet. Early the next morning, the entire fleet set sail.[26]

Word of the reverse had reached Monte Video two days before. 'Of all the defeats we have ever sustained', William Eastwick opined, 'this was ... the most ignoble [and] the feeling in Monte Video was so intense, that ... insulting expressions about General Whitelocke, calling him both a coward and a traitor, were written upon the walls'.[27] With only two months to get rid of all their stock, the merchants resorted to desperate measures. 'A small portion' of the £1.5 million worth of goods they had imported was sent to Trinidad, Jamaica, Santo

Domingo, the Cape of Good Hope or Port Jackson, Australia. Others took 'the sad alternative of returning to England ... to throw themselves on the mercy of their creditors', but the bulk remained in the River Plate and a flurry of panic selling ensued. What had been a balanced market became a buyer's dream. Amongst those to profit was William Pius White, to whom Eastwick, amongst others, was obliged to sell the balance of his goods and take *Jesuit Bark* in repayment. The wealthier Monte Videans also did well. Buying as many goods as they could store, they smuggled them into the interior to be sold as far afield as Brazil and Peru. Monte Video's windfall annoyed the *porteños* intensely. The victors of La Defensa felt their rivals were reaping the rewards of a *porteño* success.[28]

On 14 July the fleet anchored off Monte Video. The next morning Whitelocke went ashore, hid in his quarters and buried himself in the one task he truly appeared to have a talent for – administration. Regulations regarding behaviour on board the transports were issued; a timetable of inspections and drills was announced; a bounty of three guineas offered to any soldier who volunteered to join the 87th or 47th, each of which needed 250 men to complete their ranks before they sailed for India as per their original orders; the ships captured on 3 February were put on sale; a note of public thanks was issued to the troops and several recommendations for promotion were processed. Sergeant-Major William Bone of the 88th, sergeants Jackson and Vinicombe of the 36th and Sergeant Bruce of the 5th were all recommended for ensigncies, while Major King of the 5th received the brevet rank of lieutenant-colonel.[29]

Some 500 miles to the northwest, in and around the towns of Córdoba, San Juan, Mendoza and La Rioja, those captured with Beresford in 1806 learnt of their imminent release. The news was greeted with joy. 'We were almost frantic with delight' Lieutenant Fernyhough recalled, '[and began] congratulating each other on the prospect of revisiting our native land'. Captain Gillepsie and his companions were equally pleased. 'The whole of us instantly ... arose, and with melody in our hearts, sang God Save the King'. The initial joy was tempered when details of the treaty arrived. Gillespie and Fernyhough were mortified, while Ensign William Gavin, held in the village of San Ignacio, 'laughed at the idea', only to have it confirmed by *porteño* newspapers. The reaction of the rank-and-file was more complex. With an abundance of well-paid employment and eligible young women, many, especially the Catholics, had decided to settle in the New World. The last thing they wanted was to return to the draconian regime imposed by the British army. Nevertheless, their overseers had their instructions and they set out for Buenos Ayres at the end of July.[30]

On 22 July Colonel Peter Kington died. Despite the efforts of Mrs O'Gorman, in whose care he had been left when the army departed for Monte Video, his leg had become infected with tetanus. Liniers, who had formed a friendship with Kington during his convalescence, had his body placed in state in the viceroy's palace until the funeral was held. As the highest-ranking British casualty of the battle, the ceremony was performed with as much gravitas as the *porteños* could muster. 'General Liniers and the principal military officers, and civil magistrates attended, with four regiments of infantry to fire over the grave, and a tablet, with a suitable inscription, was ordered, by the General, to be placed over the remains'.[31]

On 27 July General Acland and the 89th arrived at Monte Video. Their voyage had been plagued by delays. After embarking at Ramsgate a year before, a bout of opthalmia had broken out and the troops had been landed at Fort Cumberland to recover. In April they had re-embarked. While still in the Channel, the *Malabar* transport had parted company, contrary winds later prevented the rest from rounding Cape San Augustin in Brazil and a sudden storm had forced another transport to call in at Rio de Janeiro for repairs. By the time they arrived at Monte Video, the 89th had been at sea for twenty weeks.[32]

On 31 July a detachment of 'dirty, slovenly, [and] badly dressed' troops led by Colonel Elio arrived at Monte Video to oversee the transfer of power. 'To the disgust of the army, [Elio] ... was allowed to assume functions as commander' a witness recalled. The Spanish officers took advantage of the British merchants' plight to purchase the most elegant uniforms, regardless of provenance. 'It was no uncommon sight to see Dragoons in Infantry epaulets and Hussars in naval cocked hats', Monkland scoffed. On the morning of their arrival Whitelocke published a proclamation ordering all British citizens to be ready to leave on 6 September. The edict gave the lie to any lingering hopes that hostilities would recommence and on 1 August the 47th and 87th, having made up their numbers, departed for India via the Cape of Good Hope.[33] The next eight days saw a flurry of departures. On 3 August HMS *Rolla* set sail and on 8 August the 88th and 95th and the 9th and 20th Light Dragoons departed for England. In convoy were the hospital ship *Alexander*, a leaky vessel which had barely survived the voyage from the Cape one year before, and sixteen merchantmen under the protection of HMS *Unicorn* and *Thisbe*.[34]

In the first days of August a general court martial tried the deserters Liniers had rounded up in Buenos Ayres. In deference to the Frenchman's request that they not be executed, the judges sentenced all but one to transportation for life, but decided to make an example of Charles Dixon, the drummer of the East India Company who had been captured at El Retiro. On the morning of 3 September detachments from each regiment landed from the transports to watch him hang. 'It rained heavily [that morning]', Private Morley recalled. 'The troops ... were formed in a hollow square [and] the dead march beat, when the unhappy man attended by a priest and a slight escort issued from the prison ... [Dixon] ... was tied up and swung off; when lo! The rope snapped ... and he fell to the ground.' As was common in such cases, the prisoner was pardoned, but was destined to die from a fall into the hold on the voyage home.[35]

By the first week of September the prisoners taken with Beresford had begun to arrive at Buenos Ayres. Lieutenant Fernyhough's party reached the capital on horseback after just forty-four days. The rank-and-file, on the other hand, endured an epic march across the *pampas*. Hundreds deserted en route, returning to employers, wives and girlfriends in the interior. Others died or fell sick and only 578 of the original 1,200 arrived. The capital remained in uproar. Drunken gangs roamed the streets and 'the rude and indisciplined soldiery' attempted to steal what few possessions the British retained. Several of the elite, by contrast, welcomed them with open arms. Gillespie was put up by an old friend and Fernyhough was sought out by a merchant who returned the scimitar he had entrusted to him several months before. Transports had been arranged to ferry the men to Monte Video, but the officers had to pay for their berths. Gillespie hired the launch of an American brig for fourteen *pesos* and set sail on 2 September. 'Soon after ... an English gun vessel hove in sight' he recalled. 'She proved to be the *Encounter*, the same vessel in which I [had] entered [the river fourteen months before]'.[36]

In Monte Video as the date of the evacuation drew near 'all was in a state of confusion'. British merchants gathered their goods and sought ships to take them away before the handover, while others shut up shop in town, speculators snapped up final bargains and the streets heaved with soldiers and sailors buying last-minute supplies, jostled and threatened by the town's youths who had found their voice now the invaders were about to leave. While most were glad to be gone and the locals equally pleased to be rid of them, for some there was a sense of regret. Harry Smith left his lodgings 'with ... the deepest sorrow and ... lively gratitude' to the 'kind Spanish family' who had cared for him during his illness and the Cabildo wrote a letter of thanks to Colonel Gore Browne for his fair and kind-hearted governorship. Down at the pier the prize ships that the Royal Navy had been unable to sell were loaded with surplus hides, tallow and cocoa, towed out into the roads and set on fire and on 5 September the remaining troops embarked. Ensign Gavin and 250 of the 71st boarded the *Princessa*, a Spanish galleon the navy had deemed worth saving. The rest boarded the transports that had brought them to South America. Fearing they would suffer the same fate as the *peónes* Whitelocke had abandoned in Buenos Ayres, Saturnino Rodríguez Peña and Manuel Acieto Padilla, the men who had arranged Beresford's escape, departed with their entire families. Peña would be left at Brazil while Padilla sailed to England. Both were awarded a British pension of 300 pounds a year. On the morning of 7 September the last of the garrison left town and the celebrations began. Cannon were fired from Fort San Joseph and the Citadel and the people drank and danced in the streets round bonfires fuelled by ripped up British signs, while their would-be conquerors looked on from the massed transports in the roads.[37]

Epilogue

Echoes

7 September 1807 to modern day

The last of the sick and wounded left Buenos Ayres on 25 September on the *Campion* transport. With their departure the only official British presence remaining in the River Plate was a flotilla consisting of the frigate HMS *Nereide* and three cutters (HMS *Cherwell*, *Hermes* and *Olympia*) under the command of Captain Corbet, who had orders to prevent any late-coming British merchantmen falling into enemy hands. Corbet spent an uneventful three and a half months patrolling the river. Aside from occasionally chasing Spanish schooners into the shallows, the only occurrence of note was a staggeringly high rate of desertion. While HMS *Nereide* was at anchor off Ensenada on 27 November ten sailors stole the cutter, sailed in shore, set her on fire and disappeared inland chased by volleys fired by Corbet's marines. Three others fled at Maldonado on 6 November. Corbet left the river for the Cape of Good Hope on 26 January 1808.[1]

On land the celebrations continued. *Te Deums* were organised, celebratory odes composed and victory parades held throughout Spanish South America. Official congratulations were sent from Santiago, Lima and Mexico City and a gigantic gold and silver plaque memorialising the *porteños'* achievement was cast in Oruro on the Altiplano of Upper Peru. Liniers sent victory dispatches to Carlos IV and Napoleon Bonaparte and requested reinforcements and supplies to ward off the next British attack. In September titles and pensions were awarded to the heroes of La Defensa, the Plaza Mayor was renamed Victory Square and El Retiro became the Field of Glory. On 12 November 130 slaves who had taken part in the fighting were liberated. Each was awarded an annual pension of six *pesos*, while their owners received compensation of 250 *pesos* a head.[2]

The leading ships of the First Division of Whitelocke's army touched at Spithead on 5 November. Within two weeks all were accounted for with the exception of the *Alexander* hospital ship, last seen lagging behind on 20 October. With his vessel leaking badly, Captain Richard Howard had set short sail and manned the pumps. Nevertheless, the water rose in the hold and the 110 men, women and children on board panicked. Most were sick or wounded soldiers of the 5th, 36th, 38th and 87th.[3] On 22 October the water reached the orlop deck. Taking to the launch before sunset with the ship's agent and four of his crew, Howard sailed round the *Alexander* as she sank. At nightfall he ordered the chief mate and boatswain to lower the longboat. The situation on board was horrendous. Strapped into their hammocks, the most badly wounded had already drowned.

Dozens more swarmed on deck, whilst the women and children huddled together in the cabin. In the chaos a pole stove in the longboat's side and thirteen soldiers, sixteen sailors and a woman, Joanna Evans, who was clutching her thirteen-month-old baby, scrambled on board. Patching up the damage, they drifted clear and at 10.00 pm the *Alexander* 'gave a heavy lurch, and went down head foremost ... into the abyss'. All on board were drowned. Captain Howard's launch was picked up within eight days by an American merchantman bound for Salem, Massachusetts. With just four biscuits, three gallons of spirits and one pound of raisins, those on board the longboat began to starve. Seven soldiers and three sailors died and the survivors turned to cannibalism. Ten days after leaving the *Alexander*, they were spotted by a merchantman. As she came alongside, the survivors hurled the remains of the corpse they had been eating overboard.[4]

The ships of the Second Division arrived in England in late November 1807. Having separated early in the voyage, HMS *Medusa*, with Lieutenant-General Whitelocke on board, was the first to disembark. Travelling 'incog[nito]', White-locke took a carriage to Whitehall to make his report.[5] News of the surrender had preceded him by several weeks. On 14 September *The Times* had termed the defeat 'the greatest [disaster] that has been felt by this country since the commencement of the revolutionary war.' Colonel Gordon, the Duke of York's secretary, compared it to 'the destruction of the army under General [Edward] Braddock near Fort Duquense [in 1755]' and the public and papers demanded a court of inquiry. 'Such a trial is what ... the tarnished honour of the Army calls for [and] what the surviving relations of the departed heroes weep for', *The Times* opined. The government concurred. The Duke of York briefly considered trying Craufurd for his surrender at Santo Domingo, but a single scapegoat was all that was deemed necessary and when a general court martial was convened in the Royal Hospital in Chelsea on 28 January 1808 Whitelocke took the stand alone.[6]

The lieutenant-general was charged on four counts: incompetent organisation of the march from Ensenada and the attack on Buenos Ayres; losing contact with his troops during the assault; erring in his decision to attack with unloaded muskets; and capitulating unnecessarily and surrendering Monte Video without cause. The judges included some of the biggest names in the military establishment. Lieutenant-General Sir William Medows was president and amongst nineteen generals judging was the future commander-in-chief Sir David Dundas and Sir John Moore, soon to be immortalised by his death at La Coruña.[7] Whitelocke pleaded not guilty and the trial lasted thirty-one days. His staff officers and brigadier-generals gave evidence, as did the commanders of all thirteen columns aside from those sent to India. Several newspapers serialised the proceedings. *The Times* published two supplements devoted to the trial, the court transcript was published and the gallery was packed throughout. On 18 March, after the judges had made their deliberations, Medows pronounced Whitelocke guilty on three charges. That relating to unloaded muskets was discounted as a commonly-taken measure to ensure a swift attack. As the verdict was read out Whitelocke's father, present in the gallery throughout, 'cried like an infant', one contemporary recalled.

A suitable punishment was long debated. To be beaten by the South Americans was so humiliating that desperate measures were called for and Brigadier-General Craufurd 'strove hard to have [Whitelocke] shot'. A large part of public opinion was in accord and besides, such a punishment was not without precedent. In 1757 Admiral John Byng had been executed for the loss of Port Mahon in the Seven Years' War, prompting Voltaire to quip that 'it is good to kill an admiral from time to time, in order to encourage the others.' In Whitelocke's case the court was more lenient. Despite his failings, the lieutenant-general still enjoyed the best of connections and during the trial the Prince Regent had written to his wife, Mary, ensuring her that *her* husband, and *his* 'dear friend', had 'no cause for alarm.' On the afternoon of 18 March Whitelocke was sentenced to be cashiered out of the army 'and declared totally unfit ... to serve his Majesty in any Military Capacity whatsoever'. George III insisted that the sentence 'be read at the head of every Regiment in His Service, and inserted in all Regimental Orderly Books, with a view of its becoming a lasting memorial'. Still the country was not satisfied. 'Two thousand, five hundred ... have been lost', *The Times* thundered, 'a whole army disgraced and defeated by a herd of mechanics; and what is the ample vengeance ... afforded us ...? One general has been cashiered!'[8]

The reactions of those who had fought under Whitelocke were mixed. Stephen Morley and his comrades in the 5th pitied their former commander. 'I think his sentence ... must be worse than death', the private opined. Lieutenant Harry Smith felt that Major-General Gower had been the real villain, while Captain Wilkie thought that the War Office and Admiralty were to blame. 'Most likely [Whitelocke] ... did all ... [he] could, and the fault of [his] ... failure rested as much with those who [had] sent [him as with the general himself]', he explained. 'That he was unequal to the task is true; but few men are apt to confess, "when greatness is thrust upon them," that they are incapable, even if they are conscious of it'. Others were less forgiving. Craufurd's fury festered for the remainder of his volatile career; one diarist recorded how a private soldier, when visiting one of the maids in her employ, threw his hat to the floor and trampled it in disgust at the mere mention of the former general's name; and the toast 'success to grey hairs, but bad luck to Whitelocks' became popular in public houses and regimental dining rooms across Britain and beyond.[9]

Whilst Whitelocke's court martial signalled the end of his career, Sir Home Popham had emerged from his, held in Portsmouth Harbour on board HMS *Gladiator* twelve months before, with his prospects undimmed. Two charges had been made. Firstly, that Popham had left Cape Town at the mercy of the French by stripping it of all its warships, and, secondly, that his invasion had been undertaken without orders. A cocksure Popham played the crowd from the start. 'Sir Home ... appeared in perfect spirits;' *The Courier* reported on the first day of the trial, 'and as he came on deck, walked with his usual steady and undaunted air.' Popham spoke for a full day in his defence. After muddying the waters with a deliberately bewildering and convoluted explanation of tides and currents, he claimed that he had left the Cape at a season when it was impossible for a naval squadron to attack it due to the prevailing winds, then went on to defend himself against the second charge with a lengthy soliloquy on the glorious precedents of naval officers, such as admirals Rooke, Hood and Saint Vincent, who had acted without orders in the past. On the fifth day, the president, William Young, Admiral of the Blue, announced the court's decision. Although he felt that Popham's behaviour had been 'highly censurable' his only punishment was to be 'severely reprimanded'. When Popham was given a new command four weeks later the editor of *The Times* could barely contain his bile.[10]

Meanwhile, plans were afoot for a second invasion of the River Plate. As late as April 1808 10,000 troops, including the 5th, 36th, 38th, 40th, 45th, 71st, 2/95 and the 20th Light Dragoons, were earmarked for the operation which was to be led by Lieutenant-General Arthur Wellesley. The government decided that South American independence would be the primary aim, but as the final preparations were being made news arrived of a momentous rebellion in Spain. In March 1808 Napoleon had forced Carlos IV to abdicate in favour of his son, Ferdinand VII, but when he too proved difficult to manipulate, he was replaced by Joseph Bonaparte. Having a Frenchman on the throne was more than the Spanish could stomach and on 2 May 1808 an uprising broke out in Madrid. The French garrison were cut down and the rebellion spread. Napoleon responded with a full scale invasion, while the Spanish raised a temporary government, known as the *Cortes*, in Cádiz.

These events reverberated across the Atlantic. Many South Americans considered the *Cortes* an illegitimate body and insisted on setting up their own regional governments instead. In the River Plate, the situation was particularly factious. Although mutual antipathy towards the British had united the *porteños*, with Whitelocke's evacuation the old divisions came to the fore. The main fissure was between creole and Spaniard. Another existed between those who favoured free trade and those who benefitted from the restrictions imposed by Spain, and the established elite and the newly empowered proletariat were also vehemently opposed. At the centre of this whirlwind, Liniers struggled to maintain his authority. His nationality, his known leanings toward free trade and the influence of his married mistress, Anna O'Gorman, or 'La Perichona' as she was scathingly known, provided his enemies with plenty of ammunition. In Monte Video Governor Elio became openly defiant, while the Buenos Ayres Cabildo, still led by Liniers' long-term adversary Martín de Álzaga, began to plot the Frenchman's demise.

Back in Europe several British veterans of the River Plate were about to take centre stage. With the news of the uprising in Spain, Wellesley's expedition was diverted to the Peninsula. 'So … we had to go and fight for the very nation we had been but a few months before opposing' Private Lawrence recalled. The change of allegiance also affected the prisoners taken at the siege of Monte Video. The rank-and-file had been distributed amongst the prison hulks in the Thames, cramped, fetid places where deaths from illness were high, while their officers had been kept in relative comfort. Former Governor Huidobro and his wife and children resided in a private house in Reading. The rest lodged in boarding houses in Bishop's Waltham, Portsmouth and Plymouth. All were afforded the freedom of town. When the news from Madrid reached the British authorities, Huidobro and ten of his most senior officers were permitted to return to South America. The others were formed into a makeshift unit. Christened the Regiment of Buenos Ayres, or 'Colorados' due to the bright red British uniforms they wore, they were dispatched to Spain to join Joaquín Blake's Army of Galicia. On 14 July 1808 they fought at the Battle of Medina de Rioseco. The French were victorious and thirty-two of the South Americans were killed. The survivors remained in northern Spain until 1810 when thirty were allowed to return home. Amongst them were the three González de Balcarce brothers who had survived the siege of Monte Video three years before.[11]

Meanwhile, Sir Arthur Wellesley's army had landed in Portugal. Heralding its arrival on 1 August 1808 were captains Philip Roche, Robert Patrick and William Carrol. All three were veterans of the River Plate. At the Battle of Roliça on 17 August, another, Captain John Payne of the 45th, was amongst the casualties. The musket ball that had lodged in his lungs during Major Trotter's ill-fated charge through the streets of Buenos Ayres killed him as he led his men up a hill to attack the French line.[12] Several more veterans of the River Plate were killed at the Battle of Vimiero, Major Richard Vandeleur succumbed to illness at Camp Maior in Portugal in October and dozens more died on Sir John Moore's retreat to La Coruña that winter. On 17 January 1809, whilst fighting a rearguard action to buy time for the bulk of the army to evacuate, Sir David Baird was hit by fire from a French battery. He would never take the field again. The next day Patrick Carey fell overboard from a transport of the 71st. A former prisoner of the *Lady Jane Shore*, Carey had joined the British Army at Buenos Ayres and had survived the Reconquista and his subsequent imprisonment in the interior only to drown in La Coruña Bay.[13]

Whilst Carey's death passed unnoticed, other River Plate veterans achieved immortality in Spain. Perhaps the best known was Robert Craufurd. In command of the celebrated Light Division, Black Bob excelled on the retreat to La Coruña and played an active role in all of Wellesley's Peninsula campaigns until being mortally wounded at the siege of Ciudad Rodrigo in January 1812. William Carr Beresford also won considerable credit. Briefly employed as the Governor of Madeira, he was later charged with reforming the Portuguese army. Within two years the once ill-disciplined force had been transformed into a cohesive body which would serve with distinction alongside Wellesley's troops. In 1811 Beresford commanded an allied army at the Battle of Albuera, one of the bloodiest of the entire Peninsular War. Amongst those under his command was a thirty-two-year-old creole lieutenant-colonel named José de San Martín, future liberator of South America.

After leading the 71st at Copenhagen, Vimiero and La Coruña, Denis Pack also joined the Portuguese army. In 1813, with the rank of brigadier-general, he commanded the 6th Division and later fought under Wellington at the Battle of Waterloo. Pack's replacement as commander of the 71st, Henry Cadogan, led the Highlanders throughout the Peninsula until he was mortally wounded at the Battle of Vitoria in 1813. William Guard, lieutenant-colonel of the 45th at

Buenos Ayres, won Wellesley's respect for his rear-guard action following the Battle of Talavera in 1809 and went on to attain the rank of lieutenant-general, as did his major in the River Plate, Jasper Nicolls. Samuel Whittingham, White-locke's aide at Buenos Ayres, was also mentioned in dispatches for his bravery at Talavera. William Lumley commanded the cavalry in Sir John Stuart's short-lived Sicilian expedition, led the assault on the San Cristobal bastion at the Second Siege of Badajoz, played a pivotal role in the Battle of Albuera and led a cavalry detachment to victory at the Battle of Usagre before being invalided home in August 1811. Sir Samuel Auchmuty, the most senior of Whitelocke's brigadier-generals in the Plate, was appointed military commander at Madras and in 1811 led an invasion against the Dutch colony of Java. The Franco-Dutch forces (led by the same General Jan Willem Janssens whom Baird had defeated at the Cape six and a half years before) surrendered on 18 September 1812. The Bostonian was promoted to the rank of lieutenant-general as a result.

Two of the Royal Artillery officers in the River Plate also enjoyed successful careers. Captain Alexander Dickson used the experience he had gained at Monte Video to reduce the walled towns of Ciudad Rodrigo, Badajoz, Burgos and San Sebastian and the forts at Salamanca before being promoted to commander-in-chief of all artillery in the Peninsula, while Captain Augustus Frazer served as Dickson's second-in-command in Spain and led the Horse Artillery at Waterloo. Captain John Squire of the Royal Engineers was responsible for the destruction of several Spanish bridges, thus delaying the enemy during Sir John Moore's Coruña campaign, took an active role in the siege of Flushing and was employed in the construction of Torres Vedras in 1810. Squire also took part in the three sieges of Badajoz and was promoted to lieutenant-colonel when the town was finally captured on 6 April 1812. He died of fever brought on by exhaustion six weeks later.

Of the rank-and-file involved in the River Plate less is known. Private Stephen Morley of the 5th fought in the Peninsula from 1808 to 1813 when he was sent back to England as a recruiting sergeant; Norbert Landsheit served with the 20th Light Dragoons at Roliça, Coimbra and Sicily; Thomas Todd of the 71st survived Walcheren Fever to fight at Waterloo; as did William Lawrence of the 40th, who also saw action at New Orleans in the War of 1812. Private Thomas Plunkett, the rifleman who shot twenty Spaniards during the defence of Santo Domingo, fought and drank his way across Flanders, Portugal and Spain from 1808 to 1815. He is best remembered for a single piece of marksmanship in 1808 during Sir John Moore's retreat, when he killed General Auguste Colbert with a single shot from his Baker rifle at a range of 650 yards.

Charles Stirling was promoted to Vice-Admiral in 1810 and the following year was appointed commander-in-chief of the Jamaica Squadron. In the war of 1812 he harried American shipping and conducted several coastal raids around Bermuda, but was recalled to London and court martialled in 1813 on a charge of hiring out his ships to protect foreign merchantmen. Stirling's reputation was later restored, but he never saw active service again. George Murray also attained the rank of vice-admiral and was knighted in 1815. He died at home of a heart attack four years later. In 1809 Josias Rowley of HMS *Raisonnable* was appointed commodore at the Cape of Good Hope and took part in the capture of the Island of Mauritius in 1810. Amongst those under his command was Robert Corbet of HMS *Nereide*. Following his draconian regime in South America, Corbet's crew had mutinied and he fought in the Mauritius campaign as captain of HMS *Africaine*. On the night of 12 September, having suppressed yet another mutiny on his new command, he engaged two French frigates. His right foot shot off by the enemy's second broadside, Corbet was carried below. By the time his second surrendered two hours later, Corbet was dead. Some said his crew had murdered him. Others claimed that the humiliation of surrender led him to take his own life. After 1807 Sir Home Popham's career went from strength to strength. Just a few weeks after his court martial, he was appointed naval second-in-command in the Copenhagen Expedition and helped to capture the Danish fleet. In 1810 he was given a roving commission as captain of HMS *Venerable* and for two years aided the guerrillas in Spain with a series of perfectly executed raids on French fortresses on the Basque coast.

*   *   *

On 1 January 1809 the Buenos Ayres Cabildo put its plan to oust Liniers into effect. Supported by Bishop Benito Lué y Riega and the Catalan, Basque and Galician militia, they staged a *coup d'état*. Liniers was coerced into recognising a Junta modelled on that at Cádiz. The commander of the Patricios, Cornelio de Saavedra, had other ideas. Storming into the Sala Capitular with a file of soldiers with fixed bayonets, he forced the Cabildo to reinstate the Frenchman and Liniers became the puppet of the creole faction with Saavedra at its head. The Catalan, Galician and Basque militias were disbanded by the Patricios and the ringleaders of the coup, Martín de Álzaga foremost amongst them, were imprisoned in Carmen de Patagones, an isolated fort 500 miles away. The situation seemed ripe for independence. Liniers resolved to open Buenos Ayres to international trade and the creoles grew bolder in their talk of a split with Spain, but such ideas were put on hold by the unexpected arrival of a new viceroy in Monte Video in June 1809.

Hidalgo de Cisernos, a former Spanish naval captain who had commanded the *Santísima Trinidad* at Trafalgar, hoped to reassert the colonial system that had governed the River Plate for the last 300 years. His orders were to quash any notion of creole independence, stamp his authority on the Cabildos of Buenos Ayres and Monte Video and rid the region of the smugglers to whom Liniers had given free rein. The factions opposed to such measures were too strong, however, and Cisernos spent the next eleven months attempting to placate all sides instead. The Spanish militia were reinstated, Álzaga was allowed to return to Buenos Ayres, and Saavedra was promoted to full colonel. Such tactics proved counter-productive and news of continuing Spanish reverses in the Peninsula sparked another revolution in May 1810. Once more the creole faction emerged triumphant and on 25 May Cisernos was deposed by the First Junta, a creole council headed by Saavedra. When news reached Liniers, who had gone into retirement in Córdoba on Cisernos' arrival, he began raising troops and made an ill-advised march on Buenos Ayres, supported by Gutiérrez de la Concha and Colonel Santiago Allende. Desertions decimated the Frenchman's army and when the Junta mobilised against him, he fled for Upper Peru, but was captured 200 miles southeast of Córdoba and sentenced to death. Colonel Allende and de la Concha were shot by his side.[14]

Saavedra's Junta was the first of a series of short-lived dictatorships which blighted Buenos Ayres. Thousands were purged, amongst them many veterans of the British invasions. Discredited for initial resistance to the First Junta, Bishop Lué y Riega was forbidden from speaking in public and in 1811 exiled to the village of San Fernando. The following March he died after a birthday celebration. Poisoning was widely believed to be the cause. Martín de Álzaga was killed three and a half months later. Arrested for plotting the overthrow of the First Triumvirate (the third government following Cisernos' expulsion), he was sentenced to death by firing squad with thirty others in July 1812. His body was hung up in Victory Square for three days as a warning to those who dared oppose the revolution. Pascual Huidobro was also implicated in the plot. To avoid arrest the former governor of Monte Video set off for a new life across the Andes, but died of an illness whilst in Mendoza in March 1813. Three years later Juan Martín de Pueyrredón was elected Supreme Dictator of the United Provinces of the River Plate. Pueyrredón backed Jose de San Martin's liberation campaigns in Chile, which saw the region freed from the Spanish yoke, but was forced into exile in Monte Video in 1819 and would play no further role in public life.

On the far side of the Atlantic, with the Napoleonic Wars at an end, the majority of the British veterans of the River Plate had been disbanded. Most faded into obscurity, but a few high-ranking exceptions were assigned diplomatic roles overseas. In 1817, Rear-Admiral Sir Home Popham was given command of the Jamaica Squadron. Tropical illnesses weakened his health and in 1820 he requested a return to England. He died within seven weeks of going home. Samuel Whittingham, Whitelocke's aide at Buenos Ayres, was Governor General of Dominica from 1819 to 1821; William Lumley was appointed governor of Bermuda, but was dismissed in 1825 for dabbling in ecclesiastical matters; and Richard Bourke, Whitelocke's quarter-master-general, served as governor of New South Wales from 1831 to 1837. An avowed Whig, Bourke reformed the transportation system, named the town of Melbourne and died a full general in 1851.

His name tarnished by the River Plate campaign, John Leveson Gower was never given an active command again and died in 1816 at the age of forty-two. John Whitelocke survived his former second-in-command by seventeen years. On 23 October 1833 he died at Hall Barn Park in Beaconsfield, Buckinghamshire. His death passed unremarked. Harry Smith, the young rifle officer who had been wounded at the breach at Monte Video, fought throughout the Peninsular War and served in the Xhosa Wars (1834–6) at the Cape of Good Hope and the First Anglo-Sikh War (1845–6) in Northern India. Smith died a lieutenant-general in 1860 at the age of seventy-three. Perhaps the last surviving veteran of the River Plate campaign was Captain Fletcher Wilkie. Having had his memoirs published in the *United Service Magazine*, Wilkie died a lieutenant-colonel on 12 May 1862. He was ninety years old.

*   *   *

Never more than an embarrassing sideshow in a long and gruelling war, the invasions of the River Plate were soon forgotten in Britain, but in Uruguay and, to a greater extent, Argentina, memories of the Reconquista and Defensa remain very much alive. Having emerged from seven decades of intermittent internecine conflict, in the 1870s the inhabitants of the River Plate began to look back with pride at the war that had sparked their independence. Over the next six decades several books were written on the subject, culminating in Carlos Robert's magisterial effort, *Las Invasiones Inglesas*. A lull followed, only for the conflict to be rediscovered in the early 1980s. As tensions over the Falkland Islands grew, Argentina took comfort in the victory they had formerly won over the British and a final flourish of histories were published to mark the bicentennial. Today several traces of the invasions can still be seen. A plaque marks the site of the breach at Monte Video, the bagpipe banner captured by Pueyrredón at the Reconquista hangs in the National History Museum in Buenos Ayres and the flags of the 71st and Royal Marines remain on display in the atrium of Santo Domingo Church. Faded and hanging behind glass, they make for a sterile memorial, but the visitor who braves the traffic to cross the street is rewarded with a more visceral sight. Looking back one can see that the left hand tower of the church is still peppered with round shot fired on the day that the redcoats were humbled over 200 years before.

Appendix I

British Troops Numbers and Casualty Statistics

Beresford's army, 25 June, 1806
Staff, 7; Royal Engineers, 3; Royal Artillery, 36; St Helena Artillery, 102; 20th Light Dragoons, 7; 71st, 844; St Helena Infantry, 182; Marines, 340; Seamen, 1,000; Officers, 70.
Total: 1,641.

Casualties, Buenos Ayres, 12 August 1806
2 officers, 46 men killed.
8 officers, 99 men wounded.
10 men missing.
Total: 165.

Backhouse's reinforcements
Royal Artillery, 6; 38th, 811; 47th, 685; 54th, 103; 20th Light Dragoons, 191; 21st Light Dragoons, 140; Officers and Sergeants. 244.
Total: 2,180.

Auchmuty's reinforcements
Royal Artillery, 170; 40th, 1,000; 87th, 826; 95th, 300; 17th Light Dragoons, 700.
Total: 2,996.

Casualties, Monte Video, 3 February 1807
6 officers, 112 men killed.
21 officers, 257 men wounded.

Craufurd's reinforcements
5th, 836; 36th, 822; 45th, 850; 88th, 798; 95th, 364; Royal Artillery, 243; 6th Dragoon Guards (Carabiniers), 299; Officers and Sergeants, 588.
Total: 4,800.

Whitelocke's reinforcements
Horse Artillery, 130; Draft of Recuits, 500.
Total: 630.

Casualties, Buenos Ayres, 5 July 1807
15 officers, 311 men killed.
57 officers, 622 men wounded.
1,611 of all ranks taken prisoners.
3 officers, 205 men missing.
Total: 2,824.

Money

British currency: There were 12 pennies (d) in 1 shilling (s) and 20 shillings in 1 pound (£).

Spanish colonial currency: The *peso fuerte*, known to the British as 'pesos', 'hard pesos', 'hard dollars', 'dollars' or 'Spanish dollars', was the principal monetary unit throughout Spain's South American colonies. There were 8 *reales* to 1 *peso*.

Exchange rate: The rate of exchange fluctuated. On 6 February 1807 Sir Samuel Auchmuty stated that 1 *peso* was the equivalent of 4s 6d.

Daily Wages (British Army):
Infantry Private – Standard pay was 1s per day, but soldiers were charged up to 6d for subsistence. Other deductions were made for maintenance of the soldier's uniform, medical treatment, breakages and barrack damages and a regular stipend was paid to the regimental agent and for the upkeep of the Chelsea Hospital.
Infantry Drummer/Fifer/Piper – 1s 2d.
Infantry Sergeant – 1s 7d.
Infantry Surgeon – 9s 5d.
Lieutenant – 4s 8d.
Captain – 9s 5d.
Major – 14s 1d.
Colonel – 22s 6d.

Daily Wages (Royal Navy):
Ordinary Seamen – 8d per day. Sailors were not charged for rations, although deductions were made for clothing and medical treatement.
Able-seaman – 1s.
Lieutenant – 10s.
1st Lieutenant – 15s.
Commander – 17s.
Captain – £1 4s.

Wages – Buenos Ayres:
Carpenters – 10 *reales* per day.
Bricklayers – 5 *reales* per day.
Urban labourers – 4 *reales* per day
Rural labourers (*peónes*) – 8 *pesos* per month.
Ship's carpenters – 18 *reales* per day.

Sailors – 13 *pesos* per month.
Militia (Buenos Ayres and Monte Video) – 12 *pesos* per month.

Prices – Buenos Ayres:
1 *fanega* (55.5 litres) of wheat – 8 *pesos*, 6 *reales*.
1 *arroba* (11 kilogrammes) of rice – 2 *pesos*, 2 *reales*.
1 *botija* (jug) of wine – 2 *pesos*, 1 *real*.
1 *quintal* (46 kilogrammes) of salted beef – 8 *pesos*.
1 month's rent for a single room in Buenos Ayres – 8½ *pesos*.
An unskilled slave – 200 *pesos*.
A skilled slave – 400 to 600 *pesos*.
A pair of handmade shoes for an adult male – 2 *pesos*.
A shirt – 2 *pesos*.

Appendix III

Weights and Measurements

1 league = 3 miles or just under 5 kilometres.
1 yard   = 0.9144 metres.
1 mile   = 1.6 kilometres.
1 cable = 185.2 metres (a cable is a nautical measurement equivalent to 0.1 of a nautical mile).
1 cwt   = 50.8 kilogrammes (cwt or hundredweight is an old imperial measurement equivalent to 112 lb or 8 stone).
quintal = 46 kilogrammes (*quintal* is an old Spanish unit of weight).

Notes

Introduction

1. http://www.historyhome.co.uk/c-eight/france/consys.htm
2. A useful, if somewhat dated, account of the period is Arthur Bryant's *The Years of Endurance* (Collins, London, 1942).

Chapter 1: 'The Secret is Unravelled'

1. Martin, Henry, *Journal and Letters of the Rev. Henry Martyn*, Volume 1 (Seeley and Burnside, London, 1837), p. 310.
2. http://www.pbenyon.plus.com/Naval_History/Vol_IV/Vol_IV_P_272.htm
3. Parkinson, Cyril Northcote (ed.), *Samuel Walters, Lieutenant R.N.* (Liverpool University Press, Liverpool, 2005), p. 37.
4. Graham-Yooll, Andrew, *The Forgotten Colony: A history of the English-speaking communities of Argentina* (L.O.L.A., 1999), p. 39.
5. *A Full and Correct Report of the Trial of Sir Home Popham* (J. and J. Richardson, London, 1807), p. 10.
6. Hooker, William Jackson (ed.), *Botanical Miscellany, Containing Figures and Descriptions*, Volume II (Murray, London, 1831), p. 11.
7. Gillespie, *Gleaning and Remarks collected during many months residence at Buenos Ayres* (Dewhirst, London, 1818), p. 7; Parkinson (ed.), *Samuel Walters*, p. 37; *The United Service Journal and Naval and Military Magazine*, 1836, Volume 1 (Colburn, London, 1836), p. 484.
8. *The United Service Magazine*, 1836, Volume 1, p. 484; *Journal and Letters of the Rev. Henry Martyn*, Volume 1, p. 303; *A Full and Correct Report of the Trial of Sir Home Popham*, p. 14.
9. *Journal and Letters of the Rev. Henry Martyn*, Volume 1, p. 300; *The United Service Magazine*, 1836, Volume 1, p. 484; Parkinson (ed.), *Samuel Walters*, p. 38.
10. Popham, Hugh, *A Damned Cunning Fellow: The eventful life of Rear-Admiral Sir Home Popham* (Old Ferry Press, 1991), pp. 1–10.
11. *The United Service Magazine*, 1836, Volume 2, p. 195; Gleig, George Robert, *The Hussar* (G.B. Zieber, Philadephia, 1845), p. 154.
12. *A Full and Correct Report of the Trial of Sir Home Popham*, p. 10.
13. Fernyhough, *Military Memoirs of Four Brothers* (William Sams, London, 1829), p. 67.
14. Gillespie, *Gleaning and Remarks*, p. 6; Martin, *Journal and Letters of the Rev. Henry Martyn*, Volume 1, p. 296; *The Highland Light Infantry Chronicle*, 1901, July and October, p. 695; MS. Eng. Misc. d. 242, p. 132; *The United Service Magazine*, 1836, Volume 1, p. 483.
15. *The United Service Magazine*, 1836, Volume 1, p. 484.
16. 71st pay list WO 17/192.
17. *The Highland Light Infantry Chronicle*, 1901, July and October, p. 695.
18. *Journal and Letters of the Rev. Henry Martyn*, Volume 1, p. 306.
19. *Journal and Letters of the Rev. Henry Martyn*, Volume 1, p. 308.
20. Fernyhough, *Military Memoirs of Four Brothers*, p. 69.
21. Gillespie, *Gleaning and Remarks*, p. 7.
22. Gleig, *The Hussar*, pp. 148–9.
23. *Journal and Letters of the Rev. Henry Martyn*, Volume 1, p. 326; Parkinson (ed.), *Samuel Walters*, p. 37.
24. Gillespie, *Gleaning and Remarks*, p. 8.

25. Keith, George Mouat, *A Voyage to South America and the Cape of Good Hope* (Vogel, London, 1819), p. 12.
26. Gillespie, *Gleaning and Remarks*, pp. 7–8.
27. *Journal and Letters of the Rev. Henry Martyn*, Volume 1, p. 326.
28. Fernyhough, *Military Memoirs of Four Brothers*, p. 69.
29. *The United Service Magazine*, 1836, Volume 1, p. 484.
30. MS. Eng. Misc. d. 242, p. 132.
31. Fernyhough, *Military Memoirs of Four Brothers*, p. 71.
32. Gillespie, *Gleaning and Remarks*, p. 8.
33. Keith, *A Voyage to South America*, p. 13.
34. *The United Service Magazine*, 1836, Volume 1, pp. 484–5; MS. Eng. Misc. d. 242, p. 132.
35. ADM 51/1936; ADM 51/1756; *The United Service Magazine*, 1836, Volume 1, p. 485.
36. Keith, *A Voyage to South America*, p. 13.
37. ADM 51/1936.
38. Fernyhough, *Military Memoirs of Four Brothers*, p. 71.
39. *Journal and Letters of the Rev. Henry Martyn*, Volume 1, p. 339.
40. Keith, *A Voyage to South America*, p. 14.
41. Keith, *A Voyage to South America*, p. 14.
42. Hooker (ed.), *Botanical Miscellany*, p. 11.
43. Keith, *A Voyage to South America*, p. 19.
44. *The United Service Magazine*, 1836, Volume 1, p. 486.
45. Fernyhough, *Military Memoirs of Four Brothers*, pp. 71–2; *The United Service Magazine*, 1836, Volume 1, p. 486; Keith, *A Voyage to South America*, pp. 18–19.
46. *The United Service Magazine*, 1836, Volume 1, p. 486.
47. *Journal and Letters of the Rev. Henry Martyn*, Volume 1, p. 376.
48. Fernyhough, *Military Memoirs of Four Brothers*, p. 71.
49. Gillespie, *Gleaning and Remarks*, p. 8.
50. Keith, *A Voyage to South America*, p. 19.
51. ADM 51/1936; ADM 51/4437.
52. ADM 51/4437.
53. *The United Service Magazine*, 1836, Volume 1, p. 487.
54. Fernyhough, *Military Memoirs of Four Brothers*, p. 73
55. Keith, *A Voyage to South America*, p. 17.
56. Fernyhough, *Military Memoirs of Four Brothers*, p. 73; Gleig, *The Hussar*, p. 144; Keith, *A Voyage to South America*, p. 17; Gillespie, *Gleaning and Remarks*, pp. 9–10.
57. ADM 51/1936;
58. *The United Service Magazine*, 1836, Volume 1, p. 487.
59. *The United Service Magazine*, 1836, Volume 1, p. 488.
60. Fernyhough, *Military Memoirs of Four Brothers*, p. 72.
61. ADM 51/4437; Robinson, William, *Jack Nastyface: Memoirs of a Seaman* (Walalnd, 1836) quoted in Lavery, Brian, *Jack Aubery Commands* (Conway Maritime Press, London, 2005), p. 126.
62. Cannon, Richard, and Cappeler, Carl, *Historical Record of the Seventy-first Regiment, Highland Light Infantry* (Parker, Furnivall & Parker, London, 1852), p. 57; ADM 51/1936; ADM 51/2005; *The United Service Magazine*, 1836, Volume 1, p. 489; Keith, *A Voyage to South America*, p. 21; *The Morning Chronicle*, 1 March 1806.
63. Gillespie, *Gleaning and Remarks*, pp. 9–10; *Journal and Letters of the Rev. Henry Martyn*, Volume 1, p. 366.
64. Gillespie, *Gleaning and Remarks*, p. 10.
65. Gleig, *The Hussar*, p. 146.
66. *Journal and Letters of the Rev. Henry Martyn*, Volume 1, p. 359.
67. *The United Service Magazine*, 1836, Volume 1, p. 488.
68. *The United Service Magazine*, 1836, Volume 1, p. 489.
69. ADM 51/1936.

70. *The United Service Magazine*, 1836, Volume 1, p. 489.
71. Parkinson (ed.), *Samuel Walters*, p. 38.

Chapter 2: The Capture of Cape Town
 1. Fernyhough, *Military Memoirs of Four Brothers*, p. 74.
 2. Gleig, *The Hussar*, p. 149; *The United Service Magazine*, 1836, Volume 1, p. 489; Parkinson (ed.), *Samuel Walters*, p. 38.
 3. *Journal and Letters of the Rev. Henry Martyn*, Volume 1, pp. 388–9.
 4. *The Morning Chronicle*, 1 March, 1806; Gleig, *The Hussar*, pp. 150–1.
 5. Gleig, *The Hussar*, pp. 150–1; Parkinson (ed.), *Samuel Walters*, p. 38.
 6. Parkinson (ed.), *Samuel Walters*, p. 38.
 7. *Journal and Letters of the Rev. Henry Martyn*, Volume 1, p. 390.
 8. *The Morning Chronicle*, 1 March 1806; *A Full and Correct Report of the Trail of Sir Home Popham*, p. 18.
 9. Gillespie, *Gleaning and Remarks*, p. 13; Fernyhough, *Military Memoirs of Four Brothers*, p. 74; Hooker (ed.), *Botanical Miscellany*, p. 12; http://battle.blaauwberg.net/battle_of_blaauwberg_by_tim_couzens.php
10. Gillespie, *Gleaning and Remarks*, p. 14; *Journal and Letters of the Rev. Henry Martyn*, Volume 1, p. 391; Fernyhough, *Military Memoirs of Four Brothers*, p. 74.
11. Hooker (ed.), *Botanical Miscellany*, p. 12.
12. Parkinson (ed.), *Samuel Walters*, p. 39; http://battle.blaauwberg.net/battle_of_blaauwberg_by_tim_couzens.php
13. *Journal and Letters of the Rev. Henry Martyn*, Volume 1, p. 391.
14. *Journal and Letters of the Rev. Henry Martyn*, Volume 1, p. 391; *The Morning Chronicle*, 1 March 1806; HMS *Encounter* log, ADM 51/2005.
15. Oatts, Lewis Balfour, *Proud Heritage, The Story of the Highland Light Infantry*, Volume 1 (Nelson and Son, London, 1952), p. 53; *Journal and Letters of the Rev. Henry Martyn*, Volume 1, p. 392; http://battle.blaauwberg.net/battle_of_blaauwberg_by_tim_couzens.php
16. Homans, Benjamin (ed.), *Army and Navy Chronicle*, Volumes 4–5 (Homans, Washington, 1837), p. 285; PC 1/3823; Fernyhough, *Military Memoirs of Four Brothers*, pp. 84–5; http://www.napoleon-series.org/military/organization/Britain/Infantry/Regiments/c_71stFoot.html
17. Fernyhough, *Military Memoirs of Four Brothers*, p. 76.
18. Fernyhough, *Military Memoirs of Four Brothers*, p. 76.
19. *The Morning Chronicle*, 1 March 1806; *Journal and Letters of the Rev. Henry Martyn*, Volume 1, p. 392.
20. Oman, Charles (ed.), *Diary of William Gavin* (Glasgow, 1921), p. 3.
21. Gillespie, *Gleaning and Remarks*, p. 15; Hooker (ed.), *Botanical Miscellany*, p. 12; http://battle.blaauwberg.net/battle_of_blaauwberg_by_tim_couzens.php
22. Fernyhough, *Military Memoirs of Four Brothers*, p. 78; *Journal and Letters of the Rev. Henry Martyn*, Volume 1, p. 394; Homans (ed.), *Army and Navy Chronicle*, Volumes 4–5, p. 285.
23. *Botanical Miscellany*, p. 13; Gillespie, *Gleaning and Remarks*, p. 15.
24. Theal, George McCall, *History of South Africa*, Volume 5 (Cambrige University Press, Cambridge, 2010), pp. 197–200; Parkinson (ed.), *Samuel Walters*, p. 40.
25. *Botanical Miscellany*, p. 13.
26. *Journal and Letters of the Rev. Henry Martyn*, Volume 1, p. 394.
27. Fernyhough, *Military Memoirs of Four Brothers*, p. 78.
28. *The Morning Chronicle*, 1 and 21 March 1806.
29. Parkinson (ed.), *Samuel Walters*, pp. 40–1.
30. *Botanical Miscellany*, p. 14.
31. *Botanical Miscellany*, p. 14; *A Full and Correct Report of the Trial of Sir Home Popham*, pp. 22–3; *Diary of William Gavin*, p. 3; Fernyhough, *Military Memoirs of Four Brothers*, p. 78; *The Times*, 2 September 1806.
32. Keith, *A Voyage to South America*, p. 35.
33. *Botanical Miscellany*, pp. 21–4; MS. Eng. Misc. d. 242, p. 125.

34. *The United Service Magazine*, 1836, Volume 2, p. 192.
35. Keith, *A Voyage to South America*, pp. 36–7; http://v1.sahistory.org.za/pages///places/villages/westernCape/capetown/index.php?id=10&page=3.
36. *Botanical Miscellany*, p. 27.
37. *The United Service Magazine*, 1836, Volume 2, p. 190; WO 12/7855; *Diary of William Gavin*, p. 3.
38. *The United Service Magazine*, 1836, Volume 2, p. 192.
39. Gleig, *The Hussar*, pp. 154–60; *The Times*, 2 September 1806.
40. MS. Eng. Misc. d. 242, p. 126, Roberts, Carlos, *Las Invasiones Inglesas* (Emecé Editores, Buenos Aires, 2000), p. 227.
41. Gillespie, *Gleaning and Remarks*, p. 22.
42. *The United Service Magazine*, 1836, Volume 2, p. 195.
43. *The United Service Magazine*, 1836, Volume 2, pp. 193–4.
44. Adkins, Roy, *The War for all the Oceans* (Penguin, 2011), p. 189; *A Full and Correct Report of the Trial of Sir Home Popham*, p. 192.
45. MS. Eng. Misc. d. 242, pp. 128–9; Fernyhough, *Military Memoirs of Four Brothers*, p. 79; *A Full and Correct Report of the Trial of Sir Home Popham*, p. 28.
46. Fernyhough, *Military Memoirs of Four Brothers*, pp. 79–80; http://www.keepmilitarymuseum.org/private_kerley.php?&dx=3&ob=3&rpn=empire#bref19
47. Fernyhough, *Military Memoirs of Four Brothers*, pp. 80–1 and 126.
48. Gillespie, *Gleaning and Remarks*, p. 20; Fernyhough, *Military Memoirs of Four Brothers*, p. 81; ADM 51/1583.
49. *The United Service Magazine*, 1836, Volume 2, pp. 191–2; *A Full and Correct Report of the Trial of Sir Home Popham*, pp. 31–5.
50. Roberts, *Las Invasiones Inglesas*, pp. 12–16 and 31; Anon, *A Proposal For Humbling Spain, Written in 1711* (London, Roberts, 1739).
51. Bryant, Arthur, *The Years of Endurance* (Collins, London, 1942), p. 172.
52. Popham, *A Damned Cunning Fellow*, pp. 133–4.
53. Popham, *A Damned Cunning Fellow*, pp. 133–4; ADM 1/58; Add.37,884, ff.11–22, 168–9, 256–61 and 266–7.
54. *A Full and Correct Report of the Trial of Sir Home Popham*, pp. 50 and 233.
55. Grainger, John (ed), *The Royal Navy in the River Plate 1806–1807* (Scolar Press, 1996), p. 16.
56. *A Full and Correct Report of the Trial of Sir Home Popham*, p. 13.
57. *The Times*, 21 July, 1807.

Chapter 3: Into the Unknown

1. ADM 36/17373; PC 1/3823.
2. ADM 51/1583.
3. PC 1/3823.
4. ADM 51/1583.
5. MS. Eng. Misc. d. 242, p. 129.
6. *The United Service Magazine*, 1836, Volume 2, p. 195.
7. *The United Service Magazine*, 1836, Volume 2, p. 195; *A Full and Correct Report of the Trial of Sir Home Popham*, p. 35.
8. Quoted in Popham, *A Damned Cunning Fellow*, p. 164; Roberts, *Las Invasiones Inglesas*, p. 198.
9. Hathaway, Eileen (ed.), *A Dorset Rifleman: The Recollections of Benjamin Harris* (Shinglepicker Publications, 1995), p. 78; http://en.wikisource.org/wiki/Gordon,_Alexander_(1786-1815)_(DNB00); http://en.wikipedia.org/wiki/Robert_Arbuthnot.
10. Parkinson (ed.), *Samuel Walters*, p. 42.
11. ADM 51/1615.
12. Fernyhough, *Military Memoirs of Four Brothers*, pp. 82–3.
13. ADM 36/17242.
14. *A Full and Correct Report of the Trial of Sir Home Popham*, p. 38.
15. *A Full and Correct Report of the Trial of Sir Home Popham*, pp. 38–9.
16. Parkinson (ed.), *Samuel Walters*, p. 42.

17. ADM 51/2005

18. MS. Eng. Misc. d. 242, pp. 129–30.

19. *Diary of William Gavin*, p. 4.

20. WO 1/161, ff.93–5.

21. *A Full and Correct Report of the Trial of Sir Home Popham*, p. 49.

22. *Diary of William Gavin*, p. 4.

23. Homans (ed.), *Army and Navy Chronicle*, Volumes 4–5, p. 285.

24. ADM 51/1615.

25. Anon (Monkland, George), *Journal of the Secret Expedition which sailed from Falmouth under the command of Brigadier-General Craufurd* (Monkland, Bath, 1808), pp. 21–2; NAM 6807-236, *The Diary of Lt. Col. Lancelot Holland*, pp. 45–50; Morley, Stephen, *Memoirs of a Sergeant of the 5th Regiment of Foot, containing an account of his services in Hanover, South America and the Peninsula* (Ken Trotman Ltd, Cambridge, 1999), p. 27.

26. Gillespie, *Gleaning and Remarks*, p. 29; ADM 51/1615.

27. NAM 6807-236, *The Diary of Lt. Col. Lancelot Holland*, p. 46.

28. WO 1/161, ff.93–5.

29. Parkinson (ed.), *Samuel Walters*, p. 41; PC 1/3823; *The Times*, 27 January 1807; Roberts, *Las Invasiones Inglesas*, p. 111.

30. *The Gentleman's Magazine and Historical Chronicle*, Volume 75, 1805, Part 2 (J. Nichols and Son, London, 1805), p. 1172; Fernyhough, *Military Memoirs of Four Brothers*, pp. 55–61.

31. Fernyhough, *Military Memoirs of Four Brothers*, p. 108.

32. Grainger (ed.), *The Royal Navy in the River Plate 1806–1807*, pp. 28–9.

33. Parkinson (ed.), *Samuel Walters*, p. 42.

34. L/MIL/5/148, f.5; Roberts, *Las Invasiones Inglesas*, p. 111.

35. Roberts, *Las Invasiones Inglesas*, p. 157.

36. WO 12/7855.

37. ADM 51/1615.

38. Parkinson (ed.), *Samuel Walters*, p. 42.

39. ADM 51/1936; ADM 51/1615; ADM 51/4437; Parkinson (ed.), *Samuel Walters*, p. 42.

40. ADM 35/2339; Parkinson (ed.), *Samuel Walters*, p. 42.

41. ADM 51/2005.

42. DM 51/4437.

43. Beresford to Windham, 2 July 1806 – printed in *The Times*, 15 September 1806; Diary of Surgeon Thompson – quoted in Grainger (ed.), *The Royal Navy in the River Plate 1806–1807*, p. 29; Parkinson (ed.), *Samuel Walters*, p. 42.

44. ADM 51/2005.

45. Mawe, *Travels in the interior of Brazil: particularly in the gold and diamond districts* (Longman, Hurst, Rees, Orme, and Brown, 1812), p. 6.

46. Toll, Ian W., *Six Frigates* (Penguin, London, 2007), p. 97.

47. Diary of Surgeon Thompson – quoted in Grainger (ed.), *The Royal Navy in the River Plate 1806–1807*, pp. 29–30.

48. Admiral Murray's Log Book – eg.ms.3265, f.25; Popham to Marsden, 8 July 1806 – quoted in Grainger (ed.), *The Royal Navy in the River Plate 1806–1807*, pp. 42–3.

49. Newitt (ed.), *War, Revolution and Society in the Rio de la Plata 1808–1810, Thomas Kinder's Narrative* (Non Basic Stock Line, 2010), pp. 123–4.

50. *Hampshire Telegraph and Sussex Chronicle*, 22 September 1806; HMS *Narcissus* pay roll – ADM 31/17394.

51. HMS *Narcissus* muster roll – ADM 36/17242.

52. Gillespie, *Gleaning and Remarks*, pp. 40–1; Diary of Surgeon Thompson – quoted in Grainger (ed.), *The Royal Navy in the River Plate 1806–1807*, p. 30; Popham to Marsden, 8 July 1806 – quoted in Grainger (ed.), *The Royal Navy in the River Plate 1806–1807*, p. 39.

53. *Diary of William Gavin*, p. 4.

54. Homans (ed.), *Army and Navy Chronicle*, Volumes 4–5, p. 285.

55. Diary of Surgeon Thompson – quoted in Grainger (ed.), *The Royal Navy in the River Plate 1806–1807*, p. 30; HMS *Narcissus* log book – ADM 35/2339; HMS *Raisonnable* log book – ADM 51/1812.

56. Beresford to Baird, 2 July 1806, WO 1/161, f.163; Popham to Marsden, 8 July 1806 – quoted in Grainger (ed.), *The Royal Navy in the River Plate 1806–1807*, p. 39; Gillespie, *Gleaning and Remarks*, p. 41; *The Journal of Captain Pococke, Highland Light Infantry Chronicle* (Glasgow, 1939), p. 211.

57. Beresford to Windham, 2 July 1806 – printed in *The Times*, 15 September 1806.

58. Diary of Surgeon Thompson – quoted in Grainger (ed.), *The Royal Navy in the River Plate 1806–1807*, pp. 30–1.

59. PC 1/3823.

60. HMS *Encounter* log book – ADM 51/2005.

61. Diary of Surgeon Thompson – quoted in Grainger (ed.), *The Royal Navy in the River Plate 1806–1807*, pp. 30–1; HMS *Narcissus* muster roll – ADM 31/17394; HMS *Encounter* log book – ADM 51/2005; Fernyhough, *Military Memoirs of Four Brothers*, p. 90.

62. Beresford to Windham, 2 July 1806 – printed in *The Times*, 15 September 1806; Liniers to Sobremonte, 24 June 1806 – quoted in Bandera, Héctor Alberto, *Quilmes: y las Invasiones Inglesas* (El Monje Editor, 2006), pp. 28–9.

63. Popham to Marsden, 24 June 1806 – quoted in Grainger (ed.), *The Royal Navy in the River Plate*, p. 33–4.

64. ADM 51/2005; *Diary of William Gavin*, p. 4.

65. *Diary of William Gavin*, p. 9; Regimental Pay List (71st) – WO 17/192.

Chapter 4: The Viceroyalty of the River Plate

1. Coronado, Juan (ed.), *Invasiones inglesas al Rio de la Plata, documentos inéditos* (Imprenta Republicana, Buenos Aires, 1870), p. 66.

2. Popham to Marsden, 9 July 1806 – reproduced in Grainger (ed.), *The Royal Navy in the River Plate 1806–1807*, p. 44; Liniers to Sobremonte, 2 January, 1806 – reproduced in Fortin, Jorge L.R. and Fortin, Pablo (eds), *Invasionesinglesas: colección Pablo Fortin* (Editoria Cía, Lamsa, 1967), pp. 17–19; and Velasco to His Excellency the Minister of War, 1 August 1806 in Vane, Charles William (ed.), *Correspondence, Dispatches, and other Papers, of Viscount Castlereagh edited by his brother*, Volume 7 (Murray, London, 1851), p. 302.

3. Popham to Marsden, 8 July 1806 – quoted in Grainger (ed.), *The Royal Navy in the River Plate 1806–1807*, p. 39; Roberts, *Las Invasiones Inglesas*, p. 101.

4. HMS *Leda* log book – ADM 51/1583; Fortin (ed.), *Invasiones*, p. 149.

5. HMS *Leda* log book – ADM 51/1583; Admiralty court martial records – ADM 1/5375; Fortin (ed.), *Invasiones*, p. 149.

6. http://todoababor.mforos.com/1556317/4304332-bergantines-espanoles-de-guerra/?pag=4; http://es.wikipedia.org/wiki/Domingo_de_Ugalde.

7. Johnson, Lyman, *Workshop of Revolution, Plebian Buenos Aires and the Atlantic World* (Duke University Press, 2011), pp. 150–7, 245.

8. Newitt (ed.), *War, Revolution and Society ... Thomas Kinder's Narrative*; http://en.wikipedia.org/wiki/Rafael_de_Sobremonte; Beresford to Castlereagh, 11 July 1806 – WO 1/161, ff.199–201.

9. Beresford to Baird, 2 July 1806, WO 1/161, f.163; Coronado (ed.), *Invasiones*, pp. 53 and 60.

10. Velasco to His Excellency the Minister of War, 1 August 1806 – reproduced in Vane (ed.), *Correspondence, Dispatches, and other Papers, of Viscount Castlereagh*, Volume 7, p. 303; AGN Buenos Aires, Invasiones Inglesas, 26-7-7, document 29; Roberts, *Las Invasiones Inglesas*, p. 138.

11. Sánchez de Thompson, Maraquita, *Recuerdos de Buenos Ayres virreynal* (ENE Editorial, 1953), p. 125; Socolow, *The Merchants of Buenos Aires 1778–1810: Family and Commerce* (Cambridge University Press, Cambridge, 2009), p. 86; Roberts, *Las Invasiones Inglesas*, p. 131; Johnson, *Workshop of Revolution*, p. 250.

12. Almazán, Bernardo P. Lozier, *Beresford Gobernador de Buenos Ayres* (Editorial Galerna, 1994), p. 53; Sánchez de Thompson, Maraquita, *Intimidad y Política: diario, cartas y recuerdos*, p. 151; Coronado (ed.), *Invasiones*, p. 9 and 36, Johnson, *Workshop of Revolution*, p. 251

13. Coronado (ed.), *Invasiones*, p. 34–5.
14. Coronado (ed.), *Invasiones*, p. 35.
15. Anon, *An Authentic Narrative of the Proceedings of the Expedition under the Command of Brigadier-Gen. Craufurd* (London, 1808), p. 126.
16. Coronado (ed.), *Invasiones*, p. 9–12; AGN Montevideo, Legajo 50 documento 38.
17. http://www.geni.com/people/Juan-Ignacio-de-Elia-Ilarraz/6000000000405286033;
    http://genforum.genealogy.com/quintana/messages/91.html;
    http://es.wikipedia.org/wiki/Miguel_de_Azcu%C3%A9naga;
    http://www.geni.com/people/Jaime-Alsina-y-Verjes/6000000000321836732
18. Belgrano's memoirs are available online: http://www.scribd.com/doc/61088867/Manuel-Belgrano
19. Sánchez, *Recuerdos de Buenos Ayres*, p. 151.
20. Roberts, *Las Invasiones Inglesas*, p. 86.
21. Roberts, *Las Invasiones Inglesas*, pp. 100–1.
22. HMS *Encounter* log book – ADM 51/2005; Coronado (ed.), *Invasiones*, p. 34–5.
23. Coronado (ed.), *Invasiones*, pp. 14–15 and 18.
24. Coronado (ed.), *Invasiones*, pp. 9–12.
25. Coronado (ed.), *Invasiones*, pp. 7–9 and 9–12.
26. Beresford to Windham, 2 July 1806 – printed in *The Times*, 15 September 1806; Fernyhough, *Military Memoirs of Four Brothers*, p. 90.
27. Gillespie, *Gleaning and Remarks*, p. 43.
28. http://en.wikipedia.org/wiki/List_of_gun-brigs_of_the_Royal_Navy; HMS *Encounter* log book – ADM 51/2005; Fernyhough, *Military Memoirs of Four Brothers*, p. 90.
29. Coronado (ed.), *Invasiones*, pp. 7–9.
30. Surgeon Thompson's Journal – quoted in Grainger (ed.), *The Royal Navy in the River Plate 1806–1807*, p. 34.
31. Bandera, *Quilmes: y las Invasiones Inglesas*, p. 31.
32. Coronado (ed.), *Invasiones*, p. 35; Bandera, *Quilmes: y las Invasiones Inglesas*, pp. 28–37.
33. Davie, John Constanse, *Letters from Paraguay: describing the settlements of Monte Video and Buenos Ayres* (G. Robinson, 1805), p. 117.
34. Monkland, *Journal of the Secret Expedition*, p. 57.
35. Sánchez, *Recuerdos de Buenos Ayres*, p. 152.
36. Fernyhough, *Military Memoirs of Four Brothers*, p. 91; Popham to Marsden, 8 July 1806 – quoted in Grainger (ed.), *The Royal Navy in the River Plate 1806–1807*, pp. 42–3; *Diary of William Gavin*, p. 4.
37. Beresford to Windham, 2 July 1806 – printed in *The Times*, 15 September 1806.
38. Bandera, *Quilmes: y las Invasiones Inglesas*, p. 30; Coronado (ed.), *Invasiones*, pp. 12–14; Coronado (ed.), *Invasiones*, pp. 7–9.
39. Coronado (ed.), *Invasiones*, pp. 7–9.
40. HMS *Encounter* log book – ADM 51/2005.
41. Gillespie, *Gleaning and Remarks*, p. 43.
42. Arze to Sobremonte – 8.30 am, 26 June 1806 – quoted in Bandera, *Quilmes: y las Invasiones Inglesas*, p. 31.
43. Arze to Sobremonte – 8.30 am, 26 June 1806 – quoted in Bandera, *Quilmes: y las Invasiones Inglesas*, p. 31.
44. HMS *Encounter* log book – ADM 51/2005.
45. Gillespie, *Gleaning and Remarks*, p. 46.
46. Homans (ed.), *Army and Navy Chronicle*, Volumes 4–5, p. 285.
47. Gillespie, *Gleaning and Remarks*, p. 47.
48. Arze to Sobremonte – 8.30 am, 26 June 1806 – quoted in Bandera, *Quilmes: y las Invasiones Inglesas*, p. 31.
49. Coronado (ed.), *Invasiones*, pp. 18–20; Beresford to Windham, 2 July 1806 – printed in *The Times*, 15 September 1806.
50. Arze to Sobremonte – 9.30 am, 26 June 1806 – quoted in Bandera, *Quilmes: y las Invasiones Inglesas*, p. 31.
51. Beresford to Windham, 2 July 1806 – printed in *The Times*, 15 September 1806.

52. Homans (ed.), *Army and Navy Chronicle*, Volumes 4–5, p. 285.
53. Gillespie, *Gleaning and Remarks*, p. 47.
54. Gillespie, *Gleaning and Remarks*, p. 47; Beresford to Windham, 2 July 1806 – printed in *The Times*, 15 September 1806.
55. Gillespie, *Gleaning and Remarks*, pp. 47–8.
56. Homans (ed.), *Army and Navy Chronicle*, Volumes 4–5, p. 285; *Diary of William Gavin*, p. 5.
57. Coronado (ed.), *Invasiones*, pp. 31–2; Homans (ed.), *Army and Navy Chronicle*, Volumes 4–5, p. 285; Beresford to Windham, 2 July 1806 – printed in *The Times*, 15 September 1806.
58. Coronado (ed.), *Invasiones*, pp. 12–14.
59. Gillespie, *Gleaning and Remarks*, p. 48; Fernyhough, *Military Memoirs of Four Brothers*, p. 92.
60. Coronado (ed.), *Invasiones*, pp. 12–14.
61. Quoted in Fletcher, Ian, *The Waters of Oblivion: The British Invasion of the Rio de la Plata, 1806–1807* (Spellmount, Tunbridge Wells, 1991), p. 27.
62. Coronado (ed.), *Invasiones*, pp. 12–14; Fernyhough, *Military Memoirs of Four Brothers*, pp. 92–3.
63. Popham to Marsden, 8 July 1806 – quoted in Grainger (ed.), *The Royal Navy in the River Plate 1806–1807*, p. 38.
64. HMS *Encounter* log book – ADM 51/2005; *Copy of Journal of Captain Pococke, Highland Light Infantry Chronicle*, p. 193.
65. Gillespie, *Gleaning and Remarks*, p. 48; Beresford to Windham, 2 July 1806 – printed in *The Times*, 15 September 1806.
66. Roberts, *Las Invasiones Inglesas*, p. 138.
67. Coronado (ed.), *Invasiones*, pp. 33–46.
68. Coronado (ed.), *Invasiones*, pp. 33–46.
69. Graham-Yooll, *The Forgotten Colony*, pp. 34–5.
70. Newitt (ed.), *War, Revolution and Society … Thomas Kinder's Narrative*, p. 154.
71. Roberts, *Las Invasiones Inglesas*, pp. 60–5.
72. Coronado (ed.), *Invasiones*, p. 18.
73. Coronado (ed.), *Invasiones*, pp. 33–4.
74. Monkland, *Journal of a Secret Expedition*, p. 68.
75. *Diary of William Gavin*, pp. 4–5.
76. Fernyhough, *Military Memoirs of Four Brothers*, p. 93.
77. Beresford to Windham, 2 July 1806 – printed in *The Times*, 15 September 1806.
78. Gillespie, *Gleaning and Remarks*, p. 49.
79. Anon, *Trial of Lieutenant-General John Whitelocke commander-in-chief of the expedition against Buenos Ayres, by court-martial, held in Chelsea college* (T. Gillet, London, 1808), p. 40.
80. Beresford to Windham, 2 July 1806 – printed in *The Times*, 15 September 1806; Colorado (ed.), *Invasiones*, p. 134.
81. *Diary of William Gavin*, p. 5.
82. Coronado (ed.), *Invasiones*, pp. 37–8 and 23–4.
83. Coronado (ed.), *Invasiones*, pp. 33–4, 38–9 and 44–6.
84. Beresford to Windham, 2 July 1806 – printed in *The Times*, 15 September 1806.
85. *Diary of William Gavin*, p. 5; Coronado (ed.), *Invasiones*, pp. 41–3; AGN Buenos Aires, Guerra y Marina, Legajo 40, Exp. 12.
86. Newitt (ed.), *War, Revolution and Society … Thomas Kinder's Narrative*, p. 146.
87. *Diary of William Gavin*, p. 5.
88. Coronado (ed.), *Invasiones*, pp. 37–8.
89. Coronado (ed.), *Invasiones*, p. 36.
90. http://data2.archives.ca/pdf/pdf001/p000000372.pdf; Beresford to Windham, 2 July 1806 – printed in *The Times*, 15 September 1806.
91. *Diary of William Gavin*, p. 5.
92. Coronado (ed.), *Invasiones*, pp. 33–46; http://genealogiafamiliar.net/getperson.php?personID=I26344&tree=BVCZ.
93. HMS *Diadem* Log Book – ADM 35/2201.
94. Beresford to Windham, 2 July 1806 – printed in *The Times*, 15 September 1806.

95. Beresford to Baird, 2 July 1806 – WO 1/161, f.163; *Diary of William Gavin*, p. 6; Roberts, *Las Invasiones Inglesas*, p. 146.
96. Beresford to Windham, 2 July 1806 – printed in *The Times*, 15 September 1806.
97. Beresford to Castlereagh, 12 May 1807 – WO 1/162, ff.301–31 and WO 1/162, ff.339–41.
98. Sánchez, *Recuerdos de Buenos Ayres*, p. 151.
99. *Diary of William Gavin*, p. 5.

Chapter 5: The Occupation of Buenos Ayres
 1. Monkland, *Journal of the Secret Expedition*, p. 56.
 2. Fernyhough, *Military Memoirs of Four Brothers*, p. 94; Sánchez, *Recuerdos de Buenos Ayres*, p. 151; *Diary of William Gavin*, p. 5; Gillespie, *Gleaning and Remarks*, pp. 49–50. A plaque at number 271 on the renamed *Calle Florida* marks the site of Mariquita Sánchez's house.
 3. Coronado (ed.), *Invasiones*, p. 51; Johnson, *Workshop of Revolution*, p. 251; Gillespie, *Gleaning and Remarks*, p. 50.
 4. Roberts, *Las Invasiones Inglesas*, p. 149.
 5. Beresford to Baird – 2 July 1806 – WO 1/161, f.163.
 6. Popham to Marsden, 25 August, 1806. Quoted in Grainger (ed.), *The Royal Navy in the River Plate 1806–1807*, p. 60; Fortin, *Invasiones Inglesas*, p. 41; Gillespie, *Gleaning and Remarks*, p. 91; Fortin (ed.), *Invasiones Inglesas*, p. 152; Gillespie, *Gleaning and Remarks*, pp. 108–9.
 7. Gillespie, *Gleaning and Remarks*, pp. 52–3; Sánchez, *Recuerdos de Buenos Ayres*, p. 128.
 8. *Morning Post and Gazetteer*, London, 21 December 1799
 9. Gillespie, *Gleaning and Remarks*, pp. 52–3; *Diary of William Gavin*, p. 5.
10. Popham to Marsden, 6 July 1806 – printed in *The Times*, 15 September 1806.
11. HMS *Encounter* log ADM 51/2005.
12. Socolow, *The Merchants of Buenos Aires*, p. 5; Monkland, *Journal of the Secret Expedition*, p. 54; Sánchez, *Recuerdos de Buenos Ayres*, p. 132.
13. Roberts, *Las Invasiones Inglesas*, p. 157.
14. Gillespie, *Gleaning and Remarks*, p. 69; Socolow, *The Merchants of Buenos Aires*, p. 61; Johnson, *Workshop of Revolution: Plebian Buenos Ayres*, pp. 29–30; *Account of the Present State of that Province* – Printed in *The Times*, London, 25 September, 1806; Anon, *An Authentic Narrative of the Proceedings*, p. 148.
15. Gillespie, *Gleaning and Remarks*, p. 69; Socolow, *The Merchants of Buenos Aires*, p. 61; Johnson, *Workshop of Revolution: Plebian Buenos Ayres*, pp. 29–30; *Account of the Present State of that Province* – Printed in *The Times*, London, 25 September 1806.
16. Socolow, *The Merchants of Buenos Aires*, p. 25.
17. Roberts, *Las Invasiones Inglesas*, p. 33.
18. Gillespie, *Gleaning and Remarks*, p. 72.
19. Socolow, *The Merchants of Buenos Aires*, p. 21; Burkholder, Mark A. and Johnson, Lyman L., *Colonial Latin America: Second Edition* (OUP, Oxford, 1994), p. 276; for evidence of Romero's connections with White see Olney to White, 11 November 1806, in Fortin (ed.), *Invasiones Inglesas*, pp. 110–12.
20. Socolow, *The Merchants of Buenos Aires*, p. 6; Sánchez, *Recuerdos de Buenos Ayres*, p. 131; Martínez, Pedro Santos, *Las Industrias durante el Virreinato (1776–1810)* (Eudeba, 1969) – Quoted in Galeano, Eduardo, *Las Venas Abiertas de América Latina* (Siglo Veintiuno, Madrid, 1985), pp. 289–90.
21. Socolow, *The Merchants of Buenos Aires*, p. 10–11.
22. Roberts, *Las Invasiones Inglesas*, p. 128.
23. Gillespie, *Gleaning and Remarks*, p. 69.
24. Gillespie, *Gleaning and Remarks*, p. 70.
25. 'Manumission was far more common in Latin America than in the British colonies [in the Americas]' Burkholder & Johnson, *Colonial Latin America*, p. 193.
26. Untrained slaves imported from Brazil or Africa sold for an average of 200 pesos. Skilled slaves could be worth as much as 600. Johnson, *Workshop of Revolution*, p. 233.

27. Socolow, *The Merchants of Buenos Aires*, pp. 55, 76–8 and 139; Vidal, Emeric Essex, *Picturesque Illustrations of Buenos Ayres and Monte Video* (R. Ackermann, London, 1820), p. 30; Gillespie, *Gleaning and Remarks*, p. 83; Johnson, *Workshop of Revolution*, pp. 9 and 232.
28. Johnson, *Workshop of Revolution*, pp. 152–3.
29. Davie, *Letters from Paraguay*, p. 113.
30. Fernyhough, *Military Memoirs of Four Brothers*, p. 95; Anon, *An Authentic Narrative of the Proceedings*, p. 144.
31. Roberts, *Las Invasiones Inglesas*, p. 130.
32. Gillespie, *Gleaning and Remarks*, p. 81; Anon, *Notes on the Viceroyalty of La Plata* (J. J. Stockdale, London, 1808), p. 188.
33. Johnson, *Workshop of Revolution*, pp. 21–2.
34. Socolow, *The Merchants of Buenos Aires*, p. 121; Davie, *Letters from Paraguay*, p. 116.
35. Vidal, *Picturesque Illustrations of Buenos Ayres and Monte Video*, p. 27; Sánchez, *Recuerdos de Buenos Ayres*, p. 125; Johnson, *Workshop of Revolution*, pp. 26–7.
36. http://es.wikipedia.org/wiki/Fuerte_de_Buenos_Aires; Vidal, *Picturesque Illustrations of Buenos Ayres and Monte Video*, pp. 17–18; Gillespie, *Gleaning and Remarks*, p. 83.
37. Vidal, *Picturesque Illustrations of Buenos Ayres and Monte Video*, p. 15–16.
38. Grainger (ed.), *The Royal Navy in the River Plate*, p. 39.
39. Sánchez, *Recuerdos de Buenos Ayres*, p. 133.
40. Newitt (ed.), *War, Revolution and Society … Thomas Kinder's Narrative*, p. 197.
41. Villalobos R., Sergio, *El Comercio y la Crisis Colonial* (Akhilleus, Santiago, 2009), p. 46; Sánchez, *Recuerdos de Buenos Ayres*, p. 125.
42. Vidal, *Picturesque Illustrations of Buenos Ayres and Monte Video*, pp. 63–4; Newitt (ed.), *War, Revolution and Society … Thomas Kinder's Narrative*, p. 172; Monkland, *Journal of the Secret Expedition*, p. 55–6.
43. Gillespie, *Gleaning and Remarks*, p. 82.
44. *Trial of Lieutenant-General John Whitelocke*, pp. 115–16.
45. Fernyhough, *Military Memoirs of Four Brothers*, pp. 95–6.
46. Socolow, *The Merchants of Buenos Aires*, p. 74.
47. Johnson, *Workshop of Revolution*, p. 118.
48. Vidal, *Picturesque Illustrations of Buenos Ayres and Monte Video*, p. 35.
49. Anon, *An Authentic Narrative of the Proceedings*, p. 142; Johnson, *Workshop of Revolution*, p. 25.
50. Gillespie, *Gleaning and Remarks*, p. 82.
51. Johnson, *Workshop of Revolution*, p. 28.
52. Socolow, *The Merchants of Buenos Aires*, p. 137; Fernyhough, *Military Memoirs of Four Brothers*, p. 95; Monkland, *Journal of a Secret Expedition*, p. 66; Gillespie, *Gleaning and Remarks*, p. 120; *Trial of Lieutenant-General John Whitelocke*, p. 108; Burkholder & Johnson, *Colonial Latin America*, p. 214; Johnson, *Workshop of Revolution: Plebian Buenos Ayres*, p. 75.
53. Anon, *An Authentic Narrative of the Proceedings*, p. 141; British Library Manuscripts – Add.57,717, f.12 – text accompanying *Sketch of the Attack on Buenos Ayres*.
54. Vidal, *Picturesque Illustrations of Buenos Ayres and Monte Video*, p. 36; Roberts, *Las Invasiones Inglesas*, p. 131.
55. Johnson, *Workshop of Revolution*, p. 26.
56. NAM 6807-236, *The Diary of Lt. Col. Lancelot Holland*, p. 70.
57. Sánchez, *Recuerdos de Buenos Ayres*, p. 133–4.
58. Sánchez, *Recuerdos de Buenos Ayres*, p. 124–5.
59. Socolow, *The Merchants of Buenos Aires*, p. 36.
60. Socolow, *The Merchants of Buenos Aires*, p. 26.
61. Newitt (ed.), *War, Revolution and Society … Thomas Kinder's Narrative*, p. 171; Johnson, *Workshop of Revolution*, pp. 80–1.
62. Sánchez, *Recuerdos de Buenos Ayres*, p. 128; Gillespie, *Gleaning and Remarks*, p. 91; Mawe, *Travels in the interior of Brazil*, p. 41.
63. Grainger (ed.), *The Royal Navy in the River Plate*, p. 39.
64. Beresford to Castlereagh – 16 July 1806 – WO 1/161, f.207–14.

65. AGN Buenos Aires, Hacienda, Legajo 130, Ex.3279; AGN Buenos Aires, Invasiones Inglesas, 26-6-8, document 48; Roberts, *Las Invasiones Inglesas*, p. 169.
66. AO 1/502/144.
67. Vidal, *Picturesque Illustrations of Buenos Ayres and Monte Video*, pp. 15–16.
68. WO 1/161, ff.175–80.
69. AO 1/502/144.
70. Popham to Marsden, 8 and 9 July 1806. Quoted in Grainger (ed.), *The Royal Navy in the River Plate*, pp. 40 and 43–4.
71. Monkland, *Journal of the Secret Expedition*, p. 55.
72. Álzaga, Enrique Williams, *Martín de Álzaga en la Reconquista y en la Defensa de Buenos Aires (1806–1807)* (Emecé Editores, Buenos Aires, 1971), p. 78; Popham to Marsden – 8 July 1806 – quoted in Grainger (ed.), *The Royal Navy in the River Plate 1806–1807*, p. 41.
73. Beresford to Baird, 2 July 1806 – WO 1/161, f.163.
74. Popham to Marsden, 19 July 1806. Quoted in Grainger (ed.), *The Royal Navy in the River Plate 1806–1807*, p. 48.
75. *Diary of William Gavin*, p. 5.
76. Anon, 19 June 1806, Buenos Ayres, printed in *The Hampshire Telegraph and Sussex Chronicle*, 22 September, 1806.
77. Beresford to Baird, 2 July 1806 – WO 1/161, f.163.
78. Newitt (ed.), *War, Revolution and Society … Thomas Kinder's Narrative*, pp. 155–6.
79. Popham to 'The Mayor and Corporations of Birmingham' – 1 July 1806. Reproduced in *The Times*, London, 20 September 1806.
80. Roberts, *Las Invasiones Inglesas*, p. 111.
81. Popham to Marsden, 8 July 1806 quoted in Grainger (ed.), *The Royal Navy in the River Plate 1806–1807*, p. 39.
82. Gillespie, *Gleaning and Remarks*, p. 130.
83. Roberts, *Las Invasiones Inglesas*, pp. 146–56.
84. *The Hampshire Telegraph and Sussex Chronicle*, 22 September 1806; Gillespie, *Gleaning and Remarks*, p. 54; Garzón, Rafael, *Sobre Monte y Córdoba en las invasions inglesas* (Ediciones del Corredor Austral, 2000), pp. 52–3; Beresford to Castlereagh – 16 July 1806 – WO 1/161, ff.207–14.
85. *Copy of Journal of Captain Pococke, Highland Light Infantry Chronicle*, p. 193.
86. Kew National Archives – AO 1/502/144.
87. WO 1/161, ff.175–80; Popham to Marsden, 25 August 1806. Quoted in Grainger (ed.), *The Royal Navy in the River Plate 1806–1807*, pp. 59–60; Roberts, *Las Invasiones Inglesas*, p. 157.
88. Roberts, *Las Invasiones Inglesas*, p. 158.
89. Gillespie, *Gleaning and Remarks*, p. 66.
90. Socolow, *The Merchants of Buenos Aires*, pp. 124–35.
91. Gillespie, *Gleaning and Remarks*, p. 90; Popham to Marsden, 25 August 1806. Quoted in Grainger (ed.), *The Royal Navy in the River Plate 1806–1807*, p. 60; Beresford to Castlereagh, 16 July 1806 – WO 1/161, ff.207–14; Gillespie, *Gleaning and Remarks*, p. 67; Roberts, *Las Invasiones Inglesas*, p. 158.
92. Popham to Marsden, 14 July 1806 – quoted in Grainger (ed.), *The Royal Navy in the River Plate 1806–1807*, pp. 46–7; Fortin, *Invasiones Inglesas*, p. 152; AGN Buenos Aires, Invasiones Inglesas, 26-6-8, document 77.
93. AO 1/502/144; HMS *Narcissus* Muster Roll – ADM 31/17394
94. *Copy of Journal of Captain Pococke, Highland Light Infantry Chronicle*, p. 193; Homans (ed.), *Army and Navy Chronicle*, Volumes 4–5, p. 285.
95. Homans (ed.), *Army and Navy Chronicle*, Volumes 4–5, p. 285.
96. *Copy of Journal of Captain Pococke, Highland Light Infantry Chronicle*, p. 211; Newitt (ed.), *War, Revolution and Society … Thomas Kinder's Narrative*, p. 149.
97. Gillespie, *Gleaning and Remarks*, p. 101; Roberts, *Las Invasiones Inglesas*, p. 169.
98. Gillespie, *Gleaning and Remarks*, p. 121.
99. Sánchez, *Recuerdos de Buenos Ayres*, p. 126.

100. Gillespie, *Gleaning and Remarks*, p. 67–8.
101. Elissalde, Roberto L., *Historias Ignoradas de las Invasiones Inglesas* (Aguilar, Buenos Ayres, 2006), p. 43.
102. Gillespie, *Gleaning and Remarks*, p. 105; Mulhall, Michael George, *The English in South America* (Standard Office, 1878), p. 96; *Copy of Journal of Captain Pococke, Highland Light Infantry Chronicle*, p. 193.
103. *Copy of Journal of Captain Pococke, Highland Light Infantry Chronicle*, p. 193.
104. Popham to Marsden, 8 and 19 July 1806. Grainger (ed.), *The Royal Navy in the River Plate 1806–1807*, pp. 37–49.
105. *Diadem*'s Log – ADM 51/1615; Fortin, *Invasiones Inglesas*, p. 152; ADM 2339; Parkinson (ed.), *Samuel Walters*, p. 41–2; AGN Buenos Aires, Invasiones Inglesas, 26-6-8, document 48.
106. *Copy of Journal of Captain Pococke, Highland Light Infantry Chronicle*, p. 193.
107. Beresford to Castlereagh, 16 July 1806 – WO 1/161, ff.207–14.
108. Anon to Beresford – 21 September 1806 – WO 1/161, ff.243–61.
109. Socolow, *The Merchants of Buenos Aires*, pp. 134–5.

Chapter 6: The Resistance
1. http://es.wikipedia.org/wiki/Gerardo_Esteve_y_Llach; http://es.wikipedia.org/wiki/Felipe_Sentenach; Álzaga, *Martín de Álzaga en la Reconquista*, pp. 26–7.
2. Álzaga, *Martín de Álzaga en la Reconquista*, pp. 26–7 and 52–3.
3. Newitt (ed.), *War, Revolution and Society … Thomas Kinder's Narrative*, pp. 48–50; Roberts, *Las Invasiones Inglesas*, p. 167.
4. Beresford to Castlereagh, 4 May 1807 – WO 1/162, ff.257–76; Popham to Marsden, 25 August 1806 – Grainger (ed.), *The Royal Navy in the River Plate 1806–1807*, p. 60; Gillespie, *Gleaning and Remarks*, pp. 64–5; Roberts, *Las Invasiones Inglesas*, p. 167.
5. Roberts, *Las Invasiones Inglesas*, pp. 167–8.
6. Duncan, Francis, *History of the Royal Artillery*, Vol. II (Murray, London, 1879), p. 174.
7. Almazán, *Beresford Gobernador de Buenos Ayres*, p. 85; Popham to Marsden, 25 August 1806. Quoted in Grainger (ed.), *The Royal Navy in the River Plate*, p. 60; Fortin, *Invasiones Inglesas*, p. 153.
8. Popham to Marsden, 25 August 1806. Quoted in Grainger (ed.), *The Royal Navy in the River Plate 1806–1807*, pp. 59–60.
9. http://es.wikipedia.org/wiki/Combate_de_Perdriel#Chacra_de_Perdriel_.2831_de_julio.29
10. Johnson, *Workshop of Revolution*, pp. 149–57.
11. Álzaga, *Martín de Álzaga en la Reconquista*, p. 28; Colman, Oscar Tavani Pérez, *Martínez de Fontes y la fuga del General Beresford* (Editorial Dunken, Buenos Aires, 2005), p. 56.
12. Álzaga, *Martín de Álzaga en la Reconquista*, pp. 28–9 and 48–52; Roberts, *Las Invasiones Inglesas*, p. 172.
13. http://en.wikipedia.org/wiki/Pascual_Ruiz_Huidobro; Newitt (ed.), *War, Revolution and Society … Thomas Kinder's Narrative*, p. 143; Auchmuty to Windham, 26 April 1807 – WO 1/162, ff.223–6; Anon (Tucker, John), *A Narrative of the Operations of a Small British Force under the command of Brigadier-General, Sir Samuel Auchmuty* (J.J. Stockdale, London, 1807), p. 19.
14. Fortin, *Invasiones Inglesas*, pp. 149–50.
15. Fortin, *Invasiones Inglesas*, pp. 149–51; AGN Montevideo, Legajo 166, documentos, 18–21.
16. Fortin, *Invasiones Inglesas*, pp. 53 and 149–52; Roberts, *Las Invasiones Inglesas*, pp. 180 and 242.
17. http://es.wikipedia.org/wiki/Juan_Antonio_Guti%C3%A9rrez_de_la_Concha
18. Fortin, *Invasiones Inglesas*, pp. 152–3; Roberts, *Las Invasiones Inglesas*, pp. 100–1. http://es.wikipedia.org/wiki/Hip%C3%B3lito_Mordeille; http://es.wikipedia.org/wiki/Fragata_corsaria_Dromedario.
19. Álzaga, *Martín de Álzaga en la Reconquista*, p. 31.
20. Álzaga, *Martín de Álzaga en la Reconquista*, p. 31.
21. Beverina, Juan, *Las Invasiones Inglesas al Rio de la Plata, 1806–1807*, Volume I (Taller Gráfico de L. Bernard, Buenos Aires, 1939), p. 346; Coronado (ed.), *Invasiones*, p. 117; Fortin, *Invasiones Inglesas*, p. 53; AGN Montevideo, Legajo 50, documentos 37–53.

22. Garzón, *Sobre Monte y Córdoba en las invasions inglesas*, p. 62.
23. Fortin, *Invasiones Inglesas*, pp. 152–3.
24. Álzaga, *Martín de Álzaga en la Reconquista*, pp. 29–30 and 58.
25. Beresford to Castlereagh, 4 May 1807 – WO 1/162, ff.257–76
26. Gillespie, *Gleaning and Remarks*, p. 88.
27. Gillespie, *Gleaning and Remarks*, p. 89; *Copy of Journal of Captain Pococke, Highland Light Infantry Chronicle*, p. 193; Fernyhough, *Military Memoirs of Four Brothers*, p. 96.
28. Roberts, *Las Invasiones Inglesas*, p. 157.
29. 71st Muster Roll – WO 12/7855.
30. Roberts, *Las Invasiones Inglesas*, pp. 157 and 175.
31. *Copy of Journal of Captain Pococke, Highland Light Infantry Chronicle*, p. 193 and 473; http://www.nationalarchives.gov.uk/a2a/records.aspx?cat=005-dp96&cid=-1#-1.
32. WO 1/162, ff.301–31.
33. *Copy of Journal of Captain Pococke, Highland Light Infantry Chronicle*, p. 194; Roberts, *Las Invasiones Inglesas*, p. 169.
34. Fernyhough, *Military Memoirs of Four Brothers*, p. 97.
35. *Copy of Journal of Captain Pococke, Highland Light Infantry Chronicle*, p. 194.
36. Álzaga, *Martín de Álzaga en la Reconquista*, pp. 32–3.
37. http://es.wikipedia.org/wiki/Combate_de_Perdriel#Chacra_de_Perdriel_.2831_de_julio.29
38. Álzaga, *Martín de Álzaga en la Reconquista*, p. 33; Gillespie, *Gleaning and Remarks*, p. 88–9.
39. *Copy of Journal of Captain Pococke, Highland Light Infantry Chronicle*, p. 194.
40. Beresford to Castlereagh, 4 May 1807 – WO 1/162, ff.257–76.
41. HMS *Encounter* Log Book – ADM 51/2005.
42. *Copy of Journal of Captain Pococke, Highland Light Infantry Chronicle*, p. 194.
43. Coronado (ed.), *Invasiones*, p. 117.
44. AGN Montevideo, Legajo 166, documentos 18–21.
45. Coronado (ed.), *Invasiones*, p. 117.
46. HMS *Encounter* Log Book – ADM 51/2005; Beresford to Castlereagh, 4 May 1807 – WO 1/162, ff.257–76; *Copy of Journal of Captain Pococke, Highland Light Infantry Chronicle*, p. 194.
47. *Copy of Journal of Captain Pococke, Highland Light Infantry Chronicle*, p. 194; Popham to Marsden, 25 August, 1806. Quoted in Grainger (ed.), *The Royal Navy in the River Plate 1806–1807*, pp. 60–1.

Chapter 7: La Reconquista

1. *Copy of Journal of Captain Pococke, Highland Light Infantry Chronicle*, p. 195.
2. Álzaga, *Martín de Álzaga en la Reconquista*, pp. 34–5 and 66–7; Roberts, *Las Invasiones Inglesas*, p. 182; http://es.wikipedia.org/wiki/Combate_de_Perdriel#cite_ref-5; Pueyrredón to Huidobro, Colonia del Sacramento, 3 August 1806, AGN Buenos Aires, Invasiones Inglesas, 26-7-7, documento 239.
3. Fernyhough, *Military Memoirs of Four Brothers*, p. 97–8; Gillespie, *Gleaning and Remarks*, pp. 90–1; *Copy of Journal of Captain Pococke, Highland Light Infantry Chronicle*, p. 195; *Diary of William Gavin*, p. 6; Pueyrredón to Huidobro, Colonia del Sacramento, 3 August 1806, AGN Buenos Aires, Invasiones Inglesas, 26-7-7, Document 239.
4. Gillespie, *Gleaning and Remarks*, p. 90; *Copy of Journal of Captain Pococke, Highland Light Infantry Chronicle*, p. 195.
5. Beresford to Castlereagh, 4 May 1807 – WO 1/162, ff.257–76.
6. Álzaga, *Martín de Álzaga en la* Reconquista, pp. 38–40.
7. ADM 51/1583 – HMS *Leda* Log Book; *Copy of Journal of Captain Pococke, Highland Light Infantry Chronicle*, p. 211.
8. HMS *Leda* log – ADM 51/1583; Coronado (ed.), *Invasiones*, p. 117.
9. *The Morning Chronicle*, 29 January 1807; Coronado (ed.), *Invasiones*, p. 117; AGN Montevideo, Legajo 50 documentos 37–53. Two extra transports and three armed launches also joined the expedition at Colonia. AGN Montevideo, Legajo 50 documentos 37–53.
10. Newitt (ed.), *War, Revolution and Society … Thomas Kinder's Narrative*, pp. 202–3.
11. Coronado (ed.), *Invasiones*, pp. 117–18.

12. Álzaga, *Martín de Álzaga en la Reconquista*, pp. 39–40; Coronado (ed.), *Invasiones*, pp. 117–18; Roberts, *Las Invasiones Inglesas*, p. 177.
13. HMS *Encounter* log – ADM 51/2005; King to Popham, 12 August 1806 – quoted in Grainger (ed.), *The Royal Navy in the River Plate 1806–1807*, p. 54; Popham to Marsden, 25 August, 1806. Quoted in Grainger (ed.), *The Royal Navy in the River Plate 1806–1807*, pp. 61–2.
14. Gillespie, *Gleaning and Remarks*, p. 92.
15. *Copy of Journal of Captain Pococke, Highland Light Infantry Chronicle*, p. 211.
16. *Copy of Journal of Captain Pococke, Highland Light Infantry Chronicle*, p. 212.
17. Beresford to Castlereagh, 4 May 1807 – WO 1/162, ff.257–76.
18. Álzaga, *Martín de Álzaga en la Reconquista*, pp. 41–2; *Copy of Journal of Captain Pococke, Highland Light Infantry Chronicle*, pp. 212–13.
19. Gillespie, *Gleaning and Remarks*, p. 91; Fernyhough, *Military Memoirs of Four Brothers*, p. 98; *Copy of Journal of Captain Pococke, Highland Light Infantry Chronicle*, p. 212.
20. Fernyhough, *Military Memoirs of Four Brothers*, pp. 98–9.
21. The reference to the schooners' armament is taken from Liniers' report printed in Coronado (ed.), *Invasiones*, p. 119.
22. King to Popham, 12 August 1806 – quoted in Grainger (ed.), *The Royal Navy in the River Plate 1806–1807*, p. 54; HMS *Encounter* Log – ADM 51/2005; Gillespie, *Gleaning and Remarks*, p. 93.
23. HMS *Encounter* log – ADM 51/2005.
24. *Copy of Journal of Captain Pococke, Highland Light Infantry Chronicle*, p. 211; Gillespie, *Gleaning and Remarks*, pp. 93–4.
25. AGN Montevideo, Legajo 50, documentos 37–53.
26. Fortin (ed.), *Invasiones*, p. 50.
27. Roberts, *Las Invasions Inglesas*, p. 188.
28. Coronado (ed.), *Invasiones*, p. 118; *Copy of Journal of Captain Pococke, Highland Light Infantry Chronicle*, p. 212.
29. http://www.elhistoriador.com.ar/documentos/virreinato/la_invasion_inglesa_de_1806_y_la_re-conquista_de_buenos_aires.php; *The Morning Chronicle*, 29 January 1807.
30. *Copy of Journal of Captain Pococke, Highland Light Infantry Chronicle*, p. 212.
31. Fernyhough, *Military Memoirs of Four Brothers*, p. 99; http://es.wikipedia.org/wiki/Juan_de_Dios_Dozo; 71st muster roll – WO 12/7856; Letter from an officer at Maldonado, 8 December 1806, printed in *The Morning Chronicle*, 21 February 1807; *The United Service Magazine*, 1836, Volume 3, p. 505; *Copy of Journal of Captain Pococke, Highland Light Infantry Chronicle*, pp. 440–1; see also the Journal of Balfour Kennach in Konstam, *There was a Soldier*, p. 79; Velasco to His Excellency the Minister of War, 1 August 1806 – reproduced in Vane (ed.), *Correspondence, Dispatches, and other Papers, of Viscount Castlereagh*, Volume 7, p. 305.
32. *Copy of Journal of Captain Pococke, Highland Light Infantry Chronicle*, p. 212.
33. Philippart, John (ed.), *The Royal Military Calendar, or Army Service and Commission Book*, Volume 3 (A.J. Valpy, London, 1820), p. 279
34. Hudson is named in the following document – L/MIL/5/148, f.5; Beresford mentions the fact that Macdonald was on the right – Beresford to Castlereagh, 4 May 1807 – WO 1/162, ff.257–76; Pococke states that Macdonald had two guns – *Copy of Journal of Captain Pococke, Highland Light Infantry Chronicle*, p. 215.
35. *Copy of Journal of Captain Pococke, Highland Light Infantry Chronicle*, p. 212; Beresford to Castlereagh, 4 May 1807 – WO 1/162, ff.257–76.
36. Fernyhough, *Military Memoirs of Four Brothers*, p. 99; Beresford to Castlereagh, 4 May 1807 – WO 1/162, ff.257–76; *Copy of Journal of Captain Pococke, Highland Light Infantry Chronicle*, p. 213.
37. Roberts, *Las Invasiones Inglesas*, p. 188.
38. HMS *Encounter* log book – ADM 51/2005.
39. Coronado (ed.), *Invasiones*, p. 119; Álzaga, *Martín de Álzaga en la Reconquista*, pp. 43–4; *Copy of Journal of Captain Pococke, Highland Light Infantry Chronicle*, p. 213; HMS *Encounter* Log Book – ADM 51/2005.
40. *Copy of Journal of Captain Pococke, Highland Light Infantry Chronicle*, p. 213.
41. http://en.wikipedia.org/wiki/Manuela_Pedraza#cite_note-0

42. Coronado (ed.), *Invasiones*, p. 119; AGN Montevideo, Legajo 50, documentos 14–17.
43. *Copy of Journal of Captain Pococke, Highland Light Infantry Chronicle*, p. 213; King to Popham, 12 August 1806 – quoted in Grainger (ed.), *The Royal Navy in the River Plate 1806–1807*, p. 55; Coronado (ed.), *Invasiones*, p. 119; AGN Buenos Aires, Guerra y Marina Legajo 40, Exp. 44.
44. Beresford to Castlereagh, 4 May 1807 – WO 1/162, ff.257–76.
45. 71st Muster Roll – WO 12/7856; Beresford to Castlereagh, 4 May 1807 – WO 1/162, ff.257–76; Popham to Marsden, 25 August, 1806. Quoted in Grainger (ed.), *The Royal Navy in the River Plate 1806–1807*, p. 62.
46. Popham to Marsden, 25 August 1806. Quoted in Grainger (ed.), *The Royal Navy in the River Plate 1806–1807*, p. 62.
47. Roberts, *Las Invasiones Inglesas*, pp. 190–1.
48. Gillespie, *Gleaning and Remarks*, p. 95; *Copy of Journal of Captain Pococke, Highland Light Infantry Chronicle*, p. 214; Álzaga, *Martín de Álzaga en la Reconquista*, p. 44.
49. Álzaga, *Martín de Álzaga en la Reconquista*, p. 44.
50. Roberts, *Las Invasiones Inglesas*, p. 190–1.
51. Fernyhough, *Military Memoirs of Four Brothers*, pp. 101–2.
52. Álzaga, *Martín de Álzaga en la* Reconquista, pp. 44–5.
53. Fernyhough, *Military Memoirs of Four Brothers*, p. 102.
54. Roberts, *Las Invasiones Inglesas*, pp. 190–1.
55. Coronado (ed.), *Invasiones*, p. 120; Roberts, *Las Invasiones Inglesas*, p. 190.
56. Beresford to Castlereagh, 4 May 1807 – WO 1/162, ff.257–76.
57. Coronado (ed.), *Invasiones*, pp. 119–20; King to Popham, 12 August 1806 – quoted in Grainger (ed.), *The Royal Navy in the River Plate 1806–1807*, p. 56.
58. Homans (ed.), *Army and Navy Chronicle*, Volumes 4–5, p. 285.
59. Fletcher, *The Waters of Oblivion*, pp. 43–4; AGN Montevideo, Legajo 50, documentos 37–53.
60. *Copy of Journal of Captain Pococke, Highland Light Infantry Chronicle*, p. 214.
61. Popham to Marsden, 25 August 1806. Quoted in Grainger (ed.), *The Royal Navy in the River Plate 1806–1807*, p. 63; Gillespie, *Gleaning and Remarks*, p. 95.
62. Fernyhough, *Military Memoirs of Four Brothers*, p. 105.
63. Beresford to Castlereagh, 4 May 1807 – WO 1/162, ff.257–76; Fernyhough, *Military Memoirs of Four Brothers*, p. 100; AGN Montevideo, Legajo 50 documentos 14–17 and 29.
64. AGN Montevideo, Legajo 50 documento 41.
65. Roberts, *Las Invasiones Inglesas*, p. 193; AGN Montevideo, Legajo 50, documentos 14–17.
66. Fernyhough, *Military Memoirs of Four Brothers*, p. 102.
67. *Copy of Journal of Captain Pococke, Highland Light Infantry Chronicle*, p. 214–5; *Diary of William Gavin*, p. 7.
68. Álzaga, *Martín de Álzaga en la Reconquista*, pp. 44–5.
69. Álzaga, *Martín de Álzaga en la Reconquista*, p. 45; AGN Montevideo, Legajo 50 documentos 14–17.
70. Álzaga, *Martín de Álzaga en la Reconquista*, p. 45; *Copy of Journal of Captain Pococke, Highland Light Infantry Chronicle*, p. 215; AGN Montevideo, Legajo 50 documentos 2, 13 and 77.
71. Roberts, *Las Invasiones Inglesas*, p. 193.
72. Beresford to Castlereagh, 4 May 1807 – WO 1/162, ff.257–76; Gillespie, *Gleaning and Remarks*, p. 96; Fernyhough, *Military Memoirs of Four Brothers*, pp. 101–2; *Copy of Journal of Captain Pococke, Highland Light Infantry Chronicle*, pp. 214–15; *Diary of William Gavin*, p. 7.
73. Fernyhough, *Military Memoirs of Four Brothers*, p. 128; Johnson, *Workshop of Revolution*, p. 254; Gillespie, *Gleaning and Remarks*, p. 96.
74. *Copy of Journal of Captain Pococke, Highland Light Infantry Chronicle*, p. 214–15.
75. Roberts, *Las Invasiones Inglesas*, pp. 195–6.
76. AGN Montevideo, Legajo 50, documentos 14–17.
77. *Diary of William Gavin*, p. 7.
78. HMS *Raisonnable* log – ADM 36/16299; *The Times*, 28 January 1807; King to Popham, 12 August 1806 – quoted in Grainger (ed.), *The Royal Navy in the River Plate 1806–1807*, p. 54; http://www.portaldesalta.gov.ar/libros/Libro%20Las%20invasiones%20Inglesas.pdf

Chapter 8: 'For he's a jolly good fellow!'

1. *Hampshire Telegraph and Sussex Chronicle*, 22 September 1806.
2. *The Courier* and *The Times*, 15 September 1806.
3. *Hampshire Telegraph and Sussex Chronicle*, 22 September 1806; *The Times*, 22 September 1806.
4. *The Times*, 16 September 1806.
5. Quoted in Popham, *A Damned Cunning Fellow*, p. 164.
6. *The United Service Magazine*, 1836, Volume 2, p. 198.
7. *Resolutions From Manchester*, quoted in Grainger (ed.), *The Royal Navy in the River Plate 1806–1807*, p. 125; Bryant, Arthur, *Years of Victory, 1802–1812* (The Reprint Society, London, 1945), p. 232.
8. Roberts, *Las Invasiones Inglesas*, pp. 402–3.
9. Buckland, Charles Edward, *Dictionary of Indian Biography* (S. Sonrienschein, 1906), p. 130.
10. Eastwick, Robert William, *A Master Mariner: Being the Life and Adventures of Captain Robert Eastwick* (Unwin, 1891), pp. 219–20.
11. Eastwick, *A Master Mariner*, pp. 219–35; Roberts, *Las Invasiones Inglesas*, p. 250.
12. Navy Board to Popham, 28 July 1806 – Quoted in Grainger (ed.), *The Royal Navy in the River Plate 1806–1807*, p. 118; WO 1/161, ff. 243–61; Roberts, *Las Invasiones Inglesas*, pp. 245–6.
13. Quoted in Grainger (ed.), *The Royal Navy in the River Plate 1806–1807*, p. 9.
14. Quoted in Popham, *A Damned Cunning Fellow*, p. 165.
15. Grenville to Buckingham, 13 September 1806 – Quoted in Grainger (ed.), *The Royal Navy in the River Plate 1806–1807*, p. 122.
16. *Notes on the Viceroyalty of La Plata*, p. 274.
17. *Notes on the Viceroyalty of La Plata*, pp. 274–80.
18. Lawrence, William, *The Autobiography of Sergeant William Lawrence* (Dodo Press, Milton Keynes, 2010), p. 14.
19. Downing Street to Auchmuty, 14 July and 22 September 1806, WO 1/161, ff. 223–5 and 235–42.
20. Cunliffe, Marcus, *The Royal Irish Fusiliers, 1793–1950* (OUP, Oxford, 1952), p. 27; Tucker, *Narrative of the Operations of a Small Force*, p. 9; *The Times*, 15 April, 1807.
21. http://en.wikisource.org/wiki/Butler,_Edward_Gerard_(DNB00)
22. *The Times*, 3 October 1806; Parry, D.H., *The Death or Glory Boys: the Story of the Seventeenth Lancers* (Kessinger Publishing, 2010), p. 154.
23. Downing Street to Auchmuty, 22 September 1806, WO 1/161, ff. 235–42.
24. Shee to Auchmuty, 2 October 1806, Grainger (ed.), *The Royal Navy in the River Plate 1806–1807*, p. 127; Windham Papers, British Library, Add. 37,886, ff. 10–24.
25. Todd, Thomas, *Bayonets, Bugles & Bonnets* (Leonaur, 2006), p. 24; Cleland, James, *The Annals of Glasgow: comprising an accont of the public buildings, charities, and the rise and progress of the city* (J. Smith, London, 1829), p. 185.
26. Lawrence, *The Autobiography of Sergeant William Lawrence*, pp. 10–11.
27. Smith, G.C. Moore (ed.), *The Autobiography of Lieutenant-General Sir Harry Smith* (J. Murray, London, 1903) p. 359.
28. Pitt, William, *The Cabin Boy: being the memoirs of an officer in the Civil Department of H. M. Navy* (Hamilton, Adams and Co., London, 1840), pp. 119–21; Smith (ed.), *The Autobiography of Lieutenant-General Sir Harry Smith*, p. 360.

Chapter 9: Revolution!

1. *Diary of William Gavin*, p. 7.
2. Gillespie, *Gleaning and Remarks*, p. 99.
3. Gillespie, *Gleaning and Remarks*, p. 99.
4. 71st pay list – WO 17/192.
5. WO 1/162, ff. 301–31; Philippart (ed.), *The Royal Military Calendar … 1820*, p. 274.
6. Fortin, *Invasiones Inglesas*, p. 53.
7. *Copy of Journal of Captain Pococke, Highland Light Infantry Chronicle*, p. 340.
8. http://www.nocturnar.com/forum/historia/241552-robo-y-traicion-de-invasiones-inglesas.html
9. Gillespie, *Gleaning and Remarks*, p. 101.
10. *Copy of Journal of Captain Pococke, Highland Light Infantry Chronicle*, p. 337.

11. *Copy of Journal of Captain Pococke, Highland Light Infantry Chronicle*, p. 252; Roberts, *Las Invasiones Inglesas*, p. 199.
12. Roberts, *Las Invasiones Inglesas*, p. 98.
13. Roberts, *Las Invasiones Inglesas*, pp. 200–3; Fortin, *Invasiones Inglesas*, p. 80.
14. Roberts, *Las Invasiones Inglesas*, pp. 294; Johnson, *Workshop of Revolution*, pp. 149–78.
15. Elissalde, *Historias Ignoradas de los Invasiones Inglesas*, p. 43.
16. *Copy of Journal of Captain Pococke, Highland Light Infantry Chronicle*, p. 252; Fernyhough, *Military Memoirs of Four Brothers*, p. 102; *The Morning Chronicle*, 29 January 1807.
17. *Copy of Journal of Captain Pococke, Highland Light Infantry Chronicle*, pp. 252–3.
18. HMS *Diadem*'s log: ADM 51/1615.
19. Popham to the Governor of Monte Video, 15 August 1806; Popham to Marsden, 25 August 1806. Quoted in Grainger (ed.), *The Royal Navy in the River Plate 1806–1807*, pp. 57–64.
20. Fernyhough, *Military Memoirs of Four Brothers*, pp. 126–7.
21. AGN Buenos Aires, Invasiones Inglesas, 26-6-8, document 78.
22. *Copy of Journal of Captain Pococke, Highland Light Infantry Chronicle*, p. 254.
23. Gillespie, *Gleaning and Remarks*, pp. 105–6.
24. *Copy of Journal of Captain Pococke, Highland Light Infantry Chronicle*, p. 254.
25. Fletcher, *The Waters of Oblivion*, p. 49.
26. Beresford to Castlereagh, 12 May 1807 – WO 1/162, ff.301–31; Roberts, *Las Invasiones Inglesas*, p. 203.
27. *Copy of Journal of Captain Pococke, Highland Light Infantry Chronicle*, p. 254.
28. *Copy of Journal of Captain Pococke, Highland Light Infantry Chronicle*, p. 255; Gillespie, *Gleaning and Remarks*, p. 107; Fernyhough, *Military Memoirs of Four Brothers*, p. 107.
29. *Copy of Journal of Captain Pococke, Highland Light Infantry Chronicle*, p. 337.
30. Beresford to Castlereagh, 12 May 1807 – WO 1/162, ff.301–31.
31. *Copy of Journal of Captain Pococke, Highland Light Infantry Chronicle*, p. 338.
32. http://es.wikipedia.org/wiki/Francisco_Antonio_de_Escalada#Invasiones_Inglesas_.281806-1807.29
33. Socolow, *The Merchants of Buenos Aires*, p. 131.
34. Álzaga, *Martín de Álzaga en la Reconquista*, pp. 93–9 and 114–15.
35. Socolow, *The Merchants of Buenos Aires*, p. 131; http://www.museoliniers.org.ar/tour_sala_14.php; Miranda, Arnaldo Ignacio Adolfo, *Relevamiento del Archivo Parroquial de San José de Flores* (Editorial Dunken, 2006), p. 279; http://es.wikipedia.org/wiki/Esteban_Romero.
36. Newitt (ed.), *War, Revolution and Society ... Thomas Kinder's Narrative*, pp. 230–1.
37. http://www.granaderos.com.ar/articulos/art_graficocantabro.htm
38. Johnson, *Workshop of Revolution*, pp. 254 and 291.
39. Newitt (ed.), *War, Revolution and Society ... Thomas Kinder's Narrative*, pp. 230–1.
40. Johnson, *Workshop of Revolution*, p. 275.
41. Álzaga to Pereyra, 28 October 1806. Reproduced in Álzaga, *Martín de Álzaga en la Reconquista*, pp. 108–9; Johnson, *Workshop of Revolution*, p. 263.
42. Newitt (ed.), *War, Revolution and Society ... Thomas Kinder's Narrative*, pp. 230–1; Roberts, *Las Invasiones Inglesas*, p. 180; Roberts, *Las Invasiones Inglesas*, pp. 230–7 and 338.
43. Roberts, *Las Invasiones Inglesas*, p. 234.
44. *Copy of Journal of Captain Pococke, Highland Light Infantry Chronicle*, p. 440.
45. *Copy of Journal of Captain Pococke, Highland Light Infantry Chronicle*, p. 338; Almazán, *Beresford Gobernador de Buenos Ayres*, p. 85; Roberts, *Las Invasiones Inglesas*, p. 230.
46. *Copy of Journal of Captain Pococke, Highland Light Infantry Chronicle*, p. 358.
47. Fortin, *Invasiones Inglesas*, pp. 85–6 and 160; Roberts, *Las Invasiones Inglesas*, p. 229.
48. Echeverría to Echeverría, 31 January 1807, Fortin (ed.), *Invasiones Inglesas*, p. 184; de la Concha to Unquera, 8 April 1807 and Unquera to the Audiencia, 14 April 1807, Fortin, *Invasiones Inglesas*, pp. 228–30; Grainger (ed.), *The Royal Navy in the River Plate 1806–1807*, pp. 238–42.
49. AGN Montevideo, Legajo 166, documentos 18–21.
50. Popham to Marsden, 3 October 1806. Quoted in Grainger (ed.), *The Royal Navy in the River Plate 1806–1807*, pp. 86–7.

51. *Jackson's Oxford Journal*, 20 February 1807.
52. Popham to Lord Howick, 28 August 1806. Quoted in Grainger (ed.), *The Royal Navy in the River Plate 1806–1807*, pp. 65–7.
53. Philippart (ed.), *The Royal Military Calendar ... 1820*, p. 275.
54. *Copy of Journal of Captain Pococke, Highland Light Infantry Chronicle*, p. 357; Journal of Balfour Kennach in Konstam, Angus, *There was a Soldier* (Headline Book Publishing, 2009), p. 79.
55. Roberts, *Las Invasiones Inglesas*, p. 217; Fernyhough, *Military Memoirs of Four Brothers*, p. 106.
56. *Copy of Journal of Captain Pococke, Highland Light Infantry Chronicle*, p. 358.
57. http://www.irlandeses.org/argentina.pdf
58. Gillespie, *Gleaning and Remarks*, p. 110.
59. Honeyman to Popham, 9 September 1806. Reproduced in Grainger (ed.), *The Royal Navy in the River Plate 1806–1807*, pp. 74–5; HMS *Leda* muster roll – ADM 36/17373; HMS *Leda* ship's log – ADM 51/1583; Fortin (ed.), *Invasiones Inglesas*, p. 161; AGN Montevideo, Invasiones Inglesas, Legajo 167, documentos 20–26 and 46–7.
60. *Copy of Journal of Captain Pococke, Highland Light Infantry Chronicle*, p. 443; Fernyhough, *Military Memoirs of Four Brothers*, p. 109; *Diary of William Gavin*, p. 7; Roberts, *Las Invasiones Inglesas*, pp. 218 and 223.

Chapter 10: Maldonado

1. Ship's Log HMS *Protector* – ADM 51/1708; *The Times* – 8 January 1807; Cunliffe, *The Royal Irish Fusiliers*, p. 27; *Notes on the Viceroyalty of La Plata*, p. 24; British Library Manuscripts – Add.37,886, ff. 10–24.
2. Ship's Log HMS *Protector* – ADM 51/1708; Gleig, *The Hussar*, p. 163.
3. *The United Service Magazine*, 1836, Volume 2, p. 197.
4. *The Times* – 8 January 1807; Baird to Popham, 14 August 1807 and Baird to Beresford, 24 August 1807 – both reproduced in Grainger (ed.), *The Royal Navy in the River Plate 1806–1807*, pp. 79–80; British Library Manuscripts – Add.37,886, ff. 10–24.
5. *Notes on the Viceroyalty of La Plata*, p. 293; *The Gentleman's Magazine*, Volume 98, Part 2, p. 85; Popham to Howick, 4 November 1806. Reproduced in Grainger (ed.), *The Royal Navy in the River Plate 1806–1807*, p. 99.
6. Vassal, Spencer Thomas, *Memoir of the life of Lieutenant-Colonel Vassal* (Barry and Son, Britsol, 1819), pp. 1–38.
7. *The Morning Post*, 15 September 1807.
8. *The United Service Magazine*, 1836, Volume 2, p. 198.
9. 38th Pay List – WO 12/5181.
10. Ship's Log – HMS *Lancaster* – ADM 51/1611.
11. Backhouse to Windham, 13 October 1806. Reproduced in *The Times*, 8 January 1807; *The United Service Magazine*, 1836, Volume 2, p. 199.
12. Anonymous, 13 October 1806. Reproduced in *The Caledonian Mercury*, 2 February 1807.
13. Popham to Marsden, 9 October 1806. Reproduced in Grainger (ed.), *The Royal Navy in the River Plate 1806–1807*, pp. 87–91.
14. Backhouse to Windham, 13 October 1806. Reproduced in *The Times*, 8 January 1807; Gleig, *The Hussar*, p. 164; *The United Service Magazine*, 1836, Volume 2, p. 199.
15. *The United Service Magazine*, 1836, Volume 2, p. 199.
16. Parkinson (ed.), *Samuel Walters*, p. 48.
17. Parkinson (ed.), *Samuel Walters*, p. 48.
18. *The United Service Magazine*, 1836, Volume 2, p. 200.
19. HMS *Encounter* Log – ADM 51/2005.
20. *The United Service Magazine*, 1836, Volume 2, p. 200; Parkinson (ed.), *Samuel Walters*, pp. 48–9; HMS *Encounter* Log – ADM 51/2005; HMS *Lancaster* Log – ADM 51/1611; HMS *Raisonnable* Log – ADM 51/1812; HMS *Protector* Log – ADM 51/1708; Fortin (ed.), *Invasiones Inglesas*, pp. 169–70; AGN Montevideo, Legajo 167 – Servicios en la Guerra contra los Ingelses, document 15.
21. AGN Buenos Aires, Invasiones Inglesas 26-7-9, document 186.

22. *The United Service Magazine*, 1836, Volume 2, p. 200; Parkinson (ed.), *Samuel Walters*, pp. 48–9; HMS *Encounter* Log – ADM 51/2005; HMS *Lancaster* Log – ADM 51/1611; HMS *Raisonnable* Log – ADM 51/1812; HMS *Protector* Log – ADM 51/1708; Fortin (ed.), *Invasiones Inglesas*, pp. 169–70.

23. HMS *Diomede* Log – ADM 51/1615; HMS *Encounter* Log – ADM 51/2005.

24. *Notes on the Viceroyalty of La Plata*, p. 24.

25. Popham to Baird, 17 November 1807. Reproduced in Grainger (ed.), *The Royal Navy in the River Plate 1806–1807*, pp. 102–3.

26. Parkinson (ed.), *Samuel Walters*, p. 49.

27. Gleig, *The Hussar*, p. 168; HMS *Protector* Log – ADM 51/1708; HMS *Encounter* Log – ADM 51/2005; Parkinson (ed.), *Samuel Walters*, p. 51.

28. Gleig, *The Hussar*, p. 168; *The Morning Post*, 15 September 1807.

29. Gleig, *The Hussar*, p. 168–9.

30. Parkinson (ed.), *Samuel Walters*, p. 49.

31. *The United Service Magazine*, 1836, Volume 2, p. 200; Darwin, Charles, *Journal of Researches into the Natural History and Geology of the Countries Visited During the Voyage of HMS* Beagle *round the World*, Volume II (J. Murray, London, 1845), p. 50.

32. http://www.cx4radiorural.com/wr/tomo_1.pdf p. 282.

33. Backhouse's Dispatches and Major Trotter's *Return of Ordinance, Ammunition, and Stores, &c. taken from the enemy*, 30 October 1806. Reproduced in *The London Gazette*, 27 January 1807; HMS *Protector* Ship's Log – ADM 51/1708.

34. Gleig, *The Hussar*, p. 169.

35. Letter 'from an officer of the 38th Regiment of Foot, dated Maldonado, Nov. 4, 1806.' Reproduced in *The Morning Post*, 31 January 1807; 38th Pay List – WO 12/5181.

36. *The United Service Magazine*, 1836, Volume 2, p. 200.

37. Parkinson (ed.), *Samuel Walters*, p. 50; *The Morning Post*, 31 January 1807.

38. 38th Pay List – WO 12/5181.

39. HMS *Protector* Ship's Log – ADM 51/1708; HMS *Diadem* Ship's Log – ADM 51/1615.

40. AGN Buenos Aires, Invasiones Inglesas, 26-7-8, documento 186.

41. *Notes on the Viceroyalty of La Plata*, p. 139.

42. *The Morning Post*, 31 January 1807.

43. *Exposicion de los Vecinos de Maldonado al Cabildo de Montevideo sobre la Conducta de los Ingleses.* Reproduced at http://www.cx4radiorural.com/wr/tomo_1.pdf p. 283; Gleig, *The Hussar*, pp. 170–5.

44. *Exposicion de los Vecinos de Maldonado al Cabildo de Montevideo sobre la Conducta de los Ingleses.* Reproduced at http://www.cx4radiorural.com/wr/tomo_1.pdf p. 283.

45. Gleig, *The Hussar*, pp. 170–5.

46. Backhouse's Dispatches and Major Trotter's, *Return of Ordinance, Ammunition, and Stores, &c. taken from the enemy*. 30 October 1806. Reproduced in *The London Gazette*, 27 January 1807.

47. Popham to Marsden, 30 October 1806; Popham to the Commandant of the Island of Goritti, 30 October 1806 – both reproduced in Grainger (ed.), *The Royal Navy in the River Plate 1806–1807*, pp. 94–6; HMS *Raisonnable* Log – ADM 51/1812.

48. Gleig, *The Hussar*, p. 171.

49. *Exposicion de los Vecinos de Maldonado al Cabildo de Montevideo sobre la Conducta de los Ingleses.* Reproduced at http://www.cx4radiorural.com/wr/tomo_1.pdf p. 285.

50. *Exposicion de los Vecinos de Maldonado al Cabildo de Montevideo sobre la Conducta de los Ingleses.* Reproduced at http://www.cx4radiorural.com/wr/tomo_1.pdf p. 285.

51. http://es.wikipedia.org/wiki/San_Carlos_(Uruguay); Backhouse to Windham, 31 October 1806 – reproduced in Grainger (ed.), *The Royal Navy in the River Plate 1806–1807*, pp. 97–8.

52. http://es.wikipedia.org/wiki/San_Carlos_(Uruguay)

53. Parkinson (ed.), *Samuel Walters*, p. 52.

54. *The United Service Magazine*, 1836, Volume 2, pp. 200–1.

55. *The United Service Magazine*, 1836, Volume 2, p. 487.

56. *The Morning Chronicle*, 27 January, 1807.

57. *The Caledonian Mercury*, Edinburgh, 2 February 1807.

58. *The Aberdeen Journal*, 11 February 1807.
59. *Parte de Ruiz Huidobro sobre la Toma de Montevideo por los Ingleses.* Reproduced at http://www.cx4radiorural.com/wr/tomo_1.pdf p. 292; Fortin (ed.), *Invasiones Inglesas*, p. 171.
60. Fortin (ed.), *Invasiones*, pp. 89 and 91; *Parte de Ruiz Huidobro sobe la toma de Montevideo por los Ingleses al Principe de la Paz.* Reproduced at http://www.cx4radiorural.com/wr/tomo_1.pdf p. 291.
61. Other reports claim the British column amounted to 400 infantry and eighty hussars – Fortin (ed.), *Invasiones Inglesas*, p. 172. Although Landsheit refers to 'two light field pieces' these are not mentioned in any of the Spanish accounts, but mention is made of the British firing *esemeriles* (swivel guns). AGN Buenos Aires, Invasiones Inglesas, 26-7-8, documentos 388–392.
62. Tucker, *A Narrative of the Operations of a Small British Force*, p. 20.
63. Gleig, *The Hussar*, p. 183.
64. Darwin, Charles, *Journal of Researches into the Natural History and Geology of the Countries Visited During the Voyage of HMS* Beagle *round the World*, Volume II (J. Murray, London, 1845), pp. 51–4; AGN Buenos Aires, Invasiones Inglesas, 26-7-8, documentos 388–392.
65. Gleig, *The Hussar*, pp. 185–6.
66. AGN Buenos Aires, Invasiones Inglesas, 26-7-8, documentos 388–392.
67. AGN Buenos Aires, Invasiones Inglesas, 26-7-8, documentos 388–392.
68. Pay List – 20th Light Dragoons – WO 12/1422; Gleig, *The Hussar*, p. 162.
69. AGN Buenos Aires, Invasiones Inglesas, 26-7-8, documentos 411.
70. AGN Buenos Aires, Invasiones Inglesas, 26-7-8, documentos 388–392.
71. Fortin (ed.), *Invasiones*, pp. 91–2; Gleig, *The Hussar*, pp. 186–7; José Prego de Oliver, *A la Gloriosa Memoria del Teniente de Fragata D. Augustin Agreu* – reproduced at http://www.archive.org/stream/3324749.1-5/3324749.1-5_djvu.txt; *The Journal of Captain Pococke, Highland Light Infantry Chronicle*, p. 474; *Boletin Historico del Ejercito, Nros. 255–258*, pp. 58–9 – reproduced at http://www.ejercito.mil.uy/cge/dptoeehh/Libros/Boletin%20Historico/116%20Bolet%C3%ADn%20Hist%C3%B3rico%20N%C2%BA%20255%20-%20258%20-%20a%C3%B1o%201978.pdf; Fletcher, *The Waters of Oblivion*, p. 56; Pay List – 20th Light Dragoons – WO 12/1422; Pay List – 38th Foot – WO 12/5181; AGN Buenos Aires, Invasiones Inglesas, 26-7-8, documento 186.
72. *Boletin Historico del Ejercito, Nros. 255–258* (Uruguay), p. 59.
73. Fortin (ed.), *Invasiones*, pp. 91–2; Gleig, *The Hussar*, pp. 186–7; José Prego de Oliver, *A la Gloriosa Memoria del Teniente de Fragata D. Augustin Agreu* – reproduced at http://www.archive.org/stream/3324749.1-5/3324749.1-5_djvu.txt; *The Journal of Captain Pococke, Highland Light Infantry Chronicle*, p. 474; *Boletin Historico del Ejercito, Nros. 255–258*, pp. 58–9 – reproduced at http://www.ejercito.mil.uy/cge/dptoeehh/Libros/Boletin%20Historico/116%20Bolet%C3%ADn%20Hist%C3%B3rico%20N%C2%BA%20255%20-%20258%20-%20a%C3%B1o%201978.pdf; Fletcher, *The Waters of Oblivion*, p. 56; Pay List – 20th Light Dragoons – WO 12/1422; Pay List – 38th Foot – WO 12/5181; AGN Buenos Aires, Invasiones Inglesas, 26-7-8, documentos 411.
74. Memorandum by Popham – 9 November 1806. Reproduced in Grainger (ed.), *The Royal Navy in the River Plate 1806–1807*, p. 100; Parkinson (ed.), *Samuel Walters*, p. 54.
75. Rear-Admiral Stirling's Journal. Entry for 3 December 1806. Reproduced in Grainger (ed.), *The Royal Navy in the River Plate 1806–1807*, p. 180; AGN Buenos Aires, Invasiones Inglesas, 26-7-8, documentos 379–380.
76. 20th Light Dragoons pay roll – WO 12/1422; 38th Foot pay roll – WO 12/5181; 47th Foot pay roll – WO 12/5880.
77. Gleig, *The Hussar*, p. 177; 21st Light Dragoons – WO 12/1447.
78. *The United Service Magazine*, 1836, Volume 2, pp. 201–2; Rowley to Popham, 8 November 1806 and Downman to Popham, 11 November 1806. Both reproduced in Grainger (ed.), *The Royal Navy in the River Plate 1806–1807*, pp. 100–1; Duncan, *History of the Royal Artillery*, vol. II, p. 172.
79. *The United Service Magazine*, 1836, Volume 2, pp. 201–2.
80. Popham to the Commissioners for Victualing, 28 October 1806 and 2 November 1806. Reproduced in Grainger (ed.), *The Royal Navy in the River Plate 1806–1807*, pp. 94 and 98

81. List of Neutrals at anchor in Maldonado Roads. Reproduced in Grainger (ed.), *The Royal Navy in the River Plate 1806–1807*, p. 108.
82. HMS *Lancaster* log – ADM 51/1611; *List of Neutrals at anchor in Maldonado Roads* and Popham to Stirling, 6 December 1806. Reproduced in Grainger, *The Royal Navy in the River Plate 1806–1807*, pp. 108 and 183.
83. Stirling's Journal – entry dated 4 December 1806; Popham to Stirling, December 1806. Reproduced in Grainger (ed.), *The Royal Navy in the River Plate 1806–1807*, pp. 181–2 and 183–4.
84. *Exposicion de los Vecinos de Maldonado al Cabildo de Montevideo sobre la Conducta de los Ingleses.* Reproduced at http://www.cx4radiorural.com/wr/tomo_1.pdf p. 287.
85. Pay Lists – 38th Regiment – WO 12/5181; 47th Regiment – WO 12/5880; 20th Light Dragoons -WO 12/1422; 21st Light Dragoons – WO 12/1447; Fortin (ed.), *Invasiones Inglesas*, pp. 172–8; AGN Buenos Aires, Invasiones Inglesas, 26-7-9, documentos 3, 9, 17 and 38
86. *Narración Anonima de los episodios de la toma de Maldonado por los Ingleses* and *Diario de un Inhabitante de Monte Video*, both reporduced in Fortin (ed.), *Invasiones Inglesas*, pp. 93 and 175.
87. Parkinson (ed.), *Samuel Walters*, p. 54; HMS *Diadem* log book – ADM 51/1756
88. Hardy, Horatio Charles, *A Register of Ships Employed in the Service of the Honourable the United East India Company From the Year 1760 to 1810* (Black, Perry and Kingsbury, London, 1811), pp. xx, 223, 229.
89. *The United Service Magazine*, 1836, Volume 2, p. 487.
90. Ralfe, James, *The Naval Biography of Great Britain, consisting of Historical Memoirs*, Volume III (Whitmore & Fenn, London, 1828), pp. 73–83.
91. Ralfe, *The Naval Biography of Great Britain*, Volume III, pp. 83–4.
92. Stirling to Marsden, 12 December 1806. Reproduced in Grainger (ed.), *The Royal Navy in the River Plate 1806–1807*, pp. 192–4.
93. This paragraph is based on a series of letters written by both commanders, Stirling's Journal and both commanders' communications with their superiors, all of which are reproduced in Grainger (ed.), *The Royal Navy in the River Plate 1806–1807*, pp. 183–98.
94. Fortin (ed.), *Invasiones Inglesas*, pp. 174 and 178; AGN Montevideo, Legajo 167, documentos 38–44.
95. Pay Lists – 38th Regiment – WO 12/5181; 47th Regiment – WO 12/5880; 20th Light Dragoons – WO 12/1422; 21st Light Dragoons – WO 12/1447.
96. *The Morning Chronicle*, London, 21 February 1807.
97. Auchmuty to Windham, 7 February 1807. WO 1/162, ff.55–59.
98. Carlos E. Chabot and María A. Díaz de Guerra, *Francisco Dionisio Martínez*, p. 5 http://www.smu.org.uy/dpmc/hmed/historia/articulos/f-martinez2.pdf; Fortin (ed.), *Invasiones Inglesas*, p. 181.
99. Gleig, *The Hussar*, pp. 179–80.
100. *The United Service Magazine*, 1836, Volume 2, p. 201.
101. Gleig, *The Hussar*, pp. 180–2; Fortin (ed.), *Invasiones Inglesas*, p. 181.
102. Grainger (ed.), *The Royal Navy in the River Plate 1806–1807*, p. 173; Eastwick, *A Master Mariner*, pp. 226–7.
103. Popham to Baird, 16 December 1806, Grainger (ed.), *The Royal Navy in the River Plate 1806–1807*, pp. 196–7.
104. Stirling to Popham, December 1806. Quoted in Popham, *A Damned Cunning Fellow*, p. 163.
105. Parkinson (ed.), *Samuel Walters*, p. 55; HMS *Lancaster* log, ADM 51/1611.
106. Fletcher, *The Waters of Oblivion*, p. 144; 71st pay list – WO 17/192.
107. *The United Service Magazine*, 1836, Volume 2, p. 487; Gleig, *The Hussar*, p. 188.
108. *The United Service Magazine*, 1836, Volume 2, p. 487.

Chapter 11: The Siege of Monte Video

1. Stirling's Journal – entries for 9 and 10 January 1807. Reproduced in Grainger (ed.), *The Royal Navy in the River Plate 1806–1807*, p. 200.
2. Todd, *Bayonets, Bugles & Bonnets*, p. 24.

3. Stirling's Journal – entries for 9 and 10 January 1807. Reproduced in Grainger (ed.), *The Royal Navy in the River Plate 1806–1807*, p. 200; Auchmuty to Windham, 7 January 1807, WO 1/162, ff.55–59.
4. Stirling's Journal – entry for 15 January 1807. Reproduced in Grainger (ed.), *The Royal Navy in the River Plate 1806–1807*, p. 203.
5. Stirling's Journal – entries for 9 and 10 January 1807. Reproduced in Grainger (ed.), *The Royal Navy in the River Plate 1806–1807*, pp. 200–1.
6. Gleig, *The Hussar*, pp. 189–90.
7. Gleig, *The Hussar*, p. 192.
8. HMS *Diadem* log book – ADM 51/1756.
9. *The United Service Magazine*, 1836, Volume 2, p. 487.
10. HMS *Diadem* log book – ADM 51/1756.
11. Parkinson (ed.), *Samuel Walters*, p. 55; HMS *Raisonnable* log book – ADM 51/1812.
12. HMS *Daphne* log book – ADM 51/4434.
13. Roberts, *Las Invasiones Inglesas*, pp. 271–2 and 288.
14. What was known as Carretas Point in the colonial period is now referred to as Punta Gorda. The modern day Carretas Point is three miles to the west.
15. Stirling's Journal – entry for 15 January 1807. Reproduced in Grainger (ed.), *The Royal Navy in the River Plate 1806–1807*, p. 202.
16. Stirling's Journal – entry for 15 January 1807. Reproduced in Grainger (ed.), *The Royal Navy in the River Plate 1806–1807*, pp. 202–3; AGN Montevideo, Legajo 167, documentos 138–144.
17. HMS *Ardent* log book – ADM 51/1629.
18. Tucker, *Narrative of the Operations*, pp. 5–6.
19. *Parte de Ruiz Huidobro sobre la Toma de Montevideo por los Ingleses.* Reproduced at http://www.cx4radiorural.com/wr/tomo_1.pdf p. 292.
20. *The United Service Magazine*, 1836, Volume 2, p. 489; Roberts, *Las Invasiones Inglesas*, p. 274.
21. Pitt, *The Cabin Boy*, p. 123.
22. Stirling's Journal – entry for 16 January 1807. Reproduced in Grainger (ed.), *The Royal Navy in the River Plate 1806–1807*, p. 204–5.
23. *The United Service Magazine*, 1836, Volume 2, p. 490; Tucker, *Narrative of the Operations*, p. 6; Smith, *The Autobiography of Lieutenant-General Sir Harry Smith*, Appendix 1. Diary entry for 16 January 1807. Reproduced at http://digital.library.upenn.edu/women/hsmith/autobiography/appendices.html#I
24. Pay list, 2/95, WO 12/9578; Tucker, *Narrative of the Operations*, p. 35.
25. Gleig, *The Hussar*, pp. 192–3.
26. Parkinson (ed.), *Samuel Walters*, p. 56.
27. *Parte de Ruiz Huidobro sobre la Toma de Montevideo por los Ingleses.* Reproduced at http://www.cx4radiorural.com/wr/tomo_1.pdf pp. 292–3.
28. Stirling's Journal – entry for 17 January 1807. Reproduced in Grainger (ed.), *The Royal Navy in the River Plate 1806–1807*, p. 205.
29. Tucker, *Narrative of the Operations*, p. 6.
30. Stirling's Journal – entry for 17 January 1807. Reproduced in Grainger (ed.), *The Royal Navy in the River Plate 1806–1807*, p. 205.
31. HMS *Diadem* log – ADM 51/1756; Roberts, *Las Invasiones Inglesas*, p. 291.
32. Stirling's Journal – entry for 17 January 1807. Reproduced in Grainger (ed.), *The Royal Navy in the River Plate 1806–1807*, pp. 205–6.
33. Fletcher, *The Waters of Oblivion*, p. 63.
34. Tucker, *Narrative of the Operations*, pp. 7–8; Auchmuty to Castlereagh, 6 February 1807, reproduced in Tucker, *Narrative of the Operations*, p. 28; Gleig, *The Hussar*, pp. 194–5; Smith, *The Autobiography of Lieutenant-General Sir Harry Smith*, Appendix 1. Diary entry for 19 January 1807; AGN Montevideo, Legajo 167, documentos 70–88.
35. *Notes on the Viceroyalty of La Plata*, p. 78; Anon, *An authentic narrative of the proceedings of the expedition*, p. 104; Mawe, *Travels in the interior of Brazil*, pp. 16–17.
36. Roberts, *Las Invasiones Inglesas*, pp. 36–40.

37. *Notes on the Viceroyalty of La Plata*, p. 78; Anon, *An authentic narrative of the proceedings of the expedition*, p. 104; Mawe, *Travels in the interior of Brazil*, pp. 16–17; AGN Montevideo, Legajo 167, documentos 70–73.
38. Stirling's Journal – entry for 19 and 20 January 1807. Reproduced in Grainger (ed.), *The Royal Navy in the River Plate 1806–1807*, pp. 206–7; Tucker, *Narrative of the Operations*, p. 9; Auchmuty to Castlereagh, 6 February 1807, reproduced in Tucker, *Narrative of the Operations*, p. 28; Roberts, *Las Invasiones Inglesas*, p. 275.
39. *Parte de Ruiz Huidobro sobre la Toma de Montevideo por los Ingleses*. Reproduced at http://www.cx4radiorural.com/wr/tomo_1.pdf p. 300; AGN Montevideo, Legajo 167, documentos 20–26; AGN Montevideo, Legajo 166, documentos 18–21.
40. *The United Service Magazine*, 1836, Volume 2, p. 492.
41. Lawrence, *The Autobiography of Sergeant William Lawrence*, p. 13; NAM 6807-236, *The Diary of Lt. Col. Lancelot Holland*, p. 62; Monkland, *Journal of the Secret Expedition*, p. 63; Anon, *An authentic narrative of the proceedings of the expedition*, pp. 102–3.
42. Stirling's Journal – entry for 27 January 1807, reproduced in Grainger (ed.), *The Royal Navy in the River Plate 1806–1807*, p. 213; Lecocq, 20 January 1807, *Parte Oficial de la Salida del dia 20.* Reproduced at http://www.cx4radiorural.com/wr/tomo_1.pdf p. 277; *Parte de Ruiz Huidobro sobre la Toma de Montevideo por los Ingleses*. Reproduced at http://www.cx4radiorural.com/wr/tomo_1.pdf pp. 293–4; Lecocq, 20 January 1807; Newitt (ed.), *War, Revolution and Society … Thomas Kinder's Narrative*, p. 136; http://en.wikipedia.org/wiki/Francisco_Javier_de_Viana; http://www.euskonews.com/0302zbk/kosmo30201.html
43. *The United Service Magazine*, 1836, Volume 2, p. 491; Tucker, *Narrative of the Operations*, p. 16.
44. Cannon, Richard, *Historical Record of the Eighty-Seventh Regiment, or the Royal Irish Fusiliers* (Parker, Furnivall, and Parker, 1853), pp. 10–11; Lecocq, 20 January 1807, *Parte Oficial de la Salida del dia 20.* Reproduced at http://www.cx4radiorural.com/wr/tomo_1.pdf p. 278; Gleig, *The Hussar*, p. 190.
45. *Capture of Monte Video*. Report by 'a Correspondent on the spot' printed in *The Times*, 15 April 1807; Lawrence, *The Autobiography of Sergeant William Lawrence*, p. 13.
46. Tucker, *Narrative of the Operations*, p. 9; Mullaly, Reginald, Brian, *The South Lancashire Regiment: Prince of Wales's Volunteers* (White Swan Press, 1952), p. 58.
47. Auchmuty to Castlereagh, 6 February 1807, reproduced in Tucker, *Narrative of the Operations*, p. 28.
48. Tucker, *Narrative of the Operations*, p. 9.
49. AGN, Montevideo, Legajo 167, documentos 20–26.
50. Newitt (ed.), *War, Revolution and Society … Thomas Kinder's Narrative*, p. 136;
51. Todd, *Bayonets, Bugles & Bonnets*, p. 25; AGN Montevideo, Legajo 167, documentos 156–160.
52. AGN, Montevideo, Legajo 167, documentos 70–73.
53. *The United Service Magazine*, 1836, Volume 2, p. 491.
54. Todd, *Bayonets, Bugles & Bonnets*, pp. 25–6.
55. Lecocq, 20 January 1807, *Parte Oficial de la Salida del dia 20.* Reproduced at http://www.cx4radiorural.com/wr/tomo_1.pdf p. 278.
56. Stirling's Journal – entry for 20 January 1807. Reproduced in Grainger (ed.), *The Royal Navy in the River Plate 1806–1807*, p. 206; HMS *Daphne* log – ADM 51/4434.
57. Gleig, *The Hussar*, pp. 199–200; AGN Montevideo, Carpeta 167, paginas 156–160.
58. Lecocq, 20 January 1807, *Parte Oficial de la Salida del dia 20.* Reproduced at http://www.cx4radiorural.com/wr/tomo_1.pdf p. 278; AGN Montevideo, Legajo 156, carpeta 2, pagina 9.
59. HMS *Ardent* log – ADM 51/1629.
60. Stirling's Journal – entry for 26 and 27 January 1807 reproduced in Grainger (ed.), *The Royal Navy in the River Plate 1806–1807*, pp. 212–3; HMS *Raisonnable* log – ADM 51/1812; AGN Montevideo, Legajo 167, documentos 20–26.
61. HMS *Diadem* log – ADM 51/1756.
62. http://www.nam.ac.uk/inventory/objects/results.php?shortDescription=&event=&campaign= &associatedName=&unit=&placeNotes=&productionNotes=&keyword=&page=286

63. 40th Foot pay list – WO 12/5327.
64. *Notes on the Viceroyalty of La Plata*, p. 300.
65. Tucker, *Narrative of the Operations*, pp. 9–10; Lecocq, 20 January 1807, *Parte Oficial de la Salida del dia 20*. Reproduced at http://www.cx4radiorural.com/wr/tomo_1.pdf pp. 278–9.
66. Todd, *Bayonets, Bugles & Bonnets*, p. 26.
67. Lawrence, *The Autobiography of Sergeant William Lawrence*, p. 14.
68. Tucker, *Narrative of the Operations*, p. 11; *Trial of Lieutenant-General John Whitelocke*, p. 87.
69. *Parte de Ruiz Huidobro sobre la Toma de Montevideo por los Ingleses*. Reproduced at http://www.cx4radiorural.com/wr/tomo_1.pdf p. 295.
70. Roberts, *Las Invasiones Inglesas*, pp. 36–7.
71. Newitt (ed.), *War, Revolution and Society … Thomas Kinder's Narrative*, p. 143; Fortin, *Invasiones Inglesas*, pp. 84–9; Velasco to His Excellency the Minister of War, 1 August 1806 – reproduced in Vane (ed.), *Correspondence, Dispatches, and other Papers, of Viscount Castlereagh*, Volume 7, p. 306; Roberts, *Las Invasiones Inglesas*, p. 291.
72. Fortin, *Invasiones Inglesas*, pp. 93–6; Fraga, Rosendo, *El Batallón Buenos Aires en la Guerra de la Reconquista Española* (Instituto de Historia Militar Argentina, 2007), pp. 2–3.
73. *Parte de Ruiz Huidobro sobre la Toma de Montevideo por los Ingleses*. Reproduced at http://www.cx4radiorural.com/wr/tomo_1.pdf p. 296.
74. Fraga, *El Batallón Buenos Aires en la Guerra de la Reconquista Española*, pp. 2–6; Roberts, *Las Invasiones Inglesas*, p. 291.
75. Stirling's Journal – entries for 20 and 21 January 1807. Reproduced in Grainger (ed.), *The Royal Navy in the River Plate 1806–1807*, pp. 206–7.
76. Stirling's Journal – entries for 20 and 21 January 1807. Reproduced in Grainger (ed.), *The Royal Navy in the River Plate 1806–1807*, pp. 206–7.
77. AGN, Montevideo, Legajo 167, documentos 62–68.
78. *Parte de Ruiz Huidobro sobre la Toma de Montevideo por los Ingleses*. Reproduced at http://www.cx4radiorural.com/wr/tomo_1.pdf p. 300.
79. Auchmuty to Castlereagh, 6 February 1807, reproduced in Tucker, *Narrative of the Operations*, p. 29.
80. *The United Service Magazine*, 1836, Volume 2, p. 492; Parkinson (ed.), *Samuel Walters*, p. 56.
81. HMS *Diadem* log book – ADM 35/2201; Stirling's Journal – entries for 21 January 1807. Reproduced in Grainger (ed.), *The Royal Navy in the River Plate 1806–1807*, p. 208.
82. Stirling's Journal – entry for 22 January 1807. Reproduced in Grainger (ed.), *The Royal Navy in the River Plate 1806–1807*, pp. 208–9; Stirling's Dispatches, 8 February 1807, reproduced in Tucker, *Narrative of the Operations*, p. 42; HMS *Encounter* log – ADM 51/2005; HMS *Staunch* log – ADM 51/4036.
83. Parkinson (ed.), *Samuel Walters*, p. 56; HMS *Diadem* log book – ADM 51/1756.
84. Stirling's Journal – entry for 23 January 1807. reproduced in Grainger (ed.), *The Royal Navy in the River Plate 1806–1807*, p. 209; Eastwick, *A Master Mariner*, p. 235.
85. Stirling's Journal – entry for 24 January 1807. Reproduced in Grainger (ed.), *The Royal Navy in the River Plate 1806–1807*, pp. 209–10. HMS *Leda* log – ADM 51/1583.
86. *The United Service Magazine*, 1836, Volume 2, p. 492.
87. Lawrence, *The Autobiography of Sergeant William Lawrence*, p. 14.
88. Todd, *Bayonets, Bugles & Bonnets*, p. 26.
89. HMS *Daphne* log – ADM 51/4434.
90. Fortin (ed.), *Invasiones Inglesas*, p. 184.
91. AGN Montevideo, Invasiones Inglesas, Legajo 167, documentos 62–6.
92. HMS *Leda* log – ADM 51/1583; Stirling's Journal – entry for 25 January 1807. Reproduced in Grainger (ed.), *The Royal Navy in the River Plate 1806–1807*, p. 212.
93. *The United Service Magazine*, 1836, Volume 2, p. 492.
94. Stirling's Journal – entry for 25 and 27 January 1807. Reproduced in Grainger (ed.), *The Royal Navy in the River Plate 1806–1807*, pp. 212–3.
95. AGN Montevideo, Legajo 167, documentos 20–26.

96. Stirling's Journal – entry for 25 January 1807. Reproduced in Grainger (ed.), *The Royal Navy in the River Plate 1806–1807*, p. 212.
97. *Parte de Ruiz Huidobro sobre la Toma de Montevideo por los Ingleses*. Reproduced at http://www.cx4radiorural.com/wr/tomo_1.pdf p. 300.
98. HMS *Raisonnable* log – ADM 51/1812; HMS *Daphne* log – ADM 51/4434.
99. Stirling's Journal – entry for 26 and 27 January 1807. Reproduced in Grainger (ed.), *The Royal Navy in the River Plate 1806–1807*, pp. 212–13.
100. Mullaly, *The South Lancashire Regiment*, pp. 58–9; Tucker, *Narrative of the Operations*, p. 13; 87th pay list – WO 12/8955; 17th Light Dragoons pay list – WO 12/1315.
101. Auchmuty to Castlereagh, 6 February 1807, reproduced in Tucker, *Narrative of the Operations*, p. 30.
102. Stirling's Journal – entry for 1 February 1807. Reproduced in Grainger (ed.), *The Royal Navy in the River Plate 1806–1807*, p. 214; Roberts, *Las Invasiones Inglesas*, p. 289.
103. Stirling's Journal – entry for 1 February 1807. Reproduced in Grainger (ed.), *The Royal Navy in the River Plate 1806–1807*, p. 215.
104. Fraga, *El Batallón Buenos Aires en la Guerra de la Reconquista Española*, pp. 2–3; *Parte de Ruiz Huidobro sobre la Toma de Montevideo por los Ingleses*. Reproduced at http://www.cx4radiorural.com/wr/tomo_1.pdf p. 296.
105. Liniers to Sobremonte, 2 February 1807, Fortin (ed.), *Invasiones Inglesas*, p. 134.
106. Álzaga to Chirvechez, 31 January 1806. Reproduced in Álzaga, *Martín de Álzaga en la Reconquista*, pp. 113–14; Liniers to Huidobro, 30 January 1807 – WO 1/162, f.167.
107. Fortin (ed.), *Invasiones Inglesas*, p. 184 and 188.
108. AGN Montevideo, Invasiones Inglesas, Legajo 167, documentos 13–18 and 20–26; Roberts, *Las Invasiones Inglesas*, p. 289.
109. Echeverría to Echeverría, 31 January 1807, Fortin (ed.), *Invasiones Inglesas*, p. 184
110. Anon, *An authentic narrative of the proceedings of the expedition*, p. 104.
111. *The United Service Magazine*, 1836, Volume 2, p. 492.
112. Stirling's Journal – entry for 31 January 1807. Reproduced in Grainger (ed.), *The Royal Navy in the River Plate 1806–1807*, p. 214.
113. HMS *Staunch* log – ADM 51/4036; HMS *Lancaster* log, ADM 51/1611; AGN Montevideo, Legajo 167, documentos 13–18.
114. Stirling's Journal – entry for 31 January 1807. Reproduced in Grainger (ed.), *The Royal Navy in the River Plate 1806–1807*, p. 214; *Parte de Ruiz Huidobro sobre la Toma de Montevideo por los Ingleses*. Reproduced at http://www.cx4radiorural.com/wr/tomo_1.pdf p. 295; AGN Montevideo, Legajo 167, documentos 62–8.
115. *The United Service Magazine*, 1836, Volume 2, p. 493.
116. Parkinson (ed.), *Samuel Walters*, p. 56.
117. Anon, *An Authentic Narrative of the Proceedings*, p. 104.
118. Stirling's Journal – entry for 31 January 1807. Reproduced in Grainger (ed.), *The Royal Navy in the River Plate 1806–1807*, pp. 214–15.
119. Monkland, *Journal of the Secret Expedition*, p. 63.
120. Tucker, *Narrative of the Operations*, p. 15; *The Diary of Lancelot Holland*, entry for 15 June 1807, p. 60, NAM 6807-236; Anon, *An Authentic Narrative of the Proceedings*, pp. 103–5.
121. Fortin (ed.), *Invasiones Inglesas*, p. 142; Liniers to Sobremonte, 2 February 1807, Fortin (ed.), *Invasiones Inglesas*, p. 134.
122. Roberts, *Las Invasiones Inglesas*, p. 289.
123. *Parte de Ruiz Huidobro sobre la Toma de Montevideo por los Ingleses*. Reproduced at http://www.cx4radiorural.com/wr/tomo_1.pdf pp. 296–7.
124. Vassal, *Memoir of the life of Lieutenant-Colonel Vassal*, p. 27.
125. Tucker, *Narrative of the Operations*, p. 20.
126. *The United Service Magazine*, 1836, Vol. 2, p. 493; http://en.wikipedia.org/wiki/Mathias_Everard.
127. Tucker, *Narrative of the Operations*, p. 24.
128. Fortin (ed.), *Invasiones Inglesas*, p. 143; Huidobro to Liniers, 2 February 1807 – WO 1/162, ff.171–3, AGN Montevideo, Legajo 167, documentos 132–4.

129. http://www.euskonews.com/0302zbk/kosmo30201.html
130. *Parte de Ruiz Huidobro sobre la Toma de Montevideo por los Ingleses.* Reproduced at http://www.cx4radiorural.com/wr/tomo_1.pdf pp. 295–6; Fraga, *El Batallón Buenos Aires en la Guerra de la Reconquista Española*, pp. 2–6; *Memorandum for the Cabinet, relative to South America*, 1 May 1807. Reproduced in Vane (ed.), *Correspondence, Dispatches, and other Papers, of Viscount Castlereagh*, Volume 7, pp. 317–18; Fernyhough, *Military Memoirs of Four Brothers*, p. 127.
131. *The United Service Magazine*, 1836, Volume 2, p. 494; Gleig, *The Hussar*, pp. 204–5.
132. Gleig, *The Hussar*, pp. 204–5.
133. *The United Service Magazine*, 1836, Volume 2, p. 494.
134. Anon, *An Authentic Narrative of the Proceedings*, p. 106; http://en.wikipedia.org/wiki/Mathias_Everard
135. *The Scots Magazine and Edinburgh Literary Miscellany*, Volume 69, Part 1 (Archibald Constable & Co., Edinburgh, 1807), p. 398.
136. Eastwick, *A Master Mariner*, p. 228.
137. Tucker, *Narrative of the Operations*, p. 20.
138. Anon, *An Authentic Narrative of the Proceedings*, pp. 106–7; Smith (ed.), *The Autobiography of Lieutenant-General Sir Harry Smith*, Chapter 1. Reproduced at http://digital.library.upenn.edu/women/hsmith/autobiography/peninsular.html
139. *Capture of Monte Video.* Report by 'a Correspondent on the spot' printed in *The Times*, 15 April 1807.
140. AGN Montevideo, Legajo 167, documentos 13–18 and 132–4.
141. Anon, *An Authentic Narrative of the Proceedings*, p. 107; *The United Service Magazine*, 1836, Volume 3, p. 505; Philippart (ed.), *The Royal Military Calendar*, Third Edition, Volume 4, 1820, p. 175.
142. *The United Service Magazine*, 1836, Volume 2, p. 495.
143. Letter from Sergeant B. Matthews – printed in *The Lancaster Gazette*, 25 April 1807.
144. *The United Service Magazine*, 1836, Volume 2, p. 495.
145. Letter from Sergeant B. Matthews – printed in *The Lancaster Gazette*, 25 April 1807.
146. Tucker, *Narrative of the Operations*, p. 18.
147. 40th regiment pay list, WO 12/5327.
148. Lawrence, *The Autobiography of Sergeant William Lawrence*, p. 15.
149. AGN Montevideo, Legajo 167, documentos 13–18.
150. HMS *Diadem* log – ADM 51/1756.
151. Letter from Sergeant B. Matthews – printed in *The Lancaster Gazette*, 25 April 1807.
152. Anon, *An Authentic Narrative of the Proceedings*, p. 107; Fernyhough, *Military Memoirs of Four Brothers*, p. 127.
153. *The United Service Magazine*, 1837, Part 2, p. 234.
154. 87th Regiment pay list, WO 12/8955; Cunliffe, *The Royal Irish Fusiliers*, p. 28.
155. Hathaway (ed.), *A Dorset Rifleman – The Recollections of Rifleman Harris*, p. 109.
156. Anon, *An Authentic Narrative of the Proceedings*, p. 107.
157. AGN Montevideo, Legajo 167, documentos 156–160.
158. *A letter from the Illustrious Cavildo, to Colonel Gore Browne, Commandant of the City of Monte Video*, 27 August 1807. Reproduced in *Notes on the Viceroyalty of La Plata*, pp. 278–81; Roberts, *Las Invasiones Inglesas*, p. 285.
159. Lawrence, *The Autobiography of Sergeant William Lawrence*, pp. 15 and 17.
160. Tucker, *Narrative of the Operations*, p. 19.
161. Lawrence, *The Autobiography of Sergeant William Lawrence*, p. 15; Anon, *An Authentic Narrative of the Proceedings*, p. 107; *The United Service Magazine*, 1837, Part 2, p. 234; Eastwick, *A Master Mariner*, p. 220.
162. HMS *Leda* log – ADM 51/1583.
163. Tucker, *Narrative of the Operations*, pp. 42–5; AGN Montevideo, Legajo 166, documentos 18–21.
164. *The United Service Magazine*, 1836, Volume 2, p. 496.
165. Tucker, *Narrative of the Operations*, p. 34.

166. 40th Regiment pay list – WO 12/5327; 87th Regiment pay list – WO 12/8955.
167. Fraga, *El Batallón Buenos Aires en la Guerra de la Reconquista Española*, pp. 2–6; Fortin (ed.), *Invasiones*, pp. 72–3.

Chapter 12: Captive!

1. Gillespie, *Gleaning and Remarks*, p. 126; Fernyhough, *Military Memoirs of Four Brothers*, p. 109; *The Journal of Captain Pococke, Highland Light Infantry Chronicle*, p. 443.
2. Gillespie, *Gleaning and Remarks*, pp. 128–30; *Journal of Captain Pococke, Highland Light Infantry Chronicle*, p. 443.
3. Gillespie, *Gleaning and Remarks*, pp. 133–4.
4. *The Journal of Captain Pococke, Highland Light Infantry Chronicle*, p. 444.
5. Gillespie, *Gleaning and Remarks*, pp. 136–7.
6. Fernyhough, *Military Memoirs of Four Brothers*, p. 109; Gillespie, *Gleaning and Remarks*, p. 138.
7. *The Journal of Captain Pococke, Highland Light Infantry Chronicle*, p. 444.
8. Fernyhough, *Military Memoirs of Four Brothers*, pp. 110–11.
9. Gillespie, *Gleaning and Remarks*, pp. 141–2; *The Journal of Captain Pococke, Highland Light Infantry Chronicle*, p. 474.
10. *The Journal of Captain Pococke, Highland Light Infantry Chronicle*, pp. 473–6 and 547.
11. Pitt, *The Cabin Boy*, p. 124–5.
12. Beresford to Castlereagh, 12 May 1807 – WO 1/162, ff. 301–31; *Journal of Captain Pococke, Highland Light Infantry Chronicle*, p. 475.
13. Gillespie, *Gleaning and Remarks*, pp. 150–1; *Journal of Captain Pococke, Highland Light Infantry Chronicle*, p. 475; AGN Buenos Aires, Invasiones Inglesas, 26-6-8, documentos 52 and 54.
14. Philippart (ed.), *The Royal Military Calendar … 1820*, pp. 276–81.
15. Fernyhough, *Military Memoirs of Four Brothers*, p. 114.
16. Beresford to Castlereagh, 12 May, 1807 – WO 1/162, ff. 301–31.
17. *The Journal of Captain Pococke, Highland Light Infantry Chronicle*, p. 549.
18. Gillespie, *Gleaning and Remarks*, p. 162.
19. http://en.wikipedia.org/wiki/Robert_Arbuthnot
20. Beresford to Castlereagh, 12 May 1807 – WO 1/162, ff. 301–31; *Notes on the Viceroyalty of La Plata*, p. 266.
21. Johnson, *Workshop of Revolution*, pp. 257.
22. Fortin (ed.), *Invasiones Inglesas*, pp. 133 and 185; Álzaga to Chirvechez, 26 January 1807. Álzaga, *Martín de Álzaga en la Reconquista*, p. 112.
23. Auchmuty to Windham, 6 March 1807, WO 1/162, ff. 107–15.
24. Johnson, *Workshop of Revolution*, pp. 255–6.
25. Fortin (ed.), *Invasiones*, p. 185; Velasco to His Excellency the Minister of War, 1 August 1806 – reproduced in Vane (ed.), *Correspondence, Dispatches, and other Papers, of Viscount Castlereagh*, Volume 7, p. 309; Roberts, *Las Invasiones Inglesas*, p. 295.
26. Fletcher, *The Waters of Oblivion*, pp. 71–2.
27. Velasco to His Excellency the Minister of War, 1 August 1806 – reproduced in Vane (ed.), *Correspondence, Dispatches, and other Papers, of Viscount Castlereagh*, Volume 7, pp. 308–9.
28. Colman, *Martínez de Fontes y la fuga del Genera Beresford*, pp. 93–116; http://es.wikipedia.org/wiki/Saturnino_Rodr%C3%ADguez_Pe%C3%B1a; http://es.wikipedia.org/wiki/Manuel_Aniceto_Padilla; Velasco to His Excellency the Minister of War, 1 August 1806 – reproduced in Vane (ed.), *Correspondence, Dispatches, and other Papers, of Viscount Castlereagh*, Volume 7, p. 310; Beresford to Castlereagh, 12 May 1807 – WO 1/162, ff. 301–31; Liniers to Sobremonte, 29 November, 1806, reproduced in Fortin (ed.), *Invasiones Inglesas*, pp. 107–8; Roberts, *Las Invasiones Inglesas*, pp. 296–9; http://en.wikipedia.org/wiki/Henry_Blackwood
29. Colman, *Martínez de Fontes y la fuga del Genera Beresford*, pp. 93–116.
30. Beresford to Castlereagh, 12 May 1807 – WO 1/162, ff. 301–31.
31. Colman, *Martínez de Fontes y la fuga del Genera Beresford*, pp. 93–116; Beresford to Castlereagh, 12 May 1807 – WO 1/162, ff. 301–31; *Notes on the Viceroyalty of La Plata*, p. 267.

32. Colman, *Martínez de Fontes y la fuga del Genera Beresford*, pp. 93–116; Beresford to Castlereagh, 12 May 1807 – WO 1/162, ff.301–31; *Notes on the Viceroyalty of La Plata*, p. 267.
33. *The Times*, London, 3 June 1807; Roberts, *Las Invasiones Inglesas*, p. 299.
34. Pitt, *The Cabin Boy*, p. 125; *Notes on the Viceroyalty of La Plata*, pp. 268–9; *The United Service Magazine*, 1836, Volume 3, p. 211.

Chapter 13: The Occupation of Monte Video
 1. *The United Service Magazine*, 1836, Volume 3, p. 211.
 2. *The United Service Magazine*, 1836, Volume 3, p. 211.
 3. *A letter from the Illustrious Cavildo, to Colonel Gore Browne, Commandant of the City of Monte Video*, 27 August, 1807. Reproduced in *Notes on the Viceroyalty of La Plata*, p. 280.
 4. *The United Service Magazine*, 1836, Volume 3, p. 214.
 5. WO 1/162, ff.41–2.
 6. Gleig, *The Hussar*, p. 209; *The Times*, London, 4 June 1807.
 7. Todd, *Bayonets, Bugles & Bonnets*, p. 27.
 8. *The United Service Magazine*, 1836, Volume 3, p. 509.
 9. Fraga, *El Batallón Buenos Aires en la Guerra de la Reconquista Española*, p. 6; Auchmuty to Windham, 26 April 1807, WO 1/162, ff.223–29; Rear-Admiral Stirling's Journal. Entry for 5 February 1807. Reproduced in Grainger (ed.), *The Royal Navy in the River Plate 1806–1807*, p. 219
10. *The Times*, 27 April 1807.
11. Eastwick, *A Master Mariner*, pp. 229–30; Lawrence, *The Autobiography of Sergeant William Lawrence*, p. 17.
12. Foulkes, Nicholas, *Dancing into Battle* (Phoenix, 2007), p. 203.
13. Monkland, *Journal of the Secret Expedition*, p. 47; *The United Service Magazine*, 1836, Volume 3, p. 506.
14. Philippart (ed.), *The Royal Military Calendar*, Third Edition, Volume 5, 1820, p. 172.
15. 47th Regiment Pay List, WO 12/5880.
16. Vassal, *Memoir of the life of Lieutenant-Colonel Vassal*, pp. 33–8.
17. 87th Regiment Pay Roll – WO 12/8955.
18. Smith (ed.), *The Autobiography of Lieutenant-General Sir Harry Smith*, p. 359.
19. Stirling to Marsden, 9 March 1807 – Grainger (ed.), *The Royal Navy in the River Plate 1806–1807*, pp. 228–30.
20. *The Southern Star*, Monte Video, 23 and 30 May 1807; Auchmuty to Windham, 7 February 1807, WO 1/162, ff.55–9; Rear-Admiral Stirling's Journal. Entry for 4 February, 1807. Reproduced in Grainger (ed.), *The Royal Navy in the River Plate 1806–1807*, p. 218; WO 1/162, ff.211–15.
21. *The United Service Magazine*, 1836, Volume 3, p. 211.
22. *The United Service Magazine*, 1836, Volume 3, p. 508.
23. 87th Regiment pay list, WO 12/8955; 47th Pay list, WO 12/5880; 40th Pay List, WO 12/5327; 20th Light Dragoons Pay List, WO 12/1422; 38th Pay List, WO 12/5181; 2/95 Pay List, WO 12/9578.
24. Lawrence, *The Autobiography of Sergeant William Lawrence*, pp. 17–18.
25. *The Southern Star*, Monte Video, 30 May 1807.
26. Auchmuty to Windham, 2 March 1807, WO 1/162, ff.67–71.
27. *The United Service Magazine*, 1836, Volume 3, p. 211.
28. Eastwick, *A Master Mariner*, p. 230.
29. *The Southern Star*, Monte Video, 23 May 1807.
30. Roberts, *Las Invasiones Inglesas*, p. 316.
31. Auchmuty to Windham, 6 March 1807, WO 1/162, ff.107–15.
32. NAM 6807-236, *The Diary of Lt. Col. Lancelot Holland*, pp. 4 and 20; Add.37,886, ff.10–24.
33. Various correspondence quoted and summarised in Grainger (ed.), *The Royal Navy in the River Plate 1806–1807*, pp. 115–278.
34. Grainger (ed.), *The Royal Navy in the River Plate 1806–1807*, p. 115; Baring (ed.), *The Diary of the Right Hon. William Windham, 1784 to 1810*, pp. 467–8; *General Whitelocke Vanquished*, PDF – available at:http://whitlockfamilyassociation.com.s3.amazonaws.com/sources/references/R0887.pdf.

35. Stirling to Marsden, 9 March 1807 – Grainger (ed.), *The Royal Navy in the River Plate 1806–1807*, p. 228–30.
36. Marshal, John, *Royal Naval Biography: or, Memoirs of the services of all the flag-officers*, Volume IV, Part 1 (Longman, Hurst, Rees, Orme and Brown, London, 1833), p. 4.
37. Stirling to Marsden, 9 March 1807 – Grainger (ed.), *The Royal Navy in the River Plate 1806–1807*, pp. 228–30.
38. Rear-Admiral Stirling's Journal. Entry for 6 April 1807. Reproduced in Grainger (ed.), *The Royal Navy in the River Plate 1806–1807*, p. 236.
39. *Notes on the Viceroyalty of La Plata*, pp. 155 and 158; AGN Buenos Aires, Invasiones Inglesas, 26-7-9, documento 224.
40. Gleig, *The Hussar*, p. 209; Stirling to Marsden, 9 March 1807 – Grainger (ed.), *The Royal Navy in the River Plate 1806–1807*, pp. 228–30.
41. Auchmuty to Windham, 6 March 1807, WO 1/162, ff.107–15; Stirling to Marsden, 9 March 1807 – Grainger (ed.), *The Royal Navy in the River Plate 1806–1807*, pp. 228–30.
42. Beresford to Castlereagh, 12 and 28 May 1807. WO 1/162, ff.301–31 and 355–358.
43. *The United Service Magazine*, 1836, Volume 3, p. 212.
44. Stirling to Marsden, 22 March 1807, Grainger (ed.), *The Royal Navy in the River Plate 1806–1807*, p. 232–3.
45. Browne to Windham, 25 April 1807, Windham Papers, British Library, Add. 37,886 ff.253–5.
46. Stirling to Marsden, 9 March 1807 – Grainger (ed.), *The Royal Navy in the River Plate 1806–1807*, pp. 228–30.
47. Campbell to Auchmuty, 20 March 1807, WO 1/162, ff.175–8.
48. Auchmuty and Stirling to 'persons possessing the supreme authority in Buenos Ayres', 26 February 1807, WO 1/162, ff.119–21.
49. Campbell to Auchmuty, 20 March 1807, WO 1/162, ff.175–8.
50. De la Concha to Unquera, 8 April 1807, Fortin, *Invasiones Inglesas*, pp. 228–9.
51. HMS *Staunch* log book, ADM 51/4036.
52. AGN Buenos Ayres, Invasiones Inglesas, 26-7-9, documentos 458–9.
53. HMS *Encounter* log book, ADM 51/2005; HMS *Staunch* log book, ADM 51/4036; Haultain, Charles, *The New Navy List, containing the names of all the commissioned officers in Her Majesty's Fleet*, p. 168 (London, Smipkin, Marshall and Co., 1844).
54. HMS *Encounter* log book, ADM 51/2005; HMS *Staunch* log book, ADM 51/4036.
55. Whitelocke to Windham, 12 June 1807, WO 1/162, ff.387–8; HMS *Pheasant* log book, ADM 51/1696.
56. HMS *Paz* ship's log, ADM 51/4484; HMS *Pheasant* ship's log, ADM 51/1696.
57. Lawrence, *The Autobiography of Sergeant William Lawrence*, p. 18.
58. Darwin, Charles, *Journal of Researches into the Natural History and Geology of the Countries Visited During the Voyage of HMS* Beagle *round the World*, pp. 184–5; Lawrence, *The Autobiography of Sergeant William Lawrence*, p. 18; NAM 6807-236, *The Diary of Lt. Col. Lancelot Holland*, p. 64; Roberts, *Las Invasiones Inglesas*, p. 321.
59. HMS *Diomede* log – ADM 51/1700; HMS *Raisonnable* log – ADM 51/1812.
60. Proclamation of the Cabildo of Buenos Ayres, 9 April 1807, Álzaga, *Martín de Álzaga en la Reconquista*, pp. 128–9.
61. http://www.revisionistas.com.ar/?p=5444; Newitt (ed.), *War, Revolution and Society … Thomas Kinder's Narrative*, p. 44.
62. http://www.revisionistas.com.ar/?p=5444; Newitt (ed.), *War, Revolution and Society … Thomas Kinder's Narrative*, p. 44; Grainger (ed.), *The Royal Navy in the River Plate 1806–1807*, pp. 238–42.
63. HMS *Pheasant* log – ADM 51/1696; Auchmuty to Windham, 26 April 1807, WO 1/162, ff.233–4; Account by Domingo Matheu at http://www.revisionistas.com.ar/?p=5444; Lawrence, *The Autobiography of Sergeant William Lawrence*, pp. 18–19; Smith (ed.), *The Autobiography of Lieutenant-General Sir Harry Smith*, p. 6; Gleig, *The Hussar*, pp. 230–1; *Notes on the Viceroyalty of La Plata*, p. 301; AGN Buenos Aires, Invasiones Inglesas, 26-7-9. Document 555.

64. Stirling to Marsden, 26 April and 1 May 1807, Grainger (ed.), *The Royal Navy in the River Plate 1806–1807*, pp. 244–6; Fraga, *El Batallón Buenos Aires en la Guerra de la Reconquista Española*, pp. 6–10.

Chapter 14: General Whitelocke

1. *Notes on the Viceroyalty of La Plata*, pp. 285–90; *General Whitelocke Vanquished*, PDF- available at: http://whitlockfamilyassociation.com.s3.amazonaws.com/sources/references/R0887.pdf.; Add.37885, ff.112–14; http://books.google.com/books?id=BwkyCWhj_GkC&pg=PA84#v= onepage&q&f=false; Paget Papers, II, 276. Quoted in Bryant, *Years of Victory*, p. 244.
2. *Notes on the Viceroyalty of La Plata*, pp. 285–90; *General Whitelocke Vanquished*, PDF- available at: http://whitlockfamilyassociation.com.s3.amazonaws.com/sources/references/R0887.pdf.; Add.37885, ff.112–14; http://books.google.com/books?id=BwkyCWhj_GkC&pg=PA84#v= onepage&q&f=false
3. Downing Street to Whitelocke, 5 March 1807, Add.37,886, ff.145–52.
4. *The United Service Magazine*, 1836, Volume 3, pp. 212–13.
5. Parkinson (ed.), *Samuel Walters*, p. 60.
6. *The United Service Magazine*, 1836, Volume 3, p. 213; Monkland, *Journal of the Secret Expedition*, p. 45; *Notes on the Viceroyalty of La Plata*, pp. 291–3.
7. Gleig, *The Hussar*, p. 208–9.
8. *The United Service Magazine*, 1836, Volume 3, pp. 211–12; Fortin (ed.), *Invasiones*, p. 186.
9. Whitelocke to Windham, 16 and 20 June 1807, WO 1/162, ff.403–5 and 407–12; *The Times*, 23 October 1807; Anon, *An Authentic Narrative of the Proceedings*, pp. 116–17; *Trial of Lieutenant-General John Whitelocke*, pp. 23–4, 34, 47 and 63.
10. *Trial of Lieutenant-General John Whitelocke*, pp. 29 and 35.
11. *Trial of Lieutenant-General John Whitelocke*, p. 23.
12. *Trial of Lieutenant-General John Whitelocke*, pp. 24, 35 and 78–9.
13. *Trial of Lieutenant-General John Whitelocke*, pp. 12 and 18.
14. Mawe, *Travels in the interior of Brazil*, pp. 1–35.
15. *Trial of Lieutenant-General John Whitelocke*, pp. 24, 35 and 78–9.
16. Whitelocke to Windham, 16 and 20 June 1807, WO 1/162, ff.403–5 and 407–12; *The Times*, 23 October 1807; Anon, *An Authentic Narrative of the Proceedings*, pp. 116–17; NAM 6807-236, *The Diary of Lt. Col. Lancelot Holland*, p. 63; *Trial of Lieutenant-General John Whitelocke*, p. 17; Extract of a letter, dated Monte Video, 20 July 1807', *The Times*, 23 October, 1807.
17. *The Southern Star / La Estrella del Sur*, Montevideo, 1807. Reproducción Facsimilar (Montevideo, 1942); http://webcache.googleusercontent.com/search?q=cache:http://www.histarmar.com.ar/ AcademiaUruguayaMyFl/200AniosInvInglesas/17-ColoniabajobanderaBritanica.htm
18. Todd, *Bayonets, Bugles & Bonnets*, pp. 27–31.
19. Street to the Senior Officer Commanding off Buenos Ayres, 4 June 1807, Grainger (ed.), *The Royal Navy in the River Plate 1806–1807*, p. 250; Unquera to the Audiencia, 14 April 1807, Fortin, *Invasiones Inglesas*, pp. 229–30; http://es.wikipedia.org/wiki/Goleta_Corsaria_%E2%80%9CMosca_ de_Buenos_Aires%E2%80%9D
20. Douglas to Street, 3 June 1807, Grainger (ed.), *The Royal Navy in the River Plate 1806–1807*, pp. 248–9; HMS *Dolores* log – ADM 51/1926.
21. Smith (ed.), *The Autobiography of Lieutenant-General Sir Harry Smith*, Chapter 1 – reproduced at http://digital.library.upenn.edu/women/hsmith/autobiography/peninsular.html
22. AGN Buenos Aires, Invasiones Inglesas, 26-7-9, documentos 555, 564, 620, 634 and 640.
23. Palmer to Stirling, 8 June 1807, Grainger (ed.), *The Royal Navy in the River Plate 1806–1807*, p. 250.
24. HMS *Pheasant* log book, ADM 51/1696.
25. Lawrence, *The Autobiography of Sergeant William Lawrence*, p. 19; 9th Light Dragoons Pay List – WO 12/877.
26. Lawrence, *The Autobiography of Sergeant William Lawrence*, pp. 19–20; Smith (ed.), *The Autobiography of Lieutenant-General Sir Harry Smith*, chapter 1; Pack to Whitelocke, 8 June 1807, and General Orders, 10 June 1807, Philippart (ed.), *The Royal Military Calendar ... 1820*, pp. 283–6;

Anon, *An Authentic Narrative of the Proceedings*, pp. 111–12; http://www.revisionistas.com.ar/
?p=5444

27. The Audiencia of Buenos Ayres to Liniers, 18 June 1807, Official protest against Elio signed by
seventeen officers of the Patricios Regiment, 22 August 1809. Fortin, *Invasiones Inglesas*,
pp. 233–5.

28. Lawrence, *The Autobiography of Sergeant William Lawrence*, pp. 19–20; Smith (ed.), *The Autobiography of Lieutenant-General Sir Harry Smith*, chapter 1; Pack to Whitelocke, 8 June 1807, and
General Orders, 10 June 1807, Philippart (ed.), *The Royal Military Calendar … 1820*, pp. 283–6;
Anon, *An Authentic Narrative of the Proceedings*, pp. 111–12; http://www.revisionistas.com.ar/
?p=5444

29. Pay List 21st Light Dragoons WO 12/1447; Pay List 17th Light Dragoons WO 12/1315.

30. Anon, *An Authentic Narrative of the Proceedings*, p. 116; *The Southern Star / La Estrella del Sur*,
Montevideo, 27 June 1807.

31. Landsheit, *The Hussar*, p. 231.

32. Anon, *An Authentic Narrative of the Proceedings*, pp. 113–14.

33. NAM 6807-236, *The Diary of Lt. Col. Lancelot Holland*, p. 60.

34. Craufurd to Windham, 27 March 1807, Add.37886, ff.143–4.

35. Craufurd to Windham, 27 March 1807, Add.37886, ff.143–4.

36. Parkinson (ed.), *Samuel Walters*, p. 60; NAM 6807-236, *The Diary of Lt. Col. Lancelot Holland*,
pp. 3–4.

37. NAM 6807-236, *The Diary of Lt. Col. Lancelot Holland*, p. 61.

38. *The United Service Magazine*, 1842, Part 2, p. 236.

39. *The Trial of Lieutenant-General John Whitelocke*, pp. 64–5 and 84.

40. *The Trial of Lieutenant-General John Whitelocke*, pp. 64–5.

41. HMS *Protector* log – ADM 51/1911.

42. Fernyhough, *Military Memoirs of Four Brothers*, p. 87; *Diary of William Gavin*, p. 8; Gillespie,
Gleaning and Remarks, pp. 209–42; AGN Buenos Aires, Invasiones Inglesas, 26-7-10, documentos
33–35.

43. NAM 6807-236, *The Diary of Lt. Col. Lancelot Holland*, p. 62.

44. NAM 6807-236, *The Diary of Lt. Col. Lancelot Holland*, p. 62; Anon, *An Authentic Narrative of the
Proceedings*, p. 117; Monkland, *Journal of the Secret Expedition*, p. 27; Pitt, *The Cabin Boy*, p. 127.

45. NAM 6807-236, *The Diary of Lt. Col. Lancelot Holland*, p. 63.

46. Pitt, *The Cabin Boy*, p. 127.

47. NAM 6807-236, *The Diary of Lt. Col. Lancelot Holland*, p. 63.

48. Whitelocke to Windham, 20 June 1807, WO 1/162, ff.407–12.

49. HMS *Diadem* log book ADM 51/1756.

50. Murray to Grenville, 19 June 1807, Grainger (ed.), *The Royal Navy in the River Plate 1806–1807*,
pp. 290–2; Anon, *An Authentic Narrative of the Proceedings*, p. 117. The garrison was composed
of the 47th Foot, two companies of the 38th, two squadrons of light dragoons from the 20th and
21st regiments, a company of artillery, 213 marines from the fleet and the Royal British South
American Militia.

51. Stirling to Marsden, 22 June 1807, Grainger (ed.), *The Royal Navy in the River Plate 1806–1807*,
p. 292; HMS *Nereide* log book ADM 51/1941.

52. *The United Service Magazine*, 1842, Part 2, p. 236.

53. Pitt, *The Cabin Boy*, p. 127.

54. *The Diary of Lieutenant-Colonel Richard Bourke*, Add.37887, ff.43–50.

55. NAM 6807-236, *The Diary of Lt. Col. Lancelot Holland*, p. 64; Monkland, *Journal of the Secret
Expedition*, p. 28.

56. HMS *Saracen* log book ADM 51/1712; Pitt, *The Cabin Boy*, p. 127; HMS *Diadem* log book
ADM 51/1756.

57. Holland to Cathcart, no date, p. 2 – NAM 6807-236.

58. *The Diary of Lieutenant-Colonel Richard Bourke*, Add.37887, ff.43–50; NAM 6807-236, *The Diary of
Lt. Col. Lancelot Holland*, pp. 64–6; HMS *Saracen* log book ADM 51/1712.

Chapter 15: The Advance on Buenos Ayres

1. *Letter from a Merchant of Buenos Ayres*. Printed in *The Times*, 13 November 1807.
2. *Letter from a Merchant of Buenos Ayres*, printed in *The Times*, 13 November 1807; *Fragmento de un Diario de la Defensa de Buenos Aires*, reproduced in Álzaga, *Martín de Álzaga en la Reconquista*, pp. 172–6; Mulhall, *The English in South America*, p. 118; *Acuerdo de M. I. Cabildo*, reproduced in Álzaga, *Martín de Álzaga en la Reconquista*, pp. 129–63; http://en.wikipedia.org/wiki/Juan_Bautista_ Azopardo.
3. Monkland, *Journal of the Secret Expedition*, p. 63; *Trial of Lieutenant-General John Whitelocke*, p. 150.
4. Garzón, *Sobre Monte y Córdoba en las Invasioens Inglesas*, p. 99, Roberts, *Las Invasiones Inglesas*, pp. 223 and 234–5; Monkland, *Journal of the Secret Expedition*, pp. 46–7.
5. *Letter from a Merchant of Buenos Ayres*, printed in *The Times*, 13 November 1807; NAM 6807-236, Lord Cathcart letter, p. 6.
6. *Trial of Lieutenant-General John Whitelocke*, p. 48.
7. Anon, *A Narrative of the Expedition to, and the Storming of Buenos Ayres by the British Army commanded by Lieutenant-General Whitelocke by an officer attached to the expedition* (S. Robinson, Bath, 1807), p. 21; Roberts, *Las Invasiones Inglesas*, p. 235.
8. *Relacion del Ataque y Defensa de Buenos Ayres en el Mes de Julio 1807*, reproduced in Fortin, *Invasiones Inglesas*, pp. 257–8.
9. *Letter from a Merchant of Buenos Ayres*, printed in *The Times*, 13 November 1807.
10. HMS *Saracen* log ADM 51/1712; HMS *Dolores* log ADM 51/1926; HMS *Flying Fish* log ADM 51/4449; HMS *Medusa* log ADM 51/1708; HMS *Fly* log ADM 51/1652; HMS *Encounter* log ADM 51/2005; Anon, *An Authentic Narrative of the Proceedings*, p. 120.
11. NAM 6807-236, p. 66.
12. *The United Service Magazine*, 1842, Part 2, p. 236.
13. Anon, *An Authentic Narrative of the Proceedings*, p. 121; NAM 6807-236, pp. 66–8; *The Diary of Lieutenant-Colonel Richard Bourke*, Add.37887, ff.43–50.
14. HMS *Saracen* log ADM 51/1712.
15. Anon, *An Authentic Narrative of the Proceedings of the Expedition against Buenos Ayres, under the command of Lieut. Gen. Whitelocke by an Irish officer* (R. Smith, Dublin, 1808), p. 80.
16. NAM 6807-236, pp. 66–8.
17. Anon, *An Authentic Narrative of the Proceedings*, p. 122.
18. NAM 6807-236, pp. 66–8.
19. *The United Service Magazine*, 1836, Part 3, p. 214.
20. *Trial of Lieutenant-General John Whitelocke*, p. 12; Todd, *Bayonets, Bugles & Bonnets*, p. 31.
21. NAM 6807-236, pp. 66–8.
22. *The United Service Magazine*, 1836, Part 3, p. 215.
23. NAM 6807-236, pp. 66–8.
24. Monkland, *Journal of the Secret Expedition*, p. 29.
25. Morley, *Memoirs of a Sergeant*, p. 28.
26. *Bourke's Diary*, Add.37887, ff.43–50.
27. *Trial of Lieutenant-General John Whitelocke*, pp. 54 and 86.
28. *Letter from a Merchant of Buenos Ayres*, printed in *The Times*, 13 November 1807.
29. Roberts, *Las Invasiones Inglesas*, pp. 224 and 236. Martín de Pueyrredón, the founder of the First Hussars was absent. Ordered to seek reinforcement from Spain, at the time of Whitelocke's attack he was in Brazil en-route to Europe.
30. *Relacion del Ataque y Defensa de Buenos Ayres en el Mes de Julio 1807*, reproduced in Fortin, *Invasiones Inglesas*, pp. 257–8.
31. Letter by an Anonymous Officer, *The Times*, 23 October 1807.
32. *The United Service Magazine*, 1842, Part 3, p. 65.
33. NAM 6807-236, pp. 68–9.
34. *The United Service Journal*, 1837, Part 2, p. 234.
35. NAM 6807-236, pp. 68–9; *Relacion del Ataque y Defensa de Buenos Ayres en el Mes de Julio 1807*, reproduced in Fortin, *Invasiones Inglesas*, pp. 258–9; http://es.wikipedia.org/wiki/Milicias_creadas_ en_Buenos_Aires_durante_las_Invasiones_Inglesas; Morley, *Memoirs of a Sergeant*, pp. 28–9.

36. *The United Service Magazine*, 1836, Part 3, p. 213.
37. *Trial of Lieutenant-General John Whitelocke*, p. 68.
38. *The United Service Magazine*, 1836, Part 3, p. 214.
39. *Trial of Lieutenant-General John Whitelocke*, pp. 19, 49 and 62.
40. NAM 6807-236, p. 69.
41. NAM 6807-236, p. 69.
42. Todd, *Bayonets, Bugles & Bonnets*, p. 31.
43. *Relacion del Ataque y Defensa de Buenos Ayres en el Mes de Julio 1807*, reproduced in Fortin, *Invasiones Inglesas*, pp. 258–9.
44. NAM 6807-236, pp. 69–70.
45. Lumley's evidence, *Trial of Lieutenant-General John Whitelocke*, p. 51.
46. Monkland, *Journal of the Secret Expedition*, p. 30; Anon, *An Authentic Narrative of the Proceedings*, pp. 123–4.
47. *Bourke's Diary*, Add.37887, ff.43–50; *Trial of Lieutenant-General John Whitelocke*, pp. 24, 64–5.
48. *Relacion del Ataque y Defensa de Buenos Ayres en el Mes de Julio 1807*, reproduced in Fortin, *Invasiones Inglesas*, p. 258.
49. *Bourke's Diary*, Add.37887, ff.43–50; *Trial of Lieutenant-General John Whitelocke*, pp. 25, 29, 89 and 91.
50. *Trial of Lieutenant-General John Whitelocke*, p. 93.
51. *Trial of Lieutenant-General John Whitelocke*, p. 56.
52. *Trial of Lieutenant-General John Whitelocke*, pp. 56 and 69.
53. *The United Service Magazine*, 1836, Part 3, p. 215.
54. Monkland, *Journal of the Secret Expedition*, p. 31.
55. http://es.wikipedia.org/wiki/Milicias_creadas_en_Buenos_Aires_durante_las_Invasiones_Inglesas# Quinteros_y_Labradores; http://es.wikipedia.org/wiki/Antonio_Luciano_de_Ballester; *Relacion del Ataque y Defensa de Buenos Ayres en el Mes de Julio 1807*, reproduced in Fortin, *Invasiones Inglesas*, p. 259; Newitt (ed.), *War, Revolution and Society . . . Thomas Kinder's Narrative*, Appendix A, p. 231.
56. Monkland, *Journal of the Secret Expedition*, p. 31.
57. Lawrence, *The Autobiography of Sergeant William Lawrence*, p. 23.
58. NAM 6807-236, p. 71.
59. NAM 6807-236, p. 71.
60. Monkland, *Journal of the Secret Expedition*, p. 32.
61. Anon, *A Narrative of the Expedition to, and the Storming of Buenos Ayres*, p. 7; NAM 6807-236, p. 71.
62. Monkland, *Journal of the Secret Expedition*, p. 33.
63. Monkland, *Journal of the Secret Expedition*, p. 32.
64. NAM 6807-236, p. 71.
65. Downing Street to Whitelocke, 5 March 1807, Add.37,886, ff.145–52.
66. *Trial of Lieutenant-General John Whitelocke*, p. 45.
67. NAM 6807-236, p. 72.
68. Monkland, *Journal of the Secret Expedition*, pp. 32–3; NAM 6807-236, p. 73; *Trial of Lieutenant-General John Whitelocke*, pp. 18 and 52.
69. *Trial of Lieutenant-General John Whitelocke*, p. 40.
70. HMS *Fly* log – ADM 51/1652; *Acuerdo de M. I. Cabildo*, reproduced in Álzaga, *Martín de Álzaga en la Reconquista*, p. 131.
71. *Relacion del Ataque y Defensa de Buenos Ayres en el Mes de Julio 1807*, reproduced in Fortin, *Invasiones Inglesas*, p. 259; *The United Service Magazine*, 1842, Part 3, p. 65; Monkland, *Journal of the Secret Expedition*, p. 33; *Letter from a Merchant of Buenos Ayres*, printed in *The Times*, 13 November 1807; *Acuerdo de M. I. Cabildo*, reproduced in Álzaga, *Martín de Álzaga en la Reconquista*, pp. 134–5; Velasco to Buonaventura, Jul 12 1807 – reproduced in Vane (ed.), *Correspondence, Dispatches, and other Papers, of Viscount Castlereagh*, Volume 7, pp. 396–402.
72. Anon, *An Authentic Narrative of the Proceedings*, p. 126; Monkland, *Journal of the Secret Expedition*, p. 32; NAM 6807-236, p. 72.

73. Monkland, *Journal of the Secret Expedition*, p. 32; *Trial of Lieutenant-General John Whitelocke*, pp. 13 and 68.
74. *Trial of Lieutenant-General John Whitelocke*, p. 40; *Relacion del Ataque y Defensa de Buenos Ayres en el Mes de Julio 1807*, reproduced in Fortin, *Invasiones Inglesas*, p. 259.
75. Monkland, *Journal of the Secret Expedition*, pp. 32–3; NAM 6807-236, p. 72; *Trial of Lieutenant-General John Whitelocke*, p. 51.
76. *Bourke's Diary*, Add.37887, ff.43–50.
77. *Trial of Lieutenant-General John Whitelocke*, p. 46.
78. *Letter from a Merchant of Buenos Ayres*, printed in *The Times*, 13 November 1807; AGN Buenos Aires, Guerra y Marina, Legajo 40, Exp. 12–13; Roberts, *Las Invasiones Inglesas*, p. 341; Velasco to Buonaventura, Jul 12 1807 – reproduced in Vane (ed.), *Correspondence, Dispatches, and other Papers, of Viscount Castlereagh*, Volume 7, pp. 399–400.
79. *Relacion del Ataque y Defensa de Buenos Ayres en el Mes de Julio 1807*, reproduced in Fortin, *Invasiones Inglesas*, p. 259.
80. Roberts, *Las Invasiones Inglesas*, p. 338.
81. Monkland, *Journal of the Secret Expedition*, p. 33.
82. *The United Service Magazine*, 1842, Part 3, pp. 65–6.
83. Lawrence, *The Autobiography of Sergeant William Lawrence*, p. 23; Anon, *A Narrative of the Expedition to, and the Storming of Buenos Ayres*, p. 7.
84. *Trial of Lieutenant-General John Whitelocke*, pp. 73–4.
85. *Bourke's Diary*, Add.37887, ff.43–50.
86. NAM 6807-236, p. 73; Anon, *A Narrative of the Expedition to, and the Storming of Buenos Ayres*, p. 8.
87. *Relacion del Ataque y Defensa de Buenos Ayres en el Mes de Julio 1807*, reproduced in Fortin, *Invasiones Inglesas*, pp. 259–60.
88. *Trial of Lieutenant-General John Whitelocke*, p. 76; Roberts, *Las Invasiones Inglesas*, p. 340.
89. *Bourke's Diary*, Add.37887, ff.43–50; *Trial of Lieutenant-General John Whitelocke*, p. 56.
90. *Bourke's Diary*, Add.37887, ff.43–50; *Trial of Lieutenant-General John Whitelocke*, p. 56.
91. *Trial of Lieutenant-General John Whitelocke*, p. 70.
92. NAM 6807-236, p. 73; Monkland, *Journal of the Secret Expedition*, pp. 33–4; Anon, *An Authentic Narrative of the Proceedings*, pp. 128–9; Anon, *A Narrative of the Expedition to, and the Storming of Buenos Ayres*, p. 8; *The United Service Magazine*, 1842, Part 3, pp. 65–6; *Trial of Lieutenant-General John Whitelocke*, pp. 52–3.
93. NAM 6807-236, p. 73; *Trial of Lieutenant-General John Whitelocke*, pp. 41–2.
94. *Trial of Lieutenant-General John Whitelocke*, p. 13; Monkland, *Journal of the Secret Expedition*, p. 34; Anon, *An Authentic Narrative of the Proceedings*, p. 129.
95. NAM 6807-236, p. 74.
96. *Trial of Lieutenant-General John Whitelocke*, p. 41.
97. Roberts, *Las Invasiones Inglesas*, pp. 341–3; Monkland, *Journal of the Secret Expedition*, pp. 34–5; Velasco to Buonaventura, July 12 1807 – reproduced in Vane (ed.), *Correspondence, Dispatches, and other Papers, of Viscount Castlereagh*, Volume 7, pp. 396–402.
98. *The United Service Magazine*, 1842, Part 3, p. 66.
99. *Trial of Lieutenant-General John Whitelocke*, p. 41; Monkland, *Journal of the Secret Expedition*, p. 34; Anon, *An Authentic Narrative of the Proceedings*, p. 129; Anon, *A Narrative of the Expedition to, and the Storming of Buenos Ayres*, pp. 8–9.
100. http://es.wikipedia.org/wiki/Combate_de_Miserere
101. NAM 6807-236, p. 74 and Lord Cathcart letter, p. 4; Smith (ed.), *The Autobiography of Lieutenant-General Sir Harry Smith*, chapter 1; Anon, *An Authentic Narrative of the Proceedings*, pp. 130–2; Monkland, *Journal of the Secret Expedition*, pp. 34–5; Anon, *A Narrative of the Expedition to, and the Storming of Buenos Ayres*, pp. 8–10; *The United Service Magazine*, 1842, Part 3, p. 66; Gower's Dispatch, *The Times*, 14 Sept 1807; Anonymous Account of a British Officer, *The Times*, 23 October 1807; *Trial of Lieutenant-General John Whitelocke*, pp. 41–2 and 52–3; *Relacion del Ataque y Defensa de Buenos Ayres en el Mes de Julio 1807*, reproduced in Fortin, *Invasiones Inglesas*, pp. 260–1; Santa Coloma to Olaguer Feliú, 1 August 1807, reproduced in

Álzaga, *Martín de Álzaga en la Reconquista*, pp. 189–93; AGN Buenos Aires, Guerra y Marina Legajo 40, Exp. 44.

102. Anon, *A Narrative of the Expedition to, and the Storming of Buenos Ayres*, p. 12; Roberts, *Las Invasiones Inglesas*, p. 353.

103. AGN Buenos Aires, Invasiones Inglesas, 26-7-9, documento 3331.

104. NAM 6807-236, p. 74 and Lord Cathcart Letter, p. 4; Smith (ed.), *The Autobiography of Lieutenant-General Sir Harry Smith*, chapter 1; Anon, *An Authentic Narrative of the Proceedings*, pp. 130–2; Monkland, *Journal of the Secret Expedition*, pp. 34–5; Anon, *A Narrative of the Expedition to, and the Storming of Buenos Ayres*, pp. 8–10; *The United Service Magazine*, 1842, Part 3, p. 66; Gower's Dispatch, *The Times*, 14 September 1807; Anonymous Account of a British Officer, *The Times*, 23 October 1807; *Trial of Lieutenant-General John Whitelocke*, pp. 41–2 and 52–3; *Relacion del Ataque y Defensa de Buenos Ayres en el Mes de Julio 1807*, reproduced in Fortin, *Invasiones Inglesas*, pp. 260–1.

105. Pay Roll 45th Regiment WO 12/5726; Pay Roll 88th Regiment WO 12/9028.

106. *The United Service Journal and Naval and Military Magazine*, 1837, Part 2, p. 234; Hart, H. G., *The New Annual Army List for 1845* (Murray, Lodnon, 1845), p. 227.

107. *Trial of Lieutenant-General John Whitelocke*, p. 141.

108. *Trial of Lieutenant-General John Whitelocke*, pp. 68 and 94.

109. *Trial of Lieutenant-General John Whitelocke*, p. 90; Cannon, Richard, *Historical Record of the Eighty-eighth Regiment of Foot, Or Connaught Rangers* (Parker, Furnivall & Parker, London, 1838), p. 9.

110. NAM 6807-236, p. 74.

Chapter 16: The Western Suburbs

1. *The United Service Magazine*, 1842, Part 3, p. 67.

2. *The United Service Magazine*, 1842, Part 3, p. 67.

3. Anon, *A Narrative of the Expedition to, and the Storming of Buenos Ayres*, p. 21; Liniers to Cabildo, 3 July, 1807. Reproduced in Fortin, *Invasiones Inglesas*, p. 243.

4. The *Acuerdo de M. I. Cabildo*, reproduced in Álzaga, *Martín de Álzaga en la Reconquista*, pp. 139–41 is the source for the story concerning Agustini. Another explanation for his behaviour exists. According to Bernardo Velasco, the intendant of Paraguay who served as a major-general in *La Defensa*, Agustini was bribed to desert his post by internal elements who desired a British victory as a stage on the path to independence. See Velasco to His Excellency the Minister of War, 1 August 1806 – reproduced in Vane (ed.), *Correspondence, Dispatches, and other Papers, of Viscount Castlereagh*, Volume 7, p. 313; AGN Buenos Aires, Guerra y Marina Legajo 40, Exp. 44.

5. http://www.historiadelpais.com.ar/inva_defensa.htm; AGN Buenos Aires, Guerra y Marina Legajo 40, Exp. 44.

6. *Relacion del Ataque y Defensa de Buenos Ayres en el Mes de Julio 1807*, reproduced in Fortin, *Invasiones Inglesas*, pp. 261–2; *Letter from a Merchant of Buenos Ayres*. Printed in *The Times*, 13 November 1807; Santa Coloma to Olaguer Feliú, 1 August 1807, reproduced in Álzaga, *Martín de Álzaga en la Reconquista*, pp. 189–93; *Fragmento de un Diario de la Defensa de Buenos Aires*, reproduced in Álzaga, *Martín de Álzaga en la Reconquista*, pp. 172–6; Mulhall, *The English in South America*, p. 118; *Acuerdo de M. I. Cabildo*, reproduced in Álzaga, *Martín de Álzaga en la Reconquista*, pp. 139–41; *An Authentic Narrative of the Proceedings*, pp. 145–6.

7. *Relacion del Ataque y Defensa de Buenos Ayres en el Mes de Julio 1807*, reproduced in Fortin, *Invasiones Inglesas*, pp. 261–2; *Letter from a Merchant of Buenos Ayres*. Printed in *The Times*, 13 November 1807; Santa Coloma to Olaguer Feliú, 1 August 1807, reproduced in Álzaga, *Martín de Álzaga en la Reconquista*, pp. 189–93; *Fragmento de un Diario de la Defensa de Buenos Aires*, reproduced in Álzaga, *Martín de Álzaga en la Reconquista*, pp. 172–6; Mulhall, *The English in South America*, p. 118; *Acuerdo de M. I. Cabildo*, reproduced in Álzaga, *Martín de Álzaga en la Reconquista*, pp. 139–41; Anon, *A Narrative of the Expedition to, and the Storming of Buenos Ayres*, pp. 13–14; *An Authentic Narrative of the Proceedings*, pp. 147–8 and 157; *Trial of Lieutenant-General John Whitelocke*, p. 108; AGN Buenos Aires, Guerra y Marina Legajo 40, Exp. 44; Roberts, *Las Invasiones Inglesas*, p. 346.

8. HMS *Diadem* log book – ADM 51/1756; HMS *Encounter* log book – ADM 51/2005.

9. Monkland, *Journal of the Secret Expedition*, p. 36.
10. NAM 6807-236, p. 75.
11. *Trial of Lieutenant-General John Whitelocke*, p. 67.
12. *Trial of Lieutenant-General John Whitelocke*, pp. 86–7.
13. *Acuerdo de M. I. Cabildo*, reproduced in Álzaga, *Martín de Álzaga en la Reconquista*, pp. 144–5.
14. *Trial of Lieutenant-General John Whitelocke*, pp. 86–7.
15. *Trial of Lieutenant-General John Whitelocke*, pp. 86–7.
16. Elio to Gower, 3 July 1807. Reproduced and translated in *Trial of Lieutenant-General John Whitelocke*, p. 227.
17. Anon, *A Narrative of the Expedition to, and the Storming of Buenos Ayres*, p. 21; *Trial of Lieutenant-General John Whitelocke*, p. 115, Monkland, *Journal of the Secret Expedition*, p. 41; http://www.reconquistaydefensa.org.ar/_historia/terciogallegos/terciogallegos.htm
18. *Letter from a Merchant of Buenos Ayres*. Printed in *The Times*, 13 November 1807; *Relacion del Ataque y Defensa de Buenos Ayres en el Mes de Julio 1807*, reproduced in Fortin, *Invasiones Inglesas*, p. 262; *Acuerdo de M. I. Cabildo*, reproduced in Álzaga, *Martín de Álzaga en la Reconquista*, pp. 146–7; *An Authentic Narrative of the Proceedings*, pp. 146, 158 and 164; *Trial of Lieutenant-General John Whitelocke*, pp. 115 and 150.
19. *An Authentic Narrative of the Proceedings*, p. 146; Holland to Lord Cathcart, p. 6, NAM 6807-236.
20. *Bourke's Diary*, Add.37887, ff.43–50; *Trial of Lieutenant-General John Whitelocke*, p. 57.
21. *Trial of Lieutenant-General John Whitelocke*, p. 83; Anon, *A Narrative of the Expedition to, and the Storming of Buenos Ayres*, pp. 11–12.
22. Mawe, *Travels in the interior of Brazil*, p. 37.
23. *Trial of Lieutenant-General John Whitelocke*, p. 85.
24. NAM 6807-236, Lord Cathcart letter, p. 9.
25. *The United Service Magazine*, 1842, Part 3, p. 67; Anon, *A Narrative of the Expedition to, and the Storming of Buenos Ayres*, pp. 16–17.
26. 2/95th Pay List – WO 12/9578; 88th Foot Pay List – WO 12/9028.
27. *The United Service Magazine*, 1829, part 1, p. 577; Anon, *A Narrative of the Expedition to, and the Storming of Buenos Ayres*, pp. 10–12; Pay List 36th Foot – WO 12/5034; Monkland, *Journal of the Secret Expedition*, p. 36.
28. Anon, *A Narrative of the Expedition to, and the Storming of Buenos Ayres*, pp. 10–11; Anon, *An Authentic Narrative of the Proceedings*, p. 135; Philippart (ed.), *The Royal Military Calendar*, Third Edition, Volume 5, 1820, p. 379.
29. *Trial of Lieutenant-General John Whitelocke*, pp. 57 and 83; Anon, *A Narrative of the Expedition to, and the Storming of Buenos Ayres*, pp. 11–12; *The United Service Magazine*, 1842, Part 3, p. 68.
30. *Trial of Lieutenant-General John Whitelocke*, p. 83.
31. *Trial of Lieutenant-General John Whitelocke*, pp. 20, 33 and 77; Whittingham, Ferdinand, *A Memoir of the Services of Sir Samuel Ford Whittingham* (Longmans, Green and Co., London, 1868), p. 15; NAM 6807-236, p. 75.
32. *Trial of Lieutenant-General John Whitelocke*, pp. 20, 33 and 77; Whittingham, *A Memoir of the Services of Sir Samuel Ford Whittingham*, p. 15; NAM 6807-236, p. 75.
33. *Trial of Lieutenant-General John Whitelocke*, p. 134.
34. *Trial of Lieutenant-General John Whitelocke*, pp. 20, 33 and 77; Whittingham, *A Memoir of the Services of Sir Samuel Ford Whittingham*, p. 15; NAM 6807-236, p. 75.
35. *Trial of Lieutenant-General John Whitelocke*, p. 129.
36. *Trial of Lieutenant-General John Whitelocke*, p. 50.
37. *Trial of Lieutenant-General John Whitelocke*, pp. 42–3.
38. *Trial of Lieutenant-General John Whitelocke*, p. 105.
39. *Trial of Lieutenant-General John Whitelocke*, p. 76.
40. Roberts, *Las Invasiones Inglesas*, p. 352.
41. *Bourke's Diary*, Add.37887, ff.43–50.
42. *Trial of Lieutenant-General John Whitelocke*, pp. 57–8.
43. Anon, *An Authentic Narrative of the Proceedings*, pp. 174–5; *Trial of Lieutenant-General John Whitelocke*, p. 135.

44. Roberts, *Las Invasiones Inglesas*, p. 352.
45. *Trial of Lieutenant-General John Whitelocke*, pp. 80–1; Add.37,887, f.86.
46. *Acuerdo de M. I. Cabildo*, reproduced in Álzaga, *Martín de Álzaga en la Reconquista*, pp. 148–50.
47. *Trial of Lieutenant-General John Whitelocke*, p. 50.
48. *Fragmento de un Diario de la Defensa de Buenos Ayres*, reproduced in Álzaga, *Martín de Álzaga en la Reconquista*, pp. 175–6.
49. Anon, *A Narrative of the Expedition to, and the Storming of Buenos Ayres*, p. 13.
50. Anon, *An Authentic Narrative of the Proceedings*, pp. 136–7; Monkland, *Journal of the Secret Expedition*, p. 37; 36th Pay List – WO 12/5034.
51. Philippart (ed.), *The Royal Military Calendar*, Third Edition, Volume 5, 1820, p. 379.
52. 88th Pay Lists – WO 12/9028; Anon, *An Authentic Narrative of the Proceedings*, pp. 136–7.
53. 88th Pay List – WO 12/8955; *Trial of Lieutenant-General John Whitelocke*, pp. 57–8.
54. Monkland, *Journal of the Secret Expedition*, p. 36.
55. *Trial of Lieutenant-General John Whitelocke*, p. 92.
56. *Bourke's Diary*, Add.37887, ff.43–50.
57. *Trial of Lieutenant-General John Whitelocke*, p. 140.
58. Anon, *An Authentic Narrative of the Proceedings*, p. 155.
59. *Trial of Lieutenant-General John Whitelocke*, pp. 57–8.
60. *Trial of Lieutenant-General John Whitelocke*, p. 117.
61. Anon, *An Authentic Narrative of the Proceedings*, p. 139.
62. *Trial of Lieutenant-General John Whitelocke*, p. 70.
63. Anon, *An Authentic Narrative of the Proceedings*, p. 137; Monkland, *Journal of the Secret Expedition*, p. 37.
64. *Trial of Lieutenant-General John Whitelocke*, p. 50.
65. Cannon, *Historical Record of the Eighty-eighth*, p. 13; Anon, *A Narrative of the Expedition to, and the Storming of Buenos Ayres*, p. 17; *Trial of Lieutenant-General John Whitelocke*, pp. 121–2; *The Times*, 23 October 1807.

Chapter 17: The Battle of Buenos Ayres

1. Morley, *Memoirs of a Sergeant*, p. 30.
2. HMS *Diadem* log, ADM 51/1756.
3. *Trial of Lieutenant-General John Whitelocke*, pp. 108–14; Todd, *Bayonets, Bugles and Bonnets*, p. 32.
4. *Trial of Lieutenant-General John Whitelocke*, pp. 122–4.
5. *Bourke's Diary*, Add.37887, ff.43–50.
6. Whittingham, *A Memoir of the Services of Sir Samuel Ford Whittingham*, p. 16.
7. Álzaga, *Martín de Álzaga en la Reconquista*, p. 150.
8. *The Gentleman's Magazine*, January to June 1822, Volume XCII, First Part, p. 182; *Trial of Lieutenant-General John Whitelocke*, pp. 122–4.
9. Anon, *An Authentic Narrative of the Proceedings*, pp. 157–61.
10. Todd, *Bayonets, Bugles and Bonnets*, p. 32; *Trial of Lieutenant-General John Whitelocke*, pp. 132–4.
11. Major King's account, NAM 6403-14.
12. *Trial of Lieutenant-General John Whitelocke*, pp. 123–5.
13. Anon, *An Authentic Narrative of the Proceedings*, pp. 155–6.
14. *Trial of Lieutenant-General John Whitelocke*, pp. 125–8; *The United Service Magazine*, 1836, Volume 3, pp. 503–4.
15. Cannon, *Historical Record of the Eighty-eighth*, p. 13; Anon, *An Authentic Narrative of the Proceedings*, p. 164; Monkland, *Journal of the Secret Expedition*, p. 46; *Trial of Lieutenant-General John Whitelocke*, pp. 107–8; Major King's account, NAM 6403-14.
16. Anon, *A Narrative of the Expedition to, and the Storming of Buenos Ayres*, pp. 20–1; Monkland, *Journal of the Secret Expedition*, pp. 46–7.
17. *Notes on the Viceroyalty of La Plata*, p. 277; *Trial of Lieutenant-General John Whitelocke*, pp. 107–8.
18. *Trial of Lieutenant-General John Whitelocke*, pp. 145–6.
19. *Trial of Lieutenant-General John Whitelocke*, pp. 138–9 and 228; Philippart (ed.), *The Royal Military Calendar*, Third Edition, Volume 5, 1820, p. 379.

20. *Trial of Lieutenant-General John Whitelocke*, pp. 122–3; Anon, *A Narrative of the Expedition to, and the Storming of Buenos Ayres*, p. 28; Anon, *An Authentic Narrative of the Proceedings*, pp. 155–6.

21. *Trial of Lieutenant-General John Whitelocke*, pp. 123–5; Anon, *A Narrative of the Expedition to, and the Storming of Buenos Ayres*, pp. 28–9; Anon, *An Authentic Narrative of the Proceedings*, pp. 157–61.

22. Todd, *Bayonets, Bugles and Bonnets*, p. 32; 71st Regiment Pay List – WO 17/192; *Trial of Lieutenant-General John Whitelocke*, pp. 132–4; http://books.google.co.uk/books?id=u28CAAAAMAAJ&pg=PA185&dq=lieutenant+colonel+henry+cadogan+buenos+ayres&hl=en&sa=X&ei=Ftu8T-_5K9PdgQemwqCyDw&ved=0CEwQ6AEwBA#v=onepage&q=lieutenant%20colonel%20henry%20cadogan%20buenos%20ayres&f=true

23. *Trial of Lieutenant-General John Whitelocke*, p. 132.

24. *Trial of Lieutenant-General John Whitelocke*, pp. 125–8 and 132–4; *The United Service Magazine*, 1842, Part 3, pp. 68–9; NAM 6807-236, *The Diary of Lt. Col. Lancelot Holland*, pp. 77–9; Anon, *An Authentic Narrative of the Proceedings*, pp. 152–4.

25. *Trial of Lieutenant-General John Whitelocke*, pp. 107–8.

26. *The United Service Magazine*, 1836, Volume 3, pp. 503–4; *The United Service Magazine*, 1837, Volume 2, pp. 267–8; Anon, *A Narrative of the Expedition to, and the Storming of Buenos Ayres*, pp. 20–1; Monkland, *Journal of the Secret Expedition*, pp. 46–7.

27. *Trial of Lieutenant-General John Whitelocke*, pp. 107–9 and 116–17; Major King's account, NAM 6403-14.

28. Anon, *A Narrative of the Expedition to, and the Storming of Buenos Ayres*, pp. 21–7; Monkland, *Journal of the Secret Expedition*, pp. 42–6; *Trial of Lieutenant-General John Whitelocke*, pp. 118–19.

29. *Trial of Lieutenant-General John Whitelocke*, pp. 125–8 and 132–4; *The United Service Magazine*, 1842, Part 3, pp. 68–9; NAM 6807-236, *The Diary of Lt. Col. Lancelot Holland*, pp. 77–9; Anon, *An Authentic Narrative of the Proceedings*, pp. 152–4.

30. Monkland, *Journal of the Secret Expedition*, p. 42; Anon, *An Authentic Narrative of the Proceedings*, pp. 157–61; *Trial of Lieutenant-General John Whitelocke*, pp. 123–5.

31. Monkland, *Journal of the Secret Expedition*, p. 42; Anon, *An Authentic Narrative of the Proceedings*, pp. 157–61; *Trial of Lieutenant-General John Whitelocke*, pp. 123–5; AGN Buenos Ayres, Invasiones Inglesas 26-6-12, document 106.

32. Whittingham, pp. 16–19; *Trial of Lieutenant-General John Whitelocke*, pp. 148 and 151–2; *Bourke's Diary*, Add.37887, ff.43–50.

33. *Trial of Lieutenant-General John Whitelocke*, pp. 107–9 and 116–17; Major King's account, NAM 6403-14; Morley, *Memoirs of a Sergeant*, pp. 31–7.

34. *The United Service Magazine*, 1836, Volume 3, pp. 503–4; *Trial of Lieutenant-General John Whitelocke*, pp. 115–16; Monkland, *Journal of the Secret Expedition*, pp. 46–7; Anon, *An Authentic Narrative of the Proceedings*, pp. 163–4; Anon, *A Narrative of the Expedition to, and the Storming of Buenos Ayres*, pp. 20–1; AGN Buenos Aires, Invasiones Inglesas, 26-6-12, document 221.

35. *The United Service Magazine*, 1836, Volume 3, pp. 503–4; *Trial of Lieutenant-General John Whitelocke*, pp. 107–8; Cannon, *Historical Record of the Eighty-Seventh Regiment, or the Royal Irish Fusiliers*, p. 12; Pitt, *The Cabin Boy*, pp. 128–31.

36. Álzaga, *Martín de Álzaga en la Reconquista*, p. 151; *Relacion del Ataque y Defensa de Buenos Ayres en el Mes de Julio 1807*, reproduced in Fortin, *Invasiones Inglesas*, p. 263; Roberts, *Las Invasiones Inglesas*, p. 356; AGN Buenos Aires, Invasiones Inglesas, 26-6-12, document 130.

37. *The United Service Magazine*, 1836, Volume 3, pp. 503–4; Monkland, *Journal of the Secret Expedition*, pp. 75–6.

38. *Trial of Lieutenant-General John Whitelocke*, pp. 145–6; *Notes on the Viceroyalty of La Plata*, p. 296; *The Times*, London, 22 September 1807; 9th Light Dragoons Pay List, WO 12/877.

39. *Trial of Lieutenant-General John Whitelocke*, pp. 132–4 and 138–9; Todd, *Bayonets, Bugles and Bonnets*, pp. 32–3; Monkland, *Journal of the Secret Expedition*, pp. 40–1; Roberts, *Las Invasiones Inglesas*, p. 360.

40. *Trial of Lieutenant-General John Whitelocke*, pp. 145–6 and 155–6

41. *Trial of Lieutenant-General John Whitelocke*, pp. 125–8 and 132–4; NAM 6807-236, *The Diary of Lt. Col. Lancelot Holland*, pp. 77–9; *The United Service Magazine*, 1842, Part 3, pp. 68–9; Monkland, *Journal of the Secret Expedition*, pp. 39–40.

42. *Trial of Lieutenant-General John Whitelocke*, pp. 132–4 and 138–9; Todd, *Bayonets, Bugles and Bonnets*, pp. 32–3; Monkland, *Journal of the Secret Expedition*, pp. 40–1; Roberts, *Las Invasiones Inglesas*, p. 360.

43. *Trial of Lieutenant-General John Whitelocke*, pp. 118–19 and 123–5; Anon, *An Authentic Narrative of the Proceedings*, pp. 157–61; *The Times*, 23 October 1807; AGN Buenos Ayres, Invasiones Inglesas 26-6-12, document 106.

44. *Trial of Lieutenant-General John Whitelocke*, pp. 123–5; Anon, *An Authentic Narrative of the Proceedings*, pp. 157–61; *The Times*, 23 October 1807; AGN Buenos Ayres, Invasiones Inglesas 26-6-12, document 106.

45. *Trial of Lieutenant-General John Whitelocke*, pp. 122–3; Anon, *An Authentic Narrative of the Proceedings*, pp. 155–6, Roberts, *Las Invasiones Inglesas*, p. 357.

46. Roberts, *Las Invasiones Inglesas*, pp. 365–6; Álzaga, *Martín de Álzaga en la Reconquista*, p. 151.

47. *Trial of Lieutenant-General John Whitelocke*, pp. 118–19; Anon, *A Narrative of the Expedition to, and the Storming of Buenos Ayres*, pp. 21–2.

48. *Trial of Lieutenant-General John Whitelocke*, pp. 118–19; Anon, *A Narrative of the Expedition to, and the Storming of Buenos Ayres*, pp. 21–2; Monkland, *Journal of the Secret Expedition*, pp. 42–6.

49. *Trial of Lieutenant-General John Whitelocke*, pp. 118–19; Anon, *A Narrative of the Expedition to, and the Storming of Buenos Ayres*, pp. 23–7; Monkland, *Journal of the Secret Expedition*, pp. 42–6; Philippart (ed.), *The Royal Military Calendar*, Third Edition, Volume 5, 1820, p. 379.

50. *Trial of Lieutenant-General John Whitelocke*, pp. 107–9, 116–17 and 117–18; Major King's account, NAM 6403-14.

51. *Trial of Lieutenant-General John Whitelocke*, pp. 125–8 and 132–4; *The United Service Magazine*, 1842, Part 3, pp. 68–9; NAM 6807-236, *The Diary of Lt. Col. Lancelot Holland*, pp. 77–9; Anon, *An Authentic Narrative of the Proceedings*, pp. 152–4; Monkland, *Journal of the Secret Expedition*, pp. 39–40; Fortin, *Invasiones Inglesas*, p. 263.

52. *Trial of Lieutenant-General John Whitelocke*, pp. 125–8 and 132–4.

53. *Trial of Lieutenant-General John Whitelocke*, pp. 125–8 and 132–4; NAM 6807-236, *The Diary of Lt. Col. Lancelot Holland*, pp. 77–9; *The United Service Magazine*, 1842, Part 3, pp. 68–9; Monkland, *Journal of the Secret Expedition*, pp. 39–40.

54. *Trial of Lieutenant-General John Whitelocke*, pp. 107–9, 116–17 and 117–18; Major King's account, NAM 6403-14.

55. *Trial of Lieutenant-General John Whitelocke*, pp. 118–19 and 121; Anon, *A Narrative of the Expedition to, and the Storming of Buenos Ayres*, pp. 23–7; Monkland, *Journal of the Secret Expedition*, pp. 42–6; Philippart (ed.), *The Royal Military Calendar*, Third Edition, Volume 5, 1820, p. 379; AGN Buenos Aires, Guerra y Marina, Legajo 40, Exp. 44.

56. *Trial of Lieutenant-General John Whitelocke*, pp. 118–19 and 121; Anon, *A Narrative of the Expedition to, and the Storming of Buenos Ayres*, pp. 23–7; Monkland, *Journal of the Secret Expedition*, pp. 42–6; Philippart (ed.), *The Royal Military Calendar*, Third Edition, Volume 5, 1820, p. 379; AGN Buenos Aires, Guerra y Marina, Legajo 40, Exp. 44.

57. NAM 6807-236, *The Diary of Lt. Col. Lancelot Holland*, pp. 77–9; *The United Service Magazine*, 1842, Part 3, pp. 68–9; Monkland, *Journal of the Secret Expedition*, pp. 39–40; *Trial of Lieutenant-General John Whitelocke*, pp. 125–8 and 132–4; Anon, *A Narrative of the Expedition to, and the Storming of Buenos Ayres*, pp. 30.

58. *Trial of Lieutenant-General John Whitelocke*, pp. 107–9, 116–17 and 118–19; Major King's account, NAM 6403-14; Morley, *Memoirs of a Sergeant*, pp. 31–7; Fortin, *Invasiones Inglesas*, p. 263.

59. *Trial of Lieutenant-General John Whitelocke*, pp. 118–19 and 121; Anon, *A Narrative of the Expedition to, and the Storming of Buenos Ayres*, pp. 22–7; Monkland, *Journal of the Secret Expedition*, pp. 42–6; Philippart (ed.), *The Royal Military Calendar*, Third Edition, Volume 5, 1820, p. 379; AGN Buenos Aires, Guerra y Marina, Legajo 40, Exp. 44; *The Times*, 14 and 21 September 1807; Pay list of 36th, WO 12/5034.

60. AGN Montevideo, Legajo 166, documentos, 18–21; Roberts, *Las Invasiones Inglesas*, pp. 388–9; Monkland, *Journal of the Secret Expedition*, pp. 42–6; Anon, *A Narrative of the Expedition to, and the Storming of Buenos Ayres*, pp. 32.

61. *Trial of Lieutenant-General John Whitelocke*, pp. 152–3; Whittingham, *A Memoir of the Services of Sir Samuel Ford Whittingham*, pp. 16–19.

62. NAM 6807-236, *The Diary of Lt. Col. Lancelot Holland*, pp. 77–9; *The United Service Magazine*, 1842, Part 3, pp. 68–9; Monkland, *Journal of the Secret Expedition*, pp. 39–40; *Trial of Lieutenant-General John Whitelocke*, pp. 125–8 and 132–4; Anon, *A Narrative of the Expedition to, and the Storming of Buenos Ayres*, pp. 30; Roberts, *Las Invasiones Inglesas*, p. 362; Fortin, *Invasiones Inglesas*, p. 263.

63. NAM 6807-236, *The Diary of Lt. Col. Lancelot Holland*, pp. 77–9; *The United Service Magazine*, 1842, Part 3, pp. 68–9; Monkland, *Journal of the Secret Expedition*, pp. 39–40; *Trial of Lieutenant-General John Whitelocke*, pp. 125–8 and 132–4; Anon, *A Narrative of the Expedition to, and the Storming of Buenos Ayres*, pp. 30.

64. Whittingham, *A Memoir of the Services of Sir Samuel Ford Whittingham*, pp. 16–19.

65. NAM 6807-236, *The Diary of Lt. Col. Lancelot Holland*, pp. 77–9; *The United Service Magazine*, 1842, Part 3, pp. 68–9; Monkland, *Journal of the Secret Expedition*, pp. 39–40; *Trial of Lieutenant-General John Whitelocke*, pp. 125–8 and 132–4; Anon, *A Narrative of the Expedition to, and the Storming of Buenos Ayres*, pp. 30; Letter from an officer, 22 July 1807, *Caledonian Mercury*, 9 October 1807.

66. Whittingham, *A Memoir of the Services of Sir Samuel Ford Whittingham*, pp. 16–19; Morley, *Memoirs of a Sergeant*, pp. 31–7; Monkland, *Journal of the Secret Expedition*, pp. 48; HMS *Protector* Log, ADM 51/1911.

67. *Trial of Lieutenant-General John Whitelocke*, pp. 99 and 153–4; *Bourke's Diary*, Add.37887, ff.43–50.

68. Roberts, *Las Invasiones Inglesas*, p. 366.

69. Anon, *A Narrative of the Expedition to, and the Storming of Buenos Ayres*, pp. 32–3; *Trial of Lieutenant-General John Whitelocke*, p. 100; Morley, *Memoirs of a Sergeant*, pp. 35–6; Roberts, *Las Invasiones Inglesas*, p. 359; Monkland, *Journal of the Secret Expedition*, pp. 48.

70. Todd, *Bayonets, Bugles and Bonnets*, pp. 32–3; *The United Service Magazine*, 1842, Part 3, pp. 68–9; *Notes on the Viceroyalty of La Plata*, p. 296; Anon, *An Authentic Narrative of the Proceedings*, pp. 166; *The Diary of Lt. Col. Lancelot Holland*, pp. 77–9; Monkland, *Journal of the Secret Expedition*, p. 85.

71. Roberts, *Las Invasiones Inglesas*, pp. 363–4; 45th Pay List, WO 12/5726.

Chapter 18: Surrender

1. *Trial of Lieutenant-General John Whitelocke*, pp. 100–1, 155 and 160; Whittingham, *A Memoir of the Services of Sir Samuel Ford Whittingham*, pp. 19–20.

2. Monkland, *Journal of the Secret Expedition*, p. 48; *Trial of Lieutenant-General John Whitelocke*, p. 107; HMS *Nereide* Log, ADM51/1941; HMS *Protector* Log, ADM 51/1911; Murray to Marsden, 8 July 1807, reprinted in Grainger (ed.), *The Royal Navy in the River Plate 1806–1807*, p. 310.

3. *Trial of Lieutenant-General John Whitelocke*, pp. 101 and 109; Anon, *A Narrative of the Expedition to, and the Storming of Buenos Ayres*, p. 33; Liniers to Whitelocke, 5 July 1807, Add.37,877, f.84.

4. *Trial of Lieutenant-General John Whitelocke*, pp. 94–5, 101–2; *Bourke's Diary*, Add.37887, ff.43–50.

5. *Trial of Lieutenant-General John Whitelocke*, pp. 160 and 228; Monkland, *Journal of the Secret Expedition*, pp. 38–9; Whittingham, *A Memoir of the Services of Sir Samuel Ford Whittingham*, p. 20; Fortin (ed.), *Invasiones*, pp. 244–6; Wylly, Harold Carmichael, *History of the 1st and 2nd Battalions, the Sherwood Foresters, Nottinghmashire and Derbyshire Regiment, 45th Foot, 95th Foot, 1740–1914* (Butler & Tanner, 1929), p. 125; Pay Roll of the 45th Regiment, WO 12/5726.

6. Anon, *An Authentic Narrative of the Proceedings*, p. 167; Monkland, *Journal of the Secret Expedition*, p. 49; NAM 6807-236, *The Diary of Lt. Col. Lancelot Holland*, p. 80; HMS *Protector* Log, ADM 51/1911; Murray to Marsden, 8 July 1807, reprinted in Grainger (ed.), *The Royal Navy in the River Plate 1806–1807*, p. 310.

7. *Trial of Lieutenant-General John Whitelocke*, pp. 94–5, 101–2 and 150–1; *Bourke's Diary*, Add.37887, ff.43–50.

8. *The Gentleman's magazine*, Volume XIX, 1843, p. 319.

9. *Trial of Lieutenant-General John Whitelocke*, p. 107.

10. *Trial of Lieutenant-General John Whitelocke*, pp. 94–5, 101–2 and 109–10.

11. Monkland, *Journal of the Secret Expedition*, p. 49.

12. *Trial of Lieutenant-General John Whitelocke*, pp. 94–5, 101–2, 128, 141 and 144.

13. Monkland, *Journal of the Secret Expedition*, pp. 50–1; Pitt, *The Cabin Boy*, p. 132; Morley, *Memoirs of a Sergeant*, p. 37; Major King's account, NAM 6403-14; Murray to Marsden, 8 July 1807, reprinted in Grainger (ed.), *The Royal Navy in the River Plate 1806–1807*, p. 310.

14. Whittingham, *A Memoir of the Services of Sir Samuel Ford Whittingham*, p. 21; Anon, *A Narrative of the Expedition to, and the Storming of Buenos Ayres*, p. 34; Pay roll of the 87th, WO 12/8955.

15. *Bourke's Diary*, Add.37887, ff.43–50; *Trial of Lieutenant-General John Whitelocke*, p. 141; *The Diary of Lt. Col. Lancelot Holland*, p. 80.

16. Monkland, *Journal of the Secret Expedition*, pp. 46 and 49.

17. *Trial of Lieutenant-General John Whitelocke*, p. 96; *Bourke's Diary*, Add.37887, ff.43–50

18. *Trial of Lieutenant-General John Whitelocke*, p. 158; *The Diary of Lt. Col. Lancelot Holland*, p. 80; Anon, *A Narrative of the Expedition to, and the Storming of Buenos Ayres*, p. 34; Monkland, *Journal of the Secret Expedition*, pp. 52 and 85; Velasco to Buonaventura, 12 July 1807 – reproduced in Vane (ed.), *Correspondence, Dispatches, and other Papers, of Viscount Castlereagh*, Volume 7, p. 399.

19. *Trial of Lieutenant-General John Whitelocke*, p. 158; *The Diary of Lt. Col. Lancelot Holland*, p. 80; Anon, *A Narrative of the Expedition to, and the Storming of Buenos Ayres*, p. 34; Monkland, *Journal of the Secret Expedition*, p. 49; *The United Service Magazine*, 1842, Part 3, p. 70; Newitt (ed.), *War, Revolution and Society … Thomas Kinder's Narrative*, p. 158; Roberts, *Las Invasiones Inglesas*, p. 371.

20. *The Diary of Lt. Col. Lancelot Holland*, pp. 80–1; Monkland, *Journal of the Secret Expedition*, p. 52; 71st pay list WO 17/192; *Notes on the Viceroyalty of La Plata*, pp. 296–7.

21. Monkland, *Journal of the Secret Expedition*, pp. 52 and 70; Anon, *A Narrative of the Expedition to, and the Storming of Buenos Ayres*, p. 32; *Bourke's Diary*, Add.37887, ff.43–50; *Trial of Lieutenant-General John Whitelocke*, pp. 141–2 and 155; HMS *Nereide* log, ADM 37/1422; Whittingham, *A Memoir of the Services of Sir Samuel Ford Whittingham*, p. 22; *The United Service Magazine*, 1836, Volume 3, p. 508.

22. Monkland, *Journal of the Secret Expedition*, pp. 52 and 70; Anon, *A Narrative of the Expedition to, and the Storming of Buenos Ayres*, p. 32; *Bourke's Diary*, Add.37887, ff.43–50; *Trial of Lieutenant-General John Whitelocke*, pp. 141–2 and 155; HMS *Nereide* log, ADM 37/1422; Whittingham, *A Memoir of the Services of Sir Samuel Ford Whittingham*, p. 22; *The United Service Magazine*, 1836, Volume 3, p. 508; Mawe, *Travels in the interior of Brazil*, pp. 37–8.

23. Morley, *Memoirs of a Sergeant*, p. 37; Anon, *An Authentic Narrative of the Proceedings*, p. 173; 9th Light Dragoons, Pay List, WO 12/877; 45th Pay List WO 12/5726; 1/95 Pay List, WO 12/9521; *The United Service Magazine*, 1836, Volume 3, p. 504.

24. Morley, *Memoirs of a Sergeant*, p. 37; Anon, *An Authentic Narrative of the Proceedings*, pp. 173 and 203; 9th Light Dragoons, Pay List, WO 12/877; 45th Pay List WO 12/5726; 1/95 Pay List, WO 12/9521; *The United Service Magazine*, 1836, Volume 3, p. 504.

25. Parkinson (ed.), *Samuel Walters*, p. 61; *The Diary of Lt. Col. Lancelot Holland*, pp. 81–2.

26. Whitelocke to Windham 23 July 1807, WO 1/162, ff.507–14; 5th Regiment Pay List, WO 12/2296 Newitt (ed.), *War, Revolution and Society … Thomas Kinder's Narrative*, pp. 156–7; Whittingham, *A Memoir of the Services of Sir Samuel Ford Whittingham*, p. 22.

27. Parkinson (ed.), *Samuel Walters*, p. 61; Eastwick, *A Master Mariner*, pp. 234–7;

28. Eastwick, *A Master Mariner*, pp. 234–7; *The Times*, 22 October 1807; Mawe, *Travels in the interior of Brazil*, p. 16; Roberts, *Las Invasiones Inglesas*, pp. 315–17.

29. Whittingham, *A Memoir of the Services of Sir Samuel Ford Whittingham*, p. 25; *The United Service Magazine*, 1836, Volume 3, p. 510; General Orders, Monte Video, 19 July 1807, WO 12/8955; Morley, *Memoirs of a Sergeant*, p. 38; Cannon, *Historical Record of the Eighty-eighth*, p. 14; 36th Pay List, WO 12/5034; Monkland, *Journal of the Secret Expedition*, p. 42; Lawrence, *The Autobiography of Sergeant William Lawrence*, p. 24.

30. Gillespie, *Gleaning and Remarks*, pp. 264–7; Fernyhough, *Military Memoirs of Four Brothers*, pp. 124–5; *Diary of William Gavin*, p. 9; Konstam, *There was a Soldier*, pp. 79–82; AGN Buenos Aires, Invasiones Inglesas, 26-7-10, documents 86, 90, 92–3, and 94.

31. *Notes on the Viceroyalty of La Plata*, p. 297; Anon, *An Authentic Narrative of the Proceedings*, p. 208.

32. Letter to Windham, 24 July 1807, WO 1/162, ff. 515–17; Whitelocke to Castlereagh, 29 July 1807, WO 1/162, ff. 519–22; Acland to Windham, 24 July 1807, reproduced in Grainger (ed.), *The Royal Navy in the River Plate 1806–1807*, pp. 319–20.

33. *The Times*, 22 September 1807; Whittingham, *A Memoir of the Services of Sir Samuel Ford Whittingham*, p. 26; Anon, *An Authentic Narrative of the Proceedings*, pp. 206–7.

34. *Caledonian Mercury*, 9 November 1807; Whitelocke to Castlereagh, 10 September 1807, WO 1/162, ff. 523–38; Monkland, *Journal of the Secret Expedition*, pp. 70–1.

35. Anon, *An Authentic Narrative of the Proceedings*, pp. 203–4; Morley, *Memoirs of a Sergeant*, p. 38; Monkland, *Journal of the Secret Expedition*, pp. 75–6 and 97.

36. Gillespie, *Gleaning and Remarks*, pp. 276–8; Fernyhough, *Military Memoirs of Four Brothers*, pp. 125–6; *Diary of William Gavin*, p. 9.

37. Gillespie, *Gleaning and Remarks*, pp. 279–84; *Diary of William Gavin*, p. 9; Mawe, *Travels in the interior of Brazil*, pp. 45–6; Lawrence, *The Autobiography of Sergeant William Lawrence*, p. 24; Murray to Marsden, 8 September 1807, reproduced in Grainger (ed.), *The Royal Navy in the River Plate 1806–1807*, pp. 327–9; Smith (ed.), *The Autobiography of Lieutenant-General Sir Harry Smith*, chapter 1; Whitelocke to Castlereagh, 10 September 1807, WO 1/162, ff. 523–38; Mulhall, *The English in South America*, p. 105; Monkland, *Journal of the Secret Expedition*, pp. 77–8.

Epilogue: Echoes

1. Carrol and Hamilton, *General Return of the British Prisoners*, WO 1/162, f. 571; Pitt, *The Cabin Boy*, pp. 136–9; HMS *Nereide* Log Book, ADM 37/1422.

2. Roberts, *Las Invasiones Inglesas*, pp. 394–7.

3. *The Times*, 18 Nov 1807; *The United Service Magazine*, 1836, Volume 3, pp. 510–11; *Essex Institute historical collections*, Volume 57 (Salem, Massachusetts, 1921), pp. 199–201; 5th Regiment Pay List, WO 12/2296; 38th Regiment Pay List, WO 12/5181.

4. *The Times*, 18 November 1807; *The United Service Magazine*, 1836, Volume 3, pp. 510–11; *Essex Institute historical collections*, pp. 199–201; 5th Regiment Pay List, WO 12/2296; 38th Regiment Pay List, WO 12/5181.

5. *The Times*, 26 October 1807; Lawrence, *The Autobiography of Sergeant William Lawrence*, p. 25; Monkland, *Journal of the Secret Expedition*, pp. 75–6 and 81; Morley, *Memoirs of a Sergeant*, p. 38; *Diary of William Gavin*, p. 9.

6. *The Times*, 14 September and 12 November 1807; Hathaway (ed.), *A Dorset Rifleman – The Recollections of Rifleman Harris*, p. 33; Roberts, *Las Invasiones Inglesas*, p. 391.

7. Archer, Jeremy, *General Whitelocke – Vanquished at Buenos Aires in 1807*. Published in *The British Army Review*, ref 8871 (August 1993), pp. 37–44; *A Dorset Rifleman – The Recollections of Rifleman Harris*, p. 33; Roberts, *Las Invasiones Inglesas*, p. 394.

8. Archer, Jeremy, *General Whitelocke – Vanquished at Buenos Aires in 1807*. Published in *The British Army Review*, ref 8871, pp. 37–44; Hathaway (ed.), *A Dorset Rifleman – The Recollections of Rifleman Harris*, p. 33; Roberts, *Las Invasiones Inglesas*, p. 341.

9. Hathaway (ed.), *A Dorset Rifleman -The Recollections of Rifleman Harris*, p. 33; Morley, *Memoirs of a Sergeant*, p. 41; Smith (ed.), *The Autobiography of Lieutenant-General Sir Harry Smith*, chapter 1; *The United Service Magazine*, 1836, Volume 2, p. 198; Bryant, *Years of Victory, 1802–1812*, p. 244.

10. *The Times*, 29 April 1807; Popham, *A Damned Cunning Fellow*, pp. 166–75.

11. For more details on the Buenos Ayres Regiment see Fraga, *El Batallón Buenos Aires en la Guerra de la Reconquista Española*.

12. *United Service Magazine*, 1843, part 3, p. 425; Roberts, *Las Invasiones Inglesas*, pp. 421–35; Lawrence, *The Autobiography of Sergeant William Lawrence*, p. 26.

13. *Diary of William Gavin*, p. 5.

14. Johnson, *Workshop of Revolution*, pp. 286–7.

Bibliography

Archives

Archivo General de la Nación, Buenos Aires, Argentina
Criminales, Legajos 54, 55, 57
Guerra y Marina, Legajos 40, 44,
Hacienda, Legajo 129, 130, 131, 132, 133, 140
Invasiones Inglesas 26-6-8, 26-6-12, 26-7-7, 26-7-8, 26-7-9, 26-7-10

Archivo Nacional, Montevideo, Uruguay
Caja 50, 156 – Invasion Inglesa, Defensa de la Plaza de Montevideo y toma de la Plaza de Montevideo
  por los ingleses.
Caja 165, 166, 167 – Servicios en la guerra contra los ingleses.
Caja 455 – Certificados de viudedad.
Caja 242 – La Reconquista.

Bodleian Library, Oxford, England
Ms. Eng. Misc. d. 242 (Thompson) – Journal of Surgeon Richard Thompson (R.N. – HMS *Narcissus*,
  1806)

British Museum, London, England
Asia, Pacific and Africa Collections:
  L/MAR/B/156 E-F – Ship's Log, Georgina East India Packet, 1806.
Manuscripts Department:
  Add. Ms. 37,886 and 37,887 – The Papers of William Windham M.P. – Includes various docu-
    ments and correspondence with officers in the River Plate, including Lieutenant-Colonel
    Bourke's Diary, July 1807.
  Add. Ms. 41,580, ff.47–63 – Miscellaneous Documents and Letters relating to General White-
    locke's 1807 Invasion of the River Plate, including the letters of Lieutenant George Henry
    Dansey, 88th Regiment of Foot, 1806–7.
  Add. Ms. 57,717 – Maps of Attacks on Buenos Aires, 1807.
  Eg. Ms. 3265 – The Letter Book of Rear-Admiral George Murray, 1806–7.

National Archives, London, England
Audit Office.
  AO 1/540/329 – Commissary P. Home's Audit List for troops at Maldonado, South America,
    1806–8.
  AO 1/5375 – Commissary R. Hill's Audit for troops at Buenos Ayres, South America, 1806.
Admiralty Office:
  ADM 1/59 – Admiralty In Letters, 1806–7.
  ADM 1/5374-5383 and ADM 2/1122 – General Courts Martial Records, 1806–1808.
  ADM 35/2970 – Pay Roll, HMS *Nereide*, 1806–7.
  ADM 36/14081, 16297, 16299, ADM 37/648 – Muster Rolls, HMS *Raisonnable*, 1801–8.
  ADM 36/17280 – Muster Roll, HMS *Lancaster*, 1806–7.
  ADM 37/101 – Muster Roll, HMS *Africa*, 1807.
  ADM 37/1086 – Muster Roll, HMS *Polyphemus*, 1807.
  ADM 37/1142 – Muster Roll, HMS *Ardent*, 1807.

ADM 37/1427 – Muster Roll, HMS *Daphne*, 1807.

ADM 37/2970 – Muster Roll, HMS *Nereide*, 1806–7.

ADM 51/1583, 4465 – Ship's Log, HMS *Leda*, 1806–7.

ADM 51/1597 – Ship's Log, HMS *Narcissus*, 1806.

ADM 51/1611 – Ship's Log, HMS *Lancaster*, 1806–7.

ADM 51/1615, 1756 – Ship's Log, HMS *Diadem*, 1806–8.

ADM 51/1637 – Ship's Log, HMS *Spencer*, 1805–7.

ADM 51/1652, 1673 – Ship's Log, HMS *Fly*, 1806–7.

ADM 51/1661, 1712 – Ship's Log, HMS *Saracen*, 1806–7

ADM 51/1696 – Ship's Log, HMS *Pheasant*, 1806–7.

ADM 51/1700 – Ship's Log, HMS *Diomede*, 1806–7.

ADM 51/1708, 1911 – Ship's Log, HMS *Protector*, 1806–8.

ADM 51/1789 – Ship's Log, HMS *Rolla*, 1806–7.

ADM 51/1925–6 – Ship's Log, HMS *Dolores*, 1806–7.

ADM 51/1936, 1812 – Ship's Log, HMS *Raisonnable*, 1806–8.

ADM 51/1941, 52/3848, 52/4195 – Ship's Log, HMS *Nereide*, 1806–8.

ADM 51/2005 – Ship's Log, HMS *Encounter*, 1805–8.

ADM 51/4449 – Ship's Log, HMS *Flying Fish*, 1806–7.

ADM 51/4484 – Ship's Log, HMS *Paz*, 1807.

ADM 352/285 – Map of Coastline of River Plate (Spanish with additions by P. Parker and John Engledue, 1807).

ADM 354/235 – Miscellaneous Admiralty Records (Held at the National Maritime Museum, Caird Library, Greenwich) – Details on capture of Master William Wesley Pole of HMS *Leda* at Fort Santa Teresa, April 1806.

Asia Pacific and Africa Collection:

L/MIL/5/148 – Details on prize money awarded to the officers and men of the St Helena Regiment, East India Company for prizes captured at Buenos Ayres 1806.

Colonial Office:

CO 324/68 – Correspondence with Buenos Aires and Monte Video, 1806–7.

Privy Council Records:

PC 1/3823 – Records of disputes concerning the division of prize money captured at Buenos Aires, 1806.

Prerogative Court of Canterbury Records:

PROB 31/1014/384 – Last Will and Testament of James Byre, Paymaster, 17th Light Dragoons.

War Office:

WO 1/161 and 162 – War Office in Letters, includes various correspondence from the River Plate 1806–7.

WO 12/357 – Pay Roll, 6th Dragoon Guards, 1807.

WO 12/877 – Pay Roll, 9th Light Dragoons, 1807.

WO 12/1315 – Pay Roll, 17th Light Dragoons, 1807.

WO 12/1422 – Pay Roll, 20th Light Dragoons, 1806–7.

WO 12/1447 – Pay Roll, 21st Light Dragoons, 1806–7.

WO 12/2296 – Pay Roll, 5th Regiment of Foot, 1806–8.

WO 12/5034 – Pay Roll, 1st Battalion, 36th Regiment of Foot, 1807.

WO 12/5180–2 – Pay Roll, 1st Battalion, 38th Regiment of Foot, 1806–7.

WO 12/5326–5327 – Pay Roll, 1st Battalion, 40th Regiment of Foot, 1806–7.

WO 12/5880 – Pay Roll, 1st Battalion, 47th Regiment of Foot, 1806–7.

WO 12/7847–7856 – Pay Roll, 1st Battalion, 71st Regiment of Foot, 1775–1807.

WO 12/8955 – Pay Roll, 1st Battalion, 87th Regiment of Foot, 1806–7.

WO 12/9028 – Pay Roll, 1st Battalion, 88st Regiment of Foot, 1807.

WO 12/9521 – Pay Roll, 1st Battalion, 95th Rifle Regiment, 1806–7.

WO 12/9578 – Pay Roll, 2nd Battalion, 95th Rifle Regiment, 1807.

WO 17/192 – Regimental Returns – 1st Battalion, 71th Regiment of Foot, 1806–7.

WO 71/206–212 – General Courts Martial Records, 1806–1808.
WO 76/177–8 – Service Records of Officers of the 40th Regiment of Foot.
WO 78/788 – Royal Engineers' Plan of Fortress at Buenos Ayres, 1806.
WO 97/563, 830, 833 – Individual Service Records.
WO 164/517 – Prize Money Lists, Buenos Ayres, 1806.
MR 1/19914 – Plan of Capture of Buenos Ayres, 1806.
MR 1/199 – Plan of Whitelocke's Attack on Buenos Ayres, 1807.
MPHH 1/195/1–4 – Royal Engineers' maps and plans of Whitelocke's march and attack on Buenos Ayres, 1807.

National Army Museum, London, England
NAM 6807-236 – Typescript extract from the diary of Colonel Lancelot Holland dealing with his service as deputy-quarter-master-general of the expedition to the River Plate in 1807.
NAM 6403-14 – Typescript copy of account of attack on Buenos Ayres, 1807 by Maj. H. King, 5th Foot.

Published Primary Sources
Álzaga, Enrique Williams, *Martín de Álzaga en la Reconquista y en la Defensa de Buenos Aires (1806–1807)* (Emecé Editores, Buenos Aires, 1971).
Anon, *A Full and Correct Report of the Trial of Sir Home Popham* (J. and J. Richardson, London, 1807).
Anon, *A Narrative of the Expedition to, and the Storming of Buenos Ayres by the British Army commanded by Lieutenant-General Whitelocke by an officer attached to the expedition* (S. Robinson, Bath, 1807).
Anon, *An Authentic Narrative of the Proceedings of the Expedition under the Command of Brigadier-Gen. Craufurd* (London, 1808).
Anon, *An Authentic Narrative of the Proceedings of the Expedition against Buenos Ayres, under the command of Lieut. Gen. Whitelocke by an Irish officer* (R. Smith, Dublin, 1808).
Anon, *A Proposal For Humbling Spain, Written in 1711* (London, Roberts, 1739).
Anon (Monkland, George), *Journal of the Secret Expedition which sailed from Falmouth under the command of Brigadier-General Craufurd* (Monkland, Bath, 1808).
Anon (Tucker, John), *A Narrative of the Operations of a Small British Force under the command of Brigadier-General, Sir Samuel Auchmuty* (J. J. Stockdale, London, 1807).
Anon, *Trial of Lieutenant-General John Whitelocke commander-in-chief of the expedition against Buenos Ayres, by court-martial, held in Chelsea college* (T. Gillet, London, 1808).
Anon, *Truth and reason, versus Calumny and Folly; In which the leading Circumstances of General Whitelocke's conduct in South America are Examined* (London, Kerlay & Bowdery, 1807).
Cleland, James, *The Annals of Glasgow: comprising an accont of the public buildings, charities, and the rise and progress of the city* (J. Smith, London, 1829).
Coronado, Juan (ed.), *Invasiones inglesas al Rio de la Plata, documentos inéditos* (Imprenta Republicana, Buenos Aires, 1870).
Davie, John Constanse, *Letters from Paraguay: describing the settlements of Monte Video and Buenos Ayres* (G. Robinson, 1805).
Darwin, Charles, *Journal of Researches into the Natural History and Geology of the Countries Visited During the Voyage of HMS Beagle round the World*, Volume II (J. Murray, London, 1845)
Duncan, Francis, *History of the Royal Artillery*, Volume II (Murray, London, 1879).
Eastwick, Robert William, *A Master Mariner: Being the Life and Adventures of Captain Robert Eastwick* (Unwin, 1891).
Essex Institue historical collections, Volume 57 (Salem, Massachusetts, 1921).
Fernyhough, *Military Memoirs of Four Brothers* (William Sams, London, 1829).
Fortin, Jorge L. R. and Fortin, Pablo (eds), *Invasionesinglesas: colección Pablo Fortin* (Editoria Cía, Lamsa, 1967).
Gillespie, *Gleaning and Remarks collected during many months residence at Buenos Ayres* (Dewhirst, London, 1818).
Gleig, George Robert, *The Hussar* (G.B. Zieber, Philadephia, 1845).
Grainger, John (ed.), *The Royal Navy in the River Plate 1806–1807* (Scolar Press, 1996).

Hardy, Horatio Charles, *A Register of Ships Employed in the Service of the Honourable the United East India Company From the Year 1760 to 1810* (Black, Perry and Kingsbury, London, 1811).

Hathaway, Eileen (ed.), *A Dorset Rifleman: The Recollections of Benjamin Harris* (Shinglepicker Publications, 1995).

Haultain, Charles, *The New Navy List, containing the names of all the commissioned officers in Her Majesty's Fleet*, p. 168 (London, Smipkin, Marshall and Co., 1844).

Hooker, William Jackson (ed.), *Botanical Miscellany, Containing Figures and Descriptions*, Volume II (Murray, London, 1831).

Keith, George Mouat, *A Voyage to South America and the Cape of Good Hope* (Vogel, London, 1819).

Konstam, Angus, *There was a Soldier* (Headline Book Publishing, 2009).

Larrouy, P. Antonio, *Documentos del Archivo General de Tucumán – Invasiones Inglesas y Revolucion, Tomo 1* (Buenos Aires, Juna A. Alsina, 1910).

Lawrence, William, *The Autobiography of Sergeant William Lawrence* (Dodo Press, Milton Keynes, 2010).

Marshal, John, *Royal Naval Biography: or, Memoirs of the services of all the flag-officers*, Volume IV, Part 1 (Longman, Hurst, Rees, Orme and Brown, London, 1833).

Martin, Henry, *Journal and Letters of the Rev. Henry Martyn*, Volume 1 (Seeley and Burnside, London, 1837).

Mawe, *Travels in the interior of Brazil: particularly in the gold and diamond districts* (Longman, Hurst, Rees, Orme, and Brown, 1812).

Morley, Stephen, *Memoirs of a Sergeant of the 5th Regiment of Foot, containing an account of his services in Hanover, South America and the Peninsular* (Ken Trotman Ltd, Cambridge, 1999).

Newitt (ed.), *War, Revolution and Society in the Rio de la Plata 1808–1810, Thomas Kinder's Narrative* (Non Basic Stock Line, 2010).

Pitt, William, *The Cabin Boy: being the memoirs of an officer in the Civil Department of H. M. Navy* (Hamilton, Adams and Co., London, 1840).

Philippart, John (ed.), *The Royal Military Calendar, or Army Service and Commission Book*, Volume 3 (A. J. Valpy, London, 1820).

Ralfe, James, *The Naval Biography of Great Britain, consisting of Historical Memoirs*, Volume III (Whitmore & Fenn, London, 1828).

Sánchez de Thompson, Maraquita, *Recuerdos de Buenos Ayres virreynal* (ENE Editorial, 1953).

Sánchez de Thompson, Maraquita, *Intimidad y Política, Diarios, Cartas y Recuerdos* (2004).

Smith, G. C. Moore (ed.), *The Autobiography of Lieutenant-General Sir Harry Smith* (J. Murray, London, 1903).

Todd, Thomas, *Bayonets, Bugles & Bonnets* (Leonaur, 2006).

Tucker, John, *A Narrative of the operations of a small British Force …* (1807).

Vane, Charles William (ed.), *Correspondence, Dispatches, and other Papers, of Viscount Castlereagh edited by his brother*, Volume 7 (Murray, London, 1851).

Vassal, Spencer Thomas, *Memoir of the life of Lieutenant-Colonel Vassal* (Barry and Son, Britsol, 1819).

Vidal, E.E., *Picturesque Illustrations of Buenos Ayres and Monte Video …* (1820).

Parkinson, Cyril Northcote (ed.), *Samuel Walters, Lieutenant R.N.* (Liverpool Univeristy Press, Liverpool, 2005).

Vidal, Emeric Essex, *Picturesque Illustrations of Buenos Ayres and Monte Video* (R. Ackermann, London, 1820).

Whittingham, Samford, *A Memoir of the Services …* (1865).

Newspapers and Magazines

The Aberdeen Journal (1807).

The Army and Navy Chronicle (1837).

The British Army Review (1993).

The Caledonian Mercury (1807).

The Gentleman's Magazine and Historical Chronicle (1805).

The Hampshire Telegraph and Sussex Chronicle (1807).

The Highland Light Infantry Chronicle (1893–1896, 1901, 1920, 1939).

Jackson's Oxford Journal (1807).
The Lancaster Gazette and General Advertiser (1807).
The London Gazette (1807).
The Morning Post (1807–1808).
The Morning Post and Gazetteer (1799).
The Morning Chronicle (1806–1807).
The Royal Military Calendar (1820).
The Scots Magazine and Edinburgh Literary Miscellany (1807).
The Southern Star (Montevideo, 1807).
The Times (1806–1808).
The United Service Journal and Naval and Military Magazine (1829, 1836, 1837, 1842, 1843).

Selected Secondary Sources
Adkins, Roy, *The War for all the Oceans* (Penguin, 2011).
Almazán, Bernardo P. Lozier, *Beresford Gobernador de Buenos Ayres* (Editorial Galerna, 1994).
Álzaga, Enrique Williams, *Fuga de General Beresford* (Buenos Aires, 1965).
Bandera, Héctor Alberto, *Quilmes: y las Invasiones Inglesas* (El Monje Editor, 2006).
Beverina, Juan, *Las Invasiones Inglesas al Rio de la Plata, 1806–1807* (Taller Gráfico de L. Bernard, Buenos Aires, 1939).
Buckland, Charles Edward, *Dictionary of Indian Biography* (S. Sonrienschein, 1906).
Burkholder, Mark A. and Johnson, Lyman L., *Colonial Latin America: Second Edition* (OUP, Oxford, 1994).
Bryant, Arthur, *The Years of Endurance* (Collins, London, 1942).
Bryant, Arthur, *Years of Victory, 1802–1812* (The Reprint Society, London, 1945).
Cannon, Richard, and Cappeler, Carl, *Historical Record of the Seventy-first Regiment, Highland Light Infantry* (Parker, Furnivall & Parker, London, 1852),.
Cannon, Richard, *Historical Record of the Eighty-Seventh Regiment, or the Royal Irish Fusiliers* (Parker, Furnivall, and Parker, 1853).
Cannon, Richard, *Historical Record of the Eighty-eighth Regiment of Foot, Or Connaught Rangers* (Parker, Furnivall & Parker, London, 1838).
Capdevila, Arturo, *Las Invasiones Inglesas* (Buenos Aires, 1938).
Chasteen, John Charles, *Americanos* (Oxford, OUP, 2008).
Colman, Oscar Tavani Pérez, *Martínez de Fontes y la fuga del General Beresford* (Editorial Dunken, Buenos Aires, 2005).
Compton Herbert, *A Master Mariner. Being the Life and Adventures of Captain Robert William Eastwick* (London, 1891).
Corbelini, Enrique C., *La Revolucion de Mayo y sus antecedents desde las invasions inglesas* (Buenos Aires, 1950).
Cronica General Del Uruguay, *Las Invasiones Inglesas*, Vol. 2, No. 1 (Montevideo, n.d.).
Craufurd, Alexander, *General Craufurd and his Light Division* (Uckfield, The Naval & Military Press, 2011)
Cunliffe, Marcus, *The Royal Irish Fusiliers, 1793 1950* (OUP, Oxford, 1952).
Dalton, Maj-Gen J. C., *Buenos Aires and Montevideo, 1806 and 1807*. Journál of the Royal Artillery Vol. 54 (Woolwich, 1926–7).
Destefani, Laurio H., *Los Marinos en Las Invasiones Inglesas* (Buenos Aires, 1975).
Elissalde, Roberto L., *Historias Ignoradas de las Invasiones Inglesas* (Aguilar, Buenos Ayres, 2006).
Fletcher, Ian, *The Waters of Oblivion: The British Invasion of the Rio de la Plata, 1806–1807* (Spellmount, Tunbridge Wells, 1991).
Foulkes, Nicholas, *Dancing into Battle* (Phoenix, 2007).
Fraga, Rosendo M., *El Batallón Buenos Aires en la Guerra de la Reconquista Española* (Buenos Aires, Instituto de Historia Militar Argentina, 2007).
Galeano, Edurado, *Las Venas Abiertas de América Latina* (Siglo Veintiuno, Madrid, 1985),.
Garzón, Rafael, *Sobre Monte y Córdoba en las invasions inglesas* (Ediciones del Corredor Austral, 2000).

Graham-Yooll, Andrew, *The Forgotten Colony: A history of the English-speaking communities of Argentina* (L.O.L.A., 1999).

Groussac, Paul, *Santiago Liniers, Conde de Buenos Aires, 1753–1810* (Buenos Aires, 1907).

Holmes, Richard, *Redcoat: The British Soldier in the Age of the Horse and Musket* (London, Harper Collins, 2001).

Homans, Benjamin (ed.), *Army and Navy Chronicle*, Volumes 4–5 (Homans, Washington, 1837).

Hood, Theodore, *The Life of General the Right Honourable Sor David Baird* (London, 1833).

Howard, Dr Martin, *Wellington's Doctors* (Staplehurst, Spellmount, 2002).

Johnson, Lyman, *Workshop of Revolution, Plebian Buenos Aires and the Atlantic World* (Duke University Press, 2011).

Lavery, Brian, *Jack Aubery Commands* (Conway Maritime Press, London, 2005).

López, Manuel Castro, *El Tercio de Galicia en Las Defensas de Buenos Aires* (Buenos Aires, 1911).

Lynch, John, *Spanish Colonial Administration, 1782–1810. The Intendant System in the Viceroyalty of the Rio de la Plata* (London, 1958).

Macksey, Piers, *British Victory in Egypt* (London, Tauris PArke Paperbacks, 2010).

Martínez, Pedro Santos, *Las Industrias durante el Virreinato (1776–1810)* (Eudeba, 1969).

Miranda, Arnaldo Ignacio Adolfo, *Relevamiento del Archivo Parroquial de San José de Flores* (Editorial Dunken, 2006).

Muir, Rory, *Tactics and Experience of Battle in the Age of Napoleon* (Yale YUP, 1998).

Mulhall, Michael George, *The English in South America* (Standard Office, 1878).

Mullaly, Reginald, Brian, *The South Lancashire Regiment: Prince of Wales's Volunteers* (White Swan Press, 1952).

Oatts, Lewis Balfour, *Proud Heritage, The Story of the Highland Light Infantry*, Volume 1 (Nelson and Son, London, 1952).

Oman, Charles (ed.), *Diary of William Gavin* (Glasgow, 1921).

Parry, D. H., *The Death or Glory Boys: the Story of the Seventeenth Lancers* (Kessinger Publishing, 2010).

Popham, Hugh, *A Damned Cunning Fellow: The eventful life of Rear-Admiral Sir Home Popham* (Old Ferry Press, 1991).

Puentes, Gabriel A., *Don Francisco Javier de Elio en la Rio de la Plata* (Buenos Aires, 1966).

Reginald, Brian, *The South Lancashire Regiment: Prince of Wales's Volunteers* (White Swan Press, 1952),.

Roberts, Carlos, *Las Invasiones Inglesas* (Emecé Editores, Buenos Aires, 2000),.

Robinson, William, *Jack Nastyface: Memoirs of a seaman* (Walalnd, 1836).

Sagui, Francisco, *Los ultimos cuatro años de la Domincaion Española en la antiguo Virreinato del Rio de la Plata* (Buenos Aires, 1874).

Salas, Alberto, *Diario de Buenos Aires, 1806–1807* (Buenos Aires, Editorial Sudamericana, 1981).

Socolow, *The Merchants of Buenos Aires 1778–1810: Family and Commerce* (Cambridge University Press, Cambridge, 2009).

Taylor, Stephen, *Storm and Conquest* (Faber & Faber, London, 2007).

Theal, George McCall, *History of South Africa*, Volume 5 (Cambrige University Press, Cambridge, 2010).

Toll, Ian W., *Six Frigates* (Penguin, London, 2007).

Villalobos R., Sergio, *El Comercio y la Crisis Colonial* (Akhilleus, Santiago, 2009),.

Wilson, Ben, *Decency & Disorder* (Faber & Faber, London, 2007).

Wylly, Harold Carmichael, *History of the 1st and 2nd Battalions, the Sherwood Foresters, Nottinghamshire and Derbyshire Regiment, 45th Foot, 95th Foot, 1740–1914* (Butler & Tanner, 1929).

Index

Abascal Battery (Buenos Ayres), 157, 193
Abascal, Viceroy José Fernando de, 132, 157
Abercrombie, Sir Ralph, xiv, 19, 86
Abreu Orta, Lieutenant Augustín, 62, 102–4
Acland, Brigadier-General Wroth Palmer, 154, 155, 214, n.271
Adamson, Lieutenant Peter (71st), 56, 129, 154
Agustini, Captain Francisco, 63, 72–3, 93, 157, 174–5, 192, 197, 200, 207, n.264
Allemand, Admiral Zacharie, 6
Allende, Colonel Santiago, 106–7, 110–11, 113, 224
Alsina y Vereyes, Colonel Jaime, 34
Álzaga, Martín de: background and character, 49, 61; in build-up to Reconquista, 61, 63; bides his time while Liniers rises to power, 89; undermines Liniers, 90; raises money for militia, 92; reflects on fall on Monte Video, 131; and Beresford's escape, 132; in La Defensa, xii, xii, 174, 197; and Whitelocke's surrender, 204, 206, 207; latter career and death, 220, 223–4
Arbuthnot, Captain Robert (20th Light Dragoons), 23, 28, 55, 68, 128, 131
Argentina: foundation of, 225
Arnau, Pedro, 63–4
Arroyo Maldonado (near Buenos Ayres), 71
Arroyo Maldonado (near Maldonado), 105
Arroyo San Pedro, 151
Artillery Park (Monte Video), 115, 122–5
Arze, Sub-Inspector / Brigadier-General Pedro de: during Beresford's attack on Buenos Ayres, 33, 35 9; during the siege of Monte Video, 118, 121–2; as prisoner of war, 127, 134, 201
Auchmuty, Brigadier-General Sir Samuel: background and appointment as commander, 85–6; advance on Monte Video, 109–14; and siege of Monte Video, 116–27; as governor of Monte Video, 134–42; sends troops to Colonia, 142; ignored by Whitelocke, 148; during Whitelocke's advance on Buenos Ayres, 154, 160, 170; gives opinion on Whitelocke's plan of attack on Buenos Ayres, 180; in the suburbs of Buenos Ayres,

181–2; in La Defensa, xii, 183, 187–8, 190, 194, 198, 203–5; during surrender negotiations, 206, 208; latter career, 222
Austerlitz, Battle of, xiv
Australia, 25, 135, 137, 213
Azcuénaga, Colonel Miguel Ignacio de, 34, 38–41, 49
Azopardo, Captain Juan Bautista, 150, 174, 184

Backhouse, Lieutenant-Colonel Joseph (47th): background and character, 96; reaction to news of Beresford's defeat, 97; discusses strategy with Popham, 97; in first attempt on Monte Video, 97; at Maldonado, 98, 100–8, 129–30; during advance on Monte Video, 109–10, 113; at Canelones, 140, 153
Baird, Major-General Sir David: background, 5; on voyage to Cape, 9; at the Cape, 12–15, 17–19; at Battle of Blaauwberg, 15–16; decision to invade the River Plate, 21–3; prize money, 57; reinforces Beresford, 54, 95–6; latter career and death, 221
Balbiani, Colonel César: background, 96, 157; in La Defensa, 169–70, 174, 205; as a hostage, 211
Balcarce brothers, the, 118, 127, 221
Ballester, Lieutenant-Colonel Antonio Luciano de, 165
Barreda, Mariana Sánchez, 57, 89
Batavian troops, 15–16
Bayntun, Captain Henry (R.N.), 210
Belgrano, Captain Manuel, 3, 132
Beresford, Major-General William Carr: and attack on Cape, 12, 15, 17; background and character, 22; on voyage to River Plate, 24–6; debates whether to attack Buenos Ayres, 28–9; assumes rank of major-general, 30; on advance on Buenos Ayres, 35–42; as governor of Buenos Ayres, 43, 47, 53–60, 63–6, 67; and skirmish at Perdriel 67–8, in Reconquista, 70–8; negotiates surrender with Liniers, 78–9, 88; as prisoner of war, 89–91, 95, 128–33; escape from captivity, 140, 154;

returns to England, 140, 142; latter career, 221
Blaauwberg, battle of, 15–16
Blainey, Lieutenant Thomas (R.N.), 118, 143
Blue Water Policy, xv, 5, 20
Bonaparte, Napoleon, 217
Borrás, Captain Miguel, 100
Bourke, Lieutenant-Colonel Richard: opinion on British prospects in the River Plate, 140; performs reconnaissance for landing site for Whitelocke's advance, 149; discusses possible bombardment of Buenos Ayres with Whitelocke, 155; during advance on Buenos Ayres, 160, 163–4, 167–9; opinion of Whitelocke's plan of attack, 179, 181; during Whitelocke's attack on Buenos Ayres, 184; during surrender negotiations, 207–9, 211–12, latter career, 224
Bowles, Sergeant H. (40th), 117
Bradford, Lieutenant-Colonel Thomas, 150
British Army – cavalry units (1st Battalion unless otherwise stated): 6th Dragoon Guards (Carabiniers), 153, 161, 167, 169, 178, 182, 188, 195; 9th Light Dragoons, 86, 137, 142, 151, 153, 155, 161, 167, 169, 182, 188, 195, 212, 214; 20th Light Dragoons, 3, 6, 11, 12, 18, 22, 55, 96, 97, 103, 104, 136, 214, 220, 222; 21st Light Dragoons, 104, 152
British Army – infantry units (1st Battalion unless otherwise stated): 2nd, 19; 21st, 3; 24th, 3, 14–16; 36th, 153, 161–7, 169, 170, 178, 181, 182, 184, 188, 190–1, 195, 197–8, 200–2, 204, 213, 217, 220; 38th, 3, 96–7, 100, 104–5, 109, 123–5, 136, 160, 162, 178, 184, 188, 191, 193–4, 204, 217, 220; 40th, 86, 109, 116–17, 119, 120, 123–5, 135–6, 142, 150, 152, 155, 161, 163–5, 181, 195, 206, 220, 222; 45th, 86, 153, 161, 164, 169, 178, 182, 184, 188, 190, 192, 199, 202, 204, 205, 206, 211, 212, 220, 221; 47th, 96, 100, 105, 107, 109, 136, 160, 188, 195, 213, 214; 54th, 19, 96, 107, 123; 59th, 3, 12, 14, 16–18; 71st, 3, 5, 13–19, 22–5, 28, 30, 36–40, 43, 47, 55–7, 63, 65, 67–8, 70, 72–5, 77–9, 86, 88, 93–4, 102, 109, 119, 129–130, 154, 160, 168, 184, 189, 191, 195–6, 199, 204, 210–11, 215, 220–2, 225; 2/71, 6, 75; 72nd, 3, 13, 16–17, 21; 74th, 11; 83rd, 3, 17, 96; 87th, 86, 109, 114, 120, 123, 125–7, 135–6, 160, 162, 164, 181–3, 186, 188, 190–1, 193–4, 204–5, 209–10, 213–14, 217; 88th, 153, 161–4, 167–70, 173, 178, 181–4, 189–190, 192, 196–9, 203–7, 211, 213–14;

89th, 147, 154–5, 214; 93rd, 3, 14; 1/95, 153–4, 159, 165, 173, 181, 192, 200, 203, 205, 214; 2/95, 86, 111, 113, 117, 126, 135–6, 155, 161, 165, 172, 178, 192, 205, 214, 220
British militia – The Royal British South American, 150, n.260
Brookman, Captain William (71st), 86, 109, 160, 184, 189, 211
Browne, Colonel Gore (40th): as commander of the 40th, 86, 109, 113, 116, 123; 126; as governor of Monte Video, 134, 140, 155, 215
Brownrigg, Lieutenant-Colonel Henry Fox, 103–4, 109, 116, 123–4, 135, 142
Buenos Ayres: early ideas for British attack on, 20; Sobremonte's preparations for defence of, 31–4; Beresford's capture of, 43
British occupation of, 43–66; founding and early history, 47–9; inhabitants of, 49–50; physical description of, 50–2; social life and culture of, 52–3; Reconquista, 67–80; militia raised in, 92–4; rivalry with Monte Video, 93, 118; Liniers' preparations for defence of, 157–9; preliminary battles in the suburbs, 171–82; la Defensa, 183–205
bullring, the (Buenos Ayres), 51, 73, 157, 176, 188, 190, 193–4, 196, 204–10
Burne, Lieutenant-Colonel Robert (36th), 191, 198, 200–1
Burrell, Captain Percy (6th Dragoon Guards), 195
Butler, Colonel Sir Edward Gerald, 86, 182, 188

Cabildo Abierto, 89, 131
Cabildo of Buenos Ayres, 49–51, 54, 56, 60–3, 68, 71–2, 76, 89–95, 118, 130–2, 137, 142, 174, 220, 223
Cabildo of Monte Video, 110, 115, 126, 134, 137, 215
Cadogan, Lieutenant-Colonel Henry, 189–90, 195–7, 221
Cádiz, 48, 49, 59, 61–2, 64, 220
Campbell, Brigade Major Sir John, 155, 172, 190
Campbell, Lieutenant-Colonel Robert (71st), 56, 67, 70, 129
Campbell, Major Donald (40th), 116, 123–5, 141, 163–4
Campo, Viceroy Nicolás de, 49
Canelones, 140, 153
Cape of Good Hope, the, 8

Cape San Augustin, 8
Cape Town, 5, 12–23, 96–7
Carey, Private John (71st), 47, 221
Carlos II, king of Spain, 48
Carlos IV, king of Spain, 34, 49, 58, 61, 220
Carmichael, Captain Lewis (R.A.), 122–3
Carretas Point (Montevideo), 62, 110, n.251
Carrol, Captain William Parker (88th), 173, 207–9, 211, 221
Castelli, Juan José, 132
Castro, Francisco Antonio de, 62, 65, 93, 114, 126
Catamarca, 50
Cathedral (Buenos Ayres), 50, 75, 77, 89, 93, 197, 208
Cerpa, Corporal Juan Pedro, 67–8
Cevallos, Viceroy Pedro de, 48–9, 59, 61, 97, 142
Chamber of the Board of Trade, the, 83
Chamberlayne, Lieutenant Edwin (R.N.), 118, 133
Chawner, Lieutenant Edward (95th), 111
Chico Bank, 29
Chile, 28, 50, 84, 137, 153, 157, 224
Cisneros, Viceroy Hidalgo de, 223–4
Citadel, the (Monte Video), 115, 118–21, 123, 125–6, 215
Ciudad Rodrigo, siege of, xii, 221–2
Cochabamba, 50, 131
Colbert, General Auguste, xiii, 222
Colegio de Huérfanas (Buenos Ayres), 52
Colegio de San Carlos (Buenos Ayres), 53
Colombo, Captain Pablo, 115–16, 120–1
Colonia del Sacramento: history of, 48, 142; in Reconquista, 57, 60, 63, 65, 69, 73; British occupation of, 142–3, 151–2, 155
Constantia wine, 18
Conway, Brigade Major Charles, 202
Corbet, Captain Robert (R.N.), 155, 212, 217, 223
Corbrera, Josef, 151
Córdoba, 39, 47, 50, 53, 54, 63, 131, 213, 224
Cordova, Lieutenant José de, 111
Cork, 3
Corporal punishment, 10, 18, 19, 23, 97, 134, 212
Corrales de Miserere: Liniers' occupation of during Reconquista, 71; battle of (3/7/1807), 171–3; Whitelocke's occupation of during La Defensa, 175–9, 193, 195
Corrientes, 50
Cortes, the, 220
Courier, the, 83, 84, 219
Crauford, Arthur, 136

Craufurd, Brigadier-General Robert: in Defensa, xi–xii; appointed commander of Chilean expedition, 137; diverted to the River Plate, 137–8; in Monte Video, 153–5; character and background, 153; during Whitelocke's advance on Buenos Ayres, 159–63, 165–7, 169–71; at battle of Corrales, 172–3; in the western suburbs of Buenos Ayres, 175–6, 178–180; in La Defensa, 183–4, 189–90, 192, 195–6, 199, 201–2; surrenders, 203; as prisoner of war, 204–6, 209; after truce, 211–12; nearly court martialled for surrender, 218; pushes for Whitelocke to be shot, 219; latter career and death, 221
Crookshank, Captain William (38th), 117
Crosse, Captain Joshua (36th), 178, 181, 188, 191, 200–1
Crosse, Lieutenant Robert (36th), 165
Crossing of the Line, the, 8

Dalrymple, Major John (40th), 123, 125
Davie, Lieutenant-Colonel Humphrey (5th), 164, 191, 193, 198–9, 201
Deane, Major John Thomas Fitzmaurice, 28, 58, 83, 106, 149
Defensa, la: 183–205; British casualties, 205; Spanish / creole casualties, 205
De la Concha, Captain Juan Gutiérrez: background, 62; in build-up to Reconquista, 62–3, 65, 69, 71, 73; in the Reconquista, 76–7; organises naval forces in the River Plate, 93–4, 141, 150; transports Colonel Elio's troops to Colonia, 143; in la Defensa, 157, 176, 194; latter career and death, 224
Desertion: at Cape Town, 18, 23; under Beresford at Buenos Ayres, 63, 93; under Backhouse at Maldonado, 105, 107; under Auchmuty at Monte Video, 120, 136; British deserters fighting for the enemy, 123, 135, 168, 191, 194, 199, 210; and Spanish / creole militia, 151, 207, 221; under Whitelocke at Buenos Ayres, 202, 212, 214; from the Royal Navy in the River Plate, 212, 217; amongst the British prisoners of war, 214
Dickson, Captain Alexander (R.A.), 86, 120, 122, 222
Donnelley, Captain Ross (R.N.), 8, 24, 26, 28–9, 38–9, 58, 87, 114
Douglas, Lieutenant G. (R.N.), 150–1
Dozo, Juan de Dios, 60, 64
Downman, Captain Hugh (R.N.), 98, 142
Drake, Sir Francis, 21

Duckworth, Vice Admiral (R.N.), 64
Duff, Lieutenant-Colonel Alexander (88th), 182, 183–4, 189, 192, 197
Dundas, Henry, 20
Dunn, William, 25
Dutch East India Company, 17, 18
Duval, Pedro, 50, 52, 57, 160, 162

East India Company, 3, 9, 72, 84, 194, 214
East Indiamen: in general, 5; *Britannia*, 5, 9; *Earl Spencer*, 105; *Globe*, 11; *Lady Jane Shore*, 47, 79, 135, 221; *the Pitt*, 3; Sir *Steven Lushington*, 105 Eastwick, William, 84–5, 107, 119, 136, 212–13
Ebrington, Captain Blake (20th L.D.), 103
Echart, Private Jacob (71st), 63, 67–70
Edmonds, Captain Joshua (R.N.), 29, 98
Eygpt, British campaign in, 5, 19, 22, 86, 96, 97, 109
Elder, Captain George (95th), 125–6, 161, 172–3
Elía, Colonel Juan Ignacio de, 33
Elio, Colonel Francisco Javier de: background, 142; in attack on Colonia, 142–3, 151–2; in la Defensa, 157, 166, 169, 171, 174–6, 198–9; in surrender negotiations, 203, 209; takes command of Monte Video, 214, 220
English Bank, 26, 28
Espina, Lieutenant Miguel, 122
Estebe y Llach, Gerado, 59–63, 73, 75, 207
Evans, Assistant-Surgeon Jason (71st), 30, 89
Everard, Lieutenant Mathias (2d), 123–4
Execution, 50, 70, 100, 135, 211, 214, 219, 224

Falklands Islands, the, 94, 114, 115, 225
Ferdinand VII, king of Spain, 220
Fernyhough, Lieutenant John (R.N.), 25
Fernyhough, Lieutenant Robert (R.M.): speculates about destination of Popham's expedition, 5; on voyage to Cape, 6–7, 9–10, 12, 14–17, 19, 23, 25; during occupation of Buenos Ayres, 56, 64, 71; during the Reconquista, 74, 77; on Beresford's surrender, 79; as a prisoner of war, 90, 94–5, 129, 213–15
Figueroa, Vicente, 116
Fitzpatrick, Lieutenant Timothy (40th), 117
Flores Island, 97–8, 110, 150
Fothergill, Captain William (R.N.), 96–8
Fort Amsterdam, 18
Fort (Buenos Ayres): and Sobremonte, 33, 34, 42; under British occupation, 43, 47, 53–4,

56, 58, 61, 64–5, 67–74, 76, 78; description of 51; Beresford's surrender of, 79; in la Defensa, 175, 192, 195, 197, 200–2; British prisoners of war held in, 203, 205
Fort San Jospeh (Monte Video), 119, 123–5, 215
Fort Santa Teresa, 31
Foster, Captain Andrew (24th), 14–16
Frazer, Captain Augustus (R.A.), 154, 160–4, 167, 170–1, 175–6, 184, 207–8, 222
French naval vessels: *Atalante*, 15; *Volontaire*, 19
French Revolutionary War, xiv, 17, 86
Freemasons, 57
Funchal, 7

Galves Bridge, 33, 36, 38, 39, 43, 92, 159, 161, 166, 167, 169–170, 174, 182, 206
Gama, Colonel Pio de, 92
García, Captain Pedro, 69
Gardener, Major Thomas (95th), 86, 109, 111, 152, 172, 175, 178
Garro, José de, 48
Gavin, Ensign William (71st): in South Africa, 15; on voyage to River Plate, 24; During Beresford's invasion, 39–41; in Reconquista, 67; as prisoner of war, 79, 88, 95, 215
George III, king of England, 134, 219
Gianninni, Colonel Eustaquio, 33–4, 38–41
Gillespie, Captain Alexander (R.M.): speculates on destination of Popham's mission, 5; on voyage from Cork, 6, 7; at Salvador, 10–11; at Cape Colony 18; during Beresford's invasion, 36–7, 40; during British occupation of Buenos Ayres, 47, 50–1, 56–7, 64, 70–1; during Reconquista, 76, 78; as a prisoner of war, 90–2, 94, 128–9, 131, 213, 215
Gorda Point, 150
Gordon, Ensign Alexander (3d Guards), 23, 28, 42
Gorriti Island, 98, 101, 105, 110
Gower, Major-General John Leveson: character and background, 148; during Whitelocke's advance on Buenos Ayres, 160, 162, 165–71; refuses to let Craufurd advance into central Buenos Ayres, 172–3; in western suburbs of Buenos Ayres, 175–6; and plan of attack on Buenos Ayres, 178–82; orders men to advance with unloaded muskets, 183; falls out with Whitelocke during la Defensa, 193; and Whitelocke's surrender, 207–9; blamed for British defeat, 219; latter career, 224
Graham, Ensign John (71st), 5, 6
Grant, Colonel (72d), 16

Grau, Lieutenant Jose, 62, 142 Grenville, Lord Thomas, 85, 138
Guard, Lieutenant-Colonel William, 184, 188, 190, 192, 199–200, 203, 221–2
Guemes, Martín Miguel de, 80
Gutierrez, Ventura, 100
Gwyn, Major William (45th), 169

Halliday, Surgeon (E.I.C.), 38
Hamilton, Captain Nicholas (5th), 211
Herrick, Lieutenant (R.N.), 71, 76
Hodson, Captain Benjamin (E.I.C.), 91
Hodson, Capain Charles (E.I.C.), 91
Honeyman, Captain Robert (R.N.), 22, 26, 31, 94–5, 119
Hottentots (Khoikhoi), 13, 15, 17
Hottentot Kloof, 16
Howard, Captain Richard, 102, 217–18
Howick, Lord, 94
Hudson, Captain Benjamin (E.I.C.), 72, 77
Huidobro, Pascual Ruiz: warns Sobremonte of danger of foreign invasion, 32; background and character, 49, 61–2; in build-up to Reconquista, 61–2, 64; negotiates with Popham over Beresford's release, 90, 94; repels Popham and Backhouse's attempt against Monte Video, 98; during siege of Montevideo, 110–1, 113, 115, 117–18, 120–3; as prisoner of war, 126–7, 143, 220–1; latter career and death, 224
Hyder Ali, 5, 86

India, British colonies in, 3, 5, 21, 39, 85–6, 96, 106, 139, 153, 213–14, 218, 224
Iremonger, Major William (88th), 183–4, 189

Janssens, Lieutenant-General Jan Wilem, 14–7, 222
Jasca, second Lieutenant Juan, 123–4
Joubert, Second-Lieutenant Pedro, 40
Joyce, Captain John (R.N.), 164

Kennedy, Sergeant Peter (71st), 72
Kennett, Captain George (R.E.), 22, 26, 28, 40, 56–7, 70, 76, 89
Khoikhoi, 17
King, Captain William (R.N.), 29, 35, 41, 69, 71, 74, 108
King, Major Henry (5th), 182, 184, 191, 193, 198, 200–1, 209, 213

Kington, Colonel Peter (6th Dragoon Guards), 183, 188, 195, 202, 205, 211, 213

Lady Jane Shore, 47, 79, 135, 221
Landel, Lieutenant George (R.M.), 36
Landsheit, Sergeant Norbert (20th Light Dragoons): background, 6; on voyage to Cape Colony, 6; on learning of Beresford's defeat, 97; at Maldonado, 101, 103–5, 107–8, 109; on advance on Monte Video, 113, 116; latter career, 222
Lane, Lieutenant-Colonel William (E.I.C), 25, 38
Larrañaga, Chaplain Dámaso Antonio, 71
Lasala, Lieutenant Cándido de, 194
Las Conchas (hamlet), 32, 60, 69–71
Las Conchas (river), 69
Las Piedras, 110, 115, 117, 135, 137, 140
Lawrence, Private William (40th): background, 86; leaves England, 86–7; during siege of Monte Video, 117, 126; during Auchmuty's occupation of Monte Video, 135–6; at Colonia, 151–2; on Whitelocke's advance on Buenos Ayres, 165, 168; latter career, 220, 222
Le Blanc, Captain Henry (71st), 14, 24, 28, 30, 36–8, 56, 76, 102, 129–130
Lecocq, General Bernardo, 115–17, 127
L'Estrange, Lieutenant Edmund (71st), 40–1
Le Sueur, Colonel, 13–5
Light Battalion, the, 109, 113, 116–17, 123–5, 152, 155, 172
Light Brigade, the, 155, 159, 160, 162–3, 165, 167, 170–3
Lima, 47–8, 53, 157, 217
Liniers, Captain Santiago de: occupies Ensenada prior to Beresford's invasion, 32; Background, 59–60; plans to overthrow the British, 60; seeks aid of Governor Huidobro in Monte Video, 62; on advance to Buenos Ayres prior to Reconquista, 63, 65, 69–71; occupies El Retiro, 71 4; in Reconquista, 75–7; negotiates surrender with Beresford, 79, 88–91; appointed military commander in chief at Buenos Ayres, 89; forced into changing surrender agreement, 91; raises new militia army, 92, 137, 150; in command of relief column sent to aid Monte Video, 121; possibility of his collusion in Beresford's escape, 132; his lack of authority in Buenos Ayres, 141; in build-up to La Defensa, 149, 159; during Whitelocke's advance, 161, 165–6; plans to give battle

outside Buenos Ayres, 166–9; and battle at Corrales, 171–3; loses hope, 174; returns to Buenos Ayres, 176; rejects summons to surrender, 181; in la Defensa, xii, 197, 203, 207; negotiates terms of British surrender, 204, 206–7, 209–10; facilitates prisoner exchange, 210–14; celebrates British defeat, 217; latter career, 220, 223; death, xiii, 224
Lloyd, Colonel Evan (17th L.D.), 86
Lobos Island, 26, 98, 105
López, Captain Lorenzo, 68
Loris, Captain Augustin de, 101
Los Olivos, 61, 159, 161, 175
Lospard's Bay, 12
Lué y Riega, Bishop Benito: during Beresford's occupation, 42; background, 49; appears to befriend British, 56, 68; secretly opposes British, 60; actions during British occupation, 63, 70–1; pledges money for raising of militia army, 92; during la Defensa, xii, 176; latter career and death, xiii, 223–4
Lucas, Ensign Thomas (71st), 6, 75, 88, 91
Luján, 55, 57, 62, 65, 67, 128–30, 132–3
Lumley, Brigadier-General William: character and background, 109; during advance on Monte Video, 113; and occupation of Monte Video, 134; attempts to gather horses for advance on Buenos Ayres, 148–9; on South American horses, 149; in Whitelocke's advance on Buenos Ayres, 154, 161–5, 169–173; in western suburbs of Buenos Ayres, 175, 178, 181; on Whitelocke's plan of attack, 179–81; in Whitelocke's attack on Buenos Ayres, 183, 191–2, 198, 200–2; after surrender, 212; latter career, 222, 224
Luxton, Sergeant William (40th), 120

Macdonald, Lieutenant Alexander (R.A.), 72, 74, 76–7
Mackenzie, Captain Alexander (R.M.), 78, 88, 90
Maciel, Francisco Antonio, 62, 127
Madeira, 6–7, 137, 221
Madrid, 220
Mahon, Colonel Thomas (9th Light Dragoons), 153–4, 160–1, 164–5, 167, 206, 211
Maldonado: description of, 98; British attack on, 99–101; British occupation of, 101–8; evacuation of, 109–10
Marshall, Private Thomas (20th L.D.), 104
Martín Garcia Island, 143, 150
Martin, Reverend Henry, 3, 5–8, 12, 16

Martínez, Captain Manuel, 35
Martínez, Captain José, 104
Martínez, second Lieutenant Francisco, 100
Martínez, Sergeant Pablo, 118
Matorras Brook, 50, 190
Matthews, Sergeant Benjamin (38th), 125
Mawe, John, 149, 176, 179, 211–12
McCarthy, Private Michael (71st), 93, 168
Mcleod, Major Norman (95th)
Melo, Viceroy Pedro, 49
Mendoza, 50, 213, 224
Mendoza, Pedro de, 47
Merced, la (Church, Buenos Ayres), 51, 76, 175, 191
Merchants (British): of the East India Company, 3; merchant fleets encountered on the high seas, 6; and trade with Buenos Ayres, 20, 25, 53, 54–5, 84–5, 97, 110, 137; goods for sale in Buenos Ayres, 84; attempts to defraud insurers, 118; profiteering during siege of Monte Video, 119, 121; in Monte Video, 136–7, 150, 208, 212–15
Merchants (Spanish and creole): internal divisions between, 49; contraband trade; international trade, 48–9; internal trade, 50; and taxation / treatment under British occupation, 55; and positive attitude to British occupation, 56, 58, 132; and support for expulsion of British, 62, 65, 89, 92, 114; seized by British, 64, 94–5, 126
Merchants (U.S. and other international), 38–9, 58, 94, 105, 110, 123, 130, 135
Merchant Ships: *Anna* (British), 84–5, 108, 119; *Aurora* (British), 212; *Bankege* (Portuguese), 28, 57; *Buen Viage* (Spanish), 57; *El Carmen* (Spanish), 94; *Emmanuel* (French?), 26; *Flor del Cabo* (Portuguese), 133; *Francisco de Paula* (Spanish), 57; *Justina* (British), 25, 29, 55, 74, 76, 80; *La Denia* (Spanish), 57; *Lord Chesterfiled* (British), 150, 155, 160; *Rolla* (U.S.A.), 108; *Santo Cristo del Grao* (Spanish), 64; *Superb* (U.S.A.), 105
Michelena, Lieutenant Juan Ángel de, 141
Miller, Lieutenant George (95th): on conditions on board the British transports, 154; on Whitelocke's advance 161, 168, 170–1; in the western suburbs, 174, 178; during la Defensa, 199–201; as prisoner of war, 203, 205, 211
Miller, Major Francis (87th), 114, 116, 123, 125, 190–1
Milne, Lieutenant William (R.N.), 126
Ministry of All the Talents, the, 85, 94, 108, 147

Miranda, Francisco de, 20, 84, 132
Miranda, Ensign José María, 77
Mitchell, Lieutenant William (71st), 41, 68, 74–5, 89
Monkland, Captain George (36th): on Whitelocke's advance to Buenos Ayres, 164–8; in the western suburbs, 173; during la Defensa, 191, 198, 206; on Whitelocke's surrender, 209–11, 214
Monte Video: initial plans for occupation of, 20; Popham seeks intelligence on, 22; description of, 28, 29; reinforced by Sobremonte, 28, 31,33; Popham's blockade of, 29, 57, 90, 94–5; Popham's plans to capture, 57, 97–8; troops raised for Reconquista, 60–3; rivalry with Buenos Ayres, 93; siege of, 113–23; description of, 113–14; storming of, 123–7; British occupation of, 134–43, 148, 150; trade under British occupation, 136–7; evacuation of, 212–15
Moore, Lieutenant-General Sir John, 218, 221–2
Mordeille, Hipólito: background, 62; involvement in Reconquista, 62, 69, 78; raises militia regiment at Monte Video, 110; during British advance on Monte Video, 111, 113; advises surrender of Monte Video, 121; and assault on Monte Video, 123, 125; death, 127
Moreno, Mariano, 132
Morley, Private Stephen (5th), 160, 209, 214, 219, 222
Morris, Robert, 25, 74, 76
Mossel Bay, 17
Muñoz, Lieutenant Rodrigo, 33
Murray, Lieutenant Thomas (71st), 55, 78
Murray, Rear-Admiral Sir George Murray, 137, 140, 153, 159, 167, 208, 210, 222–3
Mysore, 5

Napoleon Bonaparte, xiv, 34, 53, 85, 148, 218, 220
Nicolls, Captain W. D. (R.A.), 160, 162–3
Nicolls, Major Jasper (45th), 184, 188, 190, 204, 207, 209–10, 222
Nuevo Coliseo Theatre (Buenos Ayres), 33, 49, 57, 64
Nugent, Lieutenant-Colonel John (38th), 178, 191, 193–4, 198

Ogilvie, Captain James (R.A.): on voyage to River Plate, 22, 28; on Beresford's advance

to Buenos Ayres, 37–8, 40–1; and occupation of Buenos Ayres, 54, 63, 67–8; and la Reconquista 72; as prisoner of war, 128–9; murder of 130
O'Gorman, Anna (also see Perichon, Ana), 60, 211, 213, 220
Olavarría, Antonio de, 65, 67–8
Olondriz, Lieutenant-Colonel Juan de, 38, 40
Ortiz Bank, 26, 155

Pack, Lieutenant-Colonel (later colonel) Denis (71st): description of, 14; at Cape Colony, 14; on voyage to River Plate, 28; during Beresford's advance on Buenos Ayres, 37, 40; during occupation of Buenos Ayres, 57, 67–8, 70; and la Reconquista, 72; pushes for attack on Liniers' troops at El Retiro, 73; as prisoner of war, 79, 94, 128, 130; escapes captivity, 133, 154; and occupation of Colonia, 142–3; at Battle of San Pedro, 151–2; and Whitelocke's advance on Buenos Ayres, 166; and doubts about Whitelocke's plan of attack, 179–180; during la Defensa, 183–4, 189–90, 196, 201; and Craufurd's surrender, 203; as prisoner of war, 210; latter career, 221
Padilla, Captain Manuel Aniceto, 131–3, 150, 215
Palmer, Captain John (R.N.), 111, 113, 143
Pan de Azucar, 106
pampero, 26, 113
Paraguay, 48, 50, 59, 122, 131, 157
Patten, Robert (governor of Saint Helena), 20, 23–5
Payne, Captain John (45th), xi–xii, 199–200, 221
Pazos, Captain José de, 199
Pedraza, Manuela Hurtado de, 73
Peña, Captain Saturnino Rodríguez, 131–2, 211–12, 215
peones, 50, 160, 163–4, 215, 222
Perdriel, Chacra de: description of, 61, 67; used as base by Catalan patriots, 61, 63; battle of, 67–8
Perez, Juan José, 55
Perichon, Ana (also O'Gorman, Anna), 60, 211, 213, 220
Peru, 22, 47, 93, 132, 137, 157, 213
Piedad Church, 172
Pigot, Major George (9th Light Dragoons), 151, 195
Pinedo, Colonel Augustín, 76

Pitt, Midshipman William (R.N.), 87, 194, 209, 212

Pitt the Younger, William: and connections with Popham, 5, 20–1, 25; and Blue Water Policy, 5, 20; and interest in South America, 20, 85; death of, 25, 80, 94

Plunkett, Private Thomas (95th), xii–xiii, 196, 199, 222

Plymouth, 86, 220

Pococke, Captain Samuel (71st): character of, 63–4; during Beresford's occupation of Buenos Ayres, 63–5, 68, 70; at the Battle of Perdriel, 67; and negative opinion of Popham, 71; during Reconquista, 73, 79; as a prisoner of war, 88–91, 93, 128–9

Pooler, Surgeon John (71st), 30, 89

Popham, Commodore Sir Home: background and character, 3–5, 39, 86; and telegraph system, 5, 102; practises combined operations in Cork, 5; on voyage to Cape, 6, 11; at Madeira, 6–7; assumes the rank of commodore, 7–8; and the 'Sea Battalion', 8, 22; at Salvador, 9; during attack on Cape Colony, 12–14; and occupation of Cape Town, 17–19; and capture of *Volontaire*, 19; and prize money, 19, 30, 57; and plans to attack South America, 19–21; and preparations for voyage to River Plate, 22–3; and voyage to the River Plate, 24–6; at Saint Helena, 24–5; and reaction to the death of Pitt, 25, 80; in the River Plate, 26–30;debates whether to attack Buenos Ayres or Monte Video, 28–9; and occupation of Buenos Ayres, 47, 53–7, 69, 74; and trade with Buenos Ayres, 54; blockades Monte Video, 57–8, 62, 94–5; and build-up to la Reconquista, 69, 74; and avarice, 71, 89; reaction in England to his initial success, 83–5; attempts to secure Beresford's release, 90, 94; and attempt against Monte Video, 97–8; at Maldonado, 98–102, 104–5; and replacement by Rear-Admiral Stirling, 106–8; returns to England, 108; court martial, 219–20; latter career, 220, 223–4

Portsmouth, 20, 84, 86–7, 107, 137, 143, 147, 219–20

Potosí, 21, 50

Powell, Captain Henry, 126

Princeps & Saunders, 25

Prisoners of war: British, 5, 72, 79, 88–91, 94–5, 128–33, 137, 141, 152–3, 198, 202–12, 214–15, 221, 226; Malay, 17; Dutch, 17–18; Portuguese, 28; Spanish, 64,
100–1, 105, 117, 120, 126–7, 134–5, 141, 151–2, 173, 191–2, 194, 200, 202–6, 220–1

Privateers: *Kitty* (British), 105; *La Mosca de Buenos Ayres* (Spanish), 150; *Napoleon* (French), 15

Prize money, 17, 19, 21, 23, 28, 30, 57, 71, 102, 148

Pueyrredón, Juan Martín de: background, 60; gathers troops for Reconquista, 60, 62, 65–6; at Perdriel, 67–8; in build-up to Reconquista, 69, 74–5; in Reconquista, 78; persuades Sobremonte not to enter Buenos Ayres, 89, 91–2; raises militia unit, 93; sent to Europe, 261; latter career, 224

Querandíes, 47–8

Quinta Riglos, 191, 193, 204

Quinta Zuloaga, 184, 188, 191

Quintana, Brigadier José Ignacio de la, 42, 49

Quintana, Colonel Nicolás de la, 33–5, 38, 118, 127

Quintana, Lieutenant Hilarión José de la, 71–2, 78–9

Rancheria Barracks, 43, 56, 61, 63, 65, 76, 175, 189, 195

Ratones Island, 114, 120, 126

Real de San Carlos, 143, 155

Reconquista, la: 67–80; British casualties, 88–9, 226

Recova, la (Buenos Ayres), 51, 72, 77–8

Reducción, 33, 35–6, 38–9, 47, 166–70

Rennie, Captain Charles (40th), 124

Residencia, la, 51, 157, 173, 175–6, 178, 184, 188, 190, 196, 207, 209, 211

Retiro, el (Park in Buenos Ayres), 51, 54, 71–3, 88–9, 149, 157, 175–6, 178, 184–8, 190–1, 193–4, 198, 201–12, 214, 217

Revoredo, Sergeant Isidoro, 117, 120

Rhea, 103, 129

Riachuelo Brook, 33, 38–40, 70, 92, 149, 167–71, 176, 206

Riobo, Roque, 62

Rio de Janeiro, 28, 94–5, 105, 135, 214

Rio Grande, 32, 97–8, 135

River Plate, the: description of and difficulties of navigation, 26–8; naval combat in, 65–6, 69, 71, 93–4, 94–5, 120, 139–40, 141–2, 150–1, 217

Robin Island, 12

Roche, Captain Philip Keating (17th L.D.), 117, 175–6, 221

Rodney, Admiral Sir George (R.N.), 5
Rodríguez, Martín, 93, 161, 165, 175, 195, 197
Roliça, battle of, xii, 178, 221–2
Romero, Tomás Antonio, 50, 56–7
Rosendo, Corporal Pedro, 78
Ross, Major David (38th), 125
Rowley, Captain Josias (R.N.), 8, 29, 94, 120,
   164, 223
Royal Marines, 3, 5–6, 14–15, 29, 36–7, 54, 69,
   72, 78, 83, 100, 114–15, 134, 217, 225, 226
Royal Navy Ships-of-War: HMS *Adamant*, 18;
   HMS *Ardent*, 87, 108, 110, 113; HMS *Africa*,
   153, 210; HMS *Africaine*, 223;
   HMS *Belliqueux*, 3, 14; HMS *Charwell*, 87,
   108, 110, 118, 133, 140–2, 155; HMS *Dart*,
   6; HMS *Daphne*, 87, 110, 119–20;
   HMS *Diadem*, 3, 5–7, 9–12, 14, 19, 23–4,
   26, 28–9, 57, 69, 71, 90, 98, 102, 104, 108,
   110, 113, 122; HMS *Diomede*, 3, 9, 12, 23,
   26, 29, 57, 94, 97–8, 110, 142; HMS *Dolores*,
   71, 74, 76, 79, 140, 142, 150–1, 156, 159;
   HMS *Encounter*, 3, 10, 14, 23–4, 26, 28–30,
   35–6, 38, 47, 57, 65, 71, 98, 111, 116, 119,
   140–1, 154, 156, 215; HMS *Espoir*, 3, 12;
   HMS *Fly*, 137, 149, 153, 156, 159; HMS
   Flying Fish, 153, 155, 159; HMS *Gladiator*,
   219; HMS *Haughty*, 153, 156; HMS *Howe*,
   96, 102, 109, 113, 143; HMS *Hyaena*, 3;
   HMS *Lancaster*, 96–8, 104–5, 110, 136, 143;
   HMS *Leda*, 3, 8–10, 12, 14, 22, 26, 31, 58,
   69, 71, 74, 80, 94–5, 97, 110, 119–20, 135;
   HMS *Medusa*, 95–6, 108, 119, 135, 155–6,
   218; HMS *Olympia*, 140, 142, 155–6, 217;
   HMS *Paz*, 140, 142, 154, 156; HMS
   Pheasant, 87,106, 110–11, 140, 142, 156;
   HMS *Polyphemus*, 153; HMS *Protector*, 7–8,
   10, 14, 17, 96, 98, 118, 140, 142–3, 150,
   204; HMS *Narcissus*, 3, 5, 8, 17, 19, 23–4,
   26, 28–9, 35–6, 38, 47, 56, 58, 83; HMS
   Nereide, 137, 153, 155–6, 167, 206, 208, 212,
   217; HMS *Raisonnable*, 6–8, 11, 19, 23, 28–9,
   80, 94–5, 102, 104, 110, 120; HMS *Rolla*,
   135, 155–6, 212, 214; HMS *Sampson*, 105–6;
   HMS *Saracen*, 153–4, 156, 212; HMS
   Staunch, 108, 119, 122, 140–3, 150, 154;
   HMS *Thisbe*, 143, 148, 155–6, 214; HMS
   Unicorn, 87, 108, 214; HMS *Venerable*, 223
Royal Navy Transports: *Adamant*, 96;
   Alexander, 96, 102, 214, 217–18; *Caledonia*,
   96; *Campion*, 217; *Royal Charlotte*, 96–8;
   Columbine, 96–7; *Diadem*, 96; *Fanny*, 96–8;
   Hero, 96–8; *King George*, 3, 8–9; *Malabar*,
   214; *Melantho*, 23, 54, 70, 96; *Ocean*, 23, 4,
   28; *Polly*, 96; *Pretty Lass*, 96; *Princessa*, 215;

Rolla, 96–8; *Triton*, 23, 69, 97–8; *Walker*, 23,
   58, 69; *Willington*, 23, 102
Royal Philippine Company, the, 51, 53, 148
Rundell, Lieutenant Francis (54th), 107
Russell, William, 28–30

Saavedra, Colonel Cornelio de, 92, 195, 223–4
Saint Helena, 20, 23–6, 96
Saint Helena Regiment, 25, 37–8, 43, 63, 67,
   70, 72–3, 77, 88, 91, 94, 129, 226
Saldanha Bay, 12
Salt River, 16
Salta, 50, 80
Salvador (Saö Salvador da Bahia), 8–11, 20, 28,
   31
Salvañach, Lieutenant Cristobal, 78
Sampson, Lieutenant (E.I.C.), 70
Sánchez, Ensign Manuel, 33
Sánchez de Thompson, Mariquita, 34, 43, 52
Santa Coloma, Don Antonio Gaspar de, 39, 49,
   92
Santa Lucia, 140, 152–3
Santiago de Chile, 137, 157, 217
San Carlos, 100–5
San Francisco Church (Buenos Ayres), 175
San Francisco Church (Monte Video), 61
San Ignacio Church (Buenos Ayres), 76, 195
San Isidrio, 71
San Juan, 50, 213
San Juan Gate (Monte Video), 115, 120, 122
San Martín, José de, 221, 224
San Miguel Church (Buenos Ayres), 175, 182,
   184, 189, 192, 197
San Pedro, battle of, 151–2
San Pedro Gate (Monte Video), 63, 115, 123,
   125, 127
San Pedro y Pazos, Second-Lieutenant
   Leonardo, 40
San Sebastian Battery (Monte Video), 115,
   120–5
Sans, Sergeant Manuel, 122, 125
Santa Bárbara Beach (Monte Video), 114, 118.
Santa Catalina Church (Buenos Ayres), 193,
   198, 201–2
Santa Caterina Island, 31, 58
Santo Domingo, battle of, 64
Santo Domingo Church (Buenos Ayres), 51,
   60, 190, 192, 196, 199–204, 225
Sarratea, Martína, 59–60
Sarratea, Martín, 60
Sea Battalion, 6, 8, 11, 14–15, 22, 25–6, 29,
   35–6, 41–2, 54–5, 72, 83, 90
Selkirk, Lord, 20

Sentenach, Felipe de, 59–64, 68, 73, 75, 77–8, 93, 121

Ships (see Royal Navy Ships, Spanish Navy Ships, East Indiamen, Privateers and Merchant Ships)

Siège en Forme, 118, 120

Simon's Bay, 18, 96

Sinclair, Sir John, 85

Slavery: in South Africa, 15, 17; and slave traders, 21, 26, 38, 50, 52–3, 56, 58, 62; in Buenos Ayres, 31, 49–50, 55–6, 175, 192, 197, 202, 217, 228; in Algiers, 59; in Monte Video, 62, 113–5, 117, 120, 122, 125–6, 150

Smith, Lieutenant Harry (95th), 86, 124, 135, 215, 219, 224

Sobremonte y Núñez del Catillo, Rafael de: background and character, 31–2, 49; prior to Beresford's invasion, 31–4; during Beresford's advance on Buenos Ayres, 33–4, 38; flees to Córdoba, 42, 55; raises army in Córdoba, 63; advances on Buenos Ayres, 69, 89; advised not to return by the Buenos Ayres Cabildo, 89, 91–2; and defence of Monte Video, 110–13, 117, 119, 135, 137, 140; arrested by order of the Buenos Ayres Cabildo, 131

Socorro Church (Buenos Ayres), 204

South America: British plans for invasion of, 19–21

South Tower (Monte Video), 115, 119, 121–5, 134

Southern Star, The, 150

Spanish Army Units: Blandengues, 33, 35, 38, 63, 65, 73, 100–1, 118, 132, 152; Buenos Ayres Horse Artillery, 33, 35–7; *Cuerpo de Invalidos*, 33–4, 157; Regiment of Buenos Ayres, 221

Spanish militia units: Arribeños, 92–3, 132, 171–2, 175; Buenos Ayres Cavalry Volunteers, 33–6; Buenos Ayres Infantry Volunteers, 33–4, 43; Carabineros de Carlos IV (cavalry), 93; Cazadores (cavalry), 93; Cazadores Correntinos (light infantry), 92; Cordoban Volunteers (cavalry), 102–4, 106; Cuerpo de Gallegos, 92, 176, 194, 223; Escuadron de Labradores y Quinteros (cavalry), 93, 165, 168; Galician and Asturian Volunteers (Monte Video), 62, 110; Granaderos, 92; Húsares del Gobierno, 110–1, 123, 125, 134; Hussars of Pueyrredón / First Hussars (cavalry), 93, 161–3, 165, 175, 195, 197; Migueletes (cavalry), 93; Miñones, 62–3, 72, 74, 76–8, 90, 110, 115, 127, 142, 157, 175; Monte Video Cavalry Volunteers, 95, 103–4, 117, 120–1; Monte Video Infantry Volunteers (France, Navarre and Vizcana), 62, 71, 77, 79, 110, 116; Patriotas de la Unión (artillery), 93, 121, 132, 142, 152, 207; Regimiento de Indios, Morenos y Pardos (Artillery), 93; Regimiento de Indios, Morenos y Pardos (Infantry), 92; Regimiento de Patricios, 92, 118, 151–2, 157, 175–6, 189, 195, 223; Regiment of Buenos Ayres, 118; Tercio de Asturianos and Vizcainos, 92, 171–2, 223; Tercio de Andaluces, 92, 175, 189; Tercio de Catalanes, 92, 223; Tercio de Montañeses, 92; Urbanos, 34, 38

Spanish Navy in the River Plate, 31–2, 93–4, 141, 150, 166, 215

Spanish Navy ships: *Dos Hermanas*, 166; *Joaquina*, 31; *La Mosca de Buenos Ayres*, 150; *Nuestra Señora del Carmen*, 32; *Princessa*, 215; *Reconquista*, 166; *Remedios*, 141; *San* Antonio, 141

Squire, Captain John (R.E.), 118, 159, 172, 176, 207–8, 222

Stellenbosch, 17

Stewart, Lieutenant (R.N.), 95, 143

Stirling, Rear-Admiral Charles (R.N.): appointment, background and character, 85–7, 106; wrests control of the fleet from Popham, 106–8; during siege of Monte Video, 109–13, 116–22; and consolidation of naval control of the River Plate, 139–40; during Whitelocke's advance on Buenos Ayres, 154; latter career, 222–3

Stanhope, Captain Leicester (6th D.G.), 211

St. Leger Hill, Lieutenant Dudley (95th), 126

Street, Lieutenant Benjamin (R.N.), 119, 122, 140–1, 143, 150–1

Tabares, Sergeant Gerónimo, 33, 35

Table Bay, 12, 17, 19, 22, 24

Table Mountain, 17–18

Talbot, Lieutenant James (R.N.), 29, 35–6, 65–6, 69, 116, 119, 140–2

Tast, Bartolome, 63–4

Terrada, Captain Juan Florencio, 37, 40, 92

Thompson, Captain John (R.N. captain of the Port of Buenos Ayres), 56, 64, 74, 76, 79

Thompson, Captain John (R.N. captain of HMS Fly), 159, 194, 204, 206

Thompson, Martín Jacobo, Captain of the Port of Buenos Ayres, 33

Thompson, Surgeon Richard (R.N.), 5, 7, 17–18, 26–30, 35

Three Kings, the (Inn, Buenos Ayres), 37, 53, 56, 70, 91, 95
Times, The, 21, 83–4, 150, 218–20
Tipu Sultan, the, 84
Tobacco Administration Company, the, 51, 53
Todd, Private Thomas (71st): background, 109, 116–17; arrival at Maldonado, 109; reflections on his first experience of combat, 116–7; and siege of Monte Video, 116–17, 119; and occupation of Monte Video, 134, 150; and Whitelocke's advance, 160, 162; and la Defensa, 189; as prisoner of war, 195, 205; latter career, 222
Tolley, Major Henry (71st), 128, 154, 188, 207, 209
Torrens, Lieutenant-Colonel Francis, 168, 179–80, 193, 202, 204
Torres, Friar Gregorio, 60, 93
Trafalgar, battle of, 6, 8. 18, 25, 90. 150, 153, 223
Travers, Major Robert (95th), 160, 170–1, 173, 195–6
Treacher, Lieutenant (R.N.), 143
Trigo, Juan, 68
Trinidad Island (South Atlantic), 26, 97
Trotter, Major William (83d): during la Defensa, xi–xii, 199–201; background and character, 96–7; and capture of Maldonado, 100; and advance on Monte Video, 109; and siege of Monte Video, 117, 124; and occupation of Colonia, 142–3; and Battle of San Pedro, 152; death, xii, 221
Tucumán, 50
Tucker, Major John, 113, 123, 126
Turner, Major Charles, 124

Upper Peru, 28, 48–50, 53, 131, 217, 224

Valencia, Tomás, 61
Valenciennes, xiv
Vandeleur, Major Richard (88th), 183–4, 189, 192–3, 196–7, 199, 202, 221
vaquería, 48
Varela, Captain Jacobo, 176, 194
Vasquez, Cadet Juan, 41
Vassal, Lieutenant-Colonel Spencer (38th): background and character, 89; at Maldonado, 100–1; at Monte Video, 109, 123–5; death, 135
Velasco, General Bernardo de, 131, 157, 168–9, 174, 211
Vera Brook, 50, 207

Vértiz y Salcedo, Viceroy Juan José de, 49
Viana, Sergeant Major Francisco Javier de, 115, 121, 123, 126–7
Viceroyalty of the River Plate: foundation of, 48; administration of, 48–9; and trade and contraband, 49–50
Villeneuve, Admiral Pierre-Charles, 6
Vinicombe, Sergeant William (36th), 200, 213
Viscount Grey, 85

Waldeck infantry, 15–16, 18, 67
Walters, Lieutenant Samuel (R.N.), 102
Warnes, Lieutenant Ignacio, 38
Washington, George, 84
Waterloo, battle of, 178, 221–2
Wayne, Captain T., 21, 26
Wellesley, Lieutenant-General Arthur, 138, 220–2
West Indies, British colonies in, xiv, 3, 6–7, 96, 132, 138, 183
White, William Pius: background, 38–9, 50, 52; and occupation of Buenos Ayres, 42, 55, 60; attempts to arrange peaceful handover of Buenos Ayres, 74–5; as British spy, 130, 149; during Whitelocke's advance on Buenos Ayres, 160, 169, 180–1; and aftermath of the British defeat, 213
Whitelocke, Lieutenant-General John: appointment of, 139, 153; background and character, 147, 162, 164, 176, 212; orders, 147–8; and preparations for attack on Buenos Ayres, 148–150, 154, 163; and doubts about plan of attack, 154–5, 166–70, 183–4; and relationship with Craufurd, 154, 162; and advance on Buenos Ayres, 161–2, 164, 166–70, 176; in western suburbs, 176, 178–182; and plan of attack, 178–82; during attack on central Buenos Ayres, 193, 195–6, 202, 204, 206; contemplates surrender, 206–8; and surrender negotiations, 209–10; and evacuation of Buenos Ayres, 210–2; and evacuation of Monte Video, 213–14; and court martial, 218–19; death, 224
Whittingham, Captain Samford, 180–1, 193, 202–4, 206–7, 210, 212, 222, 224
Wildlife in the Viceroyalty of the River Plate, 26, 39, 48, 74, 98, 103, 105, 128–9, 150, 166
Wilgres, Captain Edward (R.A.), 143
Wilkie, Captain Fletcher (38th); character, 3; at Cork, 3, 5; on voyage to the Cape, 7, 9–11; at Cape Colony, 18, 22, 97; in the River Plate, 97–8; at Maldonado, 100, 102, 105–6, 108, 110; on attack on Monte Video, 111,

118, 120, 122, 124–5, 127; and occupation of Monte Video, 134, 136, 148; on Whitelocke's advance to Buenos Ayres, 162, 164; in attack on El Retiro, 184, 191, 193, 195; on Whitelocke's surrender, 209, 219, latter career and death, 225
Willaumez, Admiral Jean-Baptiste, 6, 19
Wilson, Colonel Sir Robert, 18

Windham, William, 94, 138, 147, 153, 155
Wynberg, 17

Yorke, General (R.A.), 3, 8–9

Zuñiga, Lieutenant Victorio Garciade, 77